Semantic Web Programming

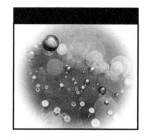

Semantic Web Programming

John Hebeler
Matthew Fisher
Ryan Blace
Andrew Perez-Lopez

WILEY

Wiley Publishing, Inc.

Semantic Web Programming

Published by
Wiley Publishing, Inc.
10475 Crosspoint Boulevard
Indianapolis, IN 46256
www.wiley.com

Copyright © 2009 by Wiley Publishing, Inc., Indianapolis, Indiana

Published simultaneously in Canada

ISBN: 978-0-470-41801-7

Manufactured in the United States of America

10 9 8 7 6 5 4 3 2

Library of Congress Cataloging-in-Publication Data is available from the publisher.

About the Authors

John Hebeler is an avid, aging, yet still excited explorer of new technologies for the development of large-scale, distributed systems. In the last five years, he has focused on the Semantic Web and emergent, distributed systems. He has published several papers, has co-written a P2P networking book, and presents at major technical conferences around the world. He is currently pursing his PhD in Information Systems at the University of Maryland. He is a division scientist for BBN technologies.

Matthew Fisher has over fifteen years experience in the fields of software and systems development. He has worked in a wide range of engineering environments, ranging from small technology startups and research and development companies to large Fortune 50 firms. He regularly contributes to the Semantic Report and has been involved with conferences such as OWLED, ISWC, and the Semantic Technology Conference. Matthew is a principal systems engineer at Progeny Systems and holds a BS in Computer Science from Penn State University and a MS in Computer Science from George Mason University.

Andrew Perez-Lopez is a software developer who has worked at BBN Technologies since 2005 on large-scale information integration systems using the Semantic Web technologies discussed in this book. He holds an MS in Computer Science from Virginia Tech and an BA in Cognitive Science from the University of Virginia.

Ryan Blace has been a Semantic Web developer and BBN Technologies employee for five years. He works on multiple large-scale Semantic Web–based knowledge management systems for the government and commercial sectors. Ryan holds a BS in Computer Engineering from the University of Maryland and is pursuing his master's in Computer Science at Virginia Tech.

When not spending late nights on his computer hacking away, Ryan spends his time cycling, mountain biking, and instructing at car club track days.

About The Technical Editors

Mike Dean (reviewer/editor) is principal engineer at BBN Technologies, where he has worked since 1984. He started working with Semantic Web in 2000, as a principal investigator in the DARPA Agent Markup Language (DAML) program. He was co-editor of the W3C OWL Reference, a co-author of SWRL, and has developed various Semantic Web tools, data sets, and applications. He currently provides technical direction for a number of Semantic Web projects at BBN. He holds a BS in Computer Engineering from Stanford University.

Mike Smith (technical editor) is a senior engineer at Clark & Parsia LLC, a software development and consulting firm specializing in the development and application of artificial intelligence technologies. Mike is a member of the W3 OWL WG, participates actively in the OWL community, and publishes content at http://clarkparsia.com/weblog/. He is one of the primary developers of Pellet, the open-source OWL reasoner, and frequently contributes to the Protégé and OWL API projects. He holds BS and MS degrees in Systems and Information Engineering from the University of Virginia.

Credits

Executive Editor
Robert Elliott

Development Editor
Christopher J. Rivera

Technical Editor
Michael Smith

Production Editor
Melissa Lopez

Copy Editor
Linda Recktenwald

Editorial Manager
Mary Beth Wakefield

Production Manager
Tim Tate

Vice President and Executive Group Publisher
Richard Swadley

Vice President and Executive Publisher
Barry Pruett

Associate Publisher
Jim Minatel

Proofreader
Corina Copp and Jen Larsen, Word One

Indexer
Ted Laux

Cover Image
Tony Sweet/ Digital Vision/ Getty Images

Acknowledgments

The idea for this book grew over two years with the support of many BBN folks but especially Pete Pflugrath, our Semantic Web visionary; Ted Benson, an all-round awesome dude who motivated us to take on this challenge; Dana Moore, whose ideas and enthusiasm are simply limitless; and Mike Dean, whose boundless knowledge and expertise in all things technological is simply an inspiration to us all.

Strong support went well beyond BBN to include Walt Kitonis, Mike MacKay and Fred Vignovich of Progeny Systems and Gary Sikora for his advocacy of Semantic Web solutions in industry. Also to Tom Dietz, vice president of iJet, a truly rare and special person whose confidence in our abilities never wavered even when ours did.

A special thank-you to Mike Smith for his detailed technical reviews that gave the book its high quality and for keeping us on the leading edge of the rapidly advancing Semantic Web. And thanks to all the folks at Wiley publishing, especially Bob Elliott (our executive editor), whose initial belief in the project made it all possible, and Christopher Rivera (our editor), whose patience and whip kept us in line and writing throughout the entire process.

Contents

Foreword

Our group at BBN Technologies has been working at the forefront of the Semantic Web since 2000, first as part of the DARPA Agent Markup Language (DAML) program and then in developing a variety of tools, data sets, and applications for other government and commercial customers. The authors and technical editor of this book are current or former members of this group, which has grown to about 30 employees. *Semantic Web Programming* reflects our backgrounds as software developers, the experience we've gained over the past eight years, and a number of hard-won insights.

The Semantic Web is an international effort to represent data (including World Wide Web data currently designed for human users) in formats amenable to automated processing, integration, and reasoning. Data is king, and it provides even greater value when it's connected with other data sources to create a linked data web. Current applications include data integration from mash-ups to the enterprise, improved search, service composition, intelligent agents, desktop and mobile applications, and collaboration.

Catalyzed by U.S. and EU research programs, the growing community includes the W3C Semantic Web Activity, a host of large and small vendors, several Semantic Web and Semantic Technology conference series, and a large number of open-source developers and projects.

While Web 3.0 is in many ways an appropriate moniker for the Semantic Web, the Semantic Web has always emphasized Web 2.0 social networking and collaboration aspects through FOAF, RSS 1.0, various semantic wiki projects, and participatory collections such as MusicBrainz. Semantic Web ontologies provide more structure than Web 2.0 tags, microformats, and folksonomies, while retaining much of their flexibility.

Semantic Web standards including RDF, OWL, and SPARQL continue to evolve based on usage. A wide range of high-quality tools, many of them open source, have been developed for different programming environments. The Linking Open Data initiative has addressed a critical need by providing foundational data for many applications and continues to grow. Many tools and applications are now highly scalable.

Developers often benefit from seeing other people's code. Throughout this book, we've taken a pragmatic approach, with lots of examples and an application that spans multiple chapters.

We hope that you'll also find that Semantic Web technologies provide an effective means of addressing current and upcoming computing challenges and that you'll enjoy working with them as much as we have.

Mike Dean
Ann Arbor, Michigan
November 2008

Introduction

Semantic Web Programming takes the Semantic Web directly and boldly into solving practical, real-world problems that flexibly deliver real value from our growing ability to access information and services from our laptop to the enterprise to the World Wide Web. The chapters form a solid, code-based path addressing information and service challenges. As the code examples build, we pragmatically explore the many technologies that form the Semantic Web, including the knowledge representations such as microformats, Resource Description Framework (RDF), RDF Schema (RDFS), the Web Ontology Language (OWL) including its latest release OWL 2 and Semantic Web Rule Language (SWRL), Semantic Web programming frameworks such as Jena, and useful Semantic Web tools. We explore these technologies, not as ends in themselves but rather for their role and merits in solving real problems. Thus, your learning is based on results—the results that each technology brings to address your application challenges.

Semantic Web Programming benefits from our many years of experience in developing large-scale Semantic Web solutions, building Semantic Web tools, and contributing to the Semantic Web standards. We know this stuff! This background provides you with not only an understanding of this new powerful technology but the ability to apply it directly to your real-world application and information challenges.

Overview of the Book and Technology

The Semantic Web offers a powerful, practical approach to gain mastery over the multitude of information and information services. Semantics offer the leverage to make *more* information *better* and not overwhelmingly worse. This requires new data representations that improve our ability to capture and share knowledge and new programming constructs and tools to make this information work for your application.

This book explores it all through actual data formats, working code, and tools. We take a *developer* perspective aimed at application results. We focus the explanations and justifications on what you need to build and manage your Semantic Web applications. The multitude of working code examples throughout the book provides the credibility and insights that truly augment the background and explanatory text. In many cases, the code does the talking. We strongly recommend that you get *hands on* and adjust the examples to your needs. This will help you gain the understanding and perspective necessary to put the Semantic Web to work for you immediately.

How This Book Is Organized

The book has 15 chapters organized in four parts. Also included is an extensive set of references in the appendices for the key technologies.

Part 1: "Introducing Semantic Web Programming," covers Chapters 1 and 2. This section quickly introduces you to Semantic Web programming. Chapter 1, "Preparing to Program a Semantic Web of Data," covers the main Semantic Web concepts and their relationship with one another. This establishes your Semantic Web developer vocabulary. Chapter 1 also points out the advantages and programming impacts; it ends with some compelling examples of the Semantic Web in use today. Chapter 2, "Hello Semantic Web World," dives right into working code with an exhaustive Hello Semantic World Web program. The example takes you from setting up your development environment to using reasoners. The explanations are brief because this chapter is merely an introduction to the rest of the book. This section is critical if you are new to the Semantic Web. Seasoned readers may choose to skim these two chapters.

Part 2, "Foundations of Semantic Web Programming," covers Chapters 3 through 7. Two main areas drive a Semantic Web application: knowledge representation and application integration. This section focuses on the former—representing and manipulating knowledge. Chapter 3, "Modeling Information," establishes the data model through RDF. Chapter 4, "Incorporating Semantics," adds an ontology to create a knowledge model using RDFS and OWL 2. Chapter 5, "Modeling Knowledge in the Real World," exercises the working ontology via application frameworks and reasoners. Chapter 6, "Discovering Information," dives into the knowledge model to extract useful information through search, navigation, and formal queries via SPARQL. Chapter 7, "Adding Rules," rounds out the knowledge representation through an exploration of the semantic rule languages, including the W3C standard SWRL.

Part 3, "Building Semantic Web Applications," covers Chapters 8 through 11. This section deals with the second main area—integrating the knowledgebase with an application that acts upon it. This part provides a solid programming base for the Semantic Web. Chapter 8, "Applying a Programming Framework," fully explores Semantic Web frameworks with extensive examples from the Jena Semantic Web Framework. The chapter ends with an outline of our FriendTracker Semantic Web application. This example spans the next three chapters as we explore methods to integrate, align, and output data and information in many formats and locations. Chapter 9, "Combining Information," focuses on integrating the information into a knowledge model from sources such as relational databases, web services, and other formats. Chapter 10, "Aligning Information," focuses on aligning the data along ontological concepts to unify the disparate information. Chapter 11, "Sharing Information," outputs the information into many formats, including RDFa, microformats, SPARQL endpoints, and more. All along we add to the FriendTracker application to directly demonstrate the programming concepts.

Part 4, "Expanding Semantic Web Programming," covers chapters 12 through 15. Here we build on your solid base of knowledge representation and Semantic Web application development to expand into powerful, useful areas, including semantic services, time and space, Semantic Web architectures and best practices, and unfolding Semantic Web tools that are almost here. Chapter 12, "Developing and Using Semantic Services," adds semantics to services to allow them to participate in the Semantic Web. Chapter 13, "Managing Space and Time," adds space and time considerations to your knowledge representations. Chapter 14, "Applying Patterns and Best Practices," is a retrospective of sorts. It builds on everything we covered so far in the book by presenting a series of architecture patterns for constructing various Semantic Web applications. Chapter 15, "Moving Forward," concludes the book by peering into the future. It focuses on four critical, evolving areas for the Semantic Web: ontology management, advanced integration and distribution, advanced reasoning, and visualization. This provides a solid view into what is on its way in the actively evolving Semantic Web.

Who Should Read This Book

The book provides a comprehensive, practical view for developing applications that use the Semantic Web. The Semantic Web takes advantage of the multitude of distributed information and services that exist in the World Wide Web, the business enterprise, and your personal resources. Therefore, many technical readers would benefit from this book whether you focus on the entire application or only the information.

Developers gain first-hand experience with the many code examples throughout the book. These include both applications developers and information developers who focus on data in its many forms, from database schemas to XML formats. This book provides all the tools, background, and rich examples to jump-start your applications.

Architects gain insights into the role of the Semantic Web within a larger application. The Semantic Web offers many benefits to any system that uses information—which is just about any system—and can quickly extend your system's capabilities to better leverage available information and services. The overall applications serve the system architect, whereas the detailed information and data management areas benefit information architects responsible for data formats and data processing.

Technical management gains insight into the power, risks, and benefits of the Semantic Web. The Semantic Web is a strategic technology—one that truly provides a solution with a significant advantage. It offers a new approach to extremely tough but lucrative challenges that employ vast amounts of information and services. Awareness of the Semantic Web is required for any solution that depends on dynamic information and service resources. The code examples provide credibility to the technology and insights into its own challenges for better planning.

Tools You Will Need

We highly recommend that you reinforce your learning by downloading and customizing the numerous coding examples throughout the book. All the software tools are open source and readily available from the World Wide Web. We include all necessary links and instructions. Your computer is compatible with all of these tools as long your operating system supports a Java 1.5 virtual machine. That's it! As we cover each tool in the book, we provide download, installation, and configuration instructions. In addition, we summarize all the tools with instructions in Appendix F.

What's on the Website

The book comes with an extensive website companion at `http://semwebpro-gramming.org`. Here you can access all related articles, complete code examples, and ontologies, as well as have an opportunity to get involved in the ongoing discussions and activities. The site also contains any book and code updates to reflect the continual expansion and evolution of the Semantic Web. We welcome comments on the book and examples.

Our site includes an active blog and wiki awaiting your contributions and insights. The wiki is a semantic wiki and offers a SPARQL endpoint. Feel free to register for either the blog or the wiki or both and enter questions or get in on the discussion. We find that the best learning occurs through your questions—ask away.

Summary (From Here, Up Next, and So On)

Semantic Web programming is an exciting, powerful new approach to better use the vast information and services available. With all of this power and excitement come a new vocabulary, new tools, and new insights into building working applications. The chapters ahead provide a smooth, expanding path to reveal, in a practical way, methods to build effective Semantic Web applications—applications that incorporate the rich, dynamic information and service landscape accessible today. Let's get going.

Introducing Semantic Web Programming

The goal of this section is to quickly introduce you to Semantic Web programming. This section establishes a launchpad from which you can begin your exploration.

Chapter 1 defines the Semantic Web and the components and concepts critical to programming with it. It identifies, from the programmer's perspective, the characteristics and advantages of the Semantic Web that can be leveraged to provide innovative solutions to common problems. The chapter discusses the many roadblocks, myths, and hype that emerge with any new area of technology like the Semantic Web.

This leads to a brief history of the Semantic Web, which provides a useful perspective on its solid foundations. The Semantic Web is not a flash in the pan but rather an evolutionary step in our ability to share and use information. Finally, the chapter ends by presenting a series of example Semantic Web applications. These examples introduce some of the terms, structures, and programming considerations that you will see throughout the rest of the book. After Chapter 1, you will be ready to jump right into Semantic Web programming.

Chapter 2 is your opportunity to say a solid "Hello" to the Semantic Web. The chapter presents a tour of the canonical "Hello World" example application from the perspective of the Semantic Web. It demonstrates how a Semantic Web knowledge model can integrate with an application and be used to separate domain-specific business logic from the program itself. The tour extends a common example-saying hello to your friends. These "Hellos" build through code examples that touch on the main topics of the book. After quickly establishing your development environment, the tour takes you through setting up an ontology, adding data from multiple sources, aligning different data sources, reasoning, rules, querying, and finally outputting results in various formats. It's a whirlwind tour that gives you a taste of what is to come.

Together, the two chapters in this section provide a quick taste of the book and prepare you to move into the depth of the chapters ahead.

Preparing to Program a Semantic Web of Data

"The Semantic Web is not a separate Web but an extension of the current one, in which information is given well-defined meaning, better enabling computers and people to work in cooperation."

—Tim Berners-Lee

Welcome to Semantic Web programming—a powerful way to access, use, and share information. Our approach gets you programming quickly through hands-on, practical examples. We maintain a programmer's perspective, not a philosopher's perspective, throughout the book. We focus on applying the Semantic Web to real-world solutions rather than long justifications and explanations.

First, we need to establish a Semantic Web programming foundation. This foundation orients you to this new technology with its jargon and its attitude. The foundation also provides a justification for your learning investment, an investment we do not take lightly.

Our approach and examples come from years of building Semantic Web applications. Our applications employ the Semantic Web to make useable sense out of large, distributed information found throughout the World Wide Web.

The objectives of this chapter are to:

- Form a useful, pragmatic definition of the Semantic Web
- Identify the major components of a Semantic Web application and describe how they relate to one another
- Outline how the Semantic Web impacts programming applications
- Detail the roadblocks, myths, and hype regarding the often misunderstood and misused term *Semantic Web*

- Understand the origin and foundation of the Semantic Web
- Gain exposure to different, real-world solutions that employ the Semantic Web

Semantic Web programming introduces many new terms and approaches that are used throughout the book. This chapter offers a preliminary definition, one on which each chapter expands.

The concept map in Figure 1-1 outlines the chapter. Two main legs establish the key areas: the Semantic Web and Programming in the Semantic Web.

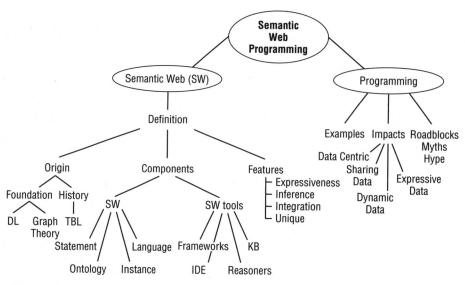

Figure 1-1 Semantic Web concept map

We start with the definition leading to the Semantic Web's components, features, and origins. Then we examine its programming implications.

Defining the Semantic Web

A definition for the Semantic Web begins with defining *semantic*. Semantic simply means *meaning*. Meaning enables a more effective use of the underlying data. Meaning is often absent from most information sources, requiring users or complex programming instructions to supply it. For example, web pages are filled with information and associated tags. Most of the tags represent formatting instructions, such as `<H1>` to indicate a major heading. Semantically, we know that words surrounded by `<H1>` tags are more important to the reader than other text because of the meaning of H1. Some web pages add basic semantics for search engines using the <META> tag; however, they are merely isolated keywords and lack linkages to provide a more meaningful context. These semantics are weak and limit searches to exact matches. Similarly, databases contain data and limited semantic *hints*, if well-named tables and columns surround the data.

Semantics give a keyword symbol useful meaning through the establishment of relationships. For example, a standalone keyword such as *building* exists on a web page devoted to ontologies. The <META> tag surrounds the *building* keyword to indicate its importance. However, does *building* mean constructing an ontology or ontologies that focus on constructing buildings? The awkwardness of the previous sentence points out the difficulty in simply expressing semantics in English. Semantics are left for the human reader to interpret. However, if the keyword relates to other keywords in defined relationships, a web of data or context forms that reveals semantics. So *building* relates to various other keywords such as *architect*, *building plans*, *construction site*, and so on—the relationships expose semantics. If a formal standard captures the arrangement of terms, the terms adhere to specified grammar rules. It is even better if the terms themselves form an adopted standard or language. The two standards together, grammar and language, help incorporate meaning, or semantics. As this contextual web of grammar rules and language terms expands through relationships, the semantics are further enriched.

The Semantic Web is simply a web of data described and linked in ways to establish context or semantics that adhere to defined grammar and language constructs.

Programmatically, your application can add semantics through programming instructions; however, there is no formal standard for such programmed semantics. In addition, aggregation, sharing, and validation are usually difficult or not possible. The semantics are lost in a maze of if/else programming statements, database lookups, and many other programming techniques. This makes it difficult to take advantage of this rich information or even to recognize it all. The nonstandard, dispersed way of programmatic semantic capture places restrictions on it and makes it unnecessarily complex, essentially obfuscated. Standing alone, the meaning of various terms such as *building* is simply lost.

The Semantic Web addresses semantics through standardized connections to related information. This includes labeling data unique and addressable. Thus, your program can easily tell if this *building* is the same as another *building* reference. Each unique data element then connects to a larger context, or *web*. The web offers potential pathways to its definition, relationships to a conceptual hierarchy, relationships to associated information, and relationships to specific instances of *building*. The flexibility of a web form enables connections to all the necessary information, including logic rules. The pathways and terms form a domain vocabulary or ontology. Semantic Web applications typically use many ontologies, each chosen for a required information area. The applications can choose to standardize on specific ontologies and translate to ones employed by other applications. Advanced Semantic Web applications could automatically align vocabularies using advanced information techniques that logically employ the many paths within the Semantic Web. Thus, the rich relationships and the many relationship types each contribute to establish semantics—the Semantic Web.

Figure 1-2 illustrates the difference between a stranded keyword, plane, and a Semantic Web of data related to the keyword, plane. The figure uses a graph perspective for easier visualization of the relationships.

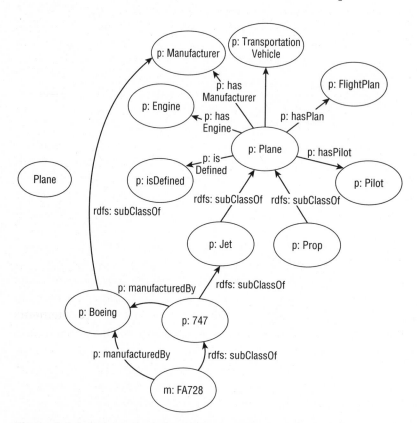

Figure 1-2 Isolation versus the Semantic Web

Shortly we will outline all the major components of the Semantic Web. For now, the fundamental building block of the Semantic Web is a *statement*. This might sound too generic and basic, but this simplicity creates many possibilities. Throughout the book, we explore all types of statements contained in the Semantic Web, statements that describe concepts, logic, restrictions, and individuals. The statements share the same standards to enable sharing and integration, which take advantage of the semantics.

The Semantic Web is best understood in comparison to the World Wide Web (WWW). Table 1-1 compares the two. Rather than being a substitute for the WWW, the Semantic Web extends it through useable, standardized semantics that draw deeply on academic research in knowledge representation and logic to approach the goal of ubiquitous automated information sharing.

Table 1-1 Comparison of WWW and SW

FEATURE	WWW	SEMANTIC WEB
Fundamental component	Unstructured content	Formal statements
Primary audience	Humans	Applications
Links	Indicate location	Indicate location and meaning
Primary vocabulary	Formatting instructions	Semantics and logic
Logic	Informal/nonstandard	Description logic

The WWW consists primarily of content for human consumption. Content links to other content on the WWW via the Universal Resource Locator (URL). The URL relies on surrounding context (if any) to communicate the purpose of the link that it represents; usually the user infers the semantics. Web content typically contains formatting instructions for a nice presentation, again for human consumption. WWW content does not have any formal logical constructs. Correspondingly, the Semantic Web consists primarily of statements for application consumption. The statements link together via constructs that can form semantics, the meaning of the link. Thus, link semantics provide a defined *meaningful* path rather than a user-interpreted one. The statements may also contain logic that allows further interpretation and inference of the statements.

The flexibility and many types of Semantic Web statements allow the definition and organization of information to form rich expressions, simplify integration and sharing, enable inference, and allow meaningful information extractions *while* the information remains distributed, dynamic, and diverse. Simply put, the Semantic Web improves your application's ability to effectively utilize large amounts of diverse information on the scale of the WWW. This is accomplished through a structured, standardized approach for describing information so as to allow rich information operations.

Semantic relationships form the Semantic *Web*. The relationships include definitions, associations, aggregations, and restrictions. A graph helps visualize a collection of statements. Figure 1-3 shows a small graph of statements.

Statements and corresponding relationships establish both concepts (e.g., a Person has a birth date; note the double lines) and instances (e.g., John is a friend of Bill). Statements that define concepts and their relationships form an *ontology*. Statements that refer to individuals form instance data. Statements can be asserted or inferred. The former requires the application to create the statement directly, to assert the statement (solid lines). The latter requires a reasoner to infer additional statements logically (dashed lines). That John is an associate of Bill is inferred from the asserted statements. Future chapters cover these concepts in more detail.

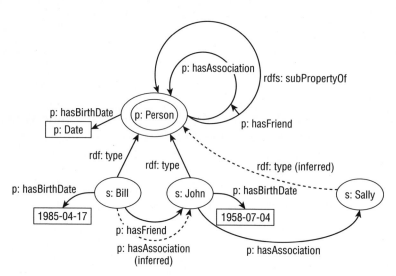

Figure 1-3 Example graph

Semantic Web statements employ a Semantic Web vocabulary and language to identify the different types of statements and relationships. Various tools and application frameworks use the statements through an interpretation of the vocabulary and language. Exploring and applying these tools and frameworks in relationship with the Semantic Web keywords is the focus of this book.

The Semantic Web offers several languages. Rather than have one language fit all information and programming needs, the Semantic Web offers a range from basic to complex. This provides Semantic Web applications with choices to balance their needs for performance, integration, and expressiveness.

A set of statements that contribute to the Semantic Web exists primarily in two forms; knowledgebases and files. Knowledgebases offer dynamic, extensible storage similar to relational databases. Files typically contain static statements. Table 1-2 compares relational databases and knowledgebases.

Table 1-2 Comparison of Relational Databases and KnowledgeBases

FEATURE	RELATIONAL DATABASE	KNOWLEDGEBASE
Structure	Schema	Ontology statements
Data	Rows	Instance statements
Administration language	DDL	Ontology statements
Query language	SQL	SPARQL
Relationships	Foreign keys	Multidimensional
Logic	External of database/triggers	Formal logic statements
Uniqueness	Key for table	URI

Relational databases depend on a schema for structure. A knowledgebase depends on ontology statements to establish structure. Relational databases are limited to one kind of relationship, the foreign key. The Semantic Web offers multidimensional relationships such as inheritance, part of, associated with, and many other types, including logical relationships and constraints. An important note is that the language used to form structure and the instances themselves is the same language in knowledgebases but quite different in relational databases. Relational databases offer a different language, Data Description Language (DDL), to establish the creation of the schema. In relational databases, adding a table or column is very different from adding a row. Knowledgebases really have no parallel because the regular statements define the structure or schema of the knowledgebase as well as individuals or instances. This has many advantages that we will explore in future chapters.

Take a look at the Semantic Web. Go to `http://www.geonames.org` and build a query. The application consists of many integrated information sources. The application is based on the ontology at `http://www.geonames.org/ontology`. Your Semantic Web application could also tap directly into this source and instantly gain access to this large, dynamic knowledgebase. These queries go well beyond simple tag or keyword searching and, therefore, provide a more focused extraction into a large information base.

One last area to consider is the Semantic Web's relationship with other technologies and approaches. The Semantic Web *complements* rather than *replaces* other information applications. It extends the existing WWW rather than competes with it. The Semantic Web offers powerful semantics that can enrich existing data sources, such as relational databases, web pages, and web services, or create new semantic data sources. All types of applications can benefit from the Semantic Web, including standalone desktop applications, mission-critical enterprise applications, and large-scale web applications/services. The Semantic Web causes an evolution in the current Web to offer richer, more meaningful interactions with information. Our solutions throughout the book touch on these areas to illustrate the many ways the Semantic Web can enhance your software solutions.

Identifying the Major Programming Components

A Semantic Web application consists of several discrete components. Future chapters examine each one in detail and the programming examples make extensive use of each. First, we must define each one, note its purpose, and outline how the components contribute to form effective Semantic Web solutions. Some we have already introduced. They fall into two major categories: major Semantic Web components and the associated Semantic Web tools.

Figure 1-4 illustrates the major components surrounded by tools.

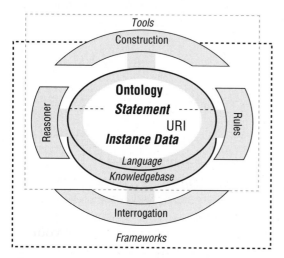

Figure 1-4 Major Semantic Web components

The core components consist of a Semantic Web statement, a Uniform Resource Identifier (URI), Semantic Web languages, an ontology, and instance data.

Statement: The statement forms the foundation of the Semantic Web. Each statement consists of multiple elements that typically form a *triple*. The triple consists of a subject, predicate, and object (e.g., John isType Person). The simplicity belies the aggregated complexity, as a solution combines thousands, even billions of these formal statements. Statements define information structure, specific instances, and limits on that structure. Statements relate to one another to form the data web that constitutes the Semantic Web. The simple approach achieves powerful, flexible expressions.

URI: A Uniform Resource Identifier provides a *unique* name for items contained in a statement *across the entire Internet*. Thus, each component of a statement—subject, predicate, and object—contains a URI to affirm its identity throughout the entire WWW. This eliminates naming conflicts, ensures that two items are the same or not, and can also provide a path to additional information. A URI provides an expansive namespace—key to addressability regardless of scale. A URI could include a Uniform Resource Locator (URL), which may be dereferenced for useful additional information, or an abstract Uniform Resource Name (URN). Thus, the URI can also offer an accessible location contained within the URL. This extends to Internationalized Resource Identifiers (IRIs) covered in Chapter 3.

Language: Statements are expressed in accordance with a Semantic Web language. The language consists of a set of keywords that provide instruction to the various Semantic Web tools. In keeping with the variety and dynamics of the Internet, there are several languages for you to choose from. The languages offer various degrees of complexity and semantic expressiveness. Therefore your Semantic Web solutions can balance performance requirements and expressiveness. Higher levels of expressiveness often demand additional processing and storage resources. Future chapters cover all the terms contained in each language and their purposes.

Ontology: An ontology consists of statements that define concepts, relationships, and constraints. It is analogous to a database schema or an object-oriented class diagram. The ontology forms an information domain model. Many rich ontologies exist for incorporation into your applications. Your applications can use them directly or adapt them to your specific needs. An ontology may capture depth in areas such as finance and medicine, or capture breath in describing common objects, or present a hybrid of depth and breath. An effective ontology encourages communication across applications within the ontology's perspective. Of course, your Semantic Web solutions can create an ontology from scratch, but this isn't our recommendation. Instead, it is best when a Semantic Web application taps into the existing ontologies covering many domains. Using or augmenting an existing ontology leverages a well-thought-out and tested information domain and provides your solution with higher quality and greater development speed. Your added statements can focus on forming the ontology for your specific problem domain while leveraging ontologies from elsewhere.

Instance Data: Instance data is the statements containing information about specific instances rather than a generic concept. *John* is an instance, whereas *person* is a concept or class. This is analogous to objects/instances in an object-oriented program. Interestingly enough, instance data need not bind to the ontology (although in many cases this is quite useful). Instance data forms the bulk of the Semantic Web. An ontology containing the concept *person* may be used by millions of instances of *person*.

In order to exercise the Semantic Web, you need tools and frameworks. Tools come in four types: construction tools to build and evolve a Semantic Web application, interrogation tools to explore the Semantic Web, reasoners to add inference to the Semantic Web, and rules engines to expand the Semantic Web. Semantic frameworks package these tools into an integrated suite.

Construction tools: These tools allow you or your application to construct and integrate a Semantic Web through the creation or import of statements for the ontology and instances. Several GUI-based tools allow you to see and explore your data web to form a useful Semantic Web editor. Several programming suites outline an application-programming interface (API) to integrate with your program.

Interrogation tools: These tools navigate through the Semantic Web to return a requested response. There are various interrogation methods ranging from simple graph navigation, to search, to a full query language. Effective interrogation surfaces the usefulness of the Semantic Web.

Reasoners: Reasoners add inference to your Semantic Web. Inference creates logical additions that offer classification and realization. Classification populates the class structure, allowing concepts and relationships to relate properly to others, such as a *person* is a *living thing, father* is a *parent, married* is a type of *relationship*, or *married* is a *symmetric relationship*. Realization offers the same, for example, the *John H* instance is the same as the *J H* instance. There are several types of reasoners offering various levels of reasoning that future chapters explore. Reasoners often plug into the other tools and frameworks. Reasoners leverage asserted statements to create logically valid ancillary statements.

Rules engines: Rules engines support inference typically beyond what can be deduced from description logic. They add a powerful dimension to the knowledge constructs. Rules enable the merging ontologies and other larger logic tasks, including programming methods such as count and string searches. Rules engines are driven by rules that can be considered part of the overall knowledge representation. Each rule engine adheres to a given rule language. Future chapters explore several of the available rules engines.

Semantic frameworks: These package the tools listed above to work as an integrated unit. Our book focuses on open-source alternatives for both a graphic integrated development environment (IDE) and an application programming interface (API). This allows you to get started programming immediately. There are also several excellent commercial semantic frameworks.

Statements, URIs, languages, ontologies, and instance data make up the Semantic Web, the connected semantic information. Semantic Web tools build, manipulate, interrogate, and enrich the Semantic Web. The book explores both in parallel with growing sophistication with each chapter.

Determining Impacts on Programming

In order for your applications to take full advantage of the Semantic Web and its tools, your applications must adapt to its expectations and impacts. We organize the programming impacts into four categories.

Web data–centric: Your Semantic Web application should place data at its center. Data is key.

Semantic data: Your Semantic Web application should place meaning directly within the data rather than within programming instructions or pushed out for user interpretation.

Data integration/sharing: Your Semantic Web application should attempt to access and share rich information resources throughout the WWW when appropriate, including taking advantage of the many existing data sources.

Dynamic data: Your Semantic Web application should enable dynamic, run-time changes to the structure and contents of your information.

These four impacts potentially change the way you design and program an application. They guide your solution to make optimal use of the Semantic Web. Figure 1-5 illustrates the four programming impacts.

Establishing a Web Data–Centric Perspective

Most applications are centered on programming instructions. They revolve around the program: if/then, while, for, int .... A Semantic Web application is just the opposite. It is all about the data. The richness of Semantic Web data lightens the programming burden. This decouples the data from the programming instructions and produces a cleaner, more flexible solution. The programming instructions focus on programmatic chores while leaving complex information representation within the Semantic Web.

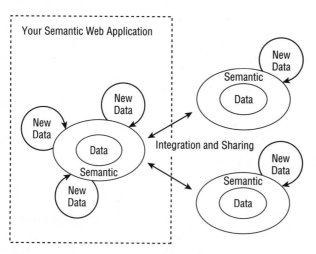

Figure 1-5 Four programming impacts of the Semantic Web

The Semantic Web application is web-centric; it takes advantage of the scale, diversity, and distribution found on the WWW. Many current applications struggle with these issues. They are unable to take full advantage of the WWW and thus remain trapped behind firewalls, serving in a limited, isolated capacity. The Semantic Web takes advantage of the size and diversity of WWW through the establishment of standard, expressive information. It was designed to take advantage of the quantity, diversity, and distribution found in the WWW.

Your programming perspective advances from a small, often-isolated, program-centered perspective (and in this case even enterprise computing could be considered small) to a global, interdependent, web-centered data perspective.

Expressing Semantic Data

The Semantic Web employs a set of new information standards, standards that others can share. As participation and adoption grow, your applications can quickly incorporate new, rich information sources. Standards in the WWW released useful content, mostly for humans. Standards applied in open-source software released powerful programs, many of which became application standards, such as the Apache Web Server. Now Semantic Web standards open up useful, rich information.

The rich standards in the Semantic Web extend well beyond syntax into forming a semantic standard. Syntax enables technical operations through the identification of the actual content. Syntax distinguishes data but not knowledge. Another part of the program—or often the end user—provides the meaning.

Syntax identifies special data items. The syntax of HTML identifies special data items called *tags*. Tags have proven helpful in many information-rich areas like photos and web pages. A single concept can have many tags. Tags can be ambiguous, and it is often difficult to discern what a specific tag means. Tags are often atomic and isolated; a *boat* tag is completely independent from a *yacht* tag. Without semantics, a boat tag and yacht tag reveal no similarities. The Semantic Web goes *beyond tags*. The Semantic Web connects these concepts through its web to improve the semantics and construct an expansive context for application consumption.

The Semantic Web enables *higher levels of information expressiveness*. Limits on information expressiveness challenge programming solutions. Variables, structures, relational tables, and so on all have their limits and peculiarities. Databases, for example, typically constrain the type of data (e.g., integer) but not its use (e.g., only on Fridays) or range (e.g., values between 5 and 9). Applications must absorb this lack of expressiveness through additional programming instructions. Thus, valuable knowledge is distributed haphazardly between data storage and programming instructions due to its inherent limitations. This often leads to brittle, inflexible code and misinterpretations, multiple interpretations, and errors. The Semantic Web offers extensive methods to define information, its relationships to other information, its conceptual heritage, and logical formation. This allows your program to capture more of its intelligence in one standardized way—the Semantic Web.

Relationships take on a primary role in the Semantic Web. In fact, they are the very fabric of the Semantic Web. Object-oriented solutions make relationships secondary to the objects themselves. Relationships do not exist outside of an object. Relationships are dependent on their associated object class. Relationships cannot be repurposed for other classes. Relationships in the Semantic Web exist distinct from the concepts that they join. Relationships are free to join any collection of statements. This allows relationships to have inheritance and restriction rules of their own. For example, a social network relationship within the Semantic Web could offer an `associatedWith` relationship that contains a subrelationship `ownsBy` and another subrelationship `friendOf`. Figure 1-6 illustrates an example graph of these relationships.

Due to the inheritance of the `associatedWith` relationship, an application could query for all `associatedWith` data. This would include both people and, in this case, cars.

Similarly, statements that refer to instances, or instance statements, are also held in distinct regard. Instances are somewhat analogous to objects in an object-oriented solution. An object in an object-oriented solution is dependent on its defined class. In fact, the object is defined as an instance of its associated class. The object's identity emerges directly from its classes. An object is bound for its lifetime to its class. The Semantic Web offers flexibility with instances. An instance is not permanently bound to any class or set of classes. In fact, an instance can have no class at all and merely stand alone as an instance statement or be associated with multiple classes. This allows the application to add instances before it understands their connections to classes. Your application can dynamically change the association of an instance with its class. Your application can also assign multiple classes to a given instance. This allows the flexibility to form and capture information independent from class definitions. These assignments of instances to class can occur at any time.

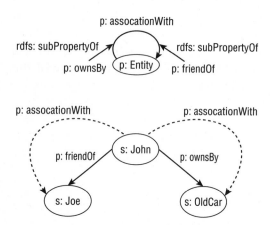

Figure 1-6 Semantic Web relationships

Fundamentally, the Semantic Web offers a new way to describe and share information, a description that flexibly contains and reveals its semantics.

Sharing Data

The ability to exchange information greatly increases the information's value. Easy information exchanges allow the applications to use the best, most up-to-date information rather than forming the information from scratch. Easy exchange also leads to real reuse.

The Semantic Web enables semantic *machine readability* for exchanging information between applications. Semantic machine readability goes beyond the mere exchange of bits to exchange meaning. This is especially important for large, distributed data exchanges typical of the WWW. Large data integration belies significant challenges in data friction and data failures. These challenges represent the part of the *integration iceberg* that is below the surface, large and hidden from the original integration task. Similar to an iceberg's hidden mass, these challenges often reveal themselves at stressful, challenging times.

Data friction results from the misalignment of the data due to different technologies and data models. For instance, an Oracle database has a table that refers to a *Person*, and a MySQL database has a corresponding table that refers to an *Individual*. One information source is centered on *work organizations*; another application is centered on *members*. Each data source maintains its own perspective based on its needs. Neither is wrong, but integrating them creates friction that's usually ameliorated through extensive and complex translation programming code. Semantic Web solutions reduce this friction through semantics that relate similar concepts using Semantic Web statements. This externalizes the friction, allowing the Semantic Web to directly address it.

Data failures result from missing data, conflicting data, and incorrect data. Large integrations are full of data failures. The semantics and logic structure that form the Semantic Web add missing data as well as the identification and sometimes correction of data errors and data conflicts. The flexibility of the Semantic Web allows these corrections to occur continuously as the data is integrated or modified. Continuous correction allows the resolution of data failures to occur gracefully throughout the data's life. There is no need for one big data cleanup activity usually demanded in other data approaches. The Semantic Web produces more useful, shareable, and up-to-date data resources. It pragmatically deals with the realities of large-scale data integration.

Naming represents a challenge to sharing information. A name identifies the information and possibly its location. Many computer resources, such as data in a database, have a name, a table name, a variable name, or the like. A useful name distinguishes it from other related resources. The related resources occupy a *namespace* where all names promise uniqueness. In order to leverage the WWW namespace, a resource must establish uniqueness across the entire WWW or else face limitations with related resources. Many namespaces limit scope even within the WWW. For example, AOL buddies maintain a namespace distinct from Yahoo buddies. Each buddy remains unique only to its associated Instant Messaging service. Semantic Web artifacts are *inherently* unique across the full span of the Internet. In addition, names are even more useful if they provide information as to the resource's location. A URL provides both a unique name and a location (along with the possibility of additional information). Elements within the Semantic Web are uniquely identified with Uniform Resource Identifiers (URIs), which can also contain a resolvable location, if so desired.

Machine readability, data friction and data failure management, and unique, resolvable names foster a much smoother path to large-scale data integration and sharing than other approaches.

Making Data Dynamic and Flexible

Dynamic change is a tenet of the WWW. It is continuous and often unexpected. Yet many applications are frozen and trapped by their initial requirements. This is especially true with data and its representations. Many data representations are, therefore, perpetually designed to address yesterday's requirements. Freeing that data from traditional approaches is possible, but it comes at a high price, increased complexity. A typical workaround to deal with change reuses database strings for new and sometimes multiple purposes. One application uses the database string field for status information for its customers in the database. Another application uses the same string field for pending adjustments to its customers. Sooner or later the two incompatible approaches collide or surrender to the increasing complexity. The technique works for a short time but eventually implodes. Properly designed Semantic Web applications allow the inclusion of new data at any time. This allows the Semantic Web application to gracefully align with current needs and avoids the traditional workarounds found in brittle designs.

The Semantic Web enables information to *figure things out* through inference. Imagine information that adds information to itself, by itself. This is a power that few information technologies offer. Once information has been properly described, a reasoner can infer new relationships. For example, say your information contains the following two facts; *John is a male, a male is a type of person*. The system could infer that *John is a person*. Thus, a query requesting all persons would return *John*. Of course, this is a simple, straightforward example, but it serves to illustrate one of the principal benefits of encoding the semantics of data along with the raw values themselves. A reasoner can also identify logical contradictions within your information. For instance, if you made the claim that men and women are mutually exclusive groups, and somewhere was the datum that John is a female, then the reasoner could use the information from above to recognize contradictory data. Of course, this is obvious and simple, but as the statements get more numerous, complex contradictions are much more difficult to identify.

Inference makes each data item more valuable, because it can have an effect on the creation of new information. This can be both positive and negative. Each new piece of information has the capacity to add a great deal of new information via inference, but that means that extra care must be taken to validate new information. The inference process, just like all computer systems, is vulnerable to the "garbage in, garbage out" phenomenon, but inference amplifies this concern.

The Semantic Web provides meaningful links between related bits of information, a new form of *information navigation*. This semantic metadata allows a new type of information discovery and flexibility. You could start at one point in the Semantic Web and explore it following a particular set of relationships. For example, you could start at information about a friend, then follow the relationship to her friends to find out their interests. One friend of your friend might have an interest new to you, so you could follow a link to a definition of the interest. Maybe it sounds interesting, and you've found a new hobby—and possibly a new friend, too! Naturally you can follow links on web pages to do this already. But the Semantic Web offers the possibility of having a program do it just as easily. Traditional searching and querying serve as a nice complement to this sort of semantic navigation.

The Semantic Web is dynamic. An application can add information at any point. Concepts can evolve at any time to become more useful or precise. The WWW is a lively place, and the Semantic Web provides technologies to leverage that change rather than avoid it. When amplified by the power of inference, one new statement could ripple through the knowledgebase to transform it into a more useful form. Similarly, that statement could be removed, and the information would be back to its original state.

Finally, the Semantic Web is inclusive. The Semantic Web's ability to express information flexibly makes it ideal to incorporate other forms of data. The Semantic Web can include semantic translation rules and statements allowing the incorporation of other types of data from relational databases, XML web services, and even simple comma-separated lists. Future chapters illustrate each of these techniques. Therefore, these Semantic Web techniques can unify and enrich other information sources and services. This is vital capability, because much of the valuable information on the Internet, in the enterprise, or on your laptop is *not* currently part of the Semantic Web.

The Semantic Web impacts require a new perspective in developing applications, a perspective based on a data-centric model leveraging large amounts of diverse, distributed data that contains greater expressiveness, easier sharing, and greater flexibility.

Avoiding the Roadblocks, Myths, and Hype

The new programming perspective must overcome the various misunderstandings already present in the nascent Semantic Web. Roadblocks, myths, and hype cloud your ability to move straight into programming, sometimes stopping you altogether. If not affecting you, they may block the way for your team or organization to take advantage of the Semantic Web. Sometimes the largest hurdles are the ones we make up.

Semantic Web Roadblocks

Roadblocks can stop programming efforts dead in their tracks before they gain momentum. We deal with three: web-centric development; taking comfort in dirty, conflicting data; and dealing with the dynamic addition of new data.

Technically the Semantic Web demands a new perspective on information. Think how relational database technology creates a *data perspective*, a perspective based on the low-level details of tables, columns, rows, and keys. Now you must establish a Semantic Web data perspective. This perspective has two parts: data-centric programming and distributed information programming.

We previously covered web data–centric impact, but unfortunately it can also become a roadblock to using the Semantic Web effectively.

In addition, information is never all in one place. Traditional approaches seek to provide integration via the Extract, Transform, and Load (ETL) approach. This involves a laborious process of acquiring the information, transforming it, and finally integrating it into some single, unified store. This approach has several problems: it does not scale; it incurs latency, leading to incorrect information; it is error prone; it doesn't handle change well; and it has a single point of failure. The small scope of most traditional applications reduces the seriousness of these challenges, but the applications remain constrained by them. Integrating via Semantic Web programming means creating an interface with the real source and not usually copying it. Real-time semantic translations allow your solution to scale while maintaining up-to-date information. Accordingly, Semantic Web solutions must also deal with performance issues and resource failures due to the distributed nature of the Semantic Web.

The second roadblock is the failure to recognize dirty, noisy data as an advantage. The WWW is full of data, lots of it. Some of it is useful, some of it is not, and some of it is just plain wrong. Traditional solutions that attempt to incorporate such data try to *fix* and *correct* the data prior to using it. Subscribing programs assume the data is clean and correct. Again, a small application may actually correct all its data, but that is simply not a possibility for the global information space of the WWW. Instead, large data integration produces dirty, noisy information with apparent conflicts, duplication, and errors. In order to *fix it*, your program would first have to know the truth. Unfortunately, often in the WWW there is no ground truth, no overriding authority. Rather than mount the quixotic struggle to right all the wrongs, a Semantic Web application can operate effectively within this global mess. A Semantic Web application creates concepts that it considers useful for its needs. These concepts can incorporate dirty information or not. For example, a Semantic Web application could collect vendor feedback scores from several sites and create a *reputation* concept for vendors. The concept can choose to include information or not, depending on your concerns and values for a given situation. Conflicting information could be incorporated into the concept, possibly lowering the confidence in the reputation. Likewise, supporting information could increase the confidence. The flexibility of the semantics enables applications to define reputation in different ways and manage conflicting information. This flexibility allows an application to incorporate all or some of the relevant information and map it to its specific concept. Traditional applications fail to offer such flexibility or take advantage of this flexibility. Similarly, a Semantic Web application can handle missing data or incorrect data, as you shall see when we cover reasoning and related topics.

The dynamic flexibility of the Semantic Web can also form a roadblock. A Semantic Web application is not nailed down like traditional applications. The dynamic nature requires your application to manage change. Your Semantic Web application must remain open to possibilities, at any time. Remaining open is not a perspective easily gained. A Semantic Web application is designed to handle new, incoming information. As mentioned previously, this information could be conflicting or contain errors. A Semantic Web application maintains a nimble, agile view to data. It is not as fixed and controlled as traditional database applications. Many upcoming examples will help to provide a more concrete view of this important perspective.

So beware of these roadblocks: programming instructions over the creation of statements for the Semantic Web, trying to gather all the data into one place, and fearing the dynamics that the Semantic Web allows. Heeding these road-blocks causes Semantic Web solutions that mimic the constraints of traditional systems and thereby fail to gain the full advantages of the Semantic Web.

Semantic Web Myths

Several myths can also impede your efforts. They were founded in the development of traditional systems: developing one data model, developing one data view, and the inability to accept change à la the human acceptance myth.

Building the *one* of anything has been the scourge of technical progress. Have you been involved in building the *one* corporate database, the *one* enterprise framework, the *one* perfect web service? One of the biggest myths of the Semantic Web and one sure to undermine its success is the pursuit of the one big information model. We have seen several efforts stumble over this unachievable challenge with lengthy debates (*is a thing an object?*). Do not fall into this trap. It is the black hole of the Semantic Web, where effort goes in and nothing ever comes out. Even in some other universe where it works, it ultimately won't scale anyway. The Semantic Web is designed to support a multitude of distributed information sources with a multitude of perspectives. Your solutions need to maintain this perspective; *you should too*. The Semantic Web mirrors the WWW itself, so a Semantic Web application seeks to leverage the Web's vast distributed information. This small paragraph will not stop the insanity of others from pursuing the one perfect model, but hopefully it will stop you. If you hear someone discussing the one big data model, run!

The next myth, which aligns perfectly with the one model, is the one view. The Semantic Web allows a solution to provide deep customized views into information. This freedom is at the very heart of the Semantic Web. Rather than be a straightjacket of control, an effective Semantic Web application allows any view for information analysis. Accordingly, this multiple-information perspective aligns perfectly with agile methods. Even in a limited-scope information source, it is unlikely that your initial design will work perfectly. The same ability to absorb other information sources easily works to absorb your future changes. This also stops the initial paralyzing steps of nailing the perfect, albeit limited, information model. This perspective allows you to get started quickly and then adapt and evolve as the development unfolds. Accordingly, this also encourages a decoupled, modular design. Multiple views also help manage the dirty-data phenomena. What is one person's data dirt may provide someone else with a useful insight.

In addition, both the one information model and the one view suffer from a further myth, Not Invented Here (NIH). The Semantic Web encourages just the opposite. A Semantic Web solution should first look for existing semantic sources and then add customizations. Only the last resort creates an information source from scratch.

Finally, the acceptance myth: Change is difficult, and we have never experienced a Semantic Web implementation that was instantly accepted. New technologies, especially those dealing with sensitive data, scare people, as they should. Change also scares people. You need to address this up front and prepare for resistance. As with all new technologies and approaches, there is risk; however, risk works both ways: positive and negative. Positive risk may provide your application with a real advantage compared with traditional approaches. Negative risk may saddle your application with extra training and support costs. Simply play up the positives by taking advantage of the Semantic Web and work to mitigate the disadvantages. Face this directly and honestly to maximize the benefits while realizing that nothing is a silver bullet.

Semantic Web Hype

Hype dooms a technology, for it overpromises (lies), and in doing so, it disappoints, just as we need to invest and learn it. As with any major technology, the Semantic Web is full of hype, some positive and some negative. Much of the hype comes from its artificial intelligence (AI) roots. In the 1980s, AI had everyone excited about the friendly computer agent that would achieve a level of sentience. Videos demonstrated computers of the future that offered human insights and capabilities. This, of course, didn't happen and produced a cynical view of powerful AI research. AI had stunning successes, but much of this was buried under the disappointment caused by the hype. Adding semantics through relationships and logic does not achieve AI. The Semantic Web did, however, incorporate excellent AI research of the past decades. The Semantic Web offers a useful improvement in leveraging information. It is an evolutionary step in making our information work harder for us. In ways, the Semantic Web helps fulfill some of the AI goals by providing a rich, expressive data form that is machine readable, but the Semantic Web will not achieve sentience anytime soon.

Hype can also make a complex technology seem too simple. Tough, challenging problems demand complex technical solutions. Would you want your MRI performed by a hacked Visual Basic script? Complexity is valuable as long as it remains focused on the problem. Unnecessary complexity in the solution makes the problem's complexity that much more difficult. Modern computer languages have removed much of the complexity of the underlying computer resources so that applications can step up to more complex solutions. Similarly, the Semantic Web has removed much of the complexity of forming and exchanging complex information. It has not removed the complexity of the information itself but rather enabled its capture. Rocket science is still rocket science, but now information about it can be more easily expressed, shared, and reasoned over. The Semantic Web reduces unnecessary complexity to focus on the necessary complexity, that of managing all the information and knowledge we produce.

Finally, hype can overpromise the inherent challenges in using a new technology. Our efforts in the real world took us into areas of the Semantic Web that have never been applied to real solutions. We braved this world so that you don't have to. That doesn't mean that it is all finished. Much remains to be done, and it is our hope that you will contribute to its advancement. The Semantic Web is improving with large investments across the globe, but it is not without its growing pains. That is simply the truth in working with any new, emerging, and evolving technology. Do not expect a perfect world with respect to tools, frameworks, and the semantic language itself. You may hit some bumps, but hang in there; it will be worth it.

Understanding Semantic Web Origins

The origin of the Semantic Web comes from the quest to externalize knowledge. Despite a long history of advancements, the quest remains for us today. We have tried in so many ways and yet remain frustrated with our efforts. Read *Gödel, Escher, Bach: An Eternal Golden Braid* by Douglas R. Hofstadter (Basic Books, 1999) if you want some reassurance that the human brain processes information in ways we simply don't understand. It is no surprise we have trouble translating information to a machine. The computer demands exactness and precision, two areas that humans often fudge. Herein lies the dilemma: Computers can do useful things only if we explain those things in excruciating, precise, and consistent detail. This struggle has produced many types of data, information, and even knowledge formats. Commonly we can refer to them as forms of knowledge representation. They include network databases, relational databases, tree structures, objects, messages, and the like. Along this path, we collectively have learned what works and what doesn't work for different problems. Often it is not an absolute answer but a contextual one. The Semantic Web is no different. It does not so much replace these approaches as give you a new approach. It embraces a new form of knowledge representation, a knowledge representation that leverages and improves on some previous methods.

The Semantic Web gained wide visibility following an article in *Scientific American* by Tim Berners-Lee, James Hendler, and Ora Lassila (`http://www.sciam.com/article.cfm?id=the-semantic-web`). The article outlined a pragmatic vision to improve the value of the information contained in the World Wide Web. It foretold many of the characteristics noted previously: machine readability, easy information integration, information inference, unique naming, and rich representations, among others. This led the authors to make a bold statement: "The Semantic Web can assist the evolution of human knowledge as a whole." Bold but possible, given the current extent of information on the World Wide Web. We know that many answers to our questions are out there, but due to the current human-only readable form of the data, they remain only a tantalizing possibility. How many web pages can you digest to form an answer? How many do you need to read to gather all the little pieces that together form the answer you seek?

The Semantic Web did not emerge out of just one seminal paper, but many. The Semantic Web is based on sound, proven information techniques built on centuries of scholarly contributions. Two major disciplines contributed to the Semantic Web: graph theory and description logic.

Graph theory is at the heart of the Semantic Web. A graph represents nodes and relationships. Stepping back from the WWW, you can recognize a graph-like structure or web through its many hyperlinks. Graph origins predate, by quite a bit, the World Wide Web and even computer technology more generally. Graph theory started with a seminal paper from 1736: "The Seven Bridges of Königsberg," by Leonhard Euler, the famous mathematician. This paper provided a solution to a basic question. Is there a route that allows the traveler to cross each of the seven bridges of Königsberg once and return to the starting point? The answer is *no*, and he solved it using a new branch of math, graph theory. With graph theory, he could *prove* that it is not possible. His graphs imply the answer. The only other approach is brute force—*try each path*. This is not only a tedious, exhausting method, but it leaves the questioner with troubling doubts, for it is possible that an untried path does exist. The search for a traveling route forms the foundation of establishing routes to useful information on the Web. Semantic Web solutions tap directly into the mathematical advantages that graph theory offers. This leads to data processing efficiencies.

Description logic also goes back, but not quite as far. Several papers outline the basics in the 1980s. Description logic holds the rules to construct valid, useful knowledge representations, knowledge representations that are decidable, representations that can actually produce an answer. Undecidable representations result in representations that wrap around themselves, never reaching any conclusions. It derives from first-order logic. It defines expressions that are, well, *logical*, a formalism for representing knowledge (see *An Introduction to Description Logics* by Daniele Nardi and Ronald J. Brachman (Cambridge University Press, 2002). Description logic resulted from years of AI research aimed at capturing rich knowledge in an explicit, externalized form. Description logic makes information explicit rather than tacit. Tacit information is what gets diffused in traditional applications via if/else, special values, and shortcuts, because only humans really understand it (and we have trouble articulating it). The externalized form reveals the information for verification, integration, reasoning, and interrogation. Description logic includes many types of relationships beyond inheritance to provide the flexibility to form rich, complex concepts that maintain defendable logic. These external forms researched and proved in description logic translate into Semantic Web constructs. Thus, your Semantic Web programs can now take full advantage of description logic. Your Semantic Web application can tap directly into this powerful expression of information.

Why mention this history? Good ideas are good ideas, ideas that take many forms over the ages. The Semantic Web is the latest manifestation of graph theory and description logic. Your Semantic Web applications form instances of these advancements. Your programming efforts in the Semantic Web spring from this solid theoretical ground. You can defend your pursuit and your solutions. How many others could refer to a work from 1736 and exercise useful nuggets from AI? Semantic Web solutions incorporate advanced information theory. The pursuit of paths through bridges and information itself led to the new technologies that underlie the Semantic Web.

The Semantic Web is built not only on mathematical theories but also on fundamental Internet technologies and philosophies. The success of the WWW has taught us not to go it alone, at least if a technology wants to survive. Build success on other proven successes. The Semantic Web is no different. The Semantic Web supports the inclusive and evolutionary nature of the WWW. The Semantic Web layer cake illustration in Figure 1-7 demonstrates some key dependencies such as URLs and XML that form the foundation of the Semantic Web.

Figure 1-7 also shows that future Semantic Web capabilities will deal with trust and providence. Semantic Web applications also utilize Internet services such as DNS and even traditional relational database technologies found in implementations such as Oracle and MySQL. More fundamental than that, the Semantic Web depends on existing information sources, the more semantic the better. Successful Semantic Web solutions reach out to many diverse sources to fulfill their larger information need. This fits with the recently formed Web 2.0 philosophy, a philosophy based on extensive integration and user contributions. Examples include Google maps, MySpace.com, Flickr.com, and Facebook.com. Semantic Web solutions make the most of available technologies. In addition, like any Web 2.0 technology, the Semantic Web benefits with each new additional application and information source. It benefits from the virtuous cycle of wide-scale contributions that established Web 2.0.

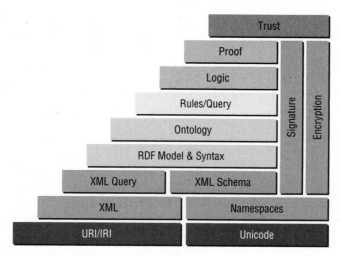

Figure 1-7 Semantic Web layer cake

The origin of the Semantic Web begins with our pursuit of externalizing what we know. It benefited from key advancements in graph theory and description logic to produce a viable knowledge representation that values existing technologies, applications, and data sources.

Exploring Semantic Web Examples

Now we'll demonstrate some actual Semantic Web information sources and applications. The following examples highlight some of the advantages of the Semantic Web applications. The examples include a variety in order to highlight key semantic features.

Semantic Wikis (*semantic-mediawiki.org*)

Wikis collaboratively build useful websites; however, the easy creation of content, web pages, and links belies the difficulty of fully leveraging the content. Wikis depend heavily on human-entered links. Content becomes stranded or just plain lost if the link doesn't exist on an obvious page. The links themselves are almost nonsensical due to their automatic, dynamic creation. Semantic wikis allow the collaborators to enter semantics. This allows a user to query the wiki or semantically navigate to find information rather than just depending on the native links. In addition, applications can query the content and reuse it. This is vital as the wiki grows beyond a few pages. Since the wiki participates in the Semantic Web, inference and other tools can add to its value. The contributors enter semantic properties, and the associated values are bound to the entered content. The Semantic wiki can export the semantics to a file or an external application. This book was developed using a semantic wiki for collaboration and discussion. Figure 1-8 illustrates a basic query to find content.

Figure 1-8 Semantic wiki

There are several rapidly evolving semantic wikis. They hold the promise to manage and leverage large amounts of user created content.

Twine (*www.twine.com*)

Twine is all about relationships, information relationships. From these relationships, other relationships, such as social relationships, emerge. The result is a *knowledge network*. It employs the Semantic Web to construct and manage many of these relationships. You can easily add information and meta-information from all types of sources, such as RSS feeds, emails, blogs, and direct file downloads. Figure 1-9 illustrates a twine about the ontologies.

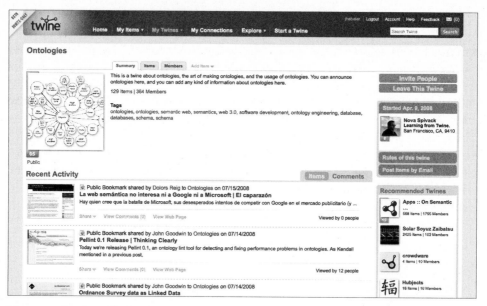

Figure 1-9 Twine relationships

Figure 1-10 illustrates adding information to an existing twine, in this case the BBN Semantic Web twine.

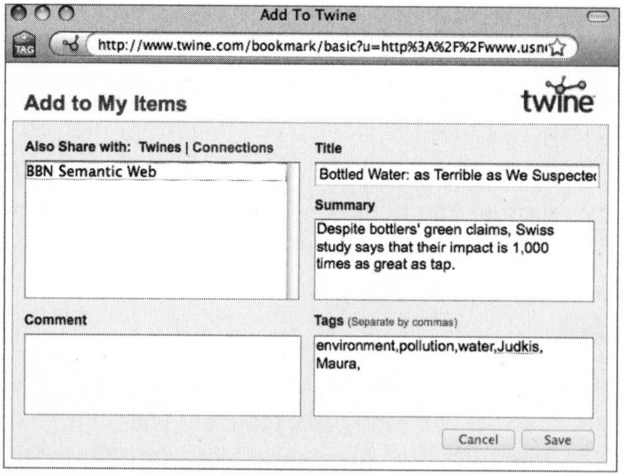

Figure 1-10 Contributing to a twine

The FOAF Project (*www.foaf-project.org*)

FOAF is not so much an application as an ontology used by many applications, including major ones discussed later in this book. The Friend of a Friend (FOAF) project was one of the first to recognize the simple power of social networks. The FOAF project offers tools to relate people through a model that contains typical social attributes such as a name, email address, interests, and the like. Tools allow you to create a model describing yourself (see `www.ldodds.com/foaf/foaf-a-matic`). The following code below is a FOAF file in TURTLE format (more on that later) describing some fictitious folks we explore in the next chapter. It contains basic information and their relationships to each other. Believe it or not, this basic start is a solid foundation for forming rich social networks. Future sections expand on this concept, including the next chapter that builds a Hello World semantic application.

```
<http://org.semwebprogramming/chapter2/people>
        rdf:type foaf:PersonalProfileDocument ;
        admin:errorReportsTo
                <mailto:leigh@ldodds.com> ;
        admin:generatorAgent
                <http://www.ldodds.com/foaf/foaf-a-matic> ;
        foaf:maker <http://org.semwebprogramming/chapter2/people#me> ;
        foaf:primaryTopic <http://org.semwebprogramming/chapter2/people#me> .


<http://org.semwebprogramming/chapter2/people#me>
        rdf:type foaf:Person ;
        foaf:depiction <http://semwebprogramming.org/semweb.jpg> ;
        foaf:family_name "Web" ;
        foaf:givenname "Semantic" ;
        foaf:homepage <http://semwebprogramming.org> ;
        foaf:knows
<http://org.semwebprogramming/chapter2/people#Reasoner> ,
<http://org.semwebprogramming/chapter2/people#Statement> ,
<http://org.semwebprogramming/chapter2/people#Ontology> ;
        foaf:mbox <mailto:dataweb@gmail.com> ;
        foaf:name "Semantic Web" ;
        foaf:nick "Webby" ;
        foaf:phone <tel:410-679-8999> ;
        foaf:schoolHomepage <http://www.web.edu> ;
        foaf:title "Dr" ;
        foaf:workInfoHomepage
                <http://semwebprogramming.com/dataweb.html> ;
```

```
foaf:workplaceHomepage
        <http://semwebprogramming.com> .

<http://org.semwebprogramming/chapter2/people#Reasoner>
    rdf:type foaf:Person ;
    rdfs:seeAlso <http://reasoner.com> ;
    foaf:mbox <mailto:reason@firefox.com> ;
    foaf:name "Ican Reason" .
<http://org.semwebprogramming/chapter2/people#Statement>
    rdf:type foaf:Person ;
    rdfs:seeAlso <http://statement.com> ;
    foaf:mbox <mailto:mstatement@adobe.com> ;
    foaf:name "Makea Statement" .

<http://org.semwebprogramming/chapter2/people#Ontology>
    rdf:type foaf:Person ;
    rdfs:seeAlso <http://ont.com> ;
    foaf:mbox <mailto:ont@gmail.com> ;
    foaf:name "I. M. Ontology" .
```

The FOAF project encourages everyone to create and publish his or her FOAF model. Model readers can then recognize and incorporate this information into a contact list or a search response. Many existing web pages contain FOAF information.

RDFa and Microformats

Similar to FOAF, microformats and RDFa are also formats employed by many applications. These enter semantics directly into a typical XHTML web page. This demonstrates description data sharing using semantic formats. Tools integrated into the browser recognize these semantics and offer capabilities to use the semantics information. Although a small step, it is a step in the right direction. The lack of semantics on a basic web page makes search much more difficult. Microformats are a big improvement over screen scraping, which is a very brittle approach to obtaining information. A microformat could describe a contact as including a FOAF model, an event, resumes, job offerings, and much more. There are dozens of standard microformats, each for different types of information. See www.microformats.org for an extensive list. The Firefox extension, Semantic Radar, inspects web pages for semantic content and indicates this content via icons on the Firefox status bar. The web page illustration, Figure 1-11, contains several icons in the lower right that provide links to the underlying RDF files, including a FOAF description. The second illustration, Figure 1-12, is the Ontology Online website.

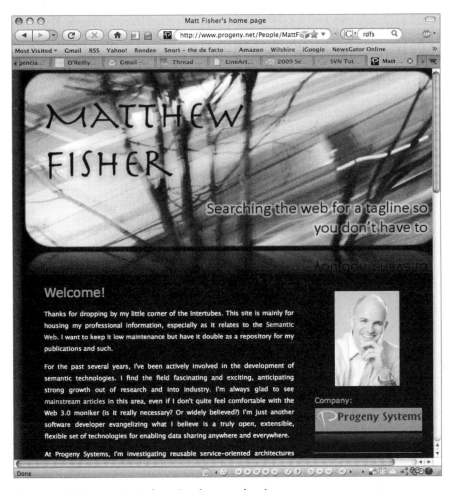

Figure 1-11 Semantic Radar microformat plug-in

Semantic Radar provides a path to the semantic information. A partnering application could take this information and populate your calendar, your contact list, or your social networks. There is no easy way to accomplish this simple knowledge transfer without an agreed-upon semantics.

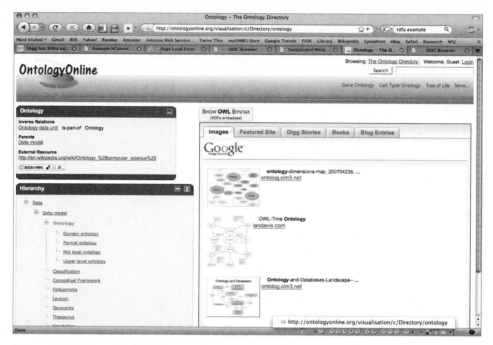

Figure 1-12 Semantic Radar example

Semantic Query Endpoint (*dbpedia.org/sparql*)

A semantic query endpoint offers the ultimate information exposure: a URL that answers your questions formed from a standard semantic query language, SPARQL. We focus on semantic query languages with SPARQL (SPARQL Protocol and RDF Query Language) in Chapter 7, "Adding Rules" but just note that the full power of that query can be directly exposed via the Web. This forms a Semantic Web offering. Without all the background, you can still give it try (`dbpedia.org/sparql`). Figure 1-13 illustrates a query response.

Semantic Search (*www.trueknowledge.com*)

Search is made much more powerful with the addition of semantics. Although still in beta, True Knowledge moves into this space. Others include www.opencalais.com and www.powerset.com. Figure 1-14 demonstrates the power of semantic search.

Some semantic wikis also offer up their content via a SPARQL endpoint.

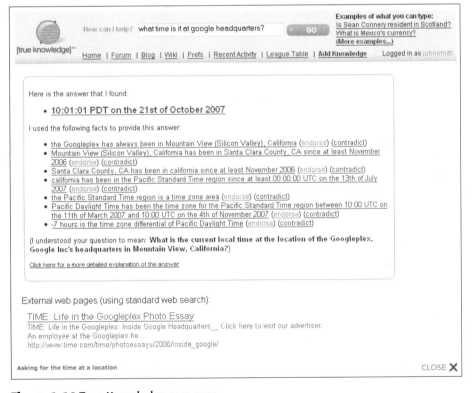

Figure 1-13 dppedia–SPARQL endpoint

Figure 1-14 True Knowledge response

Okay, that gives you a taste of the possibilities ahead. On to forming your first Semantic Web application, the Hello Semantic World Tour, in the next chapter.

Summary and Onward

Your Semantic Web conceptual foundation is now established. The Semantic Web offers a new, more powerful way to create and share information. Its logical and standardized definition enables advanced information processing such as inference and validation. The Semantic Web requires a new programming perspective, one that turns distributed, confusing, and massive information into real solutions.

The Semantic Web has its fair share of roadblocks, myths, and hype. Seeing past these helps ensure a positive programming experience with a successful outcome. The Semantic Web is solidly grounded on graph theory and description logic. It provides a knowledge representation that is defendable and worthy of your investment.

Semantic Web programming consists of core components: statements, the URI, an ontology, and instance data managed and formed through the various construction tools, interrogation tools, reasoners, and rules.

Now, get programming—say hello to the Semantic Web Tour.

Notes

1. W3C Semantic Web Activity home page, http://www.w3.org/2001/sw/, which is ground zero for the Semantic Web URLs

2. "Expressiveness and Tractability in Knowledge Representation and Reasoning," Hector J. Levesque and Ronald J. Brachman

3. "Ontology Driven Architectures and Potential Uses of the Semantic Web in Systems and Software Engineering," eds. Phil Tetlow and Jeff Z. Pan (W3C Working Group, 2003)

4. An Introduction to Description Logics, Daniele Nardi and Ronald J. Brachman (Cambridge University Press, 2002)

5. "Ontology-Driven Software Development in the Context of Semantic Web: An Example Scenario with Protégé/OWL," Holger Knublach

6. "An Introduction to Model Driven Architecture," Alan Brown (IBM, 2004)

7. "A Semantic Web Primer for Object-Oriented Software Developers" (W3C Working Group, 2006)

## CHAPTER 2

Hello Semantic Web World

"Hello? Operator! Give me the number for 911!"
—Homer Simpson

Now we step directly into Semantic Web programming, saying hello to a web of data. We start with a simple hello to the Semantic Web itself and then expand to its friends via its web of data. Thus, rather than a one-shot "hello world," you'll get a hands-on tour of Semantic Web programming—a Hello Semantic Web World tour.

This tour forms a programming introduction to the rest of the book. It gets you started in code, with a code-based foundation. This gives you the immediate ability to experiment with actual programming examples. Of course, you might not understand everything at this point, nor should you expect to. The examples in this chapter provide an initial glimpse into what is ahead in the rest of the book. Hopefully, the Hello Semantic Web World tour will be a fun, insightful, and pragmatic start into Semantic Web programming.

We strongly recommend not just reading the code but running it too. You can customize it as you like or just skip to detailed description in the chapters ahead. This not only gets your hands into code but validates that your environment is set up correctly so that you can follow along with the rest of the book.

The objectives of this chapter are:

- Set up a Semantic Web programming environment.
- Illustrate a basic Semantic Web "hello world" program.
- Gain initial Semantic Web programming experience.
- Illustrate examples of the key operations involved in Semantic Web programming.

Setting Up Your Semantic Web Development Environment

First we need to set up your development environment. This environment forms the foundation for most of the examples in the book. Here we keep it simple and straightforward. Please refer to the appendix if you run into any problems or have questions not answered in this direct treatment. Here is an overview of the environment:

- Compiling and execution tools: Java 1.6 Software Development Kit (SDK)

- Code-editing tools: Eclipse Integrated Development Environment 3.4 (IDE)

- Ontology editing tool: Protégé Ontology Editor 4.0 Alpha

- Semantic Web Programming Framework: Jena Semantic Web Framework 2.5.6

- Ontology Reasoner: Pellet 1.5.2

Within the Semantic Web community, most of the tools that have been developed to date use the Java programming language, and this book does so as well. Therefore, our examples require a Java Software Development Kit (Java SDK). We assume that readers are familiar with Java. The SDK provides you with compiling tools and a runtime virtual machine to run Java programs. We recommend the latest release of Java, which at the time of this writing is Java 1.6. (Sun also refers to v1.6 as v6.0.) The examples also work with Java 1.5. If you don't have the Java SDK already, go to the Java download site (`http://java.sun.com/javase/downloads/index.jsp`) and install the latest update to JDK 6.

In addition to the SDK, you will need an editor. You can use any Java editor you like, but all of the examples in this book make use of the Eclipse platform's Integrated Development Environment (IDE). It is an excellent and widely used software package, and it is freely available (`http://www.eclipse.org/downloads/moreinfo/java.php`). While our examples are oriented toward Eclipse, none of them depend on Eclipse, so feel free to use your preferred editor.

You will need to create, edit, and combine ontologies using an ontology editor. These files can also be hand-coded in a standard text editor, but an ontology editor offers many conveniences and features specific to ontologies. We use version 4 of the freely available Protégé ontology editor (`http://protege.stanford.edu/download/protege4/installanywhere/`).

In order to manipulate an ontology programmatically, you need a Semantic Web programming framework. This contains the libraries to allow your programs to interact with Semantic Web data, such as ontologies and instance data, and to allow you to take advantage of reasoners and query languages. For this purpose, we use the Jena Semantic Web framework version 2.5.6 (`http://downloads.sourceforge.net/jena/Jena-2.5.6.zip`). To help you as you follow the examples in this book, you might want to explore the Jena website; it contains documentation, tutorials, and a support area. The standard Jena download also includes extensive documentation. The documentation resides in the `doc` directory underneath the directory where you unzipped Jena.

The Jena framework download includes several reasoners. You don't need to worry about downloading and installing these reasoners separately. In addition to the reasoners provided in Jena, we also use the Pellet 1.5.2 reasoner (`http://pellet.owldl.com`).

We chose these tools in part due to their adoption, maturity, and effectiveness but also because they are freely available, open-source software. Many other open-source and commercial tools are also excellent, but we chose these tools to focus on working code examples rather than a tool survey.

That completes all the components you require for most of our examples throughout the book. Figure 2-1 illustrates and summarizes how the pieces fit together. Appendix F supplies detailed information on these components.

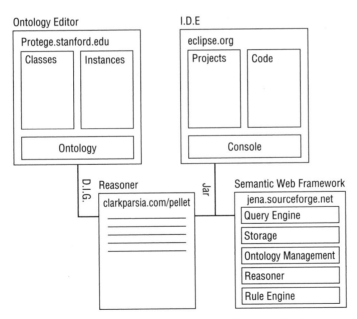

Figure 2-1 Semantic Web Software Development Environment

Now that all of the software has been installed, you have two development tools: Eclipse for Java and Protégé for ontologies. You also have two sets of libraries: Jena for Semantic Web interactions and Pellet as an independent reasoner. Now we'll show you how to exercise the environment with the Semantic Web Hello World tour.

Programming the Hello Semantic Web World Application

The Semantic Web offers quite a bit, and a simple hello is only the start. We expand the example throughout this chapter to form a Semantic Web Hello World tour that illustrates key Semantic Web programming concepts and capabilities. The purpose of these examples is to show you *what* can be done, expressed in a simple, direct way. Future chapters dive into the details. This gets your coding started. You need not understand all the details at this point. You can follow along knowing that more explanation will come in the chapters ahead. As we explore the specifics in future chapters, this tour provides you with a programming foundation that will improve your retention and understanding of the later, more detailed chapters.

Our hello tour takes a very literal approach to saying hello to the Semantic Web. In this example, we pretend that the Semantic Web is a person to whom we want to say hello. Suppose there are two sets of data describing the "friends" of the Semantic Web. Consider each data set as coming from a different Personal Information Manager (PIM). PIMs contain information about the owning person, in this case the Semantic Web, and the Semantic Web's associates. It is not unusual to have more than one data source and format due to the many websites and applications that track PIM information. Examples of PIMs include Facebook.com, Myspace.com, a gmail.com contact list, and Microsoft Outlook. Each one has information about the owner and the owner's associates in its own format. Our Semantic Web Hello World tour wants to say hello to all the Semantic Web's friends contained in both data sets. This example not only illustrates the basic programming needs but also exposes you to the methods for extracting, integrating, and evolving ontologies.

First we establish the project. Open up your IDE and create a new Java project. Our example uses the project name HelloSemanticWeb, and all project files are available at our book website. Make sure to set the Java Runtime Environment (JRE) correctly to version 1.6. Figure 2-2 illustrates, in Eclipse, making a new Java project.

Next we create a new `HelloSemanticWeb` class. In order to keep the example simple, this class will hold all the necessary program code. Make sure to check the "public static void main(String[] args)" box. This enables this class to start the program with the call to the `main` function and thus output in the traditional Hello World text window. Figure 2-3 illustrates, in Eclipse, the creation of the new class.

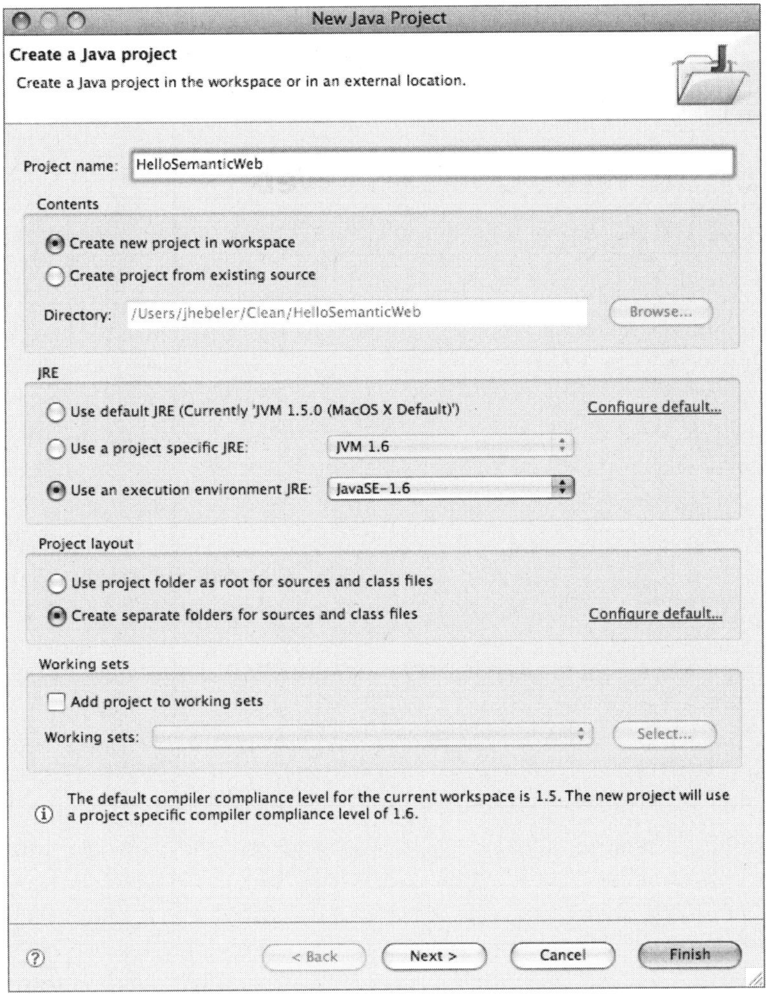

Figure 2-2 New project

Finally, we need to add the Jena and Pellet libraries to our new project. Select the Project Properties menu item from the top Eclipse menu. This opens a new Properties window. Select Java Build Path within the Properties window. Then select the Libraries subwindow. Select Add External JARs. This allows you to enter all the necessary JAR or library files from the Jena Semantic Web framework. Since we are exercising quite a bit in the Hello tour, just add them all. Go to the directory where you unzipped Jena, and select all the JAR files in the `lib` directory. Repeat for the Pellet `lib` directory. Note for Pellet that you do not need to include the Jena libraries that are included in the Pellet download. You need only `pellet.jar`. Your included JARs should look similar to those in Figure 2-4.

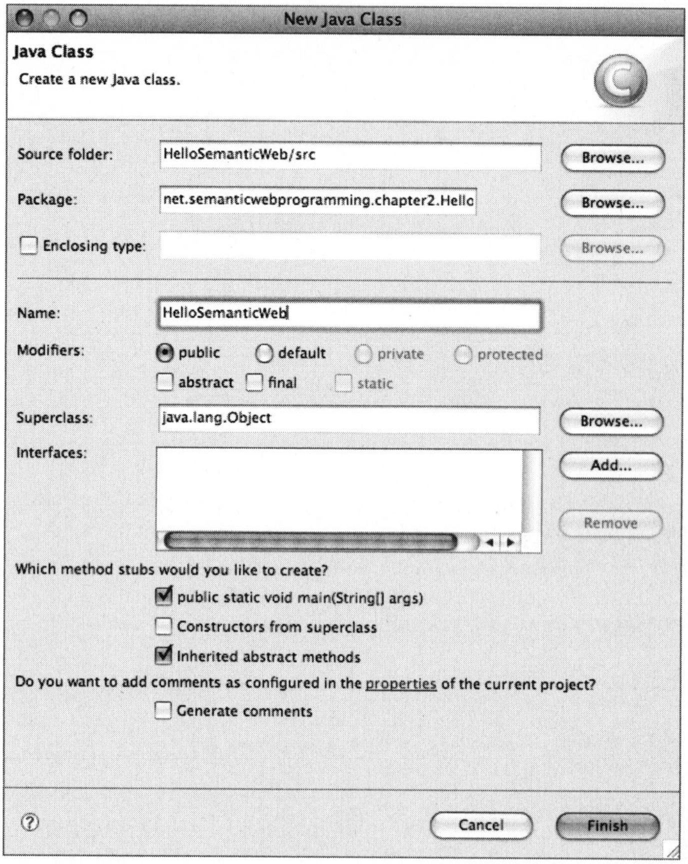

Figure 2-3 New class

This completes the setup of your Semantic Web project environment. You are now ready to add code and make your application say hello.

As stated earlier, we designed a Semantic Web Hello World program that provides a tour of Semantic Web programming. We use Hello World to guide us though the many possibilities. Our Hello Semantic Web World tour has six major stops:

1. Say hello to the Semantic Web.

2. Say hello to some friends of the Semantic Web.

3. Expand the friend list to include friends from a different source.

4. Say hello to all the Semantic Web's friends.

5. Say hello to a restricted list of only friends with email addresses.

6. Say hello to a restricted list of only friends with gmail.com addresses.

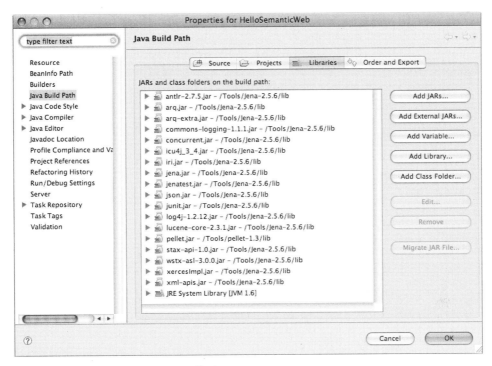

Figure 2-4 External libraries (JAR files)

Along the way, the tour will have some false stops to help illustrate why the program requires additional steps.

We will explore and query the instance data (the friends), align the instance data to ontologies, integrate multiple data sets and ontologies, reason across the data, and establish restrictions and rules, all demonstrated in code. Each tour stop implements four major steps: acquiring a structured storage space or model, populating the model with Semantic Web data, possibly processing the data including querying the data, and finally outputting the appropriate data—the hellos. Much of this is similar to building a relational database application.

We plan to say hello to the Semantic Web, and for that we need to create instance data in a format compatible with the Semantic Web. This FOAF-a-Matic (http://www.ldodds.com/foaf/foaf-a-matic) site provides a fill-in form that generates a Semantic Web instance data of people and their associates. You can save the data in a file. It only scratches the surface of the full FOAF ontology, but it is sufficient for our purposes and many others.

The FOAF ontology contains social information that you can share and search. The range of data it supports is consistent with what might be provided by a PIM. It contains information such as an owner's name (in this case, Semantic Web), email address, work, and people known by the owner (in this case, friends of the Semantic Web). We populated a FOAF graph for the fictitious owner, Semantic Web. This provides us with the information to say hello to the Semantic Web. Many folks already use FOAF to allow easy exchange of contact information. Throughout the book, we extend and enrich this social ontology in lots of interesting ways. This step provides us with some useful Semantic Web data.

Before we use the FOAF data from the FOAF-a-Matic in our application, we examine it in Turtle format. More information about different formats for Semantic Web data can be found in Chapter 3, "Modeling Information." It is slightly edited to focus on the key portions. The complete code is available at our website.

```
@prefix rdfs:    <http://www.w3.org/2000/01/rdf-schema#> .
@prefix foaf:    <http://xmlns.com/foaf/0.1/> .
@prefix admin:   <http://webns.net/mvcb/> .
@prefix owl:     <http://www.w3.org/2002/07/owl#> .
@prefix xsd:     <http://www.w3.org/2001/XMLSchema#> .
@prefix rdf:     <http://www.w3.org/1999/02/22-rdf-syntax-ns#> .
@prefix swp2:    <http://semwebprogramming.org/2009/ont/chp2#>.
< swp2:me>
      rdf:type foaf:Person ;
      foaf:depiction <http://semwebprogramming.org/semweb.jpg> ;
      foaf:family_name "Web" ;
      foaf:givenname "Semantic" ;
      foaf:homepage <http://semwebprogramming.org> ;
      foaf:knows < swp2:Reasoner> , < swp2:Statement> , < swp2:
        Ontology> ;
      foaf:name "Semantic Web" ;
      foaf:nick "Webby" ;
      foaf:phone <tel:410-679-8999> ;
      foaf:schoolHomepage <http://www.web.edu> ;
      foaf:title "Dr" ;
      foaf:workInfoHomepage
              <http://semwebprogramming.com/dataweb.html> ;
      foaf:workplaceHomepage
              <http://semwebprogramming.com> .

< swp2:Reasoner>
      rdf:type foaf:Person ;
      rdfs:seeAlso <http://reasoner.com> ;
      foaf:mbox <mailto:reason@hotmail.com> ;
      foaf:name "Ican Reason" .

< swp2:Statement>
      rdf:type foaf:Person ;
      rdfs:seeAlso <http://statement.com> ;
```

```
      foaf:mbox <mailto:mstatement@gmail.com> ;
      foaf:name "Makea Statement" .

< swp2:Ontology>
      rdf:type foaf:Person ;
      rdfs:seeAlso <http://ont.com> ;
      foaf:mbox <mailto:ont@gmail.com> ;
      foaf:name "I. M. Ontology" .
```

This collection of statements does not constitute an ontology, although it refers to the various ontologies or vocabularies in the prefix portion at the top. An ontology has information regarding classes and their relationships. This data only refers to potential ontologies elsewhere.

These Semantic Web statements produced by the FOAF-a-Matic describe the person, Semantic Web, and friends. The statements form relationships. For example, the first grouping under #me declares information regarding the owner, the Semantic Web. The grouping of statements provides information about the owner's name, telephone number, and the like. The code also contains three smaller groupings describing the people known by Mr. Semantic Web. For each person, "Ican Reason," "Makea Statement," and "I. M. Ontology," the document contains a name and email address. We will use just these statements to say our initial hellos. Note that the actual instance URI is not the same as the name. Ican Reason is merely a name associated with the URI `swp2:Reasoner`. The resource `swp2:Reasoner` could have many names or no name at all. Figure 2-5 outlines the FOAF Instance Graph.

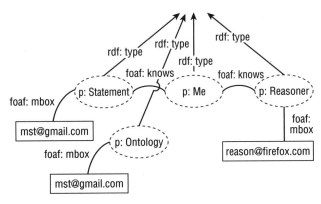

Figure 2-5 FOAF Instance Graph

We are now going to programmatically create a place to load this data—a model—and then load the above Semantic Web data into the model. This allows us to query for information such as a list of friends. Once we have the query response, we can issue our hellos. Here is the initial code to load the graph. As with all our examples, our website provides the complete source.

```
public class HelloSemanticWeb {
            static String defaultNameSpace = "
http://semwebprogramming.org/2009/ont/chp2:#";

  private Model _friends = null;

  public static void main(String[] args) throws IOException {

  HelloSemanticWeb hello = new HelloSemanticWeb();

    //Load my FOAF friends
    System.out.println("Load my FOAF Friends");
    hello.populateFOAFFriends();
    //...
  }
// ...
  private void populateFOAFFriends(){
    friends = ModelFactory.createOntologyModel();
    InputStream inFoafInstance =
        FileManager.get().open("Ontologies/FOAFFriends.rdf");
    friends.read(inFoafInstance,defaultNameSpace);
    inFoafInstace.close();
  }
```

The start of the file contains all the necessary imports, but we left these out of the code sample for brevity. The Eclipse IDE suggests the necessary imports automatically. The first line in the sample declares the class, HelloSemanticWeb. This is followed by two variables that contain the default namespace in setting up a URI and a model to hold the Semantic Web friends. We selected a resolvable URI based on the book's website. Once initialized, the _friends model holds the web of data shown in Figure 2-5. We create an instance of the class, HelloSemanticWeb, and then call one of its methods, populateFOAFFriends(), to populate the _friends model. The first step creates the model, ModelFactory.createOntologyModel(). Next, we read into the model the contents of our file from the FOAF-a-Matic created previously.

Now the graph outlined earlier in Figure 2-5 is in the _friends model and ready for processing, including questioning to generate our initial hellos.

In the next section of code, we say hello to the Semantic Web itself. The data does not contain any semantics yet, so we need to match actual characters. In the first case, we match on the Semantic Web itself, referred to as me in our automatically generated file.

```
// Say Hello to myself
public static void main(String[] args) {
// ...
System.out.println("\nSay Hello to Myself");
hello.mySelf(hello.friends);
// ...
}
// ...
private void mySelf(Model model){
//Hello to Me - focused search
runQuery
    (" select DISTINCT ?name where{ swp2:me foaf:name ?name  }", model);
}
.
.
.
private void runQuery(String queryRequest, Model model){
StringBuffer queryStr = new StringBuffer();
// Establish Prefixs
queryStr.append("PREFIX swp2" + ": <" + defaultNameSpace + "> ");
queryStr.append("PREFIX foaf" + ": <" +
                  "http://xmlns.com/foaf/0.1/" + "> ");
//Now add query
queryStr.append(queryRequest);
Query query = QueryFactory.create(queryStr.toString());
QueryExecution qexec = QueryExecutionFactory.create(query, model);
//Run Select
try {
    ResultSet response = qexec.execSelect();
    while( response.hasNext()){
        QuerySolution soln = response.nextSolution();
        RDFNode name = soln.get("?name");
        if( name != null ){
          System.out.println( "Hello to " + name.toString() );
        }
        else
          System.out.println("No Friends found!");
      }
  } finally { qexec.close();}
}
```

The query searches for an exact match on swp2:me, which leads to Semantic's web name, Semantic Web. Note that swp2:me is the actual instance of a foaf:Person. That instance has a property that contains its name. The instance is not the same as its name. This allows an instance to have no name or several names. Other instances could have the same name but not be the same resource, which is swp2:me.

As mentioned before, the data in the model, so far, has no notion of semantics because it does not contain an ontology. Thus, we query for exact matches on data.

The code also includes the general function to run a query and output the appropriate hellos. This method repeats throughout the Semantic Web Hello World tour. Much of the query method is due to the logistics of setting up the query. This includes establishing the prefixes so the code doesn't repeat the long URI strings. The query portion actually involves just two steps: creating the query and then executing it. The method `QueryExecutionFactory()` creates the query, and the `execSelect()` method executes the query. We then iterate through the result set to list the hello candidates, saying hello to the returned values. There are many other ways to extract information, as we shall see in the coming chapters. We stick to the query format for consistency.

Running this results in the following output:

```
Load my FOAF Friends
Say Hello to Myself
Hello to Semantic Web
```

Now that we have said hello to the Semantic Web, we say hello to all its friends obtained through our FOAF-a-Matic. This code snippet shows the expansion of the query by following a path outlined in the graph.

```
private void myFriends(Model model){
    //Hello to just my friends - navigation
    runQuery(" select DISTINCT ?myname ?name where{
            swp2:me foaf:knows ?friend.
            ?friend foaf:name ?name } ", model);
}
```

The query simply follows or navigates the relationships as it connects the Semantic Web with its friends. The query matches on the resource, `swp2:me`, and the property, `foaf:knows`. This identifies the friends. We then follow the friends to obtain their names. Any statement that contains these two elements matches the query request. The object, `?name`, is the variable that produces the desired names. This is who the program offers the greeting, hello, to. Chapter 6, "Discovering Information," goes into extensive detail about queries and other ways to sort through the Semantic Web.

Running this snippet results in the following output:

```
Say Hello to my FOAF Friends
Hello to I. M. Ontology
Hello to Ican Reason
Hello to Makea Statement
```

Now things get interesting because we want to add additional friends from a *different* source—a source based on an entirely different view of the world, a different vocabulary as seen in the URIs. Instead of taking the ontology from elsewhere on the Web, which is usually the first choice, we use Protégé to create a *People* ontology and associated instances of people. This forms a second vocabulary. Protégé allows us to create classes, class inheritance relationships, and even instances. The first two contribute to establishing the semantics. Figure 2-6 illustrates the addition of the new class for `individuals`. You select the class `Thing`. Then click the upper-left button in the same window to create a new class that is a subclass to `Thing`. This pops up a box that allows you to label the new class, **Individual**.

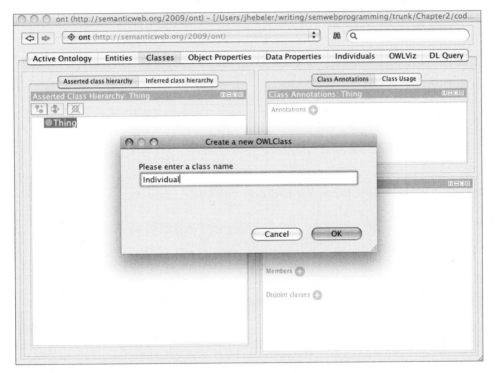

Figure 2-6 Using Protégé to create a new ontology class

Protégé also allows the creation of new properties. Here we add `people:hasName` (Figure 2-7) and `people:hasFriend` (Figure 2-8). The former is a data property because it associates individuals with literals. The latter, `people:hasFriend`, is an object property because it relates two resources such as individuals. Relationships exist outside of resources and thus can be used in multiple ways. This forms a simple ontology with classes and relationships.

Next we add a couple new friends based on the People ontology and relate them to one another. You can also add the properties for each instance on the lower-right side, such as their name and associations. Figure 2-9 illustrates Protégé containing three instances with their properties: one for the Semantic Web itself and two new friends.

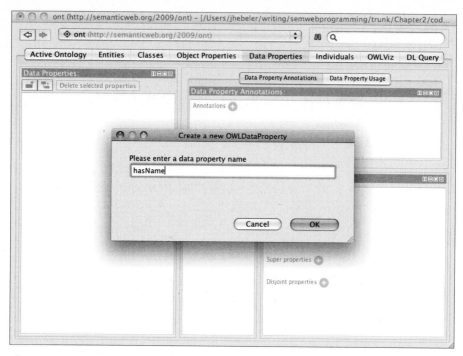

Figure 2-7 Using Protégé to create a new data property

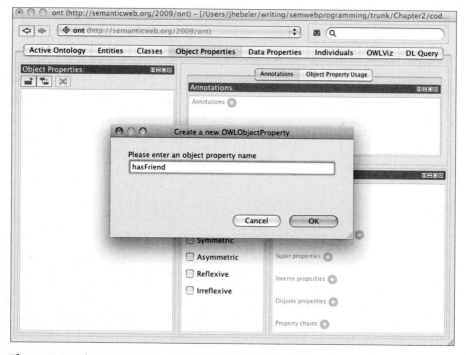

Figure 2-8 Using Protégé to create a new object property

Figure 2-9 Protégé adding new instances

Once we complete our additions in Protégé, we save the project. This also creates a file containing the ontology and instances. We could then load the file into the model as before, but we take an extra step of separating the ontology statements from the instance statements. One file, `additionalFriends.owl`, contains only the new instances or friends. An additional file, `additionalFriendsSchema.owl`, contains the semantics or classes and relationship types. This parallels the treatment with the FOAF data and enables more efficient reasoning. You do not need to do this for your example. We note the reason for this in the upcoming examples.

```
//Add my new friends
System.out.println("add my new friends");
hello.populateNewFriends();
.
.
.
private void populateNewFriends() throws IOException {
InputStream inFoafInstance =
    FileManager.get().open("Ontologies/additionalFriends.owl");
friends.read(inFoafInstance,defaultNameSpace);
inFoafInstance.close();
}
```

Here we are going to add only the new friends or the instances we created using Protégé. The code is identical to the previous population of FOAF friends except the file is different. Now the `_friends` model contains two sets of friends based on two different vocabularies or schemas. If we run `hello.myFriends()` a second time, it still says hello only to the same set of friends—the new ones are missing from the hello greeting. This is due to using two different, incompatible definitions or syntax formats for describing the friends. The first one used the FOAF ontology. The one we created used our new People ontology.

Examine the new file of instances we created via Protégé to see why the new friends did not get the hello greeting.

```
:Individual_5
      rdf:type :Individual ;
      :hasFriend :Individual_6 , :Individual_7 ;
      :hasName "Sem Web" .

:Individual_6
      rdf:type :Individual ;
      :hasFriend :Individual_5 ;
      :hasName "Web O. Data" .

:Individual_7
      rdf:type :Individual ;
      :hasFriend :Individual_5 ;
      :hasName "Mr. Owl" .
```

We have added to the Semantic Web here with an alias, "Sem Web," and his two friends. Note that whereas friends in the previous graph used `foaf:person`, this graph refers to them as `people:Individuals`. (Note that the People ontology is the default namespace, so it is not listed in this code.) Even though in these two friend-tracking ontologies the ideas are *semantically* equivalent, they have a *syntactic* difference. This difference causes the original `helloFriends` query to not find any of these friends, much less identify "Sem Web" as the same as Semantic Web. They did not match the key relationship of `foaf:knows`. Since the syntax doesn't match, the query addresses only our original friends in the first file. The new friends are in the model but are not represented as friends compatible with FOAF.

In order to align these two different names, `foaf:Person` and `people:Individual`, we need to align the semantics. This will make them semantically the same even though they retain their syntax differences. When we are finished, the graphs will unify to produce the correct chorus of hellos. First we need a model that contains the associated ontologies of both friend instances, FOAF and People. The ontologies declare relationships to `foaf:Person` and `people:Individual`. Here we have two, the FOAF ontology and our People ontology. Figure 2-10 graphs the key portions of FOAF and People ontologies.

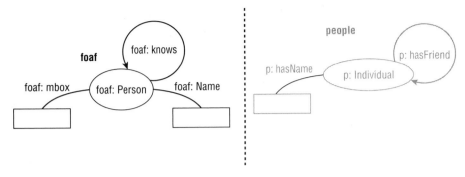

Figure 2-10 Graph of FOAF subset and People ontologies

We create a new model to hold the ontologies and then populate them as follows:

```
Model schema = null;

// Add the ontologies
System.out.println("\nAdd the Ontologies");
hello.populateFOAFSchema();
hello.populateNewFriendsSchema();
   .
   .
   .

private void populateFOAFSchema(){
        schema = ModelFactory.createOntologyModel();
                schema.read("http://xmlns.com/foaf/spec/index.rdf");

friends.read("http://xmlns.com/foaf/spec/index.rdf");
}

   private void populateNewFriendsSchema() throws IOException {
        InputStream inFoafInstance =
     FileManager.get().open("Ontologies/additionalFriendsSchema.owl");
        friends.read(inFoafInstance,defaultNameSpace);
        inFoafInstance.close();
   }
```

Remember, we separated these new *friend* statements into two files; one containing the new instances (friends) and one containing the ontology or schema. The latter is stored in the file `additionalFriendsSchema.owl`, which is loaded in the code above. Now the models contain both ontologies and both sets of instance data.

Although the new ontologies detail the relationships within each ontology, they do not contain any statements as to how the ontologies relate to one another. This requires additional statements to align the two ontologies. These additions bridge the two ontologies in key areas, allowing our query to include all friends instead of just those from one or the other ontology. This ontology alignment is not strictly necessary. If the query was changed to incorporate the knowledge of how the two ontologies relate to one another, it would return all the friends, but this approach couples the query to each added data set. This is a complex and brittle approach because every addition of new data requires rewriting the queries.

The use of ontologies and associated alignment statements allows a Semantic Web program to incorporate new ontologies and data incrementally as the application and its users learn about them. Thus, you can add ontologies together (and instance data) and adjust them over time. You do not need to have a priori knowledge of how the alignment occurs. This is exactly what our tour does. You can actually add alignment statements during the running of your Semantic Web application. As you will see, this is a tremendous benefit in handling the integration of Semantic Web data. We are doing just that in our example. First, we add the two files of instance data based on different vocabularies. This does not break the existing query, but it also does not expand its capability at returning friends. Next, we add statements to align the two ontologies. The program can dynamically add alignment when needed. While awaiting the alignment statements, the original query works as before without any problems or complications.

Quickly you can see the similarities between the two ontologies. We take advantage of the similarities between the two ontologies and relate them to one another by extending the ontology model that now contains both. We add statements to the ontology that express the following observations.

`people:Individual` is equivalent to `foaf:Person`.

`people:hasName` is equivalent to `foaf:name`.

`people:hasFriend` is a subproperty of `foaf:knows`.

We have two choices: make the pair fully equivalent or make one a specialization of the other. Consider the semantic choices in choosing a specialization relationship over an equivalent relationship. A `foaf:Person` and a `people:Individual` refer to the same concept and hence are equivalent. A `foaf:knows` relationship between two people indicates some knowledge of a person but not necessarily a friendship with that person. Therefore, we make `people:hasFriend` a specialization of `foaf:knows`. Each of these statements allows inferences that relate instances of type `foaf:Person` and `people:Individual`. We shall see the impact of these inferences shortly.

There is one other concern the instance data presents. Both data sets describe the same instance or person, the Semantic Web. There are two distinct references to the Semantic Web with two different names: ''Semantic Web'' and "Sem Web." We need to relate these two resources to each other with an additional statement that makes the instances equivalent. Thus, the Semantic Web concept becomes consistent across both data sets.

The following code creates four statements that align the two data sets and adds them to the schema model as previously instructed. There are several ways to add statements. This code illustrates the programmatic method for adding statements. You could also use Protégé to create the statements and read in the statements as accomplished earlier from the Protégé saved file.

```
// State that :individual is equivalentClass of foaf:Person
Resource resource =
schema.createResource(defaultNameSpace + "Individual");
Property prop = schema.createProperty("owl:equivalentClass");
Resource obj = schema.createResource("foaf:Person");
schema.add(resource,prop,obj);

 //State that :hasName is an equivalentProperty of foaf:name
 resource = schema.createResource(defaultNameSpace + "hasName");
 prop = schema.createProperty("owl:equivalentProperty");
 obj = schema.createResource("foaf:name");
 schema.add(resource,prop,obj);

 //State that :hasFriend is a subproperty of foaf:knows
 resource = schema.createResource(defaultNameSpace + "hasFriend");
 prop = schema.createProperty("rdfs:subPropertyOf");
 obj = schema.createResource("foaf:knows");
 schema.add(resource,prop,obj);
 //State that sem web is the same person as Semantic Web
 resource = schema.createResource("swp2:#me");
 prop = schema.createProperty("owl:sameAs");
 obj = schema.createResource("http://swp2:#Individual_5");
 schema.add(resource,prop,obj);
```

The first new statement aligns the class `foaf:Person` with the class `people:Individual` by declaring them equivalent. It creates the resources for the subject and object along with the property. It then adds the statement to the model. The second statement aligns the property `foaf:name` with the property `people:hasName` by also declaring their equivalence. The third statement aligns `foaf:knows` with `people:hasFriend` by declaring `people:hasFriend` to be a subproperty of `foaf:knows`. The fourth and final statement declares the two instances of the Semantic Web to be the same. Figure 2-11 illustrates the additional statements that align the ontologies.

Regardless of how many friends the Semantic Web may have, if they are expressed according to either of these two ontologies, a query requesting the Semantic Web's friends returns them all. This occurs with the addition of only the first three statements. Keep in mind that the data need not be in the same file or same location. In addition, the alignment statements can be kept separate in a different file or location. This allows you to maintain different alignment files for different alignment missions (more on that later). Any data read into the model that conforms to these two ontologies allows the program to identify all the friends. Moreover, should more data become available expressed in a new ontology, only the relations between the various ontologies need to align the additional data. More work is still needed to produce all the necessary hellos. These statements relate only the ontologies to each other and not the instances (friends, in our case). They provide the logical foundation to add statements that equate the instance data. Thus `Ican Reason` remains only a `Foaf:Person` and not a `People:Individual`. Alas, our query would still not say hello to any of the new friends.

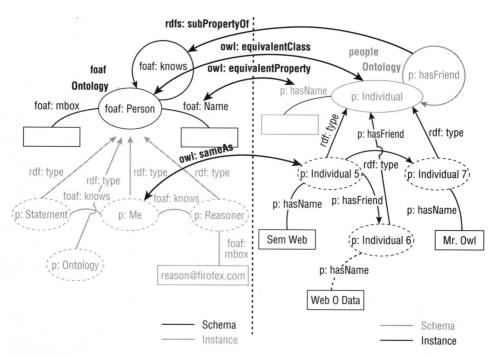

Figure 2-11 Ontology alignment

A reasoner, like one Jena includes, supplies the additional inferred statements or entailments. In fact, Jena has several reasoners and also supports the ability to interface with external third-party reasoners. Chapter 4, "Incorporating Semantics," covers this topic in more detail, but for now we will use Jena's default OWL reasoner. The following function details the acquisition and execution of the reasoner. The reasoner examines the ontology statements and, based on its reasoning ability, adds inferred or entailed statements. The reasoner stays bound to the model, and future statement additions will also produce appropriate entailments. The reasoner, given the additional alignment statements shown previously, adds statements that make each instance of a `foaf:Person` a `People:Individual` and so on. Whereas there was previously one statement referring to `Ican Reason` as a `foaf:person`, there are now additional statements that declare `Ican Reason` a `people:Individual` also. A query could use either concept to acquire `Ican Reason`. The following code details the methods to acquire and bind the Jena reasoner to the model:

```
private void bindReasoner(){
   Reasoner reasoner = ReasonerRegistry.getOWLReasoner();
   reasoner = reasoner.bindSchema(schema);
   inferredFriends =
       ModelFactory.createInfModel(reasoner, friends);
}
```

The method acquires the Jena OWL reasoner and then binds it to the schema we saved earlier. This schema or ontology separation allows some precalculations to improve performance of the reasoning. It then creates a model bound to the reasoner based on the `_friends` model. This extends the `_friends` model to include all the entailments inferred from the ontology, including our added statements and entailments from any future additions. This also allows the program to return to the original model, which does not contain any entailments.

You can also try out the external reasoner Pellet instead of Jena's internal reasoner. The following snippet shows the code for using Pellet:

```
private void runPellet( ){
   Reasoner reasoner = PelletReasonerFactory.theInstance().create();
   reasoner = reasoner.bindSchema(schema);
   inferredFriends = ModelFactory.createInfModel(reasoner, friends);
}
```

The Pellet reasoner implements the same interface as the Jena reasoner. This allows a program to easily use different reasoners for different purposes, a topic further explored later in Chapter 4, "Incorporating Semantics".

Finally, we are ready to extend our hello to everyone in the Semantic Web model. The following code contains the output with hellos that include the two new friends. Note, we run the exact same query as before:

```
Run a reasoner
Finally - Hello to all my friends!
Hello to I. M. Ontology
Hello to Ican Reason
Hello to Makea Statement
Hello to Mr. Owl
Hello to Web O. Data
```

The combination of the two ontologies and instances creates an interesting anomaly. This is revealed by running the hello to just the Semantic Web again.

```
Hello to Semantic Web
Hello to Sem Web
```

The model maintains one Semantic Web `foaf:Person` (also equivalent to `people:Individual`) but now with two names. This is not unusual. The model now contains the knowledge that there is only one Semantic Web that it knows of. It just happens to have two names. Since this ontology does not limit the number of names, the model can contain as many names as desired, but they all are related to the same `foaf:Person` resource. The ontology statements we added previously overcome the syntax differences between the statements regarding the owner, the Semantic Web.

Now we'll go in the opposite direction. Instead of adding friends, we create subsets of friends—subgroups of the friends we already have. We outline steps to constrain the hello greetings to a selected subset of friends. The hello tour illustrates two such subsets: email friends and email friends who use a Gmail address. Email friends have at least one email address, so we could send the hello via email. Gmail friends have an email address in the gmail.com domain.

Email friends need only be a `foaf:Person` (remember that `people:Individual` is equivalent) and have a `foaf:mbox` relationship. There are several ways to achieve this, but we want the ontology to contain this information. Therefore, we create a special concept, or class, that forms a restriction. Restrictions outline the logic for membership within the restricted class and are described in detail in Chapter 4. Restrictions have lots of interesting uses, including declaring a collection of instance statements associated with a class through inference. The following code outlines the restriction for email friends:

```
people:EmailPerson
      rdf:type owl:Class ;
      rdfs:subClassOf foaf:Person;
      owl:equivalentClass
            [ rdf:type owl:Restriction ;
              owl:minCardinality " 1 "^^xsd:nonNegativeInteger ;
              owl:onProperty foaf:mbox
            ] .
```

The restriction notes that in order to be a member of the class `people:EmailPerson` you must have at least one `foaf:mbox`. All of the original friends have email addresses, and so they would all be entitled to be of type `people:EmailPerson`. We also restrict it to a specialization of `foaf:Person` (and hence `People:Individual`) to avoid other concepts that have email addresses that are not people, such as a laser printer. Now we read in the restriction to the reasoner-bound model and query for email friends. This results in correctly identifying friends with email addresses. We could use this list to send out emails. The restriction is no different from other Semantic Web statements. You could create the restriction with Protégé, Jena program steps, or simply a text editor.

In order to restrict our friends further, we want only friends with gmail.com email addresses. This goes beyond the ontology constructs because we actually need a method to perform a partial string match, although this construct is now possible in OWL 2, as we show in Chapter 5. For now, we want to demonstrate a simple rule. We want to match an email address that contains the string `gmail.com`. We could also use methods in a query, as you will see in Chapter 7. Nevertheless, for the purposes of this example, we will use a Semantic Web rule. Rules expand or increase ontology expressivity.

Like reasoners, there are many rule engines, each with its own rule language. For simplicity's sake, in this example we use Jena Rules. We establish a rule that finds gmail.com email addresses and creates a statement that associates the instance subject with a `GmailPerson` ontology class. This is similar to what the reasoner did before, but rather than follow the ontology logic, it follows the specified rule. Rules are excellent vehicles for transformation between two ontologies and are fully explored in Chapter 10, "Aligning Information." An individual resource may be an instance of multiple classes.

```
private void runJenaRule(Model model){
String rules = "[emailChange:
   (?person foaf:mbox ?email),strConcat(?email,?lit),
   regex( ?lit, "(.*@gmail.com)')
   -> (?person rdf:type> People:GmailPerson)]";

Reasoner ruleReasoner = new GenericRuleReasoner(Rule.parseRules(rules));
ruleReasoner = ruleReasoner.bindSchema(schema);
inferredFriends = ModelFactory.createInfModel(ruleReasoner, model);
}
```

The string `rules` contains the rule. Here the rule finds statements with a `foaf:mbox` and then tests the `foaf:mbox` entry for `gmail.com` using a rule method, `regex()`. If both conditions are true, `foaf:mbox` and `gmail.com`, a statement is added to the model that relates the matched person instance with the class, `person:GmailPerson`. Thus, a query looking for `GmailPerson` would return all `foaf:Persons` that have a gmail.com address. As noted before, your program needs only to bind the reasoner to the appropriate model. Once bound, the reasoner continually fires when necessary. So if a new friend was added with a gmail.com address, the reasoner would follow the rule and also make the friend a `person:GmailPerson`.

```
Hello to Makea Statement
Hello to I. M. Ontology
```

Now after all that, we make sure we can still send out a hello to all our friends. Say hello to all the Semantic Web friends again. This ensures us that we haven't placed incorrect or unintended logic that confused our friend list. It is always a good idea to have requirement questions that help ensure the integrity of the model as changes are made.

```
Hello to I. M. Ontology
Hello to Ican Reason
Hello to Makea Statement
Hello to Mr. Owl
Hello to Web O. Data
```

Yes, it works! We produced a single program that incorporates multiple, incompatible data sets that we unified and adapted to fulfill all our hello desires.

SLASH VS. NUMBER SIGN VOCABULARIES

You may have noticed that two types of references exist in declaring a namespace for Semantic Web vocabularies. Examine the prefixes in the code above that outline the various vocabularies. The FOAF ontology uses a slash (/). The People ontology, the one we created, uses a number sign (#). The URI specification refers to the number sign as a fragment identifier. See `http://www.ietf.org/rfc/rfc3986.txt`. Both are acceptable and work properly with the Semantic Web and a web browser. However, they behave differently with a browser. Whereas slash details a page on the web, a number sign details a location on a web page.

So which do you use? We recommend that small, relatively static vocabularies use the number sign. The number sign allows the entire vocabulary to fit in one file, with the number sign delineating the various classes, relationships, and the like. Large, dynamic vocabularies use the slash. This allows individual components to exist on many pages.

Summary

We have covered a lot of territory quickly with basic explanations. In fact, we touched on almost every major topic in the book—a rather big hello. We loaded ontology and instance data, queried it, added more instance data, bound the instances to ontologies, and then aligned the ontologies. We used a reasoner to infer information into models based on the ontologies, and finally we went the other way and restricted the hellos to a subset of the initial data. First, we restricted it to friends with email addresses and then only to friends with gmail.com email addresses using a special class construct and a rule engine. Along the way we glimpsed many of the techniques and issues we will expand on in the coming chapters. Table 2-1 summarize each tour stop.

Table 2-1 Semantic Web Hello World Tour Summary

HELLO TOUR STOP	TECHNIQUE	NOTES
Hello to the Semantic Web	Searched for me	Added FOAF instances
Hello to Semantic Web friends	Searched/navigated for friends of me	
Attempt a hello to all friends, new and old	Added new people friends	New friends not semantically aligned; no hellos
Attempt to say hello to all	Added both FOAF and People ontologies	New friends still not semantically aligned; no hellos
Attempt to say hello to all	Added alignment statements	Ontology aligned but not the instances; missing reasoner
Hello to all friends—success	Bounded reasoner to data	Instances now aligned through the extra statements from the reasoner
Limit hello to email friends	Created a class based on a restriction	Produced a subset of friends
Limit hello to gmail.com friends	Created a rule and bounded a rule engine	Produced a more refined subset based on a string match
Say hello to all friends	Same original query	Assured all data and logic are intact

Now that you have a brief programming foundation, you can start building on it. The next part of the book takes you into the knowledge model itself and its associated constructs. That is followed by full applications that build on the FOAF ontology and beyond. We hope you enjoyed the tour. We trust you were able to gain some hands-on experience. This will prove helpful in the chapters ahead.

Foundations of Semantic Web Programming

There are two primary aspects to Semantic Web programming: knowledge representation and application integration. This section focuses on the former—representing and manipulating knowledge using the resource description framework (RDF) data model, ontologies (OWL), queries, rules, and reasoning. Each of the five chapters in this section builds the foundations of knowledge representation in the Semantic Web.

Chapter 3 establishes the data model of the Semantic Web: the Resource Description Framework (RDF). The chapter highlights the key differences between RDF and other traditional data representations like XML or relational databases, pointing out the distinction between syntax and semantics. RDF provides a flexible and highly expressive data model onto which the Semantic Web is built. All information in an RDF model can be conceptualized as statements about resources. These statements are much like statements in the English language—they have subjects, predicates, and objects. This chapter presents the features and limitations of RDF and introduces its abstract structure as well as its numerous concrete syntaxes.

Chapter 4 uses the OWL Web Ontology Language to add semantics to the RDF data model. OWL provides a vocabulary of terms that can be used in RDF statements. These terms have special semantics associated with them that are used to give meaning to the data they describe.

Semantics provide rich meaning such as taxonomical relationships between terms, model restrictions, and logical assertions. This chapter is about semantics in the Semantic Web, and it covers the second version of the OWL Web Ontology Language (OWL 2). RDF Schema (RDFS) is covered as a subset of the OWL 2 vocabulary.

Chapter 5 bridges the gap between the abstract world of OWL knowledge modeling and the real world. The chapter begins by exploring the tools and technologies that implement OWL semantics and how they integrate to create a Semantic Web framework. A number of real world knowledgebase, reasoner, and triple store projects are discussed and their relative merits compared. Next, the profiles of OWL 2 are described and a programming example is presented that compares the side effects of various levels of reasoning (none, RDFS, and OWL) on the information that is derived from an example ontology. The chapter concludes with a detailed look at working with ontologies, including application-ontology integration and ontology reuse and sharing.

Chapter 6 takes a close look at retrieving useful information from the Semantic Web. There are three general methods of retrieval: search, navigation, and query. Each method has its proper use and relative merits. Search provides a way to identify and retrieve information using an approximate match and is useful when you don't know exactly what it is you are looking for. Navigation enables information discovery through a process of traversing the relationships that exist between pieces of information, much like a Web surfer explores the World Wide Web by traversing the hyperlinks that connect Web pages.

Finally, querying involves the retrieval of precise sets of information using the SPARQL Query Language for RDF. The bulk of this chapter is spent exploring the features of SPARQL.

Chapter 7 presents rules in the Semantic Web. Rules can be used to create additional formalisms in a knowledge model that can't necessarily be represented using an ontology. The chapter presents the Semantic Web Rule Language (SWRL) as the de facto rule language for the Semantic Web. SWRL can be used to model implications (if-then statements) that can be used to express domain knowledge, map between the concepts of various ontologies, or translate data. Rules extend your capabilities beyond OWL representations which is useful form various ontology transformations.

## CHAPTER 3

Modeling Information

"It's not what you think, it's how you think."
—Anonymous

In this chapter, we expand the discussion from Chapter 1 into some of the fundamental technologies and approaches for dealing with information in applications for the Semantic Web.

On the Semantic Web, information is modeled primarily with a set of three complementary languages: the Resource Description Framework (RDF), RDF Schema (RDFS), and the OWL Web Ontology Language. RDF defines the underlying data model and provides a foundation for the more sophisticated features of the higher levels of the Semantic Web layer cake. Semantic Web information modeling with RDF is the main subject of this chapter. In this chapter we discuss the problem of information sharing and present the model adopted by Semantic Web technologies as one solution to this problem. You'll learn about the important underlying concepts of RDF and how to write your own RDF documents in some of the most popular formats, and you will write a short program to read and write RDF.

In summary, in this chapter you will:

- Learn about information sharing in general
- Explore the Semantic Web approach to information sharing, RDF
- Learn about popular RDF encodings
- Write a program using Java to manipulate RDF data

Modeling Information in Software

In software systems, information modeling is of the utmost importance. The attributes of real-world objects that you choose to capture in your software and the way that you choose to represent them largely determine the operations that your system can perform and the questions that it can answer. In a semantic system this is even more important, because by modeling concepts and objects with sufficient rigor, it is possible to reuse data from one application in another.

All but the simplest software must be designed with an information model of some sort. The character of the information model depends on the aims of the program and the context for which it is designed. For instance, consider a simple application that manages a collection of mailing addresses. One approach is to model the information as a set of related objects. You might expect a `Person` class and an `Address` class, each with various appropriate data members. An alternate approach, contrasted in Figure 3-1, is to use a relational model and to think of a Person table and an Address table, each with appropriate columns for values, and a link table to define the relationships between them.

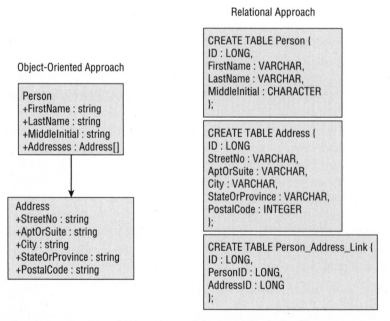

Figure 3-1 Two approaches to modeling people and addresses

Each type of information model presents its own set of advantages and dis-advantages. For instance, an object model is very flexible, and it can be directly coupled with behaviors in object-oriented programming languages. A relational model, on the other hand, easily translates to use in a relational database, which can offer superlative scalability, fast querying, transactions, and persistence across sessions. Often a single software system will support several representations of its information precisely in order to exploit the strengths of each. A good example of this is database-backed software, which uses a relational model for data storage and retrieval but loads information into objects for business processing. Semantic Web technologies are based on an information model that is designed to facilitate easy data sharing and interoperability.

Sharing Information: Syntax and Semantics

The problem of sharing data between systems can be broken into two important subproblems: the syntactic sharing problem and the semantic sharing problem. The syntactic aspect of the data-sharing problem involves gaining access to the shared data, while the semantic aspect involves incorporating that information into the data structures of the consuming system.

Consider the case of two people who are trying to communicate with each other. There are many ways to communicate, and depending on the circumstances, they may choose one approach or another. They could speak or write to each other, but they could also use Morse code, semaphore flags, or even something more exotic, like smoke signals. Finding a common medium for communication is analogous to the syntactic aspect of sharing data. It is a very important first step in the information-sharing problem. If one person decides to sit down for a chat, but the other is planning to send smoke signals, they will have a hard time exchanging ideas!

Once a proper medium is chosen, the two people must agree on a shared language, or encoding, for their ideas. A language is a way of mapping the ideas in our heads into a form that can be communicated with others. To communicate, people must agree on a medium and a common language. If two people speak different languages, they will not be able to understand each other, even if they have both decided to communicate via, for example, spoken words. Finding a mutually intelligible encoding of concepts within the common medium is analogous to the semantic data-sharing problem.

To illustrate the difference between syntax and semantics, consider three approaches to information representation and the implications for sharing data. In each case, the scenario is a simple one: Two software systems each maintain information about a common domain. The first system, the producer, has information that the second, the consumer, wishes to incorporate.

Serialized Objects

The first approach is the simplest and most straightforward: binary object serialization. With binary object serialization, the producer generates objects that represent the data that is to be shared, and the data values in these objects are then directly serialized as ordered collections of bytes.

This technique, while easy to implement for the producer, can be properly integrated only with a great deal of insight on the part of the consumer. The consuming system must know the exact details of the producer's data structures merely to address the syntactic data-sharing problem. The semantic data-sharing problem creates additional challenges. The consumer must know all of the object data members of the producer and precisely how each maps to the corresponding data structure within the consumer, if it even exists. The amount of foreknowledge required significantly impacts the utility of this method of sharing information.

Relational Databases

A relational database can offer significant improvements over serialized objects for exchanging information, but this approach is not without its own short-comings. Relational databases are usually distinct, reusable components that are not concerned with the main business logic of a software system. This has led to the standardization of APIs for interacting with them, for instance, Open Database Connectivity (ODBC) or Java Database Connectivity (JDBC). In addition, most relational databases support Structured Query Language (SQL) queries as a means to retrieve the data they contain. Use of one of these APIs and SQL can greatly reduce the complexity of the syntactic data-sharing problem. Software written to issue SQL queries against one database can often be adapted to use a second database without major changes.

There are still difficulties, however. Even with the use of a standard API and SQL, the syntactic sharing problem still exists. ODBC and JDBC provide a standard software interface, but each database vendor provides its own product—and even version-specific driver implementations. Without knowing a priori whether the producer is using Oracle or Microsoft SQL Server, for example, the consumer cannot easily access the producer's database.

In addition to the syntactic challenges, the semantic problem remains. Without a detailed understanding of the database schemata and table definitions, it can be very challenging to integrate even the simplest databases.

Extensible Markup Language (XML)

XML is currently a very popular and effective way of exchanging information. XML languages conform to a well-defined syntax that is compatible with many widely available parsers. XML can provide an effective solution to the syntax problem for data sharing. In spite of the strict constraints on XML's structure, the lack of reserved keywords or predetermined vocabulary of terms makes it flexible enough to be used for a wide variety of applications.

Despite its flexibility, XML does not address the semantic data sharing problem. It is true that it is possible to define custom elements and to use XML Stylesheet Transformations (XSLTs) to convert one syntax to another, but XML elements and attributes have no meaning by themselves. Also, XSLTs are highly syntax-specific and therefore very fragile. If anything should change about either the producer's or the consumer's XML format, the stylesheets would need to be updated. Even a very minor change, like reordering two tags, could create a great deal of work for system developers. Without any means of encoding the meaning of and the relationships between XML elements, there is no way to determine the impact of a change in order or terminology.

These three data-sharing solutions—binary object serialization, relational databases, and XML—show a progression through time and sophistication dealing solely with the syntactic data-sharing problem. Even today, the task of merging two XML documents is a significant amount of work. This is because the focus of these interoperability efforts has not been on the semantic data-sharing problem. This is understandable because the syntactic data-sharing problem must be overcome before the semantic data sharing problem can even become an issue. What would the structure of the tables of a relational database matter if there were no way to issue it queries? Once there is agreement on a communication medium, then the work can begin on a way to express ideas. Progress on the semantic data-sharing problem comes from the realization that, in practical terms, the distinction between data and metadata is an illusion.

Metadata and Data in Information Sharing

Data and metadata are different. Data is values, individual atoms of information, and metadata describes the relationship between those atoms and other data. In applications, the amount of data typically dwarfs the amount of metadata. Metadata also usually changes much less frequently than data. A complex database might have tens or hundreds of tables but could easily have millions or tens of millions of records, and it could be updating those records weekly or even daily.

Take, for instance, the case of a database for Ultra-Mart's chain of retail stores. Suppose Ultra-Mart uses its customer loyalty cards to maintain information about customers and what they buy. The database keeps track of information about customers (maybe name, gender, age, and address) and their purchases (say, item UPC, quantity, price at checkout, and date of purchase). In this case, the metadata in the database would represent information about each of these fields—that name should be a string of characters, but that price should be a number, for instance. With the fields suggested so far, there would be on the order of ten values of metadata. The data, on the other hand, would be all of the values in the tables described by the metadata. That means information about all of Ultra-Mart's thousands of customers and then about each of the millions of purchased items per day. This relationship between data and metadata is very common, and typically relational databases are used in these situations because of their impressive performance characteristics.

However, recall that for all of the strengths of relational databases, they still present semantic information-sharing challenges. Seen from the perspective of the information-sharing problem, data and metadata are really two halves of the same whole. Values without metadata from a producing system cannot be incorporated into a consuming system. Similarly, collections of metadata without values are rarely of any use. Usually the melding of data and metadata takes place in the application developer's head, but automated information sharing cannot depend on a human in the loop. To allow computers to share information automatically, data and metadata must be grouped together. In a sense, without metadata, there is nothing to talk about, and without data, there is nothing to say.

The combination of data and metadata greatly reduces the information-sharing problem at the semantic level. Together data and metadata make information portable because the relationships among data values remain independent from their storage. Treating metadata as data also simplifies the implementation of tools, since a single representation can be used for both types of information. Metadata as data also gives a new degree of flexibility because existing information can be augmented with additional metadata as easily as adding new values. These are powerful advantages for an information-sharing approach, and they are compelling reasons to choose the Semantic Web approach for information interchange.

The Semantic Web Information Model: The Resource Description Framework (RDF)

On the Semantic Web, information is represented as a set of assertions called *statements* made up of three parts: subject, predicate, and object. Because of these three parts, statements are also sometimes referred to as *triples*. The three elements of a statement have meanings that are analogous to their meanings in normal English grammar. The subject of a statement is the thing that statement describes, and the predicate describes a relationship between the subject and the object. To clarify, consider the following Listing 3-1 about the authors of this book.

```
Andrew knows Matt.
Andrew's surname is Perez-Lopez.
Matt knows John.
Ryan works with John.
```

Listing 3-1 Information about the authors

Figure 3-2 is a graphical representation of that small set of information. Assertions of this form naturally form a directed graph, with subjects and objects of each statement as nodes, and predicates as edges. This is the data model used by the Semantic Web, and it is formalized in the language called the Resource Description Framework (RDF).

NOTE Throughout the book, we will be using diagrams to visualize RDF graphs. We will adopt the following common conventions: Resources are represented by ovals, literals are represented by rectangles, and predicates are represented by arrows. The direction of the arrow always points from the subject of a statement to the object of the statement.

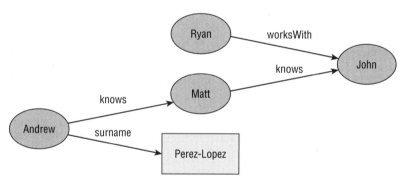

Figure 3-2 A graph representation of the sentences from Listing 3-1

Nodes: Resources and Literals

The nodes of an RDF graph are the subjects and the objects of the statements that make up the graph. There are two kinds of nodes: resources and literals. Literals represent concrete data values like numbers or strings and cannot be the subjects of statements, only the objects. Resources, in contrast, represent everything else, and they can be either subjects or objects.

In RDF, resources can represent anything that can be named. A resource is, in fact, nothing but a name—a name that represents an object, act, or concept. Resource names take the form of Internationalized Resource Identifiers.

INTERNATIONALIZED RESOURCE IDENTIFIERS

The Internationalized Resource Identifier (IRI) is an extension of the more familiar Uniform Resource Identifier (URI) that provides an encoding for Unicode character sets. In light of the similarity between IRIs and URIs, and the greater familiarity of most people with the latter, we will use the term IRI and URI interchangeably throughout this book.

IRIs are an essential part of the underlying infrastructure of the World Wide Web. An IRI is simply a standardized way of naming resources. Some IRIs include information about how to access such a resource on the Internet, and this subclass of IRIs is referred to as the Uniform Resource Locator, the URLs with which we are all familiar.

In general, IRIs take the following form:

```
scheme ":" [ "//" authority "/" ] [ path ] [ "?" query ] [ "#" fragment ]
```

where the scheme describes what type of IRI it is, and the subsequent portions more completely name the resource. The following examples of URIs should make this clear:

```
http://www.semwebprogramming.com:80/index.html
ftp://server.example.com/foo
gopher://gopher.floodgap.com/1/v2
mailto:person@example.net
urn:isbn:978-0553283686
```

While some of these IRIs may look more familiar than others, all are valid. Note that while IRIs often contain information that would allow an application to retrieve the resource, such as the server name or port, they need not. The last IRI is a Uniform Resource Name (URN) that describes a book by its International Standard Book Number (ISBN), but the book is not a resource that is resolvable on the Web. In general then, the IRI scheme provides a vast hierarchical namespace for resources of various kinds, which may be—but are not necessarily—accessible via the Web.

IRIs provide a foundation for a data-sharing infrastructure because they all exist within a single universal namespace. This means that every statement with a named resource as its subject unambiguously describes that particular resource, regardless of where the statement is asserted. Whereas a particular row in a database table is identified with a primary key unique to one table within one database, an IRI is a name that is universally unique. An IRI remains valid in any context, which means that information expressed in RDF is much more portable than information expressed in other ways.

In the previous figure, all of the resources are people, but consider the graph in Figure 3-3.

In the statement shown in this graph, the subject is Andrew, and the object is SoftwareEngineer. While *Andrew* is a person, *software engineer* is more abstract;

it is a concept. This generalized notion of resource allows statements in RDF to describe almost anything, including concrete objects and abstract concepts.

Figure 3-3 Resources can represent people, like Andrew, or concepts, like software engineer

Edges: Predicates

Predicates, also called *properties*, represent the connections between resources; predicates are themselves resources, however, and RDF statements can be made about predicates just as they can about any other resources. Like subjects, predicates are represented as IRIs. In the previous figures, we labeled resources without full IRIs for convenience sake, but now we will show the graph from Figure 3-2 as a graph with IRIs (see Figure 3-4). Because these full IRIs can clutter up a diagram for the rest of the chapter, we will use prefixes unless there is a particular reason to highlight the full IRI.

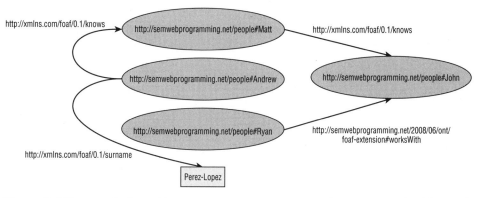

Figure 3-4 The graph from Figure 3-2, now more accurately represented with IRIs for each resource

One special type of predicate defined by RDF is `type`. The `rdf:type` predicate is used to group resources together. In Figure 3-3, we drew the distinction between `Andrew` as a person and `SoftwareEngineer` as a concept. That was an assumption based on knowledge that we, as humans, have but that was not represented in the graph. To be more accurate, we should assert that Andrew is a person with a statement that gives Andrew a type. In Figure 3-5, the resource `Andrew` is associated via the `rdf:type` predicate with a resource that represents the notion of a Person.

Figure 3-5 Andrew is designated as being of type `foaf:Person`

RDF supports a very permissive notion of type. Even though type is a special predicate defined in RDF, it is really just a predicate like any other. That is, the fact that there is a statement that asserts that Andrew is of type `Person` does not in any way preclude there being other statements about Andrew's type. Any resource can have any assertions made about it, including many or no `rdf:type` assertions.

Exchanging Information with RDF

RDF is a data model optimized for sharing and interchange. This ease of interchange arises from some of the characteristics of RDF that we've explored in the previous section, primarily the simple structure of the basic unit of RDF graphs, the graph structure of RDF, and the global namespace provided by the use of URIs.

Graphs do not have roots. Some other representations, for example, XML, are tree based. In an XML document, the root element of the tree has a special significance because all of the other elements are oriented with respect to the document root. When trying to merge two trees, it can be difficult to determine what the root node should be because the structure of that tree is so important to the overall significance of the data. In an RDF graph, by contrast, no single resource is of any inherent significance as compared to any other. That makes it easier, because combining graphs is conceptually the same as placing them next to one another.

The triple itself is a powerful tool for information integration. Triples are just collections of URIs and literals, and each URI and literal inherently has a global scope. The use of global names is critically important because it means that triples can always be merged without name translations. Since each constituent statement in a graph can be used without translation, entire graphs can be transported and combined without any translation, which is a great advantage when exchanging data.

Since RDF statements need no translation when moving from one system to another, they are valid in any context. They are completely self-contained assertions of information, and as such they are independent from one another. This independence means that the order in which they are encountered is irrelevant.

Statements as Points

One way to think about RDF statements is as points in an abstract three-dimensional space. Each axis would represent either the subject, predicate, or object of a statement and would be populated with every possible URI and literal, as shown in Figure 3-6. In this representation, a statement can be depicted as a point defined by its subject, predicate, and object. Each point represents a small atom of information, and each collection of these points would represent an RDF graph.

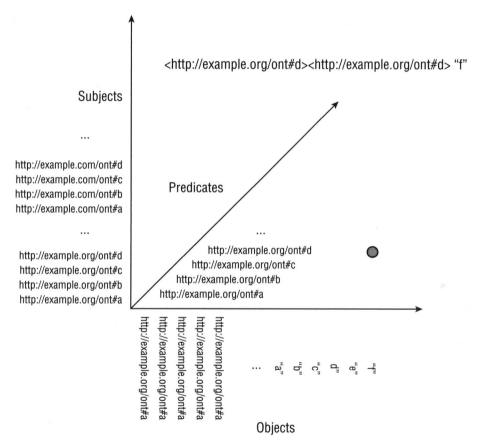

Figure 3-6 RDF statements can be thought of as points in an IRI/literal namespace. This helps illustrate some of their key characteristics.

Thinking about statements this way can illustrate some of their benefits for data sharing:

Easy merging: Points in statement space are just like points in any other n-dimensional space. Two sets of points can be overlaid on top of each other to create a richer image, just as two graphs of statements can be combined to form a richer graph.

No order: Imagine an image made of statement-space points coming into view. After all the points have been added and the image is complete, there is no way to determine any ordering as to when the different points were added.

No duplicates: If two statements have the same subject, predicate, and object, they are identical. Therefore, after a statement has been added to a collection, subsequent attempts to add that statement will contribute no additional information to the overall collection of assertions.

RDF Serializations

RDF graphs are powerful tools for representing information, but they are abstract—good for human analysis but unsuitable for application exchange. Serialization makes RDF practical for information exchange by providing a way to convert between the abstract model and a concrete format, such as a file or other byte stream. There are several equally expressive serialization formats. Three of the most popular are RDF/XML, the Terse RDF Triple Language (Turtle), and N-Triples. Turtle is the simplest and most concise; therefore we use it throughout this book.

An exhaustive discussion of the nuances of the various RDF serializations is outside of the scope of this chapter. There are many resources available on the World Wide Web, and in particular at the W3C website. Nevertheless, a practical knowledge of RDF serializations is critical to an understanding of Semantic Web technologies and how to use them effectively in real-world systems.

Since all RDF graphs have the same structure, each serialization format must represent the same constructs: statements and the URIs and literals that they comprise. Different serializations have special features to represent these constructs more conveniently, but they all describe the same information.

RDF/XML

RDF/XML is an XML syntax for representing RDF triples, and it is the only normative (standard) exchange syntax for RDF serialization. It must be supported by all well-behaved Semantic Web applications. There are other very common syntaxes, but to ensure that there is at least one syntax supported by all RDF tools, RDF/XML was selected as the official syntax. Unfortunately, even though there is a baseline format for serializing RDF, there is no canonical representation for RDF/XML. This results in differences for the same graph when serialized by different tools. It is very difficult, therefore, to compare RDF/XML documents because two documents that look very different from each other may in fact be the same. Some of the ways that RDF/XML documents can differ from one another will be explained later in this section.

This section's discussion of RDF/XML will be based on the sample RDF/XML graph shown in Listing 3-2.

```
<rdf:RDF
    xmlns:people="http://semwebprogramming.net/people#"
    xmlns:rdf="http://www.w3.org/1999/02/22-rdf-syntax-ns#"
    xmlns:foaf="http://xmlns.com/foaf/0.1/"
    xmlns:ext="http://semwebprogramming.net/2008/06/ont/
        foaf-extension#">
<!-- This is a comment. -->
  <rdf:Description rdf:about="http://semwebprogramming.net/
        people#Ryan">
    <ext:worksWith
        rdf:resource="http://semwebprogramming.net/people#John"/>
  </rdf:Description>
  <rdf:Description rdf:about="http://semwebprogramming.net/
        people#Matt">
    <foaf:knows
        rdf:resource="http://semwebprogramming.net/people#John"/>
  </rdf:Description>
  <rdf:Description
        rdf:about="http://semwebprogramming.net/people#Andrew">
    <foaf:surname>Perez-Lopez</foaf:surname>
    <foaf:knows
        rdf:resource="http://semwebprogramming.net/people#Matt"/>
  </rdf:Description>
</rdf:RDF>
```

Listing 3-2 The content from Listing 3-1, serialized as RDF/XML

Note the overall structure. All of the RDF content is contained within an `rdf:RDF` tag, which contains a series of `rdf:Description` elements. Another important item to note is the XML namespace declarations within the opening `rdf:RDF` tag. Since RDF/XML is the normative exchange syntax for RDF, the RDF document that defines RDF itself is formatted in RDF/XML. That document can be found on the Web at `http://www.w3.org/1999/02/22-rdf-syntax-ns`. By convention of the Semantic Web community, that namespace is always abbreviated `rdf`, either by XML namespaces in RDF/XML or by similar facilities offered by other serialization methods that you'll see later in the chapter.

Comments

In RDF/XML, comments are represented as in any other XML document. They begin with the sequence `<!--` , and end with the sequence `-->`. These comments are not part of the graph and are thus not "round-trippable" when parsing and reserializing an RDF/XML document.

Statements

In an RDF/XML document, statements about resources are grouped into the `<rdf:Description>` elements. Each description element has an `rdf:about` attribute, which gives the subject of all of the statements within it. Each of the subsequent elements within the description then defines the predicate and object of a statement. The name of the internal tags represents the predicate of a statement. The object is represented differently depending on whether it is a resource or a literal. The following pseudo-RDF/XML illustrates the general form.

```
<rdf:Description rdf:about="subject">
   <predicate rdf:resource="object" />
   <predicate>literal value</predicate>
</rdf:Description>
```

As an example, look at the following snippet from the RDF/XML document shown previously.

```
<rdf:Description rdf:about="http://semwebprogramming.net/
      people#Andrew">
   <foaf:surname>Perez-Lopez</foaf:surname>
   <foaf:knows rdf:resource="http://semwebprogramming.net/people#Matt"/>
</rdf:Description>
```

This excerpt expresses the graph shown in Figure 3-7.

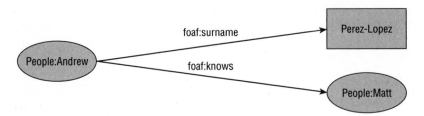

Figure 3-7 Subsection of the graph from the preceding code

Resources

Resources are treated differently depending on whether they are the subject or object of a statement. As we explained, subjects of statements are designated with the `rdf:about` attribute of a `rdf:Description` tag. Objects of statements appear in `rdf:resource` attributes of predicate tags.

RDF/XML is XML, so it uses standard XML namespace conventions to abbreviate full URIs that appear as XML elements. XML entity declarations can be used to abbreviate full URIs in XML attribute values such as for `rdf:resource`.

Literals

Literals appear as the text content of a predicate element. Literals can be assigned a datatype using standard XML Schema Datatypes (XSD). In fact, any URI can be used as a datatype for a literal, so you can create your own custom types. String literals can optionally be marked by language. The example in Listing 3-3 illustrates these features of RDF/XML:

```
<rdf:RDF
    xmlns:rdf="http://www.w3.org/1999/02/22-rdf-syntax-ns#"
    xmlns:zoo="http://example.org/zoo/"
>
<rdf:Description rdf:about="http://example.org/zoo/Animal-123456">
<zoo:numberOfLegs
    rdf:datatype="http://www.w3.org/2001/XMLSchema#int"
>4</zoo:numberOfLegs>
<zoo:scientificName>Canis lupus familiaris</
      zoo:scientificName>
<zoo:commonName xml:lang="en">Dog</zoo:commonName>
<zoo:commonName xml:lang="es">Perro</zoo:commonName>
</rdf:Description>
</rdf:RDF>
```

Listing 3-3 Literal values in RDF/XML

You can use the `xml:lang` attribute to indicate the language of the text in the associated string and use the `rdf:datatype` to indicate how to treat literal values. In the previous listing, `xml:lang` is used to distinguish the English from the Spanish version of the common name, and the `rdf:datatype` is used to mark the value 4. In contrast to typing for literals, the set of valid language tags is restricted. All language tags must be lowercased, and the codes for each language are as defined by RFC 3066 (available at `http://www.isi.edu/in-notes/rfc3066.txt`).

Shorthand and Special Features

RDF/XML allows a shorthand syntax for assigning types to resources:

```
<type rdf:about="resource" />
```

In a concrete example, consider this short RDF/XML document:

```
<rdf:RDF
    xmlns:rdf="http://www.w3.org/1999/02/22-rdf-syntax-ns#"
```

```
    xmlns:foaf="http://xmlns.com/foaf/0.1/"
    xml:base="http://semwebprogramming.net/people#"
>
<foaf:Person rdf:ID="#Ryan" />
<rdf:Description rdf:about="#Ryan">
    <rdf:type rdf:resource="http://xmlns.com/foaf/0.1/Person" />
</rdf:Description>
</rdf:RDF>
```

Even though that RDF/XML document contains a `rdf:Description` element as well as a the `<foaf:Person rdf:ID="#Ryan" />` statement, both are equivalent. They are different expressions of the same statement, which is that there is a resource called `http://example.com/people#Ryan` and that this resource is of type `foaf:Person`.

TIP A great resource for working with RDF/XML documents is the World Wide Web Consortium's RDF Validator. It can be accessed at `http://www.w3 .org/RDF/Validator/`.

TIP The definitive site on the Web for information about RDF/XML is `http://www.w3.org/TR/rdf-syntax-grammar/`.

Terse RDF Triple Language (Turtle)

The Terse RDF Triple Language, or Turtle, is another serialization syntax for RDF. Compared with other serializations, Turtle is a more human-friendly and readable syntax. Turtle is not an XML language—it was designed specifically for RDF. Because it does not have to represent a graph as a tree, it can be more concise and readable. Listing 3-4 shows the same graph used in Listing 3-2, this time serialized into Turtle.

```
@prefix foaf:     <http://xmlns.com/foaf/0.1/> .
@prefix rdf:      <http://www.w3.org/1999/02/22-rdf-syntax-ns#> .
@prefix people:   <http://semwebprogramming.net/people/> .
@prefix ext:      <http://semwebprogramming.net/2008/06/ont/foaf-
extension#> .
# This is a comment.

people:Ryan ext:worksWith people:John .
people:Matt foaf:knows people:John .
people:Andrew
      foaf:knows people:Matt ;
      foaf:surname "Perez-Lopez" .
```

Listing 3-4 The graph from Listing 3-2 serialized as Turtle

Comments

Turtle uses the # character at the beginning of a line to indicate a comment. Everything from the # symbol to the end of the line is ignored by the parser.

Statements

Turtle uses a simple format for each triple. The subject, predicate, and object are written on a line, separated by white space, and the statement is terminated with a period. Look at this line from the example:

```
people:Ryan ext:worksWith people:John .
```

In this line, `people:Ryan` is the subject, `ext:worksWith` is the predicate, and `people:John` is the object, and the statement is terminated with a period.

Turtle provides a shorthand way of writing multiple statements about the same subject. Look at the following snippet from Listing 3-4.

```
people:Andrew
       foaf:knows people:Matt ;
       foaf:surname "Perez-Lopez" .
```

In Turtle, the use of a semicolon indicates that the next two elements will be the predicate and object of a statement that has the same subject as the preceding statement. This bit of the document is equivalent to the following.

```
people:Andrew foaf:knows people:Matt .
people:Andrew foaf:surname "Perez-Lopez" .
```

The semicolon serves to reduce the effort required to write Turtle and to make it more readable.

Similar shorthand can be used for when two statements have the same subject and predicate.

```
people:Andrew foaf:knows people:Matt .
people:Andrew foaf:knows people:Ryan .
people:Andrew foaf:knows people:John .
```

A comma can be used to compact these three lines. When a comma appears at the end of a statement, it indicates that the next element is the object of a statement with the same subject and predicate as the previous statement. So the three lines about people Andrew knows can be compressed into the following Turtle.

```
people:Andrew foaf:knows people:Matt, people:Ryan, people:John .
```

Resources

In Turtle, resources are written in one of two ways. URIs appear either fully qualified and enclosed in < and > or with a predefined prefix. The previous document shows examples of both forms. Consider the following two lines:

```
@prefix ext: <http://semwebprogramming.net/2008/06/ont/foaf
  extension#> .
people:Ryan ext:worksWith people:John .
```

The first line describes a prefix declaration, which informs the Turtle parser that for this document, when ext: is encountered, it should be expanded to the full URI associated with the prefix. The prefix declaration also demonstrates how fully qualified URIs are expressed in Turtle. The second line has an example of using the prefix. That line could just as validly have been written as follows:

```
people:Ryan <http://semwebprogramming.net/2008/06/ont/foaf
  extension#worksWith> people:John .
```

Prefixes greatly reduce the clutter of the document and make Turtle much easier for people to read and write.

Literals

Literal values in Turtle are enclosed in double quotes, as in the previous example. Strings that contain double quotes can escape them with the "\n" character sequence. Strings that contain line breaks should be enclosed with three sets of double quotes, as in the following example:

```
@prefix ex: <http://example.com/> .
ex:Poem ex:hasText """Roses are red,
Violets are \"blue\",
Sugar is sweet,
And so are you.""" .
```

Turtle can also encode literals of specific XSD datatypes or languages, just like RDF/XML. Listing 3-5 shows the dog graph from Listing 3-3 expressed in Turtle:

```
@prefix zoo:  <http://example.org/zoo/> .
@prefix rdf:    <http://www.w3.org/1999/02/22-rdf-syntax-ns#> .
zoo:Animal-123456
     zoo:commonName "Dog"@en , "Perro"@es ;
     zoo:numberOfLegs
          "4"^^<http://www.w3.org/2001/XMLSchema#int> ;
     zoo:scientificName
          "Canis lupus familiaris" .
```

Listing 3-5 Literal values in Turtle

Datatypes are indicated by appending `^^<datatype URI>` to the end of the literal. Specific languages are indicated by appending `@language` to the end of a literal.

Shorthand and Special Features

Similar to RDF/XML, Turtle provides convenient shorthand for designating the type of an individual resource. In Turtle, the letter `a` is used instead of the more cumbersome `rdf:type`. As with other Turtle-specific features, this serves to make the document much easier for humans to read and write.

In the following document, both lines after the prefix declarations are equivalent:

```
@prefix rdf: <http://www.w3.org/1999/02/22-rdf-syntax-ns#> .
@prefix foaf: <http://xmlns.com/foaf/0.1/> .
@prefix : <http://semwebprogramming.net/people#> .

:Ryan a foaf:Person .
:Ryan rdf:type foaf:Person .
```

> **TIP** The authoritative site on the Web for information about Turtle is
> `http://www.w3.org/TeamSubmission/turtle/`.

N-Triples

N-Triples is a simplified version of Turtle. It uses the same syntax for comments, URIs, and literal values but imposes some simplifying restrictions. N-Triples does not support the `@prefix` directive or the `;` or `,` shorthand for statements. A statement in N-Triples is represented by a single line containing the subject, predicate, and object. N-Triples's simplicity can make it an attractive choice for serializing RDF, particularly in applications with streaming data.

For comparison, the example document from the other two serializations is repeated here in N-Triples. Because N-Triples is a line-based format, a single statement cannot span multiple lines. Strictly for purposes of demonstration, therefore, the serialization of the graph will, in this case, use a slightly different set of namespaces in order to fit it on the printed page. In Listing 3-6, the URI that in previous examples was `http://semwebprogramming.net/people#` is replaced with a shorter URI, `urn:sw:`. The FOAF extension URI of `http://semwebprogramming.net/2008/06/ont/foaf-extension#` is replaced with `urn:swprg:foaf:`, and the FOAF URI itself, `http://xmlns.com/foaf/0.1/`, is replaced with a shortened, print-friendly version, `urn:foaf:`.

```
<urn:sw:Ryan> <urn:swprg:foaf:worksWith> <urn:sw:John> .
<urn:sw:Matt> <urn:foaf:knows> <urn:sw:John> .
<urn:sw:Andrew> <urn:foaf:surname> "Perez-Lopez" .
<urn:sw:Andrew> <urn:foaf:knows> <urn:sw:Matt> .
```

Listing 3-6 Listing 3-2 serialized as N-Triples

TIP More information about N-Triples can be found on the Web at
`http://www.w3.org/TR/rdf-testcases/#ntriples`

Quick Hack

It is very important for you to know about different types of RDF serializations,
particularly since you will almost certainly need to write some by hand when
you build your Semantic Web system. A few short minutes with Java and the
Jena API yields a little application that can easily convert among RDF/XML,
N3, and N-Triples. The code in Listing 3-7 uses Jena to read in a file in a
specified RDF format (RDF/XML, N3, or N-Triples) and then writes out the
same graph to another file in a different format:

```java
package net.semwebprogramming.chapter3.RDFSerializer;

import java.io.*;
import com.hp.hpl.jena.rdf.model.Model;
import com.hp.hpl.jena.rdf.model.ModelFactory;

public class RDFSerializer {
    public static void main(String[] args) {
        String inputFileName = null;
        String outputFileName = null;
        String inputFileFormat = null;
        String outputFileFormat = null;
        FileOutputStream outputStream = null;
        FileInputStream inputStream = null;

        if(args.length != 4) {
            System.err.println("Usage: java RDFSerializer <input file> " +
                    "<output file> <input format> <output format>");
            System.err.println("Valid format strings include: RDF/XML, " +
                    "N3, and N-TRIPLES");
            return;
        }
```

(continued)

```
        inputFileName = args[0];
        outputFileName = args[1];
        inputFileFormat = args[2];
        outputFileFormat = args[3];

        try {
            inputStream = new FileInputStream(inputFileName);
            outputStream = new FileOutputStream(outputFileName);
        } catch (FileNotFoundException e) {
            System.err.println("'" + outputFileName + "' is an invalid " +
                                "file name.");
            return;
        }

        Model rdfModel = ModelFactory.createDefaultModel();
        rdfModel.read(inputStream, null, inputFileFormat);
        rdfModel.write(outputStream, outputFileFormat);

        try {
            outputStream.close();
        } catch (IOException e) {
            System.err.println("Error writing to file.");
            return;
        }
    }
}
```

Listing 3-7 Program for reading and writing RDF serialization formats using Jena

Looking at the code, the majority of it just unpacks the command-line arguments, initializes file I/O, and handles exceptions that might be thrown. Only three lines perform any RDF-specific operations.

```
Model rdfModel = ModelFactory.createDefaultModel();
rdfModel.read(inputStream, null, inputFileFormat);
rdfModel.write(outputStream, outputFileFormat);
```

The first line instructs Jena to create an empty RDF graph. The second line populates the graph with the triples from the stream, using a parser that is capable of reading the given RDF format. The `null` parameter passed to the `read` method instructs Jena to automatically convert any relative URIs that it might encounter to absolute URIs that it maintains internally. Finally, the third line serializes the RDF graph to the given stream in the specified output format.

NOTE This example results in a program that behaves just like a program called `jena.rdfcopy` that is included with the Jena distribution. It is a very useful utility when working with RDF documents in different formats. If you choose not to implement this Quick Hack, you can use `jena.rdfcopy` instead.

More RDF

Up to this point, this chapter has focused on the main concepts behind RDF, the information model for the Semantic Web, and some of the most important characteristics of that model. Nevertheless, there are a few extra ideas that need to be explained in order for you to understand all of RDF.

Blank Nodes

An RDF statement contains a subject, predicate, and object, where the subject and predicate are URIs in a global namespace and the object is either a URI or a literal. There is a special case of this rule. Not all resources are designated as URIs in the global namespace. Some resources, called *blank nodes*, conceptually have no names at all.

Blank nodes are used to represent *existential variables*. A good example of an existential variable that illustrates some of the special characteristics of blank nodes is the old adage, "There's someone special out there for everyone." In a more logic-friendly rephrasing, the saying is, "It is true that for every person, there exists a person who is a good match for the first person." In this case, the good match is a person who is an existential variable. What's important is that this other person cannot have a name because he or she can be identified only with respect to the adage. You can talk about the person, but when you do so, you must refer to him or her as "your special person" to tie the thing to the notional person described in the saying. You can say, "My special person will be nice," or "good looking," or "tall," or what have you, but it does not make sense to separate the subject of these statements from the notion of "your special person." This is because such an existential variable does not truly describe any single individual entity, but rather an abstract template of an entity.

Similarly, in RDF serializations, blank nodes can be given names, but these names are unique only within the context of the particular RDF document, and blank nodes can never be referred to outside the current document. This notion of a blank node seems like a subtle and abstract concept. How are blank nodes really used in practice? Why would it be desirable to even have blank nodes, and what are the implications of their existence on the Semantic Web information model?

The simple structure of RDF is a great advantage for information sharing, but simplicity comes at a price. RDF supports only binary predicates. That is, a statement expresses a relationship between two resources and never more than that. Say, for instance, that you wanted to express in RDF the idea of a person living in a city and state. There is no single statement that can connect a resource to both a city and a state, because RDF allows only binary predicates. You could have two predicates like `residesInCity` and `residesInState`, but that solution falls down when a person has two or more residences. At that point, because the city and state for both residences are associated with the person, it becomes impossible to determine which city belongs with which state.

The proper way to solve this problem is to create a resource that represents a residence, associate the residence with the person, and then link the city and state with the residence. Without blank nodes, however, RDF requires that this intermediary residence node have a globally resolvable name even when, as in this case, it doesn't make sense to provide such a name. Requiring URIs for such intermediary nodes is clumsy and counterintuitive.

More important, such a requirement could hinder data sharing. Consider the following two RDF documents shown in Listing 3-8, written with an RDF specification that does not permit blank nodes:

```
# First document, created by an organization that owns example.org
@prefix ex: <http://example.org/residences#> .
@prefix sw: <http://semwebprogramming.net/resources#> .

sw:Bob sw:hasResidence ex:SomeResidence .
ex:SomeResidence sw:isInCity "Arlington" ;
                 sw:isInState "VA" .

#Second document, created by an organization that owns example.com
@prefix ex: <http://example.com/bob-info#> .
@prefix sw: <http://semwebprogramming.net/resources#> .

sw:Bob sw:hasResidence ex:SomeResidence .
ex:SomeResidence sw:isInCity "Arlington" ;
                 sw:isInState "VA" .
```

Listing 3-8 RDF if blank nodes were not allowed

In this code, the only difference between the first and the second documents is the prefix defined for `ex:`. The term `SomeResidence` is used by both documents as a placeholder for some residence in Arlington. In this case, because we are forcing every resource to have a URI, both documents are using a global name, but they naturally are placing that name within a namespace that they control. When the two graphs are combined, however, it will appear as though Bob has two residences. Nothing in RDF precludes multiple URIs being used to describe the same resource, so nothing about that combination is technically wrong, but it is cumbersome. Since both graphs really don't intend to say anything about Bob's residence situation other than that one in Arlington, VA, exists, they would be better served using a blank node.

In Turtle, there is a special prefix reserved for blank nodes. A blank node may be given a node ID that starts with the _: prefix. For example, _:blanknode, _:placeholder, _:p3, _:rabbit. All are valid blank node IDs. Each node ID is unique only within the scope of a single RDF document.

Using blank nodes, the documents from Listing 3-8 can be rewritten as shown in Listing 3-9.

```
# First document, using the example.org namespace
@prefix ex: <http://example.org/residences> .
@prefix sw: <http://semwebprogramming.net/resources#> .

sw:Bob sw:hasResidence _:residence .
_:residence sw:isInCity ""Arlington" ;
            sw:isInState "VA" .

#Second document, using the example.com namespace
@prefix ex: <http://example.com/bob-info> .
@prefix sw: <http://semwebprogramming.net/resources#> .

sw:Bob sw:hasResidence _:bobshouse .
_:bobshouse sw:isInCity "Arlington" ;
            sw:isInState "VA" .
```

Listing 3-9 The documents from Listing 3-8 presented with blank nodes

When the two documents are combined, the result will be something like this:

```
@prefix sw: <http://semwebprogramming.net/resources#> .

sw:Bob sw:hasResidence _:node .
_:node sw:isInCity "Arlington" ;
       sw:isInState "VA" .
```

Turtle also provides convenient shorthand for referring to blank nodes. You can use the [and] characters to define a blank node without providing a blank node ID. All of the statements within the [and] have the blank node as the subject. Using this shorthand, the two previous graphs would be written as shown in Listing 3-10:

```
# First document, using the example.org namespace
@prefix ex: <http://example.org/residences> .
@prefix sw: <http://semwebprogramming.net/resources#> .

sw:Bob sw:hasResidence [
            sw:isInCity "Arlington" ;
            sw:isInState "VA"
            ] .

#Second document, using the example.com namespace
@prefix ex: <http://example.com/bob-info> .
@prefix sw: <http://semwebprogramming.net/resources#> .

sw:Bob sw:hasResidence [
            sw:isInCity "Arlington" ;
            sw:isInState "VA"
            ].
```

Listing 3-10 Blank nodes represented using the Turtle shorthand

Note that the node IDs in each document that used the blank nodes were different. Because conceptually those nodes don't have a name, the string value that appears in the serialized RDF version can be different every time.

The advantages of blank nodes come with some considerations. Blank nodes, as anonymous resources, cannot be referred to from outside their defining document. This can present significant challenges when trying to create links between data, a crucial goal for the Semantic Web.

Even if linking data is not an explicit concern, blank nodes can be a problem when using queries to access RDF information. These difficulties will become clearer after the explanation of querying that comes in Chapter 6, "Discovering Information." In general terms, the problem is that if a blank node is included in a query result, the node ID given to the node in the result is valid only for that query result. Therefore, subsequent queries cannot refer to the blank node directly. If you plan to use queries in your system, you may choose not to use blank nodes to represent any information you care to retrieve later.

Another problem with the limited scope of blank nodes is that it complicates merging RDF graphs. In particular, the problem arises from possible node ID conflicts. When merging graphs, software tools must ensure that each distinct blank node has a node ID that is unique within the scope of the combined document. Because RDF does not impose any ordering on statements, it can be difficult to assign these node IDs properly. This issue particularly complicates processing streams of RDF statements.

Reification

It is possible to make a statement about anything in RDF, even other statements—a statement about a statement. This is an extremely valuable tool for practical Semantic Web systems. It can be employed to qualify or annotate information in useful ways. One application might be to tag information with provenance information or with a timestamp of when it was added to a system. You might use this to group statements together or in a closed system to indicate the validity of statements.

RDF statements must always have a resource as a subject, so in order to make a statement about a statement, a resource must be used to represent an entire statement. RDF provides a special type called `rdf:Statement` to designate those resources that represent statements. The `rdf:subject`, `rdf:predicate`, and `rdf:object` predicates are used to define the statement that is being annotated. For instance, suppose you wanted to express the idea "Matt says that John knows Ryan." You could use reification like so:

```
@prefix :foaf <http://xmlns.com/foaf/0.1/> .
:Matt :asserts _:stmt .
_:stmt a rdf:Statement ;
          rdf:subject :John ;
          rdf:predicate foaf:knows ;
          rdf:object :Ryan .
```

This example uses a blank node to represent the statement resource, but a full URI could be used as well.

RDF Organizational Constructs

RDF provides several constructs for grouping information. Typically, complex information is not stored in RDF alone; richer semantic languages build on the RDF data model. Nevertheless, it is important to recognize how these RDF constructs work and how they are used.

RDF Containers

RDF defines three types of resources that are understood to be collections of resources. The first, `rdf:Bag`, is used to represent an unordered grouping of resources, while `rdf:Seq` can maintain an ordered collection. The final container type, `rdf:Alt`, is an unordered collection like `rdf:Bag`, but it is intended for a particular purpose. The `rdf:Alt` container should be used when describing a set of equivalent alternatives.

In order to associate resource with these containers, RDF defines a special set of predicates, namely, `rdf:_1`, `rdf:_2`, `rdf_3,` ... , `rdf_n`. These predicates associate a container as the subject with a resource it contains as the object. Even though `rdf:Bag`, `rdf:Seq` and `rdf:Alt` all use the `rdf:_n` predicates to establish the containment relationship with other resources, the value of n can be ignored except in the case of an `rdf:Seq` type container. The example in Listing 3-11 illustrates the different types of containers:

```
@prefix ex: <http://example.com/> .
@prefix rdf: <http://www.w3.org/1999/02/22-rdf-syntax-ns#> .
@prefix people: <http://www.semwebprogramming.net/people/> .
@prefix foaf:    <http://xmlns.com/foaf/0.1/> .

ex:Authors a rdf:Bag ;
          rdf:_1 people:Ryan ;
          rdf:_2 people:Matt ;
          rdf:_3 people:Andrew ;
          rdf:_4 people:John .

ex:Chapters a rdf:Seq ;
          rdf:_1 ex:ChapterOne ;
          rdf:_2 ex:ChapterTwo ;
          rdf:_3 ex:ChapterThree ;
          rdf:_4 ex:ChapterFour ;
          rdf:_5 ex:ChapterFive .

ex:Homepages a rdf:Alt ;
           rdf:_1 <http://www.semwebprogramming.net> ;
           rdf:_2 <http://www.semwebprogramming.org> .

ex:Book ex:writtenBy ex:Authors .
ex:Book ex:hasChapters ex:Chapters .
ex:Book foaf:homepage ex:Homepages .
```

Listing 3-11 RDF Containers – `rdf:Bag`, `rdf:Seq`, and `rdf:Alt`

In this example, there are three containers, one for a book's authors, one for its chapters, and one for its home-page URLs. The authors are stored in an unordered collection, because conceptually there is no relevance to their order. With the collection of chapters, on the other hand, order could be very important. Finally, with the collection of home pages, each is an equally valid representation for the object of the statement describing the book's `foaf:homepage`.

Numbering each one of the elements in a collection this way can be very tedious, particularly in the case of `rdf:Seq`. Inserting an element into an ordered collection might require renaming every subsequent element. For this reason, RDF serializations use the `rdf:li` predicate instead of the `rdf_n` predicates. Conceptually, each `rdf:li` predicate is in fact one of the `rdf_n` predicates, but when actually writing RDF, it is much more convenient to use the `rdf:li` predicate instead. This is also one of the only situations where the order of statements is relevant. Because a sequence represents an ordered set of resources, if you use the `rdf:li` shorthand, then the first resource of the group will become `rdf:_1`, the second `rdf:_2`, and so on.

RDF Lists

RDF lists help to group collections of resources in such a way that they will not be altered even when RDF graphs are merged. Consider the following graph:

```
@prefix ex: <http://example.com/> .
@prefix rdf: <http://www.w3.org/1999/02/22-rdf-syntax-ns#> .
@prefix people: <http://www.semwebprogramming.net/people/> .
@prefix foaf:    <http://xmlns.com/foaf/0.1/> .

ex:Authors a rdf:Bag ;
          rdf:_1 people:Ryan ;
          rdf:_2 people:Matt ;
          rdf:_3 people:Andrew ;
          rdf:_4 people:John .
ex:Book ex:writtenBy ex:Authors .
```

If it were merged with this graph

```
@prefix ex: <http://example.com/> .
ex:Authors rdf:_5 ex:SomeOtherPersonThatIsntAnAuthor
```

then the resulting graph would indicate an extra author, which might not be the desired effect. In order to express a collection that cannot be modified in this way, RDF provides the `rdf:List` construct. Listing 3-12 shows how an `rdf:List` could represent the author information in a more closed way:

```
@prefix ex: <http://example.com/> .
@prefix rdf: <http://www.w3.org/1999/02/22-rdf-syntax-ns#> .
@prefix people: <http://www.semwebprogramming.net/people/> .
@prefix foaf:    <http://xmlns.com/foaf/0.1/> .

ex:Authors a rdf:List ;
          rdf:first people:Ryan ;
          rdf:rest _:r1 .
      _:r1 a rdf:List ;
          rdf:first people:Matt ;
          rdf:rest _:r2 .
      _:r2 a rdf:List ;
          rdf:first people:Andrew ;
```

(continued)

```
         rdf:rest _:r3 .
    _:r3 a rdf:List ;
         rdf:first people:John ;
         rdf:rest rdf:nil .


ex:Book ex:writtenBy ex:Authors .
```

Listing 3-12 A List serialized in Turtle

In this example, lists are constructed with two predicates. The `rdf:first` predicate refers to the first element of a list, while the `rdf:rest` predicate refers to another list that has as its `rdf:first` resource the second resource of the overall list. This process continues recursively until the `rdf:rest` of the list is `rdf:nil`. This construct allows for collections where each element explicitly refers to the subsequent element. This prevents the order or contents from being altered as new RDF graphs are combined.

This can be a valuable tool, but it is an extremely awkward and unreadable way to represent RDF lists. Thankfully, Turtle provides very concise shorthand to represent RDF lists. The list from Listing 3-12 can be equally represented by the RDF document that follows:

```
@prefix ex:       <http://example.com/> .
@prefix foaf:     <http://xmlns.com/foaf/0.1/> .
@prefix rdf:      <http://www.w3.org/1999/02/22-rdf-syntax-ns#> .
@prefix people:   <http://www.semwebprogramming.net/people/> .

ex:Book
      ex:writtenBy (people:Ryan people:Matt people:Andrew people:John) .
```

In Turtle, lists can be written as parentheses containing white space–separated resources. This makes for much more readable RDF documents than the original syntax. The shorthand forms for containers and lists Turtle provides not only improve readability and help to make documents shorter, but they also greatly reduce the likelihood of human error. As you develop your Semantic Web applications and need to update RDF files, the verbose syntax of containers and lists make it easy to zig when you should zag, as it were. It is very easy to introduce a subtle numbering error or to forget a `rdf:rest` statement when updating in a list, particularly when the list is large, and it can be very difficult to figure out where the error occurs.

Summary

Over the course of this chapter, you've learned about the information-sharing problem in abstract terms and about how the Semantic Web model, RDF, approaches that problem. You've seen some of the strengths and weaknesses of RDF for data sharing as compared to other information models, and you've learned how information can be represented in RDF. You've seen examples of a few RDF serializations and written a short program to convert among the different formats. You've learned about the importance of integrated metadata for information portability and seen how RDF's flexibility allows it to express arbitrary statements about anything, even concepts.

In Chapter 4, "Incorporating Semantics," you'll see how to use RDF to describe groups of resources and the relationships between those groups. In Chapter 5, "Modeling Knowledge in the Real World," you'll learn how to apply the principles from this group of chapters to real problems, and you'll also be introduced to inference, one of the most powerful features of the Semantic Web.

Incorporating Semantics

"Whatever we learn has a purpose and whatever we do affects everything and everyone else, if even in the tiniest way. Why, when a housefly flaps his wings, a breeze goes round the world; when a speck of dust falls to the ground, the entire planet weighs a little more; and when you stamp your foot, the earth moves slightly off its course ... And it's much the same thing with knowledge, for whenever you learn something new, the whole world becomes that much richer."

—Norton Juster, *The Phantom Tollbooth*

In the previous chapter, you learned about the information model of the Semantic Web: the Resource Description Framework, or RDF. RDF provides a virtually limitless model for describing information. You can say anything you want *about* anything you want. The drawback of all the flexibility and expressiveness of RDF is that used alone, it lacks explicit support for specifying the meaning, or semantics, behind the descriptions.

Fortunately, the original vision for the Semantic Web considered the fact that developers and users need some way of specifying rich semantic descriptions of concepts and relationships to exchange information effectively. RDF Schema (RDFS) and the OWL Web Ontology Language provide these capabilities.

The purpose of this chapter is to provide you with the knowledge necessary to add semantics to your web of RDF data. Semantics are the key to incorporating domain knowledge into RDF data, making the descriptions richer and more meaningful.

The objectives of this chapter are:

- to understand the role of semantics in information modeling and the Semantic Web
- to introduce the elements of the OWL Web Ontology Language and how each is used to add meaning to information in the Semantic Web

This chapter is meant to be a primer for semantics in the Semantic Web and should serve as an excellent reference for the OWL Web Ontology Language. Chapter 5, "Modeling Knowledge in the Real World," builds on the contents of this chapter by discussing ontology development and management and the role of inference in the Semantic Web through an in-depth, hands-on example.

Semantics on the Web

Before diving head first into learning the technologies that will allow you to incorporate semantics into your web of data, it's important to understand why semantics are needed and how the various technologies of the Semantic Web fit together. The following sections explore the motivations behind incorporating semantics into the RDF model and how RDFS and OWL combine to provide this capability.

You'll recall from Chapter 3, "Modeling Information," that communication involves semantics and syntax. *Semantics* refers to the meaning or concepts of the information that's being shared. *Syntax* refers to the means by which the information is transferred. Consider a communication between a soccer player who has just scored a goal and her coach. The coach wishes to congratulate the player, so he gives her a high five and shouts, "Great shot!" The coach is expressing approval and congratulations. The meaning of these concepts is the semantics of the communication. The high five and verbal adulation are transfer mechanisms for communicating the semantics. They are the syntax of the communication. The player understands the communication by interpreting the syntax and its associated semantics.

Adding semantics to a web of data requires the ability to define concepts and relationships precisely in a manner that transcends syntax. Leveraging this capability is what the Semantic Web is all about, and this chapter takes the first step toward understanding and applying semantics to any web of data, even the World Wide Web (WWW).

> **NOTE** You can skip straight to the "Introduction to Ontologies" section if you are already familiar with the foundations of the Semantic Web and you want to begin learning about the OWL Web Ontology Language and ontologies.

Motivating Factors

There are many motivating factors driving Semantic Web development. These include but are not limited to: making web-based information machine understandable, providing a rich semantic model for expressing domain knowledge, and enabling cross-domain information exchange. The next couple of subsections present two specific use cases to help you better understand the goals of the Semantic Web.

Understanding the World Wide Web

The World Wide Web is one of the largest public repositories of information in the world. At the time this book was written, it was estimated that there are on the order of tens of billions of web pages (`www.worldwidewebsize.com`). That is an extraordinary amount of information. Unfortunately, most of that information is inaccessible to computers because it is designed for human consumption. Machines were designed to relay information, not to be aware of the concepts and relationships contained within it. This makes it very difficult for applications to utilize the WWW as an information source in any kind of automated manner.

It's not immediately apparent that there are limitations with the current design of the WWW. When you need some piece of information, it's relatively easy to find it. You go to a search engine like Google or Yahoo, type in a search string, and then you review the results, refining your search as you go, until you find the page you're looking for (as depicted in Figure 4-1).

Figure 4-1 Searching on the Web involves an iterative process of refining search terms based on the set of documents returned. This process relies heavily on the user's ability to quickly interpret the results

This process works as well as it does because the user is in the loop. You, the user, do the hard part. Yes, indexing the contents of pages and ranking their relevance to search terms are hard, but these tasks require computers to do what they're really good at: calculating, indexing, and sorting. The search engine is really only performing a syntax-based pattern match between your query and the contents of documents on the Internet, with some added features for improving performance and accuracy.

Unfortunately, the search engine isn't aware of the semantics of the search terms, nor does it understand the meaning of the information contained in each web page; therefore, it is unable to solve, or provide an *answer*, to the query. All it can do is to try to help *you, the user*, answer it with information from Web documents that contain terms similar to your search. Try one of the following Web searches and observe the results:

- Which 2005 model year passenger car has the best fuel economy?
- What are the 10 largest lakes in the United States of America?
- Were any American presidents born in Maryland?

For each of the listed searches, the search engine will find Web pages that are using the same language or asking the same question as your search. The search engine is helping you by pointing you to documents that are relevant to your question, but it can't answer your question directly because it doesn't understand it. Moreover, even if it could understand your question, it doesn't understand all the web pages that are on the WWW, so it has no ability to search and identify information that is relevant to the semantics of your question.

The search engine simply applies a mathematical model to the content of each web page and the words in your query. Despite the lack of semantics, search engines work remarkably well for a majority of use cases because of how easy it is for humans to review a document and determine its relevance. Automatically performing this ability using a computer involves natural language processing, which is a nontrivial challenge.

It is a bit unfair to fault search engines for not being able to answer the kinds of questions we've discussed. After all, that's not what they were designed to do. They were designed to retrieve the documents on the Web that are syntactically similar to your search terms, and they do that remarkably well. The real point of this example is to raise the question: Why aren't there popular search engines that search the Web using semantics? One of the biggest reasons is what we mentioned before. Most of the information on the Web is in purely human-readable and human-understandable form.

While improving search engine performance is not the primary goal of adding semantics to the Web, it does serve as an illustrative example of why automated information processing systems need semantics. If each web page were annotated with semantic metadata, it would make the *hard* part of the problem much easier for computers to deal with. Search engines could be aware of what information is out there and how to interpret queries and apply them to the available information to produce a real answer, rather than simply providing a pointer to relevant resources. This type of web forms a vast knowledgebase of information from which any program or anyone can extract information more easily.

Knowledge Domain Integration

Forming and capturing semantics at the WWW level can be a bit overwhelming. There is already so much data out there that it's hard to imagine annotating all of it with semantic metadata. Moreover, there is an ugly chicken-and-egg problem. It is hard to justify the development of Semantic Web applications without a Semantic Web, but there is little motivation to build the Semantic Web without having applications that actually use it. A more immediately tangible and micro-level motivation for semantics involves information sharing between specific knowledge domains.

Information sharing is fundamental to the Semantic Web. It's not only about transferring a stream of bits from one system to another but also about conveying a set of concepts between systems or across knowledge domains. When information is semantically (rather than syntactically) described, it can be shared across domain boundaries by defining the concepts of the foreign domain in terms of the concepts of the local domain. This is similar to how we learn new concepts. We describe them and understand them in terms of the concepts we're familiar with. Once these relationships between the concepts of each domain are established, anyone can take advantage of them. Figure 4-2 illustrates this concept by presenting very simple definitions of the Semantic Web and the World Wide Web and drawing relationships between the concepts of each. On the left side of the figure is a very high-level description of the WWW. On the right side is the same for the Semantic Web. The circles in the figure represent concepts, while the arrows represent relationships between concepts. The arrows that are dashed connect the concept of WWW with the concept of Semantic Web.

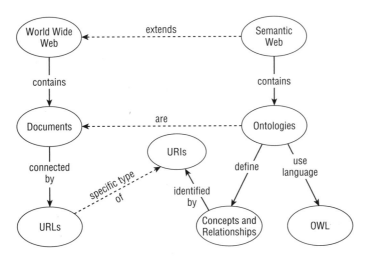

Figure 4-2 Unfamiliar information can become more understandable when you see it related to concepts you know

There is nothing groundbreaking about sharing information between groups that use different formats, languages, and schemata; however, there is a critical difference between traditional approaches and the Semantic Web approach. Take a relational database as an example. To share information between two communities that each use a different schema for its database, sharing would occur through a process of translation. A dump of data would be mapped and translated from one schema to the other. The key here is that the data is fundamentally changing. The old information that was captured in the original schema is gone, and it has been replaced with new information according to the destination schema. Any data that cannot be directly translated will be lost, and any difference in how general or specific the different schemata are will be manifest in the final product.

The Semantic Web approach to information sharing involves description. Concepts from the source knowledge domain are described in terms of the concepts of the destination knowledge domain. This is a purely additive process. In the end, the data has meaning in both domains, *and* the full context and fidelity of the data are maintained because no information has been lost through a process of translation. Even if an application does not directly understand the foreign concepts, it can use the relationships between the local and foreign concepts as a basis for interpretation.

Expressing Semantics in RDF

The Resource Description Framework (RDF) provides a way to model information but does not provide a way of specifying what that information means—its semantics. An RDF graph alone can only be interpreted as just that: a graph. The only meaning that is apparent is based solely on your ability to recognize and interpret the URIs, literals, and general structure of the graph. Despite the fact that the RDF graph in Figure 4-3 contains no explicit semantics, it is apparent that it is describing a few people who know each other.

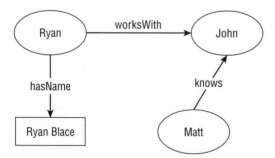

Figure 4-3 The meaning of this RDF graph is apparent because the resources and properties are recognizable. Despite this, there is no meaning in this graph beyond its structure.

It becomes much harder to make sense of what is being expressed in RDF if the contents of the graph are in a different language or are unrecognizable. Consider the RDF graph in Figure 4-4. The same exact information is represented, but the URIs are no longer recognizable. Can you still tell what the graph represents? To add meaning to RDF graphs properly, you need some means of defining a vocabulary of predefined terms with accompanying semantics for describing the information.

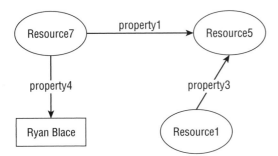

Figure 4-4 This RDF graph is the same as in Figure 4-3, only this time the resources and properties aren't human-recognizable.

Vocabularies, Taxonomies, and Ontologies

Vocabularies, taxonomies, and ontologies are all related. Each contains a set of defined terms, and each is critical to the ability to express the meaning of information. Their differences lie in their expressiveness, or how much meaning each attaches to the terms that it describes:

- A *vocabulary* is a collection of unambiguously defined terms used in communication. Vocabulary terms should not be redundant without explicit identification of the redundancy. In addition, vocabulary terms are expected to have consistent meaning in all contexts.

- A *taxonomy* is a vocabulary in which terms are organized in a hierarchical manner. Each term may share a parent-child relationship with one or more other elements in the taxonomy. One of the most common parent-child relationships used in taxonomies is that of specialization and generalization, where one term is a more-specific or less-specific form of another term. The parent-child relationships can be many-to-many; however, many taxonomies adopt the restriction that each element can have only one parent. In this case, the taxonomy is a tree or collection of trees (forest). Figure 4-5 illustrates the hierarchical structure of a taxonomy.

- An *ontology* uses a predefined, reserved vocabulary of terms to define concepts and the relationships between them for a specific area of interest, or domain. *Ontology* can actually refer to either a vocabulary, a taxonomy, or something more. Typically the term refers to a rich, formal logic-based model for describing a knowledge domain. Using ontologies, you can express the semantics behind vocabulary terms, their interactions, and context of use.

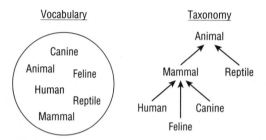

Figure 4-5 Vocabularies are simple collections of well-defined terms. Taxonomies extend vocabularies by adding hierarchical relationships between terms.

The Semantic Web uses a combination of a schema language and an ontology language to provide the capabilities of vocabularies, taxonomies, and ontologies. RDF Schema (RDFS) provides a specific vocabulary for RDF that can be used to define taxonomies of classes and properties and simple domain and range specifications for properties. The OWL Web Ontology Language provides an expressive language for defining ontologies that capture the semantics of domain knowledge.

A Vocabulary Language for RDF

As the previous chapter explains, RDF allows you to make statements about resources that are identified using URIs. These statements take the form of triples that associate a resource (subject) with a value (object) using a property (predicate). RDF provides an extremely powerful and expressive model for capturing information; however, RDF alone provides no way to capture the meaning of the information it is modeling.

The first step toward expressing the meaning of RDF information is to develop a common vocabulary, or collection of resources, that has a well-understood meaning and is used in a consistent manner to describe other resources. RDF Schema does not attempt to define these shared vocabularies; rather, it provides a language with which you can develop your own shared vocabularies. The namespaces that are used by RDFS are listed in Table 4-1 with the prefixes rdf, rdfs, and xsd.

RDFS vocabularies describe the classes of resources and properties being used in an RDF model. Using RDFS, you can arrange classes and properties in generalization/specialization hierarchies, define domain and range expectations for properties, assert class membership, and specify and interpret datatypes. All resources in RDFS are considered members of the class of all RDF resources and as such are all instances. You can further describe those instances by making statements about them using properties or by explicitly making them members of other classes defined in an RDFS vocabulary.

RDFS is one of the fundamental building blocks of ontologies in the Semantic Web and is the first step toward incorporating semantics into RDF. The specific constructs of RDFS will be covered as part of the larger discussion of ontologies in this chapter.

An Ontology Language for the Web

The OWL Web Ontology Language extends the RDFS vocabulary with additional resources that can be used to build more expressive ontologies for the Web. OWL introduces added restrictions regarding the structure and contents of RDF documents in order to make processing and reasoning more computationally decidable. OWL uses the RDF and RDFS, XML Schema datatypes, and OWL namespaces. The OWL vocabulary itself is defined in the namespace `http://www.w3.org/2002/07/owl#` and is commonly referred to by the prefix `owl`. OWL 2 extends the original OWL vocabulary and reuses the same namespace. The full set of namespaces used in OWL and their associated prefixes are listed in Table 4-1.

Table 4-1 Namespaces Used in the OWL Web Ontology Language

NAMESPACE	PREFIX
`http://www.w3.org/1999/02/22-rdf-syntax-ns#`	`rdf`
`http://www.w3.org/2000/01/rdf-schema#`	`rdfs`
`http://www.w3.org/2001/XMLSchema#`	`xsd`
`http://www.w3.org/2002/07/owl#`	`owl`

These prefixes will be used in all examples without necessarily being defined explicitly.

The original OWL documents became a World Wide Web Consortium (W3C) recommendation in February 2004, after almost three years of academic and industry development. At the time of this writing, development is underway on the second version of OWL, with completion expected in mid-2009. OWL 2 is a backwards-compatible extension of OWL that adds a set of new capabilities motivated by feedback from the users of the original version.

In this book, all discussion regarding OWL is oriented toward OWL 2; however, OWL 2–specific topics and capabilities will be explicitly identified as such.

When working with ontologies, you can choose which elements of RDFS and OWL you want to use. It is very common to build an OWL ontology using only a small subset of the OWL language elements (if any at all). This is perfectly acceptable. The language was developed to be flexible, and it should be used in the most reasonable and pragmatic manner possible. To help users make these decisions, there are a number of predefined subsets, or profiles, of OWL that provide varying levels of expressivity with tradeoffs in computational complexity.

The set of valid OWL documents is a subset of the set of valid RDFS documents. In other words, OWL introduces extra vocabulary and structure assumptions that are not explicitly present in RDFS. Regardless of the subset of language elements you use in your system, you should base your knowledge model on OWL. If you instead build a system around RDFS and later decide to switch to OWL, you may be in for a headache. Tools that are built for the restrictions and vocabulary of OWL may not be compatible with your RDFS-based system and knowledge model.

The rest of this chapter focuses on ontologies in the Semantic Web, including critical assumptions and principles of OWL and an in-depth exploration of the elements of ontologies and their uses.

Introduction to Ontologies

OWL ontologies are used to model domain knowledge. This encompasses significantly more than the simple structure of an RDF graph or the list of defined terms and hierarchical structure of an RDFS vocabulary. Ontologies are the core element of the Semantic Web, and as such they are the primary focus of the remainder of this chapter. We begin by reviewing their characteristics, assumptions, and structures.

Distributed Knowledge

Semantic Web technologies are designed to make the World Wide Web more machine-understandable. Resources on the Web are inherently distributed, and as a result, the resource descriptions contained on the Semantic Web are also distributed. OWL supports this kind of distributed knowledge model because it is built on RDF, which allows you to declare and describe resources locally or refer to them remotely. OWL also provides a mechanism for importing and reusing ontologies in a distributed environment. We'll discuss that later in the section on ontology headers.

To provide a foundation on which to make valid inferences in the distributed knowledge model of the Semantic Web, we must make two important assumptions: the open world assumption and the no unique names assumption.

Open World Assumption

Because of the inherently distributed knowledge model of the Semantic Web, OWL makes an *open world assumption*. This assumption has some significant impacts on how information is modeled and interpreted. The open world assumption states that the truth of a statement is independent of whether it is known. In other words, not knowing whether a statement is explicitly true does not imply that the statement is false. The closed world assumption, as you might expect, is the opposite. It states that any statement that is not known to be true can be assumed to be false. Under the open world assumption, new information must always be additive. It can be contradictory, but it cannot remove previously asserted information.

As an example of the open world versus the closed world, consider the relational database that stores customer information for the local Ultra-Mart. The absence of a record for Ryan Blace in the Customer table (depicted in Figure 4-6) implies that Ryan Blace is not, in fact, a customer of Ultra-Mart. This is because the database assumes that it represents a complete knowledge model. There is no information relevant to the database that is not already contained in it. In this case, the system has a scoped (or closed) world. In the Semantic Web, the absence of a statement that says that the resource representing Ryan Blace is a customer of Ultra-Mart does not imply anything about his status as a customer.

Customers		
Name	Phone_Number	Last_Visit
John Smith	(703) 555-2134	June 8, 2008
Andrew Hebeler	(410) 555-7623	July 14, 2008
Mike Fisher	(202) 555-2944	August 7, 2007
Matt Dean	(703) 555-5417	June 11, 2008

Figure 4-6 Applying the open world assumption, the example implies that the system is not aware of whether or not there is a customer named Ryan Blace. With a closed world assumption, you can infer that there is no customer with the name Ryan Blace.

Most systems operate with a closed world assumption. They assume that information is complete and known. For many practical applications this is a safe, and often necessary, assumption to make. However, a closed world assumption can limit the expressivity of a system in some cases because it is more difficult to differentiate between incomplete information and information that is known to be untrue. Returning to the example of Figure 4-6, there is no straightforward way to model the fact that Mike Smith may or may not be an employee. In a system that makes a closed world assumption, there are only two things in the world: employees and not employees.

Abiding by the open world assumption impacts the kind of inference that can be performed over the information contained in your model. In OWL, it means that reasoning can be performed only over information that is known. The absence of a piece of information cannot be used to infer the presence of other information. This impact is real, and you must be aware of it as you begin to work with the logical constructs and inference capabilities of OWL ontologies. Correct inference of OWL semantics in the distributed world of the Semantic Web relies on the adherence to the open world assumption.

No Unique Names Assumption

The distributed nature of description in the Semantic Web makes it unreasonable to assume that everyone is using the same URI to identify a specific resource. Rather, it is often the case that a resource is being described by multiple users in multiple locations, and each of those users is using his or her own URI to represent the resource. A simple example of this situation is the fact that people commonly have multiple email addresses, home pages, blogs, and social networking profiles. Each of these can serve as an identifier for an individual, but they are all different.

The *no unique names assumption* states that unless explicitly stated otherwise, you cannot assume that resources that are identified by different URIs are different. Once again, this assumption is quite different from those of many traditional systems. In most database systems, for instance, all information is known, and assigning a unique identifier, such as a primary key that is consistently used throughout the system, is possible. Like the open world assumption, the no unique names assumption impacts inference capabilities related to the uniqueness of resources. Redundant and ambiguous data is a common issue in information management systems, and the no unique names assumption makes these issues easier to handle because resources can be made the same without destroying any information or dropping and updating database records.

Overview of Ontology Elements

OWL ontologies are commonly stored as documents on the Web. Each document consists of an optional ontology header, annotations, class and property definitions (more formally referred to as *axioms*), facts about individuals, and datatype definitions. Because OWL is based on the RDF model, there is no explicit distinction between the ontology and the data the ontology is used to describe. A less-formal way of saying this is that there is no official partition that exists between ontologies and instances. Partitioning is arbitrary and does not affect the meaning of the information; however, it is a common practice to maintain ontologies separately from the data they describe.

Ontologies optionally contain headers that define and describe the resource representing the ontology itself. Annotation properties add nonsemantic descriptive information to resources. Ontologies are composed of three fundamental semantic building blocks: classes, individuals, and properties. A *class* is a set of resources. An *individual* is any resource that is a member of at least one class. A *property* is used to describe a resource. Finally, ontologies can contain datatype definitions that describe ranges of values.

Ontology Header

An ontology header is a resource that represents the ontology itself. The header describes the ontology and typically contains comments, labels, versioning information, and ontology import statements. Import statements are important because tools use them to determine what other ontologies are referred to by the current document and are needed to fully comprehend the concepts and relationships described in the current ontology.

Classes and Individuals

An OWL *class* is a special kind of resource that represents a set of resources that share common characteristics or are similar in some way. A resource that is a member of a class is called an *individual* and represents an instance of that class. In OWL, individuals can become members of classes both directly (by asserting their membership explicitly) and indirectly (by defining the membership conditions for a class such that it can be inferred that a resource is a member of that class). In Figure 4-7, the Person resource is a class and Ryan and Andrew are individuals.

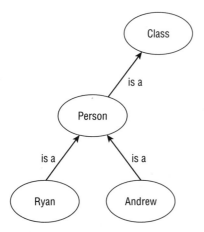

Figure 4-7 Classes in OWL represent groups of similar resources. In this example, Ryan and Andrew are instances of the Person class.

Properties

A *property* in OWL is a resource that is used as a predicate in statements that describe individuals. There are two main types of properties in OWL: object properties that link individuals to other individuals, and datatype properties that link individuals to literal values. In Figure 4-8, Ryan and Andrew now have datatype properties that specify their names. They are connected to each other by the object property knows.

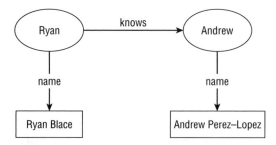

Figure 4-8 Properties are used to describe resources, and they are one of two primary types: object properties or datatype properties.

Annotations

Annotations are statements (triples) that have annotation properties as predicates. Annotation properties are similar to normal OWL properties, but they have no associated semantics and are primarily used in human user interfaces. The two most common annotation properties are rdfs:label and rdfs:comment. Many tools are designed to interpret and use the common predefined annotation properties when presenting information to users.

Datatypes

Datatypes in OWL represent ranges of data values. Some common datatypes are integer, string, and time. OWL 2 allows you to define your own complex datatypes that are explicitly enumerated or defined using facet restrictions (value range restrictions).

The addition of custom datatypes in OWL 2 is substantial because it allows you to model new concepts that you couldn't in OWL 1. Using facet restrictions, you can define a datatype that represents the correct range for a dose of medicine as between 50 and 70 mL or create a datatype that represents the range of legal driving ages in the United States as greater than or equal to 16. These datatypes can then be used when describing how classes and properties interact.

Elements of an Ontology

Now that you've explored the concept of semantically describing resources on the World Wide Web and received a cursory glance of the Web Ontology Language, it's time to explore the details of OWL. The following section looks at the various constructs of OWL that are used in ontology descriptions of domain-specific knowledge, including those that are reused and extended from RDFS.

We begin with some introductory material covering annotations and ontology declarations. We then move into basic classification, class membership, and property-based description. Finally, we explore the more complex features of the language, including defining datatypes, using property restrictions, defining classes using enumerations and set operators, and working with equality in OWL. After studying this section, you will have the knowledge necessary to understand and build OWL ontologies for your own domain.

> **NOTE** This section explores the RDFS language elements as they are used and extended in OWL, rather than addressing them in detail separately as part of a discussion of RDFS alone. All ontology discussions and examples use the second version of OWL (OWL 2), and all constructs specific to OWL 2 are identified as such.

> **W3C SEMANTIC WEB ACTIVITY RESOURCES**
>
> The World Wide Web Consortium (W3C) maintains detailed project pages for the OWL Web Ontology Language, Resource Description Framework, RDF Schema specifications, and other Semantic Web–related resources. These pages contain all work, past and present, performed by the various working groups who have contributed to W3C Semantic Web activities. These resources can be found at the W3C Semantic Web Activity home page, at http://www.w3c.org/2001/sw.

OWL 2 Typing

Resources in an ontology can be typed as individuals (instances of a class), as classes, or as properties. OWL 2 specifies a series of constraints about how resource types can be assigned in an ontology that dictates how URIs can be used and reused as different types. As we have already briefly introduced, the specific resource types in an ontology are individual, class, datatype, object property, datatype property, and annotation property. The constraints on how each type can be applied to a URI are as follows:

- Object, datatype, and annotation properties must be disjoint.
  No URI can be typed as more than one kind of property.

- Classes and datatypes must be disjoint. No URI can be typed as both a class and a datatype.

These restrictions apply to the reuse of URIs that are part of the OWL vocabulary. These restrictions allow a single URI to be used to refer to more than one type of entity in an OWL ontology. In the OWL documentation, this is referred to as *metamodeling*. One common form of metamodeling is the reuse of a URI to represent both a class and an individual. For more information on entity declarations and typing in OWL 2, refer to the OWL 2 Web Ontology Language Structural Specification and Functional-Style Syntax document on the W3C website.

Ontology Header

The *ontology header* is a description of the resource that represents the ontology itself. There is no requirement than an ontology document must contain an ontology header, but it is good form. The ontology header may contain annotations such as versioning and compatibility information as well as labels and comments. The header may also contain a set of ontology import statements.

The property `owl:imports` specifies the set of ontologies that are referred to in the importing ontology. Import statements provide tools with the information necessary to build a complete model of all resources referred to in an ontology. The extent to which imports are used is dependent on the tool. Some reasoning engines require complete information and will import the full transitive closure of all imported ontologies (all ontologies imported directly, plus all imported by those that are imported directly, and so on), while other tools, such as browsers and editors, may be flexible in how they handle imports.

The versioning properties, `owl:priorVersion`, `owl:backwardCompatible With`, and `owl:incompatibleWith`, provide a basis for version management. Ontology versioning is a sticky subject in general in the Semantic Web and will be revisited later in the chapters that focus on practical applications.

Ontology headers usually contain annotation properties that describe the ontology. The following RDF shows a sample ontology header definition that provides an import statement and an annotation property specifying a comment about the ontology. Notice that the subject of the ontology declaration used only the prefix `ex:`. The namespace of the ontology document is `http://example.org/`. We use that URI in the ontology declaration because we are referring to the ontology itself, using the ontology's URI.

```
@prefix ex: <http://example.org/ >.

ex: rdf:type owl:Ontology;
    rdfs:comment "This is an example ontology";
    owl:imports <http://example.org/example-import>.
```

Annotations

Annotations are statements that describe resources using annotation properties. Annotation properties are semantics-free properties. These properties can be used to describe any resource or axiom in an ontology, including the ontology itself. Class, property, and individual annotations are made by creating a statement that uses the annotation property as the predicate of the statement.

Axiom annotations are slightly more complicated because their exact structure depends on the type of axiom that is being described. For example, if the axiom being described is a statement, then a reification object is created and the annotation is made. There are a number of other ways that axiom annotations can be made, but most annotations are made about classes, properties, and individuals, and so this discussion of axiom annotations is intentionally brief. For more information about axiom annotations, consult the OWL 2 Web Ontology Language Structural Specification and Functional Syntax document on the W3C website.

Table 4-2 lists the annotation properties that are predefined in OWL. The most commonly used are `rdfs:label`, `rdfs:comment`, and `owl:versionInfo`. Each of these annotation properties can be used to make annotations about classes, properties, individuals, and axioms.

Table 4-2 Annotation Properties Defined in OWL

PROPERTY	DESCRIPTION OF USE
rdfs:label	A label, or terse description of the subject resource.
rdfs:comment	A comment about the subject resource.
owl:versionInfo	Information about the subject ontology or resource version. Frequently used to embed source control metadata.
rdfs:seeAlso	Used to specify that another resource may hold more information about the subject resource. Not commonly used.
rdfs:isDefinedBy	Used to specify that another resource defines the subject resource. Not commonly used.

You can define an additional annotation property by declaring an instance of the class `owl:AnnotationProperty`. Because annotation properties have no semantic meaning, you cannot define subproperty, inverse property, or domain and range relationships for them. Annotation properties are primarily used by tools and applications to interact with humans.

Basic Classification

One of the most basic ways to describe an object is to place it into a category, or class, of things with which it shares common features. In OWL, you can define classes and specify membership in those classes using the resources `owl:Class` and `rdf:type`. The resource `owl:Class` represents the class containing all OWL classes. Every class in OWL must be a member of `owl:Class`, and every resource that has an `rdf:type` of `owl:Class` is a class. The resource `rdf:type` is a property that assigns class membership to a specific resource.

Classes and Individuals

The members, or instances, of a class are referred to in OWL as individuals. The set of individuals that are members of a class is considered its *class extension*. Containment in an OWL class extension does not preclude an individual from being a member of any other class. An OWL class has intrinsic meaning beyond its class extension. This implies that two classes can have exactly the same class extension but still represent unique classes, and no assumptions can be made otherwise. This concept is important because it emphasizes that class extension equivalence is not a sufficient condition for class equivalence. Two classes may have the same extension in a particular context; however, if they are different concepts, their extensions may diverge in a different context.

As the following RDF excerpt illustrates, you can use the resources `owl:Class` and `rdf:type` to state that `ex:Canine` and `ex:Human` are classes and that `ex:Daisy` is a canine and `ex:Ryan` is a human. In this example, `ex:Daisy` is an individual and a member of the class `ex:Canine`. The example is a very simple representation of a class that contains no description or information beyond a URI. All we know about `ex:Canine` from this example is that it is a class and that it has at least one member, `ex:Daisy`:

```
@prefix ex: <http://example.org/>.

# Canine and Human are owl classes
ex:Canine rdf:type owl:Class.
ex:Human rdf:type owl:Class.

# Daisy is an instance of the class Canine
ex:Daisy rdf:type ex:Canine.

# Ryan is an instance of the class Human
ex:Ryan rdf:type ex:Human.
```

An OWL class definition consists of some optional annotations followed by zero or more constructs that restrict the membership of the class. These restrictions represent descriptions of the class and form the basis of the class definition. The various forms of class restriction include subclass relationships, explicit membership enumeration, property restrictions, and class-based set operations. Each of these is discussed throughout the following sections.

CAUTION It is common for software developers to think that individuals in OWL are analogous to the objects of object-oriented programming (OOP), because they are both instances of classes. While this assumption won't get you into too much trouble, there are subtle differences between the two concepts. First, objects in OOP derive all their information from their class types. The types of an object do not depend on its characteristics; rather, its characteristics depend on its types. In OWL, classes describe sets of individuals that share common characteristics. The types of an OWL individual do not necessarily dictate its structure; rather, OWL individuals can have any structure, regardless of their types.

rdfs:SubClassOf

One of the simplest ways of restricting the membership of a class is to create a taxonomic relationship between it and other classes using the property `rdfs:subClassOf`. Consider the following statement that asserts that `Class1` is a subclass of `Class2`: `(Class1 rdfs:subClassOf Class2)`. The statement implies that:

- `Class1` is a specialization of `Class2`.
- Each member of `Class1` must be a valid member of `Class2` (it must pass all membership restrictions specified by `Class2`).
- Membership in `Class1` implies membership in `Class2`.
- The properties of `Class2`, including membership restrictions, are subsumed (inherited) by `Class1`.

Now consider the following example, which extends our previous sample ontology by asserting that the classes `ex:Canine` and `ex:Human` are each `rdfs:subClassOf` a new class, `ex:Mammal`. Each class is now defined as a specialized form of the class `ex:Mammal`. All of the members of the classes `ex:Canine` and `ex:Human` are now implicitly also members of the class `ex:Mammal`:

```
@prefix ex: <http://example.org/>.

ex:Mammal rdf:type owl:Class.

# Canine is a subclass of Mammal
ex:Canine rdf:type owl:Class;
          rdfs:subClassOf ex:Mammal.

# Human is a subclass of Mammal
ex:Human rdf:type owl:Class;
```

```
            rdfs:subClassOf ex:Mammal.

# Both Daisy and Ryan are implicitly members of the class Mammal
ex:Daisy rdf:type ex:Canine.
ex:Ryan rdf:type ex:Human.
```

To understand the implications of the subclass-of relationship in a knowledge management environment, consider a database with a schema that represents humans and canines as two separate tables. Applications that wish to extract the set of all mammals from the database must combine entries from both the human and the canine tables. The semantics of the relationship between humans and canines has been captured in the application, not the schema. A developer understood that humans and canines are each mammals and wrote a query that combined the two tables to produce the desired result.

Using an ontology, you can extract the semantics of this relationship out of the application and put them where they belong: in the knowledge model. This way, applications can utilize the knowledge model to determine how to satisfy a request for all mammals. This approach simplifies application development because the application is effectively decoupled from the knowledge model. Additional subclasses of mammals, for example, felines, can be added to the knowledgebase and knowledge model without requiring application changes. In the case of the database, the applications and any queries that previously assumed that the set of mammals was composed of all canines and humans would have to be extended to include felines.

Instance versus Subclass

Developers often confuse the distinction between the subclass-of relationship and the instance-of relationship. This confusion stems from the fact that you may want a concept to represent a class or an instance depending on the conceptual context in which it is being considered.

In the example, `ex:Mammal` is a class because it represents the set of all mammals in existence. The resource `ex:Canine` represents a specific subset of those mammals, and `ex:Daisy` is one of the members of that subset. If instead `ex:Mammal` represented the set of all the *kinds* of mammals that exist, it would no longer make sense for `ex:Canine` to be its subclass. Rather, `ex:Canine` would be one of the specific individuals that make up that set.

The important difference between the two relationships is that a subclass represents a subset of the members of the parent class, while an instance represents an individual member of a class. The following example illustrates this difference by adding a new class hierarchy to the sample ontology:

```
@prefix ex: <http://example.org/>.
...
ex:Breed rdf:type owl:Class.
ex:LargeBreed rdf:type owl:Class;
              rdfs:subClassOf ex:Breed.
ex:SmallBreed rdf:type owl:Class;
              rdfs:subClassOf ex:Breed.

ex:GoldenRetriever rdf:type ex:LargeBreed.
ex:Chihuahua rdf:type ex:SmallBreed.
```

The class `ex:Breed` represents the set of all dog breeds, which is further subdivided into the subclasses `ex:LargeBreed` and `ex:SmallBreed`. At this point, you may be tempted to add a few breeds such as `ex:GoldenRetriever` and `ex:Chihuahua` as subclasses of `ex:LargeBreed` and `ex:SmallBreed`, respectively; however, this is conceptually incorrect. Golden retrievers and Chihuahuas are not subsets of breeds; they are breeds. They should be members of the subclasses `ex:LargeBreed` and `ex:SmallBreed`, not subclasses of them.

TIP The key question to ask when determining whether a resource is an instance or a subclass of a specific class is: Is this resource a member of this class, or is it a subset of the members of this class? Understanding how the concepts in question are related is critical to answering this question.

owl:Thing and owl:Nothing

In OWL, there are two fundamental classes from which all other classes are derived: `owl:Thing` and `owl:Nothing`. The resource `owl:Thing` represents the class of all individuals, and every resource that is an instance of a class is implicitly a member of `owl:Thing`. The resource `owl:Nothing` represents the empty class, a class that has no members. Looking at this from a taxonomic point of view (shown in Figure 4-9), `owl:Thing` is the most generalized class possible, and `owl:Nothing` is the most specific class possible (it is so exclusive that no thing can be considered a member).

Defining and Using Properties

OWL properties are used to establish relationships between resources. The two fundamental classes of OWL properties are:

`owl:ObjectProperty`—The class of all relationships between individuals

`owl:DatatypeProperty`—The class of all relationships between an individual and a literal value

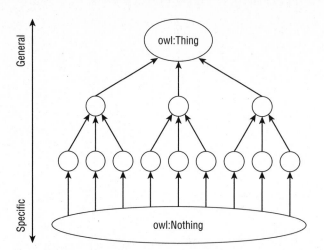

Figure 4-9 No class can be more general than `owl:Thing` or more specific than `owl:Nothing` because every OWL class is implicitly a subclass of `owl:Thing`, and `owl:Nothing` is implicitly a subclass of every OWL class.

The following example demonstrates the basic definition and use of properties in ontologies. First, two new properties are created, `ex:name` and `ex:breed`, using the resources `owl:DatatypeProperty` and `owl:ObjectProperty`, respectively. Second, the properties specify that `ex:Daisy` has a name, ``Daisy``, and a breed, `ex:GoldenRetriever`:

```
@prefix ex: <http://example.org/>.
...
#name is a datatype property because it refers to literals
ex:name rdf:type owl:DatatypeProperty.

#breed is an object property because it refers to an individual
ex:breed rdf:type owl:ObjectProperty.

ex:Daisy ex:name "Daisy";
        ex:breed ex:GoldenRetriever.

ex:Ryan ex:name "Ryan Blace".
```

Property Domain and Range

OWL allows you to describe the domain and range relationships between properties and classes or datatypes using the properties `rdfs:domain` and `rdfs:range`:

   `rdfs:domain`—Specifies the type of all individuals who are the
      subject of statements using the property being described

rdfs:range—Specifies the type of all individuals or the datatype of all literals that are the object of statements using the property being described

Domain and range specify the class memberships of individuals and the datatypes of literals, and they are globally asserted relationships. This is significant because it means that all future use of the resource, regardless of context, will be subject to the domain and range specified for the property. In general, global domain and range assertions can introduce inflexibility and should be used with caution.

As an example, consider the sample ontology. You could further define Daisy and assert that the most general concept in your ontology, ex:Mammal, is the domain of the property ex:name. This is fine in the limited ontology; however, suppose you want later to describe a bird, or an organization, or a landmark, none of which is an ex:Mammal. You couldn't reuse the ex:name property without implying that those individuals were of type ex:Mammal, which is certainly not your intention.

Describing Properties

OWL provides a number of ways to describe (or add semantics to) properties. The first two involve describing a property in terms of another, and the rest involve making a property a member of a class of properties that have a special meaning in OWL.

rdfs:subPropertyOf

As with classes, properties can be arranged into taxonomies using the property rdfs:subPropertyOf. To explain the implications of a subproperty relationship, consider the following statement that asserts that Property1 is a subproperty of Property2: (Property1) rdfs:subPropertyOf (Property2). The statement asserts the following:

- Property1 is a specialization of Property2.
- Any two resources related using Property1 are implicitly related by Property2.

Consider the following RDF, which defines a new property, ex:registered Name, that is used to specify Daisy's official registered name. ex:registered Name is a specialization of ex:name. To add that information to the ontology, you assert that ex:registeredName rdfs:subPropertyOf ex:name. This relationship implies that Daisy's ex:registeredName, "Morning Daisy Bathed in Sunshine", is also her ex:name:

```
@prefix ex: <http://example.org/>.
...
```

```
#registered name is a subproperty of name
ex:registeredName rdf:type owl:DatatypeProperty;
                  rdfs:subPropertyOf ex:name.

#the subproperty relationship implies that Daisy's registered
#name is also one of her names
ex:Daisy ex:registeredName "Morning Daisy Bathed in Sunshine".
```

Top and Bottom Properties

For each class of properties, both object and datatype, there are two corresponding special properties defined in OWL. These two properties are the top and bottom properties that represent the most general and most specific properties from which all other properties are derived. The specific properties are:

- `owl:topObjectProperty`
- `owl:bottomObjectProperty`
- `owl:topDataProperty`
- `owl:bottomDataProperty`

Each of the top properties represents the most general property. The role of `owl:topObjectProperty` is that it connects all possible pairs of individuals. The role of `owl:topDataProperty` is that it connects all possible individuals with all literals. Each of the bottom properties represents the most specific property. The role of `owl:bottomObjectProperty` is that it connects no pairs of individuals, and `owl:bottomDataProperty` does not connect any individual with a literal.

Inverse Properties

Properties assert directed relationships, from domain to range or subject to object. Sometimes the existence of a relationship in one direction implies that another relationship exists in the opposite, or inverse, direction. The following pairs are examples of inverse relationships:

- identifies—is identified by
- has child—has parent
- has part—is a part of

OWL allows you to assert that a property is the inverse of another using the property `owl:inverseOf`. Consider the following statement that asserts that `Property1` is the inverse of `Property2`: (`Property1 owl:inverseOf Property2`). This statement implies the following:

- `Property1` represents a relationship that is the inverse of `Property2`.

- The existence of a statement (`Entity1 Property1 Entity2`) implies the existence of the statement (`Entity2 Property2 Entity1`).

- The existence of a statement (`Entity2 Property1 Entity1`) implies the existence of the statement (`Entity1 Property2 Entity2`).

To better understand the `owl:inverseOf` property and its implications, apply it to the ongoing Daisy example. The following RDF excerpt shows the addition of two new properties: `ex:hasOwner` and `ex:owns`. The example asserts that `ex:hasOwner owl:inverseOf ex:owns` and that `ex:Daisy ex:hasOwner ex:Ryan`. These statements imply the existence of the statement `ex:Ryan ex:owns ex:Daisy`:

```
@prefix ex: <http://example.org/>.
...
ex:hasOwner rdf:type owl:ObjectProperty.
ex:owns rdf:type owl:ObjectProperty.

#has owner is the inverse of owns
ex:hasOwner owl:inverseOf ex:owns.

ex:Daisy ex:hasOwner ex:Ryan
```

Both the domain and range of the `owl:inverseOf` relationship must be object properties. Datatype properties cannot have inverses because literal values cannot be the subjects of statements. It would not make sense for `owl:DatatypeProperty ex:name` to have an inverse property `ex:isNameOf` because a literal, such as `''Daisy''`, cannot be the subject of a statement.

Disjoint Properties

OWL 2 provides a couple of constructs for specifying that two properties are disjoint. When we say that two properties, `property1` and `property2`, are disjoint, it means that no two statements can exist where the subjects and objects of each statement are the same, and the first statement has `property1` as the predicate while the second statement has `property2` as the predicate. The first of the two disjoint property constructs is a relationship that can be established between properties: `owl:propertyDisjointWith`. The following RDF example illustrates the use of `owl:disjointPropertyWith` to specify that the two properties `ex:hasMother` and `ex:hasFather` are disjoint properties:

```
@prefix ex: <http://example.org/>.
...
ex:hasMother rdf:type owl:ObjectProperty.
ex:hasFather rdf:type owl:ObjectProperty.

ex:hasMother owl:propertyDisjointWith ex:hasFather.
```

The second method is a construct used to identify that sets of properties are pair-wise disjoint. This construct uses the class `owl:AllDisjointProperties` and the property `owl:members`. The following RDF demonstrates making the same properties disjoint using this alternate construct:

```
@prefix ex: <http://example.org/>.
...
ex:hasMother rdf:type owl:ObjectProperty.
ex:hasFather rdf:type owl:ObjectProperty.

[] rdf:type owl:AllDisjointProperties;
   owl:members (
       ex:hasMother
       ex:hasFather
   ).
```

Notice here that the disjoint property set is an anonymous instance. OWL requires that instances of `owl:AllDisjointProperties` remain unnamed. Although the example used to demonstrate disjoint properties uses two object properties, datatype properties can also be made disjoint. The syntax for datatype properties is exactly the same as that for object properties.

Property Chains

OWL 2 introduces a very interesting construct called a *property chain*. The idea is to use a chain of properties that connects a set of resources as the subproperty in an `rdfs:subPropertyOf` relationship. A simple example will make this concept clear.

Consider the `hasUncle` relationship, where your uncle is the brother of one of your parents. The relationship can be defined only in terms of two properties that occur in an ordered chain connecting three individuals. So far, you've learned to describe properties only in terms of one other property at a time. Using a property chain, you can represent an ordered chain of properties and then use it as the subproperty in a subproperty-of relationship. Using the uncle example, you would first define a property chain representing the parent relationship followed by the brother relationship. Next, you would assert that the property chain was `rdfs:subPropertyOf` a property `ex:hasUncle`. This would have the effect of expressing that the existence of the property chain connecting two resources implies the existence of the `ex:hasUncle` property. The following RDF uses property chains to express the relationship `ex:hasUncle` using OWL:

```
@prefix ex: <http://example.org/>.
...
# Define each of the relationships
```

```
ex:hasUncle rdf:type owl:ObjectProperty.
ex:hasParent rdf:type owl:ObjectProperty.
ex:hasBrother rdf:type owl:ObjectProperty.

# Describe the uncle relationship situation
exRyan ex:hasParent ex:Jean.
ex:Jean rdf:type ex:Human;
        ex:hasBrother ex:Doug.

# Define that the property chain is a
# subproperty of the uncle relationship
[] rdfs:subPropertyOf ex:hasUncle;
   owl:propertyChain (
     ex:hasParent
     ex:hasBrother
     ).
```

Property chains can be as long as you need them to be. Expressing the relationship great-grandmother would be similar to expressing the uncle relationship, only it would involve three mother properties in a chain. An important restriction on the use of property chains is that they can be used only as part of a subproperty relationship and they can appear only in the subproperty position of such a relationship. They cannot be used in any other property relationships such as an inverse, equivalent, or disjoint relationship.

Symmetric, Reflexive, and Transitive Properties

OWL provides a number of property classes that provide additional semantics to property descriptions. The first five we will discuss are `owl:Symmetric Property`, `owl:AsymmetricProperty`, `owl:ReflexiveProperty`, `owl:Irre flexiveProperty`, and `owl:TransitiveProperty`. The final two are `owl: FunctionalProperty` and `owl:InverseFunctionalProperty`. Asymmetric, reflexive, and irreflexive properties are new in OWL 2.

Each property class is a subclass of `owl:ObjectProperty`, with the exception of `owl:FunctionalProperty`. Table 4-3 contains definitions for each kind of property.

An `owl:SymmetricProperty` is its own inverse. A less precise but simpler way to think of symmetric properties is that they are bidirectional relationships. The existence of the relationship in one direction (subject to object) implies that the same relationship exists in the opposite direction (object to subject) as well. Some example symmetric properties include `equals`, `adjacent to`, and `has spouse`.

An `owl:AsymmetricProperty` can never exist as a bidirectional relationship. No two individuals A and B can be related (A p B) and (B p A) by an asymmetric property p. Example asymmetric properties include `has mother` and `is greater than`.

Table 4-3 Classes of OWL Properties

PROPERTY CLASS	DEFINITION
owl:SymmetricProperty	(A p B) implies the statement (B p A).
owl:AsymmetricProperty	(A p B) implies there is no statement (B p A).
owl:ReflexiveProperty	Implies the statement (A p A), for all A.
owl:IrreflexiveProperty	Implies there is no statement (A p A), for all A.
owl:TransitiveProperty	(A p B) and (B p C) implies the statement (A p C).
owl:FunctionalProperty	(A p x) and (C p y) implies that x = y.
owl:InverseFunctionalProperty	(A p B) and (C p B) implies that A = C.

In each example, A, B, and C represent individuals, x and y represent resources (literals or individuals), and p represents a property of the corresponding type.

An owl:ReflexiveProperty relates all individuals to themselves. In mathematics, the equals operator (=) is reflexive, because every number is equal to itself. Knows is a reflexive property because it is assumed that everyone knows himself or herself. Use reflexive properties carefully, because they have global impact; the mere definition of a reflexive property is enough to imply that every individual is related to itself using that property. Once a reflexive property is defined, you will never have to use the property explicitly because it will already be implicitly asserted for every individual.

An owl:IrreflexiveProperty is a property that never relates an individual to itself. In mathematics, the greater than (>) and less than (<) operators are irreflexive. Has uncle and has mother are examples of irreflexive properties. It is incorrect to assume that a property is irreflexive simply because it is not reflexive, because properties can be reflexive, irreflexive, or neither.

The example in Table 4-3 is the most straightforward way to explain properties of type owl:TransitiveProperty. For any individuals A, B, and C and a transitive property p, (A p B) and (B p C) implies (A p C). Transitive properties are commonly used to describe *part-of-a-whole* and *contains* relationships. For example, the United States of America *contains* Virginia, which *contains* Arlington. If you declare that *contains* is a transitive property, then it is implied that the United States *contains* Arlington.

Functional and Inverse Functional Properties

An object or datatype property is functional if it is a member of the class owl:FunctionalProperty. When a property is functional, it can associate only a single unique value with a particular individual. Date of birth is a good example of a functional property because an individual can have only one birthday, but two people can share the same birthday. An example of a functional object property is has biological mother because a person can have only one mother, but siblings can share the same mother. The semantics of functional properties are such that if a person has two functional properties, each with different individuals as the objects of the statements, it implies that the two objects are the same. Using the has biological mother example, if Bob has a biological mother Sue and a biological mother Susan, it is inferred that Sue is the same person as Susan. Functional properties do not make any assertions about the uniqueness of the subjects of statements; this is the role of inverse-functional properties.

An object property is inverse-functional if it is a member of the class owl:InverseFunctionalProperty. In a statement with a predicate of this type, the object uniquely identifies the subject. No two individuals can have the same value for that property; however, an individual can have more than one unique value. Take the property has email address as an example. Assume for this example that no two people can have the same email address. If the property has email address is inverse-functional and two people share the same value for the property, it either implies an error or indicates that the two are actually the same person. In contrast to functional properties, it is completely valid for one person to have multiple email addresses. A common inverse-functional property you may be familiar with is a relational database primary key, which serves as a unique identifier for a record in the scope of a database table.

Keys

OWL 2 introduces the concept of *keys*, which are similar to inverse functional properties in that they describe a relationship between individuals and properties such that the values of the properties uniquely identify the individuals. Although they are similar, keys are unique from inverse functional properties in the following ways:

- Keys are class-specific.
- Keys can specify one or more property expressions that combine to uniquely identify the subject they describe.
- Keys apply only to named individuals.

More precisely, a key describes a set of properties whose values in statements with an individual of the specified class as the subject uniquely identify that subject. OWL contains the property owl:hasKey, which is used to associate a specific class with a set of properties that are the keys for instances of that class. The following example RDF illustrates the use of keys to specify that the properties `ex:hasOwner` and `ex:name` together uniquely identify instances of the class `ex:Pet`:

```
# has owner and name uniquely identify canines
ex:Canine owl:hasKey (
    ex:name
    ex:hasOwner
    ) .
```

Sometimes tables in relational databases have multiple keys that combine to form a primary key or unique identifier for each row. This concept is similar to keys in OWL. For a given class (table), there is a set of properties (field) whose values uniquely identify an instance of the class (record). Keys are particularly significant to use cases for the Semantic Web in which data from disparate sources is integrated. Disparate data sources often have identifiers that are not globally unique. Once multiple sources are aggregated, more than the local identifier alone is needed to generate a globally unique identifier.

Datatypes

Datatypes represent ranges of data values that are identified using URIs. OWL allows you to use a number of predefined datatypes, most of which are defined in the XML Schema Definition (`xsd`) namespace. The full set is too long to list here, but a subset of the most commonly used datatypes is listed here:

Numeric—`xsd:integer, xsd:float, xsd:real, xsd:decimal`

String—`xsd:string, xsd:token, xsd:language`

Boolean—`xsd:Boolean`

URI—`xsd:anyUri`

XML—`rdf:XMLLiteral`

Time—`xsd:dateTime`

For more information on any of these datatypes, consult the OWL 2 Syntax document on the W3C website.

In addition to the predefined datatypes, OWL 2 introduces the ability to define your own. There are two ways to define a datatype: you can create a custom data range, or you can define a datatype in terms of other datatypes. The following sections introduce these methods.

Datatype Restrictions

OWL allows you to define your own datatypes by creating instances of the class `rdfs:Datatype` and associating one or more facet restrictions with the instance. A *facet restriction* is a way of describing a set of values for a specific datatype that makes up the range of valid values. An example of a simple instance of data range is all integers greater than 5. In this example, *integer* is the datatype of the range and the facet restriction is *greater than 5*. A single data range can have more than one facet restriction, allowing you to build complex ranges. All of the available facets are presented and described in Table 4-4.

Table 4-4 Facets Supported by OWL

FACET	DESCRIPTION
xsd:length	*N* is the exact number of items (or characters) allowed.
xsd:minLength	*N* is the minimum number of items (or characters) allowed.
xsd:maxLength	*N* is the maximum number items (or characters) allowed.
xsd:pattern	A regular expression that defines allowed character strings.
xsd:minInclusive	Values must be greater than or equal to *N*.
xsd:minExclusive	Values must be strictly greater than *N*.
xsd:maxInclusive	Values must be less than or equal to *N*.
xsd:maxExclusive	Values must be strictly less than *N*.
xsd:totalDigits	The number of digits must be equal to *N*.
xsd:fractionDigits	*N* is the maximum number of decimal places allowed.

N refers to the value portion of the facet restriction.

The following RDF demonstrates how to define two example data ranges using facets. The first data range represents all integers greater than 5 and less than or equal to 10, commonly represented by the notation (5, 10]. Notice that multiple restrictions are combined into a list in order to fully describe the range. The second example represents Social Security numbers. Each data range is created as an anonymous resource because OWL does not allow data ranges to be named:

```
@prefix ex: <http://example.org/>.
...
#integers in the range (5, 10]
[]
    rdf:type rdfs:Datatype;
    owl:onDatatype xsd:integer;
    owl:withRestrictions (
        [
            xsd:maxInclusive 10;
```

```
            ]
        [
            xsd:minExclusive 5;
            ]
        ).
#valid social security numbers
[]
    rdf:type rdfs:Datatype;
    owl:onDatatype xsd:string;
    owl:withRestrictions (
        [
            xsd:pattern "[0-9][0-9][0-9]-[0-9][0-9]-[0-9][0-9][0-9][0-9]";
            ]
        ).
```

NOTE The examples are temporarily diverting from the ongoing ontology example for this discussion of datatypes, but we'll apply custom datatypes to the example ontology during the discussion of property restrictions in the next section.

Defining Datatypes in Terms of Other Datatypes

OWL provides a couple of additional methods of creating your own datatypes. You can use one of the OWL set operator constructs `owl:intersectionOf`, `owl:unionOf`, or `owl:datatypeComplementOf` to define a new datatype. Also, you can define a datatype as consisting of an enumeration of values using `owl:oneOf`. The following RDF demonstrates each of these kinds of datatype descriptions:

```
@prefix ex: <http://example.org/>.
...
# Integers other than 0 using union-of
[] rdf:type rdfs:Datatype;
   owl:unionOf (
       [
           rdf:type rdfs:Datatype;
           owl:onDatatype xsd:integer;
           owl:withRestrictions (
               [
                   xsd:maxExclusive 0;
                   ]
               )
           ]
       [
           rdf:type rdfs:Datatype;
           owl:onDatatype xsd:integer;
           owl:withRestrictions (
```

```
                [
                    xsd:minExclusive 0;
                ]
            )
        ]
    ).


# Combining complement-of and intersection-of to create
# the strings that don't match social security numbers
[] rdf:type rdfs:Datatype;
    owl:intersectionOf (
        xsd:string
        [
            rdf:type rdfs:Datatype;
            owl:datatypeComplementOf [
                rdf:type rdfs:Datatype;
                owl:onDatatype xsd:string;
                owl:withRestrictions (
                    [
                        xsd:pattern
                            "[0-9][0-9][0-9]-[0-9][0-9]-[0-9][0-9][0-9][0-9]";
                    ]
                )
            ]
        ]
    ).


# The prime numbers less than ten using one-of
[] rdf:type rdfs:Datatype;
    owl:oneOf (2 3 5 7).
```

The first example creates a union of the ranges of integer values that are greater than zero and less than zero. The second example combines the use of the datatype complement-of set operator and the intersection-of set operator to create a datatype that is all strings that do not match the pattern for a social security number. In this example, it would not be enough to simply take the complement of the strings that match the social security number pattern because that datatype would represents *all values* that are not strings that match the social security number pattern. Such a datatype includes all integers, floats, decimals, and so on. To make sure that the datatype includes only strings that do not match the social security number pattern, the intersection of the complement and all xsd:string values is specified.

The final example demonstrates that you can specify that a data range is one of a set of specified values. In this case, the data range is prime numbers less than 10, and the values are 2, 3, 5, and 7.

Negative Property Assertions

The most common use case for properties is to specify the existence of some relationship between an individual and something else—either a literal or another individual. OWL 2 introduces a new way to use properties in which an assertion is made that no relationship exists, for a particular property, between an individual and something else. In the following RDF example, a negative property assertion is made that specifies that the individual ex:Daisy does not have the owner ex:Amber:

```
@prefix ex: <http://example.org/>.
...
[] rdf:type owl:NegativePropertyAssertion;
    owl:sourceIndividual ex:Daisy;
    owl:assertionProperty ex:hasOwner;
    owl:targetIndividual ex:Amber.
```

Negative property assertions can be made for both object and datatype properties. The specification changes slightly with owl:targetValue replacing owl:targetIndividual. The following RDF example demonstrates the use of a negative property assertion to specify that the individual ex:Daisy does not have the name Rudiger:

```
@prefix ex: <http://example.org/>.
...
[] rdf:type owl:NegativePropertyAssertion;
    owl:sourceIndividual ex:Daisy;
    owl:assertionProperty ex:name;
    owl:targetValue "Rudiger".
```

Notice that negative property assertions are in fact instances of the class ex:NegativePropertyAssertion. These instances cannot be named according to the OWL specification.

Negative property assertions are useful because without them, it is inconvenient at best to try to model that a specific relationship does not exist between an individual and a value. A consequence of the open-world assumption is that in order for something to be known, it has to be stated either explicitly or implicitly as the result of interpreting the semantics of OWL. Consider that you don't know Daisy's breed, but you know for a fact that she is not a Chihuahua. Without negative property assertions, you would have to create an extra property in your ontology in order to capture this information. You might have an ex:breed property and an ex:notBreed property. This negative assertion construct gives you a way to reuse elements of your ontology for more than one purpose.

Property Restrictions

So far, we have only discussed how to describe properties in the global context. Property descriptions (`rdfs:subPropertyOf`, `owl:inverseOf`) and property types (symmetric, reflexive, transitive, and so on) are each global descriptions of properties. It is also useful to be able to describe properties within the context of a specific class. This is the purpose of property restrictions. Using property restrictions, you can specify how a property is to be used when it is applied to an instance of a particular class.

A property restriction describes the class of individuals that meet the specified property-based conditions. The restriction is declared using the construct `owl:Restriction`, and the property to which the restriction refers is identified using the property `owl:onProperty`.

Restrictions are applied to a particular class by stating that the class is either a subclass (`rdfs:subClassOf`) or the equivalent class (`owl:equivalentClass`) of the restriction. `owl:equivalentClass` is a construct that states that two classes are the same and have the same class extension. We discuss this class relationship in the later section "Equivalence in OWL." When a class is related to a restriction using the subclass-of relationship, the restriction specifies conditions necessary for membership in the class. That is, all members of the class must meet the conditions specified by the restriction. When a class is related to a restriction using the equivalent-class relationship, the restriction specifies conditions that are not only necessary but also sufficient to assert that an individual is a member of the class. That is, class members must meet the conditions of the restriction *and* any individual who meets the conditions of the restriction is implicitly a member of the class. A single class can contain many restrictions. When this is the case, each restriction is applied independently of the others to create a set of conditions that are each either necessary or sufficient for membership in the class.

There are two kinds of property restrictions: value and cardinality. In addition, OWL 2 introduces the concept of qualified cardinality restrictions, which combine cardinality and value restrictions. These will be described in the following subsections. After each description, we will apply some restrictions to our ongoing sample ontology.

Value Restrictions

OWL provides three types of value restrictions for specifying the range of a property when it is used with an instance of a particular class: `owl:allValuesFrom`, `owl:someValuesFrom`, and `owl:hasValue`. Table 4-5 contains concise explanations of each kind of restriction.

Table 4-5 Semantics of Value Restrictions

RESTRICTION	INTERPRETATION
owl:allValuesFrom	For all instances, if they have the property, it must have the specified range.
owl:someValuesFrom	For all instances, they must have at least one occurrence of the property with the specified range.
owl:hasValue	For all instances, they must have an occurrence of the property with the specified value.

This table is derived from an example contained in the OWL Web Ontology Language Guide—http://www.w3.org/TR/owl-guide.

The first restriction in the following RDF excerpt defines a restriction that the property ex:registeredName has a range of datatype xsd:string, when it is used with the class ex:Canine. This means that anytime the property ex:registeredName is used with an instance of the class ex:Canine, it must have a value with the datatype xsd:string. When an individual is a member of the class ex:Canine but does not meet this restriction, it is not a valid member of the class.

The second example restriction in the following code uses an equivalent-class restriction to state that every instance of ex:Canine must have at least one ex:breed that is an instance of the class ex:Breed and that any individual that meets these conditions is implicitly an instance of the class ex:Canine. It is important to note that this is not the same as saying that the range of ex:breed is ex:Breed. According to this example, it would be completely valid for an instance of ex:Canine to have an ex:breed of ex:Human, as long as there is at least one ex:breed property that does point to an instance of ex:Breed. Moreover, the lack of at least one ex:breed property that points to an instance of ex:Breed does not mean that the information is invalid; rather, the open world assumption asserts that a property that satisfies the condition of the restriction exists somewhere; you just aren't aware of what it is yet:

```
@prefix ex: <http://example.org/>.
...
# registeredName must always have a range of xsd:string
# when it is used to describe a Canine
ex:Canine rdfs:subClassOf [
        rdf:type owl:Restriction;
        owl:onProperty ex:registeredName;
        owl:allValuesFrom xsd:string
        ].

# Any individual with a breed that is an instance of
# the class Breed is implicitly a Canine
ex:Canine owl:equivalentClass [
```

```
rdf:type owl:Restriction;
owl:onProperty ex:breed;
owl:someValuesFrom ex:Breed
].
```

```
# annotating this property with a comment
# that average weight is in pounds (lbs)
ex:averageWeight rdf:type owl:DatatypeProperty;
                  rdfs:comment "Average weight in pounds (lbs)".
```

NOTE This and the rest of the examples create restrictions as anonymous resources using the bnode syntax of Turtle (the square brackets [ ]). The OWL specification requires that restrictions cannot be named and must be defined using anonymous resources. This is a reasonable condition because restrictions are relevant only to the context of the class in which they are defined and never need to be referred to.

To help explain the final kind of value restriction, owl:hasValue, we're going to add a new class, ex:PetsOfRyan, to the sample ontology. There are two conditions that must be met to be a member of this class. The first is that all members must be mammals, and the second is that each member must be owned by Ryan. The concept of ownership and the class of mammals are already defined, so all that is needed is to construct a class that uses those concepts to restrict its membership. The following RDF contains the class definition for ex:PetsOfRyan. The first part of the definition states that ex:PetsOfRyan is a subclass of ex:Mammal. The second part of the definition contains a value restriction that asserts that every instance of ex:PetsOfRyan must have a property ex:hasOwner that has a value of ex:Ryan. This restriction does not preclude an instance of ex:PetsOfRyan from having another owner who is not ex:Ryan; it merely asserts that one of the owners has to be ex:Ryan:

```
@prefix ex: <http://example.org/>.
...
ex:Mammal rdf:type owl:Class.
ex:hasOwner rdf:type owl:ObjectProperty.
...
ex:PetsOfRyan rdf:type owl:Class;
              rdfs:subClassOf ex:Mammal;
              rdfs:subClassOf[
                  rdf:type owl:Restriction;
                  owl:onProperty ex:hasOwner;
                  owl:hasValue ex:Ryan
                  ].
```

```
# cleans is an object property
ex:cleans rdf:type owl:ObjectProperty.
```

```
# Feline is a subclass of Mammal
```

```
# and Mini is a Feline who cleans herself
ex:Feline rdf:type owl:Class;
          rdfs:subClassOf ex:Mammal.
ex:Mini rdf:type ex:Feline;
        ex:cleans ex:Mini.

# Self cleaners are all individuals who clean themselves
ex:SelfCleaner rdf:type owl:Class;
                    owl:equivalentClass [
                        rdf:type owl:SelfRestriction;
                        owl:onProperty ex:cleans
                        ].
```

There is one final type of value restriction that is different from the others, called a self-restriction. This restriction takes a single parameter, the property on which the restriction applies, and is used to refer to the class of all individuals that are related to themselves using that property. In addition, the class representing a self-restriction is different from other restrictions and is identified by the URI owl:SelfRestriction. The preceding example contains a class called ex:SelfCleaner, which is defined as the set of all individuals who clean themselves. In the example, Mini is a member of the class ex:Feline and Mini cleans herself. This implies that Mini is a member of the class ex:SelfCleaner.

Cardinality Restrictions

Cardinality restrictions give you the ability to specify in very precise terms how many times a property can be used to describe an instance of a class. OWL provides the cardinality restrictions listed in Table 4-6.

Table 4-6 Semantics of Cardinality Restrictions

RESTRICTION	INTERPRETATION
owl:minCardinality	There must be at least N properties.
owl:maxCardinality	There can be at most N properties.
owl:cardinality	There are exactly N properties.

N refers to the value of the cardinality restriction. (N must be nonnegative.)

Going back to the example ontology, the members of the class ex:Canine can have a maximum of one registered name and must have at least one breed. As the following RDF illustrates, we can capture these conditions using cardinality restrictions. The first restriction states that each member of the class ex:Canine must have at most one property, ex:registeredName. The second restriction states that each member must have at least one property, ex:breed.

```
@prefix ex: <http://example.org/>.
...
ex:Canine rdfs:subClassOf [
        rdf:type owl:Restriction;
        owl:onProperty ex:registeredName;
        owl:maxCardinality 1
        ].

ex:Canine rdfs:subClassOf [
        rdf:type owl:Restriction;
        owl:onProperty ex:breed;
        owl:minCardinality 1
        ].
```

Cardinality and value restrictions can be combined to create more interesting class membership conditions. The example that follows is the most complex class description so far. This example uses the combination of a value restriction with a custom datatype and a cardinality restriction to specify that the class ex:LargeBreed is a subclass of ex:Breed *and* that all instances of the class must have at least one property, ex:averageWeight, *and* that all values of that property must be greater than or equal to 50. Each instance of ex:LargeBreed must have at least one ex:averageWeight property, and all of the values for that property must be greater than or equal to 50:

```
@prefix ex: <http://example.org/>.
...
# Large breeds must have average
# weight greater than or equal to 50 lbs
ex:LargeBreed rdf:type owl:Class;
              rdfs:subClassOf ex:Breed;
              rdfs:subClassOf [
                  rdf:type owl:Restriction;
                  owl:minCardinality 1;
                  owl:onProperty ex:averageWeight
                  ];
              rdfs:subClassOf [
                  rdf:type owl:Restriction;
                  owl:onProperty ex:averageWeight;
                  owl:allValuesFrom [
                      rdf:type rdfs:Datatype;
                      owl:onDatatype xsd:real;
                      owl:withRestrictions (
                          [
                              xsd:minInclusive 50.0;
                          ]
                      )
                  ]
              ].
```

The example RDF contains a description of ex:LargeBreed that is restricted in such a way that all members of that class must meet each of those restrictions. The conditions are necessary for class membership. What if you wanted to make those conditions together both necessary and sufficient for membership in the ex:LargeBreed class? Previous examples have used equivalent-class relationships to do just that; however, in this situation, this approach will not have the desired effect. In the previous example, to assert that the cardinality restriction is an equivalent-class relationship would imply that any individual with at least one property, ex:averageWeight, is a member of the class ex:LargeBreed. This implication would occur regardless of whether the other restrictions were met or not. This is because each of the restrictions is applied to the description of ex:LargeBreed independently of one another. Such behavior is clearly not the intention of this class definition. You will revisit this example in the section on defining classes using set operations to demonstrate how to create class descriptions similar to ex:LargeBreed where the restrictions are both necessary and sufficient for class membership.

Qualified Cardinality Restrictions

OWL also provides the notion of qualified cardinality restrictions. These restrictions combine elements of cardinality and value restrictions to allow you to specify not only the number of expected properties but also their range. OWL includes the qualified cardinality restrictions listed in Table 4-7.

Table 4-7 Semantics of Qualified Cardinality Restrictions

RESTRICTION	INTERPRETATION
owl:minQualifiedCardinality	There must be at least N properties that each point to an instance of C.
owl:maxQualifiedCardinality	There can be at most N properties that each point to an instance of C.
owl:qualifiedCardinality	There are exactly N properties that point to an instance of C.

N refers to the value and C refers to the class of the qualified cardinality restriction. (N must be nonnegative.)

As an example, consider you have the property ex:hasBiologicalParent, and you want to model the fact that any ex:Canine has two biological parents, one male and one female. Using standard cardinality restrictions, the only way you could actually restrict the class so that an instance of ex:Canine has exactly one male parent and one female parent would be to define properties that represent the hasMother and hasFather relationships.

While this doesn't seem like a significant issue, consider the same problem when describing a complex system such as the components of an automobile. A single `hasComponent` property is much more tractable than hundreds of component-specific properties.

Using qualified cardinality restrictions, you can specify a cardinality restriction that applies only when the property of the restriction has a range that is an instance of a specific class. The following example demonstrates the use of a qualified cardinality restriction that specifies that an `ex:Canine` must have two `ex:hasBiologicalParent` properties, and that one must point to an instance of type `ex:Male` and one must point to an instance of type `ex:Female`. The first restriction asserts that a canine must have exactly two biological parents. The second asserts that a canine must have exactly one biological parent that is male. Finally, the third asserts that a canine must have exactly one biological parent that is female:

```
@prefix ex: <http://example.org/>.
. . .
ex:Canine rdf:type owl:Class;
ex:Male rdf:type owl:Class.
ex:Female rdf:type owl:Class.
ex:hasBiologicalParent rdf:type owl:ObjectProperty.
. . .
ex:Canine rdfs:subClassOf [
          rdf:type owl:Restriction;
          owl:cardinality 2;
          owl:onProperty ex:hasBiologicalParent
          ];
      rdfs:subClassOf {
          rdf:type owl:Restriction;
          owl:qualifiedCardinality 1;
          owl:onProperty ex:hasBiologicalParent;
          owl:onClass ex:Male
          ];
      rdfs:subClassOf {
          rdf:type owl:Restriction;
          owl:qualifiedCardinality 1;
          owl:onProperty ex:hasBiologicalParent;
          owl:onClass ex:Female
          ]
      ].
```

While this example deals with a qualified cardinality restriction that is applied to object properties and the classes of the individuals to which they refer, qualified cardinality restrictions can be constructed for datatype properties as well. The only difference is that instead of using the property `owl:onClass` to identify the class to which the restriction refers, you use the property `owl:onDataRange` to identify a range of data values for the restriction.

The semantics of datatype property–qualified cardinality restrictions are the same as those for object properties.

Advanced Class Description

OWL provides a few more methods for describing classes. You can explicitly enumerate the members of a class, and you can describe the class membership in terms of other classes using the set operators union-of, intersection-of, and complement-of. Finally, you can define that the memberships of any two classes are disjoint.

Enumerating Class Membership

OWL allows you to define a class by explicitly enumerating its instances, as demonstrated in the following example, by adding the new class `ex:FriendsOfDaisy` to the ongoing ontology example. `ex:FriendsOfDaisy` represents all of Daisy's canine friends, and for this example you will list each member of the class explicitly. Listing the membership of a class in this manner completely specifies the class extension of `ex:FriendsOfDaisy`. No individual that is not listed in the enumeration can become a member of this class. In addition, an individual that is included in a class membership enumeration is implicitly a member of that class:

```
@prefix ex: <http://example.org/>.
...
ex:Daisy rdf:type ex:Canine.
...
ex:Cubby rdf:type ex:Canine.
ex:Amber rdf:type ex:Canine.
ex:London rdf:type ex:Canine.

# Each friend of Daisy's is explicitly included in this class
ex:FriendsOfDaisy rdf:type owl:Class;
                  owl:oneOf (
                  ex:Cubby
                  ex:Amber
                  ex:London
                  ).
```

Set Operators

OWL provides three set operations that can be used to describe the membership of a class in terms of the extensions of other classes. These are `owl:intersectionOf`, `owl:unionOf`, and `owl:complementOf`. Table 4-8 defines the behavior of each set operation. Each operation is analogous to its set theory counterpart. Intersection-of and union-of each operate on the extensions of a list of class expressions, while complement-of operates on the extension of a single class expression. Each set operation establishes an equivalent-class relationship with the class that it is describing. This means that whatever set of instances the operation identifies as its result is implicitly the same as the extension of the described class.

Table 4-8 The Semantics of Set Operators

SET OPERATION	INTERPRETATION
`owl:intersectionOf`	Individuals that are instances of all classes A, B, and C
`owl:unionOf`	Individuals that are instances of at least one class A, B, or C
`owl:complementOf`	Individuals that are not instances of class A

A, B, and C are class expressions (class reference, class definition, restriction, etc.).

The following RDF demonstrates the use of each of the set operators when defining classes. The first example revisits the class descriptions that described the class ex:PetsOfRyan and asserted conditions necessary for inclusion in that class. Set operators are slightly different from most of the descriptions you have used to this point. They describe conditions that are both necessary and sufficient for class membership. By redefining ex:PetsOfRyan using owl:intersectionOf, we can correctly assert that anything that is both an ex:Mammal and is described by the property ex:hasOwner with a value of ex:Ryan is implicitly a member of ex:PetsOfRyan.

The second example demonstrates the use of owl:unionOf to describe a new class, ex:FriendsOfRyan, as the combined class extensions of a class that enumerates its membership as only Daisy, the class ex:FriendsOfDaisy, and the restriction that describes all individuals who have an ex:isFriendsWith relationship with ex:Ryan.

The final example uses owl:complementOf to define the membership of a final class ex:EnemiesOfRyan as the complement of the membership of ex:FriendsOfRyan:

```
@prefix ex: <http://example.org/>.
...
# Example 1—intersection of
ex:PetsOfRyan rdf:type owl:Class;
            owl:intersectionOf (
              ex:Mammal
              [
                rdf:type owl:Restriction;
                owl:onProperty ex:hasOwner;
                owl:hasValue ex:Ryan
```

```
                        ]
                    ).

# Example 2—union of
ex:isFriendsWith rdf:type owl:ObjectProperty.

ex:FriendsOfRyan rdf:type ex:Class;
        owl:unionOf (
          [
            rdf:type owl:Class;
            owl:oneOf (
              ex:Daisy
            )
          ]
          ex:FriendsOfDaisy
          [
            rdf:type owl:Restriction;
            owl:onProperty ex:isFriendsWith;
            owl:hasValue ex:Ryan
          ]
        ).

#Example 3—complement of
ex:EnemiesOfRyan rdf:type owl:Class;
          owl:complementOf ex:FriendsOfRyan.
```

Disjoint Classes

OWL supports the notion of disjoint classes. When two classes are related using the property owl:disjointWith, no instance of either class can be an instance of both classes. More precisely, the sets representing each class's extension share no members (are disjoint). Returning to the example ontology, you can assert that the classes ex:Canine and ex:Human are disjoint because no instance of ex:Canine can also be an instance of ex:Human, and no instance of ex:Human can be an instance of ex:Canine. The following example illustrates how to add this new information to the ontology:

```
@prefix ex: <http://example.org/>.
...
# canine and human are disjoint classes
ex:Canine owl:disjointWith ex:Human.

ex:Animal rdf:type owl:Class.
ex:Bird rdf:type owl:Class;
        rdfs:subClassOf ex:Animal.
ex:Lizard rdf:type owl:Class;
        rdfs:subClassOf ex:Animal.
ex:Feline rdf:type owl:Class;
        rdfs:subClassOf ex:Animal.
```

```
# Each of the classes is pair-wise disjoint
_: rdf:type owl:AllDisjointClasses;
   owl:members (
      ex:Bird
      ex:Lizard
      ex:Feline
      ex:Canine
      ).

# Each of the classes is pair-wise disjoint
# and Animal is the union of those classes
ex:Animal owl:disjointUnionOf (
           ex:Bird
           ex:Lizard
           ex:Feline
           ex:Canine
           ).
```

OWL provides a shortcut for defining that a set of classes is pair-wise disjoint, using the construct `owl:AllDisjointClasses` and the property `owl:members`. The preceding example asserted that the subclasses of `ex:Animal` are pair-wise disjoint. Sometimes you may want to define that a class is the union of a set of disjoint classes. You can define the class `ex:Animal` to say that it is exactly the class that is the union of all of its disjoint subclasses. OWL provides the notion of a disjoint union, specified using the property `owl:disjointUnionOf`, which points to a collection of classes.

The drawback to the use of a disjoint union to define a superclass is that any future attempt to incorporate a new subclass of `ex:Animal` will require you to redefine the disjoint union to include the new subclass. The benefit of such a specification is control—you can essentially close or limit the membership of a superclass so that it can have only members that are members of the disjoint subclasses.

Equivalence in OWL

Early in this chapter you explored a motivation for the Semantic Web that involves being able to define concepts in one knowledge domain in terms of the concepts of another. You've already explored many of the ways to do this, but you've not yet covered how to state explicitly whether two concepts, properties, or individuals are equivalent. This section briefly explores the various properties and associated semantics that OWL provides for stating equivalence between resources. They are:

- `owl:sameAs`
- `owl:differentFrom`

- owl:equivalentClass
- owl:equivalentProperty

Equivalence among Individuals

As discussed in the beginning of this chapter, OWL uses a no unique names assumption. In order to deal with the various names (URIs) that a single individual can have as a result of the assumption, OWL provides the property owl:sameAs for asserting that two individuals with different URIs are the same. The example we used in our discussion of the no unique names assumption involved two URIs, mailto:rblace@bbn.com and http://example.org/people#rblace, that each refer to the same individual, the person Ryan Blace. To establish that these two URIs represent the same thing, you can assert the statement (mailto:rblace@bbn.com owl:sameAs http://example.org/people#rblace). Once this relationship is established, the two individuals are treated as though they are the same.

OWL also provides a property that indicates that two URIs refer to different individuals, owl:differentFrom. This property is very important, because the combination of the open world assumption and the no unique names assumption results in an environment where there are very few situations in which you can assume that resources identified by different URIs are different.

To reduce the number of statements required to assert that a large set of individuals is pair-wise different, OWL also provides the construct owl:AllDifferent and the property owl:distinctMembers. These two resources allow you to define a collection of individuals that are pair-wise different:

```
@prefix ex: <http://example.org/>.
...
ex:Daisy rdf:type ex:Canine.
ex:Cubby rdf:type ex:Canine.
ex:Amber rdf:type ex:Canine.
ex:London rdf:type ex:Canine.
...
[] rdf:type owl:AllDifferent;
   owl:distinctMembers (
      ex:Daisy
      ex:Cubby
      ex:Amber
      ex:London
      ).
```

Equivalence among Classes and Properties

In addition to equivalence properties for individuals, you can use `owl:equivalentClass` to assert that two classes are equivalent and `owl:equivalentProperty` to assert that two properties are equivalent.

When you assert that two classes are equivalent, the two classes are treated as a single resource from then on. All class restrictions and the class extensions are shared between the two classes. This implies that all individuals who are members of either class will implicitly become members of the other class as well. When you assert that two properties are equivalent, the property descriptions are combined. Every statement that uses one of the properties as a predicate implicitly exists with the other equivalent property as a predicate as well.

Earlier sections in this chapter presented the concepts of disjoint classes and properties. Specifying that two classes are disjoint is one way to specify that they are different; however, classes can be different but still share overlapping or identical extensions. The semantics of disjoint properties are different from disjoint classes, but the idea is similar. Stating that properties are disjoint is a very strong way of saying that they are different. Two properties can be different and not be disjoint. Later chapters will explore the topic of ontology mapping in depth by building a system that integrates multiple knowledge domains.

Summary

This chapter explored the role of semantics in information modeling and the Semantic Web. We presented a thorough overview of the OWL Web Ontology Language and reviewed a number of examples illustrating the use of the various semantic constructs in the language. Chapter 5, "Modeling Knowledge in the Real World" builds on the foundation of this chapter by exploring the practical considerations you will have to make as you incorporate semantics into your own applications.

Modeling Knowledge in the Real World

"Welcome to the real world"
—Morpheus, *The Matrix*

Most of the discussion so far about RDF, OWL, and ontologies has been very abstract. To this point, you've learned what they are, but not as much about how to use them in practical applications and how to utilize the information they enable you to model.

This chapter is about using OWL ontologies in the real world. In it, you learn about:

- How ontologies fit into practical applications
- The concept of inference and how it is critical to the implementation of the semantics of OWL
- Profiles of OWL, their purposes, and how they can be used to provide desirable computational characteristics to systems using OWL
- Critical design principles for information-management applications

Exploring the Components of the Semantic Web

OWL ontologies allow you to describe things using explicit semantics. In Chapter 4, we often said that the semantics of various OWL constructs *imply* other information. For example, a statement asserting that two classes are related using `rdfs:subClassOf` implies that all members of the subclass are also members of the superclass. Returning to the example in Chapter 4,

Daisy is a member of the class `ex:Canine` because it is explicitly stated in the following RDF excerpt:

```
@prefix ex: <http://example.org/>.

ex:Mammal rdf:type owl:Class.

# Canine is a subclass of Mammal
ex:Canine rdf:type owl:Class;
        rdfs:subClassOf ex:Mammal.

# Daisy is implicitly a member of the class Mammal
ex:Daisy rdf:type ex:Canine.
```

The semantics of the `rdfs:subClassOf` relationship between `ex:Canine` and `ex:Mammal` implies that Daisy is also a member of the class `ex:Mammal`. In this example, the fact that Daisy is a canine is explicit. The fact that she is also a mammal is implicit, or implied by the semantics of the ontology.

OWL is merely an ontology language; it is not an application. As such, OWL alone doesn't really do anything. OWL is a tool for specifying semantics and defining knowledge models. Real-world applications must implement the features of OWL to utilize the descriptive power of its semantics. To provide these capabilities, many Semantic Web applications use a framework of integrated components to provide the storage and retrieval of RDF information, as well as the interpretation of OWL semantics. We have already touched on this subject in the introduction to this book, but now we will go into depth exploring these frameworks and their components.

Semantic Web frameworks are used for many different purposes, including database translation and integration, domain knowledge modeling, validation, analysis, and even simply the storage and retrieval of information. Regardless of their purpose, most frameworks provide the ability to create and manipulate a *knowledgebase*. A knowledgebase is a software component that represents a collection of information that is ontologically described, processed, and accessed in a Semantic Web application. To provide this capability, a framework is composed of a set of tools, including an *RDF store* (often referred to as a *triple store* or *graph store*), an *access API* or *query processor*, and a *reasoning engine* (or *reasoner*). Each of these components plays a critical role in providing the storage and retrieval of RDF data, as well as the interpretation of the semantics of OWL ontologies and instance data.

While many Semantic Web frameworks are developed and released as complete packages, they usually allow developers to customize each component to optimize the framework for a specific set of requirements. For example, the Jena Semantic Web Framework, which we will explore in greater depth throughout this chapter and the rest of this book, provides interfaces for you to incorporate your own RDF storage mechanism or your own reasoning engine.

The Sesame RDF Framework provides a stack-based interface model that allows you to insert your own layers, providing custom storage and inference.

Developers have a large number of component implementations to choose from when customizing these frameworks because the components of the Semantic Web are built upon open standard interfaces, languages, and protocols. The following subsections explore the concepts, technologies, and tools necessary to apply Semantic Web technology to problems in the real world, beginning with Semantic Web frameworks.

Semantic Web Frameworks

Most Semantic Web frameworks are a collection of integrated tools that allow you to create and work with a knowledgebase. The framework is the set of tools; the knowledgebase is the capability or concept of what they achieve. These frameworks are usually composed of three basic kinds of components, as depicted in Figure 5-1: storage, access, and inference. Each element is interconnected because there is often a lot of interaction among these various components. Storage components are repositories of RDF statements that store information. Access components are usually query processors or application programming interfaces (APIs) that provide the retrieval and modification of information, and inference components are reasoning engines that apply interpretation of OWL semantics to the information in the knowledgebase.

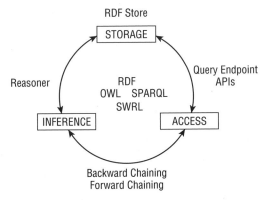

Figure 5-1 A Semantic Web framework (and knowledgebases in general) usually consists of three fundamental components: storage, access, and inference.

Fundamentally, a knowledgebase is a collection of facts (statements). The components of a Semantic Web framework serve to store, provide access to, and infer about these facts. Facts can be explicit or implicit. Explicit facts are those that have been directly asserted in the knowledgebase. Implicit facts are entailments, facts whose existence is implied by the combination of explicit facts and the semantics of ontologies and rules in the knowledgebase. Entailments are derived by the reasoning component of the knowledgebase. Depending on implementation, entailments may be stored directly in the underlying storage mechanism or they may be derived as needed when information is retrieved from the knowledgebase. Knowledgebase implementations may perform inference automatically or not, and they can perform inference internally within the knowledgebase or through an external process.

The modular design of most Semantic Web frameworks allows developers to customize the various aspects of the framework to optimize the knowledgebase for a specific set of requirements. For example, if the application requires a very fast system that can operate over large volumes of data with minimal support for the semantics of OWL, the knowledgebase should integrate a highly scalable persistent RDF store with a fast retrieval implementation and a minimal inference component. If the requirements call for complete OWL inference capabilities but are not as concerned with scalability and large volumes of data, a very lightweight in-memory RDF store may be used in combination with a powerful reasoning engine. These types of tradeoffs are common when building Semantic Web applications because increasingly complex ontologies are often accompanied with increasing computational requirements to compute all entailments.

Storing and Retrieving RDF

All Semantic Web frameworks require storage and access mechanisms, but not all frameworks include scalable, high-performance RDF stores. A framework's storage and access mechanism can range from a small in-memory model with a retrieval API to a server-based RDF store capable of storing billions of statements with a query processor that can handle hundreds of concurrent queries. The implementation of a Semantic Web framework storage component is usually transparent to a user because the user interacts with it only through the access component. The implementations of access components are usually transparent as well, because most lie behind standardized interfaces.

RDF Store Implementations

RDF stores persist the statements contained in an RDF graph. Efficiently storing and accessing RDF is an area of significant research interest because the flexible model of RDF does not work well with traditional relational storage models that rely on well-defined, static structural expectations to improve performance. Relational database-based RDF stores use tables to store subject, predicate, and object triples. They often assume the presence of RDF, RDFS, and OWL vocabularies in order to provide faster retrieval of common statements. Figure 5-2 shows an excerpt of the structure of the

Sesame RDF Framework's MySQL-based RDF store, which is illustrative of common approaches to implementing a triple store using a relational database.

Table: triples

id	subj	pred	obj	explicit
1	1	1	2	0
53	1	1	16	0
101	1	20	1	0
9	1	21	16	0
25	1	22	17	0
94	2	1	16	0
87	2	1	17	0
136	2	19	2	0
123	2	19	16	0
70	3	1	16	0
71	3	1	17	0
46	3	1	27	0
134	3	19	3	0
121	3	19	16	0
47	3	19	18	0
2	4	1	2	0
54	4	1	16	0
102	4	20	4	0
14	4	21	7	0
30	4	22	16	0
3	5	1	2	0

Table: resources

id	namespace	localname
17	2	Class
28	2	Container
30	2	ContainerMembershipProperty
27	2	Datatype
18	2	Literal
16	2	Resource
23	2	comment
21	2	domain
25	2	isDefinedBy
24	2	label
29	2	member
22	2	range
26	2	seeAlso
19	2	subClassOf
20	2	subPropertyOf
51	3	Amber
39	3	Breed
33	3	Canine
48	3	Chihuahua
50	3	Daisy
47	3	GoldenRetriever

Figure 5-2 Example relational database–based triple store implementation. This example is based on the MySQL-based RDFS triple store distributed with the Sesame RDF Framework.

Two tables from the database are shown: triples and resources. The triples table contains a list of every statement in the knowledgebase and whether it is an explicit statement or an entailment. The resources table contains a list of every instance of rdf:Resource that is in the knowledgebase and its namespace and local name (which together make up its URI). Querying an RDB-based triple store can be inefficient, requiring multiple joins and scans of entire tables. When the ontology that describes the data in a triple store is known a priori, performance can be boosted using column indices and additional tables that are specific to the elements of that ontology.

Graph model–based RDF stores have been developed as a data structure that more directly models the structure of RDF data and mitigates some of the performance problems of relational model–based stores. Given a particular statement, a graph-based store provides an efficient means to locate statements that share the same resources (subject, predicate, or object) because by design they are stored with a high degree of locality (that is, they are stored close to each other). Common implementations of graph-based RDF stores use statement lists that are linked such that every statement sharing the same resource as its subject, predicate, or object is arranged in a continuous linked list, or they use special indexed data structures to link statements that are adjacent (connected) in the RDF graph. These provide mechanisms for quickly traversing every statement that contains a particular resource as its subject, predicate, or object. This feature of the design is similar to the column indices and additional tables of the RDB approach; however, the graph-based implementation is more general purpose and does not require advanced knowledge of the data that is to be stored within it.

Retrieving Information in a Knowledgebase

There are a number of ways to retrieve the information contained in a knowledgebase. First, you can navigate the information using a browser that allows you to walk the graph of interconnected resources as you would traverse the World Wide Web. The Sesame RDF Framework is packaged with one such browser, shown in Figure 5-3, which provides a way to browse from resource to resource using lists of statements that have each resource as the subject, predicate, or object of the statement. This is a straightforward method of inspecting the contents of a knowledgebase for humans. It allows a user to see how a resource or statement fits into the larger graph of RDF. This can be extremely useful when little is known about the structure of the data or when trying to debug a system, because the full context of every resource can be assessed quickly. The concept of browsing a distributed graph of RDF information is covered in more depth in Chapter 6, "Discovering Information."

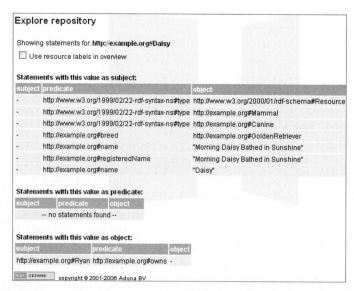

Figure 5-3 The Sesame RDF Framework browser interface allows you to browse the repository of resources using the statements in which they are contained.

Browsing is less useful for automated systems because it is an unfocused and imprecise approach to inspecting data. The example in Figure 5-3 shows a knowledgebase that contains the example ontology from Chapter 4, "Incorporating Semantics." The browser is currently showing all statements that contain the resource `http://example.org#Daisy`. As you can see, the browser shows a list of all statements that have that resource as the subject, predicate, or object.

Most Semantic Web frameworks provide an API for programmatically accessing and manipulating the contents of the knowledgebase; however, there is no single, commonly accepted RDF/OWL API, which makes these APIs hard to use as a universal access mechanism for knowledgebases. APIs are used to integrate programmatically the various components of a framework or to integrate a knowledgebase into an external application without relying on the use of queries.

The final and most commonly used method of accessing the information in a knowledgebase is via a query interface. The SPARQL Protocol and Query Language is the recommended query language of the Semantic Web. SPARQL is discussed at length in Chapter 6, but for now we'll discuss it in terms of the query-processing aspect of a knowledgebase. Query processors accept SPARQL queries and then issue them against the underlying RDF store of the knowledgebase to produce a result set in either RDF or tabular form. SPARQL query processors can act as servers, accepting queries from remote clients, or as part of an API. Either way, they take queries and produce result sets reflecting the contents of the knowledgebase.

Realizing the Semantics of OWL

The main benefit of using OWL is the ability to define semantics that enrich information. As discussed before, a knowledgebase needs to apply an inference component to interpret semantics and *realize* the enriched information. Applications that perform inference are often referred to as *reasoning engines*, or *reasoners*. A reasoning engine is a system that infers new information based on the contents of a knowledgebase. This can be accomplished using rules and a rule engine, triggers on a database or RDF store, decision trees, tableau algorithms, or even programmatically using hard-coded business logic.

Many Semantic Web frameworks perform inference using rules-based reasoning engines. These engines combine the assertions contained in a knowledgebase with a set of logical rules in order to derive assertions or perform actions. Rules comprise two parts, modeling an if-then statement. The first part is the condition for the rule, and the second part is conclusion of the rule. Rules can be used to express much of the semantics of OWL and as a tool for users to express arbitrary relationships that cannot otherwise be modeled in OWL. There are many different kinds of rules depending on the application.

Some languages allow only conjunctive rules (A and B imply C), while others allow disjunctive rules (A or B imply C). In addition, some languages allow negation as failure (not A implies B) in rules, while others do not.

A rule establishes that any time a set of statements matches the conditions of the rule, the statements in the conclusion of the rule are implicit in the knowledgebase. As an example, consider the two rules listed here that capture the semantics of the `rdfs:subClassOf` relationship between classes:

```
[IF]
  ?class1 rfds:subClassOf ?class2
  AND
  ?instance rdf:type ?class1
[THEN]
  ?instance rdf:type ?class2

[IF]
  ?class2 rfds:subClassOf ?class1
  AND
  ?class3 rfds:subClassOf ?class2
[THEN]
  ?class3 rdf:type ?class1
```

The first rule expresses that instances of a class are also members of the superclasses of that class. The second rule expresses that `rdfs:subClassOf` is a transitive property. This example uses a notional rule language to illustrate the point. In the example, variables are identified using the ? symbol. Rules and rule languages are discussed at length in Chapter 7, "Adding Rules," with special focus on the Semantic Web Rule Language (SWRL).

Often the inference capability is integrated directly into the knowledgebase and is transparent to users. In some applications, inference is implemented as an external component that is manually initiated and the entailments of which are manually added to the knowledgebase. The latter approach can be used as a method of mitigating the computational cost of performing inference if it negatively impacts the overall performance of the knowledgebase.

There are two primary methods of executing inference in a rule-based reasoner: *forward chaining* and *backward chaining*. Some systems combine the two methods and are referred to as *hybrid* reasoners. In the following sections, we review the major differences between forward and backward chaining inference methods and explore the benefits and drawbacks to each approach.

Understanding Forward Chaining Inference

In forward chaining inference, all entailments (implied facts) are asserted directly to the repository. Forward chaining occurs whenever new facts are added and the entailed statements are immediately added to the knowledgebase as part of the same operation. As a result, the knowledgebase always contains all explicitly asserted facts as well as all implicitly asserted facts. For-ward chaining is named as such because inference is performed by working forward from the data and rules in the knowledgebase toward the entailments they imply. Figure 5-4 demonstrates the process of forward chaining inference. Initially, the only explicit facts in the knowledgebase are Fact 1 and Fact 2. Fact 1 entails the existence of Facts 3, 4, and 5. When Fact 6 is added, the process of forward chaining will lead to the entailment of Facts 7, 8, 9, and ultimately 10.

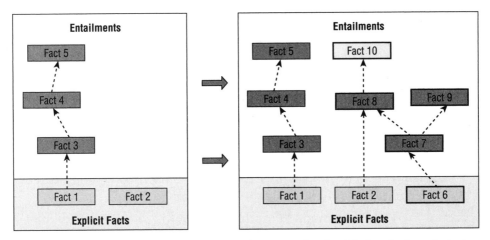

Figure 5-4 Forward chaining derives all entailments as data is added to the knowledgebase. The forward chaining process continues as long as there are more facts to be entailed.

Each time a new explicit fact is added, any new entailments are derived. After the addition is complete, it requires no additional work to determine whether the knowledgebase contains Fact 10 because it has already been added to the knowledgebase through the forward-chaining process. However, as this example illustrates, a lot of other facts have also been added to the knowledgebase as well. If you care only about the existence of Fact 10, you've made the knowledgebase larger than necessary and have spent extra time inferring facts that you don't need. Consider the following example.

```
@prefix ex: <http://example.org/>.
...
ex:hasOwner rdf:type owl:ObjectProperty.
ex:owns rdf:type owl:ObjectProperty.

#has owner is the inverse of owns
ex:hasOwner owl:inverseOf ex:owns.

ex:Daisy ex:hasOwner ex:Ryan
```

We've defined that the property ex:hasOwner is the inverse of ex:owns. As soon as you add the statements in the example to the knowledgebase, all entailments will be derived and added as well. In this example, the statements (ex:Daisy ex:hasOwner ex:Ryan) and (ex:hasOwner owl:inverseOf ex:owns) imply the existence of the statement (ex:Ryan ex:owns ex:Daisy). Thus, the forward-chaining method of inference will add the statement (ex:Ryan ex:owns ex:Daisy) directly to the knowledgebase's underlying storage mechanism.

The forward-chaining method of inference increases storage size and overhead associated with insertion and removal operations in an attempt to improve retrieval performance in a knowledgebase. All of the implied facts are derived and stored, even if none is ever needed or used. This translates into not only wasted space but also wasted computation time spent deriving the facts. In addition, the extra statements lead to a larger knowledgebase, which can diminish the performance benefits of using forward chaining in the first place. Despite these drawbacks, forward chaining is an approach that's optimized for retrieval. Since all entailments have been derived as data and added to the store, no additional inference is necessary when performing retrieval operations. In conditions where data expansion is less of an issue, or where the contents of a store are relatively static, forward-chaining inference can provide more efficient retrieval with little negative impact.

Using forward chaining can be problematic if you require the ability to remove previously asserted statements. Because the system is continually adding entailments to the knowledgebase as facts are asserted, the retraction of a previously asserted statement could result in a situation in which a statement exists in the knowledgebase even though it shouldn't (that is, it was previously asserted as an entailment of the fact that has since been retracted). Revisiting the previous code snippet to remove the statement (ex:hasOwner owl:inverseOf ex:owns) would mean that the entailed statement (ex:Ryan ex:owns ex:Daisy) is no longer implied by the facts in the knowledgebase. This issue is mitigated somewhat by the fact that knowledgebase implementations are supposed to adhere to the open-world assumption of the Semantic Web and not to remove previously asserted facts; nevertheless, as we discussed in Chapter 4, "Incorporating Semantics," this adherence is not always practical or even desirable.

The issue introduced here is critical to the task of *truth maintenance* in knowledgebases. Truth maintenance involves assuring that as facts are asserted and retracted, the existence of all entailed facts is still valid. Improper truth maintenance can quickly lead to an inconsistent knowledgebase that includes invalid entailments or contradictory information. Figure 5-5 illustrates what happens during the process of truth maintenance when a fact is removed. In this case, Fact 6 is removed, which leads the removal of all of the facts that were originally entailed as a result of its addition. After the removal, the knowledgebase no longer contains any of the facts that were entailed by the addition of Fact 6. This example is a simplification of the many situations and conditions that have to be considered when removing facts from a knowledgebase. Multiple facts may cause the same entailments, and removed facts may be entailments themselves. Because of the complexity of the interrelations between explicit and implicit facts in the knowledgebase, it can be a very complicated task to keep track of it all so that a fact can be removed properly.

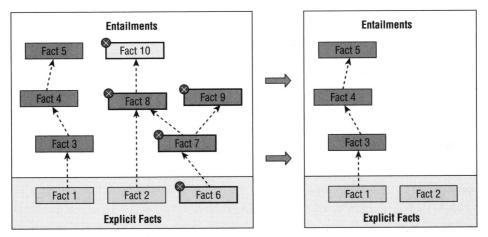

Figure 5-5 As facts are added, new facts are entailed. When a fact is removed, all facts that are no longer implied must be removed. Removing Fact 6 leads the removal of Facts 7, 8, 9, and 10.

Although the concept of truth maintenance is reasonably straightforward, the challenge lies in implementing it in a manner that provides desirable performance characteristics. Most knowledgebase solutions either don't perform truth maintenance or they take a very simple approach and purge all entailed facts any time one or more facts are removed. When entailments are purged, the knowledgebase must then re-perform forward chaining over the entire knowledgebase to derive all entailments. The drawback to not performing truth maintenance is that the knowledgebase may contain facts that it shouldn't, which may lead to unknown consequences. The drawback to purging all entailments is that for any knowledgebase of significant size or number of rules, the overhead to re-perform entailment is significant.

Alternate approaches to truth maintenance have been proposed that attempt to maintain a record of the entailment dependencies between facts so that upon removal, the reasoner can quickly identify and remove all facts that were entailed only by the existence of the fact that is to be removed. This approach gets complicated quickly because implicit facts can be entailed by complex reasoning chains involving numerous facts and rules. In addition, facts may exist both explicitly and implicitly. Maintaining adequate records can introduce unwanted overhead associated with record keeping, bloat the size of a knowledgebase, and introduce a complex process of "unwinding" the entailments when facts are removed.

Understanding Backward Chaining Inference

Backward chaining is the other primary method of executing inference in a reasoning engine. In backward chaining, reasoning is performed by attempting to derive the conditions of the goal set of facts (the condition of a rule or the pattern of a query) by applying the logic of the system backwards until the conditions can be satisfied by explicit facts in the knowledgebase. The process is depicted in Figure 5-6. Once again, the goal is to determine if the knowledgebase contains Fact 10. The process of backward-chaining inference determines whether Fact 10 can be derived from the explicit facts that are in the knowledgebase. It does this by determining what facts lead to the entailment of Fact 10. In this cast, Fact 8 implies Fact 10. Now the reasoning process must determine whether Fact 8 can be derived. Fact 8 is implied by the combination of Fact 2 and Fact 7. Fact 2 already explicitly exists, so the process must determine whether Fact 7 can be derived. Fact 7 is implied by Fact 3, which is explicitly in the knowledgebase. Thus, Fact 10 is contained in the knowledgebase. If any of those facts had been missing along the way, it would have indicated that Fact 10 is not in the knowledgebase.

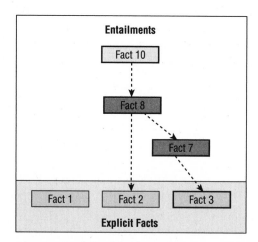

Figure 5-6 Backward chaining uses entailment to expand queries as a method to determine whether or not queries can be satisfied. When the query is complete, the entailed information is not persisted in the knowledgebase.

Backward-chaining inference is attractive because entailments are made as necessary to verify whether or not certain facts exist. It avoids the unnecessary expansion of facts in a knowledgebase and does not add any overhead to the operations of the insertion or removal of statements. Once facts are derived through backward chaining, they are not persisted in the knowledgebase as they are in forward chaining (although they may be cached to improve performance). Depending on the use case in which it is applied, backward chaining may be more efficient from a computation and storage perspective because inference is performed only as needed and unused statements are not being stored. One major advantage of backward chaining is that it vastly simplifies truth maintenance because only explicit statements are persisted in the knowledgebase, and the removal of an already asserted statement has no impact on the other statements in the knowledgebase.

There are drawbacks to backward chaining as well. It trades insertion and removal overhead for access overhead. This means that access to information in the knowledgebase using an API or query interface involves more computation and cost because it is then that entailments are derived. In many knowledgebase systems, query time is one of the most critical performance metrics. Without caching, a backward-chaining system may be very inefficient if it has to satisfy the same queries over and over because it will perform the same process of entailment repeatedly.

Choosing the Right Inference Method

Choosing the right inference method is often a matter of assessing requirements and constraints and determining which method works the best for a given application. Most frameworks provide forward-chaining knowledgebases because they are easier to implement, and the additional size and computational requirements during insertion and removal operations are acceptable. Forward chaining prioritizes query performance over insertion and removal performance, and in most applications, queries are the most common operation performed.

Backward chaining is often desirable when ontologies are volatile or when knowledgebase modifications (including statement removals) are frequent. This is because backward chaining does not do anything to the underlying stored information, and any modifications to that information can be made without regard for the inference method. Backward chaining can be a necessity when working with distributed reasoning systems in which no centralized knowledgebase exists. In these situations, there is no knowledgebase in which forward chaining can take place and entailments can be stored, so queries must be expanded and distributed using a backward chaining–based approach.

Common Frameworks and Components

There are a number of mature, open-source Semantic Web frameworks available today. Arguably the most widely used are the *Jena Semantic Web Framework* (http://jena.sourceforge.net) and *Sesame RDF Framework* (http://www.openrdf.org). Each of these is written in Java and includes an

API as well as a number of plug-ins and tools for working with RDF and OWL. Sesame can be directly deployed as a servlet in a servlet container such as Apache Tomcat (Apache Tomcat is an open-source servlet container and can be found at `http://tomcat.apache.org`), communicating via HTTP; and Jena can be stood up as a server by combining it with a tool like the Joseki SPARQL Server for Jena (`http://www.joseki.org`).

We use Jena in all of the programming examples included in this book for a number of reasons. First, Jena is one of the most commonly used frameworks available. Second, we use it in many of our own Semantic Web projects. Third, it's free—and it's written for Java, which is also free (and who doesn't like free stuff?). For the sake of fairness, Sesame is also an excellent, commonly used, free framework that we use in many of our own projects and that would likely suit your needs. For consistency's sake, however, we decided to choose only one framework to help you get familiar with Semantic Web programming. This spares you from having to master the nuanced details of a number of different tools and applications. We've mentioned Sesame and Jena, but there are many other open source frameworks out there, including those listed in Table 5-1.

Table 5-1 Frameworks for Programming in the Semantic Web

FRAMEWORK	DESCRIPTION
4Suite	4Suite is an open-source XML and RDF processing library for Python. More information about the project can be found at `http://www.4suite.org`.
Jena	Widely used Semantic Web framework for Java. Provides a SPARQL interface, RDF and OWL APIs, and inference support. Provides multiple storage and reasoning mechanisms and also allows the integration of custom mechanisms. More information about the Jena Semantic Web Framework can be found at `http://jena.sourceforge.net`.
Sesame	Widely used RDF framework and server. Provides a SPARQL interface and an HTTP server interface. Is packaged with multiple storage and reasoning mechanisms and also allows the integration of custom mechanisms. More information about the Sesame RDF Framework can be found at `http://www.openrdf.org`.
OWL API	OWL API and implementation for Java. Provides OWL API that is built on the functional syntax of OWL 2 and contains a common interface for many reasoners. More information about the OWL API can be found at `http://owlapi.sourceforge.net`.

(continued)

Table 5-1 (*continued*)

FRAMEWORK	DESCRIPTION
RAP RDF API	RAP is an open-source RDF API and software suite for storing, querying, and manipulating RDF in PHP. The project can be found at `http://sourceforge.net/projects/dfapi-php`.
Redland	Collection of RDF libraries for C, with bindings for various other languages. Provides RDF API, parsers, and query interfaces. More information about Redland can be found at `http://librdf.org`.
LinqToRDF	Semantic Web framework for .NET built on the Microsoft Language-Integrated Query (LINQ) Framework (language-independent query and data processing system). More information about the LinqToRDF project can be found at `http://code.google.com/p/linqtordf`.

The OWL API is an open-source project that's developing a Java API for programming with OWL 2. Redland is a collection of RDF libraries written in C with language bindings for various other languages, including Ruby, PHP, Python, and Perl. Finally, LinqToRDF is a smaller project aimed at developing a Semantic Web/RDF framework for the Microsoft .NET Framework based on the Language-Integrated Query (LINQ) package for .NET.

Almost all of the frameworks discussed are packaged with their own RDF store implementations, retrieval components, and inference engines, and they also allow the integration of custom mechanisms. For this purpose, there are a number of projects aimed solely at providing high-performance components that can be integrated into these frameworks. The following subsections present some of the more common and useful RDF stores, retrieval components, and reasoners.

RDF Store Implementations

Many of the Semantic Web frameworks (including Jena and Sesame) allow you to plug in your own RDF store implementation. There are a number of RDF stores to pick from. The following is a short compilation of the most widely used and mature projects:

AllegroGraph: This RDF store is available in a number of forms ranging from a free scaled-down version to a full licensable version. AllegroGraph is available in both Java and Lisp implementations and provides a SPARQL interface and reasoning based on RDFS. AllegroGraph can be found at `http://agraph.franz.com/allegrograph`.

Mulgara: This is an open-source, Java RDF store with a SPARQL query processor that replaces the project previously known as Kowari. Mulgara can be downloaded at `http://www.mulgara.org`.

OpenLink Virtuoso: This provides both open-source and commercial versions of an RDB-based RDF store. It supports embedding SPARQL into SQL as a method of accessing RDF data that is stored in the knowledgebase. More information can be found at `http://virtuoso.openlinksw.com`.

Oracle 11g: Oracle first introduced support for RDF and rules in Oracle Database 10g Release 2. The 11g release includes support for a subset of OWL, transactions, and security. Limited information is available about its performance and scalability. Oracle 11g information can be found at the Oracle website: `http://www.oracle.com`.

OWLIM: This Java-based repository is packaged as a Sesame Storage and Inference Layer (SAIL) and supports inference using RDFS and a subset of OWL. Two versions of OWLIM are available. The first is an open-source, in-memory model with a persistence mechanism and is called Swift OWLIM. A commercial version called Big OWLIM is also available under license. Big OWLIM uses a proprietary file-based storage mechanism that is more scalable than the Swift OWLIM version. Information about both versions of OWLIM can be found at `http://www.ontotext.com/owlim`.

Parliament: This is a C++-based RDF store implementation that utilizes efficient disk-based storage and limited inference capabilities. Jena and Sesame integration packages are available. At the time of this writing, Parliament is en route to becoming an open-source RDF store. Information about Parliament can found at `http://asio.bbn.com`. (Some of the authors of this book work for BBN Technologies.)

Retrieval Components

Most Semantic Web frameworks, such as Jena and Sesame, provide a SPARQL endpoint as well as APIs for accessing the information in the knowledgebase. There are not a lot of standalone components that provide retrieval for Semantic Web frameworks. One of the few worth mentioning is the Joseki project (`http://www.joseki.org`), which provides an HTTP servlet-based SPARQL endpoint for Jena. In many of our distributed Semantic Web projects, we use either Sesame or Jena combined with Joseki as an HTTP-based SPARQL endpoint.

Reasoning Engines

FaCT++: An open-source, C++-based reasoner supporting a large subset of OWL DL, FaCT++ can be found at `http://owl.man.ac.uk/factplusplus`.

Hermit: This Java-based OWL reasoner is based on a new tableau reasoning algorithm. It can be integrated into Protégé and Java applications using the OWL API. Downloads and information can be found at `http://www.hermit-reasoner.com`.

KAON2: This is a Java-based framework for working and reasoning with OWL DL ontologies. It supports reasoning over a large subset of OWL DL. Documentation and downloads can be found at `http://kaon2.semanticweb.org`.

Pellet: This is an open-source, Java-based OWL DL reasoning engine that supports a majority of the constructs of OWL, including those introduced in OWL 2. Pellet is developed and commercially supported by Clark and Parsia. We use Pellet as our reasoner of choice throughout the examples in this book because it is a mature, well-supported reasoner that supports the latest features of OWL. Pellet can be downloaded at `http://pellet.owldl.com`.

RacerPro: This commercially available reasoner supports a large subset of OWL DL. More information about Racer-Pro can be found at `http://agraph.franz.com/racer`.

Vampire: This award-winning, commercially licensable, first-order logic theorem prover has been the subject of investigations looking into its applicability as an OWL-DL reasoner (*Using Vampire to Reason with OWL*, Tsarkov, Riazanov, Bechhofer, and Horrocks, University of Manchester, 2004).

Knowledgebase Performance

Knowledgebases vary in form from local, in-memory solutions with limited inference support to distributed, server-based solutions supporting the full inference of OWL DL. A knowledgebase lies at the center of most Semantic Web applications. Thus, understanding the performance profile of that knowledgebase and matching performance expectations with the components in use is a critical design consideration.

A number of metrics are useful for measuring the performance of a knowledgebase. Two of the most commonly used are query duration and load time. *Query duration* is the amount of time it takes for a knowledgebase to return the result set for a particular query. *Load time* is the amount of time it takes to add some information to the knowledgebase, including any entailments that occur as part of this operation. Other useful metrics include the supported level of reasoning, reasoning correctness (soundness and completeness), memory footprint, disk space requirements, and deletion duration. Trends observed in these metrics over varying knowledgebase sizes and concurrent loads all provide useful insight into the overall performance profile.

Knowledgebase performance and scalability are areas of concern for developers and researchers alike. Current technologies are relatively new and immature in comparison to relational databases, which have been in development for over 30 years. To make matters worse, knowledgebases usually *do* more than traditional databases, introducing a much more flexible and inference-based knowledge model. To cope with these conditions, it is often necessary to take steps to manage the scale of the knowledgebase and to mitigate performance and scalability issues that may emerge.

LEHIGH UNIVERSITY BENCHMARK

To track the progression of knowledgebase performance and to benchmark and compare various implementations, the Semantic Web and Agent Technologies Lab at Lehigh University developed the Lehigh University Benchmark (LUBM). The benchmark was quickly adopted by numerous projects as a way of advertising performance gains and has since become the de facto standard for OWL knowledgebase system benchmarking.

The benchmark system includes a test harness, a data generator, and a set of sample queries. The data generator is used to create data sets of fixed sizes based on an ontology included with the benchmark. The sample queries vary in complexity and result size. The test harness runs each query against each data set and gathers a set of metrics designed to assess various aspects of the completeness and performance of the knowledgebase. The primary metrics of the benchmark include data set load time and query response time. In addition, the benchmark performs checks to verify that the results of queries have returned the expected results, verifying the soundness and completeness of the inference performed by each knowledgebase.

Even with the frameworks available and the amount of research going into knowledgebase development, implementing the full specification of OWL in a Semantic Web application is not feasible. The full, unrestricted specification of OWL (referred to as OWL Full) is not decidable; that is, there is no algorithm capable of providing complete inference over a complex OWL Full ontology and a large knowledgebase. To ease the burden on Semantic Web tools developers, OWL contains a number of profiles, or subsets of the full language, that give up some expressive power in exchange for more attractive and feasible computational characteristics. The next section introduces each profile and discusses when it is appropriate to use each.

Exploring the Profiles of OWL

Both the original OWL specification and OWL 2 provide profiles, or sublanguages of the language that give up some expressiveness in exchange for computational efficiency. These profiles introduce a combination of modified or restricted syntax and nonstructural restrictions on the use of OWL. In the original OWL specification, there were three species of OWL: OWL Full, OWL DL, and OWL Lite. OWL Full was the full, unrestricted OWL specification. OWL DL introduced a number of restrictions on the use of OWL Full, including the separation of classes and individuals. These restrictions were designed to make OWL DL decidable. OWL Lite was essentially OWL DL with a subset of its language elements.

The intention of introducing OWL Lite was to provide application and tool developers with a development target, or starting point for supporting the features of OWL 1. Unfortunately, OWL Lite was regarded mostly as a failure because it eliminated too many of the useful features of OWL 1 without introducing enough of a computational benefit to make the reduced features attractive. OWL DL was more successful; however, the fact that it is decidable does not guarantee that even correct implementations will have desirable performance when dealing with nontrivial knowledge-bases. Knowing that a reasoning algorithm will, theoretically, finish is less useful if it won't do so before the heat death of the universe (`http://en.wikipedia.org/wiki/Heat_death_of_the_universe`). This is not to say that OWL DL reasoning often takes eons to complete (the heat death reference is a slight exaggeration); rather, it is to assert the point that decidability is not necessarily in sync with practicality. OWL Full was introduced primarily for compatibility with RDF and RDF Schema.

OWL Full and OWL DL

OWL Full is not a sublanguage of OWL; rather, it is the full OWL language. So far, our discussion of OWL has been about OWL Full. It is a pure extension of RDF. As a result, every RDF document is a valid OWL Full document, and every OWL Full document is a valid RDF document. The important point to make here is that OWL Full maintains the ability to *say anything about anything*. With the flexibility comes a tradeoff in computational efficiency. As we have said before, OWL Full is not decidable. There are no known algorithms that can produce all the entailments of the semantics of a complex OWL Full knowledgebase.

OWL DL is so named because it provides many of the capabilities of *description logic* (hence, OWL *DL*), an important subset of *first-order logic*. It contains the entire vocabulary of OWL Full but introduces the restriction that the semantics of OWL DL cannot be applied to an RDF document that treats a URI as both an individual and a class or property. This and some additional restrictions make OWL DL decidable. As we mentioned before, decidability provides only that there exists an algorithm that provides complete reasoning. It does not say anything about the performance of such an algorithm or whether it will complete in an acceptable or realistic amount of time. As we progress in this book, we may not adhere to any particular profile of OWL; however, we will always stay within the restrictions of OWL DL.

The Profiles of OWL

The main purpose of an OWL profile is to produce subsets of OWL that trade some expressivity for better computational characteristics for tools and reasoners. The profiles were developed with specific user communities and implementation technologies in mind. At the time of this writing, there are three standardized profiles of OWL: OWL EL, OWL QL, and OWL RL. Each profile is defined by restricting OWL DL and is covered in following sections.

> **NOTE** It is important to understand the implications of OWL profiles. You will rarely, if ever, work with OWL Full. OWL DL and the OWL profiles are what make it feasible to implement and work with OWL.

OWL EL

The OWL EL profile is designed to provide *polynomial-time computation* for determining the consistency of an ontology and mapping individuals to classes. That is, the relationship between ontology size and the time required to perform the operation can be represented by the formula $f(x)=x^a$. The purpose of this profile is to provide the expressive features of OWL that many existing large-scale ontologies (from various industries) require while also eliminating unnecessary features. Features are pruned to reduce the computational complexity of many common reasoning tasks. The ontologies for which this profile is designed tend to rely heavily on huge collections of classes that are organized taxonomically.

OWL EL is a syntactic restriction on OWL DL. We will list some of the more significant allowed and disallowed elements in this subsection; however, there are other restrictions on the use of OWL EL that are not covered in this section. You can review the full list of features that are included and not included in this and the other profiles in the OWL 2 Profiles document located on the W3C OWL website located at `http://www.w3.org/2007/OWL/wiki/Profiles`.

Class description is limited to the following methods:

- Class declarations
- Subclass-of relationships
- Intersection-of set operations
- Some-values-from, has-value, and self-exists restrictions
- Enumerations containing exactly one individual

Disallowed class descriptions include the following:

- Cardinality and all-values-from restrictions
- Union-of, disjoint union, and complement-of set operations

Disallowed property descriptions include the following methods:

- Disjoint and inverse property relationships
- Irreflexive, functional, symmetric, and asymmetric property types

While the restrictions of OWL EL may seem limiting, carefully consider which features of OWL you will need and how they balance with your performance requirements. Often you will find that there is a small subset of the features of OWL that are most important to your requirements, and the others can be sacrificed in order to achieve better performance. OWL EL is ideal for users who want to classify instances using a rich taxonomy and are willing to sacrifice some expressivity when it comes to properties. Despite the limitations on restrictions, OWL EL supports property domain and range descriptions, which can be used to regain some of the functionality of those restrictions.

OWL QL

The OWL QL profile is designed to enable the satisfiability of conjunctive queries in *logspace* with respect to the number of assertions in the knowledge-base that is being queried. That is, the relationship between knowledgebase size and the time required to perform the operation can be represented by the function $f(x) = \log(a)$. As with OWL EL, this profile provides *polynomial-time computation* for determining the consistency of an ontology and mapping individuals to classes.

This profile was based on work involving the virtual integration of databases. The idea was to develop a profile of OWL that allows for efficient query expansion such that a query can be translated, expanded, and issued directly against the underlying storage mechanism, whether it is SQL, RDF, or any other implementation. In this way, the implementation of QL semantics is conceptually similar to the process of backwards chaining presented earlier in this chapter. As a result of the focus toward database integration, the modeling capabilities of OWL QL are similar to that of the Unified Modeling Language (UML) or Entity-Relationship (ER) models.

OWL QL restricts how subclass relationships can be constructed by limiting the ways that you can define the superclass of the relationship. Specifically, subclass axioms can use only the following language elements:

- Explicitly defined classes
- Some-values-from restrictions
- Complement-of and intersection-of set operations

Disallowed class and property descriptions include:

- Cardinality, has-value, and all-values-from restrictions

- Union-of set operations
- Property chains
- Transitive, reflexive, irreflexive, asymmetric property types
- Inverse-functional property types

OWL QL is ideal for users who want to model the information contained in existing databases. These use cases include database exposure and integration efforts. Once again, we haven't necessarily covered all of the restrictions that are present in OWL QL. For complete coverage of the profile, refer to the OWL 2 Profiles document on the W3C OWL website.

OWL RL

The OWL RL profile is designed to be as expressive as possible while allowing implementation using rules and a rule-processing system. Part of the design of OWL RL is that it only requires the rule-processing system to support conjunctive rules. Conjunctive rules are those that have only axioms that are connected using logical AND. A sample conjunctive rule is "IF A AND B THEN C AND D." The restrictions of the profile eliminate the need for a reasoner to infer the existence of individuals that are not already known in the system, keeping reasoning deterministic.

Like the other profiles, OWL RL makes syntactic restrictions on OWL DL. Most of the changes are related to how and where class expressions can be used. Classes defined as the subclass in an expression can only be described using the following methods:

- Explicit class definition
- One-of, some-values-from, and has-value restrictions
- Intersection-of and union-of set operations

Classes defined as the superclass in an expression can only be described using the following methods:

- Explicit class definition
- All-values-from and has-value restrictions
- Max-cardinality restrictions with a value of zero or one
- Intersection-of set operations

Finally, classes defined as the equivalent class in an expression can only be described using these methods:

- Has-value restrictions
- Intersection-of set operations

Demonstrating OWL Inference

Now that you've learned about ontologies, knowledgebases, and the role that inference plays in realizing the semantics of OWL, it's time to put everything together into a working example. This section presents a hands-on example of enabling various levels of inference in a knowledgebase containing a simple OWL ontology. The knowledgebase used in this example is a Jena model, and the ontology is the example from Chapter 4 involving humans and canines. There are three levels of inference to consider: no inference, RDFS, and the OWL inference provided by Pellet. We will first review the ontology and the application, and then we'll review the results of running the application at each inference level, illustrating the differences between the information in the resulting knowledge models. This example can be downloaded in its entirety from the book's website.

The Ontology

First let us review the ontology we will be using for this example.

```
@prefix ex: <http://example.org#>.
@prefix rdf: <http://www.w3.org/1999/02/22-rdf-syntax-ns#>.
@prefix rdfs: <http://www.w3.org/2000/01/rdf-schema#>.
@prefix owl: <http://www.w3.org/2002/07/owl#>.

ex:Mammal rdf:type owl:Class.

ex:Human rdf:type owl:Class;
        rdfs:subClassOf ex:Mammal.

ex:Canine rdf:type owl:Class;
        rdfs:subClassOf ex:Mammal;
        owl:equivalentClass [
            rdf:type owl:Restriction;
            owl:onProperty ex:breed;
            owl:someValuesFrom ex:Breed
            ].

ex:PetOfRyan rdf:type owl:Class;
            owl:intersectionOf (
                ex:Mammal
                [
                    rdf:type owl:Restriction;
                    owl:onProperty ex:hasOwner;
                    owl:hasValue ex:Ryan
                    ]
                ).
```

```
ex:Breed rdf:type owl:Class.
ex:LargeBreed rdf:type owl:Class;
              rdfs:subClassOf ex:Breed.
ex:SmallBreed rdf:type owl:Class;
              rdfs:subClassOf ex:Breed.

ex:name rdf:type owl:DatatypeProperty.
ex:registeredName rdf:type owl:DatatypeProperty;
                  rdfs:subPropertyOf ex:name.
ex:breed rdf:type owl:ObjectProperty.
ex:hasOwner rdf:type owl:ObjectProperty.
ex:owns rdf:type owl:ObjectProperty;
        owl:inverseOf ex:hasOwner.

ex:GoldenRetriever rdf:type ex:LargeBreed.
ex:Chihuahua rdf:type ex:SmallBreed.

ex:Ryan rdf:type ex:Human;
        ex:name "Ryan Blace";
        ex:owns ex:Daisy.

ex:Daisy rdf:type ex:Canine;
        ex:name "Daisy";
        ex:registeredName "Morning Daisy Bathed in Sunshine";
        ex:breed ex:GoldenRetriever.

ex:Amber rdf:type ex:Mammal;
        ex:name "Amber";
        ex:breed ex:GoldenRetriever.
```

This example ontology contains elements of RDFS and OWL. No specific profile is adhered to; however, the ontology stays within OWL DL. In this example, we've defined a number of classes and a few properties, as well as some individuals (which normally wouldn't be included in an ontology). To keep the ontology succinct, no labels or comments are included. First we include simple class definitions for ex:Mammal and ex:Human, which is a subclass of ex:Mammal.

```
ex:Mammal rdf:type owl:Class.

ex:Human rdf:type owl:Class;
        rdfs:subClassOf ex:Mammal.
```

Then we define the class ex:Canine as a subclass of ex:Mammal and equivalent to the class of instances for which there is at least one ex:breed property with a value that is an instance of the class ex:Breed.

```
ex:Canine rdf:type owl:Class;
        rdfs:subClassOf ex:Mammal;
```

```
owl:equivalentClass [
    rdf:type owl:Restriction;
    owl:onProperty ex:breed;
    owl:someValuesFrom ex:Breed
    ].
```

Next, `ex:PetOfRyan` is defined using the intersection-of set operator. The class definition states that an instance is a member of the class if it is an instance of the class `ex:Mammal` and it has a property `ex:hasOwner` that has a value of `ex:Ryan`.

```
ex:PetOfRyan rdf:type owl:Class;
             owl:intersectionOf (
                 ex:Mammal
                 [
                     rdf:type owl:Restriction;
                     owl:onProperty ex:hasOwner;
                     owl:hasValue ex:Ryan
                     ]
                 ).
```

After that, we define a simple hierarchy of breed classes, `ex:Breed`, and two subclasses, `ex:LargeBreed` and `ex:SmallBreed`. Then we define a datatype property, `ex:name`, and three object properties: `ex:breed`, `ex:hasOwner`, and `ex:owns`. The only really interesting things here are that we've defined `ex:registeredName` to be a subproperty of `ex:name` and `ex:owns` to be the inverse of `ex:hasOwner`.

The final part of this ontology defines a number of individuals. The first two are `ex:GoldenRetriever`, which is an instance of `ex:LargeBreed`, and `ex:Chihuahua`, which is an instance of `ex:SmallBreed`. The last three are `ex:Ryan`, `ex:Daisy`, and `ex:Amber`.

The Example Application

We will take a look at the application we are going to use to demonstrate the various inference levels in action on the knowledge model we just went through. The purpose of this example is to illustrate the effect of various inference levels on a knowledge model but not to teach you how to program in Java or how to use Jena. Therefore, we'll explain the relevant features of Jena enough to communicate specific pieces of the application but not much more. We explore Jena in detail later in the book.

The source code for the example application is shown in the following snippet, abridged to make it easier to read and understand. The website accompanying this book contains the full, unabridged source code for this example. We've omitted package and import statements as well as most of the error checking and validation code. The application takes four parameters: an input file, the input file format (N3, RDF/XML, N-Triple, or Turtle), an output file, and the inference level (none, rdfs, or owl). When it runs, it loads the input file into a Jena model and applies the specified inference level to the knowledge model. Then it prints a summary of each individual and those statements in the model that describe it.

```java
public class InferenceExample
{
    public static void main(String[] args)
    {
        String inputFileName = args[0];
        String inputFileFormat = args[1];
        String outputFileName = args[2];
        String reasoningLevel = args[3];

        FileInputStream inputStream = null;
        PrintWriter writer = null;
        try
        {
            inputStream = new FileInputStream(inputFileName);
        } catch (FileNotFoundException e) {}
        try
        {
            writer = new PrintWriter(outputFileName);
        } catch (FileNotFoundException e) {}

        //create the jena default model
        OntModel model = null;
        if("none".equals(reasoningLevel.toLowerCase()))
        {
            model = ModelFactory.createOntologyModel(
                OntModelSpec.OWL_DL_MEM);
        }
        else if("rdfs".equals(reasoningLevel.toLowerCase()))
        {
            model = ModelFactory.createOntologyModel(
                OntModelSpec.OWL_DL_MEM_RDFS_INF);
        }
        else if("owl".equals(reasoningLevel.toLowerCase()))
        {
            Reasoner reasoner =
                PelletReasonerFactory.theInstance().create();
            Model infModel = ModelFactory.createInfModel(
                reasoner, ModelFactory.createDefaultModel());
            model = ModelFactory.createOntologyModel(
                OntModelSpec.OWL_DL_MEM, infModel);
        }
```

```
     //load the facts into the model
     model.read(inputStream, null, inputFileFormat);

     //Iterate over the individuals, print statements about them
     ExtendedIterator iIndividuals = model.listIndividuals();
     while(iIndividuals.hasNext())
     {
         Individual i = (Individual)iIndividuals.next();
         printIndividual(i, writer);
     }
     iIndividuals.close();

     writer.close();
     model.close();
 }

 public static void printIndividual(
     Individual i, PrintWriter writer)
 {
     //print the local name of the individual (to keep it terse)
     writer.println("Individual: " + i.getLocalName());

     //print the statements about this individual
     StmtIterator iProperties = i.listProperties();
     while(iProperties.hasNext())
     {
         Statement s = (Statement)iProperties.next();
         writer.println("   " + s.getPredicate().getLocalName()
             + " : " + s.getObject().toString());
     }
     iProperties.close();
     writer.println();
 }
}
```

This application takes an input ontology and outputs the individuals in the knowledge model, including any statements about them, after one of the three inference levels has been applied. The first thing the application does is extract the parameters from the arguments to the main() method. Next, it creates an input stream for the input file and a print writer for the output file. Once all the setup is complete, the interesting part begins. Depending on the inference mode, the application creates the Jena OntModel in one of three ways, each explained shortly.

The code snipped here shows that in no inference mode ("none"), the program creates a basic ontology model using the OWL_DL_MEM OntModelSpec. This specifies that Jena should load the RDF, RDFS, and OWL ontologies but perform no inference in the model.

```
if("none".equals(reasoningLevel.toLowerCase()))
{
    model = ModelFactory.createOntologyModel(
        OntModelSpec.OWL_DL_MEM);
}
```

As the next snippet shows, the model is created using the OWL_DL_MEM_RDFS_INF OntModelSpec when it is run in RDFS mode. This model will also be loaded with the RDF, RDFS, and OWL ontologies; however, it will perform RDFS inference over the model using Jena's internal reasoning engine. This means that inference should be performed over all elements of the RDFS vocabulary (property and class hierarchies, domain, range, and so on).

```
else if("rdfs".equals(reasoningLevel.toLowerCase()))
{
    model = ModelFactory.createOntologyModel(
        OntModelSpec.OWL_DL_MEM_RDFS_INF);
}
```

The final mode, OWL, involves more setup than the previous two modes. First, we create a new Reasoner instance using the PelletReasonerFactory. Then, we create a Jena inference model using the Jena ModelFactory, providing as parameters the Pellet reasoner and a newly created, empty Jena model. Finally, we create our actual Jena OntModel, which wraps the Pellet inference model we just created and once again loads the RDF, RDFS, and OWL ontologies. The result is a Jena ontology model that will perform inference using the Pellet OWL reasoner.

```
else if("owl".equals(reasoningLevel.toLowerCase()))
{
    Reasoner reasoner =
        PelletReasonerFactory.theInstance().create();
    Model infModel = ModelFactory.createInfModel(
        reasoner, ModelFactory.createDefaultModel());
    model = ModelFactory.createOntologyModel(
        OntModelSpec.OWL_DL_MEM, infModel);
}
```

Finally, after creating the model in one of the three ways, we load the ontology into the model using model.read(...). Inference occurs automatically, so no explicit action has to be taken to ensure that entailments are derived. In the following snippet, we read the ontology from an input stream containing the ontology, specify no base namespace for the ontology (the second parameter, which is null), and pass in the string representing the input file format—in our case, Turtle.

```
model.read(inputStream, null, inputFileFormat);
```

The final part of the application involves iterating over the list of all individuals in the model, and printing them and all statements for which they are the subject in a summary form to the output file.

The Results

Now we're ready to run the application in each of the three modes, observing and juxtaposing the consequences of each inference level on the information in the knowledge model.

Performing No Inference

Running the application with no inference over the example ontology results in the output file contained in the following example. Resources in the output file, other than those that are the objects of statements, are abbreviated by the application to make it easier to read. With no inference, we expect to see exactly the set of individuals and statements that are expressed in the example ontology. No additional statements are present, because no additional statements are being inferred.

```
Individual: Chihuahua
   type : http://example.org#SmallBreed

Individual: GoldenRetriever
   type : http://example.org#LargeBreed

Individual: Daisy
   breed : http://example.org#GoldenRetriever
   registeredName : Morning Daisy Bathed in Sunshine
   name : Daisy
   type : http://example.org#Canine

Individual: Ryan
   owns : http://example.org#Daisy
   name : Ryan Blace
   type : http://example.org#Human

Individual: Amber
   breed : http://example.org#GoldenRetriever
   name : Amber
   type : http://example.org#Mammal
```

The result is as expected. The output contains only the information that is explicitly contained in the ontology. No new statements are inferred as a result of the semantics of the ontology. This example alone is not very interesting, but it provides a baseline to which we can compare the RDFS and OWL inference modes.

Performing RDFS Inference

Now we will look at the results of running the same application, only in RDFS inference mode. We expect to see inference as a result of the RDFS semantics in our ontology. In this case, subclass and subproperty relationships will take effect. The file generated by running the application in RDFS mode is shown in the following code. Statements that are new when compared to the results in the preceding example are shown in bold to make them easier to identify.

```
Individual: Chihuahua
    type : http://example.org#SmallBreed
    type : http://example.org#Breed

Individual: GoldenRetriever
    type : http://example.org#LargeBreed
    type : http://example.org#Breed

Individual: Daisy
    breed : http://example.org#GoldenRetriever
    registeredName : Morning Daisy Bathed in Sunshine
    name : Daisy
    type : http://example.org#Canine
    name : Morning Daisy Bathed in Sunshine
    type : http://example.org#Mammal

Individual: Ryan
    owns : http://example.org#Daisy
    name : Ryan Blace
    type : http://example.org#Human
    type : http://example.org#Mammal

Individual: Amber
    breed : http://example.org#GoldenRetriever
    name : Amber
    type : http://example.org#Mammal
```

Immediately you can see that there is a difference between this output file and the one generated with no inference. The output includes inferences that occur as a result of the taxonomic relationships between classes and properties. These include the facts that a Chihuahua and Golden Retriever are also breeds, that Daisy's registered name is also a name, that Daisy is not only a canine but also a mammal, and that Ryan is not only a human but also a mammal. These are all the result of the semantics of constructs from the RDFS namespace.

Some of these entailments occur because a subclass relationship causes an instance to become a member of a superclass. The others are inferred because a subproperty relationship causes a new property to be added to an instance.

Since we are providing only RDFS inference, we still don't see any new information entailed by OWL semantics, including the fact that Amber is a canine or that the inverse relationship that exists between `ex:owns` and `ex:hasOwner` means that Daisy has the owner Ryan.

Performing OWL Inference

The final example we'll take a look at involves applying the full set of OWL semantics that Pellet supports to the knowledge model. Here we should see all implicit statements, as Pellet supports all of the OWL and RDFS constructs that we've used in our example ontology. The following example contains the output of the final inference example run, in OWL mode. The statements that are new are compared to the results from the previous example in bold.

```
Individual: Chihuahua
   type : http://example.org#SmallBreed
   type : http://www.w3.org/2002/07/owl#Thing
   type : http://example.org#Breed
   sameAs : http://example.org#Chihuahua

Individual: Ryan
   name : Ryan Blace
   owns : http://example.org#Daisy
   type : http://example.org#Human
   type : http://www.w3.org/2002/07/owl#Thing
   type : http://example.org#Mammal
   sameAs : http://example.org#Ryan

Individual: Daisy
   name : Morning Daisy Bathed in Sunshine
   name : Daisy
   hasOwner : http://example.org#Ryan
   breed : http://example.org#GoldenRetriever
   registeredName : Morning Daisy Bathed in Sunshine
   type : http://www.w3.org/2002/07/owl#Thing
   type : http://example.org#Mammal
   type : http://example.org#PetOfRyan
   type : http://example.org#Canine
   sameAs : http://example.org#Daisy

Individual: GoldenRetriever
   type : http://www.w3.org/2002/07/owl#Thing
   type : http://example.org#Breed
   type : http://example.org#LargeBreed
   sameAs : http://example.org#GoldenRetriever
```

```
Individual: Amber
  name : Amber
  breed : http://example.org#GoldenRetriever
  type : http://www.w3.org/2002/07/owl#Thing
  type : http://example.org#Mammal
  type : http://example.org#Canine
  sameAs : http://example.org#Amber
```

This time there are a lot of new statements in the knowledge model. All of the inferences of the RDFS inference example are still present. In addition, all of the individuals are now members of the class `owl:Thing`. This is because we are now in the realm of OWL semantics, where all instances are members of the `owl:Thing` class. An artifact worth mentioning is that all instances are `owl:sameAs` themselves. Depending on the implementation of an inference engine, you may see statements like these that are technically valid, even if they are less than useful.

Taking a closer look, Daisy now correctly has the owner Ryan. Now that the has-owner relationship correctly exists between Daisy and Ryan, the class `ex:PetOfRyan` is correctly being interpreted, and Daisy is a member of it because she has the property `ex:hasOwner` with a value of `ex:Ryan`. Finally, now that the OWL semantics are correctly being interpreted, Amber is implicitly a canine because she has a property `ex:breed` that points to an instance of the class `ex:Breed`.

This exercise demonstrates the semantics of RDFS and OWL in action. RDFS introduces the taxonomic structure of properties and classes, allowing you to take advantage of automatic propagation of statements and class membership. OWL adds a lot more expressivity using restrictions and advanced class and property descriptions. An ontology that contains OWL constructs can still be used by an application that is applying only RDFS or even no inference; nevertheless, you will not be able to realize all of the semantics of the ontology unless you use an inference level that supports the constructs you used in the ontology. The project for the programming example we just explored is available on the website that accompanies this book. It is designed to accept any valid ontology, so feel free to play around with the ontology and see the side effects for yourself.

Working with Ontologies

Working with Semantic Web applications and ontologies can seem like unfamiliar territory to developers who are used to working with other, more traditional information management systems. Semantic Web technologies enable users to share and reuse the same data sets across multiple platforms and applications. They accomplish this through two critical design principles: decoupling the knowledge model from the application and integrating knowledge models through reuse and extension. The following sections explore these two design principles and how you can implement them in your Semantic Web applications.

Decoupling the Knowledge Model from the Application

Decoupling the knowledge model from the application is critical to enabling data sharing and reuse between users and applications. Knowledge models built for a specific application often contain application-specific concepts or are built to consider the application's implementation. This tightly coupled approach may improve application performance or simplify the design of the model, but it limits the user's ability to move data between applications and environments. One approach to solving this issue is to translate the data from application to application; however, if the model contains or requires application-specific elements, this is a challenging task.

Even if it were trivial to translate between the knowledge models of various applications, there are still potential complications. The limited expressivity of traditional knowledge models like relational databases and XML schemas has forced developers to supplement these models with application-layer business logic. For example, a database schema is primarily a structural representation of data. It contains very little information about the semantics of the data. The interpretation of the information is contained in the queries that execute against the database and the logic that interprets the query results. While databases provide some features for expressing additional business logic directly (stored procedures and query views), most of the time it is introduced as part of the application itself. This means that part of the knowledge model is actually embedded in the application. To move to a different application means losing part of the model or requires the re-implementation of the business logic. This often leads to situations in which users are stuck with a specific application even if it is obsolete or inferior to an alternative because the data is so tightly coupled with that application (see Figure 5-7).

As we said before, the goal is to build a knowledge model that is independent of the applications that use it. All of the business logic in the model should be captured in the model itself and not in the applications. This creates a conflict. You can't require all applications to operate off of a common knowledge model, just as you can't require all users of various knowledge domains to share the same knowledge model. The solution is to use application-specific ontologies as interfaces between the user's knowledge model and the application. Each application supports its own (or, preferably, a standard) knowledge model, and developers can integrate their own knowledge models using the various mapping capabilities provided by OWL and SWRL, some of which we have already discussed and others that will be presented throughout the remainder of this book. This is similar to how component-based systems use programming interfaces and adapters to achieve integration.

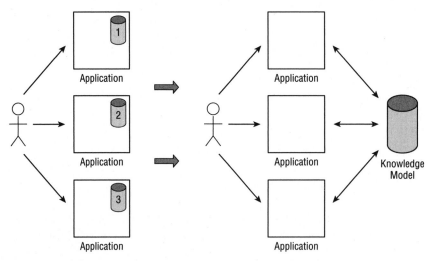

Figure 5-7 Developers can use ontologies and rules to move business logic from applications into the user's knowledge model.

What this all means to you as a developer is that you need to learn to move business logic out of applications and into knowledge models using ontologies and rules. You must learn to design well-scoped ontologies that prioritize the requirements of the user rather than the requirements of applications. The remainder of this chapter addresses these goals.

Sharing across Domain and Application Boundaries

Sharing information across knowledge domains and applications is made possible by establishing relationships between the concepts in each. You may not be familiar with the term *strigiformes* but, if you learn that strigiformes is the biological order that contains all the species of owls (see Figure 5-8), you should have a pretty good idea of what the term means. The concept *strigiformes* is conveyed by defining it in terms of concepts that you probably do understand: *biological order* and *species of owls*. This kind of information sharing and interpretation can occur only if these interdomain relationships and concept mappings exist a priori or are manually added as they are needed.

The amount of effort required to integrate two knowledge domains (or applications) is directly proportional to the number of distinct, disconnected concepts in each. The process can involve simple mapping between identical concepts, the establishment of subclass or subproperty relationships, or

operations as complicated as mathematical calculations or string manipulations. Some of these relationships can be established using ontology
constructs, but others require the use of a rule language like the Semantic
Web Rule Language (SWRL).

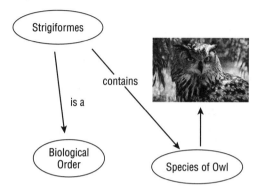

Figure 5-8 *Strigiformes* is a term most people don't recognize. Add the fact that strigiformes
is the biological order that contains all of the species of owls, and it is suddenly a
well-defined concept.

To ease domain integration, you should strive to minimize the number of
concepts that are disconnected between domains. One of the easiest ways to do
this is to reuse or extend existing ontology concepts. If an ontology is missing
some content or expressivity that you need, you can extend the ontology to
satisfy your needs. Only if you absolutely must should you create your own
ontology from scratch. When you create a new, unique ontology, it is completely disjoint from the other ontologies already out there. Any conceptual
connection to other ontologies must be manually added. Your goal in ontology
development should be to create a connected web of concepts and relationships, and this can be accomplished if you reuse and extend existing ontologies
as much as possible and create new ones only when absolutely necessary.

What Is a Foundational Ontology?

When you reuse or extend an ontology, you are using that ontology as a basis
for your domain-specific ontology. An ontology that serves as that basis is
often referred to as a *foundational ontology*, or an *upper ontology*. A foundational
ontology is an ontology that contains objects and concepts that transcend
the boundaries of a single knowledge domain. These ontologies can simplify
information exchange by creating an environment in which the terminologies
of disparate knowledge domains are all rooted in a common space. Any
ontology can be used as a foundational ontology; however, it is common
that they are designed with reuse and extension in mind. Some foundational

ontologies contain a loosely scoped set of high-level, general terms that can be used across knowledge domain boundaries, while others are focused more narrowly on a specific area of interest and provide concepts at various levels of granularity within that area.

Foundational ontologies create an environment in which different knowledge domains share common sets of root concepts and are able to enrich the ontology both in breadth and specificity as necessary for each specific application. When this is achieved, the various domains can share information at the foundational ontology level regardless of how each ontology has been extended.

As an example, consider the scenario depicted in Figure 5-9. The two Internet applications, Jabber (`http://www.jabber.org`) and Facebook (`www.facebook.com`) deal with instant messaging between users and social networks, respectively. Jabber focuses on connecting two users so that they can communicate. Facebook focuses on the interpersonal relationships and communications that exist between friends and their interests. If each application independently developed an ontology describing the data it contains, the resulting ontologies would undoubtedly be disjoint. They may share some of the same ideas and concepts, but the terminology and namespaces used would be almost certainly different. Consider the knowledge model excerpts in Figure 5-9. A client on Jabber is referred to as a *User*. Users are connected using the property `hasContact`. A User has a *jabberId*, a *name*, and a *status*. Facebook shares many of the same concepts but uses different terminology. A client is a *Person*. People are connected by the property `hasFriend`. A Person has a *username* and a *name* and *is* doing something. A Jabber User is very similar to the concept of a Facebook Person, and the relationship `hasContact` is similar to `hasFriend`.

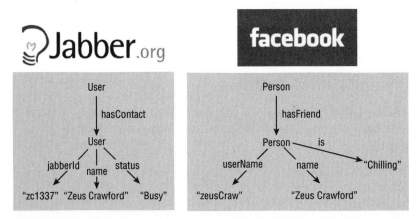

Figure 5-9 Knowledge models developed independently representing Jabber and Facebook would most likely be completely disjoint even though they share many of the same concepts.

Now consider if the two sites developed knowledge models based on a common set of foundational ontologies. The areas of conceptual overlap that are apparent between the two domains would be connected by a common set of concepts. Even if the concepts are relatively general, they provide a high-level mapping between the two domains that would otherwise be separate.

Common Foundational Ontologies

Over the years, many ontologies have been developed and shared that provide an excellent basis for extension and reuse. So far we've really talked only about extending foundational ontologies, implying that they provide only a high-level representation of the concepts you are interested in. This is not always the case. There are a number of ontologies that take the opposite approach, providing an in-depth representation of a narrowly scoped area of interest. With this kind of ontology, you may not necessarily extend the concepts they contain; rather, you may simply reuse the concepts directly, or generalize them. The following is a list of projects whose goal is to provide one or more ontologies or vocabularies that can be used as a reference or a basis for reuse or extension as you begin to develop your own ontologies. The ontologies listed are not necessarily OWL specific; however, OWL translations are available for each.

- Basic Formal Ontology (BFO)
- Cyc and OpenCyc
- Descriptive Ontology for Linguistic and Cognitive Engineering (DOLCE)
- Dublin Core Metadata Initiative
- Friend of a Friend (FOAF)
- GeoRSS
- Suggested Upper Merged Ontology (SUMO)
- OWL Time

BFO

The Basic Formal Ontology (BFO) project maintains an ontology that is oriented toward scientific research. BFO consists of a number of subontologies that can be categorized as either SNAP or SPAN ontologies. *SNAP* ontologies express concepts useful for describing snapshots of things that are either enduring (they are not affected by the passage of time) or are instantaneous. *SPAN* ontologies express concepts useful for describing things that span across time and for which temporal context is important. The BFO website (`http://www.infomis.org/bfo`) contains the OWL BFO ontology as well as information about the project and documentation.

Cyc and OpenCyc

Cyc is a large artificial intelligence (AI) project that is developing a comprehensive ontology and associated knowledgebase of objects and concepts related to everyday life. The goal of the project is to build a knowledgebase that can be used by AI applications to reason about the world in order to mimic human behavior. OpenCyc is the open-source subproject of Cyc and has a public knowledgebase at its website (`http://sw.opencyc.org`), allowing users to search for the terms it contains. Figure 5-10 shows the summary results of a search for the term *Automobile*. The OpenCyc website has a Semantic Web–specific page that contains an automatically translated OWL version of the OpenCyc ontology. Because the original ontology is not captured in OWL, some expressivity is lost in the translation to OWL.

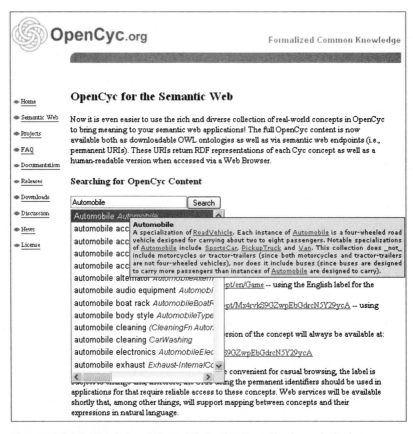

Figure 5-10 A search for *Automobile* in the OpenCyc knowledgebase.

DOLCE

DOLCE (`http://www.loa-cnr.it/DOLCE.html`) is a comprehensive ontology that spans many domains and fields of research. The DOLCE project maintains an ontology that expresses objects and concepts relevant to natural language and cognitive science.

SUMO

The Suggested Upper Merged Ontology (SUMO) is a collection of domain ontologies that are used for various research applications, including linguistics and reasoning. The project is hosted at `http://www.ontologyportal.org`.

Dublin Core Metadata Initiative

The Dublin Core Metadata Initiative (`http://dublincore.org`) is a project whose goal is to develop metadata standards for a wide range of applications, including document and multimedia description. The project maintains a registry of metadata terms that can be browsed or searched, as shown in Figure 5-11. The terms are primarily oriented toward simple and common descriptive metadata, including title, type, description, authorship, and timestamp information, and are often used as annotation properties in OWL.

Figure 5-11 The Dublin Core Metadata Initiative maintains a repository of widely applicable metadata terms at `http://dcmi.kc.tsukuba.ac.jp/dcregistry/`.

FOAF

The FOAF project (http://www.foaf-project.org) maintains the Friend of a Friend ontology, which expresses information relevant to sharing information about friends on the World Wide Web. The ontology contains classes and properties for capturing personal information, email addresses, online account and instant messaging information, as well as online documents and images. Following is a sample description of an individual using the FOAF ontology, generated using the FOAF-a-Matic web application located at http://www.ldodds.com/foaf/foaf-a-matic.

```
@prefix: <http://test#> .
@prefix rdfs: <http://www.w3.org/2000/01/rdf-schema#> .
@prefix foaf: <http://xmlns.com/foaf/0.1/> .
@prefix admin: <http://webns.net/mvcb/> .
@prefix rdf: <http://www.w3.org/1999/02/22-rdf-syntax-ns#> .

:me rdf:type foaf:Person ;
    foaf:family_name "Crawford" ;
    foaf:givenname "Zeus" ;
    foaf:homepage <http://www.zeuscrawford.net> ;
    foaf:name "Zeus Crawford" ;
    foaf:title "Mr" .
```

The goal of the FOAF project is to provide a means to capture your online life in an application-independent and website-independent manner in order to break down the walls that divide the various communities on the Web. The example shows a declaration of a foaf:Person, with some common properties about that individual including foaf:name, foaf:title, and foaf:homepage. Other properties that could be added to this entry are usernames for various messaging applications and social-networking websites as well as links to other foaf:Person instances that Zeus Crawford is friends with. We'll reference and revisit FOAF throughout the examples in this book.

GeoRSS and OWL-Time

GeoRSS (http://georss.org) is a vocabulary of terms that can be used in RDF documents to represent geospatial information. The primary purpose of the project is to provide a common vocabulary of geospatial terms for use in RSS feeds. OWL-Time (http://www.w3.org/TR/owl-time) is a set of OWL ontologies that express a number of concepts relevant to representing temporal information in OWL. Some of the concepts that the ontology can be used to describe include instants in time, durations, and time zones. We'll visit modeling and working with the concepts of space and time in more detail in Chapter 13, "Managing Space and Time."

Finding Ontologies to Reuse or Extend

We've introduced some common foundational ontologies that you can reuse or extend in your own projects. There are plenty of other ontologies out there that you may want to take advantage of if none of the ones we've discussed are suitable for your purposes. Fortunately, a number of tools are available to help you find them. These tools are usually characterized as registries, repositories, or search engines.

An ontology *registry* is an application where users can go and register their ontologies to share with others. Usually the registry maintains a description of the ontology, some statistics about its contents, and a link to the ontology. Registries don't provide ontology storage; they simply act as directories that users can browse or search in order to find ontologies. A repository is a lot like the phone book. It contains a searchable list of ontologies and information on how to find them.

An ontology *repository* takes a more centralized approach by introducing ontology storage and management. Not only does the repository allow users to search and locate ontologies, but the repository stores a local copy of each ontology and allows users to upload multiple versions of each. It may also provide ontology-editing capabilities. There are a number of ontology repositories on the Web. Some of them are general purpose, but most have a specific focus or area of interest. For example, the TONES Ontology Repository (`http://owl.cs.manchester.ac.uk/repository`) is maintained to provide tool developers a central location to find test ontologies. You can browse the repository using various metrics and filters, as shown in Figure 5-12.

An example of a domain-specific ontology repository is BioPortal (`http://bioportal.bioontology.org`). BioPortal is a repository for biomedical ontologies. It provides the ability to browse, search, and visualize the concepts contained in its ontologies. Figure 5-13 shows the results of a search for *influenza* that eventually led to the visualization of the concept *Influenzal pneumonia*.

Registries and repositories each require users to actively push their ontology out into the world. Ontology search engines take a more automated approach, crawling the Web using URIs and hyperlinks, searching for and indexing the ontologies they find. One of the most prominent ontology search engines on the Web today is Swoogle (`http://swoogle.umbc.edu`). Swoogle allows you to search an index of ontologies using plain-text queries as you would with any information-retrieval system like Google or Yahoo. We will discuss Swoogle again as part of our discussion of exploring the Semantic Web in Chapter 7; however, it is useful to draw attention to the distinction between an ontology search engine and an ontology-enhanced search engine. An ontology search engine is used to locate ontologies. An ontology-enhanced search engine uses ontologies to enhance the process of locating and ranking web pages that are relevant to a search.

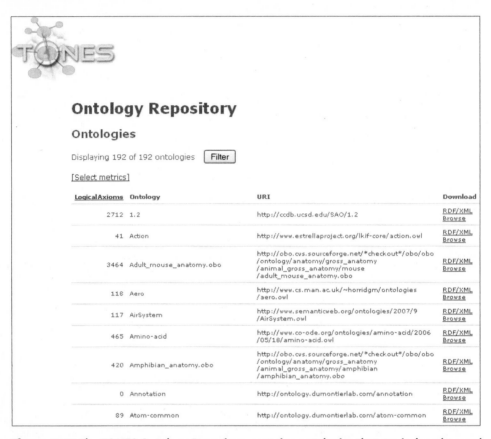

Figure 5-12 The TONES Ontology Repository contains ontologies that are indexed according to a number of metrics and can be searched using various filters.

OPEN ONTOLOGY REPOSITORY

The Open Ontology Repository is a project aimed at creating an ontology repository architecture that provides full life-cycle support for the use of ontologies throughout the world. The goal is to provide a deployable server framework that businesses and organizations can use to support the creation, searching, and sharing of ontologies. Additional features include version management and ontology language translation services. More information can be found about the Open Ontology Repository project at
`http://www.openontologyrepository.org`.

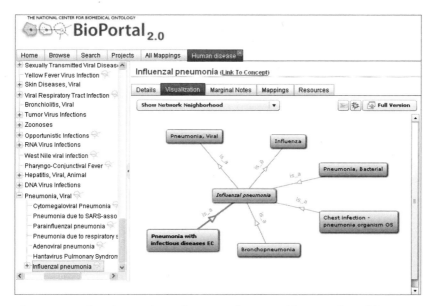

Figure 5-13 The BioPortal ontology repository provides search and browse capabilities as well as visualization tools and ontology mappings.

Choosing the Right Foundational Ontologies

As we've said, many of the foundational ontologies we are discussing are not Semantic Web–or OWL-specific and were developed using a variety of ontology languages and for a variety of reasons. In most cases, OWL translations are available; however, you may encounter situations in which there is no OWL representation of an ontology you would like to use. In these cases, it is good practice to use the foundational ontology as a reference for modeling your ontology so that the models will at least be consistent in design.

In our experiences working with ontologies, we have found that a foundational ontology is most useful if it tries to achieve either a wide-breadth or a deep-depth representation of a well-scoped area of interest, but not both. We have found that ontologies that try to express everything in the world to a great level of detail are intractable unless we work only with subsets of the concepts they contain.

When working with ontologies, it is critically important to avoid overrepresenting your knowledge domain. Because the ontology model is inherently flexible and extensible, you don't have to worry about including and describing every piece of information you may ever be interested in. Rather, you should focus on your current requirements and simply try to avoid anything that might limit or interfere with your future modeling requirements.

Summary

In this chapter, you learned about a number of topics that are critical to using OWL in the real world. We discussed knowledgebases and their components, including storage mechanisms, query processors, and inference engines. We introduced you to a number of common components and frameworks that you can use in your own applications. You learned that Jena and Pellet are two of the components that are used throughout this book.

After your introduction to knowledgebases and inference, you learned about the importance of having profiles of OWL, which trade some expressivity for desirable computational characteristics and will help tool developers and programmers like you make applications that meet real-world performance requirements. Next you saw a detailed example that integrates the Pellet inference engine with the Jena Semantic Web Framework to demonstrate OWL semantics against the sample ontology that was built in Chapter 4.

We ended the chapter by exploring some important ontology design principles, including the importance of ontology reuse, the role of foundational and application ontologies, and a number of commonly used foundational ontologies. Finally, you learned how you can go about finding ontologies on the Web, which you can reuse in your Semantic Web applications. As you move ahead into the next chapters, you will continue to learn about the critical components of the Semantic Web so that you will have all the tools you need to program with the Semantic Web.

Discovering Information

*"All truths are easy to understand once they are discovered; the point is to
discover them."*
—Galileo Galilei

Information discovery concerns the different ways we can find information
that is stored in RDF statements. There is no single method for locating
information in the Semantic Web that works in all situations. Depending upon
whether we know *exactly* what we are searching for and where the data might
exist, and if we are aware of how the data is structured, we could discover the
answers through navigation, searching, or querying.

Navigation is the simplest form of information discovery, where we have a
tool to retrieve and visualize RDF data and, triple by triple, we dereference
URIs to locate additional triples with no particular plan or goal in mind.
Dereferencing a URI is the process of requesting and receiving a URI resource's
representation (for example, a web page). This process repeats until we run out
of triples or inclination. When we navigate, we may or may not be concerned
with finding an answer because we might not have a question in mind;
navigation can be thought of as *free discovery*. Semantic Web browsers are one
means of navigation and will be explored in this chapter.

Searching builds on navigation by not only having a goal, such as searching
for information on Chinese restaurants, but also relying upon more than just
our navigation tool to find information manually. Searching doesn't have to
be limited to search engines, although they are good examples of common
search implementations. Focusing on keyword searching, the use of keywords
requires the user to have a goal (we can't perform keyword searching without
some criteria or input), and searching allows us to leverage all the Semantic

Web documents and data stores that have been previously indexed by the engine. This type of information discovery might include not knowing where to find this knowledge or how much of it is available in a semantic format.

Querying is the final form of information discovery that allows for complex, explicit, and structured questions to be posed, and the resulting information either succeeds or fails to answer those questions. Querying is based on formal syntax and semantics and, unless explicitly told to do so, does not return approximate information or supply answers that are "good enough." This type of information discovery tends to be the most difficult because it isn't always easy or efficient to develop the optimal query. Much like software development, we may *think* our query should be performing correctly, yet we're not seeing the results we're expecting. We will explore querying through SPARQL, a W3C-based RDF query language.

In this chapter, you investigate each form of information discovery: *navigating, searching*, and *querying*. This chapter focuses on querying using the SPARQL query language and all its various components. We chose this focus because querying requires learning a query language, its syntax, and usage. By the end of the chapter, you will gain familiarity with and get comfortable using the various types of information discovery as well as building and executing SPARQL queries. In this chapter, you will learn about:

- Navigating, searching, and querying
- Understanding and using each type of information discovery
- Querying with SPARQL

Navigating the Semantic Web

We remember first discovering and surfing the Internet; with every hyper-linked click we would find another wellspring of information, browsing to all sorts of topics not knowing where the hours went. This *drunkard's walk* for information wasn't always effective, but it provided a good starting point for getting a sense of what information was available, where it could be found, and how much of it existed. Navigating does not need to be goal-oriented, as we are merely exploring the RDF landscape, and hence there is no requirement for returning or finding any information of interest.

For the Internet, we use a web browser for navigation. For the Semantic Web, we can use a Semantic Web browser. Browsing the Semantic Web seems a little odd at first. For most of the book, we have talked about how the Semantic Web is focused on machine-based accessibility and semantic artifacts that aren't primarily for user consumption. Yet it is extremely useful to have a tool that visualizes RDF data for debugging, data verification or, in our case, free discovery. It is important that you are aware of Semantic Web browsers and their use so you can gain a sense of how much interconnected RDF data and other RDF-based languages, such as OWL, are available today on the Internet.

In addition to Semantic Web browsers, there are also RDF browsers. The former dereferences resolvable URIs, enabling a continuous exploration of browser-accessible triples, while the latter visualizes RDF triples typically based on a local RDF data store. There is not universal agreement on this distinction as some technologists still refer to both as RDF browsers. Several options are available, such as the Tabulator Extension for Firefox (`http://dig.csail.mit.edu/2007/tab/`), OpenLink's RDF Browser (`http://demo.openlinksw.com/DAV/JS/rdfbrowser/index.html`), and Disco (`http://www4.wiwiss.fu-berlin.de/bizer/ng4j/disco/`), to name a few. We'll demonstrate Disco, built at Freie Universität Berlin, for our exploration.

Disco has a simple interface that displays triples in a table-based layout, as shown in Figure 6-1. In addition, Disco provides easy access to provenance information by displaying the source graph for each triple, detailed in the Sources column on the right-hand side.

Navigation requires us to have a starting point. In this case, we're starting with Matt's FOAF information, as displayed in Figure 6-1. After entering the FOAF URI into Disco (notice the inclusion of fragment identifier #me), we quickly get an overview of Matt (we will assume this FOAF file is accurate and provides only truthful information about Matt Fisher, ignoring the larger aspects of trust and security). We see that he knows several people and has listed the web pages for his workplace, home page, and other items such as the nearest airport. We see what Matt looks like based on the `foaf:depiction` object resource that resolves to a PNG image. After we've finished exploring this knowledge, we decide to learn more about what Matt is interested in, so we follow the `foaf:topic_interest` link to `http://dig.csail.mit.edu/data#DIG`. You may get different results online since DIG's data is offered through MIT's resources and might change over time.

Disco next displays information about DIG, also known as the Decentralized Information Group, its members, logo, URI, and home page, as shown in Figure 6-2. We've learned quite a bit at this point following only two URIs. In fact, in the case of Figure 6-2, Disco automatically dereferenced six URIs (noted at the bottom of the figure under the Sources heading) to populate this page and has used the triples found at these websites to display incoming URIs. In other words, Disco is displaying triples where `http://dig.csail.mit.edu/data#DIG` is both the subject and object resource across multiple RDF data stores. Notice the unusual is includes of property shows DIG as the subject instead of the object for

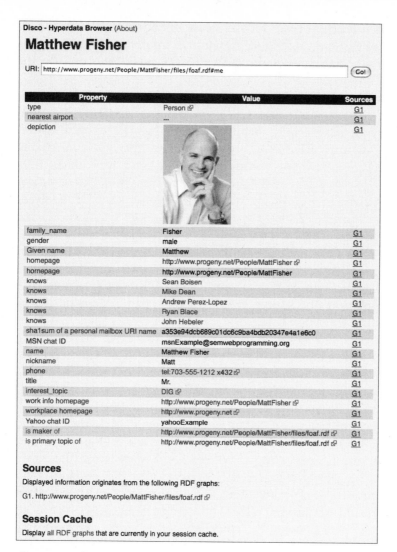

Figure 6-1 The Disco browser interface

property http://www.w3.org/2001/04/roadmap/org#includes, for easier viewing in Disco's tabular format. These additional references expand the potential direction we can browse because we see not only all resources that http://dig.csail.mit.edu/data#DIG relates to but also some of the resources that relate to http://dig.csail.mit.edu/data#DIG. Note that this page doesn't show all known triples in the world that reference http://dig.csail.mit.edu/data#DIG, only those in our session cache (that is, all graphs and their triples that have been dereferenced by Disco so far).

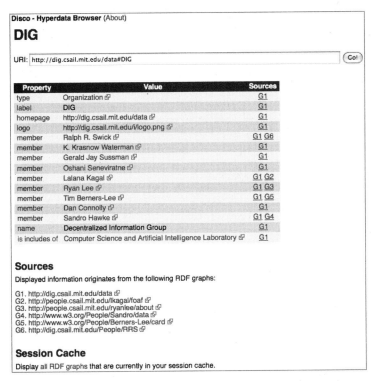

Figure 6-2 Disco displays information about DIG

Looking for more information, we click on Tim Berners-Lee's name from the DIG data, which leads us to Tim's FOAF file and some personal information, much like we discovered about Matt. We could continue this journey by repeatedly following links to additional sources of RDF data. This cycle ends when we decide that there is no more information we want to gather or if a particular URI is dereferenced but contains no RDF data. In the latter case, we can return to an earlier Disco page and traverse other URIs. Chances are we'll run out of interest before we run out of RDF links.

In summary, we learned a little about Matt Fisher, Tim Berners-Lee, DIG, and the names of some people who work at DIG. We weren't out specifically to target any of these things; our free discovery of RDF data led us to them. Like throwing a wide net into the sea, we started at a URI and began to follow the data, not sure where it would take us or what we would learn. The resulting information could be used to tell us how to contact Matt, who to call at DIG for a job interview, or what the various hobbies are of the folks who work at DIG. Our discovery is limited only by the quantity and quality of data people publish in RDF. Note that this type of navigation is dependent on the fact that URIs are resolvable (i.e., when they are dereferenced, some usable data is returned). Plenty of RDF stores don't have resolvable URIs (for example, using `www.example.org` as a hostname) and therefore won't work for browser-based navigation.

Unfortunately, navigation can quickly become cumbersome as information discovery becomes a regular chore. In addition, there simply isn't sufficient time to navigate through enough data sources to solve questions when we have them. In these cases, we need to graduate to searching.

Searching the Semantic Web

Searching goes beyond navigating because users are typically looking for answers (goal-oriented), and more automation is involved (moving beyond simple URI dereferencing in a browser to relying on some computer agent for results). When we search, we would like to take advantage of any data preprocessing a system has completed in advance, such as discovering, sorting, filtering, indexing, and storing. By entering a set of search parameters, we are loosely defining what information we wish to retrieve and how we wish to retrieve it (the parameters and their capabilities are highly dependent on the functionality of the search agent).

In this section, we'll be using Swoogle (`http://swoogle.umbc.edu/`) as our search agent. Swoogle was developed at the University of Maryland, Baltimore County (UMBC) and contains some of the main features used by major Internet search engines. Swoogle employs crawlers to discover Semantic Web documents, indexes document metadata, and calculates an *ontology rank*, a measure of a document's importance in the Semantic Web space. We won't be investigating the mechanics of Swoogle in this section, but you can find additional information at `http://ebiquity.umbc.edu/_file_directory_/papers/116.pdf`. Other semantic search engines include SWSE (`http://swse.deri.org/`), Sindice (`http://www.sindice.com/`), Watson (`http://watson.kmi.open.ac.uk/WatsonWUI/`), and Falcons (`http://iws.seu.edu.cn/services/falcons/objectsearch/index.jsp`).

When we were navigating, our examples focused on traversing instance data. We could have followed class and property definitions just as easily. Search engines are a great way to locate metadata such as ontology models and definitions. Searching for metadata is useful toward encouraging knowledge reuse: We don't want to create ontologies, vocabularies, or any type of RDF data model without initially verifying the existence of similar or identical models. Reuse not only saves time but also promotes growth of the Semantic Web by linking existing data together, enriching the existing web of data.

If, for example, we were interested in extending the FOAF ontology to include genealogical attributes about a person, such as siblings, parents, and grandparents, it would be wise to see what similar RDF models have already been produced. Swoogle can do that with a search for properties that include the terms *brother*, *sister*, *father*, and *grandfather*, as shown in Figure 6-3.

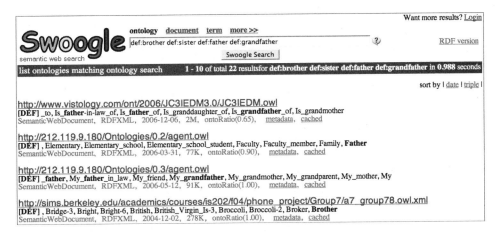

Figure 6-3 Searching Swoogle for genealogical definitions

The use of the `def:` constraint states that we are strictly looking for class or property definitions that include the terms *brother*, *sister*, *father*, and *grandfather*. Several dozen Semantic Web documents were found at the time of this search, and, as we refine our query, it is likely that our results will become smaller and increasingly relevant. There are additional Swoogle parameters for improving search results, such as limiting the potential document pool to OWL files, defining a date and time window for valid documents, or making reference to ontologies of a particular size or specific URIs.

For example, since we started with the idea of expanding FOAF, we could verify if other data modelers had followed a similar vein by using the search string

```
def:brother def:sister def:father def:grandfather
url:"http://xmlns.com/foaf/0.1"
```

This search returns nothing, yet takes us a step closer toward realizing the need to create a new FOAF-based genealogy ontology. Finding this information through navigation techniques alone could never be as effective.

Searching is only as useful as the keywords on which it is based. In addition, there is no one Semantic Web search engine that has indexed every URI-accessible RDF document and RDF store, and it is possible that a particular engine isn't crawling the proper data store. There are instances where we *know* where the data might be housed and we want to ascertain, with 100 percent accuracy, the existence of some particular data set. What we need is a transition from keywords into more explicit syntax, like that provided by a query language, as well as the ability to define the data stores in which to search, independent of the search engine.

Querying the Semantic Web

Querying the Semantic Web requires a language that recognizes RDF as the fundamental syntax. From this base, querying RDF-based languages such as OWL from a pure RDF perspective does not require special procedures or language features. SPARQL is a recursive acronym for SPARQL Protocol and RDF Query Language and is pronounced "sparkle." SPARQL is a W3C Recommendation and is the language we'll use for the rest of the chapter. There are other RDF query languages, such as RDQL (RDF Data Query Language) and SeRQL (Sesame RDF Query Language, pronounced "circle"), but we'll be limiting the discussion to SPARQL because of its W3C standardization, the wide community support, and the large number of publicly available endpoints. An *endpoint*, also called a *processor*, is a service (although not necessarily a web service) that accepts and processes SPARQL queries and returns results in different formats depending on the query form (query forms will be discussed in more detail later in the chapter). Those endpoints that are available via HTTP should follow the SPARQL protocol (`http://www.w3.org/TR/rdf-sparql-protocol/`).

Note that SPARQL is both a query language *and* a protocol. Most people focus on the query language since it defines the syntax in which to frame queries. The protocol is used to describe how a SPARQL client (such as one accessible via a web browser) talks to a SPARQL endpoint/processor (such as `http://dbpedia.org/sparql`) both in an abstract sense and using a concrete implementation based on WSDL 2.0. In addition, most code libraries will hide the protocol implementation, but the same cannot be said of using the language. The SPARQL Recommendation (`http://www.w3.org/TR/rdf-sparql-query/`) is the official specification for the query language. If this chapter doesn't have an answer you need, refer to the Recommendation directly.

Quickstart with SPARQL

If you are familiar with SQL, SPARQL will seem like a long-lost friend (unless you have some unpleasant memories of SQL). Before we get into the details of SPARQL, let's try a quick example to see the query language in action. Go to `http://dbpedia.org/sparql`, and you should see a page displayed similar to that in Figure 6-4. Enter the following query in the Query textbox (you will want to overwrite any existing text that appears in the textbox), and click the Run Query button.

```
# George Washington's Namesakes
SELECT ?location
WHERE {
    ?person <http://www.w3.org/2000/01/rdf-schema#label>
        "George Washington"@en.
    ?location <http://dbpedia.org/property/namedFor> ?person
    }
```

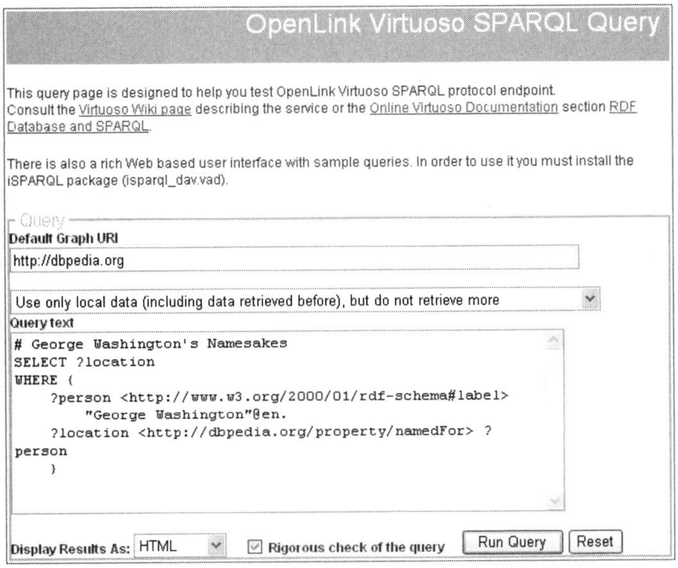

Figure 6-4 Querying DBpedia's SPARQL endpoint for all locations named after George Washington

The query asks for *all locations that have been named after George Washington.* It may not be initially clear that the SPARQL query and its English translation are expressing the same idea, but translating queries becomes easier with practice.

There are two main components to this query: the SELECT and WHERE clauses. The SELECT clause identifies which variables and their values will be returned from the query, and the WHERE clause defines the graph pattern that will be matched against the data in DBpedia's RDF repository. ?person and ?location are variables representing either resources or data types. Variables are stated in lower CamelCase, and keywords (such as SELECT and WHERE) are capitalized. These conventions are a stylistic choice, not a requirement. Also, the literal George Washington is an English-based language string (represented by the trailing en language tag), and the URI properties (label, namedFor) denote the references that connect everything together. The pound sign (#) permits full-line comments. The graph for this query is depicted in Figure 6-5.

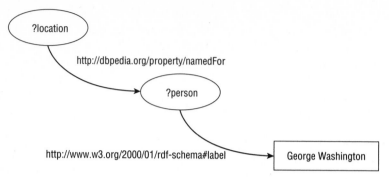

Figure 6-5 RDF graph pattern for George Washington's namesakes

Note the reuse of variable ?person. Variable usage in SPARQL is similar to typical programming languages: A variable holds one RDF resource at a time, and that variable and its value can be reused throughout a query. Variables have global scope in a query no matter how many graph patterns are used. One final note on variables: Both the question mark (?) and the dollar sign ($) are valid when indicating a variable in SPARQL, but conventionally the question mark is used.

By default, DBpedia returns an HTML table with the result set, as shown in Table 6-1. A *result set* is mapping from a set of variable(s), ?location in this case, to a set of RDF terms. Note that when you execute this query, your results may be different from those displayed in this chapter since the underlying DBpedia data can change. Information on the Internet is constantly growing and evolving over time, and you have (near) real-time access to it. Don't be alarmed that all semantic solutions are as fluid as this example. We realize not every solution needs to be centered on an open system (we've noted that closed systems work well for Semantic Web technologies), but the ability to harness global data, or even your own distributed data around the Internet, is a possibility.

Table 6-1 Washington's Namesakes

LOCATION
http://dbpedia.org/resource/Grayson_County%2C_Kentucky
http://dbpedia.org/resource/Washington_County%2C_Minnesota
http://dbpedia.org/resource/Washington_County%2C_Utah
http://dbpedia.org/resource/Washington_County%2C_Georgia
http://dbpedia.org/resource/Washington_County%2C_Idaho
http://dbpedia.org/resource/Washington_County%2C_Ohio
http://dbpedia.org/resource/Washington_Parish%2C_Louisiana
http://dbpedia.org/resource/Washington_County%2C_Kentucky

Returning to our example, we could view the results as XML instead of HTML. To view the XML output, select XML from the Display Results As drop-down list box on the lower-left-hand side of the query interface, as shown in Figure 6-4. The details of how SPARQL results are serialized in XML can be found at `http://www.w3.org/TR/rdf-sparql-XMLres/`. The following results are a subset of the previous result set but displayed in XML (modified for readability):

```
<?xml version="1.0" ?>
<sparql xmlns="http://www.w3.org/2005/sparql-results#"
xmlns:xsi=http://www.w3.org/2001/XMLSchema-instance"
xsi:loc="http://www.w3.org/2001/sw/DataAccess/rf1/result2.xsd">
  <head>
    <variable name="location"/>
  </head>
  <results distinct="false" ordered="true">
    <result>
      <binding name="location">
        <uri>http://dbpedia.org/resource/Grayson_County%2C_Kentucky
        </uri>
      </binding>
    </result>
    <result>
      <binding name="location">
        <uri>http://dbpedia.org/resource/Washington_County%2C_Minnesota
        </uri>
      </binding>
    </result>
  ...
  </results>
</sparql>
```

A couple of notes:

- These results are not ordered. If the same query were run again, it would be acceptable to return the same values in a different order.

- The term *binding* is used to relate a variable to an IRI, a blank node, or a literal. A variable has no bindings if there are no results for that particular variable. In this example, the variable `location` is *bound* to RDF resources that represent Grayson County, Kentucky, and Washington County, Minnesota.

Here are some variations of the same query that do *not* return any bindings for the variable `?location`. Try them out at `http://dbpedia.org/sparql`.

```
# There are no triples in which the exact label, "George Washington"
# exists in DBpedia (i.e. every reference to "George
# Washington" has a language tag).  This pattern matching failure
# is due to SPARQL's default entailment as discussed in the
# section entitled, "SPARQL entailment"
```

```
SELECT ?location
WHERE {
    ?person <http://www.w3.org/2000/01/rdf-schema#label> "George
Washington".
    ?location <http://dbpedia.org/property/namedFor> ?person
    }


# There are no triples that state that George Washington was named
# in honor of some location
SELECT ?location
WHERE {
        ?person   <http://www.w3.org/2000/01/rdf-schema#label>   "George
Washington".
    ?person <http://dbpedia.org/property/namedFor> ?location
    }
```

Four Foundational Query Forms

SPARQL supports four different query forms:

- SELECT–SELECT is comparable to SQL's SELECT statement. The SELECT keyword instructs endpoints to bind RDF terms (blank nodes, IRIs, or literals) to variables based on the given graph pattern (for example, the WHERE clause). Bindings are simply returned and are not part of an RDF graph. SELECT-based result sets display well in tabular form.

- CONSTRUCT–CONSTRUCT allows you to reformulate bound variables into any kind of RDF graph you can design, as long as each triple is valid (for example, no literals used in the subject or predicate position). This query form allows an easy and powerful way to transform data from one RDF graph or OWL ontology into another. Graphs returned from CONSTRUCT queries can be added to RDF repositories or combined with other RDF graphs.

- ASK–If you want to know whether a particular graph exists, ASK will respond with a boolean result of either true or false. Clients are able to probe endpoints for information without having to submit a potentially-expensive SELECT or CONSTRUCT query.

- DESCRIBE–DESCRIBE returns an RDF graph determined solely by the processor with limited query input from a client. DESCRIBE is an interesting case since the client does not need to be intimately familiar with how the data is structured. The endpoint ultimately decides what RDF data is returned to the client. DESCRIBE can be useful for building foundational information when data source awareness is not present. It is not used as heavily as the other forms.

We'll discuss the SELECT query form first, followed by RDF datasets and the use of keywords such as FROM and FROM NAMED. Next, we'll discuss common modifiers such as LIMIT, DISTINCT, and ORDER BY. All of these areas will give us a solid background before we move into the other three query forms of CONSTRUCT, ASK, and DESCRIBE.

SELECT Essentials

Returning to our earlier example with George Washington, it quickly becomes a hassle to deal with long, repetitive namespaces. SPARQL supports the use of XML namespace prefixes with the PREFIX keyword. Most of the syntax used in SPARQL, such as prefixes and graph patterns, is modeled after the Turtle/N3 serialization and is covered in more depth in Chapter 4, "Incorporating Semantics." Prefix names, such as dbprop, can be as short as a single letter but typically represent a readable shorthand description of the subsequent IRI, which must be wrapped in angle brackets.

```
# George Washington's Namesakes
PREFIX rdfs: <http://www.w3.org/2000/01/rdf-schema#>
PREFIX dbprop: <http://dbpedia.org/property/>
SELECT ?location
WHERE {
    ?person rdfs:label "George Washington"@en.
    ?location dbprop:namedFor ?person
    }
```

Listing every single variable in the SELECT clause can also be cumbersome. Just like SQL, queries do not always need to SELECT specific variables. Returning all known bindings for all variables is possible through the use of the asterisk character (*). The asterisk is available only to the SELECT and DESCRIBE query forms. If we rewrote the previous query using the asterisk, the result set would bind all declared variables: ?location and ?person.

```
# George Washington's Namesakes
PREFIX rdfs: <http://www.w3.org/2000/01/rdf-schema#>
PREFIX dbprop: <http://dbpedia.org/property/>
SELECT *
WHERE {
    ?person rdfs:label "George Washington"@en.
    ?location dbprop:namedFor ?person
    }
```

We mentioned before that the WHERE clause is the graph pattern that is compared against RDF data to find the appropriate matching RDF results. If the WHERE clause doesn't find an exact match against the RDF data store, then data is not returned.

Every line in the WHERE clause that is a complete triple must have a period at the end, except for the last line. A semicolon is valid when the subject is reused for two or more triples. A comma is valid when both the subject and predicate are reused for two or more triples. From the processor's point of view, these characters provide clear demarcation between triples since white space characters such as line breaks, line feeds, and carriage returns are valid and do not act as demarcation flags. See the following note on turtle equivalency statements for an example of the syntax.

TURTLE EQUIVALENCY STATEMENTS

Capitalizing on reusable IRIs can greatly cut down on repetitive query strings. Below is a table for quick reference on syntax usage, recapping Chapter 4's coverage of Turtle. Each row refers to an equivalent set of triples.

STANDARD	COMMON SUBJECT	COMMON SUBJECT AND PREDICATE
a :b c . d :e f .	N/A	N/A
a :b c . a :e f .	a :b c ; :e f .	N/A
a :b c . a :b f .	a :b c ; :b f .	a :b c , f .

The following example demonstrates the use of semicolons with a query for George Washington's occupation(s), any and all places where he was born, and any image(s) of him. As an aside, we stress the possibility of multiple answers because it is not safe to assume there will be a single answer to any given query. For example, we ask for any and all places George Washington was born because people can be born in a city, county, state, province, country, as well as a hemisphere.

```
# George Washington's occupation(s), birthplace(s) and image(s)
PREFIX rdfs: <http://www.w3.org/2000/01/rdf-schema#>
PREFIX dbprop: <http://dbpedia.org/property/>
PREFIX foaf: <http://xmlns.com/foaf/0.1/>
SELECT ?job ?birthLoc ?picture
WHERE {
    ?person rdfs:label "George Washington"@en;
            dbprop:occupation ?job;
            dbprop:birthPlace ?birthLoc;
            foaf:img ?picture
}
```

Sure enough, we find Mr. Washington has five known birthplaces. Notice that those five locations are repeated twice. Washington's occupations are also repeatedly listed (Table 6-2 shows the result set, substituting the prefix r for `http://dbpedia.org/resource/` and w for `http://upload.wikimedia.org/wikipedia/commons/b/b6a/`, for easier viewing).

Table 6-2 Frivolous Facts of a Founding Father

JOB	BIRTHLOC	PICTURE
r:Farmer	r:British_America	w: Gilbert_Stuart_Williamstown_Portrait_of_George_Washington.jpg
r:Farmer	r:Colony_of_Virginia	w: Gilbert_Stuart_Williamstown_Portrait_of_George_Washington.jpg
r:Farmer	r:Colonial_Beach%2C_Virginia	w: Gilbert_Stuart_Williamstown_Portrait_of_George_Washington.jpg
r:Farmer	r:Westmoreland_County%2C_Virginia	w: Gilbert_Stuart_Williamstown_Portrait_of_George_Washington.jpg
r:Farmer	r:United_States_of_America	w: Gilbert_Stuart_Williamstown_Portrait_of_George_Washington.jpg
r:Soldier	r:British_America	w: Gilbert_Stuart_Williamstown_Portrait_of_George_Washington.jpg
r:Soldier	r:Colony_of_Virginia	w: Gilbert_Stuart_Williamstown_Portrait_of_George_Washington.jpg
r:Soldier	r:Colonial_Beach%2C_Virginia	w: Gilbert_Stuart_Williamstown_Portrait_of_George_Washington.jpg
r:Soldier	r:Westmoreland_County%2C_Virginia	w: Gilbert_Stuart_Williamstown_Portrait_of_George_Washington.jpg
r:Soldier	r:United_States_of_America	w: Gilbert_Stuart_Williamstown_Portrait_of_George_Washington.jpg

Our result set seems to be returning a significant amount of duplicate data. We ran the query again with the DISTINCT modifier (described in more detail later in the chapter) to remove the duplicates.

```
# George Washington's occupation(s), birthplace(s) and image(s)
PREFIX rdfs: <http://www.w3.org/2000/01/rdf-schema#>
PREFIX dbprop: <http://dbpedia.org/property/>
PREFIX foaf: <http://xmlns.com/foaf/0.1/>
SELECT DISTINCT ?job ?birthLoc ?picture
WHERE {
    ?person rdfs:label "George Washington"@en;
```

```
dbprop:occupation ?job;
dbprop:birthPlace ?birthLoc;
foaf:img ?picture
}
```

The result set is identical to the first. It turns out that the data we're seeing for both queries is completely valid. Recall that the WHERE clause is a graph pattern and is matched to a set of RDF items one at a time. The first time the query is run, DBpedia found a unique set of bindings (called a *query solution*) to the three variables (job, birthLoc, and picture) based on the IRIs of Farmer, British_America, and Gilbert_Stuart_Williamstown_Portrait_of_George_Washington.jpg that, together, matched the WHERE clause. DBpedia found another query solution based on the IRIs of Farmer, Colony_of_Virginia, and Gilbert_Stuart_Williamstown_Portrait_of_George_Washington.jpg. Each query solution is unique, as shown in the following standard XML result set (modified and highlighted below for readability):

```
<?xml version="1.0" ?>
<sparql xmlns=http://www.w3.org/2005/sparql-results#
        xmlns:xsi=http://www.w3.org/2001/XMLSchema-instance
        xsi:loc="http://www.w3.org/2001/sw/DataAccess/rf1/result2.xsd">
  <head>
    <variable name="job"/>
    <variable name="birthLoc"/>
    <variable name="picture"/>
  </head>
      <result>
        <binding name="job">
          <uri>http://dbpedia.org/resource/Farmer</uri>
        </binding>
        <binding name="birthLoc">
          <uri>http://dbpedia.org/resource/British_America</uri>
        </binding>
        <binding name="picture">
          <uri>http://upload.wikimedia.org/wikipedia/commons/b/b6/
Gilbert_Stuart_Williamstown_Portrait_of_George_
Washington.jpg</uri>
        </binding>
      </result>

      <result>
        <binding name="job">
          <uri>http://dbpedia.org/resource/Farmer</uri>
        </binding>
        <binding name="birthLoc">
          <uri>http://dbpedia.org/resource/Colony_of_Virginia</uri>
        </binding>
```

```
        <binding name="picture">
          <uri>http://upload.wikimedia.org/wikipedia/commons/b/b6/
              Gilbert_Stuart_Williamstown-
              Portrait_of_George_Washington.jpg</uri>
        </binding>
      </result>
    ...
  </results>
</sparql>
```

Each highlighted section is a single-query solution and has three unique pairings/bindings of variable to value.

We conclude with a note about RDF collections. SPARQL supports RDF collections with Turtle syntax:

```
(collItem1 collItem2 collItem3 ...).
```

It is difficult to write a query that lists all the items in a collection because there is no support for looping or variable-length lists. It is the experience of the authors that RDF collections are not used heavily in production environments.

TIPS ON SPARQL QUERY DEBUGGING

Debugging SPARQL queries can be a challenge. It is not always easy to find why your queries aren't working quickly (language tags easily fall into this category). Here are some tips.

◆ **Dump your data.** When querying via SELECT, if you aren't seeing any bound variables or get an incomplete set of results (low precision), rewrite your query to use more variables, and add them to your SELECT statement. This will allow you to see more results after execution, a process that harkens back to the days of debugging C/C++ code with printf statements.

◆ **Simplify, simplify, simplify.** Fault detection is much easier if you remove a single line, term, or expression from your query and rerun it. This process of elimination can be tedious, but it will serve you well when frustration sets in and you are making all sorts of random changes without remembering any of them.

◆ **Verify your contents.** When querying small-to-medium RDF stores, make sure the statements you think are in the repository are actually there. For example, you could run the following query for a complete listing of triples:

```
select ?statement ?pred ?obj
where {
  ?statement ?pred ?obj
}
```

(continued)

TIPS ON SPARQL QUERY DEBUGGING *(continued)*

Note that beyond your sandbox RDF store, SPARQL endpoints on the Internet are not required to respond to this query as it can obviously eat up resources and may be tagged as a denial-of-service attack.

◆ Delete `DISTINCT` and remove `REDUCED`. In some cases, using either of these keywords masks what your graph pattern is actually returning. A query could be more complex than it needs to be, but you have to see the entire result set to be absolutely certain.

◆ Restrict result sets with `LIMIT`. While we haven't yet covered the `LIMIT` keyword in detail, it is useful in limiting the number of results that a query returns, saving time when executing queries.

RDF Datasets, FROM and FROM NAMED

Take a look at the Default Graph URI textbox on DBpedia's SPARQL page in Figure 6-6.

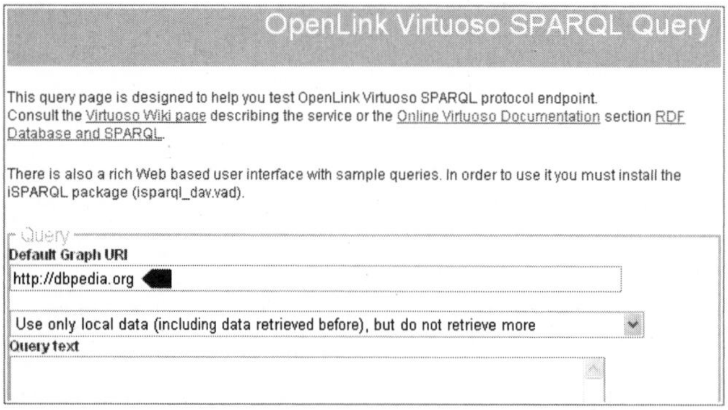

Figure 6-6 DBpedia's Default Graph URI textbox

Every SPARQL query is always run against at least one graph: the *default graph*, one or more *named graphs*, or a merged set of the default and all named graphs. The default graph is the main repository of RDF triples that is searched by an endpoint when it is presented with a query. SPARQL clients should be able to override the default graph or add to the possible set of queried data stores by providing one or more `FROM` or `FROM NAMED` clauses. In the following example, the graph that is queried is created as a result of the merger of the triples from each `FROM` clause's IRI without the default graph. We will get into more details of named graphs when we discuss them later in the chapter.

Branching out from DBpedia's default graph, let's find out anything we can about Tim Berners-Lee's friends (used because his FOAF file is rich with data). Returning to the DBpedia query page, remove the URI in the Default Graph URI textbox, select Retrieve remote RDF for all missing source graphs from the drop-down list box, and then execute this query:

```
PREFIX tbl: <http://www.w3.org/People/Berners-Lee/card#>
PREFIX foaf: <http://xmlns.com/foaf/0.1/>
PREFIX rdfs: <http://www.w3.org/2000/01/rdf-schema#>
PREFIX karl: <http://www.w3.org/People/karl/karl-foaf.xrdf#>
SELECT ?personName2 ?predicate ?object
FROM <http://www.w3.org/People/Berners-Lee/card>
FROM <http://www.w3.org/People/karl/karl-foaf.xrdf>
FROM <http://www.koalie.net/foaf.rdf>
FROM <http://heddley.com/edd/foaf.rdf>
FROM <http://www.cs.umd.edu/~hendler/2003/foaf.rdf>
FROM <http://www.dajobe.org/foaf.rdf>
FROM <http://www.isi.edu/~gil/foaf.rdf>
FROM <http://www.ivan-herman.net/foaf.rdf>
FROM <http://www.kjetil.kjernsmo.net/foaf>
FROM <http://www.lassila.org/ora.rdf>
FROM <http://www.mindswap.org/2004/owl/mindswappers>
WHERE {
    tbl:i foaf:knows ?person.
    ?person foaf:name ?personName1;
            rdfs:seeAlso ?iri.
    ?iri foaf:primaryTopic ?person2.
    ?person2 foaf:name ?personName2;
             ?predicate ?object
    FILTER(?personName1 = ?personName2).
}
```

Table 6-3 shows a few selected results from the full result set with some of the namespaces prefixed or removed for readability. The original result set consists of over 75 rows of data describing three friends who matched the ?personName2 variable.

Several points are worth discussing:

▪ This query is more complex than the previous example, but it is also more realistic. As with any query language, getting the perfect set of all the right answers (high recall, high precision) can take work and still result in some very large queries. Many tutorials never mention this side of querying.

▪ There are 11 FROM graphs in the query, but there are details for only three friends. The reason for the sparse results is because of the focused query. Our query is looking for *Tim's friends whose own FOAF files have been specifically referenced with an rdfs:seeAlso predicate and those subsequent FOAF files have used the foaf:primaryTopic predicate to reference that particular friend's FOAF identity and the friend's names, in both Tim's FOAF file and the friend's FOAF file, are identical.* The FILTER clause is new but straightforward; we'll cover it in detail later in the chapter.

▪ An issue with this query is that we have to know the IRI of every graph we want to search. This is forgivable because, in the long run, we will create the tools that will automate the crawling. The Semantic Web was built to automate searches like these. The Semantic Web Client Library (`http://www4.wiwiss.fu-berlin.de/bizer/ng4j/semwebclient/`) is a perfect example of this.

Table 6-3 Getting to Know Tim's Friends

PERSONNAME2	PREDICATE	OBJECT
Coralie Mercier	rdfs:type	foaf:Person
Coralie Mercier	foaf:name	Coralie Mercier
Edd Dumbill	rdfs:seeAlso	http://times.usefulinc.com/
Edd Dumbill	foaf:knows	http://danbri.org/foaf#danbri
Edd Dumbill	foaf:depiction	edd-shoulders.jpg
Karl Dubost	foaf:givenname	Karl
Karl Dubost	foaf:title	Mr
Karl Dubost	foaf:workInfoHome page	http://www.w3.org/People/karl

It would be helpful if we could limit any part or the entire query graph pattern to particular RDF data sets. Declaring provenance data by specifying the data store that contributed each triple could be critical in certain circumstances. *Named graphs*, the third and final type of RDF data set, handles both of these challenges.

USING THE BASE KEYWORD

Searching for Tim's friends still caused us to retype IRIs more than once. We can reduce redundancies with the use of the BASE keyword. SPARQL allows for a single base URI to be declared from which all other relative IRIs derive. We

(continued)

USING THE BASE KEYWORD *(continued)*

can't eliminate all unnecessary duplications, but in the case of the query for Tim's friends, the query could change from

```
PREFIX tbl: <http://www.w3.org/People/Berners-Lee/card#>
PREFIX foaf: <http://xmlns.com/foaf/0.1/>
PREFIX rdfs: <http://www.w3.org/2000/01/rdf-schema#>
PREFIX karl: <http://www.w3.org/People/karl/karl-foaf.xrdf#>
SELECT ?personName2 ?predicate ?object
FROM <http://www.w3.org/People/Berners-Lee/card>
FROM <http://www.w3.org/People/karl/karl-foaf-xrdf>
...
```

to

```
BASE <http://www.w3.org/People/karl/karl-foaf.xrdf>
PREFIX tbl: <http://www.w3.org/People/Berners-Lee/card#>
PREFIX foaf: <http://xmlns.com/foaf/0.1/>
PREFIX rdfs: <http://www.w3.org/2000/01/rdf-schema#>
# all relative IRIs have the BASE IRI prepended automatically
PREFIX karl: <#>
SELECT ?personName2 ?predicate ?object
FROM <http://www.w3.org/People/Berners-Lee/card>
# not an empty graph, BASE will be used
FROM <>
...
```

or

```
BASE <http://www.w3.org/People/karl/>
PREFIX tbl: <http://www.w3.org/People/Berners-Lee/card#>
PREFIX foaf: <http://xmlns.com/foaf/0.1/>
PREFIX rdfs: <http://www.w3.org/2000/01/rdf-schema#>
# all relative IRIs have the BASE IRI prepended automatically
PREFIX karl: <karl-foaf.xrdf/#>
SELECT ?personName2 ?predicate ?object
FROM <http://www.w3.org/People/Berners-Lee/card>
# all relative IRIs have the BASE IRI prepended automatically
FROM <karl-foaf.xrdf>
...
```

all of which return identical result sets.

Named graphs are possible through the use of the FROM NAMED keywords. Named graphs act just like default graphs, but there are two subtle differences. First, the SPARQL specification notes that named graphs are a pairing of the graph itself (some set of triples) to an IRI. Without both, the named graph doesn't exist. Default graphs do not have this pairing. Second, named graphs are followed by their own graph pattern, delineated by an additional pair of curly brackets ({}), scoping the possible set of matched triples. Note that this design is not the same as a *subquery*, because an entirely new query, such as a SELECT-in-a-SELECT query, is not allowed. This situation is better explained as a *subgraph* query, where we're allowed to insert a graph pattern within a larger graph pattern.

The simplest test case for using named graphs is the inclusion of an empty graph pattern (note the empty curly brackets), which should return a list of each named graph (since ?g is the only declared variable). Before executing, make sure you click the Reset button located in the lower right-hand corner of Figure 6-4 to reset all the query parameters.

```
SELECT ?g
FROM NAMED <http://www.w3.org/People/Berners-Lee/card>
FROM NAMED <http://www.koalie.net/foaf.rdf>
FROM NAMED <http://heddley.com/edd/foaf.rdf>
FROM NAMED <http://www.dajobe.org/foaf.rdf>
FROM NAMED <http://www.mindswap.org/2004/owl/mindswappers>
WHERE {
    GRAPH ?g {}
}
```

The number of graph IRIs has been cut in half for simplicity as well as protection against DBpedia's query timeout threshold. Nevertheless, this query fails in DBpedia (complaining of ?g not being assigned) unless we add a triple statement to the named graph's pattern.

```
SELECT DISTINCT ?g
FROM NAMED <http://www.w3.org/People/Berners-Lee/card>
FROM NAMED <http://www.koalie.net/foaf.rdf>
FROM NAMED <http://heddley.com/edd/foaf.rdf>
FROM NAMED <http://www.dajobe.org/foaf.rdf>
FROM NAMED <http://www.mindswap.org/2004/owl/mindswappers>
WHERE {
    GRAPH ?g {?empty1 ?empty2 ?empty3}
}
```

This query returns all five IRIs of the named graphs. All of these named graph IRIs were copied from Tim Berner-Lee's FOAF file, but you could use any resolvable IRIs in their place. Two final examples show how we can have graph patterns targeted for all named graphs or a chosen few.

Let's look at all the FOAF files of Tim's friends and see what nicknames they have. Notice the use of blank nodes, which was covered in Chapter 4. In SPARQL queries, blank nodes references (for example, _:blank1) do not correspond to an actual blank node in a graph. Rather, they act like variables in that they can be bound to any IRI, but blank nodes cannot be directly referenced like variables, such as their inclusion in a SELECT statement. See the sidebar "Utility of Blank Nodes" for more information.

UTILITY OF BLANK NODES

Blank nodes are just as useful in queries as they are in regular triple stores. They allow us to connect triples without caring about the connecting resource itself. Blank nodes aren't recognized by SELECT * or DESCRIBE * queries, meaning that even though a blank node can hold any type of RDF data, like a variable, such data will not be included in any result sets that come back, unlike a variable.

There are two ways to create a blank node: either combining an underscore, a colon, and a series of alphanumeric characters (such as _:blank_node_9) or using square brackets. Note that square brackets can have any amount of white space in-between but can be used only once. If repeated use is required, use the first type of labeled blank nodes. The following example is a quick reference on usage, where each row is equivalent.

LABELED BLANK NODES	ANONYMOUS
`_:a9 :property1 object1 .`	`[ ] :property1 object1` `OR [ :property1 object1 ]`
`_:empty6_0 :property1 object1 .` `_:empty6_0 :property2 object2 .`	`[ :property1 object1 ]` `:property2 object2 .`
`subject1 :property1 _:none .` `_:none :property2 object2 .`	`subject1 :property1 [` `:property2 object2 ] .`
`_:silent :property1 object1;` `:property2 object2;`	`[ :property1 object1;` `:property2 object2 ] .`
`_:ghost :property1 object1,` `object2;`	`[ :property1 object1,` `object2 ] .`

```
PREFIX tbl: <http://www.w3.org/People/Berners-Lee/card#>
PREFIX foaf: <http://xmlns.com/foaf/0.1/>
PREFIX rdfs: <http://www.w3.org/2000/01/rdf-schema#>
PREFIX rdf: <http://www.w3.org/1999/02/22-rdf-syntax-ns#>
SELECT *
FROM NAMED <http://www.koalie.net/foaf.rdf>
FROM NAMED <http://heddley.com/edd/foaf.rdf>
FROM NAMED <http://www.cs.umd.edu/~hendler/2003/foaf.rdf>
FROM NAMED <http://www.dajobe.org/foaf.rdf>
FROM NAMED <http://www.isi.edu/~gil/foaf.rdf>
FROM NAMED <http://www.ivan-herman.net/foaf.rdf>
FROM NAMED <http://www.kjetil.kjernsmo.net/foaf>
FROM NAMED <http://www.lassila.org/ora.rdf>
FROM NAMED <http://www.mindswap.org/2004/owl/mindswappers>
WHERE {
    GRAPH ?originGraph {
        _:blank1 foaf:knows _:blank2.
```

```
        _:blank2 rdf:type foaf:Person;
                 foaf:nick ?nickname;
                 foaf:name ?realname
    }
}
```

The results, shown in Table 6-4, are pretty modest. The named graph is given along with all the nickname/realname pairs found at that resource. We removed the uninteresting entries for the sake of brevity.

Table 6-4 Named Graph Nickname Query

ORIGINGRAPH	NICKNAME	REALNAME
http://www.kjetil.kjernsmo.net/foaf	nacho	Michael Nachbaur
http://www.kjetil.kjernsmo.net/foaf	'Moe'	Jörg Walter
http://www.kjetil.kjernsmo.net/foaf	phish108	Christian Glahn
http://www.dajobe.org/foaf.rdf	zool	Jo Walsh
http://heddley.com/edd/foaf.rdf	clurr	Claire Rowland
http://heddley.com/edd/foaf.rdf	klurr	Claire Rowland

It's also possible to target a single-named graph as we look for all the nicknames in just Tim's FOAF file. The default graph must not be queried (since we have a single named graph), so we must remove any URI in the Default Graph URI textbox before execution.

```
PREFIX foaf: <http://xmlns.com/foaf/0.1/>
SELECT ?nickname
WHERE {
    GRAPH <http://www.w3.org/People/Berners-Lee/card> {
        _:blank3 foaf:nick ?nickname
    }
}
```

As expected, this query returns a small, single-column table of four nick-names located only in Tim's FOAF file.

Query Modifiers

Before we move on to the other query forms, it is important to understand the various SPARQL modifiers and how they can improve your queries, in terms of both better results and performance. Modifiers are keywords that affect the result set that is returned from a given query, allowing queries to hone their scope and reach. We'll focus first on detailing the modifiers DISTINCT, REDUCED, ORDER BY, OFFSET, LIMIT, FILTER, OPTIONAL, and UNION by explaining their definition and usage. We'll use examples based on SELECT queries since that is where we have had the most exposure so far.

DISTINCT

The DISTINCT modifier eliminates duplicate query solutions, not individual RDF terms. Let's continue to use DBpedia but return to the last Washington query. Make sure you enter http://dbpedia.org in the Default Graph URI input box. This example binds only the picture URI and removes the DISTINCT keyword:

```
# George Washington's occupation(s), birthplace(s) and image(s)
PREFIX rdfs: <http://www.w3.org/2000/01/rdf-schema#>
PREFIX dbprop: <http://dbpedia.org/property/>
PREFIX foaf: <http://xmlns.com/foaf/0.1/>
SELECT ?picture
WHERE {
    ?person rdfs:label "George Washington"@en;
            dbprop:occupation ?job;
            dbprop:birthPlace ?birthLoc;
            foaf:img ?picture
}
```

This query still returns the same eight duplicates as before. To understand why, this query uses the *exact same* graph pattern as before (that is, the WHERE clause is identical), but our SELECT clause isn't showing all the variable bindings from before. Internal to DBpedia's SPARQL processor, there still are eight unique graph solutions that match the graph pattern, but our query's SELECT clause specifies only that the result set should contain picture bindings.

Applying the DISTINCT keyword will remove the duplication problem and return a single query solution:

```
# George Washington's occupation(s), birthplace(s) and image(s)
PREFIX rdfs: <http://www.w3.org/2000/01/rdf-schema#>
PREFIX dbprop: <http://dbpedia.org/property/>
PREFIX foaf: <http://xmlns.com/foaf/0.1/>
SELECT DISTINCT ?picture
WHERE {
    ?person rdfs:label "George Washington"@en;
            dbprop:occupation ?job;
            dbprop:birthPlace ?birthLoc;
            foaf:img ?picture
}
```

There are both good and bad issues to consider when using DISTINCT. On the good side, DISTINCT reduces our data set as well as saves our endpoint from utilizing unnecessary bandwidth. In addition, the absence of DISTINCT can be useful for aggregation, such as indirectly counting the number of triples in a result set for proper sum operations. On the bad side, using DISTINCT can hide both the amount of data found by the endpoint and obfuscate why excess time was needed to return it. Don't be tempted to add the DISTINCT keyword to cover up a poorly formed query if you aren't expecting duplicate results. Chances are you need to focus on your query pattern. We're not implying that the DISTINCT keyword isn't always necessary but rather indicating to exercise caution in its use.

REDUCED

REDUCED is an interesting modifier, as its inclusion does not compel the end-point to return a different result set from a query *without* the REDUCED keyword. It directs the SPARQL processor that if there are duplicate bindings (for example, eight bindings of http://upload.wikimedia.org/wikipedia/commons/b/b6/Gilbert_Stuart_Williamstown_Portrait_of_George_Washington.jpg to ?picture), the endpoint may reduce the result set to *any* number of solutions between at least one and the maximum possible (eight, in our Washington query). If only everything were this easy!

REDUCED gives processors the opportunity to implement DISTINCT functionality without being forced to do so (as DISTINCT requires) if it may have a negative impact on the query or query performance. It's an opportunistic result set reduction function that allows the query processor to omit duplicate query solutions if it prefers to do so. This design is a tradeoff between the cost of performing the query and handling the result set against the cost of the client processing the result set. In our experience, REDUCED is rarely used since SPARQL clients typically want consistent and repeatable results, achieved through the use of DISTINCT or no modifier at all.

ORDER BY

The modifier ORDER BY applies only to SELECT queries and directs the processor to order the result set according to one or more variables or expressions. RDF graphs, such as those returned by DESCRIBE and CONSTRUCT, are inherently unordered and are thus unaffected by ORDER BY. ASK queries return only a boolean statement, so ordering is unnecessary.

ORDER BY allows result sets to be sorted by variable bindings or expressions either in ascending or descending order based on two optional order modifiers, ASC() and DESC(). ASC() uses the less-than (<) operator for comparison of terms in ascending order, and DESC() uses the greater-than (>) operator for comparison of terms in descending order. In the case of ASC(), a set of string bindings or resources will sort alphabetically, whereas integers will sort by numerical value; DESC() performs the opposite steps. If the variable data types aren't known, SPARQL uses a combination of string collation, numeric type promotions, and subtype substitution to determine which comparison operator to employ. In addition, ORDER BY can sort on multiple variables based on the order in which they are listed, all in a single query.

ORDER BY gives developers an easy way to compare result sets to each other or to other types of data in a consistent, repeatable manner. Returning to our original Washington facts example, we'll order the results first in ascending order by birthLoc, followed by descending order by job. We don't need to wrap the birthLoc variable with the ASC() modifier because, by default, ORDER BY uses ASC():

```
# George Washington's occupation(s), birthplace(s) and image(s)
PREFIX rdfs: <http://www.w3.org/2000/01/rdf-schema#>
PREFIX dbprop: <http://dbpedia.org/property/>
PREFIX foaf: <http://xmlns.com/foaf/0.1/>
SELECT ?job ?birthLoc ?picture
WHERE {
    ?person rdfs:label "George Washington"@en;
            dbprop:occupation ?job;
            dbprop:birthPlace ?birthLoc;
            foaf:img ?picture
} ORDER BY ?birthLoc DESC(?job)
```

Our query returns the following output (see Table 6-5) as expected (the results use the prefix r for http://dbpedia.org/resource/ and w for http://upload.wikimedia.org/wikipedia/commons/b/b6/ for easier viewing).

Data Streaming with OFFSET and LIMIT

The OFFSET and LIMIT modifiers manage large result sets. So far, our sample queries have always dealt with small amounts of data (how many places can Washington have been born anyway?), easily returned in a single result set. Retrieving all results at once is not realistic or tenable for large data sets, something that should be considered given the global scope of the Semantic Web. The idea of streaming results for performance and scalability reasons was identified early on by the W3C's RDF Data Access Working Group and is satisfied with the use of the OFFSET and LIMIT keywords. The precondition for any query using OFFSET and LIMIT is the required addition of ORDER BY, since streaming depends on well-ordered and repeatable results. Thus, SPARQL's streaming capability is limited to SELECT queries, effectively barring RDF triples from being streamed. As a developer, if you need the results in an RDF graph, you will need to transform SELECT result sets into RDF statements on the client side (through an XSLT, for example) as a workaround.

Table 6-5 An Ordered Result Set

JOB	BIRTHLOC	PICTURE
r:Soldier	r:British_America	w: Gilbert_Stuart_Williamstown_ Portrait_of_George_Washington.jpg
r:Farmer	r:British_America	w:Gilbert_Stuart_Williamstown_ Portrait_of_George_Washington.jpg
r:Soldier	r:Colonial_Beach %2C_Virginia	w:Gilbert_Stuart_Williamstown_ Portrait_of_George_Washington.jpg
r:Farmer	r:Colonial_Beach %2C_Virginia	w:Gilbert_Stuart_Williamstown_ Portrait_of_George_Washington.jpg
r:Soldier	r:Colony_of_Virginia	w:Gilbert_Stuart_Williamstown_ Portrait_of_George_Washington.jpg
r:Farmer	r:Colony_of_Virginia	w:Gilbert_Stuart_Williamstown_ Portrait_of_George_Washington.jpg
r:Soldier	r:United_States_of_ America	w:Gilbert_Stuart_Williamstown_ Portrait_of_George_Washington.jpg
r:Farmer	r:United_States_of_ America	w:Gilbert_Stuart_Williamstown_ Portrait_of_George_Washington.jpg
r:Soldier	r:Westmoreland_County %2C_Virginia	w:Gilbert_Stuart_Williamstown_ Portrait_of_George_Washington.jpg
r:Farmer	r:Westmoreland_County %2C_Virginia	w:Gilbert_Stuart_Williamstown_ Portrait_of_George_Washington.jpg

OFFSET is an integer that declares the starting point from which to return results, relative to a numbering scheme based on a larger set of solutions. LIMIT is an integer that caps the number of returned query solutions. Using the two modifiers together allows for queries that will always return identical results over time (assuming the underlying RDF data doesn't change). By both looping over the number of query solutions returned and increasing OFFSET's value by that same number, eventually the entire result set can be retrieved. Loop execution stops when the number of query solutions returned is smaller than the value of LIMIT. The following pseudocode and Figure 6-7 provide additional detail.

```
limit=30 (the value is based on the capabilities of your system)
offset=0 (queries with an OFFSET of zero have no side effects)
```

```
resultCount=0
WHILE resultCount NOT LESS THAN limit
  results = executeQuery("PREFIX ... LIMIT <limit> OFFSET <offset>")
  resultCount = count(results)
  appendResults(results)
  offset = offset + resultCount
ENDWHILE
```

Note that SPARQL doesn't support or require a transactional architecture. A data store that supports transactions follows the guidelines of ACID: atomicity, consistency, isolation, and durability. In short, there is no guarantee that a particular slice of data (a *slice* is defined as a result set based on a SPARQL query with OFFSET and LIMIT parameters) will remain unchanged even if the query remains the same and is issued in quick succession (see Figure 6-7). The underlying data may be mutable to the point that it could change in the middle of the endpoint's processing of the query.

Flexible Querying with FILTER and OPTIONAL

Up to this point, we have only been able to issue SELECT queries using graph patterns that matched *exactly* the triples that exist in DBpedia. In addition, query matching was an all-or-nothing proposition; results were returned only if all the variables were bound. These constraints are highly restrictive and severely limit the data returned from an endpoint. SPARQL uses the keywords FILTER and OPTIONAL to handle these all-or-nothing scenarios, invaluable additions for real-world query development. We will cover FILTER in the following section and OPTIONAL in the next section.

FILTER

FILTER evaluates boolean expressions and removes any query solutions from the result set where the FILTER expressions return false. If the result of a FILTER evaluation is true *and* the remaining portions of the graph pattern match, then all applicable RDF data is returned. So filtering is still an all-or-nothing graph-matching situation, yet it introduces query flexibility.

All SPARQL expressions come from either a subset of the operators and functions that are based on XQuery and XPath or special operators defined specifically for SPARQL. We will not cover all of the allowable expressions in this chapter because of the overwhelming number of available operators, but they are listed in Appendix D. If you aren't knowledgeable about XQuery or XPath, we recommend that you familiarize yourself with the basics of both technologies before continuing.

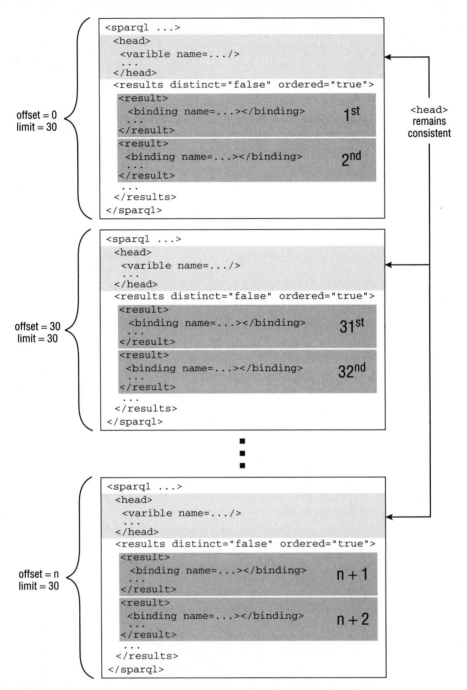

Figure 6-7 Decomposing SPARQL XML results when streaming data

The following example illustrates a simple `FILTER` example. The query will return any RDF relationships (personal, political, commercial) that are relevant during Washington's last term of office. In the United States, presidential terms are limited to four years.

```
PREFIX rdfs: <http://www.w3.org/2000/01/rdf-schema#>
PREFIX dbprop: <http://dbpedia.org/property/>
PREFIX xsd: <http://www.w3.org/2001/XMLSchema#>
SELECT ?prop ?object
WHERE {
    ?person rdfs:label "George Washington"@en;
            dbprop:presidentStart ?start;
            ?prop ?object.
    FILTER(xsd:integer(?start) + 4 <= xsd:integer(?object))
}
```

The `FILTER` clause can be located anywhere in the `WHERE` clause. The same results will be observed whether it is listed as the first or last statement. We use the casting operation of `xsd:integer` to assure correct comparison operations and to view the results as listed in Table 6-6.

SPARQL supports three major classes of operations: unary, binary, and trinary (aka ternary). Unary operations cover logical NOT as well as unary addition and subtraction (setting numeric values either positive or negative). Binary operations cover inequalities, logical AND and OR, the core mathematical functions (addition, subtraction, division, and multiplication), and REGEX for regular expressions. There is only a single trinary operator: REGEX. It differs from the binary REGEX in that the trinary form can also take flags as a parameter. All these operations and functions are laid out in Appendix D.

Through extensible value testing (`http://www.w3.org/TR/rdf-sparql-query/#extensionFunctions`), `FILTER` provides a way for SPARQL processors to extend the language by implementing new functions not currently supported in the SPARQL recommendation. This allows vendors to provide capabilities that distinguish their endpoints from competitors' without explicit requirements to be interoperable.

OPTIONAL

The `OPTIONAL` modifier allows additional bindings to be added to a result set if they are found but will not remove any query solutions if the optional bindings are not found. `OPTIONAL` clauses, just like `WHERE` clauses and `GRAPH` statements, have their own graph pattern scope, delineated by curly brackets (`{}`). By stating that certain triples are optional, a query solution can now have unbound variables without affecting other variables. `SELECT` queries will continue to return table-based result sets, but unbound variables will appear as empty cells. These cells do *not* contain a null or nil parameter; it is the absence of any value at all that makes the result set appear as such. The DESCRIBE and CONSTRUCT forms will not return or add triples that involve unbound variables.

Table 6-6 Activities in Washington's Later Years

PROP	OBJECT
http://dbpedia.org/property/presidentEnd	1797
http://dbpedia.org/property/stateStart	1794
http://dbpedia.org/property/stateStart	1795
http://dbpedia.org/property/warStart	1795
http://dbpedia.org/property/warStart	1796
http://dbpedia.org/property/treasuryStart	1795
http://dbpedia.org/property/justiceEnd	1794
http://dbpedia.org/property/justiceEnd	1795
http://dbpedia.org/property/justiceEnd	1797
http://dbpedia.org/property/postEnd	1795
http://dbpedia.org/property/postEnd	1797
http://dbpedia.org/property/warEnd	1794
http://dbpedia.org/property/warEnd	1795
http://dbpedia.org/property/warEnd	1797
http://dbpedia.org/property/justiceStart	1794
http://dbpedia.org/property/justiceStart	1795
http://dbpedia.org/property/postStart	1795
http://dbpedia.org/property/vicePresidentEnd	1797
http://dbpedia.org/property/stateEnd	1793
http://dbpedia.org/property/stateEnd	1795
http://dbpedia.org/property/stateEnd	1797
http://dbpedia.org/property/treasuryEnd	1795

We'll revisit some of those previous queries and add OPTIONAL blocks to show how they can affect our results.

Our first Quickstart looked at all locations that have been named after George Washington. We limited our search based on the property `http://dbpedia.org/property/namedFor`. It turns out there is another RDF property, `http://dbpedia.org/property/blankInfo`, that states a township in Pennsylvania is also named after George Washington (we discovered this relationship only through navigation, reiterating our point that one form of information discovery is not always enough). We didn't find this information in our initial query because we didn't know `blankInfo` was used in the same manner as `namedFor`. In fact, who knows how any of the data we search is structured? That leads into an important note: *We don't always have insight into how people store their RDF data, yet we need to be able to query it as if we did.* Adding the `OPTIONAL` modifier will broaden the query to look for other ways of discovering things that are named after George Washington. Notice that there are multiple `OPTIONAL` statements. That is because we want each pattern in each `OPTIONAL` block to stand alone. There is no relationship between `dbprop:blankInfo` and `dbprop:namedFor` such that they should be in the same graph pattern. In fact, it would reduce our results if they were together.

```
# Hopefully all of George Washington's Namesakes!
PREFIX ex: <http://www.example.com/>
PREFIX rdfs: <http://www.w3.org/2000/01/rdf-schema#>
PREFIX dbprop: <http://dbpedia.org/property/>
SELECT ?l1 ?l2 ?l3 ?l4
WHERE {
    ?person rdfs:label "George Washington"@en.
    ?l1 dbprop:namedFor ?person.
    OPTIONAL { ?l2 dbprop:blankInfo ?person }
    OPTIONAL { ?l3 ex:isNamedAfter ?person }
    OPTIONAL { ?person ex:wasFamousAndGaveNameTo ?l4 }
    }
```

Our modified query returns the data in Table 6-7 (the prefix r is used for `http://dbpedia.org/resource/` and the term `lyComCtyPa` for `http://dbpedia.org/resource/Washington_Township%2C_Lycoming_County%2C_Pennsylvania` for easier viewing).

When you run this query, it will return new data, seen under ?l2, and could have returned others as well. Since `ex:isNamedAfter` and `ex:wasFamousAndGaveNameTo` don't exist in any triples, ?l3 and ?l4 remain unbound. Yet their failure to find any matching data doesn't affect all the successful matches for ?l1 and ?l2. This means that we can now query with a less-restrictive net into the web of data and not be so concerned if exact matches aren't found. Queries can become large, as developers often add many `FILTER` and `OPTIONAL` keywords (as well as others) to find the specific data they need.

You may have noticed that the variable ?person kept its scope for the entire query. Earlier in the chapter we noted that variables have global scope. If they didn't, the query would have had to reestablish the scope by repeating the `?person rdfs:label "George Washington"@en` triple in each OPTIONAL clause.

Table 6-7 Finding More Namesakes for Washington

L1	L2	L3	L4
r:Grayson_County%2C_Kentucky	lyComCtyPa		
r:Washington_County%2C_Minnesota	lyComCtyPa		
r:Washington_County%2C_Utah	lyComCtyPa		
r:Washington_County%2C_Georgia	lyComCtyPa		
r:Washington_County%2C_Idaho	lyComCtyPa		
r:Washington_County%2C_Ohio	lyComCtyPa		
r:Washington_Parish%2C_Louisiana	lyComCtyPa		
r:Washington_County%2C_Kentucky	lyComCtyPa		

The OPTIONAL modifier can help us discover more FOAF information on Washington. Suppose that when we found a triple using `foaf:name`, there would always be either exactly three associated FOAF triples (based on `foaf:img`, `foaf:mbox`, and `foaf:family_name`) or none at all. In this case, we could state

```
PREFIX foaf: <http://xmlns.com/foaf/0.1/>
SELECT *
WHERE {
    ?person foaf:name ?name.
    OPTIONAL {
        ?person foaf:img ?img;
                foaf:mbox ?mbox;
                foaf:family_name ?fName
        }
}
```

For each query solution in our result set, either we would see `?img`, `?mbox`, and `?fName` bound in each case, or none of the three values would be bound at all. Again, this is because the OPTIONAL block is a pattern graph that must be matched exactly. A more realistic case is that we have no idea what FOAF information is available, so we place every query line in its own OPTIONAL clause.

```
PREFIX foaf: <http://xmlns.com/foaf/0.1/>
SELECT *
WHERE {
```

```
    ?person foaf:name ?name.
    OPTIONAL { ?person foaf:img ?img }
    OPTIONAL { ?person foaf:mbox ?mbox }
    OPTIONAL { ?person foaf:family_name ?fName }
}
```

There is at least one case of anomalous behavior noted by the W3C working group that created the W3C SPARQL recommendation (`http://www.w3.org/TR/rdf-sparql-query/#convertGraphPattern`). In one particular test query where a doubly-nested filter and pattern were inside an OPTIONAL block, the query could result in two different result sets.

```
PREFIX dc: <http://purl.org/dc/elements/1.1/>
PREFIX x: <http://example.org/ns#>
SELECT ?title ?price
WHERE {
    ?book dc:title ?title .
    OPTIONAL {
        {
        ?book x:price ?price .
        FILTER (?title = "TITLE 2") .
        }
    } .
}
```

We needn't worry about such edge cases in typical efforts; this was a query that came out of the W3C's RDF Data Access Working Group as a way for SPARQL endpoints to test their implementations.

UNION

UNION statements create an aggregate result set from the result sets of two graph patterns. If we consider each triple in a graph pattern as an atomic unit, a SPARQL endpoint must find the intersection of all the triples in that pattern to return any data. Membership in this result set is loosened with OPTIONAL statements and tightened with FILTER statements. UNION works well with cases of mutual exclusion and situations when returning one particular statement in a given set of statements is satisfactory. Suppose a query could separate the identity of a person from robots by requesting a resource that has a foaf:gender of *either* male *or* female *and* has a foaf:interest in `http://www.iamhuman.com` *or* `http://lovebeinghuman.org`. UNION allows the results of these two completely different graph patterns to be merged into a single result set. UNION functionality can also be mimicked with FILTER and/or OPTIONAL statements.

Here's a concrete example of differentiating humans from robots.

```
PREFIX foaf: <http://xmlns.com/foaf/0.1/>
SELECT *
```

```
WHERE {
    { ?unknown foaf:gender "male" }
    UNION
    { ?unknown foaf:gender "female" } .
    { ?unknown foaf:interest <http://www.iamhuman.com> }
    UNION
    { ?unknown foaf:interest <http://lovebeinghuman.org> }
}
```

UNION statements can also be chained together. We can now use this tactic on the previous query results found in Table 7-3. We know that each of the named graphs in that query has various ways of describing what it knows about friends. We can create several unique graph patterns based on the data in each named graph and merge the results (merging usually makes more sense with a CONSTRUCT query because we can dictate the resulting triples). Forgive the use of the historic www.mindswap.org website, as it serves a good purpose here.

```
PREFIX foaf: <http://xmlns.com/foaf/0.1/>
PREFIX rdf: <http://www.w3.org/1999/02/22-rdf-syntax-ns#>
PREFIX ms: <http://www.mindswap.org/2003/owl/mindswap#>
SELECT DISTINCT *
FROM NAMED <http://www.kjetil.kjernsmo.net/foaf>
FROM NAMED <http://www.dajobe.org/foaf.rdf>
FROM NAMED <http://heddley.com/edd/foaf.rdf>
FROM NAMED <http://www.cs.umd.edu/~hendler/2003/foaf.rdf>
FROM NAMED <http://www.koalie.net/foaf.rdf>
FROM NAMED <http://www.isi.edu/~gil/foaf.rdf>
FROM NAMED <http://www.ivan-herman.net/foaf.rdf>
FROM NAMED <http://www.lassila.org/ora.rdf>
FROM NAMED <http://www.mindswap.org/2004/owl/mindswappers>
WHERE {
    GRAPH ?originGraph {
        # This pattern now returns information for everyone except
        # www.mindswap.org.
        {
            _:blank1 foaf:knows _:blank2.
            _:blank2 rdf:type foaf:Person.
            # If we find a foaf:Person, then make sure we either
            # print the nickname and/or the name and/or the home page.
            # If we had omitted the FILTER clause, then we could
            # have returned a query solution containing ?originGraph
            # and no other information!
            OPTIONAL { _:blank2 foaf:nick ?nick }.
            OPTIONAL { _:blank2 foaf:name ?rname }.
            OPTIONAL { _:blank2 foaf:homepage ?hpage }.
            FILTER(bound(?nick) || bound(?rname) || bound(?hpage))
        }
```

```
# Here's where we grab www.mindswap.org folks of all
# stripes.  We are claiming that any friends we find
# will have triples declaring his/her name, home page and
# mailbox.
UNION {
    { _:blank3 rdf:type ms:Affiliate }
    UNION
    { _:blank3 rdf:type ms:Alumni }
    UNION
    { _:blank3 rdf:type ms:Faculty }
    UNION
    { _:blank3 rdf:type ms:Programmer }
    UNION
    { _:blank3 rdf:type ms:Researcher }
    UNION
    { _:blank3 rdf:type ms:GraduateStudent }
    UNION
    { _:blank3 rdf:type ms:UndergraduateStudent } .
    _:blank3 foaf:name ?rname;
             foaf:homepage ?hpage;
             foaf:mbox ?mbox
    }
  }
}
```

By reusing variables such as `?rname` and `?hpage`, the result set in Table 6-8 looks uniform and consistent regardless of the resources each variable binds. (The contents of Table 6-8 have been truncated and abridged for readability.)

Table 6-8 A More Perfect Union

ORIGINGRAPH	NICK	RNAME	HPAGE	MBOX
http://.../~gil/foaf.rdf		Jim Hendler		
http://.../~hendler/.../foaf.rdf	vard			
http://www.lassila.org/...			http://...	
http://www.dajobe.org/...	zool	Jo Walsh		
http://www.dajobe.org/...	jang	Jan Grant	http://...	
http://www.mindswap.org/...		Aaron Mannes	http://...	mailto: ...

We would like to leverage the knowledge that all the various mindswap RDF types to which we referred (`Affiliate`, `Faculty`, and so on) are subclasses of `Swapper` (`http://www.mindswap.org/2003/owl/mindswap`). Instead of entering seven rdf:type statements that are joined by UNION statements, we could have had a single _:blank3 rdf:type ms:Swapper triple. This is possible as long as there is a triple store with inference capabilities over our mindswap data. In this case, the ms prefix's IRI references the raw data without ever having an inference engine pass over the data.

CONSTRUCT Essentials

CONSTRUCT allows us to ask queries and obtain our results in RDF; we query using triples in a graph pattern and are returned a set of triples. All the modifiers we've discussed so far are also applicable in CONSTRUCT queries, except for DISTINCT, REDUCED, and the use of the asterisk for wildcard queries. This seems like a much more natural way of handling RDF data. Unfortunately, since we cannot order RDF data, we are limited in what we can do with the data, such as streaming or comparing and contrasting various RDF results without the need for a custom graph diff operation. Nevertheless, CONSTRUCT is well adapted for data transformation such as ontology mapping, data repurposing, and data mash-ups, areas we'll cover in upcoming chapters.

Revisiting the query used for Table 6-9, we reformulate it using CONSTRUCT. Besides the new query form, the biggest change here is that blank nodes _:blank2 and _:blank3 have been replaced with ?person. This change guarantees that ?person will contain the same IRI throughout the query, and the resulting graph will properly merge these triples based on this subject. If _:blank2 or _:blank3 were kept in the query, the blank node values would change for each triple, and certain statements would not merge properly (if, for example, http://example.org/Joe has two mailboxes, blank nodes would allow a result set of two triples with different subjects, modifying the original intent of the data, and could be fixed only by equating the two triples with an owl:sameAs statement).

```
PREFIX foaf: <http://xmlns.com/foaf/0.1/>
PREFIX rdf: <http://www.w3.org/1999/02/22-rdf-syntax-ns#>
PREFIX ms: <http://www.mindswap.org/2003/owl/mindswap#>
CONSTRUCT {
    ?person rdf:type foaf:Person;
            foaf:name ?rname;
            foaf:home page ?hpage;
            foaf:nick ?nick;
            foaf:mbox ?mbox.
    }
FROM NAMED <http://www.kjetil.kjernsmo.net/foaf>
FROM NAMED <http://www.dajobe.org/foaf.rdf>
FROM NAMED <http://heddley.com/edd/foaf.rdf>
FROM NAMED <http://www.cs.umd.edu/~hendler/2003/foaf.rdf>
FROM NAMED <http://www.koalie.net/foaf.rdf>
```

```
FROM NAMED <http://www.isi.edu/~gil/foaf.rdf>
FROM NAMED <http://www.ivan-herman.net/foaf.rdf>
FROM NAMED <http://www.lassila.org/ora.rdf>
FROM NAMED <http://www.mindswap.org/2004/owl/mindswappers>
WHERE {
    GRAPH ?originGraph {
        # This pattern now returns information for everyone except
        # www.mindswap.org.
        {
            _:blank1 foaf:knows ?person.
            ?person rdf:type foaf:Person.
            # If we find a foaf:Person, then make sure we either
            # print the nickname and/or the name and/or the home page.
            # If we had omitted the FILTER clause, then we could
            # have returned a query solution containing ?originGraph
            # and no other information!
            OPTIONAL { ?person foaf:nick ?nick }.
            OPTIONAL { ?person foaf:name ?rname }.
            OPTIONAL { ?person foaf:homepage ?hpage }.
            FILTER(bound(?nick) || bound(?rname) || bound(?hpage))
        }
        # Here's where we grab www.mindswap.org folks of all
        # stripes.  We are claiming that any friends we find
        # will have triples declaring his/her name, home page and
        # mailbox.
        UNION {
            { ?person rdf:type ms:Affiliate }
            UNION
            { ?person rdf:type ms:Alumni }
            UNION
            { ?person rdf:type ms:Faculty }
            UNION
            { ?person rdf:type ms:Programmer }
            UNION
            { ?person rdf:type ms:Researcher }
            UNION
            { ?person rdf:type ms:GraduateStudent }
            UNION
            { ?person rdf:type ms:UndergraduateStudent } .
            ?person foaf:name ?rname;
                    foaf:homepage ?hpage;
                    foaf:mbox ?mbox
        }
    }
}
```

Data transformations enable graph patterns to pull the data we need and then write a completely different CONSTRUCT graph pattern to place the variable bindings in a new RDF configuration we choose. If, for instance, we decide that the FOAF schema no longer fits our needs, we could issue a new query, listed here, that is identical to the previous query but with a different CONSTRUCT pattern. The following query returns information in RDF with respect to another friend-based schema found at www.example.com.

```
PREFIX myfriends: <http://www.example.com/2008/myfriends/>
PREFIX rdf: <http://www.w3.org/1999/02/22-rdf-syntax-ns#>
CONSTRUCT {
    ?person rdf:type myfriends:Humanoid;
            myfriends:handle ?rname;
            myfriends:homepage ?hpage;
            myfriends:informalName ?nick;
            myfriends:email ?mbox.
    ?mbox myfriends:isOwnedBy ?person.
    ?hpage myfriends:isManagedBy ?person.
    }
FROM NAMED ...
```

This example shows how we can create and transform new RDF data from existing triples. CONSTRUCT queries enable ontology transformation, data repurposing, and basic federated queries (i.e., querying data from various sources and returning a single RDF graph).

DESCRIBE Essentials

The DESCRIBE query form allows an endpoint to choose what RDF is contained in the query result set, as restricted by the WHERE clause. The client does not need to be aware of the underlying data's RDF structure for a given endpoint, and the endpoint is given more flexibility in the data it returns. To be more specific on the former point, a client *can* utilize what it knows about the data because DESCRIBE supports WHERE and FROM clauses; however, it is not required. This query form is a return to navigating as a form of information discovery, enabling clients to glean insight into one or more RDF data sets with minimal specificity.

```
PREFIX rdf: <http://www.w3.org/1999/02/22-rdf-syntax-ns#>
PREFIX dbpedia: <http://dbpedia.org/resource/>
DESCRIBE *
WHERE {
    ?person ?anyProperty dbpedia:George_Washington
}
```

Executing this query at DBpedia returns thousands of triples, while the similarly constructed query,

```
PREFIX dbpedia: <http://dbpedia.org/resource/>
DESCRIBE dbpedia:George_Washington
```

returns significantly less information! Our initial belief that providing a WHERE clause in the first query would limit the potential results over the less-restricted second query was wrong. The query

```
PREFIX rdf: <http://www.w3.org/1999/02/22-rdf-syntax-ns#>
PREFIX dbpedia: <http://dbpedia.org/resource/>
DESCRIBE *
```

fails because the asterisk indicates that the endpoint should display all query variables, yet we have not provided a WHERE clause with any variables. Don't be surprised if certain endpoints do not respond to a DESCRIBE query. Some SPARQL query processors recognize the keyword, but haven't put an implementation in place.

ASK Essentials

ASK returns boolean values of true or false in response to a query. Given a graph pattern, an endpoint can tell you whether or not the pattern exists in the underlying data store. ASK queries can be mimicked by using a SELECT query with an identical graph pattern and verifying the contents of the query result set with a boolean check in software or code. ASK is a useful query form because it allows the query processor to stop execution of a query as soon as the processor is able to respond with a boolean answer. Not only does this action reduce computational load on both the processor and the client, it also saves bandwidth because the result set is limited to a single response.

ASK supports FROM and WHERE clauses. In the following example, we will see whether Washington was president in the year 1795.

```
PREFIX rdfs: <http://www.w3.org/2000/01/rdf-schema#>
PREFIX dbprop: <http://dbpedia.org/property/>
PREFIX xsd: <http://www.w3.org/2001/XMLSchema#>
ASK
WHERE {
    ?person rdfs:label "George Washington"@en;
            dbprop:presidentStart ?startDate;
            dbprop:presidentEnd ?endDate.
    FILTER(xsd:integer(?startDate) < xsd:integer('1795') &&
            xsd:integer(?endDate) > xsd:integer('1795'))
    }
```

The XML result tells us that he was, indeed, president (modified here for readability).

```
<?xml version="1.0" ?>
<sparql xmlns=http://www.w3.org/2005/sparql-results#
        xmlns:xsi=http://www.w3.org/2001/XMLSchema-instance
```

```
        xsi:loc="http://www.w3.org/2001/sw/DataAccess/rf1/result2.xsd">
   <head></head>
   <boolean>true</boolean>
</sparql>
```

ASK queries enable the incremental development of queries. As an application determines what data does or does not exist in an RDF data store using ASK queries, it can craft a final query that will optimally require fewer resources to execute as well as return a more precise result set.

SPARQL Entailment

Entailment can be defined as follows: Given a set of statements in graph A and a set of statements in graph B, A *entails* B if every statement in B is also true in A. Entailment is illustrated as a Venn diagram in Figure 6-8.

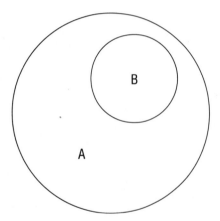

Figure 6-8 Venn diagram of entailment

Entailment is important as both a theoretical construct and a practical limitation. There are different levels of entailment in SPARQL, which are shown in Figure 6-9. Detailed definitions and proofs are available from the W3C RDF Semantics Recommendation (http://www.w3.org/TR/rdf-sparql-query/#sparqlBGPExtend); utilizing SPARQL doesn't require an in-depth understanding of the various levels of entailment other than how they can affect your query results (see Figure 6-9). We shall discuss an example next.

Entailment plays a role in determining how well a graph pattern is matched by a SPARQL endpoint. If we look at an example of D-entailment, this is a type of vocabulary entailment. Specifically, XSD typed and untyped literals are seen as equivalent (and thereby improve our ability to match statements containing literals), which isn't true under simple entailment. For example, an RDF repository might contain several literal values for George Washington.

```
"George Washington"
"George Washington"^^xsd:string
"George Washington"@en
```

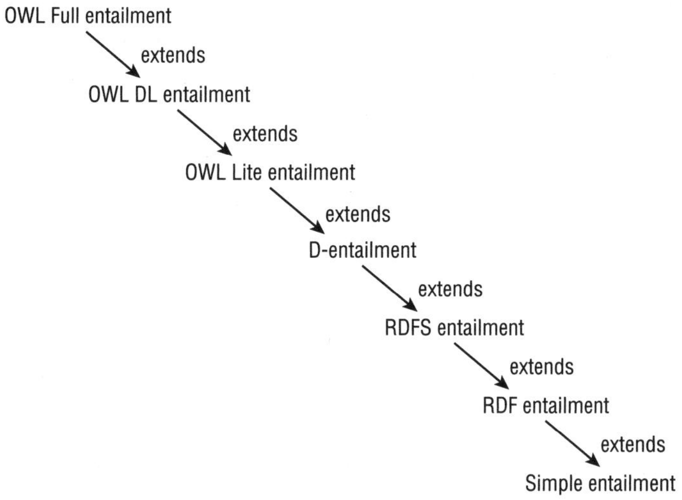

```
OWL Full entailment
        \  extends
      OWL DL entailment
              \  extends
          OWL Lite entailment
                  \  extends
              D-entailment
                      \  extends
                  RDFS entailment
                          \  extends
                      RDF entailment
                              \  extends
                          Simple entailment
```

Figure 6-9 Ordering of SPARQL entailment

Endpoints that support only simple entailment would see each of these literals as three separate and distinct values. Executing the query

```
# George Washington's Namesakes
SELECT ?location
WHERE {
    ?person <http://www.w3.org/2000/01/rdf-schema#label>
        "George Washington".
    ?location <http://dbpedia.org/property/namedFor> ?person
    }
```

returns an empty result set because there are no literals marked strictly as `"George Washington"`, even though there are literals stored as `"George Washington"@en`. A SPARQL endpoint that supports D-entailment or higher entailment would return the same results for any of the three different literals pertaining to George Washington.

These entailment limitations enable endpoints to determine their own level of query specificity and accuracy as well as the amount of inference that is permitted. Our advice is to create very precise queries; the more explicit information you can add to your queries (such as language tags), the less dependent you will be on the query-matching capabilities of your endpoint.

Unsupported Functionality

SPARQL has quite a bit of flexibility and power to retrieve relevant data, but there are some capabilities it doesn't support. Among these unsupported capabilities are the main themes of data modification, subquery support, and aggregation.

Data Modification

A significant issue is that SPARQL supports only read-only access to data without the ability to create, update, or delete triples. Some of the more prominent suggestions for data modification support include the W3C Member Submission SPARQL Update (`http://www.w3.org/Submission/2008/SUBM-SPARQL-Update-20080715/`), also referred to as *SPARUL*, and SPARQL+ (`http://arc.semsol.org/docs/v2/sparql+`). Both syntaxes continue in the same vein as SPARQL and SQL, creating implementations for keywords such as `CREATE`, `DELETE`, `DROP`, and `INSERT`. The issue for data-updating capabilities has been noted by the RDF Data Access Working Group, but it has been postponed since 2005. We won't discuss data modification through SPARQL since there isn't a clear standard on approaching this issue (yet). To be clear, RDF repositories support data creation, insertion, and deletion, but not as part of the SPARQL query language.

Subqueries

SPARQL does not support subqueries but does support nested subgraphs in queries. Subqueries allow more than one query form in a single query, for example, using a `SELECT` statement in the `WHERE` clause of another `SELECT` statement. Nested subgraphs are a different concept. They describe the use of graph patterns inside other graph patterns, such as having `OPTIONAL` blocks inside `UNION` graph patterns that are all part of a `WHERE` clause. We used several cases of subgraphs in this chapter.

Aggregation

There is no support for aggregate functions (such as `count`, `min`, `max`, `avg`, or `sum`) at the query-form level. SPARQL+ has support for some of these functions, but it is not standardized.

The items listed in this section are not comprehensive but are rather a sampling of some of the better-known issues facing SPARQL. For a full list of issues, the Working Group maintains them at the W3C at `http://www.w3.org/2001/sw/DataAccess/issues`.

Summary

From navigation to searching to querying, there are many ways to discover information. You learned about each of these forms, with a strong focus on querying the Semantic Web through SPARQL. Using readily available SPARQL endpoints, specific examples, and a detailed discussion of the query language itself, you should have a good understanding of the technology and tools that are available to find the semantic data that you need.

Adding Rules

"Hell, there are no rules here—we're trying to accomplish something."
—Thomas Edison

At this point, you've been exposed to a wide variety of knowledge representations, ranging from RDF to the latest version of OWL. Before the advent of OWL 2, OWL 1 had limits on the amount of expressivity it could offer users. One solution to this issue was to keep the OWL recommendations unaltered but support the inclusion of rules to expand the expressive nature of RDF/OWL data. In this chapter, you will learn about the need for rules to augment OWL as well as a particular rule implementation called the *Semantic Web Rule Language (SWRL)*, whose Member Submission can be found at `http://www.w3.org/Submission/SWRL/`. There will also be a short discussion of Jena rules, a rule language specifically implemented for the Jena API.

Since Semantic Web rules were first proposed in 2003 and 2004, the Semantic Web landscape has significantly changed. OWL 2, as discussed in Chapters 5 and 6, has addressed some of the shortcomings of the original OWL recommendation and implements functionality previously unavailable. In addition, the W3C chartered the *Rule Interchange Format (RIF) Working Group* to "produce a core rule language plus extensions which together allow rules to be translated between rule languages and thus transferred between rule systems." Therefore, RIF is not about developing the preeminent rule language but rather considers the more difficult issue of rule interoperability between legacy rule systems and the Semantic Web. The latter half of this chapter will introduce RIF artifacts, including the *Basic Logic Dialect (BLD)* and the *Production Rule Dialect (PRD)*, providing insight into the future of W3C-based rule development. RIF is not yet a W3C recommendation, but it is on track as some of the documents are currently in "Last Call."

In this chapter, you will:

- Learn about several Semantic Web rule proposals
- Familiarize yourself with SWRL, its syntax and examples of usage
- Increase your knowledge about Jena rules
- Learn about the direction and goals of RIF
- Gain an understanding of the main features of RIF

What Are Rules?

A *rule* is a means of representing knowledge that often goes beyond OWL 1 or is easier to understand than what can be expressed using OWL 1. Rules in the Semantic Web are typically conditional statements: if-then clauses. New knowledge is added only if a particular set of statements is true. The rest of this chapter will show you how to represent if-then clauses in the Semantic Web via SWRL and Jena rules.

Reasons for Rules

As we've discussed in earlier chapters, the Semantic Web layer cake is built on previous technologies and languages (for example, RDF, RDFS and OWL) as much as possible, expanding expressivity at each level and allowing users to use a given representation based on the amount of semantics needed for a particular application. If we step back and look at what OWL 1 lacked, it becomes clear why there has been a push for an additional level of expressivity based on user-defined rules. Let's look at some reasons for the rules.

No Support for Property Composition

An often-discussed issue with OWL 1 is the "uncle" problem, also known as *property chaining*. It is impossible to determine whether individual A has an uncle in individual B because that requires *two* pieces of information. First, does A have a known parent? Second, does that known parent have a male sibling? Rules support the concept that the existence of both of these two pieces of data results in the creation of an uncle relationship. OWL 2 partially solved this problem with property chains, which are described in Chapter 5, "Modeling Knowledge in the Real World."

Use of Built-ins

Built-ins allow for common transformations of data. For example, OWL 1 cannot check whether a URI has a datatype property that starts with the word `President` and then use that information as the basis to add some new property to the same subject, such as `isPresidentOf`. This example of pattern matching is just one simple example. Mathematical operations, conditional checks, and datatype or unit conversions are some of the other typical needs for built-ins.

Ontological Mediation

Chapter 6 covered the notion that a CONSTRUCT SPARQL statement could be used to map RDF statements from one graph model to another, expanding the possibility of mapping resources between different ontologies. This functionality is limited, however. Literals cannot be transformed (such as concatenating a _new substring to a newly discovered string), and more complex translations are difficult to express (`if A knows B and B knows C and C hasFamilyMember D, then assert D canTrust A`).

Limiting Assumptions

It is often desirable to trigger certain data operations based on the existence (or potentially the lack thereof) of information. A simple example noted previously was the case of concatenation; however, operations don't need to be limited to string transformations. They could also cover a range of operations based on mathematics, conditional verification, or datatype transformations.

Rules can be used to limit OWL's open world assumption (using a technique known as *negation as failure*, or *NAF*) or to support the unique names assumption. In the former case, imagine a rule that states:

```
If Andrew isn't known to have a brother, then assert he is brotherless
```

In the latter case, imagine another rule that states:

```
If Person1 has a name of Andy and Person2 has a name of Andrew, then
    assert Person1 and Person2 are different individuals
```

Having a separate rule for every pair of different names is hardly ideal, but the point is that rules can axiomatize a unique names assumption. There are very real use cases for supporting both the closed world and the unique names assumptions. We see this every day in database systems. There is no clear answer when one should and should not ignore the open world or unique names assumptions. It is important to know that there are times when each is appropriate and that the Semantic Web languages can support them.

Rule Languages

The *Rule Markup Language (RuleML) Initiative* focused on an XML-based markup language for various types of rules (such as business, transformational, or reactive). SWRL became a W3C Member Submission in 2004, combining work from the DARPA Agent Markup Language (DAML) program and RuleML. *Description Logic Programs (DLPs)*, as presented at the WWW 2003 conference, detailed the combination of description logics (OWL DL) and logic programs (RuleML) as a potential area of growth. The *Web Rule Language (WRL)* was submitted to the W3C in late 2005. *Semantic Web Services Language (SWSL) Rules* came out the same year, also part of a joint DAML/EU effort. Most recently, the *RIF Working Group* has been working toward a different goal, looking for rule interoperability using implementable specifications.

The de facto standard language for Semantic Web rules is SWRL. SWRL enjoys strong community recognition and tool support, has a large user base, and is based on the work of some of the best-respected researchers in the field: Ian Horrocks, Peter F. Patel-Schneider, Harold Boley, Said Tabet, Benjamin Grosof, and Mike Dean. This chapter will focus on SWRL as our model for learning Semantic Web rules.

SWRL Essentials

SWRL is based on the OWL 1 DL and OWL Lite species, using a subset of RuleML rules modeled on Horn clauses. SWRL predates OWL 2. The RuleML subset supported in SWRL includes only unary and binary predicates, a sensible choice, given OWL 1's foundation in RDF.

A *Horn clause* represents the familiar if-then conditional statement more formally referred to as *implication*. An implication is the combination of an *antecedent* (commonly referred to as the *body* and akin to an *if* clause) and a *consequent* (commonly referred to as the *head* and akin to a *then* clause). Antecedents and consequents are made up of zero or more *atoms*. An atom consists of any unary predicate (class inclusions such as "John belongs to class `Person`"), binary predicate (any type of object or datatype property), equality, inequality, or built-ins, each of which will be described in detail later in this chapter.

It seems odd that a head or body with no atoms might be considered a valid implication, but it is allowable in the SWRL Member Submission. If an antecedent has no atoms, then it evaluates to true, making all the statements in the consequent true. This is no different from using OWL to make the same assertions without a rule. In the case where the consequent has no atoms, then no assertion will ever be made, and the rule evaluates to false. This means that the empty consequent cannot be satisfied by any ontology and, by implication, neither can its antecedent, so the rule is false. If the antecedent does match any statements, then the ontology contains a logical inconsistency.

Horn clauses are any combination of statements in the antecedent that are interpreted as a *conjunction*, or intersection, of those statements. In other words, all of the statements must be simultaneously true to cause all of the atoms in the consequent to be true. Think of this as an if-then statement with multiple boolean clauses joined by logical AND operators.

```
int a, b, c;
String filename = ... ;
 ...
if (a == 5 && b > 4 && filename.startsWith("Rule")) {
    c = 22 % b;
}
```

Disjunction (a logical OR operation) is not directly supported by SWRL but can be implemented by splitting the disjunction into separate rules (a simple operation that is part of Lloyd-Topor transformations). Duplicate consequents are not an issue because RDF can handle duplicate statements. Using Java as an example, a disjunction would start like this:

```
if (a == 5 || b > 4 || filename.startsWith("Rule")) {
    c = 22 % b;
}
```

It could also be split into the following statements:

```
if (a == 5) {
    c = 22 % b;
}
if (b > 4) {
    c = 22 % b;
}
if (filename.startsWith("Rule")) {
    c = 22 % b;
}
```

SWRL's main goal was to provide expressivity not allowable by OWL 1 while maintaining compatibility with OWL's syntax, semantics, and theoretical model. As a W3C Member Submission, it became an input to the RIF Working Group.

SWRL has three different syntaxes: one abstract and two concrete flavors based on XML and RDF. The abstract syntax will be covered only for familiarization; most of the chapter's SWRL examples will be grounded in either the XML or RDF concrete serializations.

The Abstract Syntax

The abstract syntax represents SWRL using a small number of Extended Backus-Naur Form (EBNF) notations.

```
axiom ::= rule
rule ::= 'Implies(' [ URIreference ] { annotation } antecedent
    consequent ')'
```

```
antecedent ::= 'Antecedent(' { atom } ')'
consequent ::= 'Consequent(' { atom } ')'
atom ::= description '(' i-object ')'
   | dataRange '(' d-object ')'
   | individualvaluedPropertyID '(' i-object i-object ')'
   | datavaluedPropertyID '(' i-object d-object ')'
   | sameAs '(' i-object i-object ')'
   | differentFrom '(' i-object i-object ')'
   | builtIn '(' builtinID { d-object } ')'
builtinID ::= URIreference
i-object ::= i-variable | individualID
d-object ::= d-variable | dataLiteral
i-variable ::= 'I-variable(' URIreference ')'
d-variable ::= 'D-variable(' URIreference ')'
```

Don't be too concerned if you can't fully understand all of these statements. We'll discuss them in detail in the next section.

A human-readable syntax of SWRL rules can be utilized when XML or RDF is too verbose or difficult to read. An implication is represented by an arrow (→), logically connecting an antecedent to a consequent. Variables are preceded by a question mark (?), similar to SPARQL notation. Atoms are conjunctively joined with the caret mark (^). Properties and built-ins (covered later in the chapter) resemble method calls where the return value is usually assigned to a variable.

If you wanted to express a long-time nemesis in our FOAF example, it could look like the following example in our human-readable syntax (note the use of reification). ?today holds today's date:

```
Person(?p) ^ Person(?nemesis) ^
dislikes(?p, ?nemesis) ^ dislikes(?nemesis, ?p) ^
Statement(?statement) ^ subject(?statement, ?p) ^
predicate(?statement, knows) ^ object(?statement, ?nemesis) ^
startDate(?statement, ?knowsStartDate) ^
swrlb:addYearMonthDurationToDate
     (?diff, ?knowsStartDate, "P10Y0M") ^
swrlb:greaterThan(?today, ?diff)
     → hasLongTimeNemesis(?p, ?nemesis)
```

Or it could look like this:

```
Implies(
  Antecedent(
    Person(I-variable(p))
    Person(I-variable(nemesis))
    dislikes(I-variable(p)
            I-variable(nemesis))
    dislikes(I-variable(nemesis)
            I-variable(p))
```

```
      Statement(I-variable(statement))
      subject(I-variable(statement)
               I-variable(p))
      predicate(I-variable(statement)
                 I-variable(knows))
      object(I-variable(statement)
              I-variable(nemesis))
      startDate(I-variable(statement)
                 I-variable(knowsStartDate))
      swrlb:addYearMonthDurationToDate(
        D-variable(diff)
        D-variable(knowsStartDate)
        D-variable("P10Y0M"))
      swrlb:greaterThan(D-variable(today)
                        D-variable(diff)))
  Consequent(
    hasLongTimeNemesis(I-variable(p)
                       I-variable(nemesis))))

  )
```

Our nemesis example can be read, "If p and nemesis are of type Person and both p and nemesis dislike each other and p has known nemesis for over 10 years, then p is a long-time nemesis of nemesis." It is a long rule, but you'll notice the chaining that occurs from one statement to the next in the antecedent. Most rules you will write and observe will form a connected subgraph as in this example.

Note that this is just one way to state this rule, and there could be some issues with how it is implemented. This example assumes that simply because the `dislikes` property is present between p and nemesis that it implies their relationship has always been one of hostility for all the years they've known each other. This may not be true and could be clarified with finer-grained properties, such as using other properties that clearly delineate hate/like between p and nemesis instead of relying solely on how long they have known each other, or the inclusion of temporal tagging of relationships (see Chapter 13, "Managing Space and Time" for insights using concepts).

The XML Concrete Syntax

The XML syntax for SWRL is based on the OWL XML Presentation Syntax (a detailed overview is located at http://www.w3.org/TR/owl-xmlsyntax) as well as RuleML (the XML Schema can be found at http://www.ruleml.org/xsd/0.8/ruleml-datalog-monolith.xsd). Interestingly, the former syntax specification is currently released as a W3C Note (it is not part of the OWL Recommendation), and the latter is not under any sort of formal W3C purview.

The SWRL XML syntax uses the OWL XML Ontology root element and some of its subelements:

```
VersionInfo

PriorVersion

BackwardCompatibleWith

IncompatibleWith

Imports

Annotation

Class

EnumeratedClass

SubClassOf

EquivalentClasses

DisjointClasses

DatatypeProperty

ObjectProperty

SubPropertyOf

EquivalentProperties

Individual

SameIndividual

DifferentIndividuals
```

Our focus will be on the RuleML element additions.

> **NOTE** The SWRL Submission does not have any limitations or guidelines regarding either the ordering of rules or the ordering of atoms within a rule. While certain SWRL processors may utilize an approach based on file ordering (that is, rules/atoms located earlier in the file are read before rules/atoms toward the end of a file), no assumptions are made by the SWRL specification.

The following sections will cover all the SWRL XML elements defined by the SWRL schema (http://www.w3.org/Submission/SWRL/swrlx.xsd). We begin with the only two legal element extensions to the Ontology root element: var and imp. In the following examples, ruleml denotes the http://www.w3.org /2003/11/ruleml namespace and swrlx denotes the http://www.w3.org/2003 /11/swrlx namespace.

var

ruleml:var, short for *variable declaration*, is a xsd:string-based declaration of a variable. It is considered good form to start variables with a lowercase alphabetic character. For example:

```
<ruleml:var>firstVariable</ruleml:var>
```

imp

`ruleml:imp`, short for *rule implication*, defines a rule. A rule is the combination of one _head element and one _body element, whereby the _head is true if the _body is true. A rule label (_rlab) and OWL annotations (`<annotation>`) are optionally allowed.

Allowed subelements are _rlab, _body, _head, and one or more OWL annotations. For example:

```
<ruleml:imp>
  <ruleml:_rlab ruleml:href="#importantRuleName"/>
  <ruleml:_body>
    ...
  </ruleml:_body>
  <ruleml:_head>
    ...
  </ruleml:_head>
<ruleml:imp>
```

_rlab

This optional element for a rule label, has a required attribute of `href`, which takes a valid URI reference as input. For example:

```
<rule:_rlab ruleml:href="#ruleName"/>
```

_body

The _body element describes the antecedent or the *if* clause of a rule. It contains zero or more atoms (remember that zero is a special case, and typically a rule will have at least one atom), where an atom is one of the following subelements (note the change in namespace): `swrlx:classAtom`, `swrlx:datarangeAtom`, `swrlx:individualPropertyAtom`, `swrlx:datavaluedPropertyAtom`, `swrlx:sameIndividualAtom`, `swrlx:differentIndividualsAtom`, or `swrlx:builtin-Atom`. Recalling our discussion of Horn clauses, every atom of the _body statement must be true for the _head element to be true. The following example shows how conjunction is written. In this case, there are two atoms that must be satisfied before the consequent will be true.

```
<ruleml:_body>
  <swrlx:individualPropertyAtom>
    ...
  </swrlx:individualPropertyAtom>
  <swrlx:builtinAtom>
    ...
  </swrlx:builtinAtom>
<ruleml:_body>
```

_head

The _head element describes the consequent, or the *then* clause, of a rule. It contains zero or more atoms (remember that zero is a special case, and typically a rule will have at least one atom), where an atom can be described as one of the following subelements (note the change in namespace): swrlx:classAtom, swrlx:datarangeAtom, swrlx:individualPropertyAtom, swrlx:datavaluedPropertyAtom, swrlx:sameIndividualAtom, swrlx:differentIndividualsAtom, or swrlx:builtinAtom. If the _body of the rule evaluates to true, *every* atom in the _head element will be evaluated. The following example shows how conjunction is written. In this case, there are three atoms that will be asserted (this could mean these statements are added to a knowledgebase or returned as part of an RDF result set) if the antecedent evaluates to true.

```
<ruleml:_head>
  <swrlx:classAtom>
    . . .
  </swrlx:classAtom>
  <swrlx:builtinAtom>
    . . .
  </swrlx:builtinAtom>
  <swrlx: sameIndividualAtom>
    . . .
  </swrlx: sameIndividualAtom>
<ruleml:_head>
```

classAtom

A classAtom can refer to either an existing class or it can define a new class, adhering to OWL 1 semantics and syntax. It is followed by a single reference to a specific individual or a previously defined variable. If classAtom appears in a _body element, then that named individual or variable must belong to that class for the atom to be true. If it appears in the _head element, then that named individual or variable will now be an instance of that class. For example:

```
<swrlx:classAtom>
  <owlx:Class owlx:name="Person" />
  <ruleml:var>p</ruleml:var>
  <!-- p must be previously declared -->
</swrlx:classAtom>
<swrlx:classAtom>
  <owlx:Class owlx:name="Person" />
  <owlx:Individual owlx:name="#JohnHebeler" />
</swrlx:classAtom>
<swrlx:classAtom>
  <owlx:ObjectRestriction owlx:property="&foaf;mbox">
    <owlx:minCardinality value=1 />
```

```
    </owlx:ObjectRestriction>
    <ruleml:var>m</ruleml:var>
    <!-- m must be previously declared -->
  </swrlx:classAtom>
```

datarangeAtom

The `datarangeAtom` element is not defined in the OWL XML syntax specification but lists either a specific single datatype or a list of datatypes followed by a previously defined variable. If `datarangeAtom` appears in a `_body` element, then the associated variable must have that datatype or value for the atom to be true. If it appears in the `_head` element, then the variable will now have that datatype or value. For example:

```
  <swrlx:datarangeAtom>
    <owlx:Datatype owlx:name="&xsd;string" />
    <ruleml:var>name</ruleml:var>
    <!-- name must be previously declared -->
  </swrlx:datarangeAtom>
  <swrlx:datarangeAtom>
    <owlx:OneOf>
      <owlx:DataValue
      owlx:datatype="&xsd;string">John</owlx:DataValue>
      <owlx:DataValue
      owlx:datatype="&xsd;string">Matt</owlx:DataValue>
      <owlx:DataValue
      owlx:datatype="&xsd;string">Ryan</owlx:DataValue>
      <owlx:DataValue
      owlx:datatype="&xsd;string">Andrew</owlx:DataValue>
    </owlx:OneOf>
    <ruleml:var>fName</ruleml:var>
    <!-- fName must be previously declared -->
  </swrlx:datarangeAtom>
```

individualPropertyAtom

`individualPropertyAtom` relates a specific individual or variable to another specific individual or variable through an object property. Whichever individual or variable is listed first becomes the subject of the property, and whichever individual or variable is listed second becomes the object. `individualPropertyAtom` requires the use of a `property` attribute. If this atom appears in the `_body` element, then the given triple must exist for the atom to be true. If it appears in the `_head`, then that triple will be asserted. For example:

```
  <swrlx:individualPropertyAtom property="hasUncle">
    <owlx:Individual owlx:name="#JohnHebeler" />
```

```
  <owlx:Individual owlx:name="#TomHebeler" />
</swrlx:individualPropertyAtom>
<swrlx:individualPropertyAtom property="hasUncle">
  <owlx:Individual owlx:name="#JohnHebeler" />
  <ruleml:var>uncle</ruleml:var>
  <!-- uncle must be previously declared -->
</swrlx:individualPropertyAtom>
<swrlx:individualPropertyAtom property="isUncleOf">
  <ruleml:var>uncle</ruleml:var>
  <!-- uncle must be previously declared -->
  <owlx:Individual owlx:name="#JohnHebeler" />
</swrlx:individualPropertyAtom>
```

datavaluedPropertyAtom

datavaluedPropertyAtom relates a specific individual or a literal value through a datatype property. The specific individual or variable must be listed first and the literal value second. datavaluedPropertyAtom requires the use of a property attribute. If this atom appears in the _body element, then the given triple must exist for the atom to be true. If it appears in the _head, then that triple will be asserted. For example:

```
<swrlx:datavaluedPropertyAtom property="&foaf;birthday">
  <owlx:Individual owlx:name="#MattFisher" />
  <owlx:DataValue
    owlx:datatype="&xsd;string">06-01</owlx:DataValue>
</swrlx:datavaluedPropertyAtom>
```

sameIndividualAtom

This atom asserts equality between two or more specific individuals or variables (the SWRL Submission allows for zero or more specific individuals or variables, but zero or one doesn't make sense when implementing). This assertion is equivalent to using owl:sameAs between each pair of individuals and/or variables. For example:

```
<swrlx:sameIndividualAtom>
  <owlx:Individual owlx:name="#JohnHebeler" />
  <owlx:Individual owlx:name="#JohnnyHebeler" />
</swrlx:sameIndividualAtom>
<swrlx:sameIndividualAtom>
  <owlx:Individual owlx:name="#JohnHebeler" />
  <ruleml:var>person</ruleml:var>
  <ruleml:var>author</ruleml:var>
    <!-- person and author must be previously declared -->
</swrlx:sameIndividualAtom>
```

differentIndividualsAtom

This atom will assert inequality between two or more specific individuals and/or variables (the SWRL Submission allows for zero or more specific individuals and/or variables, but zero or one doesn't make sense when implementing). This assertion is equivalent to using `owl:differentFrom` between each pair of individuals and/or variables. For example:

```
<swrlx:differentIndividualAtom>
  <owlx:Individual owlx:name="#JohnHebeler" />
  <owlx:Individual owlx:name="#JohnnyHebeler" />
</swrlx: differentIndividualAtom >
<swrlx:differentIndividualAtom>
  <owlx:Individual owlx:name="#JohnHebeler" />
  <ruleml:var>person</ruleml:var>
  <ruleml:var>author</ruleml:var>
  <!-- person and author must be previously declared -->
</swrlx:differentIndividualAtom>
```

builtinAtom

The `builtinAtom` element declares built-in functions. This element requires the `builtin` attribute, which takes a URI that identifies the built-in operation. Built-ins will be covered later in this chapter, but here are some examples of syntax:

```
<swrlx:builtinAtom
 swrlx:builtin="&swrlb;greaterThanOrEqual">
  <ruleml:var>ageOfJohn</ruleml:var>
  <ruleml:var>ageOfMatt</ruleml:var>
</swrlx:builtinAtom>
<swrlx:builtinAtom swrlx:builtin="&swrlb;add">
  <ruleml:var>totalAge</ruleml:var>
  <ruleml:var>mattAge</ruleml:var>
  <ruleml:var>johnAge</ruleml:var>
  <ruleml:var>andrewAge</ruleml:var>
  <ruleml:var>ryanAge</ruleml:var>
</swrlx:builtinAtom>
```

The RDF Concrete Syntax

The RDF concrete syntax mirrors the XML syntax in its constructs, so we don't cover it with the same degree of detail in this chapter. In addition, some of our examples in the rest of this chapter use the RDF syntax, so you will gain exposure by reading those sections as well as using Protégé for the same examples.

In our experience, developers tend to represent their SWRL rules in RDF rather than XML syntax. This may be in part because RDF SWRL rules can be saved in both triple stores and ontology files like any other RDF data. In addition, the older version of Protégé, the 3.*x* series, supported a SWRL editor that serializes SWRL in the RDF format using the SWRLTab, located at `http://protege.cim3.net/cgi-bin/wiki.pl?SWRLTab`.

For more information on the RDF concrete syntax, the SWRL submission has more details. There is also an RDF schema for SWRL (`http://www.w3.org/Submission/SWRL/swrl.rdf`) as well as an OWL 1 ontology (`http://www.w3.org/Submission/SWRL/swrl.owl`).

Built-ins

SWRL built-ins expand the expressive power of SWRL and are a main motivator for the use of SWRL. The majority of the remaining sections in this chapter detail built-ins in example form, and the full list of built-ins specified in the SWRL submission appears in Appendix C. Built-ins are straightforward and mainly correspond to traditional operations available in most major programming and scripting languages. They cover the following areas:

- Comparisons
- Mathematical transformations
- List operators (not recommended since they cannot be used in OWL 1 Lite or DL)
- Modifiers for strings, dates, and times
- Boolean and URI checks
- URI construction

We cover some examples here in abstract syntax so you can become familiar with their form and function. You should use `http://www.w3.org/2003/11/swrlb` for the built-in namespace along with the recommended `swrlb` prefix.

Examples

Johnny just swiped his credit card at the grocery store. Can he purchase that pack of cigarettes? He needs to be an 18-year-old resident of the state. In this case, `?customer` refers to Johnny and `?today` holds today's date.

```
hasAddress(?creditCardMachine, ?ccAddress) ^
hasAddress(?customer, ?custAddress) ^
hasState(?ccAddress, ?ccState) ^
hasState(?custAddress, ?custState) ^
```

```
swrlb:equal(?custState, ?ccState) ^
hasBirthday(?customer, ?bDate) ^
swrlb:subtractYearMonthDurations(?diff, ?today, ?bDate) ^
swrlb:greaterThanOrEqual(?diff, "P18Y0M")
→ LegalCigaretteBuyer(?customer)
```

Create a formal greeting based on a set of personal facts.

```
foaf:Person(?person) ^
foaf:gender(?person, "female") ^
foaf:name(?person, ?name)
→ swrlb:stringConcat(?s, "Dear Ms. ", ?name, ":") ^
    hasFormalGreeting(?person, ?s)
```

DL-Safe Rules

While the discussion so far has focused on the positive aspects of SWRL's broad expressiveness, the biggest downside is the loss of decidability. It may seem counterintuitive that SWRL, which is purposely based on the decidable dialects of OWL, could so easily cause an ontology to become undecidable.

Look at the following example in the abstract syntax:

```
Person(?person) ^ friendCount(?person, ?count) ^
swrlb:add(?countByOne, ?count, 1) → friendCount(?person, ?countByOne)
```

This rule tries to increase the `friendCount` property by one. OWL 1 did not have a good way to explicitly state `count`. Instead, it is much better to generate this value dynamically through code by first executing a SPARQL query for the number of `friendCount(?x, ?y)` statements (SPARQL doesn't support a COUNT statement like SQL) and second using that number without saving it as an explicit statement. If this rule were to be run without any type of checks and balances, it would add triples forever!

The advent of *DL-safe rules* solves some of the problems regarding undecidability. DL-safe rules are those rules that bind only known instances in your knowledge base or ontology to rule variables. If there isn't instance data that specifically matches your query, then a DL-safe rule will not execute its consequent, even if the rule is perfectly valid. In the previous example, DL-safe rules are not applicable since `friendCount` is a datatype property and DL-safe rules apply to instances. Yet, this scenario doesn't discount their utility. The applicability of these rules can be confusing, so let's take a look at an example.

Using Protégé, the FOAF ontology is extended by creating a new ontology and adding the following concepts:

- Create class `Friend` that is a subclass of `FOAF Person` (see Figure 7-1).

- Create object property `isBestFriendOf` without any restrictions (see Figure 7-2).

- Create class `PopularFriend` that is not only a subclass of `Friend` but also has a restriction that any instance of `PopularFriend` must be the best friend of at least one friend (see Figure 7-3).

- Create an instance of `Friend` with a resource ID of `John` (see Figure 7-4).

- Create an instance of `PopularFriend` with a resource ID of `QuarterbackAndrew` (see Figure 7-5).

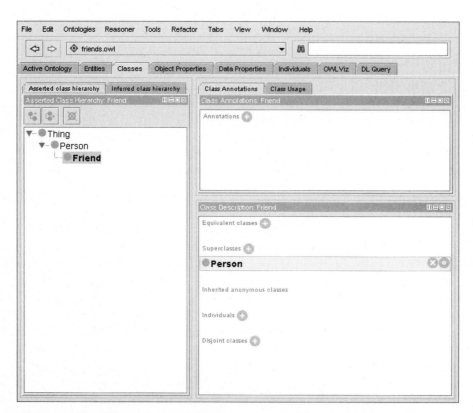

Figure 7-1 Creating the `Friend` class

At this point, we can turn on the reasoner. We are using Pellet, a popular open-source reasoner that supports decidable reasoning over OWL and is already integrated into Protégé. Choose Pellet 1.5 from the Reasoner menu item (see Figure 7-6) and then select the Inferred Axiom subtab in the Active Ontology tab to see what new information Pellet was able to infer (see Figure 7-7).

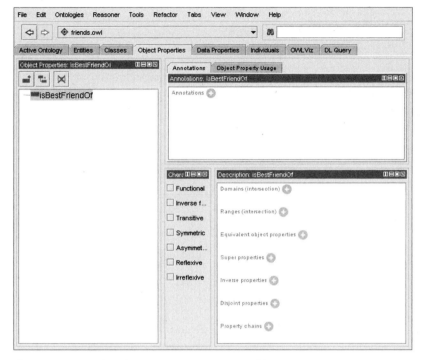

Figure 7-2 Creating the `isBestFriendOf` object property

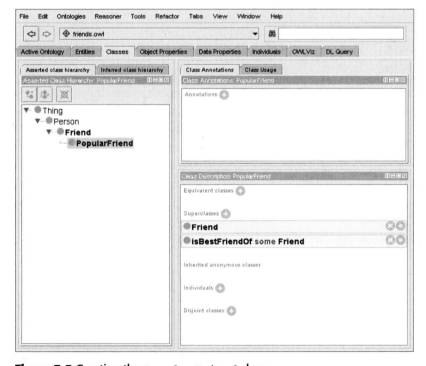

Figure 7-3 Creating the `PopularFriend` class

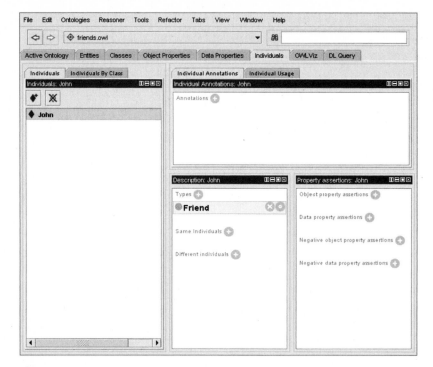

Figure 7-4 Creating `John`, a `Friend` instance

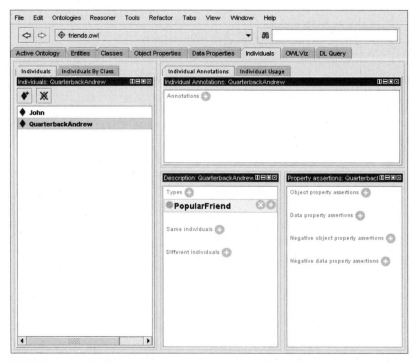

Figure 7-5 Creating `QuarterbackAndrew`, an instance of `PopularFriend`

Figure 7-6 Enabling the Pellet reasoner

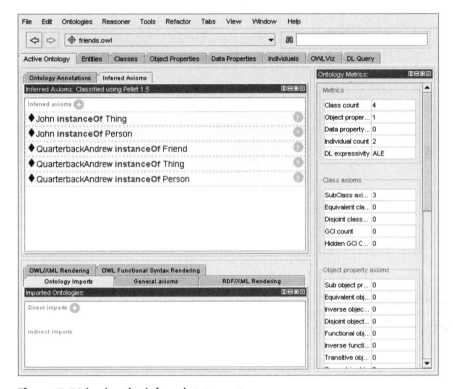

Figure 7-7 Viewing the inferred statements

The five inferred statements that are shown in Figure 7-7 are basic subclass/superclass inferred statements. We're missing one final part to our ontology: a rule that states that any `Person` that is the best friend of another `Person` belongs to a class of individuals `PotentialClassKing`. The rule, labeled `IsAPotentialClassKing`, is shown here in RDF/XML syntax. Note the explicit declaration of variables outside the `swrl:Imp` element:

```
highSchool:f1
    rdf:type swrl:Variable .
highSchool:f2
    rdf:type swrl:Variable .

highSchool:IsAPotentialClassKing
    rdf:type swrl:Imp ;
```

```
        swrl:body (
            [ rdf:type swrl:ClassAtom ;
              swrl:argument1 highSchool:f1 ;
              swrl:classPredicate foaf:Person
            ]
            [ rdf:type swrl:ClassAtom ;
              swrl:argument1 highSchool:f2 ;
              swrl:classPredicate foaf:Person
            ]
            [ rdf:type swrl:IndividualPropertyAtom ;
              swrl:argument1 highSchool:f1 ;
              swrl:argument2 highSchool:f2 ;
              swrl:propertyPredicate
                  highSchool:isBestFriendOf
            ]) ;
        swrl:head (
            [ rdf:type swrl:ClassAtom ;
              swrl:argument1 highSchool:f1 ;
              swrl:classPredicate
                  highSchool:PotentialClassKing
            ]) .
```

Protégé 4 includes a minimal SWRL editor. It can read SWRL rules and allow SWRL-enabled reasoners, like Pellet, to reason over them. If adding this rule to the ontology via some type of text editor doesn't appeal to you (don't worry, you're hardly alone), then you may want to use the latest version of Protégé 3 (such as 3.4). There is an optional tab in Protégé 3 called SWRLTab that allows rules to be displayed in the abstract syntax.

After adding this rule to our OWL file and rerunning the Pellet reasoner over the ontology, we should expect to see that QuarterbackAndrew is an instance of PotentialClassKing, but Protégé/Pellet doesn't infer it! If QuarterbackAndrew is an instance of PopularFriend, at *some* point he has to be *someone's* best friend; that's clearly required if something is a PopularFriend (this is due to the owl:someValuesFrom restriction). Add this to the fact that QuarterbackAndrew is an instance of Friend, and our statements satisfy the statements in the body of the rule.

A reasoner that didn't restrict itself to DL-safe rules would agree with all of the above and would infer that QuarterbackAndrew is an instance of PotentialClassKing. Inferring information without all the information present (that is, we don't know yet who will have QuarterbackAndrew as a best friend) can lead to undecidability. In this particular case, our rule is decidable with the limited data set we used, but a DL-safe rule engine can't know this ahead of time in every circumstance. It can guarantee decidability only by requiring all necessary data to be present at the time the rule is fired.

If we add a statement that clearly states that QuarterbackAndrew is the best friend of John (see Figure 7-8), Pellet is able to now infer that QuarterbackAndrew is, indeed, a PotentialClassKing instance (see Figure 7-9).

TIPS ON RULE DEVELOPMENT

The suggestions noted here come from both the SWRL submission as well as our own experience when writing SWRL rules.

◆ **Use named classes.** When using the `classAtom` element, using previously defined classes (either externally or in the same file) can assist rule-translation tools while enhancing readability and class reusability. Some SWRL implementations support only named classes.

◆ **Tighten your typing.** By declaring all the pertinent classes that a given variable belongs to (assuming the variable represents an individual), rule execution may slow down as a result and reduce the rule engine's ability to take advantage of inference. Plus, maintenance can become an issue. Thus, if you know that `?x` is an `Animal`, `Person`, and `Father` and there is a progressive subclass relationship among all three classes, you should limit any type atoms to just the most specific subclasses, in this case `Father`.

◆ **Limit generalized rules.** As a rule of thumb, the more variables that are present in a rule's antecedent, the more time reasoners require in evaluating these atoms.

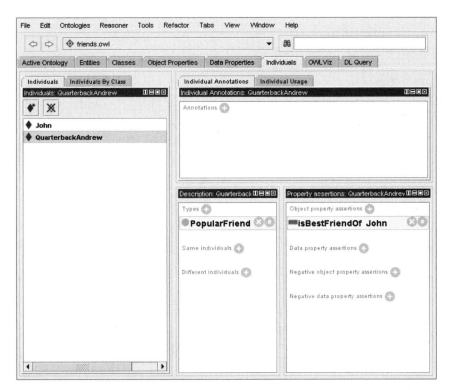

Figure 7-8 Making `QuarterbackAndrew` one of `John`'s best friends

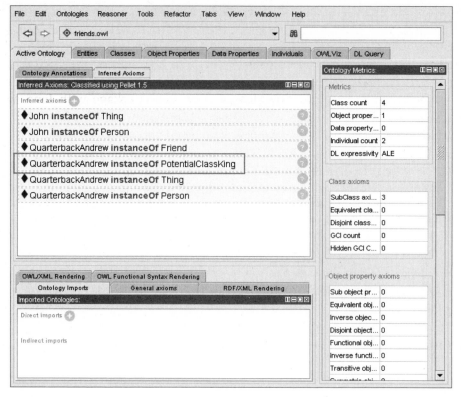

Figure 7-9 QuarterbackAndrew is now an instance of PotentialClassKing

Ontological Mediation

Some of the advantages of the Semantic Web discussed in this book include reusability, flexibility (for example, ontologists are free to define their own vocabularies, even for identical concepts across data sources), and the support of distributed knowledge (that is, no requirement of a single, one-size-fits-all knowledge representation controlled by some subset of the community). *Ontological mediation* is the idea that while the Semantic Web gives users these freedoms, there will most definitely be a need to integrate RDF data across these systems at various levels.

Semantic Web rule languages, such as SWRL, not only permit complex data integration but also naturally allow those rules to be explicitly declared in the data instead of burying them in code or database triggers or elsewhere. In this section, we'll explore Snoggle (http://snoggle.projects .semwebcentral.org), an open-source ontology-mapping tool that creates SWRL rules graphically, enabling data using one ontology to be translated into another ontology.

We won't detail the installation of Snoggle 1.1 since it uses a straightforward, self-installing `.jar` file (based on the open-source Ant Installer) that includes a wizard to assist in the process. Snoggle can be installed with or without Jena 2.4 as part of the download. You can use the Jena 2.5.6 libraries discussed in Chapter 2 if you feel comfortable setting up your classpath with all the proper links. Otherwise, feel free to download the Snoggle package with Jena so you will not have to worry about any runtime configurations. In addition, if you haven't installed the 1.6 version of the JDK yet, you must do this step first because Snoggle needs it for the required `tools.jar` archive file.

Our discussion here will not cover all of the functionality of Snoggle. If you'd like to learn more about Snoggle, it comes with a tutorial project (loaded by selecting the Help ➢ Load Tutorial Project menu item), which covers the tool in more depth.

Mapping Friends without Upsetting Any of Them

Let's look at an example of how to use Snoggle. Pretend we have a situation where we've been using a freely available ontology about people, and we've created a lot of instance data based on this ontology. But now we want to create a mapping to FOAF for the sake of compatibility. We'll start by launching Snoggle:

```
java -jar snoggle.jar
```

You should notice a GUI appear, as shown in Figure 7-10. Snoggle models mapping from a "from", or *source*, ontology to a "to", or *destination*, ontology and requires at least one ontology of each type to be identified before any rules can be created. The freely available people ontology (`http://owl.man.ac.uk/2005/07/sssw/people`), represented here with namespace `ns0`, is loaded from Ontology ➢ From Ontology ➢ Load Ontology. Next, load the FOAF RDF file (`http://xmlns.com/foaf/spec/index.rdf`) as the destination ontology via the Ontology ➢ To Ontology ➢ Load Ontology menu option. Snoggle should then look similar to Figure 7-11. Snoggle does not limit the loading of a single source or destination ontology; continued Load Ontology menu operations would simply add additional ontologies into the tool. This is particularly helpful when creating mapping rules that have the same source and destination ontology.

At this point, we can begin to create our mappings. Starting with a simple case of mapping across classes, let's state that anyone who is an `ns0:person` (a concept from our source ontology) is also a `foaf:Person` (from our destination ontology). More precisely, if any resource is an instance of `ns0:person`, that resource will also be an instance of `foaf:Person`. Drag the `ns0:person` list item from the upper-right From Ontology list box and drop it in the center canvas.

When you drag the item over the canvas, Snoggle will ask if you want the element in the head (represented by the color blue) or the body (represented by the color green) of a rule. Drop it in the body. Next, drag the `foaf:Person` list item from the To Ontology list box to the canvas, and select it for inclusion in the head. At this point, our `ns0:person` is a green gradient rectangle in the center canvas, and the `foaf:Person` is a blue gradient rectangle. You can move the shapes around in any arrangement you like. The final step involves clicking and dragging the small square at the center of the `ns0:person` element to the center of the `foaf:Person` element. An arrow connecting the two rectangles appears and completes the rule, as shown in Figure 7-12.

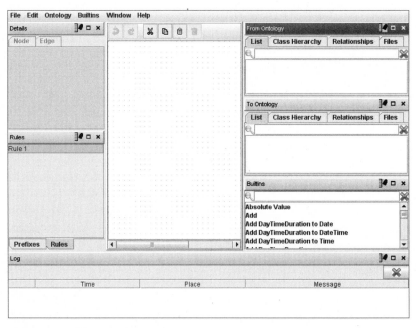

Figure 7-10 The initial Snoggle screen

Repeat these steps for as many rules as you need (several more examples are outlined), but the process isn't completed until it is serialized in a SWRL concrete format. Snoggle supports both XML and RDF serializations, which can be created by choosing File ➤ Export. SWRL files in XML are saved with the `.swrlx` extension, whereas SWRL files in RDF use the `.swrl` file extension. You should notice a message in the bottom panel of Snoggle (the logging window) that states that the resulting SWRL data passed validation as part of exporting. Snoggle also supports project files for storing metadata such as window layouts, input ontologies, and the ordering of rules as well as the rules themselves.

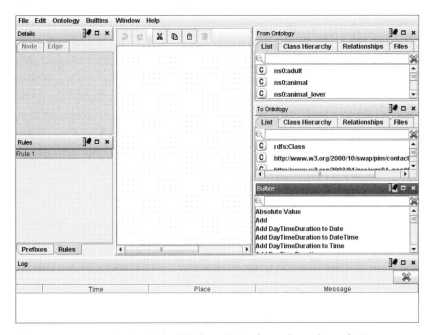

Figure 7-11 Snoggle loaded with the minimal number of ontologies

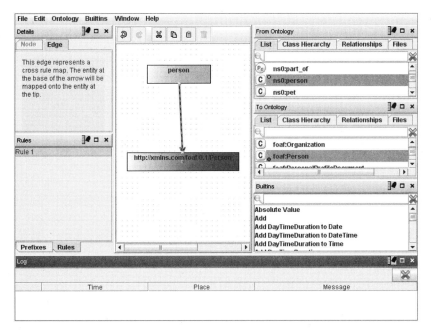

Figure 7-12 A simple class-mapping rule. In the center panel, the `person` rectangle is green, representing a rule body, while the `http://xmlns.com/foaf/0.1/Person` rectangle is blue, representing the rule head.

The Power of Rules

In the next example, we look at a more complicated rule. As shown in Figure 7-13, if there is an instance of `ns0:elderly` that has a pet identified by the `ns0:has_pet` property and stored in `var1`, then that elderly person is also of type `foaf:Person`, has a `foaf:interest` based on `var1`, and has earned the `foaf:nick[name]` property of "Crazy Pet Lady." Note that variable name of `var1` is hardly descriptive, but it is Snoggle's default naming scheme. These default names can easily be overridden by selecting the variable's shape in the center canvas and then entering a new variable name in the Node panel in the upper left.

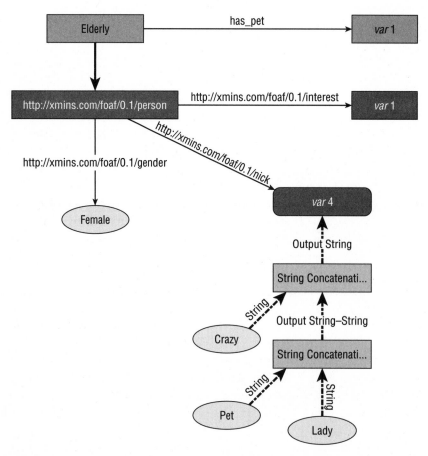

Figure 7-13 Snoggle example that includes built-ins, intra-rule variable sharing, and literal assignments

We could have gone a step further in this example and used the `rdfs:label` value of any of `var1`'s types as part of the nickname, resulting in strings like "Crazy Duck Lady" or "Crazy Cat Lady."

If you were to view the large amount of XML resulting from the serialization of this example (over 100 lines worth of RDF when viewed with carriage returns!), tools such as these make a great deal of difference toward rule generation, maintenance, validation, and adoption. They are a very important part of the adoption of the Semantic Web by a wider audience of developers.

These examples only scratch the surface of Snoggle's capability, but they should be enough to get you going on your own creation of mapping rules.

Jena Rules

Jena, the Semantic Web Framework, also supports rules, called *Jena rules*. The *Hello Semantic Web World Tour* in Chapter 2 touched on these rules to identify Gmail.com email friends. The Jena rule stated that if an email address contains the string `gmail.com`, then create a new statement that includes the owner of the email address in the `people:GmailPerson` class. As stated previously, rules add expressivity through various if-then constructs that may also include built-in functions. Jena, similar to SWRL, contains its own syntax to construct a rule and a set of built-in methods that can be used in rules.

Jena rules are bound to a rule reasoner. A rule reasoner is bound to a model or schema, as with any Jena reasoner, with the call to `bindSchema(schema)`. Once bound to a model, the rule fires in accordance to its configuration. A reasoner, including a rule reasoner, may fire in a forward-chaining mode, backward-chaining mode, or a hybrid of both. Forward rules fire whenever a new rule is added to the rule reasoner or new statements are added to the associated model. Backward rules fire whenever a query is executed on the associated model. A rule may add new statements to the model and new rules to the rule reasoner. Thus a rule may create another rule and so on. Rules fire until no matched bodies remain; however, there is no assurance that rules fire in a given order.

A Jena rule contains a list of body terms or premises (the *if* clause) and a list of head terms or conclusions (the *then* clause). Each rule can optionally have a name for convenience and a direction for hybrid rules. The rules are specified in a Jena-specific format suitable for use in a text file. This text rule example is taken from Chapter 2:

```
emailChange: (?person foaf:mbox ?email),
strConcat(?email, ?lit), regex( ?lit, '(.*@gmail.com)')
→ (?person rdf:type people:GmailPerson>)]
```

The rule is named *emailChange*. Rule names are optional. This rule contains three body terms separated by commas. Variables are preceded by question marks, similar to SPARQL and SWRL. The first term in the body matches statements that contain a `foaf:mbox` property. The second term contains a built-in rule function, `strConcat()`, to make the email variable into a literal term. The third term matches the regular expression pattern `@gmail.com` through a call to another built-in function, `regex()`. If all three terms are true, the head term is added to the model associated with the rule reasoner. Just like SWRL's human-readable syntax, the arrow (→) separates the body terms from the head terms. In this case, the forward direction of the rule indicates a forward rule that fires on rule addition and new statement addition. If the arrow is reversed, the rule is a backward rule that fires during query expansion. In backward chaining, the system looks for a match on the head term and then expands the model or query in accordance with the body terms. The head term consists of a statement that declares the resource associated with the email address is of type `people:GmailPerson`.

In addition to the rule we just discussed, the rule text file can also contain the following:

- Comment lines: `#` or `//`
- Prefixes: `@prefix pre: <URI>`
- Other rule files: `@include <URI>`

Jena supports several built-in methods that cover the following categories:

- Test for type of object
- Equality
- Math
- String concatenation
- String search
- Time
- Print
- List manipulation

As an alternative to SWRL, Jena rules provide a basic rule syntax to expand the expressiveness of an ontology. It allows the flexibility of backward or forward chaining as well as combining the two. In addition, the rule terms may contain built-in methods to perform various calculations and string manipulations.

Rule Interchange Format

Currently there is no standard rule language for the Semantic Web. To date, a wide variety of rule languages and engines, such as F-Logic, Prolog, and Jess, have already been used with the Semantic Web in one way or another. It is highly unlikely that there will ever be a single rule language for the Semantic Web. First, it is very difficult to support all the needs of the entire community. Second, working implementations, such as Jess, are satisfactory in many cases and shouldn't be excluded or ignored by the community for lack of following a specific standard. Third, research and development in the areas of rules and rule-based systems is far from complete.

The W3C initiated the RIF Working Group in 2005. Its goals are both ambitious and difficult:

- To enable and promote rule interoperability across existing systems
- To support interoperability and extensibility for *future* systems
- To create and support normative serializations based on XML

These are only the highest-level goals. For a more detailed list, see `http://www.w3.org/TR/rif-ucr/#Goals`.

None of the work produced by the RIF Working Group has yet been accepted as final recommendations by the W3C, and implementations have just begun to emerge. Next we'll focus on introducing the Working Group's effort so far and the documents that are currently available.

Delving into the Details

At the time of this writing, the Working Group has produced seven documents of particular interest.

- RIF Basic Logic Dialect (BLD), located at `http://www.w3.org/TR/2008/WD-rif-bld-20080730/`

- RIF Production Rule Dialect (PRD), located at `http://www.w3.org/TR/2008/WD-rif-prd-20081218/`

- RIF Core, located at `http://www.w3.org/TR/2008/WD-rif-core-20081218/`

- RIF Framework for Logic Dialects (FLD), located at `http://www.w3.org/TR/2008/WD-rif-fld-20080730/`

- RIF Datatypes and Built-Ins 1.0 (DTB), located at `http://www.w3.org/TR/2008/WD-rif-dtb-20081218/`

- RIF RDF and OWL Compatibility (RDF+OWL), located at `http://www` `.w3.org/TR/2008/WD-rif-rdf-owl-20080730/`

- RIF Use Cases and Requirements (UCR), located at `http://www.w3.org` `/TR/2008/WD-rif-ucr-20081218/`

The term *dialect* refers to an XML-based rule language with well-defined semantics. In general, intra-dialect compatibility isn't a requirement, but overlap and compatibility between dialects is a desirable goal. Thus, as new rule languages are defined, additional dialects may be needed to support translation to and from other dialects.

The first two dialects, BLD and PRD, are the main dialects being currently defined by the Working Group. BLD concentrates on logic programming models, mainly those defined around Horn rules (much like we've seen with SWRL), and can be seen in architectures such as deductive databases. BLD is the basis for interoperability with RDF and OWL. PRD, on the other hand, is focused on the condition-response frameworks. Given a *condition* that is found to be true, the rule should elicit a *response*. The PRD allows for actionable responses: updating a KB, emailing an administrator, or creating a log file, for example. BLD systems can have only logic statements in their conclusions (that is, *then* statements). The intersection of BLD and PRD includes what is known as the *RIF Core*, which is envisioned as being shared by all dialects, including those not yet defined.

FLD serves as the foundational framework for logical RIF dialects; its main audience is dialect creators versus the typical developer user. DTB details the datatype primitives and built-in functions and predicates supported by RIF. DTB covers the usual XML Schema datatypes and is heavily based on XPath and XQuery functions: type conversions, mathematical operations and comparisons, and string transformations. There are still shortcomings in the DTB, such as supporting comparison functions for all datatypes, but the version at the time of this writing is still an initial draft. RDF+OWL elaborates on RIF's BLD interoperability specifically with RDF data and RDFS as well as OWL. UCR outlines the requirements and several high-level common use cases demonstrating the need for rule interoperability.

The Future of RIF

The RIF Working Group' charter, originally set to expire in 2007, has been extended, and the Working Group continues to make progress toward producing W3C Recommendations. Tools supporting BLD and PRD should be available in the short term as at least two implementations are usually required before W3C specifications can progress beyond Candidate Recommendation status.

Summary

Rules are a big subject to cover, and we've tried to give you not only a working definition of what rules are but also examples of the various syntaxes to familiarize yourself with Semantic Web rules. You should have enough familiarity with SWRL and Jena to begin to experiment by adding rules to your ontologies and discovering how they affect your knowledge bases. Finally, we covered RIF, which is W3C's emerging work on rules. You've examined one of the final building blocks of the Semantic Web—good luck!

Building Semantic Web Applications

This section deals with the second major aspect; integrating the knowledgebase with an application that acts upon it. Most Semantic Web applications are built using the same fundamental principles, similar components, and variations of a basic architecture. This section builds on the foundation established so far by using the components and technologies already presented to perform tasks that are common to Semantic Web applications like integrating a knowledge model into an application, exposing data as RDF, integrating the disparate knowledge models, and sharing semantic information with the world. Each chapter explores one of these common tasks, providing numerous examples along the way. Additionally, each chapter in this section incrementally develops a large scale Semantic Web reference application called the FriendTracker to clearly illustrate the programming aspects.

Chapter 8 takes the first step towards building a Semantic Web application by presenting the integration and interactions of a Semantic Web framework and traditional applications. The chapter provides an extensive look at the complete life cycle of a Semantic Web application. Next, it presents the common frameworks and provides a complete overview of the Jena Semantic Web framework using programming examples. Finally, the chapter presents many common programming challenges and solutions such as customization and configuration, status reporting, and concurrency as they manifest in Semantic Web applications. The chapter ends by outlining the FriendTracker application, which the next three chapters build.

Chapter 9 presents the task of integrating data from various formats and representations into a RDF data model. The data sources illustrated include RESTful XML Web services, relational databases, and plain old java objects (POJOs). The Semantic Web forms a meta layer that avoids coping the information but rather provides a semantic path to the data in its native format and location. Numerous programming examples illustrate the various ways that existing technologies and data source integrate into a knowledge model. Throughout the chapter, many common issues related to data exposure and integration are discussed and potential solutions are introduced.
The chapter integrates the data sources of the FriendTracker application.

Chapter 10 tackles the issue of aligning and unifying disparate knowledge models. Whereas chapter 9 is concerned with pulling data from diverse formats and representations into a common data model, Chapter 10 pulls together the information into a single unified knowledge model. Alignment forms common concepts and relationships across the various data sources. Many approaches to unifying knowledge models are presented including using SWRL rules to map between them, OWL ontology constructs to draw relationships between classes, properties, and individuals, and direct RDF manipulation with software to work the data into a unified knowledge model. This chapter explains the FriendTracker application and ontologies and uses programming examples to illustrate how data from each of the data sources is made available to the application.

Chapter 11 completes the loop by taking the FriendTracker knowledge model and exposing it to the outside world. Many methods of exposure are discussed into the use of embeddable formats like RDFa, Microformats, and eRDF. Other more direct ways of exposing information are explored, including the establishment of a SPARQL endpoint. The chapter concludes with an example of exposing the data contained in FriendTracker in an XHTML document using RDFa.

## CHAPTER 8

Applying a Programming Framework

"It is the framework which changes with each new technology and not just the picture within the frame."

—Marshall McLuhan, Canadian communications theorist, educator, writer, and social reformer, 1911–1980

The previous chapters provided solid exposure to forming a Semantic Web of data with ontologies, rules, and such. This section presents a formal and comprehensive treatment of a Semantic Web programming framework. A framework organizes programming methods to use the rich data in the Semantic Web effectively. A framework makes the processing of the Semantic Web data come alive with all of its possibilities. The upcoming chapters apply the framework to rich domains that ingest, align, and output Semantic Web information. Operations are illustrated through the construction of the multichapter FriendTracker application. This chapter prepares for that deeper exposure by focusing specifically on the framework. Here you learn about the framework's purpose and operations in detail. Extensive coding examples are included, which are based on the Jena Semantic Web Framework. This chapter allows you to focus on the framework operations themselves without the complexity of domain applications.

In this chapter, you also learn about:

- Key concepts in a Semantic Web framework
- Available Semantic Web frameworks
- Concepts through code examples using the Jena Semantic Web Framework

■ Solutions to various programming challenges using a Semantic Web framework, such as customization, status, multithreading, and multiuser interactions

Framing the Semantic Web

The Semantic Web is all about data, useful semantic data. In order to do something with that data, you need processing. You could directly employ your brain to such a processing task, but that misses the point of the Semantic Web's machine readability. This readability requires a machine, actually an application, properly programmed to interact with the formal constructs of the Semantic Web.

Semantic Web processing comprises several key areas:

■ Referencing and managing accessible storage

■ Populating or linking Semantic Web data to the referenced storage

■ Interrogating the Semantic Web data via navigation, search, and queries

■ Reasoning via logic and rules across the Semantic Web data

■ Adapting the framework to allow substitutions and customization for optimum results in a specific application domain

In addition, the processing manages the data and various use scenarios. For example:

■ Obtaining information regarding the application's Semantic Web data such as its size and capabilities

■ Event-based programming dealing with key changes within the Semantic Web data

■ Resource management such as networking, database, and file system interactions to access and store local and remote Semantic Web data

■ Handling concurrent threads and multiple user access

You would also want the framework to offer consistent processing methods and concepts to simplify writing and debugging your code. Consistency requires common semantics and syntax across processing methods, attributes, and parameters. Effective Semantic Web frameworks do all this and more by offering a consistent and complete programming environment for the Semantic Web.

Programming languages employed by the frameworks, however, are not written in OWL (at least not yet), nor are any major languages specifically designed for the Semantic Web. Programming languages have their own perspective and capabilities. This requires a translation between Semantic Web data constructs and Semantic Web processing frameworks. Typically, Semantic Web frameworks focus on object-oriented behaviors. The frameworks translate Semantic Web statements, classes, and such data items into programming-related classes, objects, methods, and attributes of the given programming language. The two are not completely orthogonal, but there are significant differences because they have different goals: Semantic Web *knows* (semantic data); frameworks *do* (programming instructions). In a sense, the Semantic Web is the brain, whereas frameworks offer a useful programming body to apply the Semantic Web's data.

There are several excellent programming frameworks that exploit the potential of the Semantic Web, as noted in Chapter 5, "Modeling Knowledge in the Real World." Table 8-1 outlines the key characteristics and other reference material. The table notes the programming method and its semantic expressivity across the various Semantic Web language standards. This continues the discussion started in Chapter 5.

Table 8-1 Semantic Web Framework Summary

FRAMEWORK	LANGUAGE/INTERFACE	SEMANTIC LEVEL
Jena	Java	RDF to OWL 2
Sesame	Java & RESTful web service	RDF
OWL API	Java	OWL 2
RAP—RDF API	PHP	RDF
Redland	C, Python, Ruby, Perl, & PHP	RDF
LinqToRDF	.NET	RDF

Figure 8-1 illustrates our path in exploring and detailing a Semantic Web framework.

The illustrated path contains two main portions: Semantic Web data development and Semantic Web data management. Semantic Web development deals directly with data manipulation. Semantic Web data management deals with the administration of the Semantic Web data and its associated processing. We add details to the illustration.

The Semantic Web data development life cycle follows these steps:

1. Storage—The framework must acquire or reference existing space, typically in memory or a database, to store Semantic Web data. Note that your application can have multiple storage locations for performance and programmatic reasons.

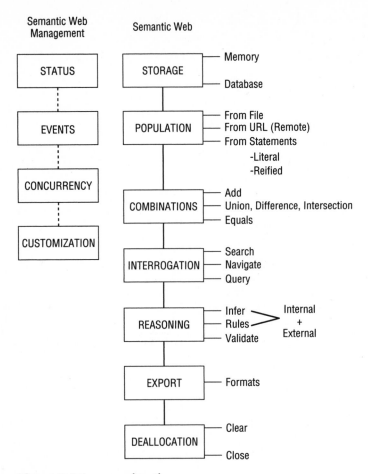

Figure 8-1 Framework path

2. Population—The framework populates the referenced storage with Semantic Web data retrieved from files, network locations, databases, and/or constructed directly.

3. Combinations—The framework combines your referenced Semantic Web data from multiple places to create additions, unions, differences, and intersections as well as test for equality between the referenced locations.

4. Reasoning—The framework allows internal and external reasoning of the Semantic Web to produce additional information based on inference. The additional information could add new statements and also indicate issues with existing statements.

5. Interrogation—The framework investigates the Semantic Web data through searching, navigation, and queries. Searching uses simple

matching. Navigation follows the path created by the various property relationships, and queries employ a formal query language.

6. Export—The framework provides methods to export the Semantic Web data in various standard formats.

7. Deallocation/close—The framework clears out the referenced storage and frees any allocated computing resources.

Semantic Web management provides:

- Information—The framework provides its size, capabilities, and characteristics of the Semantic Web data.

- Events—The framework indicates the occurrence of various events such as adding statements to the data to enable event-driven programming.

- Concurrency—The framework manages multiple threads and users manipulating the same Semantic Web data concurrently.

- Customization—The framework allows custom substitutes for specialized use such as the modification of the data storage mechanism.

Because this is a programming book and not a survey book, we dive into one of the frameworks with code examples to illustrate its programming capabilities. We selected the Jena Semantic Web Framework because it strikes a useful balance between the various Semantic Web languages, offers excellent flexibility, and is open source. We examine code examples for each of the previously mentioned operations.

The Jena Semantic Web Framework

We start our exploration with an examination of Jena's programming abstractions. Jena is implemented in the Java programming language. These Java-based abstractions translate the statements and constructs of the Semantic Web into useful programming artifacts such as Java classes, objects, methods, and attributes. Next we acquire and initialize the Jena Framework with additional details beyond the discussion in Chapter 2. Finally, we detail the major framework operations in accordance with the outlined framework exploration path. This provides you with the programming building blocks for the Semantic Web applications in the upcoming chapters.

Defining Jena Programming Concepts

The Jena Semantic Web Framework maintains a consistent treatment of the Semantic Web through its use of Java classes and variables. Table 8-2 illustrates the major Java classes and interfaces and connects them to their corresponding Semantic Web artifact. Note that the Semantic Web artifacts are data representations, whereas the Jena artifacts are object-oriented Java classes containing both data representations and corresponding methods. As you can see, they track very closely with one another.

Table 8-2 Semantic Web and Jena Framework Comparison

ARTIFACT	SEMANTIC WEB	JENA JAVA CLASS	NOTES
Subject, predicate, object	URI	`Resource, Property`	A resource can be a subject, object, or predicate.
Statement	Statement	`Statement`	Special consideration for reified statements.
Data	Ontology and instance data	`Graph` and `Model`	Graphs are a basic building block for models. They both may contain ontology and instance data.
Query and results	SPARQL and Semantic Web data	`Query` and `ResultSet`	Analogous to relational databases.
Reasoner	Reasoner	`Reasoner`	Allow multiple internal and external reasoners.
Rules	SWRL	`Reasoner`	Rule support determined by specific reasoner.
Event notification	Not applicable	`ObjectListener`	Enable event-driven processing.

The Jena Framework employs the following major Java classes (upcoming code examples cover each one in more detail):

- `Resource`—A class representing an element contained within a statement such as a subject, predicate, or object. This is analogous to an RDF resource. There also exists a Jena resource referred to as a *reified statement* that considers a triple a single resource.

- `Statement`—A Semantic Web triple containing a subject, predicate, and object. The `Statement` class allows simple interrogation of its containing components. A special statement called a reified statement contains a statement about a statement. A reified statement is an extension of a regular statement in which it is both a statement and a resource. This is a convenience that Jena provides to encapsulate the abstract concept of reification.

- Graph—Basic method for maintaining Semantic Web data. A graph allows basic add, delete, find, and contain operations. Typically, an application does not deal directly with a Graph object. The Graph interface allows the instantiation of different types of storage mechanisms. This provides low-level flexibility regarding Semantic Web storage.

- Model—A model builds on the basic graph to offer rich interactions with Semantic Web data. Your applications read, write, reason, and query Semantic Web data through access to the Jena model. The model forms the actual knowledgebase. There exist several types of model classes based on the application's needs for expressivity and reasoning. These classes include Model for basic RDF and OntModel for OWL. Your application can maintain many models concurrently for various reasons, such as performance, cache, and so on.

- Query and ResultSet—The query employs SPARQL with results returned as ResultSet. Your application iterates through the ResultSet matching on the variables used in the query.

- Reasoner—Contains the reasoner processing via either internal or external reasoning. *Internal* refers to the framework's capabilities itself, whereas *external* enables third-party reasoners access to the knowledgebase. A third-party reasoner can be either *local* using Java calls or *remote* using DIG calls. Your application binds a specific reasoner to a specific Jena model. Your application can have multiple reasoners acting upon multiple models.

In addition to offering classes for typical Semantic Web constructs, Jena offers classes to convert ontologies to Java classes. Jena offers a Java class, schemagen (yes, that is lowercase), to generate a Java class description of a Semantic Web ontology or schema. This does not convert the instance data into Semantic Web data, only the ontology statements. It is limited to the ontology or schema constructs. The schemagen Jena class constructs a Java class for each of the Semantic Web classes, allowing your application programmatic access to its underlying components.

Typically, schemagen is called directly from a command window or via an Ant script, a Java-based automated code-building tool. You need only provide a few options and the location of the ontology via a file or URL. As an example we use schemagen to generate a Java class from the FOAF ontology. Here is the command-line call.

```
java -classpath "./jena.jar:
  ./commons-logging-1.1.1.jar:./xercesImpl.jar:
  ./xml-apis.jar:./log4j-1.2.12.jar:
  ./iri.jar:./icu4j_3_4.jar"
jena.schemagen -i foaf.rdf --package
"net.semwebprogramming.chapter10.JenaExploration"
-o Foafowl.java -ontology
```

The command-line call includes the necessary classpath `.jar` files as well as several key `schemagen` options:

- `-i`—Provides the input location of the ontology. This can be either a local file or a remote URL. Here we have a local file, `foaf.rdf`.

- `--package`—Provides the package name for the created Java class.

- `-o`—Provides the name of the output file to contain the Java class.

- `--ontology`—The class uses OWL constructs as opposed to the default RDF constructs.

Running this command produces a single Java class titled `Foafowl` in accordance with the `-o` option. (Note that FOAF has only one main class.) In order to follow the proper naming convention, capitalize the output file (`schemagen` capitalizes the class name as the accepted Java convention). The following output shows a subset of the class. We need not include the entire file—you get the idea.

```
package net.semwebprogramming.chapter10.JenaExploration;
import com.hp.hpl.jena.rdf.model.*;
import com.hp.hpl.jena.ontology.*;


/**
 * Vocabulary definitions from foaf.rdf
 * @author Auto-generated by schemagen on 27 Sep 2008 14:42
 */
public class FoafOwl {
    /** <p>The ontology model that holds the vocabulary terms</p> */
    private static OntModel m_model =
      ModelFactory.createOntologyModel( OntModelSpec.OWL_MEM, null );
    /** <p>The namespace of the vocabulary as a string</p> */
    public static final String NS = "http://xmlns.com/foaf/0.1/";
    /** <p>The namespace of the vocabulary as a string</p>
     *  @see #NS */
    public static String getURI() {return NS;}
    /** <p>The namespace of the vocabulary as a resource</p> */
    public static final Resource NAMESPACE = m_model.createResource( NS );
    /** <p>Indicateshomepagethe service provide for this  account.</p> */
    public static final ObjectProperty accountServiceHomepage =
      m_model.createObjectProperty
        ("http://xmlns.com/foaf/0.1/accountServiceHomepage" );
```

```
/** <p>A location that somethingnear, for some broadly human notion of
 *  near.</p>
 */
public static final ObjectProperty based_near =
  m_model.createObjectProperty
  ( "http://xmlns.com/foaf/0.1/based_near" );
/** <p>A current project this person works on.</p> */
public static final ObjectProperty currentProject =
  m_model.createObjectProperty
  ("http://xmlns.com/foaf/0.1/currentProject" );
/** <p>A depiction of some thing.</p> */
public static final ObjectProperty depiction =
  m_model.createObjectProperty
  ( "http://xmlns.com/foaf/0.1/depiction" );
/** <p>A thing depicted in this representation.</p> */
public static final ObjectProperty depicts =
m_model.createObjectProperty( "http://xmlns.com/foaf/0.1/depicts" );
/** <p>An organization funding a project or person.</p> */
public static final ObjectProperty fundedBy =
  m_model.createObjectProperty
  ( "http://xmlns.com/foaf/0.1/fundedBy" );
/** <p>Indicates an account held by this agent.</p> */
public static final ObjectProperty holdsAccount =
 m_model.createObjectProperty
 ("http://xmlns.com/foaf/0.1/holdsAccount" );
```

The class produces a static instance of the ontology. Note the call that creates the Model object and each resource. You could use this object to refer directly to the various resources and related data through the generated method calls. For example, `Foaf.getURI()` returns the URI of the FOAF ontology. This approach provides an easy way to reach into the ontology via Java class methods rather than dealing indirectly via the various calls that instantiate the ontology method and attribute.

Now that we covered the concepts, we will put them to work.

Programming with Jena

We explore the Jena Framework by following the path previously outlined in Figure 8-1: Semantic Web data development and Semantic Web data management. This provides a systematic way to explore the framework with coding details for each area.

This section focuses on the construction of applications using the Jena Framework. We do not focus on complex application domains so as to reveal clearly Jena functionality. Future chapters apply these Jena code methods and constructs to various application domains.

In order to have complete working examples, we start by outlining the framework through high-level method calls. Don't let this scare you. We break down each method along the way. The following methods outline the path we take through the Jena Framework. We follow it directly, except we save the noted management methods for last (`// Part of Management`).

```java
public class JenaExploration {

    final private String defaultNameSpace =
        "http://semwebprogramming.org/2009/ont/chp8#";
    private OntModel _modelMem = null, _modelDB = null;
    private InfModel _jenaInferModel = null, _jenaRuleModel = null,
                    _pelletInferModel = null, _digInferModel = null;
    private JenaListener _listenerMem = null, _listenerDB = null;

    public static void main(String[] args)  {

        try {

        JenaExploration jena = new JenaExploration();

        // Initial Creation
        jena.aquireMemoryForData();
        jena.aquireDBForData();

        // Bulk Populate
        jena.addDataFromFile();
        jena.addDataFromURL();

        // Monitor Events
        jena.setEventListener();   // Part of Management

        // Populate with Statements
        jena.addDataFromStatements();
        jena.addDatafromOntology();

        jena.addLiterals();
        jena.addReifiedStatements();

        // Get Status
        jena.getModelInfo();   // Part of Management

        // Combinations
        jena.combineData();

        // Interrogation
        jena.searchAndNavigateData();
        jena.queryData();

        // Reason
```

```
        jena.reasonOverData();

        // Validate
        jena.validateData();

        // Critical region
        jena.criticalRegionWrite();    // Part of Management

        // Export the Model
        jena.writeData();

        // Create a Custom Graph for the Model
        jena.createCustomModel();  // Part of Management

        // Clear and Close
        jena.clearAndCloseData();

    }
    catch (Exception e) {
        System.out.println("Failure: " +
            e.getClass().getName() + "-" + e.getMessage());
        e.printStackTrace();
        return;
        }
    }
```

We create a new Java class, JenaExploration. The name purposely hints at the class's perspective to show the raw Jena code rather than contribute to a complex Semantic Web application. The comments outline the programming flow from forming Semantic Web storage to closing it. Next we go through each one. You can download this working example. One note before we dive into each method: The code declares global variables that set the namespace and the variables for the various models. We refer to a Model object simply as *model* in lowercase. We follow this convention for other Jena objects as well.

Also, we need to say a few words regarding Java exceptions. It is not the intention of this Jena code exploration to demonstrate a production application, but that does not give us a complete escape from exceptions. As a compromise, we handle exceptions within the main() method. As you shall see, several Jena methods (and other related methods) may throw an exception. We isolate the exception-handling code to here and meekly acknowledge its presence. As we explore the code, we note where exceptions are thrown. This reminds us of the importance of handling exceptions without complicating the Jena examples. Each method notes the exception types it throws in the method declaration. We won't dwell on them, but they are included in the code examples.

Establishing the Jena Development Environment

Hopefully you downloaded the framework according to the instructions in Chapter 2, "Hello Semantic Web World." This section supplies some additional details regarding your Jena environment. For the following references, we refer to your Jena installation directory as `JenaInstallDirectory`.

The Jena download (found at `http://jena.sourceforge.net/downloads .html`) contains a wealth of valuable information beyond the necessary Jena `.jar` files. It contains dozens of examples, major ontologies, an FAQ section, and extensive documentation including the Jena Javadocs. Links to all of this content is found by loading the `JenaInstallDirectory/readme.html` file into your browser. The download also includes a test script to exercise the many Jena functions. You can run the self-check test, and you are all set.

The only essential item from the download is the various Jena `.jar` files that contain the framework itself. These are found in the `JenaInstall Directory/lib` directory. You need to include these `.jar` files in your Java classpath when accessing the Jena Semantic Web Framework.

Establishing the Knowledgebase: Setting Up the Model

The first step in processing Semantic Web data is to find a place to refer to it. Without a location, actions such as a query cannot occur. This requires the naming and allocation of reference resources. The naming allows your application to maintain multiple, unique data locations. Your application may maintain separate areas for various reasons, including performance, security, comparisons, and the like.

For Jena, it all begins with the creation of a Model object. The `Model` class contains a reference to the Semantic Web data along with methods to manage its contents. There are several different types of models your application can request that reflect various levels of inference support. The various model types reflect the various Semantic Web languages, such as RDF, RDFS, and OWL. In addition, the model may allocate memory or database storage. We illustrate creating an OWL model residing in memory and in a database.

The code that follows illustrates creation of a memory-based OWL model. Initially, this model contains initialization data from the included specification. An OWL specification includes OWL, RDFS, and RDF schema data. Without the OWL specification, the model would be completely empty. In either case, the model does not contain any domain or application data.

```
private void aquireMemoryForData(){
    modelMem =
        ModelFactory.createOntologyModel(OntModelSpec.OWL_DL_MEM);
}
```

The static method, `ModelFactory.createOntologyModel()`, creates an empty model. The argument specifies types of entailments that occur within the model. The `OWL_DL_MEM` specifies no additional inference within the model until we bind a reasoner. If instead your application required only an RDF model, you'd substitute the `createModel()` method for the `createOntologyModel()` method. You can also create models from existing Model objects and graph-based objects. Graphs form a low-level interface to the actual storage. Your application can choose to directly implement the graph interface to allow substitution of the storage mechanism; more on that later in this chapter.

In addition to the straightforward use of the `ModelFactory`, you can also form advanced versions of the models through the creation of a ModelMaker object instead of direct creation of a model using the `ModelFactory`. Advanced models provide additional inference and storage options. This requires three steps:

1. Create the ModelMaker object.
2. Use the ModelMaker object to create a basic model.
3. Use the newly created basic model to create a more advanced model.

We perform this three-step process for two types of models: a memory model backed by file storage and a database-backed model.

The code for the memory model backed by a file store is as follows:

```
private void aquireMemoryForData(){
    ModelMaker modelMaker =
        ModelFatory.createFileModelMaker
        ("/Users/jhebeler/filestore/filesave.owl/");
    Model modeltmp = modelMaker.createDefaultModel();
    modelMem =
    ModelFactory.createOntologyModel(OntModelSpec.OWL_DL_MEM, modeltmp);
}
```

Here we create a ModelMaker object instead of directly creating a model using the `ModelFactory.createFileModelMaker()` method. The method requires the name of a file for the storage of the file. If the file already contains RDF/XML data at the model's creation, the file populates the model during its creation. When the model is closed, the contents of the model are written to the file in RDF/XML format. Note that it doesn't refresh the data stored in the file during model operations. It updates the file only when closing the model. This step creates only a basic RDF model, a limitation of a created ModelMaker. In order to create an ontology model, we use the `ModelFactory.createOntologyModel()` method as before but now provide an additional argument, the basic model we created with ModelMaker.

Next is the creation of a database-backed model. This is a bit more involved because of the logistics of establishing the database connection. The code illustrates the same three-step approach. The following code illustrates the creation of an OWL-based model stored in a MySQL relational database. Jena supports other databases including PostgreSQL, Oracle, and Microsoft SQL Server; see `http://jena.sourceforge.net/documentation.html` for additional details.

```
private void aquireDBForData()
                  throws SQLException, ClassNotFoundException {
    IDBConnection conn = null;
    Model modeltmp = null;

    Class.forName("com.mysql.jdbc.Driver");
    System.out.println("JDBC Driver found");

    String DB_URL = "jdbc:mysql://semwebprogramming.org/jenaDB";
    String DB_USER = new String("jenaUser");
    String DB_PASSWD = new String("jenaPassword");
    String DB_TYPE = new String("MySQL");

    conn = new DBConnection(DB_URL, DB_USER, DB_PASSWD, DB_TYPE);

    if(conn.getConnection() != null)  // throws exception
        System.out.println("Connection Successful");

    ModelMaker maker = ModelFactory.createModelRDBMaker(conn);

    //check to see if the model is already present
    if(conn.containsModel("FoafInstancesDB")){
        System.out.println("Opening existing model");
        modeltmp=maker.openModel("FoafInstancesDB",true); //throws
exception if not present
    }
    else {
        System.out.println("Creating new model");
        modeltmp = maker.createModel("FoafInstanceDB");
    }
    OntModelSpec spec = new OntModelSpec(OntModelSpec.OWL_MEM);
    _modelDB = ModelFactory.createOntologyModel(spec,modeltmp);
}
```

This code illustrates a connection to a MySQL database using JDBC. The first part of the method checks for and, if possible, acquires the necessary JDBC driver. Then the method declares the necessary database access information including the host address, login information, and database name (for example, jena), which is contained in the URL. We could have combined them here but kept them separate for clarity. We then establish a connection to the database and check it with the `getConnection()` method. This method generates an exception if there is no connection. Otherwise, your application might hang. We create a database ModelMaker object through the `createModelRDBMaker()` method. We check to see whether the model already exists in the database from previous interactions. The `DBConnection` object method `containsModel()` determines whether the name is set to `FoafInstancesDB`. If the data already exists, we use the `ModelMaker.openModel()` method to open the basic model. If it doesn't exist, we create a new one through the `ModelMaker.createModel()` method providing its name. Finally, we need to turn this basic model into one that supports OWL. We call the `createOntologyModel()` method providing the model already created. Thus, the three-step process is applied: obtain a ModelMaker object; create a basic model, in this case a database-backed model; and then advance the basic model to an ontology-based model. You must set up the database with appropriate access permissions prior to this method call. You do not need to create any relational tables and columns. The database itself is sufficient. Please refer to your specific relational database documentation for more information.

Populating the Model with Semantic Web Data

Now that you have a reference to storage for your Semantic Web data, you need to populate it. There are several ways to populate the model. You can populate the model from a file, from a URL, and from adding statements directly. You can also populate through other existing models, and we look at that in the next section.

Populating the model by a file or URL is straightforward. You just provide the filename with its path or the URL. Here are examples of both:

```
private void addDataFromFile() throws IOException{
    System.out.println("Loading from FOAF instance File");
    InputStream inFoafInstance =
        FileManager.get().open("Ontologies/FOAFFriends.rdf");
    _modelDB.read(inFoafInstance,defaultNameSpace);
    inFoafInstance.close();
}
private void addDataFromURL(){
    System.out.println("Loading FOAF ontology URL");
    _modelMem.read("http://xmlns.com/foaf/spec/index.rdf");
}
```

For the file, you need to create an `InputStream` and then pass that to the `read()` method. Using the Java `InputStream` enables flexibility in dealing with stored data. An `InputStream` is a base class for many other useful ways of dealing with data. See Java SDK Javadocs for more information. For the URL, you simply provide the URL. Note the possible thrown exception, `IOException`, because of missing or unavailable data.

The two methods, using files and URLs, provide a batch way to load large numbers of statements; however, this technique is useful for relatively static information. Your application may want to add statements dynamically directly to the model. For that we directly form Jena resources into Jena statements. The following code demonstrates adding a statement through the creation of resources:

```
private void addDataFromStatements(){
    System.out.println("Adding statement to model");
    // Create resources
    Resource resource = _modelDB.createResource(defaultNameSpace + "me");
    Property prop =
_modelDB.createProperty("http://www.w3.org/2002/07/owl#sameAs");
    //Property prop2 = OWL.sameAs();
    Resource obj = _modelDB.createResource(defaultNameSpace +
        "Individual_5");
    _modelDB.add(resource,prop,obj);
        // or
    _modelDB.add(resource,OWL.sameAs,obj);
}
```

We created three Jena resources. The `Jena` property is a type of Jena resource. We provide all three to the `add()` method for the model that receives the statement. Important note: If you don't execute the `add()` method, it is not added to the model. You could also include an additional step to create a Jena statement first and then add the statement through a `createStatement()` method call to the model. There are two ways to reference the property for `OWL:sameAs`. You can use the brute force method of forming the property or use the Jena premade resources. Jena contains all RDFS and OWL constructs as static resources. We add additional OWL statements in the code that follows. One final note; the `createResource()` method always returns a resource but doesn't always create one. If the resource already exists in the model, it merely returns the existing one. Therefore, you need not worry about duplicating a resource.

Jena offers an ontology-based interface that provides methods to create various OWL constructs such as `sameAs`, `equivalentClass`, and OWL restrictions. The following code adds statements via this ontology interface:

```
private void addDatafromOntology(){
    Ontology ont = _modelMem.createOntology("Memory Model");
    ont.addVersionInfo("1.0");

    OntClass people = _modelMem.createClass(defaultNameSpace + "People");
    OntClass individual =
        _modelMem.createClass(defaultNameSpace + "Individual");
    people.addEquivalentClass(individual);
```

```
OntClass friend = _modelMem.createClass(defaultNameSpace + "Friend");
friend.addSubClass(people);

OntProperty hasFriend =
    _modelMem.createObjectProperty(defaultNameSpace + "hasFriend");

// Create restriction
OntResource joe =
    _modelMem.createOntResource(defaultNameSpace + "Joe");
OntResource joseph =
    _modelMem.createOntResource(defaultNameSpace + "Joseph");
OntResource jane =
    _modelMem.createOntResource(defaultNameSpace + "Jane");

joe.addSameAs(joseph);

_modelMem.add(joe, hasFriend, jane);
}
```

The ontology methods offered by the OntClass Jena class provide annotations regarding the ontology. As mentioned in Chapter 6, annotations are not subject to reasoning. Here we set the ontology version for our ontology to 1.0. We then create two classes, People and Individual. Then we make the two classes equivalent. We declare a subclass, Friend. Lastly, we create an object property and two ontology resources, joe and joseph. We establish instance equivalence by using the addSameAs() method. Finally, we add the statement that joe has Friend jane. Note that a reasoner would infer that joseph also has the friend jane.

Jena also provides methods to create reified statements. As noted previously, reified statements are statements about statements. Jena simplifies this by also allowing a complete Jena statement to be a resource. In this case a special resource is called a reified resource. The following code creates a reified statement and then adds it to the model.

```
private void addReifiedStatements(){
    Resource resSubject = _modelMem.getResource(defaultNameSpace + "Joe");
    Property prop = _modelMem.getProperty(defaultNameSpace + "seenAt");
    Resource resObject = _modelMem.getResource(defaultNameSpace +
        "Wendys");
    Statement state = _modelMem.createStatement(resSubject, prop,
        resObject);
    Resource reifiedResource = _modelMem.createReifiedStatement(state);

    Property propseen = _modelMem.getProperty(defaultNameSpace +
        "atTime");
    _modelMem.add(reifiedResource, propseen,
            "xsd:dateTime 2008-10-26T21:32:52");
```

```
    RSIterator iter = _modelMem.listReifiedStatements();
  while(iter.hasNext()){
      ReifiedStatement rei = iter.nextRS();
      StmtIterator iter2 = rei.listProperties();
      System.out.println("Statement: " +
rei.getStatement().getSubject().toString() +
        " " + rei.getStatement().getPredicate().toString() + " " +
        rei.getStatement().getObject().toString());
      while( iter2.hasNext()){
        Statement st = iter2.nextStatement();
        System.out.println("Reified Statement: " +
          st.getPredicate().toString() + " " +
          st.getObject().toString()  );
      }
    }
  }
```

In order to create a reified statement, we first need a regular statement—the statement that we are going to make a statement about. In this case we create a statement: `Joe SeenAt McDonalds`. Now we want to note the time Joe was seen at McDonalds, which was late! In order to do this we need to create a reified statement. So we turn the statement we created into a resource through a call to the model `createReifiedStatement()` method. This returns a valid resource we can use in another statement. We create an additional property, `atTime`, and we are all set. We create the statement that contains the reified resource along with the other two resources. This notes that Joe as seen at McDonalds at 12:30 a.m., thus creating a statement about a statement. Just for completeness, the code also iterates through the statements and reified statements and prints out the results. We need two iterators: one to walk through the reified statements and one to walk through any statements related to the specified reified statement. Here we had only one, but you can have as many as you want. Keeping with the example, reified statements could note whom Joe was with, what he ordered, how much it cost, and so on, all referring to the same visit to McDonalds, which refers to only the one original statement.

Combining Semantic Web Data

You can also populate a model from other existing models. You can simply add all statements from one to the other or selectively add statements. The following code takes you through multiple ways to add statements from one model to another.

```
private void combineData(){
  Model _modelNew;
  // Add two models together model1.add(model2)
```

```
      //allows cascading
_modelMem =  (OntModel) _modelMem.add((Model)_modelDB);

// Union of two models model1.union(model2)
_modelNew = _modelMem.union(_modelDB);   //creates a new model

// Intersection of two models model1.intersection(model2)
_modelNew = _modelMem.intersection(_modelDB);  // creates a new model

// Difference of two models  model1.difference(model2)
_modelNew = _modelMem.difference(_modelDB);  // creates a new model

// Are two models equal model1.equals(model2)

if( _modelNew.equals(_modelMem)){
   System.out.println("Underlying Graph Objects are identical");
   }
if (_modelNew.isIsomorphicWith(_modelMem)){
   System.out.println("Model Statements are identical");
   }
}
```

In our example we declared a new model, _modelNew. This is not necessary. You can also use an existing model. The add() method simply copies all the statements in the parameter model modifying the model. The union() method is analogous to the add but eliminates any duplicate statements. The intersection() method produces a model with only statements that are contained in both of the models. The difference() method contains only statements that are unique to both models. Only the add() method modifies the original model. The other methods merely augment the model.

For completeness, the code also demonstrates comparisons between two models using the equals() method, which tests for the same underlying Graph objects, and using the isIsomorphicWith() method, which tests for the same statements in each model.

Interrogating Semantic Web Data

Now that we have a Jena model populated with Semantic Web data, we can interrogate the data. Jena allows three basic approaches: search, navigate, and query. Search finds identical matches within the data—a simple query really that merely matches a string without any semantics. Navigate follows the path outlined by the various relationships to find data. Navigation can be quite powerful given the description of the various relationships in Semantic Web data. Finally, query uses a formal query language; SPARQL. Previously we covered the data techniques and the SPARQL language; now we demonstrate the interrogation code using Jena.

```
private void searchAndNavigateData(){
    // Search to find me
    Resource me = _modelDB.getResource(defaultNameSpace + "me");

    // Navigate around me
    StmtIterator iter = me.listProperties();
    int count = 1;
    while (iter.hasNext()){
        System.out.println("Property " + count++ + ": " +
            iter.nextStatement().getObject());
    }
}
```

The code first starts with a search for an exact match on a Jena Resource object. It is important to note that the getResource() method operates identically to the createResource() method. In other words, it always finds the resource; if the resource doesn't exist, getResource creates it. Once we have the resource, we can use it to navigate various ways depending on the existing relationships. Here we examine all the properties of the resource. Since many properties can be related to a resource, we use an iterator to step through the entire set. In addition to the listProperties() method, there are many other list methods to navigate through the model; see the Jena Javadocs. The Jena StmtIterator specializes the standard Java iterators with extra methods to return statements and a close() method to free resources if the application does not complete the iteration.

Queries offer formal interrogation of the Semantic Web data. Jena contains a SPARQL query processor to translate SPARQL queries to a result set for a SELECT query or graphs for a CONSTRUCT query. We covered the SPARQL language in Chapter 6, so we need not repeat it here. Instead we focus on using SPARQL within the Jena framework. The code that follows does just that for a SELECT query:

```
private void queryData(){
    StringBuffer queryStr = new StringBuffer();
    // Establish Prefixes
    //Set default Name space first
    queryStr.append("PREFIX people" + ": <" + defaultNameSpace + "> ");
    queryStr.append("PREFIX foaf" + ": <" +
        "http://xmlns.com/foaf/0.1/" + "> ");

    //Now add query
    queryStr.append
        (" select DISTINCT ?name where{ people:me foaf:name ?name  }");
    Query query = QueryFactory.create(queryStr.toString());
    QueryExecution qexec = QueryExecutionFactory.create(query, _modelDB);
    try {
        ResultSet response = qexec.execSelect();
```

```
    while( response.hasNext()){
        QuerySolution soln = response.nextSolution();
        RDFNode name = soln.get("?name");
        if( name != null ){
            System.out.println( "Hello to " + name );
        }
        else
            System.out.println("No Friends found!");
        }
} finally {
    qexec.close();
}
```

This may look familiar because it is the same code we use in the Hello Semantic Web World Tour. Now we examine it a bit closer. First, we create a StringBuffer object to eventually contain the full SPARQL query. Next we place our prefix shortcuts to save us from typing in the long URIs. After that we add in the actual query. Now we have the entire query string. We use the `QueryFactory.create( )` method to create a valid Jena Query object. We use the `QueryExecutionFactory.create()` method to execute the query against the model contained in the parameters. This returns a context to the query in the form of a QueryExecution object. From the QueryExecution object we obtain the ResultSet object. It contains statements that fulfilled the query. Keep in mind that it is possible to have no statements or many statements in a ResultSet. The ResultSet object implements the Iterator interface. We step through the iterator to get the entire results. Each statement in the result requires the ResultSet to provide a QuerySolution object. Within the QuerySolution object, we request a given variable that was provided in the SPARQL query. This variable could be many possible objects, so we use the simplest possible object, an RDFNode, to receive it. We could typecast it if we know the type of the variable returned. The RDFNode object contains null if the ResultSet does not contain a binding for the specified variable.

Reasoning across Semantic Web Data

Another important aspect beyond interrogating the Semantic Web data is reasoning across the data, realizing the full power of semantics. For that we need to integrate reasoners beyond what is already present in the model. The Jena framework offers several ways to integrate reasoners. The operation is similar to creating a more advanced model from a simpler one, as illustrated earlier, such as going from an RDF file-backed model to an ontology model. We incorporate two major types of reasoners: inference reasoners and rule reasoners (although they are treated similarly within Jena). Chapter 4, "Incorporating Semantics," and Chapter 7, "Adding Rules," covered the operations and languages of both. Here we show how the Jena framework integrates the reasoners.

In addition, reasoners exists as three distinct types: internal reasoners built into the Jena framework, external reasoners offered as external Java files, and external reasoners remotely offered via the DL Information Group (DIG) interface. The DIG interface is a standardized XML interface to description logics reasoning via an HTTP interface.

We illustrate an internal Jena reasoner for inference in this code:

```
private InfModel bindJenaInferenceReasoner(){
    Reasoner reasoner = ReasonerRegistry.getOWLReasoner();
    reasoner = reasoner.bindSchema(_modelMem);
    InfModel inferredFriends =
        ModelFactory.createInfModel(reasoner, _modelDB);
    return inferredFriends;
}
```

We get the OWL reasoner contained in the Jena framework through the `ReasonerRegistry.get()` method. The ReasonerRegistry holds references to all of the Jena reasoners. We take an extra step here and bind the reasoner to a given model that holds the ontology or schema. A reasoner may interact or bind to multiple models. This allows the reasoner to reason across the schema prior to the addition of instance data. This makes no real difference when using one instance data model; however, the approach gains efficiencies when using two or more models that contain instance data for the same ontology. Then we use the `ModelFactory.createInfModel()` method to create a new model that combines the reasoner and model provided in the parameters. Here is where some of the virtualization of the Jena model comes into play. When you combine a reasoner with a model, the new inferred model contains not one but two graph-based objects. One Graph object contains the original model statements. The other graph contains only the entailments. Thus, the original model is still available to your application. Your application could retrieve statements directly from the original model if statements derived from the reasoner are to be avoided. This also allows Jena to discard entailments quickly, which may be required on large additions to the model when the reasoner must run against the new data. Thus, the graphs reflect a lower-level object that can combine to form one model. This virtualizes the Jena model to allow combinations of included graphs.

The bound reasoner chosen previously (OWLReasoner) provides OWL entailments that cover OWL constructs such as `sameAs`, `SymmetricProperty`, `maxCardinality`, and the like. Your application may not need that level of inference because of the language used, desired results, or performance considerations. There are several other native reasoners including an RDFS reasoner to support RDFS entailments and a transitive reasoner for entailments only because of symmetric and transitive properties in RDFS. See the Javadocs under ReasonerRegistry for the complete list. This allows your application to tune entailments to your needs. Your application obtains the available reasoners from the static ReasonerRegistry methods as we did previously.

Another type of Jena reasoner is its general-purpose rule engine. It contains its own rule language with useful methods to construct *if/then* rules. Here is an example of using the Jena general-purpose rule engine. The Jena rule language was briefly covered in Chapter 7.

```
private InfModel bindJenaRuleReasoner(){
    String rules =
     "[emailChange: (?person <http://xmlns.com/foaf/0.1/mbox> ?email), " +
      "strConcat(?email, ?lit), regex( ?lit, '(.*@gmail.com)') -> " +
      "(?person <http://www.w3.org/1999/02/22-rdf-syntax-ns#type> " +
      "<http://org.semwebprogramming/chapter2/people#GmailPerson>)]";

    Reasoner ruleReasoner = new
  GenericRuleReasoner(Rule.parseRules(rules));
    ruleReasoner = ruleReasoner.bindSchema(_modelMem);
    InfModel inferredFriends =
        ModelFactory.createInfModel(ruleReasoner, _modelDB);
    return inferredFriends;
}
```

The string *rules* contains the rule in the Jena rule language format. The first field provides a name of the rule, emailChange. The first part of the rule contains the *if* portion, or body. The body declares a variable, ?person. That variable must have an mbox. The mbox object is placed in another variable, ?email. Next we use a Jena rule method, strConcat(), to copy the ?email variable contents into a literal variable, ?lit. This ensures that ?lit is a literal value that is needed by the next method. We then call another Jena rule method, regex(). This method matches a string that contains "@gmail.com." If there is a person with an email address that contains gmail.com, the body, or *if* portion of the rule, is true. Thus, the head, or *then* portion, is executed or fired. This adds a new statement to the model bound to the reasoner that takes the same person contained in the ?person variable and declares that person a type of the GmailPerson class.

It is important to note the direction of the arrow between the head and body in the Jena rule. Here the direction is to the right, indicating forward chaining of the inference. You can reverse the direction to achieve backward chaining. Keep in mind that a rule can contain several subrules, which allows you to mix forward and backward chaining. There is an excellent reference document on the Jena site at http://jena.sourceforge.net/inference/ that covers additional details and provides additional examples for each reasoner.

We have now covered the reasoners internal to Jena. Next we will examine methods to integrate external reasoners. As mentioned before, external reasoners integrate into Jena through two means: via the Java class path directed to a .jar or class file or a remote DIG interface. We cover the class path file implementation first. Typically this is faster because of the lack of any networking to interact with the reasoner; however, the reasoner exists in the same application space.

First we examine an external reasoner, Pellet. Pellet is available at http://pellet.owldl.com. Pellet is Java based and therefore offers a convenient .jar-contained interface. Non-Java-based reasoners may also offer this access by providing a JNI interface. In either case, Jena enables direct access to the reasoner's capabilities. The Pellet reasoner offers OWL and SWRL inference. Along with the necessary Java .jar files, the Pellet download includes extensive documentation and examples. The following code integrates the Pellet reasoner:

```
private InfModel bindPelletReasoner(){
    Reasoner reasoner = PelletReasonerFactory.theInstance().create();
    reasoner = reasoner.bindSchema(_modelMem);
    InfModel inferredFriends =
        ModelFactory.createInfModel(reasoner, _modelDB);

    return inferredFriends;
}
```

The Pellet reasoner integrates similarly to a Jena internal reasoner. Using PelletReasonerFactory.theInstance().create() produces a Jena Reasoner object. The Reasoner object binds to a schema in just the same manner as a Jena internal reasoner. So the rest of the method is identical.

If a reasoner does not allow direct access via a Java .jar file, the Jena framework supports the DIG interface, a standard for reasoners. The DIG interface is an XML standard for access to description logic processing via the HTTP protocol. DIG's future is unclear but remains a method for remotely interacting with a reasoner. DIG is also less expressive than OWL description logic; therefore, DIG incurs some loss because of incomplete coverage—see the DIG documentation. The DIG-accessed reasoner runs as an external process that you could distribute to a different host. The Pellet reasoner, used previously, also offers a DIG interface. The following code demonstrates integrating the Pellet reasoner using the DIG interface operating on port 2009.

```
private InfModel bindDigReasoner(){
    System.out.println("Entering DIG reasoner");

    Resource conf = _modelMem.createResource();
    conf.addProperty(ReasonerVocabulary.EXT_REASONER_URL,
        _modelMem.createResource("http://localhost:8081")   );
```

```
DIGReasonerFactory drf =
   (DIGReasonerFactory) ReasonerRegistry.theRegistry().
      getFactory(DIGReasonerFactory.URI);

DIGReasoner r = (DIGReasoner)drf.create(conf);

OntModelSpec spec = new OntModelSpec(OntModelSpec.OWL_DL_MEM);
spec.setReasoner(r);

OntModel m = ModelFactory.createOntologyModel(spec,null);
m.add(_modelMem);
return m;
}
```

We first create a URI-based DIG reasoner factory. Then we create the
reasoner. We specify the reasoner's hostname and port, and we associate
the reasoner with a specification. We configure the specification of an
ontology-based model and associate the reasoner instance with it. We then
create an ontology model using the reasoner specification. Finally, we add the
original model into the newly created one using the add() method.

Reasoners allow several operations to validate the model contents. The
following code takes you through a validation report.

```
private void validateDataFromModel(InfModel infModel){
   System.out.println("Validation of "+
      infModel.getReasoner().toString());
   ValidityReport report = infModel.validate();
   // returns true if Model is logically consistent (i.e. valid)
   // and generates no warnings
   if ( report.isClean() != true ){
      Iterator<ValidityReport.Report> iter = report.getReports();
      while( iter.hasNext()){
         System.out.println
         (((ValidityReport.Report)iter).isError?"ERROR: ":"Warning:" +
            ((ValidityReport.Report)iter).description);
      }
   }
   else
   System.out.println("Model is clean");
}
```

First we print out the name of the reasoner using the inference model
getReasoner() method. Then we use the validate() method to return a
ValidityReport object. The isClean() method returns true if the model is
logically consistent and has no warnings. Inconsistencies result from instance
statements or ontology statements that are in conflict. Warnings result in
classes that can never have instances. If isClean() returns false, we create an
iterator to deal with each invalid determination. The iterator steps through

each report, first determining whether it is an error or warning and then printing out the full description.

Exporting Semantic Web Data

Now that we have useful Semantic Web data, we need to export it for others to use or maintain it for our future use. In upcoming chapters we cover dynamic ways to expose our data. For now, we export to a file. The Jena Framework offers a simple, straightforward way, as shown in the following code:

```
private void writeData() throws IOException{
   FileOutputStream outFoaf= null, outFoafInstance=null;
   outFoaf = new FileOutputStream("Ontologies/foaf.turtle");
   outFoafInstance = new FileOutputStream
         ("Ontologies/foafInstance.turtle");

   _modelMem.write(outFoaf, "TURTLE");
   _modelDB.write(outFoafInstance, "TURTLE");
   outFoaf.close();
   outFoafInstance.close();
}
```

Most of this code is acquiring a `FileOutputStream` to absorb the Semantic Web data. This can generate an `IOException`. Once we obtain a valid `FileOutputStream`, we pass it to the `write()` method along with the desired format. Here we use our preferred Turtle format. The Jena Framework also offers RDF/XML, RDF/XML-ABBREV, N-Triple, and N3 formats. The `write()` method defaults to RDF/XML if the format is blank.

Deallocating Semantic Web Data Resources

The last major step releases the references to the various resources used to manipulate your Semantic Web data. This requires only two methods: one to clear out the storage, which is optional, and one to close it down to release all resources and perform final actions. Note that you can clear the contents at any time. The following code illustrates both actions:

```
private void clearAndCloseData(){
   _modelMem.removeAll();
   _modelDB.removeAll();
   System.out.println("Closing Models");
   _modelMem.close();
   _modelDB.close();
}
```

The `removeAll()` method clears all statements in the given model. The `removeAll()` method can also take parameters to remove specified subsets of the model. The subsets include matches on a specified subject, predicate, object, or reified statement combinations. Removing reified statements uses the `removeReification()` and `removeAllReifications()` methods. It is not necessary to remove statements prior to close. It is demonstrated here in case you wish to reuse the model or part of it.

The `close()` method returns all resources associated with the model and manages any connections to storage devices, such as closing database connections or writing out file contents.

Managing Semantic Web Data

We have demonstrated a complete life cycle of using the Jena Semantic Web Framework classes and methods in dealing with Semantic Web data. This covered creation to deallocation of Semantic Web data; however, there are other areas to consider when managing and programming Semantic Web data. These include getting information regarding your Semantic Web data, event notification of changes in your Semantic Web data, dealing with concurrent operations on your Semantic Web data, and customizing the Jena Framework. These operations reflect the realities of programming in a multiuser, event-driven environment.

Getting Information Regarding Your Semantic Web Data

Information regarding your Semantic Web data or model offers useful insights into its operations. This code demonstrates a few basic areas:

```
private void getDataStatus(Model m){
    // Test of empty
    System.out.println("Model is " + (m.isEmpty()?"":"not" )+ " empty!");
    // Size of model
    System.out.println("Model Size: " + m.size());
    // Supports Transactions?
    System.out.println("Model does " +
        (m.supportsTransactions()?"":"not" )+ "support transactions.");

    // List namespaces used within Model
    NsIterator iter = m.listNameSpaces();
    int count = 1;
    while( iter.hasNext()){
        System.out.println("Namespace  " + count++ + ": " + iter.nextNs());
    }
}
```

The preceding code performed four information-gathering methods. The `isEmpty()` method returns a Boolean regarding whether there are statements in the model. The `size()` method returns the number of asserted statements or a lower bound of statements when including inferred statements. The `supportsTransactions()` method indicates whether the model handles traditional transactions. With transactions, all modifications occur atomically or not at all. The Model interface supports transactions with a `begin()` method to mark the start of the transaction modifications to the model. The end of the transaction is marked with either the `commit()` method to execute all modifications or the `abort()` method to discard all modifications. The `listNameSpaces()` method lists all the namespace abbreviations contained within the model. You can add namespace abbreviations at any time through the static class `PrefixMapping.Factory` methods that are inherited by the Jena `Model` class.

Generating Events Based on Semantic Web Data

Event-driven programming allows your program to react to events rather than loop waiting for them to occur or worse, never realizing that a critical event occurred. In addition, loop constructs incur latency waiting for the next call of the polling loop. Typically, event-driven programming allows the application to register interest in a given event with an associated callback function. This allows efficient reactions to critical programming events. For example, reasoners take advantage of events by employing callbacks to adjust entailments resulting from modifications in the model.

The Jena Framework works similarly. Your application registers a callback object for a given event of interest. The callback object includes several different event methods. The framework executes the callback method when the appropriate event occurs, possibly passing context regarding the event. The Jena Framework lets your application subscribe to the following events:

- Any object added or removed from a specified model
- A single statement added to or removed from a specified model
- A list of statements added to or removed from a specified model
- A model added to or removed from the specified model
- An array of statements added to or removed from a specified model
- Contents of a statement iterator (`StmtIterator`) added to or removed from a specified model

The Jena Framework offers a base class, `ObjectListener`, to handle callbacks. Your application need only extend this class and then register an object of this class with the specific model. Following is an example of an extension to the `ObjectListener` class:

```
public class JenaListener extends ObjectListener {
    String modelName=null;
```

```
JenaListener( Model m, String name){
    modelName = name;
}

public void notifyEvent(Model m, Object o){
    System.out.println(modelName + ": Event Occured");
}

public void addedStatement(Statement s){
    System.out.println(modelName + ": Statement added");
}
}
```

The class `JenaListener` extends the Jena class, `ObjectListener`. The constructor receives the name of the model to use in console output. The class overrides two event methods, `notifyEvent()` and `addedStatement()`. Both merely print out a message. Nevertheless, they are provided with the context of the event, allowing a more powerful operation. We need to create an object based on this class and then associate it with a model that requires events processing. The following code does just that:

```
private JenaListener _listenerMem = null, _listenerDB = null;

private void setEventListener(){
    _modelDB.register(_listenerDB);
    _modelMem.register(_listenerMem);
}
```

We created two objects based on `JenaListener` class: one associated with the memory model and one associated with the database model. We then registered the appropriate one with each model using the `register()` method. Now, every time a single statement is added to either model, the `addedStatement()` callback method for the correct model executes.

Dealing with Concurrency and Your Semantic Web Data

Concurrency within a Jena model occurs in two ways: concurrent access within the same application because of multiple threads and concurrent access from multiple applications including multiple users. We deal with each one in different ways. Concurrent operations devoid of control mechanisms such as locks can provide inconsistent, corrupt results when performing multiple operations on the model. Defects resulting from concurrent interference are hard to localize because of the intermittent nature of concurrent operations.

Concurrent activities from different threads in the same application can cause data inconsistencies because the Jena Framework is not inherently thread-safe. Jena model iterators are especially suspect: they do not make a copy; rather they keep going back to the model for each iteration. Therefore your application must take additional steps if doing concurrent operations because of multiple threads. The Jena Framework contains a basic locking approach within each model. The following code demonstrates the declaration of a critical region within model access.

```
private void criticalRegionWrite(){
    try {
        _modelMem.enterCriticalSection(Lock.WRITE);
        // Do critical stuff writing to model
    }
    finally {  // make sure you always give it up
        _modelMem.leaveCriticalSection();
    }
}
```

Each model controls a lock for either writing or reading. The enterCritical Section() method acquires a lock for the appropriate action, reading or writing. A read lock prevents other threads from creating a write lock but allows any other thread to create a read lock. A write lock prevents other threads from establishing either a read or write lock. The method blocks if the lock is not available. The leaveCriticalSection() method returns the lock and wakes up any threads awaiting a lock. The basic approach used in the Jena Framework creates possible deadlocks, so your application must always release the lock. This is accomplished by using the *finally* clause in a *try/catch* and calling the leaveCriticalSection() method. You can use a Java timer to escape from a deadlock condition if the block takes too long—or better yet, use the Java 1.5 Lock class, which allows interruptions generated by a timer. Keeping a lock for extended time periods can cause serious performance issues with the overall application.

Concurrent activities from different applications and users are not addressed directly by the Jena Framework. Rather, the Jena Framework depends on managing external threads from a web server or using database locking for such concurrent operations. The latter requires the use of a Jena model based on a transaction-supporting database. The code example uses transactions. This would provide the necessary thread protection during concurrent operations.

```
private void transactionModel() throws BackingStoreException {
    try {
        if (_modelDB.supportsTransactions() != true){
            BackingStoreException exc =
                new BackingStoreException("Does not support transactions");
            throw exc;
        }
        _modelDB.getGraph().getTransactionHandler().begin();
        // Do transaction stuff
```

```
      _modelDB.getGraph().getTransactionHandler().commit();
      }
   catch (Exception e) {
      System.out.println("Transaction aborted due to " +
            e.getMessage());
      _modelDB.getGraph().getTransactionHandler().abort();
   }
}
```

The example tests whether the model supports transactions. If so, it starts a transaction and then appropriately commits or aborts the transaction. Locking would occur automatically depending on the database configuration. Just in case of an unexpected exception, the program aborts the current transaction with the abort() method. It is not recommended to catch all exceptions but it is coded here for simplicity.

Customizing the Jena Framework

The Jena Framework allows customized implementations to provide flexibility. Remember that a model actually consists of a collection of objects that implement a Jena Graph interface. The Jena Graph interface provides a limited set of methods (see the Jena Javadocs for a complete list). Your application can create a Java class that implements the Jena Graph interface to customize graph behaviors such as altering the persistence implementation. For example, your application could align the memory to achieve certain performance efficiencies given your particular application. Creating a custom model requires two steps: the creation of the customized graph-based object and then the creation of the model based on the customized Graph object. The following example demonstrates the basic structure:

```
Model _customModel = null;

private void createCustomModel(){
   CustomGraph myGraph = new CustomGraph();
   _customModel = ModelFactory.createModelForGraph(myGraph);
}

public class CustomGraph implements Graph {

   public void close() {
   }

   public boolean contains(Triple arg0) {
      return false;
   }

   public boolean contains(Node arg0, Node arg1, Node arg2) {
```

```
        return false;
    }

    public void delete(Triple arg0) throws DeleteDeniedException {
    }

    public boolean dependsOn(Graph arg0) {
        return false;
    }

    public ExtendedIterator find(TripleMatch arg0) {
        return null;
    }

    public ExtendedIterator find(Node arg0, Node arg1, Node arg2) {
        return null;
    }

    public BulkUpdateHandler getBulkUpdateHandler() {
        return new CustomBulkUpdateHandler();
    }

    public Capabilities getCapabilities() {
        return null;
    }

    public GraphEventManager getEventManager() {
        return new CustomGraphEventManager();
    }

    public PrefixMapping getPrefixMapping() {
        return new CustomPrefixMapping();
    }

    public Reifier getReifier() {
        return new CustomReifier();
    }

    public GraphStatisticsHandler getStatisticsHandler() {
        return new CustomGraphStatisticsHandler();
    }

    public TransactionHandler getTransactionHandler() {
        return new CustomTransactionHandler();
    }

    public boolean isClosed() {
        return false;
    }
```

```
public boolean isEmpty() {
   return false;
}

public boolean isIsomorphicWith(Graph arg0) {
   return false;
}

public QueryHandler queryHandler() {
   return null;
}

public int size() {
   return 0;
}

public void add(Triple arg0) throws AddDeniedException {
}
}
```

We declare a model, _customModel. Then we declare the customized Graph object, myGraph. (Note that this is notional implementation that wouldn't do much for your Semantic Web data because it contains only empty methods.) We then use the ModelFactory.createModelforGraph() method, passing in the myGraph object. We successfully substitute a new storage behavior. All code within your application that uses the model methods remains unaware of the substitution. Here we basically created a Unix /dev/null.

Serializing Semantic Web Data

Serialization offers the ability to transmit the model via various means and then reconstitute it on its reception. Models and Graph objects are not directly serializable. Nevertheless, you can take advantage of a model's capability to export a stream into a buffer that you can serialize. The following code illustrates the serialization:

```
public byte [] exportModel(){
ByteArrayOutputStream io = new ByteArrayOutputStream();
model.write(io);
return (io.toByteArray());
}

SerializableModel serialModel =
      new SerialzableModel( model.exportModel);

public class SerializableModel implements Serializable {
      private byte graphbuf[];
```

```
SerializableModel( byte graph[]){
graphbuf = graph;
 }

public SemanticObject importModel(byte[] buf){
    ByteArrayInputStream input = new ByteArrayInputStream(buf);
    model.read(input,defaultNameSpace);
    return this;
}
```

The first method exports the model data into a `ByteArrayOutputstream`. The stream is then copied to the array. This byte array is an object variable in the new class, `SerializableModel`, which implements `Serializable`. Once it is in this form, the entire model can be stored or transmitted. The serialized data then can be reconstituted through a reverse operation.

Common App Overview: FriendTracker

Our common application puts the Jena Framework and the associated concepts to work in building an application that spans the next three chapters. Here we introduce the project and outline the upcoming chapter coverage. Each chapter covers a major aspect of using Semantic Web data with the application.

The FriendTracker application integrates several different online information sources regarding one's friends. The information merges into one Semantic Web data model where the FriendTracker can search, navigate, and query across all the sources as if they were in one model. This creates a world of possibilities: you can track your friends across multiple sites and services. In a sense, a real semantic concept of your friends emerges rather than `joe2345@aol.com` and joe on Facebook. The FriendTracker lets you keep up with your friends as they cross from one site to the next. That's not all; the FriendTracker also allows you to export the information in many formats in addition to a Semantic Web format. Thus, the FriendTracker shares the information with non-Semantic Web parties.

Of course, the main goal is not to produce a cool application but rather to show off cool Semantic Web applications. We do this using the tools outlined so far, from RDF to SPARQL to the Jena Semantic Web Framework we covered in this chapter.

The FriendTracker has three technical goals that align with the next three chapters:

■ Input data into a Semantic Web data model from several common online sources. This requires interfacing via different protocols and syntax and then performing a translation to a Semantic Web data format. The FriendTracker inputs from four diverse sources of data, including Jabber Instant Messaging via the XMPP protocol, Facebook via its Restful XML interface, upcoming.org (an event service from Yahoo) via a standard file format, and WordPress blogger via an interface into the MySQL relational database.

▪ Align the diverse semantics into one unified knowledgebase. This requires aligning the semantics across the various sources—so a friend is really a friend regardless of the specific name employed, such as friend, associate, partner, and the like. This allows seamless interrogation and reasoning across the diverse data set.

▪ Expose the semantic data in a variety of ways to make it available to other applications even outside the Semantic Web. This includes a SPARQL endpoint, RDFa, microformats, XML, and a simple HTML page.

Chapter 9, "Combining Information," focuses on getting data into the Semantic Web. Chapter 10, "Aligning Information," focuses on semantic alignment of the data so that queries can span the entire data set. Chapter 11, "Sharing Information," focuses on exposing the data and interrogation methods to others including non-Semantic Web methods.

Summary

This chapter covered the major operations of a Semantic Web framework and illustrated those operations using the Jena Semantic Web Framework. Hopefully, you played with the sample code and established confidence with the concepts and the Jena Semantic Web Framework implementation. Now you will put all those methods to work in the next three chapters as you build and understand the FriendTracker Semantic Web application.

Combining Information

"Words, so innocent and powerless as they are, as standing in a dictionary, how potent for good and evil they become in the hands of one who knows how to combine them."

—Nathaniel Hawthorne

Pieces of information, like the words of a sentence, are more useful and powerful when they are combined effectively. One of the major use cases in the Semantic Web involves virtually integrating information from multiple disparate sources. This process of integration can be decomposed into two primary steps: bringing data into a common data model (in the case of the Semantic Web, RDF) and describing the data using a common knowledge model. Once combined in a common data model, the aggregate information can be accessed and manipulated in a single model; however, the data is still described using different vocabularies. For data to be fully integrated it must be combined into a common data model and described using a common knowledge model.

As an illustrative example, consider two disjoint databases, each with a single table and a unique schema. One maintains the inventory at a store, and the other maintains records for the transactions made at that store. Combining these sources (as depicted in Figure 9-1) could be as simple as merging the two databases, each with a single table, into one database with two tables. By combining the data, it becomes a common data model and representation, the tables of a relational database, but the two sources are still disjoint conceptually. The two tables store information according to two distinct schemas. To bring the information together and do higher-order operations like reasoning and querying as though it were one contiguous body of information, it must be integrated conceptually.

Chapter 10, "Aligning Information," explores the techniques and technologies critical to the task of integrating data conceptually. This chapter focuses on combining data from various sources into the RDF model. More specifically, this chapter is all about the techniques and technologies that you can use to translate data from various formats into RDF. The first section of this chapter focuses on the general concept of combining information and translating other formats into RDF. The rest of the sections explore translating specific kinds of data sources into RDF, including XML feeds, relational databases, Java objects, and other representations and formats. Many but not all of the examples throughout this chapter are targeted directly at the data sources for Friend-Tracker. In some cases, the application of a particular exposure technique to one of the FriendTracker data sources acts as a supplemental example that extends the primary example. Each section covers diverse techniques and technologies, presents multiple hands-on examples, and discusses the benefits and drawbacks of each available option.

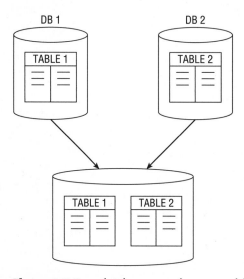

Figure 9-1 Two databases can be merged into a single database, but it's not as easy to integrate the information each contains.

The goal of these sections is not for you to become an expert in all of these technologies but rather to raise awareness of and demonstrate the application of each. The sections contain numerous hands-on programming examples and are meant to serve as a basis for extension and reuse.

The objectives for this chapter are to:

- Explore the general concept of combining information on the Semantic Web

- Introduce the various approaches to combining information and discuss the conditions under which each is most appropriate

- Work through a number of specific technology examples that expose various information sources to the Semantic Web as ontologically described RDF

- Take the first step toward establishing the FriendTracker application by demonstrating how to expose each data source as RDF

Combining Information

A huge number of formats and representations are available for use by developers and users to exchange and store information. Even among the most common, there are variations and specializations tuned to specific use cases and environments. This diversity is necessary; it exists to meet the requirements of a diverse world in which no two applications and no two environments are the same. Moreover, this diversity and competition are the driving forces behind rapid development and innovation.

Representing Information

Consider some of the most common information storage and exchange mechanisms:

- Relational databases are often used to store information in applications that must provide scalable performance under heavy user and data load.

- XML is often used as an information interchange format for applications that provide data to multiple diverse consumers.

- Comma- or tab-delimited files are often used when the data is highly volatile and users must frequently interact with and share the data.

- Proprietary file formats are often used where other more common technologies cannot adequately meet all requirements of a more standard format.

The goal of the Semantic Web is not to subvert these existing data representations. Rather, the goal is to provide tools that make it easier to integrate information across all formats and representations and schemas. RDF provides a flexible, extensible data model that eases the task of combining data sets into a common *data* model. The combination of the OWL Web Ontology Language, SWRL rules, and SPARQL query language with RDF make it easier to bring data sets together under a common *knowledge* model. These ideas are expressed in Figure 9-2.

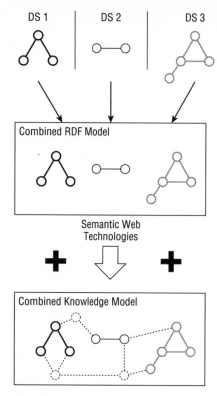

Figure 9-2 Disparate data sources can be combined into a common data model using RDF. By adding the other Semantic Web technologies, they can also be integrated into a common knowledge model.

Translating between Representations

It is challenging to translate between information representations for a number of reasons. Among these is the fact that different representations have varying levels of expressivity and make different assumptions about the underlying information. These differences arise because each representation has been designed for different users and a different environment. The consequence of these differences is that you can't always easily translate from one data representation to another; or, once you've moved to the RDF data representation, you can't always go back to the original representation without losing some expressivity. As we explore the various methods of moving between data representations, we will raise and address many of these challenges.

Following is a list of some of the more significant questions that arise during this process:

- Will any information be lost in the translation process?

- How do you maintain a record of where the translated data came from?

- Once in the new representation, is there any way to go back?
- How do you handle streaming data? Temporally and spatially varying data?
- How do you handle large volumes of data?

Addressing the Challenges of Translation

These are legitimate concerns anytime you are translating data from one representation to another. As each of the translation approaches is introduced and explained, we will raise and address these concerns.

Maintaining Fidelity

As you move data from other representations to RDF and into the Semantic Web, you will find that little detail is lost. In fact, you can gain a lot of expressivity by defining an ontology that describes the RDF data. However, there is a drawback to this condition, because attempting to translate the data back to the original representation means losing any expressivity that was gained. This issue is touched on in the upcoming subsection "Reversing the Process."

Tracking Provenance Information

When you begin to pull together data from numerous sources, it becomes increasingly important to track where that data came from. We will present a number of ways to deal with provenance in large heterogeneous data sets that range from appending metadata to individuals and property values to generating base URIs that indicate the source of the data, as demonstrated in Figure 9-3.

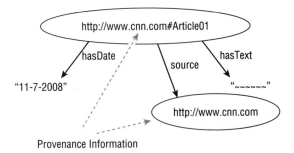

Provenance Information

Figure 9-3 Provenance information is provided using metadata and resolvable URIs. In this example, the article is clearly from CNN because the URI resolves to `http://www.cnn.com`.

Ideally, all resources have resolvable URIs that allow you to investigate the source of individuals, properties, classes, and property values and get more information about each; however, this tends to add complexity, and most of the examples we present will omit this feature.

Reversing the Process

Even if you know where the data came from, it's not always easy or even possible to go back. The transformation may involve one-way functions in which there is no straightforward way to undo or reverse the process. In addition, the data may have been augmented or enriched once it was pulled into the Semantic Web environment. If this is the case, it may not be possible to represent this new information in the source representation. This often leads to scenarios where you will move data into the Semantic Web, work with it, add depth and meaning to it, and then move back into less-expressive representations only when you have to or only temporarily in order to use a legacy application. Essentially, it can create a one-way path for data that is difficult to get around. This issue may be mitigated by asserting that data flows only one way into your Semantic Web application or that the application is read only. Otherwise, you may have to lose some of the data fidelity on the way out of the Semantic Web representations.

Handling Varying Data

Another concern with translating data is how to handle data that varies across a dimension such as time or space. Some data is static—historical records, for example. This kind of data doesn't change because it represents a piece of information with full context intact. Consider the case in which you are translating a current weather observation for your neighborhood (this will be one of the examples this chapter uses). In this case, the concept of *now* has to be codified and correctly represented with the context intact. This issue is closely connected to fundamental challenges with data representation itself, so we won't deal with it in too much detail in the coming sections; however, we'll revisit it in later chapters.

Managing Data Volume

The final question that was raised involves handling large volumes of data. As you will see in the examples you will explore, there are many different approaches to translating data that use many different technologies. Each technology has its own strengths and constraints. Among them is the ability to perform translation on a stream of data rather than having to process the entire data set at once. Unless you can subdivide your data into manageable chunks, or have enough resources available to process it all at once, you will need the ability to process the data as a stream.

Some translation techniques add additional benefits, such as the ability to perform reasoning over the data that is being processed or to perform advanced functions like string manipulation or mathematical operations. Often the features and benefits that give a method of transformation more expressiveness or power come at the cost of scalability benefits like stream processing or minimal resource requirements. Thus, managing data volume often means sacrificing some of the flexibility and features you may enjoy with a smaller data set.

The various concerns we've introduced in this section will be discussed in context in the sections that follow. Using this guidance, you will be able to select the techniques that work best for your Semantic Web programming requirements.

Introducing the FriendTracker Data Sources

FriendTracker is essentially an aggregator of information about a user's social networks. It pulls data from multiple sources of contacts and friends and events and presents all of the information in a common application. This chapter discusses the various techniques that you can employ to take data from numerous distributed data sources, each with its own format or representation or schema, and convert it into the common data model of RDF. The data sources that FriendTracker pulls information from are these:

- Facebook friend information from an XML web service
- Jabber contacts derived from the Smack Jabber client for Java
- Upcoming.org events from an XML web service
- WordPress blog entries stored in a MySQL database

Facebook provides extensive information about a user's friends and contacts but doesn't have the same depth of information regarding their real-time status or activity. Jabber can provide real-time status information about contacts but lacks the same level of biographic detail that Facebook provides. Upcoming.org provides events and activities that may be related to individuals geospatially. Finally, WordPress is a blog application that has posts from users who share common interests or activities.

Each of these data sources provides a unique perspective on an individual's social interactions. By combining them, we develop a picture of a social network that is greater than the sum of its parts.

Facebook XML Web Service

Facebook is one of the most popular social networking sites on the Internet. Once you have a Facebook account, you can establish a network of friends with whom you share pictures, messages, events, and personal information. Facebook provides a number of APIs with which applications can integrate to access a specific user's social network information. These APIs can be found at `http://developers.facebook.com`. While there is no official client API, a number of offshoot projects are developing clients for various programming languages.

The Facebook data source for FriendTracker uses a custom client API to query the web service over HTTP and retrieve the XML results as a stream. As you will see later in this chapter, the Facebook data source is exposed as RDF using XSL Transformations.

Jabber Java Client

Jabber (`http://www.jabber.org`) is a popular open-source messaging and collaboration protocol that builds on the Extensible Messaging and Presence Protocol (XMPP) to provide an open-instance messaging service. Some well-known Jabber messaging implementations include Google's chat application (GChat) and the messaging service that is integrated with Google's email service. The Jabber data source for FriendTracker uses a Java Jabber client API called Smack. Smack is maintained by Jive Software and can be found at `http://www.igniterealtime.org/projects/smack`. The Jabber data source uses Smack to access a user's contact list and then uses a streaming Turtle RDF writer to build an RDF representation of the data.

Upcoming.org XML Web Service

Upcoming.org is a website that maintains information about events and their temporal and geospatial information. The site provides an XML web service that can be accessed using HTTP to gather information about events local to a specific location. The Upcoming.org data source for FriendTracker is exposed by reading the data into custom Java classes by parsing the XML using the Document Object Model (DOM) and then using a general-purpose Java Reflection API–based RDF generator.

WordPress Relational Database

WordPress is a popular blogging application that you can download for free from `http://wordpress.org/download/`. WordPress uses a relational database to store all of its content. A PHP website queries the database to gather content and generate HTML pages to display it. The WordPress data source for FriendTracker is exposed as RDF using a tool called D2RQ. D2RQ is one of a family of tools that exposes a relational database as a virtual RDF graph. In this case, the relational database is MySQL with the WordPress schema.

Exposing XML-Based Web Services as RDF

A huge number of XML data sources are available on the World Wide Web. The prevalence of XML processing tools and XML's simplicity and flexibility have made it one of the most common formats for exchanging information. This abundance of data, even if it isn't RDF, is a great thing for you, the Semantic Web programmer; because you can take advantage of the plethora of XML technologies that are available to convert all of that XML data into ontologically described RDF.

Moving to RDF from XML is relatively straightforward because there is an XML syntax for RDF: RDF/XML. Some issues come up as a result of RDF and XML being fundamentally different data structures. XML is a tree structure made up of nodes. Each node can contain attributes that describe the node or can contain other child nodes. A node can have no children, or it can be a data node and simply store a value. XML schema can be used to describe the expected structure and data types of the nodes in an XML document. All of this can be done using RDF and OWL. Some challenges arise from the structure of XML documents. RDF represents statements that connect resources using properties in a graph-like structure. It is difficult to generate a general-purpose XML-to-RDF translator because translating structure and attribution into resources and relationships is not always straightforward. Consider the following example XML document:

```
<?xml version="1.0" ?>
<people>
   <person email="zcrawford@zeuscrawford.net" >
      <name>Zeus Crawford</name>
      <joined>1996</joined>
      <telephone>(202)555-1337</telephone>
   </person>
   <person email="darklord@semwebprogramming.net" >
      <name>Darklord Adams</name>
      <joined>1996</joined>
   </person>
</people>
```

The document contains a single element node called `people` that contains two `person` nodes. Each person has an `email` attribute, a `name` node with a text value representing the person's name, and a `joined` node specifying the date he or she joined this service. Zeus Crawford has a `telephone` node with a text value representing his telephone number. To map this XML document into an RDF representation, we need to decide how the various nodes are related.

For example, it is apparent that the `people` node represents a set of people. Each `person` node is a person who is a member of the set of people in the document. Is the collection itself relevant? Is the relationship between the collection of `people` and each individual `person` relevant? What is the best way to represent this relationship?

In this example, `person` appears to represent the type of the node (the class of objects to which it belongs). Should we treat `person` as a type or a property or both? It connects two objects, but it also identifies the type of one of the objects. These are just a few of the questions you will have to settle when you work with XML as a data source.

The following subsections focus on various approaches to generating RDF from XML data. Two approaches are presented in this section; each has its own benefits and drawbacks and may or may not be applicable based on the situation. The first approach involves translating XML into RDF using Extensible Stylesheet Language Transformations (XSLT). The second approach combines Java XML Bindings (JAXB) with the Velocity template engine to produce RDF.

Introducing the Weather.gov XML Feed

To make it easier to compare the relative merits of various approaches to exposing XML as RDF, the following examples will reuse the same XML source document. The National Oceanic and Atmospheric Administration's National Weather Service maintains a website (`http://www.weather.gov`) that contains both current and historical meteorological and hydrological data for the United States. The website contains RSS and XML feeds providing current weather observations for stations located throughout the United States. Below is a copy of the XML weather feed for a station located near the Baltimore-Washington International Airport that has been abridged for length. The full version of the XML source file can be found in each of the Chapter 9 XML-to-RDF example projects. The latest, live copy of the XML file is located on the Weather.gov website at `http://www.weather.gov/xml/current_obs/KBWI.xml`.

```
<?xml version="1.0" encoding="ISO-8859-1"?>
<current_observation version="1.0"
    xmlns:xsd="http://www.w3.org/2001/XMLSchema"
    xmlns:xsi="http://www.w3.org/2001/XMLSchema-instance"
    xsi:noNamespaceSchemaLocation=
        "http://www.weather.gov/xml/current_obs/current_observation.xsd">

    <credit>NOAA's National Weather Service</credit>
    <credit_URL>http://weather.gov/</credit_URL>
    <location>Baltimore-Washington International Airport, MD</location>
    <station_id>KBWI</station_id>
    <latitude>39.19</latitude>
```

```
    <longitude>-76.67</longitude>
    <observation_time_rfc822>
       Mon, 27 Oct 2008 12:54:00 -0400 EDT
    </observation_time_rfc822>
    <weather>Overcast</weather>
    <temp_f>50</temp_f>
    <temp_c>10</temp_c>
    <relative_humidity>43</relative_humidity>
    <wind_dir>Northwest</wind_dir>
    <wind_degrees>310</wind_degrees>
    <wind_mph>9.2</wind_mph>
    <wind_gust_mph>NA</wind_gust_mph>
    <pressure_mb>1015.5</pressure_mb>
    <dewpoint_f>28</dewpoint_f>
    <windchill_f>46</windchill_f>
    <visibility_mi>10.00</visibility_mi>
    <copyright_url>http://weather.gov/disclaimer.html</copyright_url>
</current_observation>
```

Exposing XML Using XSL Transformations

XSL Transformations (XSLT) is an XML language that is used to transform XML documents into other XML documents. The typical use pattern involves a processor that combines an XML source document with an XSLT document to generate an output XML document. The XSLT contains template rules that specify how to translate the elements of the source XML document into elements of the output document. This chapter primarily deals with features of XSLT 1.0. As a quick introduction, recall the XML weather feed from the last section and consider the XSLT document that transforms it into RDF/XML.

```
<?xml version="1.0"?>
<xsl:stylesheet xmlns:xsl="http://www.w3.org/1999/XSL/Transform"
  xmlns:rdf="http://www.w3.org/1999/02/22-rdf-syntax-ns#"
  xmlns:w="http://www.semwebprogramming.net/2009/04/weather-ont#"
  xml:base="http://www.semwebprogramming.net/weather"
  version="1.0">

  <xsl:output method="xml" version="1.0" encoding="UTF-8"
    indent="yes" />

  <xsl:template match="/">
   <rdf:RDF
     xmlns:rdf="http://www.w3.org/1999/02/22-rdf-syntax-ns#"
     xmlns:rdfs="http://www.w3.org/2000/01/rdf-schema#"
     xmlns:owl="http://www.w3.org/2002/07/owl#"
     xmlns:xsd="http://www.w3.org/2001/XMLSchema#"
     xml:base="http://www.semwebprogramming.net/weather#"
     xmlns = "http://www.semwebprogramming.net/weather#"
     >
```

```
      <xsl:apply-templates />
    </rdf:RDF>
  </xsl:template>

  <xsl:template match="current_observation">
    <w:WeatherObservation>

      <w:source rdf:resource="{credit_URL}"/>
      <w:time>
        <xsl:value-of select="observation_time_rfc822"/>
      </w:time>
      <w:location><xsl:value-of select="location"/></w:location>
      <w:latitude><xsl:value-of select="latitude"/></w:latitude>
      <w:longitude><xsl:value-of select="longitude"/></w:longitude>

      <w:temperature_f>
        <xsl:value-of select="temp_f "/>
      </w:temperature_f>
      <w:windDirection rdf:resource="#{wind_dir}"/>
      <w:wind_mph><xsl:value-of select="wind_mph"/></w:wind_mph>

      <xsl:if test="wind_gust_mph != 'NA'">
        <w:wind_gust_mph>
          <xsl:value-of select="wind_gust_mph"/>
        </w:wind_gust_mph>
      </xsl:if>

      <xsl:if test="weather">
        <w:weatherDescription>
          <xsl:value-of select="weather"/>
        </w:weatherDescription>
      </xsl:if>

      <w:copyright rdf:resource="{copyright_url}"/>
    </w:WeatherObservation>
  </xsl:template>
</xsl:stylesheet>
```

The document contains the stylesheet definition identified by the element `xsl:stylesheet`, an output definition (`xsl:output`), and two rule templates (`xsl:template`). The `xsl:stylesheet` node defines the `xsl`, `rdf`, and `w` namespaces and identifies the version of XSLT being used. The namespaces of both the input and output documents have to be defined for the XSLT processor to be able to generate the output document correctly. The `xsl:output` node optionally specifies that the output document is going to be XML, that the encoding of the output document is UTF-8, and that the output document should be produced with indenting. The XSLT defines two `xsl:template` elements that are applied to the elements of the source XML document to perform the transformation and generate the output XML document.

When the XSLT processor is run, it will parse the source XML document and then try to apply the templates contained in the XSLT document to the nodes of the XML tree, starting with the root node and traversing the tree in a depth-first manner. At each node, the templates of the XSLT are applied if the XML Path (XPath) pattern specified in the `match` attribute of the template matches the node of the source XML document. A template contains output text or XML that will be generated along with embedded XSLT tags that perform further processing. XSLT uses XPath to match a specific node or set of nodes in the source document, and then it applies the appropriate template to each of these nodes. The templates process the structure and values of the nodes to generate an output document. Various XSLT elements are used to control the logical processing of the XML nodes in the source document and to control the generation of the output XML document. The coming sections will explore many of these elements, but first it's important to spend some time introducing XPath.

Traversing XML Documents with XPath

XPath is a W3C standard language used to build path expressions that identify specific nodes or sets of nodes in an XML document. The current version of XPath is 2.0, although the examples discussed here deal only with features from 1.0. Path expressions are constructed using a series of baseline expressions combined with predicates, wildcards, and other operators. XPath path expressions resemble directory paths in traditional file systems. A path expression consists of a series of expressions separated by the / character. Each expression represents a step through the hierarchical structure of an XML document and toward the XML node or nodes that the path expression identifies. Table 9-1 lists some of the expressions that can be used in an XPath path expression and provides a description of each.

Table 9-1 Elements of an XML Path Expression

EXPRESSION	INTERPRETATION
/	When used at the beginning of a path expression, identifies the root of the document.
node-name	Identifies the node node-name.
@	Identifies the attributes of the current node.
.	Identifies the current node.
..	Identifies the parent of the current node.
//	Identifies the descendants of the current node, regardless of where they are in the document.

Path expressions are composed by concatenating the above elements with the / delimiter. Like directory paths, path expressions are interpreted relative to the current node, unless they start with /, in which case they are considered absolute paths that start with the root node of the XML document. When an XPath path expression is interpreted, the node or nodes identified by it become the current node, against which all nested relative path expressions are interpreted. Absolute path expressions are always interpreted relative to the root of the document. To help clarify how path expressions can be constructed, consider the path expressions in Table 9-2 as they are applied to the XML document from the first code example.

Table 9-2 Example Path Expressions Applied to the XML Document

PATH EXPRESSION	INTERPRETATION
/current_observation	Matches current_observation nodes that are at the root of the document
location	Matches location nodes that are anywhere among the descendents of the current node
/current_observation/latitude	Matches latitude nodes that are the children of current_observation nodes that are at the root of the document
location/../@	Matches attributes of the parent of location nodes that are anywhere among the descendents of the current node
/current_observation//wind_mph	Matches wind_mph nodes that are anywhere among the descendents of current_observation nodes that are at the root of the document

XPath provides expression predicates that can be used to identify a specific node within the XML document based on its position or value. Predicates are appended to expressions and contained within square brackets, [...], and contain comparisons and functions that further constrain the node or nodes that should match the expression. In addition, multiple path expressions can be composed using the | character, which acts as a union operator over multiple path expressions. Table 9-3 contains notional path expressions that demonstrate some of the predicates and the optional syntax.

XPath provides many more functions and features for identifying specific nodes and sets of nodes within an XML document. This section has only started to scratch the surface and should be treated as a quick introduction to open your eyes to the potential applications of this technology. For more information on XPath, there are numerous excellent online references and tutorials. The official XML Path Language reference can be found online at `http://www.w3.org/TR/xpath`.

Table 9-3 Example Path Expressions with Predicates and Unions

PATH EXPRESSION	INTERPRETATION
`nodeA[1]/nodeB`	Matches the `nodeB` node of the first `nodeA` node (Note: this indexing scheme is ones-based.)
`nodeA[last() - 1]`	Matches the second-to-last `nodeA` node
`nodeA[@attributeC]`	Matches all `nodeA` nodes that have an `attributeC` attribute
`nodeA | nodeB`	Matches `nodeA` nodes or `nodeB` nodes
`nodeA[valueD < 10]`	Matches `nodeA` nodes that have `valueD` nodes with value less than 10 (Note: in your XSLT file, you must escape the > and < characters using > and <.)

Applying XSLT to a Simple Example

Now that you've been introduced to XPath, one of the critical aspects of XSLT, it's time to return to the example XML and XSL files from the preceding examples. The XSLT processor will begin the process with the document's root node. The first of the two templates will match the root node (because the match path expression is simply the root node identifier `/`). The first template creates the `rdf:RDF` element of the output document along with all of the required namespace declarations and then calls `apply-templates`. This instructs the processor to reapply all the templates to the children of the current node, which is the root of the input document.

At this point, the processor will move onto the `current_observation` node, matching to it the second template. The second template contains a number of XSLT elements that are each used to guide the construction of the output document. It is listed here:

```
<xsl:template match="current_observation">
  <w:WeatherObservation>

    <w:source rdf:resource="{credit_URL}"/>
    <w:time>
      <xsl:value-of select="observation_time_rfc822"/>
    </w:time>
    <w:location><xsl:value-of select="location"/></w:location>
    <w:latitude><xsl:value-of select="latitude"/></w:latitude>
    <w:longitude><xsl:value-of select="longitude"/></w:longitude>
```

```
        <w:temperature_f>
          <xsl:value-of select="temp_f "/>
        </w:temperature_f>
        <w:windDirection rdf:resource="#{wind_dir}"/>
        <w:wind_mph><xsl:value-of select="wind_mph"/></w:wind_mph>

        <xsl:if test="wind_gust_mph != 'NA'">
          <w:wind_gust_mph>
            <xsl:value-of select="wind_gust_mph"/>
          </w:wind_gust_mph>
        </xsl:if>

        <xsl:if test="weather">
          <w:weatherDescription>
            <xsl:value-of select="weather"/>
          </w:weatherDescription>
        </xsl:if>

        <w:copyright rdf:resource="{copyright_url}"/>
      </w:WeatherObservation>
    </xsl:template>
```

The first thing the template does is create the `<w:WeatherObservation>` node in the output document. This creates a new individual of type `w:WeatherObservation`. The template does not bother to assign a URI to the new individual, so it remains an anonymous node in the RDF model.

> ▋**CAUTION** There is a significant reason why the `w:WeatherObservation` individual is left anonymous and not assigned a consistent URI. The instance in the generated RDF represents a snapshot in time of the current weather. Thus, the results of the conversion process will change periodically as it is run. Using consistent URIs to identify the instance could lead to a situation where multiple distinct weather observations share the same URI. If the two instances are both loaded into the same RDF model, there will be no way to tell which measurements correspond to which weather observation. By leaving the instances anonymous, they will be kept separate anytime they cohabitate an RDF model.

Among the contents of the template you will notice a number of `xsl` elements. These elements instruct the XSLT processor how to generate the output document based on the input. Take a look at the first few lines of the template.

```
<w:source rdf:resource="{credit_URL}"/>
<w:time>
  <xsl:value-of select="observation_time_rfc822"/>
</w:time>
```

These lines of the template instruct the XSLT processor to create new XML nodes in the output document for `w:source` and `w:time`. The node `w:source` is created with an attribute `rdf:resource` that has the value `"{credit_URL}"`. Also, the node `w:time` is created with a child text node that has the value `<xsl:value-of select="observation_time_rfc822"/>`. The first element here to familiarize yourself with is `<xsl:value-of>`. This element tells the processor to insert into the current position in the output document a new node with a value that matches the node in the source document that matches the `select` path expression. In this case, it will insert into the output document a new node with the value of the `observation_time_rfc822` node from the source document.

The element `<xsl:value-of>` is used to output node values into the output document. Attribute values are output using a slightly different syntax that involves the curly braces: `{...}`. This is important to note because it is a critical feature when you want to construct resource references in your output RDF/XML. If more than one node matches the select, only the first match that the parser comes across is processed. When more than one node is expected and you want to output all of them, you should use a nested loop.

Once you are comfortable with the two elements that we just introduced, most of the rest of the template is nothing unusual. It's the same basic principle applied to the other nodes in the source document that are being transformed into nodes in the output document. The lines of the template are nothing new until the two occurrences of the `<xsl:if>` element shown here:

```
<xsl:if test="wind_gust_mph != 'NA'">
  <w:wind_gust_mph>
    <xsl:value-of select="wind_gust_mph"/>
  </w:wind_gust_mph>
</xsl:if>

<xsl:if test="weather">
  <w:weatherDescription>
    <xsl:value-of select="weather"/>
  </w:weatherDescription>
</xsl:if>
```

The element `<xsl:if>` represents a conditional and allows you to perform a test on a value, processing the child commands of the element only if the test is passed. The `test` attribute identifies the condition of the element. The first conditional has a `test` attribute with the value `"wind_gust_mph != 'NA'"` and passes only when the value of the `wind_gust_mph` node is not equal to `'NA'`. The weather XML feed occasionally outputs a value of `'NA'` when no data is available for wind gust speed. The output RDF document should contain only measurements, so the XSLT should omit any values that are `'NA'`. When the test passes, the template generates a new node with the correct value in the output document.

The second conditional has a test attribute with the value `"weather"`. This test passes only when a `weather` node exists as a child of the current node. The input weather XML file sometimes omits the `weather` node, so the XSLT must test for its presence before generating anything in the output document based on it. Otherwise, the output RDF document might contain an empty literal. The `test` attribute can be any valid path expression or function that evaluates to true or false. Through XPath, XSLT supports many mathematical, boolean, as well as built-in functions that can be used as part of the test of a conditional or path expression. For more information, consult the official XSLT language specification at `http://www.w3.org/TR/xslt`.

The XSLT processor will continue the depth-first traversal of the XML tree, processing each node and generating nodes in the output document until no more nodes are unvisited. At that point, the process terminates and the output document is complete. For this weather example, the output RDF/XML document is as follows:

```
<?xml version="1.0" encoding="UTF-8"?>
<rdf:RDF xmlns:xsd="http://www.w3.org/2001/XMLSchema#"
  xmlns:w="http://www.semwebprogramming.net/2009/04/weather-ont#"
  xmlns:owl="http://www.w3.org/2002/07/owl#"
  xmlns:rdf="http://www.w3.org/1999/02/22-rdf-syntax-ns#"
  xmlns:rdfs="http://www.w3.org/2000/01/rdf-schema#"
  xmlns="http://www.semwebprogramming.net/weather#"
  xml:base="http://www.semwebprogramming.net/weather">

  <w:WeatherObservation>
    <w:source rdf:resource="http://weather.gov/"/>
    <w:time>Sun, 19 Oct 2008 14:54:00 -0400 EDT</w:time>
    <w:location>
      Baltimore-Washington International Airport, MD
    </w:location>
    <w:latitude>39.19</w:latitude>
    <w:longitude>-76.67</w:longitude>
    <w:temperature_f>57</w:temperature_f>
    <w:windDirection rdf:resource="#Northeast"/>
    <w:wind_mph>10.35</w:wind_mph>
    <w:wind_gust_mph>22</w:wind_gust_mph>
    <w:weatherDescription>Partly Cloudy</w:weatherDescription>
    <w:copyright rdf:resource="http://weather.gov/disclaimer.html"/>
  </w:WeatherObservation>
</rdf:RDF>
```

The result is an RDF/XML document that reflects the information contained in the XML source document. This example is relatively straightforward because the XML contains only a single `weather_observation` node, and the XML structure very closely resembles an object with a series of properties.

Processing becomes more complicated when the source XML document becomes more complicated, as you will see in the later example that uses XSLT to convert XML data retrieved from Facebook's RESTful API in order to integrate it into FriendTracker. As a reference, Table 9-4 describes some of the most useful XSLT elements.

Table 9-4 Other Useful XSLT Elements

ELEMENT	DESCRIPTION
apply-templates	Applies a template or all templates to the current node.
call-template	Applies a named template to the current node.
for-each	Loops through each node in a node set.
if	Applies a template if the condition is true.
choose, when, otherwise	Used in conjunction to specify a multiple-option conditional with a default value. Similar to a switch block in Java.
text	Writes text directly to the output document.

We haven't touched on a number of aspects of XSLT so far in this section. XSLT is a very powerful language, and a complete exploration of it is well out of the scope of this book. Fear not, because as we already pointed out, there are many excellent resources available on the Web that you can use to learn more about this and other related technologies, including http://www.w3.org/Style/XSL/.

Processing XML and XSLT Programmatically

So far, we've presented a full example of using XSLT to transform XML information into RDF/XML. The next step is to put this knowledge into action and build an application that combines an XML source document with an XSLT to produce an output RDF document. The example in this subsection is a simple client application that uses Java's XSLT libraries to generate RDF/XML from an input XML document and an already constructed XSLT document. The application builds an RDF/XML file and then reads the file into a Jena model in order to validate the syntax of the RDF and output it in Turtle format.

The source code for the example application is listed here. It has been abridged to make it shorter and easier to read. The exception handling has been simplified and some of the error checking has been removed. The full source code is available in the programming examples that accompany this chapter. The project for this programming example is called `WeatherToRdfWithXslt`.

```
public class WeatherToRdfWithXslt
{
    public static void main(String[] args)
    {
        String xmlFile = args[0];
        String xslFile = args[1];
        String outputFile = args[2];

        try
        {
            //create the output turtle file
            FileOutputStream outputStream =
                new FileOutputStream(outputFile);

            //get the xml file input
            URL xmlFileUrl = new URL(xmlFile);
            InputStream xmlFileInputStream = xmlFileUrl.openStream();

            //get the xsl file input
            FileInputStream xslInputStream = new FileInputStream(xslFile);

            //set up an output stream we can redirect to the jena model
            ByteArrayOutputStream transformOutputStream =
                new ByteArrayOutputStream();

            //transform the xml document into rdf/xml
            TransformerFactory factory = TransformerFactory.newInstance();
            StreamSource xslSource = new StreamSource(xslInputStream);
            StreamSource xmlSource = new StreamSource(xmlFileInputStream);
            StreamResult outResult =
                new StreamResult(transformOutputStream);

            Transformer transformer = factory.newTransformer(xslSource);
            transformer.transform(xmlSource, outResult);
            transformOutputStream.close();

            //build a jena model so we can serialize to Turtle
            ByteArrayInputStream modelInputStream =
                new ByteArrayInputStream(
                    transformOutputStream.toByteArray());

            Model rdfModel = ModelFactory.createDefaultModel();
            rdfModel.read(modelInputStream, null, "RDF/XML");
            rdfModel.write(outputStream, "TURTLE");
            outputStream.flush();
```

```
        System.out.println("Success.");
      }catch(Exception e){}
  }
}
```

Most of the first half of the application involves setting up the streams for the input and output files. After they have been created, the XSLT transform is applied by the following code:

```
TransformerFactory factory = TransformerFactory.newInstance();
StreamSource xslSource = new StreamSource(xslInputStream);
StreamSource xmlSource = new StreamSource(xmlFileInputStream);
StreamResult outResult =
   new StreamResult(transformOutputStream);

Transformer transformer = factory.newTransformer(xslSource);
transformer.transform(xmlSource, outResult);
transformOutputStream.close();
```

The first step is to get a reference to a new `TransformerFactory` object and create `StreamSource` and `StreamResult` wrapper objects for our input and output streams. The next step is to create a new `Transformer` object that will perform the XSL transformation. The `Transformer` instance must be created with a reference to the source XSLT document. After that, simply call the transform method on the `Transformer` instance, passing in the source XML document's `StreamSource` and the output XML document's `StreamResult`. To make sure the output XML document's output stream is complete, the final line in the code snippet closes the stream. At this point, the output stream `transformOutputStream` contains the output XML document. If you were to run this application with the weather input XML document and the XSLT document, the RDF/XML document would be sitting in that output stream at this point in the application.

The final step in this application is to validate the generated RDF by loading it into a Jena model and then outputting it in Turtle format. This is no different from the other examples that manipulate data using a Jena model. First the model is created. Then the source RDF/XML data is loaded. Finally the Turtle output file is generated. The code for each step is listed here:

```
//build a jena model so we can serialize to Turtle
ByteArrayInputStream
 modelInputStream = new ByteArrayInputStream(
transformOutputStream.toByteArray());

Model rdfModel = ModelFactory.createDefaultModel();
rdfModel.read(modelInputStream, null, "RDF/XML");
rdfModel.write(outputStream, "TURTLE");
outputStream.flush();
```

The only trick to this code is that the first step is to convert the OutputStream from the XSL Transformation step into an InputStream that the Jena model can read. Running this application against the input XML document and the XSLT document produces the following RDF document in Turtle. Notice that this is the same data as before, only serialized as Turtle instead of RDF/XML.

```
[]    rdf:type w:WeatherObservation ;
      w:copyright <http://weather.gov/disclaimer.html> ;
      w:latitude "39.19" ;
      w:longitude "-76.67" ;
      w:location "Baltimore-Washington International Airport, MD" ;
      w:source <http://weather.gov/> ;
      w:temperature_f "57" ;
      w:time  "Sun, 19 Oct 2008 14:54:00 -0400 EDT" ;
      w:weatherDescription
            "Partly Cloudy" ;
      w:windDirection :Northeast ;
      w:wind_gust_mph "22" ;
      w:wind_mph "10.35" .
```

The input parameters that were used to generate the output were file:conf/KBWI.xml conf/weatherRdf.xslt output.ttl. The first parameter is a relative file URL pointing at the local copy of the weather observation XML file for Baltimore-Washington International Airport, MD. The second parameter is a file location for the XSLT document that specifies the transformation. Finally, the third parameter is the file location of the output document. The first parameter can be substituted with the URL of the live XML feed, which is http://www.weather.gov/xml/current_obs/KBWI.xml.

A few details to note at this point are that the XSLT doesn't transform all of the data in the source XML file, and the output RDF doesn't contain any data types. Each of these details is easy to address by extending the XSLT to cover more of the elements of the source XML document and by adding datatype attributes to the nodes of the output RDF/XML document. Other than that, notice that the output document contains a single w:WeatherObservation object that has a series of properties, some with literal values and some with resources as values.

Applying XSLT to the Facebook Data Source

The Facebook data source for FriendTracker uses XSLT to transform an XML data feed that is acquired using Facebook's web service. The client that interfaces with the web service is contained in the FriendTracker code that accompanies the book. The client does a lot of work to authenticate with Facebook and establish a session for the user whose information is being accessed. It's not critical to the topics of the book but is available for reference for the curious.

The two pieces of the Facebook data source worth taking a look at are the XML data feed that is retrieved from the web service and the XSLT that transforms that data into RDF/XML that is then read into a Jena model and ultimately output as Turtle. The same basic code is used in the Facebook data source to process the XML and XSLT that was used in the Weather.gov example.

Following is a small excerpt from an XML feed that contains the friends of a Facebook user and all of their user information:

```
<?xml version="1.0" encoding="UTF-8"?>
<users_getInfo_response
  xmlns="http://api.facebook.com/1.0/"
  xmlns:xsi="http://www.w3.org/2001/XMLSchema-instance"
  xsi:schemaLocation="http://api.facebook.com/1.0/
  http://api.facebook.com/1.0/facebook.xsd" list="true">
  <user>
    <uid>9999</uid>
    <about_me/>
    <activities>doin cool stuff...</activities>
    <affiliations list="true">
      <affiliation>
        <nid>999999</nid>
        <name>College Park, MD</name>
        <type>region</type>
        <status/>
        <year>2004</year>
      </affiliation>
    </affiliations>
    <birthday>September 13, 1982</birthday>
    <books>Brave New World, The Phantom Tollbooth, any Tolstoy</books>
    <current_location>
      <city/>
      <state>Maryland</state>
      <country>United States</country>
    </current_location>
    <first_name>Ryan</first_name>
    <interests>Computers, cars, bikes</interests>
    <locale>en_US</locale>
    <meeting_for xsi:nil="true"/>
    <movies>Fight Club, Casino Royale, all the Bourne Films</movies>
    <music>Tool, Nine Inch Nails, George Winston</music>
    <name>Ryan Blace</name>
    <pic>http://example.org/picture1.jpg</pic>
    <political/>
    <relationship_status>Married</relationship_status>
    <sex>male</sex>
    <tv>Lost, Daily Show, Colbert Report, Formula 1 Racing</tv>
  </user>
</users_getInfo_response>
```

The XSLT that transforms this XML document can be found in the Facebook project as well. It is located at `./conf/facebook.xsl`. As we highlight different aspects of the XML feed, the corresponding sections of the XSLT will be shown and discussed. The first characteristic of the Facebook XML feed to notice is that, unlike the Weather.gov XML feed, the Facebook XML document has a base namespace. The namespace is highlighted in the following XML:

```
<?xml version="1.0" encoding="UTF-8"?>
<users_getInfo_response
   xmlns="http://api.facebook.com/1.0/"
   xmlns:xsi="http://www.w3.org/2001/XMLSchema-instance"
   xsi:schemaLocation="http://api.facebook.com/1.0/
   http://api.facebook.com/1.0/facebook.xsd" list="true">
```

The reason why this is significant is that it means that the XSLT must define that namespace and refer to it in the XPath expressions in order for the expressions to match the source XML document. The following excerpts from the Facebook XSL file will make this point clearer:

```
<?xml version="1.0"?>
<xsl:stylesheet xmlns:xsl="http://www.w3.org/1999/XSL/Transform"
   xmlns:rdf="http://www.w3.org/1999/02/22-rdf-syntax-ns#"
   xmlns:fxml="http://api.facebook.com/1.0/"
   xmlns:f="http://www.semwebprogramming.net/2009/04/fb-ont#"
   xml:base="http://www.semwebprogramming.net/friends"
   version="1.0">
...
<xsl:template match="/fxml:users_getInfo_response">
...
</xsl:template>
```

The namespace `fxml` is the same as the base namespace from the Facebook XML feed. This namespace prefix is then used in the `match` attribute of the `xsl:template` node. This is an important thing to remember and can easily lead to difficult-to-diagnose problems in the XSLT file if it is omitted. In this example, if the `match` attribute had a value of just `"/users_getInfo_response"`, the template would never match on anything.

Notice that the XML document has a number of ways that data can be either present or missing. While some nodes are simply present or not present, depending on whether they have a text value or not, there are other nodes that are present but have no text value. Some nodes have an attribute `xsi:nil` that has a value of true if there is no value. These situations are shown in the following code snippet. `<about_me/>` is a node without any text value, and `<meeting_for xsi:nil="true"/>` also has no text value but has an attribute saying it's nil.

```
<uid>9999</uid>
<about_me/>
<activities>doin cool stuff...</activities>
<meeting_for xsi:nil="true"/>
```

Since you don't want empty literals or resources in your output RDF file, the XSLT needs to take these situations into consideration. The Weather.gov XSLT merely did an existence check on nodes before generating output. The Facebook XSLT can take that one step further and check to see that the text value of the node is not empty.

```
<xsl:if test="fxml:about_me != ''">
  <f:about_me><xsl:value-of select="fxml:about_me"/></f:about_me>
</xsl:if>
```

The Facebook XML file contains a list of `user` nodes. The XSLT handles this condition by using an `xsl:for-each` element to loop over each of the nodes. The `uid` node for each user is used to generate that user's URI. This is so that the user URIs are generated in a deterministic, consistent, and unique manner. Also notice that within the list of users is a list of affiliations that users can have with other places and organizations.

```
<affiliations list="true">
  <affiliation>
    <nid>999999</nid>
    <name>College Park, MD</name>
    <type>region</type>
    <status/>
    <year>2004</year>
  </affiliation>
</affiliations>
```

These affiliations are an interesting case study in handling this kind of XML data. If you look closely, you'll see that the affiliation is a uniquely identifiable instance that is conflated with some user-specific information. The `nid` node identifies a unique identifier that refers to the object of the affiliation itself. In this case, it's the town of College Park, MD. But the `status` and `year` nodes refer to the nature of the affiliation between the user and the affiliation instance. Ideally, the information about the uniquely identifiable instance the affiliation refers to should be separate from the information that describes the nature of the affiliation.

Two options exist as to how to handle this situation. One option is to simply translate the XML exactly as it is and leave it to a higher-level processor of the data to figure out what it means. Another option is to handle it right now in the transformation to RDF. The Facebook XSLT takes the former approach, leaving it to the consumer of the data to change it as needed. The result of applying the XSLT to the example XML data presented earlier is the following Turtle file:

```
@prefix f:          <http://www.semwebprogramming.net/2009/04/fb-ont#> .
@prefix rdfs:       <http://www.w3.org/2000/01/rdf-schema#> .
@prefix fxml:       <http://api.facebook.com/1.0/> .
@prefix xsd:        <http://www.w3.org/2001/XMLSchema#> .
@prefix owl:        <http://www.w3.org/2002/07/owl#> .
@prefix rdf:        <http://www.w3.org/1999/02/22-rdf-syntax-ns#> .
@prefix :           <http://www.semwebprogramming.net/friends#>.

<http://www.facebook.com/friends#user9999>
        rdf:type f:Friend ;
        f:activities "doin cool stuff..." ;
        f:birthday "September 13, 1982" ;
        f:books "Brave New World, The Phantom Tollbooth, any Tolstoy" ;
        f:hasAffiliation
        [
          rdf:type f:Affiliation , f:region ;
          f:affiliationId :affiliation999999 ;
          f:name   "College Park, MD"
        ] ;
        f:interests "Computers, cars, bikes" ;
        f:location
        [
          rdf:type f:Location
        ] ;
        f:movies "Fight Club, Casino Royale, all the Bourne Films" ;
        f:music "Tool, Nine Inch Nails, George Winston" ;
        f:name   "Ryan Blace" ;
        f:tv     "Lost, Daily Show, Colbert Report, Formula 1 Racing" ;
        f:uid    "9999" .
```

Weighing the Benefits and the Costs of XSLT

This section illustrated that XSLT is a very powerful and flexible tool that can be used to transform XML data into RDF/XML. One of the big benefits to using XSLT is that all of the aspects of the transformation application that are sensitive to changes in the underlying XML source data are external to the application. The entire configuration that dictates how the transformation takes place is contained in an external XSLT document. Another benefit to using XSLT is that it provides a very natural method of converting XML data to RDF/XML. That's what XSLT is designed for—to transform one XML document into another. In addition, as the example application shows, it takes a minimal amount of straightforward code to programmatically perform these transformations. A final benefit is that there is a lot of tool support for working with both XML and XSLT.

In summary, the benefits of using this approach to exposing XML as RDF are as follows:

- Transformation from XML to RDF configuration is external to the application.
- It provides a powerful language for processing and transforming XML.
- RDF has an XML concrete syntax, making XSLT a natural fit.
- The code required to process the XML and XSLT is short and simple.

There are drawbacks to XSLT as well. While it is a very powerful tool, that power comes at quite a cost. To fully express the ins and outs of XSLT and XPath would take an entire book. There's quite a steep learning curve involved in mastering the technologies. Fortunately, it's relatively easy to get up and running with simple examples. Despite the fact that the configuration for the transformation application can be entirely externalized, it does require an explicit configuration. In the common use case, XSLT is not a general-purpose XML-to-RDF tool. It requires maintenance as the underlying XML source changes, and it requires a developer to generate an XSLT document that properly converts the XML to RDF/XML.

An additional drawback to the XSLT approach outlined in this section is that it is not a streaming method of generating RDF/XML. The XSLT processor utilizes a nonstreaming parser, and the application loads the RDF/XML document into a Jena model for validation. Some technologies available that are analogous to XSLT are streaming, such as the Streaming Transformations for XML (STX) project, which can be found at `http://stx.sourceforge.net`.

In summary, the drawbacks to this approach to exposing XML as RDF include:

- XSLT is quite complex and has a steep learning curve.
- It requires configuration (XSLT file) that is manually generated.
- Changes to the XML feed may require maintenance to XSLT configuration.
- XSLT alone does not provide a streaming transformation model.
- XSLT is useful only for generating RDF in the RDF/XML syntax.

One final drawback is that XSLT is not ideal for generating RDF in syntaxes other than RDF/XML. This is because XSLT is intended for transforming XML documents. Even when run in the text output mode, it is intended that the structure of the document from which the text is generated is XML.

Exposing XML Using XML Bindings and Velocity

The previous section explored the use of XML transformation as a method of generating RDF from XML data. This section takes a slightly different approach, utilizing Java XML Bindings (JAXB) to unmarshal data from an XML document into Java objects and then using the Velocity template engine to generate an RDF/XML document based on that data. Once again, the resulting RDF will be loaded into a Jena model for validation and to be converted to the Turtle syntax. In order to maintain a consistent perspective on the various technologies being utilized, this section reuses the same XML weather feed from the Weather.gov website.

This technique to exposing XML as RDF is different from the XSLT approach because it uses Java as an intermediate format for the data. This is significant because once in Java, the data can be manipulated in almost endless ways that it could not necessarily have been using XSLT. In addition, this section introduces the idea of using a template engine to generate RDF based on Java objects. Velocity is a general-purpose template engine that can be used to do this. There are a number of other similar technologies, like the JavaServer Pages Standard Tag Library (JSTL), that can be used in a similar fashion.

There are three phases to this process, illustrated in Figure 9-4. The first involves generating the Java bindings for the XML data, based on its XML schema. This involves analyzing the XML schema and generating a set of Java classes to which data that adheres to that schema can be unmarshalled. This process can be performed ahead of time and is similar to the process of building the XSLT from the previous section. Essentially, the goal is to build a framework that specifies how to move XML data into a different representation. In this case, the representation is Java objects.

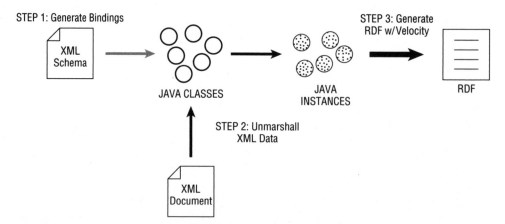

Figure 9-4 The three phases of exposing XML using JAXB and Velocity

The second phase involves unmarshalling the data from an XML input document into Java objects using the classes that were generated in the first phase. Once the objects are loaded and generated, they can be manipulated as much or as little as is desired. The third and final phase involves invoking the Velocity template engine with the set of Java objects generated in the second phase and a Velocity template file that specifies how to generate the output RDF document from the Java objects. The following subsections explore each of the phases and the technologies in each along with the application that puts them all together to convert XML data to RDF.

Generating Java Bindings for XML Data

The first step to using Java XML Bindings is to generate the bindings. Java XML Bindings are a set of Java classes that are mapped to the elements contained in an XML schema. A JAXB unmarshaller reads an XML file that conforms to a schema or schemas and then generates instances of the Java classes that were generated from the same schema. Generating the Java bindings is a relatively easy step as long as no advanced configuration is necessary. The bindings that are generated using the default parameters should be adequate for most applications.

The example project that accompanies this section is named `WeatherToRdfWithJaxb` and can be found with the other example projects for Chapter 9. The example used the JAXB Reference Implementation Project, which can be found at `http://jaxb.dev.java.net`. Full documentation as well as downloads for the implementation can be found at that website. The example project also includes the weather XML schema and pregenerated Java bindings. For the sake of completeness, the example will be presented as though the schema and bindings were not already downloaded and generated.

The only requirement for generating Java bindings is to obtain the schema for the XML data you want to generate bindings for. The XML schema can usually be found by doing some research on the website that provided the data or by resolving the URI listed in the namespace declaration in the source XML data document. Following are the first few lines from the weather XML document from the first code example in the chapter. The schema URI is in bold.

```
<?xml version="1.0" encoding="ISO-8859-1"?>
<current_observation version="1.0"
    xmlns:xsd="http://www.w3.org/2001/XMLSchema"
    xmlns:xsi="http://www.w3.org/2001/XMLSchema-instance"
    xsi:noNamespaceSchemaLocation=
      "http://www.weather.gov/xml/current_obs/current_observation.xsd">
```

Fortunately, the URI is resolvable (the importance of resolvability!). Resolving the URI yields the full schema. The following is an excerpt from that schema. The full schema can be found in the programming examples that accompany Chapter 9, located in the project under `conf/current_observation.xsd`.

```xml
<?xml version="1.0"?>
<xsd:schema xmlns:xsd="http://www.w3.org/2001/XMLSchema">
<xsd:element name="current_observation">
 <xsd:complexType>
  <xsd:sequence>
   <xsd:element name="credit" type="xsd:token" minOccurs="0"/>
   <xsd:element name="credit_URL" type="xsd:anyURI" minOccurs="0"/>
   <xsd:element name="location" type="xsd:token" minOccurs="0"/>
   <xsd:element name="station_id" type="xsd:token" minOccurs="0"/>
   <xsd:element name="latitude" type="xsd:string" minOccurs="0"/>
   <xsd:element name="longitude" type="xsd:string" minOccurs="0"/>
   <xsd:element name="elevation" type="xsd:integer" minOccurs="0"/>
   <xsd:element name="observation_time_rfc822"
                type="xsd:token" minOccurs="0"/>
   <xsd:element name="weather" type="xsd:token" minOccurs="0"/>
   <xsd:element name="temp_f" type="xsd:decimal" minOccurs="0"/>
   <xsd:element name="water_temp_f" type="xsd:decimal" minOccurs="0"/>
   <xsd:element name="wind_dir" type="xsd:string" minOccurs="0"/>
   <xsd:element name="wind_mph" type="xsd:decimal" minOccurs="0"/>
   <xsd:element name="wind_gust_mph" type="xsd:decimal" minOccurs="0"/>
   <xsd:element name="pressure_mb" type="xsd:decimal" minOccurs="0"/>
    <xsd:element name="copyright_url" type="xsd:anyURI" minOccurs="0"/>
    <xsd:element name="privacy_policy_url" type="xsd:anyURI"
                minOccurs="0"/>
  </xsd:sequence>
  <xsd:attribute name="version" type="xsd:string" default="1.0"/>
 </xsd:complexType>
</xsd:element>
</xsd:schema>
```

Understanding the schema isn't actually all that important. That's the benefit of working with JAXB—you interact with the data as Java objects, not as XML. The only entity that has to interact with the schema directly is the JAXB binding generator. Invoking the generator is pretty straightforward. For the JAXB Reference Project implementation, execute the `com.sun.tools.xjc.XJCFacade` class (located in the `jaxb-xjc.jar` file) with the following parameters:

- ▪ `-p [target package name]`
- ▪ `[XML schema]`
- ▪ `-d [target directory for generated classes]`

To regenerate the bindings in the example project, use these parameters:

```
-p net.semwebprogramming.chapter9.weather
./conf/current_observation.xsd
-d gen
```

The generator should run and output some status messages. Once it is complete, it will have generated a new source tree under the gen directory with the package net.semwebprogramming.chapter9. There should be three new class files in that package: CurrentObservation.java, ImageType.java, and ObjectFactory.java. Most of the interesting stuff is in the Current Observation.java class. The class is a normal container class that has a protected member variable for each of the XML nodes under the current_ observation node. Most of the variables have annotations associated with them that the unmarshaller will use to figure out how to unmarshal values from the XML document into the Java objects. Now that the Java binding classes are generated, it's time to unmarshal some XML data into them.

Unmarshalling XML Data into Java

The next phase after the Java XML bindings are generated is to unmarshal XML data into instances of the generated classes. Once the instances are created, they can be used just like normal Java objects. This section introduces the example application that uses JAXB to load the weather XML feed into the generated Java classes and then sends them to Velocity to be serialized using a Velocity template. The source code is listed here:

```java
public class WeatherToRdfWithJaxb
{
  public static void main(String[] args)
  {
    String xmlFile = args[0];
    String vmFile = args[1];
    String outputFile = args[2];

    try
    {
      //get the xml file input
      URL xmlFileUrl = new URL(xmlFile);
      InputStream xmlFileInputStream = xmlFileUrl.openStream();

      //get the vm file input
      FileInputStream vmFileInput = new FileInputStream(vmFile);

      //create the output file
```

```
FileOutputStream outputStream =
    new FileOutputStream(outputFile);

//unmarshal the information from xml
JAXBContext jaxbContext = JAXBContext.newInstance(
        "net.semwebprogramming.chapter9.weather");
Unmarshaller unmarshaller = jaxbContext.createUnmarshaller();
CurrentObservation currentObservation =
    (CurrentObservation)unmarshaller.unmarshal(
        xmlFileInputStream);

//execute our velocity template
VelocityEngine engine = new VelocityEngine();
engine.init();
VelocityContext velocityContext = new VelocityContext();
velocityContext.put("observation", currentObservation);

//set up an output stream that we can redirect to the jena model
ByteArrayOutputStream vmOutputStream =
    new ByteArrayOutputStream();

Writer resultsWriter = new OutputStreamWriter(vmOutputStream);
engine.evaluate(
    velocityContext,
    resultsWriter,
    "weatherRdf",
    new InputStreamReader(vmFileInput));
resultsWriter.close();

//build a jena model so we can serialize to Turtle
ByteArrayInputStream modelInputStream =
    new ByteArrayInputStream(vmOutputStream.toByteArray());

Model rdfModel = ModelFactory.createDefaultModel();
rdfModel.read(modelInputStream, null, "RDF/XML");
rdfModel.write(outputStream, "TURTLE");
outputStream.flush();

System.out.println("Success.");
} catch (Exception e) {}
```

The application takes three parameters: an XML input document URL, an input Velocity template file, and the desired output file. The first section of the code gathers the input parameters for the application and sets up the streams for the input and output documents. The code that performs the unmarshalling process follows:

```
//unmarshal the information from xml
JAXBContext jaxbContext = JAXBContext.newInstance(
    "net.semwebprogramming.chapter9.weather");
```

```
Unmarshaller unmarshaller = jaxbContext.createUnmarshaller();
CurrentObservation currentObservation =
    (CurrentObservation)unmarshaller.unmarshal(
        xmlFileInputStream);
```

First, a JAXBContext instance is created with the same namespace as the one that was used when the Java bindings were generated. Next, the JAXBContext instance is used to create a new instance of the Unmarshaller class. Finally, the actual CurrentObservation instance is unmarshalled from the input XML document by calling the unmarshal method on the instance of Unmarshaller, with the input XML document stream as the input parameter. That's all there is to it. The instance of CurrentObservation can now be manipulated just like any Java object, and it contains all of the data that was in the XML input file. The next subsection presents the part of the application that uses Velocity to generate an RDF/XML file based on the contents of the Java object that was just unmarshalled.

Introducing the Velocity Template Engine

Now that the XML data is loaded into a Java object, it's time to generate RDF using Velocity. Velocity is an open-source Java-based Apache project that provides a template language and processing engine that can be used to embed Java object data in any text output file. Velocity has many of the same features that XSLT does; however, unlike XSLT, it is not designed to generate data of any specific format or representation, and it operates on Java objects rather than XML documents.

Like many of the other technologies being discussed in this chapter, Velocity has dozens of pages of documentation and deserves a chapter itself. But the goal of this section is not to make you a master of Velocity; rather, it is to introduce the tool and demonstrate some of the capabilities it has. With that in mind, the examples will be kept quick and to the point. Picking up right where the last section left off in the source code of the JAXB-to-Velocity application, the following chunk of code is responsible for creating and executing the Velocity engine against the instance of CurrentObservation and the input Velocity template file:

```
//execute our velocity template
VelocityEngine engine = new VelocityEngine();
engine.init();
VelocityContext velocityContext = new VelocityContext();
velocityContext.put("observation", currentObservation);

//set up an output stream that we can redirect to the jena model
ByteArrayOutputStream vmOutputStream =
    new ByteArrayOutputStream();
```

```
Writer resultsWriter = new OutputStreamWriter(vmOutputStream);
engine.evaluate(
    velocityContext,
    resultsWriter,
    "weatherRdf",
    new InputStreamReader(vmFileInput));
resultsWriter.close();
```

The first two lines create and initialize an instance of `VelocityEngine`. The initialization step is critical—nothing will work if it has not been called. Immediately after the creation of the engine, an instance of `VelocityContext` is created, and the instance of `CurrentObservation` is passed into the `put` method along with the string identifier: `observation`. The instance of `VelocityContext` is used to create a context of identifier/Java object pairs that will be made accessible to the elements of the template file when it is being processed.

The next few lines of code create a new `Writer` that Velocity will use to write the result document. After that, the real magic happens. The `evaluate` method is called on the instance of `VelocityEngine`. The instance of `VelocityContext`, the output writer, a string `weatherRdf`, and a new instance of `InputStreamReader` that wraps the input Velocity template file are all passed in as parameters to that method. This one big method call is the point at which the engine merges the context with the template file and writes the results to the writer. Recall that the context contains the objects that are to be used by the template. The template contains directives that are used by the processor to generate the output document based on the contents of the Java objects in the context. By merging the two, the output document is formed and everything is done.

Before you get too curious about what the output data looks like, first take a look at the Velocity template file:

```
<rdf:RDF
  xmlns:rdf="http://www.w3.org/1999/02/22-rdf-syntax-ns#"
  xmlns:rdfs="http://www.w3.org/2000/01/rdf-schema#"
  xmlns:owl="http://www.w3.org/2002/07/owl#"
  xmlns:xsd="http://www.w3.org/2001/XMLSchema#"
  xmlns:w="http://www.semwebprogramming.net/2009/04/weather-ont#"
  xml:base="http://www.semwebprogramming.net/weather#"
  xmlns = "http://www.semwebprogramming.net/weather#" >

  <w:WeatherObservation>
    <w:source rdf:resource="$observation.CreditURL"/>
    <w:time>$observation.ObservationTimeRfc822</w:time>
    <w:location>$observation.Location</w:location>
    <w:latitude>$observation.Latitude</w:latitude>
    <w:longitude>$observation.Longitude</w:longitude>
    <w:temperature_f>$observation.TempF</w:temperature_f>
```

```
    <w:windDirection rdf:resource="$observation.WindDir"/>
    <w:wind_mph>$observation.WindMph</w:wind_mph>

#if ( $observation.WindGustMph == "NA" )
    <w:wind_gust_mph>
      $observation.WindGustMph
    </w:wind_gust_mph>
#end

#if( $observation.Weather )
    <w:weatherDescription>
      $observation.Weather
    </w:weatherDescription>
#end

    <w:copyright rdf:resource="$observation.CopyrightUrl"/>
  </w:WeatherObservation>
</rdf:RDF>
```

This template should look very familiar. It's very similar to the file that was used in the earlier example that used XSLT, only the syntax has changed to the Velocity template language. In Velocity, any variable that was placed in the `VelocityContext` instance and passed into the `evaluate` method can be dereferenced from within the template using the `$` character. Properties (getters and setters) can be accessed using the script syntax that is used in the previous template, or the full getter can be written out. The following examples are equivalent:

- `$observation.CreditURL` and `$observation.getCreditURL()`
- `$observation.Location` and `$observation.getLocation()`

Other reference methods are allowed, such as `$observation.creditURL`, and the engine will attempt to find a number of variations of the method to try to find the property to which it corresponds. Any arbitrary method that is accessible can be called directly using the full method name and parenthesis. Even methods that alter the state of the objects in the `VelocityContext` can be called with parameters. No special syntax is needed to dereference variable values from within quotation marks or in the attributes of XML nodes.

Velocity's template language supports a number of directives, including variables, conditionals, and loops. In the example template, a `#if` conditional is demonstrated. The first compares the value of `$observation.WindGustMph` to the string `"NA"`. The second checks for the existence of a value for `$observation.Weather`. The `#if` directive supports the inclusion of a `#else` clause as well. All block-based directives are terminated by a `#end` statement. For more information on the details and features of the Velocity template language, you should refer to the Apache Velocity project page at `http://velocity.apache.org`.

Generating RDF with Velocity

Returning to the task at hand, the final step in the example application is to load the RDF/XML file that is generated by the Velocity template engine into the Jena model. Once again, the Jena model will perform validation and convert the RDF/XML file to Turtle. Running the application with the input parameters `"file:conf/KBWI.xml conf/weather-rdf.vm output.ttl"` yields the following output:

```
@prefix w:      <http://www.semwebprogramming.net/2009/04/weather-ont#> .
@prefix :       <http://www.semwebprogramming.net/weather#> .
@prefix rdfs:   <http://www.w3.org/2000/01/rdf-schema#> .
@prefix owl:    <http://www.w3.org/2002/07/owl#> .
@prefix xsd:    <http://www.w3.org/2001/XMLSchema#> .
@prefix rdf:    <http://www.w3.org/1999/02/22-rdf-syntax-ns#> .


[]    rdf:type w:WeatherObservation ;
      w:copyright <http://weather.gov/disclaimer.html> ;
      w:latitude "39.19" ;
      w:location "Baltimore-Washington International Airport, MD" ;
      w:longitude "-76.67" ;
      w:source <http://weather.gov/> ;
      w:temperature_f "57" ;
      w:time    "Sun, 19 Oct 2008 14:54:00 -0400 EDT" ;
      w:weatherDescription "\n          Partly Cloudy\n        " ;
      w:windDirection <http://www.weather.gov/Northeast> ;
      w:wind_mph "10.35" .
```

This output file is almost exactly the same as what was produced in the last example with XSLT. The only strange difference is the newline characters in the `w:weatherDescription` value. We can remove those by modifying the generated Java bindings to remove extra white space when the values are set or retrieved.

Weighing the Benefits and the Costs

Using Java as an intermediate language for the XML-to-RDF translation process has many benefits, including the increased flexibility it affords. There is much more opportunity and ability to manipulate the data before it is converted to RDF because more can be done with the data once it is accessible directly from within a programming language like Java. The data can be integrated into any number of tools or processed in any number of ways. Velocity has its own advantages in that it is not as tied to XML as a destination format as XSLT is, and it has a much more concise and readable syntax than XSLT. Finally, Velocity allows you to output any arbitrary text.

In summary, the benefits of bringing the data into Java objects and then generating the output using a template engine include the following:

- This approach is very powerful and flexible. In Java, you can do anything to the data.

- Using Java as an intermediate representation makes the approach much more modular. Any number of methods for generating RDF can be swapped in.

- Velocity moves RDF generation logic from code and into configuration files.

- Velocity is very familiar to Java developers and to users of other similar template languages such as JSTL.

- Velocity enables you to generate any arbitrary text output or RDF serialization, including Turtle.

The drawbacks to this approach are nothing new. This process is not streaming because the binding process requires that all the objects from the XML be loaded at once. This process relies on having compiled binding classes that will have to be changed and redeployed if the underlying XML schema ever changes. Admittedly, this should be a rare occurrence, but it could break legacy code. Also, this approach is still not general purpose and requires a developer to not only generate Java binding classes but also generate and maintain a Velocity template file.

A concise view of these drawbacks includes the following:

- Scalability is a concern because this process is not inherently streaming.

- When using Java bindings, those bindings must change if the source XML schema changes. This leads to recompilation and redeployment.

- This approach requires the development and maintenance of Java bindings and Velocity template files.

Exposing Relational Databases as RDF

Relational databases (RDBs) represent a massive source of data for the Semantic Web. Most websites are populated by data stored in RDBs. In Tim Berners-Lee's own words: "One of the main driving forces for the Semantic Web has always been the expression, on the Web, of the vast amount of relational database information in a way that can be processed by machines" (from Relational Databases on the Semantic Web, `http://www.w3.org/DesignIssues/RDB-RDF.html`). Fortunately, RDF and OWL are apt to model much of the information that can be expressed in the Entity-Relational (ER) model that most RDBs are modeled after. A number of tools, some of them listed in Table 9-5, have been developed to expose the data contained in RDBs as virtual RDF graphs that can be navigated or queried as a SPARQL endpoint. This section will explore the use of one of these tools, called D2RQ, to expose the relational database that backs a web-based installation of the WordPress blog.

Table 9-5 Common Tools for Exposing an RDB as a Virtual RDF Graph

APPLICATION	WEBSITE
D2RQ	http://www4.wiwiss.fu-berlin.de/bizer/d2rq/
SquirrelRDF	http://jena.sourceforge.net/SquirrelRDF
OpenLink Virtuoso	http://virtuoso.openlinksw.com/

Tools like D2RQ make it easier to expose relational database data to the Semantic Web because they provide general-purpose mechanisms for mapping the tables and columns of RDBs to the classes and properties of an ontology. Most of the tools are designed to require minimal configuration, making it easy to quickly expose the database as an RDF knowledgebase.

There may be occasions when you need to generate RDF directly from the results of an SQL query or build an RDF-specific interface for a relational database. Sometimes this can happen when the RDB schema is not well defined or contains bad or inconsistent data that requires extra processing when it is being processed and converted to RDF. While this section does not contain a specific example handling that scenario, the technologies and techniques that are used throughout this chapter can be applied in such a manner.

Exposing a WordPress Blog Using D2RQ

The example in this section uses D2RQ to wrap a WordPress blog's relational database in a Jena model. The model can be queried, navigated using the Jena API, or wrapped in a Joseki SPARQL server. This is the same application that is used to expose WordPress to FriendTracker. On the website accompanying this book is an example MySQL database dump of a WordPress installation that you can download and stand up to accompany the examples of this section.

There are two steps to exposing an RDB as RDF using D2RQ. The first step involves generating a mapping file that specifies how the tables and columns of the database map to specific classes and properties in an output ontology. The tool doesn't actually generate the output ontology, but it does implicitly create one because it defines a set of classes and properties in a consistent namespace that will be used by the D2RQ processor when converting the RDB data into RDF.

The second step involves establishing a D2RQ instance that is configured with the mapping file generated in the first step and wrapping the instance in a Jena model. Once this is done, you can use the model as if it were a normal Jena RDF model. The following subsections walk through these steps using WordPress as an example database.

Creating D2RQ Mappings for the WordPress Database

D2RQ comes with a tool that automatically generates mapping files for a relational database by processing its schema. The tool can be invoked by executing the Java class d2rq.generate_mapping in the following manner:

```
d2rq.generate_mapping
      -u userName
      -p password
      -d driverClass
      -o outputFile.n3
      jdbcConnectUrl
```

As an example, consider the following command that generates mappings for a MySQL-based WordPress installation:

```
d2rq.generate_mapping
      -u exampleUser
      -p examplePassword
      -d com.mysql.jdbc.Driver
      -o outputFile.n3
      jdbc:mysql://example.com:3306/exampleBlogDb
```

The only glitch in this command is that the MySQL JDBC driver throws exceptions when it encounters a value of zero in a date column. To fix this issue, you can tell the MySQL driver to convert zero dates to null by appending ?zeroDateTimeBehavior=convertToNull to the end of the connect string. When you run this command, D2RQ will connect to the database specified and generate a default mapping file based on the schema it observes. The whole process should take only a few moments.

The resulting mapping file is too big to show in its entirety, but it is useful to take a look at a few sections of it. First, the namespace declarations:

```
@prefix map: <file:/.../mapping.n3#> .
@prefix db: <> .
@prefix vocab: <vocab/> .
@prefix d2rq: <http://www.wiwiss.fu-berlin.de/suhl/bizer/D2RQ/0.1#> .
```

The map prefix is abbreviated so it fits on one line. In the mapping file, it will be the file URL of the output filename. You can change this to whatever you want. It is only used internally to D2RQ, but it will appear as a namespace in RDF graphs that come out of D2RQ. The vocab prefix represents the namespace of the output ontology. That is, all RDF coming out of D2RQ will be described by classes and properties from the vocab prefix. This is worth changing to something unique.

To get a feel for how the mappings work, take a look at the following excerpt related to the table that stores blog posts:

```
# Table wp_posts
map:wp_posts a d2rq:ClassMap;
d2rq:dataStorage map:database;
d2rq:uriPattern "wp_posts/@@wp_posts.ID@@";
d2rq:class vocab:wp_posts;
.

map:wp_posts_post_author a d2rq:PropertyBridge;
d2rq:belongsToClassMap map:wp_posts;
d2rq:property vocab:wp_posts_post_author;
d2rq:column "wp_posts.post_author";
d2rq:datatype xsd:long;
.

map:wp_posts_post_date a d2rq:PropertyBridge;
d2rq:belongsToClassMap map:wp_posts;
d2rq:property vocab:wp_posts_post_date;
d2rq:column "wp_posts.post_date";
d2rq:datatype xsd:dateTime;
d2rq:condition "wp_posts.post_date != '0000'";
.

map:wp_posts_post_content a d2rq:PropertyBridge;
d2rq:belongsToClassMap map:wp_posts;
d2rq:property vocab:wp_posts_post_content;
d2rq:column "wp_posts.post_content";
```

CAUTION The generated URIs in the previous mapping file excerpt are based on the names of the tables and columns in the database. The URIs will appear slightly different if the database to which D2RQ is connected is different from the one used to generate this example.

This excerpt contains one instance of the d2rq:ClassMap class and three instances of the d2rq:PropertyBridge class. The d2rq:ClassMap instance with the URI map:wp_posts contains information that is used by D2RQ to map a table from the database to a class in the output ontology. The instance also contains a property value that is used to generate URIs for instances that come out of that table. The d2rq:PropertyBridge instances each contain property values that are used by D2RQ to map columns from a specific table to properties in the output ontology. If you look closely, you'll also notice that each property has datatype information that was extracted from the database schema and even reflects the directive that was passed into the JDBC connect URL telling it to treat zero dates as null (in this case, it instructs D2RQ to ignore dates that are zero).

Wrapping the D2RQ Instance in a Jena Model

Once the mappings are generated, the next step is to wrap a model around the D2RQ instance so that you can start accessing the database as RDF. D2RQ provides hooks for both Sesame and Jena. To be consistent with the other examples in this book, this example will wrap a Jena model around the D2RQ exposed WordPress database. The following application creates an instance of D2RQ with the mapping file that was just generated, wraps it in a Jena model, and then issues a SPARQL construct query. This application is contained in the `WordPressToRdfWithD2RQ` project. The results of the construct query are then serialized to an output file. The mapping file contains all of the connection configuration information, making the creation of the D2RQ model relatively simple.

```
public class WordPressToRdfWithD2RQ
{
    public static void main(String[] args)
    {
        String queryFile = args[0];
        String queryName = args[1];
        String mappingFile = args[2];
        String outputFile = args[3];
        String outputFormat = args[4];

        try
        {
            //load our queries
            QueryReader queryReader =
                QueryReader.createQueryReader(queryFile);
            String queryStr = queryReader.getQuery(queryName);
            System.out.println(queryStr);

            //create the d2rq model using the mapping file
            Model d2rqModel = new ModelD2RQ(mappingFile);

            //create the query
            Query query = QueryFactory.create(queryStr);
            QueryExecution qExec =
                QueryExecutionFactory.create(query, d2rqModel);
```

```
//execute the query
Model results = qExec.execConstruct();

//output the resulting graph
FileOutputStream outputStream =
    new FileOutputStream(outputFile);
results.write(outputStream, outputFormat);
outputStream.close();

}catch (IOException e){}
    }
}
```

As with the other examples in this chapter, we have abridged the code for readability. Extraneous comments have been removed and exception handling has been reduced. The first lines in the application read the query string from a file that contains queries using a custom `QueryReader` class. The class parses a text file with a set of queries in it and then provides a way to hash into the set of queries using a name identifier. You can add queries to the query file to change the behavior of the example. The class that is being presented in this example assumes that the query that is loaded is a construct query. There is also an example class that performs a select query instead.

Once the query has been loaded, the D2RQ instance is created and initialized. The next step is to create a new `Query` instance and `QueryExecution` so that the query can be executed against the D2RQ instance. As you may have noticed, the D2RQ instance is in fact a Jena model itself. Once the instance of `QueryExecution` is created, the only step that remains is to execute the query. This is done using the `execConstruct` method on the `QueryExecution` instance. The result of this method is a new Jena model that contains the RDF graph that is constructed by the query. Once the results are in the model, the model can be serialized.

Querying the D2RQ Exposed WordPress Database

The last step in the sample application is to take a look at the construct query that will be issued against the D2RQ virtual RDF graph. The following query retrieves posts along with the user information for each post's author.

```
PREFIX wp: <http://www.semwebprogramming.net/wordpress/ontology#>
PREFIX rdfs: <http://www.w3.org/2000/01/rdf-schema#>
PREFIX rdf: <http://www.w3.org/1999/02/22-rdf-syntax-ns#>
PREFIX xsd: <http://www.w3.org/2001/XMLSchema#>

CONSTRUCT
{
    ?user    rdf:type wp:wp_users;
```

```
                    wp:wp_users_ID ?uid;
                    ?usersProp ?usersVal.
         ?post      rdf:type wp:wp_posts;
                    wp:wp_posts_post_author ?uid;
                    ?postProp ?postVal.
    }
    WHERE
    {
         ?user      rdf:type wp:wp_users;
                    wp:wp_users_ID ?uid;
                    ?usersProp ?usersVal.
         ?post      rdf:type wp:wp_posts;
                    wp:wp_posts_post_author ?uid;
                    wp:wp_posts_post_type "post";
                    wp:wp_posts_post_status "publish";
                    ?postProp ?postVal.
    }
```

Notice that the query constructs a graph that contains all statements about both the users and the posts on the blog. The users and posts are connected by the post author's user id, as the bolded text indicates:

```
         ?user      rdf:type wp:wp_users;
                    wp:wp_users_ID ?uid;
                    ?usersProp ?usersVal.
         ?post      rdf:type wp:wp_posts;
                    wp:wp_posts_post_author ?uid;
                    wp:wp_posts_post_type "post";
                    wp:wp_posts_post_status "publish";
                    ?postProp ?postVal.
```

This means that the results of this query will contain information only for users who have authored a post. The query is designed to return all statements about posts that have the correct type and status. This is achieved by the combination of constraining the query using specific property values for post type and status and through the portions of the query that have variables for both the predicate and the value, as shown here:

```
         ?user      rdf:type wp:wp_users;
                    wp:wp_users_ID ?uid;
                    ?usersProp ?usersVal.
         ?post      rdf:type wp:wp_posts;
                    wp:wp_posts_post_author ?uid;
                    wp:wp_posts_post_type "post";
                    wp:wp_posts_post_status "publish";
                    ?postProp ?postVal.
```

Issuing this query against the WordPress database using the example application yields a result set containing RDF representation of blog posts and users in the WordPress database. The following is an excerpt of the constructed RDF graph in Turtle:

```
<file:conf/mapping.n3#wp_users/5>
        rdf:type wp:wp_users ;
        rdfs:label "wp_users #5" ;
        wp:wp_users_ID "5"^^xsd:long ;
        wp:wp_users_display_name "andrew.perez.lopez" ;
        wp:wp_users_user_email "andrew.perez.lopez@example.org" ;
        wp:wp_users_user_login "andrew.perez.lopez" ;
        wp:wp_users_user_nicename "andrewperezlopez" ;
        wp:wp_users_user_pass
                "$P$BRE7sfqcwezwImRKHJcJHktUE.edVy." ;
        wp:wp_users_user_registered
                "2008-09-29 02:01:01.0"^^xsd:dateTime .

<file/conf/mapping.n3#wp_posts/7>
        rdf:type wp:wp_posts ;
        rdfs:label "wp_posts #7" ;
        wp:wp_posts_ID "7"^^xsd:long ;
        wp:wp_posts_comment_count "0"^^xsd:long ;
        wp:wp_posts_comment_status "closed" ;
        wp:wp_posts_guid "http://semwebprogramming.org:8099/blog/?p=7" ;
        wp:wp_posts_menu_order "0"^^xsd:int ;
        wp:wp_posts_ping_status "open" ;
        wp:wp_posts_post_author "5"^^xsd:long ;
        wp:wp_posts_post_content
                "So last night I checked in the initial..." ;
        wp:wp_posts_post_date_gmt
                "2008-10-06 00:41:50.0"^^xsd:dateTime ;
        wp:wp_posts_post_modified
                "2008-10-05 20:41:50.0"^^xsd:dateTime ;
        wp:wp_posts_post_modified_gmt
                "2008-10-06 00:41:50.0"^^xsd:dateTime ;
        wp:wp_posts_post_name
                "initial-implementation-of-the-upcoming-module" ;
        wp:wp_posts_post_parent "0"^^xsd:long ;
        wp:wp_posts_post_status
                "publish" ;
        wp:wp_posts_post_title
                "Initial Implementation of the Upcoming Module" ;
        wp:wp_posts_post_type
                "post" .
```

Each post's information, along with the post's author, has been generated in the output. Each individual generated has a URI that is based on a consistent base and the primary key for the table from which the individual comes. This is important because repeated accesses to the D2RQ virtual RDF graph will result in consistent URIs, and the use of primary keys and table names guarantees that URIs will be unique within this instance of D2RQ. The result set is a reflection of the database tables and columns, which contain a good bit of application logic. This is a nice illustration of how the knowledge model and the application model can be hard to distinguish.

Weighing the Benefits and the Costs of D2RQ

The big benefit to using D2RQ is that there is minimal configuration to expose the RDB data as RDF. The mapping file is autogenerated and requires minimal adjustment. It is one of the few methods of exposing RDF that actually provides a way to dynamically issue SPARQL queries that convert only what is relevant to the query into RDF. This is the only approach that fully establishes a virtual RDF graph that is accessed and loaded lazily. Finally, the direct Jena and Sesame support provides a very quick path to application integration.

In summary, the benefits of exposing an RDB as RDF using a tool like D2RQ include the following:

- Minimal configuration that is almost completely autogenerated

- A SPARQL endpoint and direct integration with Jena and Sesame

- Minimal learning curve because all you really need to know is SPARQL and either Jena or Sesame

There are also a number of drawbacks to D2RQ. First, the generated RDF is almost an exact reflection of the underlying database schema. This may not be a good thing if the schema includes a lot of application- or performance-specific elements. The next chapter will deal with some of the issues that arise when you start to work with the knowledge model being generated through this kind of exposure process. D2RQ uses a compile-time-generated configuration file that may need to be changed if the RDB schema changes. This is mitigated by the fact that a change to an RDB schema is usually considered a big deal, and the required regeneration of the mapping file and associated queries is likely acceptable. One of the biggest drawbacks to D2RQ and other tools in its space is the simple lack of support and development. Many of the RDB-to-RDF exposure projects have slowed or stalled as they try to make the transition from government-funded research project to commercially viable product. While the projects themselves may have slowed, healthy user communities still exist and will hopefully keep the projects alive.

The drawbacks can be summarized as follows:

- Generated RDF is almost an exact reflection of database structure, which may contain application-specific and performance-specific information.

- These tools generally require a close awareness of underlying RDB schema to build useful queries.

- Changes to RDB schema may require regeneration of mappings and changes to queries.
- The level of activity surrounding D2RQ and similar projects is low.

Exposing Other Sources of Data

So far, this chapter has covered a couple of techniques for exposing XML data into the Semantic Web and exposing a relational database as a virtual RDF graph. This section introduces a few other more general methods of exposing data as RDF. The first example uses a simple streaming Turtle RDF generator that builds an RDF representation of a Jabber Java client data source for FriendTracker. The second example uses Java Reflection as a way to expose objects generated from the Upcoming.org XML web service as RDF in a general-purpose manner.

Exposing Jabber with a Custom Streaming RDF Writer

The purpose of this example is to demonstrate the use of a streaming writer to generate RDF in the Turtle syntax. The reason this example is important is that it represents a useful tool to have at your disposal when working with large volumes of data, and other more general-purpose approaches can't scale adequately to the task. The example project for this section is the same code that is used to expose the Jabber Java client data source for FriendTracker as RDF. The project is contained in the code that accompanies this chapter and is called JabberToRdf. The examples run in this section are executed with one of the authors' Google Mail accounts. The server name is `google.com`, and the username is the Google Mail email address.

There are two main parts of this example. First is a streaming Turtle writer class, `TurtleWriter`. This class provides methods for creating new individuals and then appending property values to them. The writer itself is relatively straightforward and doesn't have a lot of advanced features, but it demonstrates how a very simple concept can be used to expose a large amount of data in a scalable fashion. The second part of the example is the main application that uses the Jabber client to generate a Java representation of a user's contact list and his online status information and then iterate through that model, using the Turtle writer to generate RDF that reflects the properties and values of the data. Most of the code that performs this task is contained in a method of the `JabberToRdf` class called `retrieveFriends`. That method is shown here, with reduced exception handling and other omissions to make the code easier to read:

```java
public InputStream retrieveFriends(String server, String username,
    String password)
{
    InputStream toReturn = null;
    XMPPConnection connection = null;
    try
    {
        //create a connection
        connection = new XMPPConnection(server);

        //connect and log in
        connection.connect();
        connection.login(username, password);

        //get the contact list
        Roster roster = connection.getRoster();
        roster.setSubscriptionMode(Roster.SubscriptionMode.accept_all);
        Collection<RosterEntry> entries = roster.getEntries();

        ByteArrayOutputStream baos = new ByteArrayOutputStream();

        //create a turtle writer
        TurtleWriter writer = TurtleWriter.createTurtleWriter(baos);

        //add the prefixes for this document
        writer.addPrefix("j", "http://www.jabber.org/ontology#");
        writer.addPrefix("", "http://www.jabber.org/data#");

        for(RosterEntry entry : entries)
        {
            //open the individual
            writer.openIndividual("", entry.getUser(), "j", "Contact");

            //write their name if they have one
            if(null != entry.getName())
            {
                writer.addLiteral(
                    "rdfs", "label", entry.getName(), "xsd:string");
                writer.addLiteral(
                    "j", "name", entry.getName(), "xsd:string");
            }

            //write their presence state
            Presence p = roster.getPresence(entry.getUser());
            String type = getType(p.getType());
            String mode = getMode(p.getMode());
            String status = p.getStatus();

            if(null != type)
            {
```

```
                    writer.addReference("j", "presenceType", "j", type);
            }
            if(null != mode)
            {
                writer.addReference("j", "presenceMode", "j", mode);
            }
            if(null != status)
            {
                writer.addLiteral("j", "status", status, "xsd:string");
            }
            writer.closeIndividual();
        }
        writer.close();

        toReturn = new ByteArrayInputStream(baos.toByteArray());
    }catch (XMPPException e){}

    return toReturn;
}
```

The goal of this example is to demonstrate the use of the streaming writer, not necessarily to focus on XMPP or Jabber. With that said, the first dozen or so lines of the method establish the connection with the Jabber server and retrieve the user's contact list. The actual contact list is represented by the instance of `Roster`, and a snapshot of the contact list at a point in time can be generated by calling `Roster.getEntries()`. Jabber uses asynchronous message passing to establish the status of contacts on the contact list, so each time `getEntries()` is called, the list may be different. The example application ignores the asynchronous model and generates an RDF representation of the client's contact list (roster) at a single point in time. The unabridged source code corresponding to the code above contains a thread sleep operation that gives the client five seconds to gather status information for the contacts in the roster. Using a thread sleep in this kind of circumstance is an ugly solution and quite a hack. In any real application, a refresh period would be specified, and the data would be refreshed each time the period expired. Since it's not critical to our point, we'll leave the sleep in there for now.

Once the roster snapshot is generated, the `TurtleWriter` is created, and then each entry in the roster is processed and written. The code that creates the `TurtleWriter` is as follows:

```
ByteArrayOutputStream baos = new ByteArrayOutputStream();

//create a turtle writer
TurtleWriter writer = TurtleWriter.createTurtleWriter(baos);
```

In this particular application, the `TurtleWriter` is not being used in a truly streaming sense because all of the output is being directed into a

`ByteArrayOutputStream`. However, it could easily be tweaked into a streaming example by using a `FileOutputStream` instead. The first step in writing the output document is to establish the namespaces for the data that will be written. This includes the namespaces for both instances and for ontology elements that will be referenced.

```
//add the prefixes for this document
writer.addPrefix("j",
   "http://www.semwebprogramming.net/2009/04/jabber-ont#");
writer.addPrefix("",
   "http://www.semwebprogramming.net/jabber#");
```

This code establishes a prefix `j` that represents the ontology namespace and a blank prefix that represents the base namespace of the document. So far, the data that has been written to the output stream is basically the header for the Turtle file, including the default namespace prefixes and the ones that were added in the previous code snippet:

```
@prefix rdf: <http://www.w3.org/1999/02/22-rdf-syntax-ns#> .
@prefix rdfs: <http://www.w3.org/2000/01/rdf-schema#> .
@prefix owl: <http://www.w3.org/2002/07/owl#> .
@prefix xsd: <http://www.w3.org/2001/XMLSchema#> .
@prefix j: <http://www.semwebprogramming.net/2009/04/jabber-ont#> .
@prefix : <http://www.semwebprogramming.net/jabber#> .
```

Once the writer is initialized and the namespaces are established, it is time to iterate over each entry in the roster and write out a representative individual with types and property values. For each individual, the first step is to declare the individual as a member of a class. The code and the corresponding output that is generated are shown here:

```
//open the individual
writer.openIndividual("", entry.getUser(), "j", "Contact");

[output.ttl]
<http://www.jabber.org/data#lernerj@gmail.com>
        a <http://www.semwebprogramming.net/2009/04/jabber-ont#Contact> ;
```

The `TurtleWriter` class maintains a buffer of the last property value that was added to an open individual and writes only that last property value when there is a new property value or the individual is closed. It does this so that it can correctly determine whether it should add a terminating semicolon or period to the end of the line of Turtle, based on whether more statements are being added about a particular individual. The parameters to open an individual are the namespace prefix of the individual's base URI namespace, the URI fragment to append to that namespace to generate the individual's

URI, the prefix of the class of which the individual is a member, and finally the class itself. The individual's URI is generated based on the results of `entry.getUser()`. This is because that method returns the unique identifier for that entry. Notice that the individual URI doesn't actually use the namespace prefix when it generates the output. This is a result of the fact that the user's unique identifier is an email address and contains an @ symbol. This character is not allowed in abbreviated URIs in Turtle. These are the kinds of issues you will have to consider when you build or reuse an RDF writer of this type.

The rest of the loop writes the other properties of this individual, including name, presence type, presence mode, and status. Following is a very compressed listing of the rest of the properties that are output for the current entry in the roster:

```
writer.addLiteral("rdfs", "label", entry.getName(), "xsd:string");
writer.addLiteral("j", "name", entry.getName(), "xsd:string");
writer.addReference("j", "presenceType", "j", type);
writer.addReference("j", "presenceMode", "j", mode);
writer.addLiteral("j", "status", status, "xsd:string");
```

The `entry.getName` value is output as a literal value for both the `name` property and the annotation property `rdfs:label`. Notice that all literals are written with data types. Presence type and mode are each written as resource values for object properties, while status is written as a literal value. The reason for this is that the presence type and mode take their values from fixed enumerations. These values have meaning and semantics associated with them. Treating them as literals removes any ability to capture that meaning in an ontology. Status is a free-form text field. As such, it wouldn't be as useful to treat it as an object property and try to assign meaning to its potential values. Following is the Turtle that is generated after a complete iteration and processing of a single entry:

```
@prefix rdf: <http://www.w3.org/1999/02/22-rdf-syntax-ns#> .
@prefix rdfs: <http://www.w3.org/2000/01/rdf-schema#> .
@prefix owl: <http://www.w3.org/2002/07/owl#> .
@prefix xsd: <http://www.w3.org/2001/XMLSchema#> .
@prefix j: <http://www.jabber.org/ontology#> .
@prefix : <http://www.jabber.org/data#> .

<http://www.semwebprogramming.net/jabber#zcrawford@zeuscrawford.net >
    a <http://www.semwebprogramming.net/2009/04/jabber-ont#Contact> ;
    rdfs:label      "Zeus Crawford"^^xsd:string ;
    j:name          "Zeus Crawford"^^xsd:string ;
    j:presenceType j:Available> ;
    j:status        "Chillin..."^^xsd:string .
```

This process is repeated for each entry in the roster, and the end result is an RDF graph serialized to Turtle that represents the current state of the user's contact list. Depending on how this data is used, you may want to append some information that captures temporal context and identifies this as a snapshot in time.

This example is probably the most flexible approach that we have covered so far in this chapter. You can reuse a custom RDF writer like this to expose any data source that can be worked with in Java (or whatever language the writer is written in). This approach could easily be swapped with Velocity in the previous XML and JAXB example to generate the RDF output. In addition, the Turtle writer is entirely streaming. It does not maintain a significant amount of state information, and its performance should remain constant as data volume increases.

In summary, the benefits include:

- It is probably the most flexible and customizable approach to exposing RDF.

- Very modular, it can be used with many of the other techniques.

- The writer itself is purely streaming and can handle large volumes of data.

While the writer itself is a reusable software component, the code that uses it to generate the RDF output is not. This is the weakness of this approach. It is not a holistic, general-purpose method for exposing data as RDF. The data that is produced is determined in code, and any changes will have to be made at compile time, rather than runtime. The `TurtleWriter` class is a streaming Turtle writer; it doesn't maintain a model. This is good because it reduces the resources required to generate large amounts of data. However, there are drawbacks as well. Without a centralized model, not as much can be done with the data as it is being generated. Without any stored state reflecting what has already been written to the output stream, only the most limited reasoning can be applied, and duplicate results cannot be identified and removed. Adding any of these features increases both the overhead and the resource requirements of the writer.

To summarize, the drawbacks include:

- This approach is the most custom, and therefore it will require more work and potential recompilation if the source data changes.

- The writer is very simple. It performs no optimizations and does no data cleaning (escaping of illegal characters). These tasks, while straightforward, introduce additional overhead and may change the scaling characteristics of the writer.

- The writer does not support anonymous nodes as it is currently written. However, it could be extended to do so.

- Streaming writers gain performance at the cost of power and expressivity.

Exposing Java Objects Using Reflection

The purpose of this next example is to demonstrate the use of a fully generalized method of exposing any Java data using the Java Reflection API. The Reflection API allows programmers to take any arbitrary object and figure out what classes it is an instance of and then get information about those classes, including property names, modifiers, and attributes, as well as to make calls to those methods without requiring explicit casting.

The example project can be found, like all of the others, in the programming examples that accompany this chapter. The specific project for this example is called `JavaObjectsToRdf`. The project contains a class called `JavaObjectRdfSerializer` whose responsibility it is to construct an RDF graph from a collection of Java objects. The class uses the Java Reflection API to generate type information and property and value information for each object. As it processes each object, it adds RDF statements to a Jena model. Once the process is complete, the model is serialized to an output stream in the appropriate serialization syntax.

The `JavaObjectRdfSerializer` is created and initialized with URIs for the namespace of created individuals and the ontology namespace for generated classes and properties, a namespace identifying which Java package to limit the processing to (this prevents the processor from serializing unwanted referenced objects), and the syntax for the serialization. The class has a single public method, `void serialize(Collection<Object> objects, OutputStream outputStream)`. This method takes each method and serializes it by calling the following method:

```
private Individual processObject(Object o)
{
    Individual individual = null;

    /*
     * Determine if we should process this object
     * We don't process it if one of the following is true:
     *   1) We've already processed it
     *   2) It's not in our target package
     */
    boolean shouldProcess = true;
    shouldProcess =
        null != o
        && !_processedObjects.containsKey(o)
        && o.getClass().getPackage().getName().startsWith(_package);

    //now process it if we should
    if(shouldProcess)
    {
        //get the uri from the hashcode
```

```
      String resourceUri = String.format("%1$s%2$s", _baseUri,
o.hashCode());
      String classUri = String.format("%1$s%2$s", _ontUri, o.getClass
().getSimpleName());

      OntClass c = _model.createClass(classUri);
      individual = c.createIndividual(resourceUri);
      _processedObjects.put(o, individual);

      for(Method m : o.getClass().getMethods())
      {
         try
         {
            processMethod(o, individual, m);
         }catch (Exception e){}
      }
   }
   else if(_processedObjects.containsKey(o))
   {
      individual = _processedObjects.get(o);
   }

   return individual;
}
```

The method starts by determining whether the object that is passed in
should even be processed. It does this by checking to see whether the object's
class's package is within the scope of the packages that are being processed
and by maintaining a set of objects that have already been processed. This is
done to prevent infinite loops when two objects have references to each other.
If the object has already been processed, the method returns a reference to the
individual that was generated. After the method decides that it is processing
the object, it proceeds to create the URI for the new individual as well as a URI
for the class of which the individual is a member.

```
//get the uri from the hashcode
String resourceUri =
   String.format("%1$s%2$s", _baseUri, o.hashCode());
String classUri = String.format(
   "%1$s%2$s", _ontUri, o.getClass().getSimpleName());
```

The URI for the individual is derived from its hash code. An assumption is
made in this code that objects will have consistent and noncolliding hash codes.
In some cases this is not a safe assumption, but it works for demonstration
purposes. The class URI is derived from the simple name (without the full
package) of the object's Java class. After the two URIs are created, an OntClass
is created in the Jena model, and then a new individual is created as an instance
of the class. The next step after creating the new individual is to create all of

its property values. This is done by calling the method `processMethod(...)`, shown here:

```
private void processMethod(Object o, Individual individual, Method m)
{
    /*
     * We don't process it if one of the following is true:
     *  1) It's not a getter
     *  2) It has more than 0 parameters
     *  3) It isn't public
     */
    boolean shouldProcess = true;
    shouldProcess =
        null != m
        && m.getName().startsWith("get")
        && m.getParameterTypes().length == 0
        && Modifier.isPublic(m.getModifiers());

    if(shouldProcess)
    {
        String propertyName = m.getName().substring(3);
        Property p = _model.createProperty(
            String.format("%1$s%2$s", _ontUri, propertyName));
        Object value = m.invoke(o);

        if(null == value)
        {
            //we just want to skip these
        }
        else if(m.getReturnType().isPrimitive() || isBoxedPrimitive(value))
        {
            addBoxedPrimitiveValue(individual, p, value);
        }
        else
        {
            //add a resource
            Individual newIndividual = processObject(value);
            if(null != newIndividual)
            {
                individual.addProperty(p, newIndividual);
            }
        }
    }
}
```

The first step in this method is to determine whether to even bother processing the method. The criteria for a method to be processed are as follows:

■ The method must be a *getter*—it must start with get.

- The method must take no parameters.
- The method must be public.

If each of these criteria is met, the method will be processed. First, a new property is created in the Jena model that is based on the name of the method (everything but the `get` part). Once the property is created, the method is invoked on the object and the value is returned:

```
String propertyName = m.getName().substring(3);
Property p = _model.createProperty(
String.format("%1$s%2$s", _ontUri, propertyName));
Object value = m.invoke(o);
```

At this point, the only trick is to figure out how to interpret the value that is returned by the method. There are a couple of options. The application can treat everything as a literal value and just call the `toString(...)` method on each value to get the literal value. This is not a very good solution, however, because connections between resources will be lost and the RDF generator will generate pretty uninteresting RDF. The approach that this application takes is to try to interpret as best as it can exactly what the value is. There are two cases: Either the value is a primitive or it is an object. The two cases are really three cases, but we handle both boxed primitives and normal primitives the same way.

When the value is an object, the application recursively calls the `processObject(...)` method and then adds an object property connecting the currently being processed individual to the new one. When the value is a primitive (boxed or not), another method called `addBoxedPrimitiveValue(...)` is called. This method determines exactly what kind of primitive it is and adds it to the Jena model appropriately. Following is an excerpt from the method:

```
if(value instanceof String)
{
    i.addLiteral(p, value);
}
else if(value instanceof Integer)
{
    i.addLiteral(p, ((Integer)value).longValue());
}
else if(value instanceof Float)
{
    i.addLiteral(p, ((Float)value).floatValue());
}
else if(value instanceof Double)
{
    i.addLiteral(p, ((Double)value).doubleValue());
}
```

Applying the RDF Generator to the Weather.gov XML Feed

The following Turtle RDF file is an excerpt from the result of applying this technique to the same Weather.gov XML data feed from the earlier XML examples. The feed is once again loaded using JAXB, and the resulting objects are then fed into the `JavaObjectRdfSerializer`:

```
@prefix rdfs:  <http://www.w3.org/2000/01/rdf-schema#> .
@prefix dOnt:  <http://www.semwebprogramming.net/2009/04/weather-ont#> .
@prefix owl:   <http://www.w3.org/2002/07/owl#> .
@prefix xsd:   <http://www.w3.org/2001/XMLSchema#> .
@prefix rdf:   <http://www.w3.org/1999/02/22-rdf-syntax-ns#> .

dOnt:ImageType
    rdf:type owl:Class .

<http://www.semwebprogramming.net/weather#31384576>
    rdf:type dOnt:ImageType ;
    dOnt:Link "http://weather.gov"^^xsd:string ;
    dOnt:Title "NOAA's National Weather Service"^^xsd:string ;
    dOnt:Url "http://weather.gov/images/xml_logo.gif"^^xsd:string .

dOnt:CurrentObservation
    rdf:type owl:Class .

<http://www.semwebprogramming.net/weather#32486590>
    rdf:type dOnt:CurrentObservation ;
    dOnt:CopyrightUrl "http://weather.gov/disclaimer.html"^^xsd:string ;
    dOnt:Credit "NOAA's National Weather Service"^^xsd:string ;
    dOnt:CreditURL "http://weather.gov/"^^xsd:string ;
    dOnt:DewpointC "-3.0"^^xsd:double ;
    dOnt:DewpointF "27.0"^^xsd:double ;
    dOnt:DewpointString "27 F (-3 C)"^^xsd:string ;
    dOnt:DisclaimerUrl "http://weather.gov/disclaimer.html"^^xsd:string ;
    dOnt:HeatIndexString "NA"^^xsd:string ;
    dOnt:IconUrlBase
        "http://weather.gov/weather/images/fcicons/"^^xsd:string ;
    dOnt:IconUrlName "sct.jpg"^^xsd:string ;
    dOnt:Image <http://www.semwebprogramming.net/weather#31384576> ;
    dOnt:Latitude "39.19"^^xsd:string ;
    dOnt:Location
        "Baltimore-Washington International Airport, MD"^^xsd:string ;
    dOnt:Longitude "-76.67"^^xsd:string ;
    dOnt:ObUrl
        "http://www.nws.noaa.gov/data/METAR/KBWI.1.txt"^^xsd:string ;
    dOnt:ObservationTime
        "Last Updated on Oct 19, 2:54 pm EDT"^^xsd:string ;
    dOnt:ObservationTimeRfc822
        "Sun, 19 Oct 2008 14:54:00 -0400 EDT"^^xsd:string ;
    dOnt:PressureIn "30.33"^^xsd:double ;
```

```
dOnt:PressureMb "1027.0"^^xsd:double ;
dOnt:PressureString "30.33\" (1027.0 mb)"^^xsd:string ;
dOnt:PrivacyPolicyUrl
    "http://weather.gov/notice.html"^^xsd:string ;
dOnt:RelativeHumidity "32"^^xsd:long ;
dOnt:StationId "KBWI"^^xsd:string ;
dOnt:SuggestedPickup "15 minutes after the hour"^^xsd:string ;
dOnt:SuggestedPickupPeriod "60"^^xsd:long ;
dOnt:TempC "14.0"^^xsd:double ;
dOnt:TempF "57.0"^^xsd:double ;
dOnt:TemperatureString "57 F (14 C)"^^xsd:string ;
dOnt:TwoDayHistoryUrl
     "http://www.weather.gov/data/obhistory/KBWI.html"^^xsd:string ;
dOnt:Version "1.0"^^xsd:string ;
dOnt:VisibilityMi "10.0"^^xsd:double ;
dOnt:Weather "Partly Cloudy"^^xsd:string ;
dOnt:WindDegrees "50"^^xsd:long ;
dOnt:WindDir "Northeast"^^xsd:string ;
dOnt:WindGustMph "22.0"^^xsd:double ;
dOnt:WindMph "10.35"^^xsd:double ;
dOnt:WindString
   "From the Northeast at 10 Gusting to 22 MPH"^^xsd:string ;
dOnt:WindchillC "13"^^xsd:long ;
dOnt:WindchillF "55"^^xsd:long ;
dOnt:WindchillString "55 F (13 C)"^^xsd:string .
```

A few observations are worth pointing out with this result. All of the properties are exposed without explicitly being handled. This is different from the other approaches to exposing the Weather.gov data feed. Also, full datatype information is there for all of the values. The other approaches could also have included this; however, this time the application figured it out without requiring any manual configuration. Notice that there is more than one instance in the output and that they are connected by an object property (highlighted in the example in bold).

In summary, the benefits of the technique include:

- The technique is fully generalized and requires no configuration.

- Datatype information is intact without any extra configuration.

- It provides a very quick way to get Java data into RDF.

- It is very modular because this technique can process any data that can be loaded into Java objects.

There are a number of drawbacks to this approach. The processor in this example is very primitive and is built on some assumptions about the structure of the data it is processing. However, with some work this technique could become a very robust solution. Just as one example, the Java Reflection API provides access to class and property annotations that could be used by this system to determine which classes and properties should be exposed and how. Despite those weaknesses, the example should illustrate how powerful a method like this can be.

The drawbacks include:

- The technique is so generalized that little customization can be performed without introducing it at the Java level.

- This implementation is very simplistic and is missing a lot of features, like using annotations to configure the output behavior.

Applying the RDF Generator to the Upcoming.org XML Feed

As a final example and an introduction to one of the other FriendTracker data sources, consider the Upcoming.org data source (the project can be found with the other FriendTracker projects). Upcoming.org provides an XML web service, just like Facebook. In this application, a Document Object Model is used to parse the XML feed and load it into Java objects. DOM is just another method of parsing XML, like using Java XML bindings. It wasn't covered in the earlier XML section, but it is another useful tool to be familiar with when working with XML. The DOM builds an in-memory representation of the XML document that can be traversed and manipulated. An in-depth discussion of the DOM is out of scope for this chapter, but example code is contained in the Upcoming.org project.

Using DOM, the Upcoming.org data source builds a collection of Java objects representing events. These objects are then processed using the same Java Reflection API–based RDF generator that we just applied to the Weather.gov XML feed. Consider the following RDF that was generated by querying the data source for events near Washington, D.C.

```
@prefix rdfs:    <http://www.w3.org/2000/01/rdf-schema#> .
@prefix dOnt:    <http://www.upcoming.org/ontology#> .
@prefix owl:     <http://www.w3.org/2002/07/owl#> .
@prefix xsd:     <http://www.w3.org/2001/XMLSchema#> .
@prefix rdf:     <http://www.w3.org/1999/02/22-rdf-syntax-ns#> .

<http://www.upcoming.org/events#24267421>
  rdf:type dOnt:VEvent ;
  dOnt:CategoryId "10"^^xsd:string ;
  dOnt:DatePosted "2008-10-16 08:19:20"^^xsd:string ;
  dOnt:Description
    "Morton's Steakhouse Hosts Argentinean Wine Dinner"^^xsd:string ;
  dOnt:EndTime "21:00:00"^^xsd:string ;
  dOnt:GeocodingAmbiguous "false"^^xsd:boolean ;
  dOnt:GeocodingPrecision "address"^^xsd:string ;
```

```
dOnt:Id "1236354"^^xsd:string ;
dOnt:Latitude "38.8604"^^xsd:double ;
dOnt:Longitude "-77.0497"^^xsd:double ;
dOnt:MetroId "171"^^xsd:string ;
dOnt:Name
    "Morton's The Steakhouse: Argentinean Wine Dinner"^^xsd:string ;
dOnt:StartDate "2008-11-07T05:00:00Z"^^xsd:dateTime ;
dOnt:StartTime "18:30:00"^^xsd:string ;
dOnt:TicketFree "0"^^xsd:string ;
dOnt:TicketPrice
    "$130 per person (inclusive of tax and gratuity)"^^xsd:string ;
dOnt:TicketUrl "http://www.mortons.com"^^xsd:string ;
dOnt:UserId "204308"^^xsd:string ;
dOnt:VenueAddress "1631 Crystal Square Arcade"^^xsd:string ;
dOnt:VenueCity "Arlington, VA"^^xsd:string ;
dOnt:VenueCountryCode "us"^^xsd:string ;
dOnt:VenueCountryId "1"^^xsd:string ;
dOnt:VenueCountryName "United States"^^xsd:string ;
dOnt:VenueId "39086"^^xsd:string ;
dOnt:VenueName "Morton's The Steakhouse (Crystal City)"^^xsd:string ;
dOnt:VenueStateCode "dc"^^xsd:string ;
dOnt:VenueStateId "9"^^xsd:string ;
dOnt:VenueStateName "District of Columbia"^^xsd:string ;
dOnt:VenueZip "22202"^^xsd:string .
```

The purpose of this example is not to cover DOM but rather to introduce another FriendTracker data source and to illustrate the point that the technologies of this chapter can be mixed and matched to expose data as RDF in any number of ways.

Summary

This chapter has presented a multitude of different technologies and techniques that you can use to expose data from all kinds of formats and representations to the Semantic Web as RDF with some primitive ontology description. No formal ontology was produced for any of the data sources, but classes and properties were generated in the resulting RDF. This means that a data source ontology can be built on top of that exposed data to add semantics to the RDF that was produced. This chapter is all about pulling all of these disparate data sources together into a common data model: RDF. The next chapter will deal with managing how the semantics of the various data sources combine and integrate.

Although this chapter dealt with many different sources of data, there are too many different sources to cover them all. Some of the data you will want to expose may already be in a representation that is very close to RDF.

A number of formats are similar to RDF or have semantic annotations. RDFa and Microformats are two such technologies. The trick to pulling these formats into your Semantic Web application is to process them using an appropriate parser. In the case of RDFa, the data is already RDF; it's just a matter of getting it into a syntax you can use or into a model you can access. Microformats are slightly different because they aren't RDF. They are a set of simple data formats that are based on widely used and accepted standards and vocabularies. To convert Microformats data to RDF, you can utilize any of the techniques covered in this chapter. All you need is a parser that can give you access to the data, and then you can transform it as you wish to build RDF using the techniques discussed in this chapter.

The important lesson to take away from this chapter is that there are tons of tools, techniques, and technologies that you can use to convert data from any format or representation into RDF so you can get it into the Semantic Web. Once it is in the RDF model, you can combine it, augment it with an ontology, translate it with SWRL rules, and query it with SPARQL. The key is to make it accessible as RDF. Some of the techniques for doing so are more generalized than others. Some of the techniques require stricter assumptions about the stability and consistency of data. These are all factors that you will have to consider when you set out to expose your data. Now that all of this data is exposed as RDF, it's time to draw connections between the knowledge models of each. This is the next critical step in integrating data sources in the Semantic Web.

## CHAPTER 10

Aligning Information

"The newest computer can merely compound, at speed, the oldest problem in the relations between human beings, and in the end the communicator will be confronted with the old problem, of what to say and how to say it."

—Edward R. Murrow

In the preceding chapters, you have learned about theoretical and practical knowledge modeling with RDF and OWL, inference and reasoners, Jena, triple stores, SPARQL, and SWRL. This chapter combines all of these threads to describe the task of information integration and explains the role that such integration plays in Semantic Web applications using the FriendTracker application. Specifically, in this chapter, you will:

- Learn about data source ontologies, domain ontologies, application ontologies, and the role they play in Semantic Web applications

- Learn about the FriendTracker application and get an introduction to data-oriented software design

- Learn about ontology alignment and how that process leads to truly integrated information

- See several concrete examples of different practical techniques for ontology alignment in the context of the FriendTracker application

Data Source, Domain, and Application Ontologies

In Chapter 9, "Combining Information," you learned how to transform data from a variety of sources into RDF data for the Semantic Web. Even after all of the data is represented in RDF, however, it is still not integrated in a meaningful sense because the information from each source is expressed in a vocabulary specific to that source. These vocabularies are referred to as *data source ontologies*, and they make it difficult to exploit the data they express. If the consumer of the information is not aware of the particulars of each of the data source ontologies, then he or she cannot make use of information from that source. Even though the information has been combined, it has not been integrated because the relationships between the concepts remain undefined.

Every community sees the world according to a particular perspective and has different interests and concerns. When you, for example, get a bill from your credit card company, you care about how much you owe and when it is due. You pay little attention to the return address or how much it cost the company to mail it. The U.S. Postal Service, on the other hand, cares only about the source, destination, and postage of the correspondence and is utterly indifferent to the contents. Moreover, when you send a letter, you think of the postage stamp as an expenditure, whereas the Postal Service sees that same stamp as a source of revenue. Which things are important, and even what they mean, is, therefore, very much dependent on a particular context, or *domain*. A *domain ontology* is a description of the concepts within a domain and the relationships among those concepts. Integrating information for the Semantic Web involves establishing connections and relationships between the concepts of a data source ontology and those of the domain ontology.

The process of drawing connections and associations between two ontologies is called *ontology alignment*. To align one ontology with another is to overlay the web of concepts described in the first with those of the second so that parallels can be made between them. This process is at the heart of information integration on the Semantic Web.

When actually building applications that use Semantic Web data, it is not enough to establish mappings between data source ontologies and a domain ontology. Just as each data source supports a particular view of the entities it describes, so too does a piece of software. String length, for instance, is something that a data source that's producing RDF might not be concerned with but that a consuming application might be. In general, software is built on data structures and assumptions that may not be easily compatible with the richer semantics of any particular domain ontology. Addressing this challenge leads to the notion of an *application ontology*. An application ontology is a domain ontology that represents the perspective of a software application. In this chapter, we use the application ontology of FriendTracker as the domain ontology to which we map the concepts of the data source ontologies.

Aligning Ontologies

To convert information from one ontological representation to another, there must be a set of mappings between the two ontologies. Determining these mappings is called *aligning* the ontologies. This can be a very challenging task.

Ontologies can be large, with tens, hundreds, or even thousands of classes and properties. Trying to take stock of such a complex framework of concepts can be daunting. There is active research into techniques to automate the process, but at this point, the task must ultimately be done by humans. While current tools can calculate class name and graph similarity metrics to try to give suggestions, they cannot yet consistently align ontologies automatically. Some of the research in the field of automated ontology alignment is described in Chapter 15, "Moving Forward."

There are two main approaches to manual ontology alignment. The first involves establishing a mapping between two ontologies by mapping each to a third shared ontology. Typically a foundational ontology is used in this case. This can be a very helpful approach if mappings to align one ontology with the foundation ontology already exist. Even if both ontologies have to be aligned with the foundation ontology, future mapping tasks are made easier. Nevertheless, it involves extra work in the short term, and if the concepts of the foundation ontology are not able to capture all the meaning of one of the ontologies precisely, that extra significance is lost in translation. It is worth noting again the guidance to reuse ontologies whenever possible. One of the main benefits of ontology reuse comes in the potential to reuse mappings between ontologies.

The second approach to manual ontology alignment dispenses with the intermediary and simply aligns the two ontologies directly with each other. This is more straightforward, involves less up-front work, and helps ensure that a precise alignment is possible. This is the way the ontologies are aligned in the FriendTracker application.

Once two ontologies have been aligned and a proper mapping between their concepts determined, the system must be made to perform that translation at runtime. Several approaches are typically used in real-world applications to accomplish this. We present examples of some of these techniques in the context of FriendTracker later in the chapter. These techniques are not mutually exclusive; depending on the size of the ontology, or the expression of the concepts themselves, these approaches can be used in concert with each other to achieve the translation.

Ontology Constructs

OWL supports many constructs that make it easy to express relationships among concepts. Relationships between concepts in different ontologies can be used to infer the desired results. Some of the most useful features include `owl:equivalentClass`, `owl:equivalentProperty`, `owl:sameAs`, and `owl:inverseOf`. In addition, the `rdfs:subClassOf` and `rdfs:subPropertyOf` predicates provide very useful semantics. Consider the following example:

```
@prefix rdf: <http://www.w3.org/1999/02/22-rdf-syntax-ns#> .
@prefix rdfs: <http://www.w3.org/2000/01/rdf-schema#> .
```

```
@prefix owl: <http://www.w3.org/2002/07/owl#> .
@prefix : <http://semwebprogramming.org:8099/2009/chapter10/ex1-1#> .


:HomeDweller a owl:Class .

:Mother rdfs:subClassOf :HomeDweller .
:Father rdfs:subClassOf :HomeDweller .
:Son rdfs:subClassOf :HomeDweller .
:Daughter rdfs:subClassOf :HomeDweller .


:hasChild a owl:ObjectProperty .
:hasSon rdfs:subPropertyOf :hasChild .
:hasDaughter rdfs:subPropertyOf :hasChild .
```

This small ontology describes the people who might live together in a home. A second ontology describes familial relationships:

```
@prefix rdf: <http://www.w3.org/1999/02/22-rdf-syntax-ns#> .
@prefix rdfs: <http://www.w3.org/2000/01/rdf-schema#> .
@prefix owl: <http://www.w3.org/2002/07/owl#> .
@prefix : <http://semwebprogramming.org:8099/2009/chapter10/ex1-2#> .


:Relative a owl:Class .

:Mother rdfs:subClassOf :Relative .
:Father rdfs:subClassOf :Relative .
:Child rdfs:subClassOf :Relative .


:hasParent a owl:ObjectProperty .
```

The relationships between these two sets of concepts can be expressed in OWL. Consider the following set of statements:

```
@prefix rdf: <http://www.w3.org/1999/02/22-rdf-syntax-ns#> .
@prefix rdfs: <http://www.w3.org/2000/01/rdf-schema#> .
@prefix owl: <http://www.w3.org/2002/07/owl#> .
@prefix ex1: <http://semwebprogramming.org:8099/2009/chapter10/ex1-1#> .
@prefix ex2: <http://semwebprogramming.org:8099/2009/chapter10/ex1-2#> .

ex1:Mother owl:equivalentClass ex2:Mother .
ex1:Father owl:equivalentClass ex2:Father .

ex1:Son rdfs:subClassOf ex2:Child .
ex1:Daughter rdfs:subClassof ex2:Child .

ex1:hasChild owl:inverseOf ex2:hasParent .
```

In this mapping, the Father and Mother classes from each ontology have been declared to be equivalent to each other. That implies that any individual who is a member of the Father class in either ontology is also asserted to be a Father in the other ontology, and the same for Mothers. The Son and

Daughter classes have been set as `rdfs:subClassOf` the `Child` class, meaning that membership in the `Son` or `Daughter` class implies membership in the `Child` class, but that membership in the `Child` class by itself does not imply anything. Finally, the `hasChild` property of the first ontology has been declared as the inverse of the `hasParent` of the second ontology. Because the `hasSon` and `hasDaughter` predicates from the first ontology are `rdfs:subClassOf` the `hasChild` predicate, in a model with all three ontologies the statements

```
:James a ex1:Father ;
    ex1:hasSon :David .
```

actually imply the following set of statements:

```
:James a ex1:Father ;
    a ex2:Father ;
    ex1:hasChild :David ;
    ex1:hasSon :David .
:David ex2:hasParent :David .
```

This example shows how mapping can be accomplished with ontology statements, but it also illustrates some of the challenges associated with ontology alignment more generally. Because the second ontology does not have a notion of gender as it relates to children, the `Son` and `Daughter` concepts from the first ontology cannot be expressed in the second.

Translation via Rules

Rules can be used to express mappings between ontologies. This approach works particularly well in combination with ontology constructs that support mapping. Rule-based ontology mapping is nice because rules can be updated or tweaked without having to rebuild the application, and also because rules can be easily reused and shared. The ease with which rules can be shared means that you are more likely to find already-created mappings if you take a rule-based approach. Rule-based approaches have some shortcomings, however. As discussed in Chapter 7, "Adding Rules," there is not yet a single rule language that enjoys universal support. SWRL is the closest candidate, but many popular frameworks do not support it. Jena, for instance, has its own rule engine and does not support SWRL. Jena can be used with the Pellet reasoner to add SWRL support, but at the time of this writing even Pellet does not provide complete support for all of the SWRL built-ins.

Explicit Translation

This approach is the most direct, and it could be characterized as the "brute-force" approach. Equivalences and transformations between the ontologies are explicitly encoded in software and then invoked whenever required. With large ontologies, this can be a very difficult and tedious task, and as is the case with most difficult and tedious software, it is also prone to error. The resulting mapping is also very inflexible because it is fixed at compile time. However, this approach is simple to understand, and representing the mappings as procedures allows developers to take advantage of the wealth of tools that already exist for software development and debugging. Also, the decrease in the flexibility of the mapping is offset by an increase in expressivity.

Ad Hoc Approaches to Translation

The best approach does not always fall so clearly into one of the previous categories. Depending on the situation, sometimes an entirely different method is used. Sometimes an Extensible Stylesheet Language Transformation (XSLT) is appropriate or the use of a templating engine like Velocity. Sometimes translation need not be done explicitly as a separate step and can be done implicitly as part of a SPARQL query. For example, returning to the previous examples, the following SPARQL query returns all of the individuals of the `Son` and `Daughter` classes from the first ontology as individuals of the `Child` class from the second ontology.

```
PREFIX ex1: <http://semwebprogramming.org:8099/2009/chapter10/ex1-1#>
PREFIX ex2: <http://semwebprogramming.org:8099/2009/chapter10/ex1-2#>
CONSTRUCT {
  ?person a ex2:Child .
  ?person2 a ex2:Child .
}
WHERE {
  OPTIONAL { ?person a ex1:Son } .
  OPTIONAL { ?person2 a ex1:Daughter } .
}
```

The best approach for any mapping task must be determined on a case-by-case basis. The FriendTracker application demonstrates several of these translation techniques.

FriendTracker

FriendTracker is an application that makes use of many of the techniques and tools described throughout this book and illustrates how they can be used in a practical way. FriendTracker allows users to view information about their friends' online personas and other associated information from several online sources. The data sources supported by FriendTracker are those described in the previous chapter, namely personal information from Facebook and Jabber, local events and activities from Upcoming.org, and posts from WordPress blogs.

When the FriendTracker window appears, it presents the user with a list of his or her friends. When the user selects a contact, more detailed information about that person appears along with any blog posts he or she has authored. If FriendTracker can determine the person's hometown, it presents a set of events taking place in and around that location. Selecting an event plots its location on a map. Figure 10-1 shows the FriendTracker window with a friend and event selected.

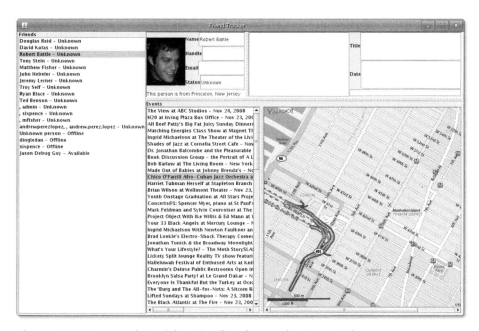

Figure 10-1 A screenshot of the FriendTracker application window

The goal of FriendTracker is to aggregate information from several different online sources, so it is designed to be very extensible with respect to its information access. In the UML class diagrams shown in Figures 10-2 and 10-3, you can see the information managed by FriendTracker and how the sources of friends, events, and blog posts are abstracted from the rest of the system.

Instances of classes that implement one of the -Source interfaces (Friend Source, EventSource, and PostSource) can be added to a SourceCollection instance, which then delegates requests it receives to these underlying sources. This separation makes it relatively easy to add a new source of information to FriendTracker: Implement one or more -Source interfaces, and then add the source to the SourceCollection. A flexible design makes sense regardless of whether the application is Semantic Web–oriented. Using Semantic Web data, however, makes the implementation of a system like this easy.

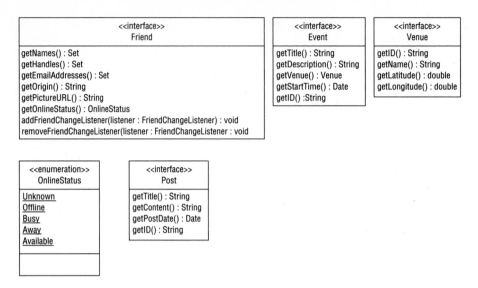

Figure 10-2 UML diagram of FriendTracker data objects

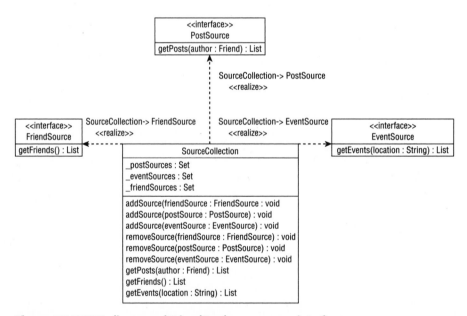

Figure 10-3 UML diagram of FriendTracker -Source interfaces

Underlying FriendTracker is an application ontology that mirrors the Java classes used by the program. The ontology defines properties and classes for all of the information that is represented in the Java objects supplied by the -Sources. A helper class called JenaSource, backed by a Jena model, serves as a bridge between the ontology and the rest of the software. The JenaSource class can create and populate FriendTracker data objects (`Friends`, `Events`, and `Posts`) based on data within its model so long as that data is encoded according to the FriendTracker application ontology. Assuming that there is useful information available encoded in the data source ontologies, all that is required of an implementation of a new -Source interface is to establish a proper conversion from the data source ontology to the FriendTracker ontology (see figure 10-4).

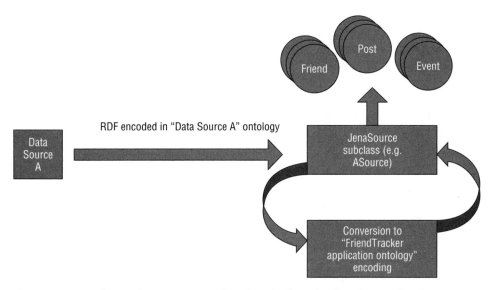

Figure 10-4 Implementing a -Source interface in the FriendTracker application

In the FriendTracker application, the classes `UpcomingEventSource`, `WordPressSource`, `FacebookFriendSource`, and `JabberFriendSource` all implement one or more of the -Source interfaces, and all subclass the `JenaSource` class.

In order to better understand the ontology alignment in FriendTracker, consider the FriendTracker application ontology:

```
# This file describes the application ontology employed by the
# FriendTracker UI.  Each of the properties and classes below can be
# populated by at least one of the data sources of FriendTracker:
# Facebook, Jabber, Upcoming, or WordPress

@prefix rdf: <http://www.w3.org/1999/02/22-rdf-syntax-ns#> .
@prefix rdfs: <http://www.w3.org/2000/01/rdf-schema#> .
@prefix owl: <http://www.w3.org/2002/07/owl#> .
@prefix xsd: <http://www.w3.org/2001/XMLSchema#> .
@prefix foaf: <http://xmlns.com/foaf/0.1/> .
@prefix time: <http://www.w3.org/2006/time#> .
@prefix geo: <http://www.w3.org/2003/01/geo/wgs84_pos#> .
```

```
@prefix : <http://semwebprogramming.org:8099/ont/friendtracker-ont#> .

# Friends represent people, and can come from Facebook, Jabber,
# or WordPress
:Friend a owl:Class ;
        rdfs:subClassOf foaf:Person .

# Online status information is available from both Facebook and Jabber
:OnlineStatus a owl:Class ;
                owl:oneOf (:Unknown :Available :Busy :Away :Offline) .
[] a owl:AllDifferent ;
    owl:distinctMembers (:Unknown :Available :Busy :Away :Offline) .

# This predicate will be used for both people and events.
:isNamed a owl:DatatypeProperty .

#   This predicate is a string which describes a location
#   (City, state, country, etc.)
:isFrom a owl:DatatypeProperty ;
        rdfs:range xsd:string .

# An OnlineStatus representing a person's online status.
:hasStatus a owl:ObjectProperty ;
            rdfs:range :OnlineStatus ;
            rdfs:domain :Friend .

# A URL of a picture of a person or venue
:hasPic a owl:DatatypeProperty .

# This field is provided by Jabber and WordPress
:hasEmailAddress a owl:DatatypeProperty ;
                 rdfs:range xsd:string ;
                 rdfs:domain :Friend .

# This field is provided by Jabber and WordPress
:hasHandle a owl:DatatypeProperty ;
            rdfs:range xsd:string ;
            rdfs:domain :Friend .

# This predicate ties people to blog posts
:hasPost a owl:ObjectProperty ;
          rdfs:range :Post ;
          rdfs:domain :Friend .

# An event has a name, a start time, and a venue
:Event a owl:Class ;
        rdfs:subClassOf [ a owl:Restriction ;
                          owl:onProperty :occursAt ;
                          owl:minCardinality "1"
                        ] ,
```

```
                              [ a owl:Restriction ;
                                owl:onProperty :isNamed ;
                                owl:minCardinality "1"
                              ] ,
                              [ a owl:Restriction ;
                                owl:onProperty :hasVenue ;
                                owl:minCardinality "1"
                              ] .
# A venue is a named point in space where an event takes place
:Venue a owl:Class ;
        rdfs:subClassOf geo:Point ,
                              [ a owl:Restriction ;
                                owl:onProperty :isNamed ;
                                owl:minCardinality "1"
                              ] .
# Associates an event with a Venue
:hasVenue a owl:ObjectProperty ;
          rdfs:range :Venue ;
          rdfs:domain :Event.

:hasDescription a owl:DatatypeProperty ;
                rdfs:range xsd:string .

# Used for both events and blog posts
:occursAt a owl:ObjectProperty ;
          rdfs:range time:Instant .

# Represents a blog post
:Post a owl:Class ;
      rdfs:subClassOf [ a owl:Restriction ;
                        owl:onProperty :hasTitle ;
                        owl:cardinality "1"
                      ] ,
                      [ a owl:Restriction ;
                        owl:onProperty :hasContent ;
                        owl:cardinality "1"
                      ] ,
                      [ a owl:Restriction ;
                        owl:onProperty :occursAt ;
                        owl:cardinality "1"
                      ] .
:hasTitle a owl:DatatypeProperty ;
          rdfs:range xsd:string .

:hasContent a owl:DatatypeProperty ;
            rdfs:range xsd:string .
```

Looking through the ontology, note the similarity between the classes and properties to those of the FriendTracker Java objects. There are, for instance, corresponding classes for Friend, Event, and Post. These OWL classes are designed to translate directly into the classes of objects (and in the case of `OnlineStatus`, an enumeration) that will be used in the application. There is some overloading of properties—the `occursAt` predicate is used for both the time of an event and the publication time of a blog post. There need not be a class or property for each class and relationship in the Java, so long as the ontology is capable of unambiguously representing the information used to build objects. This close correlation between the Java objects and the OWL constructs is typical of application ontologies.

Aligning Ontologies with OWL and SWRL

One of the important information sources for the FriendTracker application is Facebook. The following is the ontology describing the output of the Facebook data source. The classes and properties to be mapped into the FriendTracker ontology are in bold print.

```
@prefix f:        <http://www.facebook.com/ontology#> .
@prefix rdfs:     <http://www.w3.org/2000/01/rdf-schema#> .
@prefix xsd:      <http://www.w3.org/2001/XMLSchema#> .
@prefix owl:      <http://www.w3.org/2002/07/owl#> .
@prefix rdf:      <http://www.w3.org/1999/02/22-rdf-syntax-ns#> .
# Affiliation class and properties
f:Affiliation a owl:Class .

f:name a owl:DatatypeProperty .
# Location class and properties
f:Location a owl:Class .

f:city a owl:DatatypeProperty .
f:country a owl:DatatypeProperty .
f:state a owl:DatatypeProperty .
# Friend class and properties (f:name is used for Affiliations
# and Friends as well)
f:Friend a owl:Class .

f:interests a owl:DatatypeProperty .
f:books a owl:DatatypeProperty .
f:birthday a owl:DatatypeProperty .
f:activities a owl:DatatypeProperty .
f:movies a owl:DatatypeProperty .
f:music a owl:DatatypeProperty .
f:picture a owl:DatatypeProperty .
f:tv a owl:DatatypeProperty .
f:political a owl:DatatypeProperty .

f:location a owl:ObjectProperty .
f:hasAffiliation a owl:ObjectProperty .
```

Some of the information from Facebook does not have a place in the Friend-Tracker ontology. For instance, FriendTracker does not maintain information about TV or movies, so that information cannot be expressed in its ontology and cannot be mapped. Looking back at the relevant portions of the FriendTracker ontology, it is clear that there are a few direct correspondences:

```
@prefix rdf: <http://www.w3.org/1999/02/22-rdf-syntax-ns#> .
@prefix rdfs: <http://www.w3.org/2000/01/rdf-schema#> .
@prefix owl: <http://www.w3.org/2002/07/owl#> .
@prefix xsd: <http://www.w3.org/2001/XMLSchema#> .
@prefix foaf: <http://xmlns.com/foaf/0.1/> .

@prefix : <http://semwebprogramming.org/2009/ftracker#> .

#  Friends represent people, and can come from Facebook, Jabber,
#  or WordPress
:Friend a owl:Class ;
        rdfs:subClassOf foaf:Person .

#  This predicate will be used for both people and events.
:isNamed a owl:DatatypeProperty .

#  This predicate is a string which describes a location (City,
#  state, country, etc.)
:isFrom a owl:DatatypeProperty ;
        rdfs:range xsd:string .

#  A URL of a picture of a person or venue
:hasPic a owl:DatatypeProperty .
```

The one sticking point is the location. In the Facebook ontology, the location is represented as a bnode with `city`, `state`, and `country` properties. In the FriendTracker ontology, the `isFrom` property represents the origin location as a string. The relationship between the Facebook `Friend` class and the FriendTracker `Friend` class, as well as the other properties, can be expressed with `owl:equivalentClass` and `owl:equivalentProperty` statements, but the location predicate requires a SWRL rule. Using the SWRL `stringConcat` built-in, the rule can format the values of the `city` and `state` properties into a `<City>`, `<State>` form that is appropriate for FriendTracker. The following code shows the ontology statements and rule that map from the Facebook data source ontology to the FriendTracker application ontology:

```
# Standard import statements
@prefix rdf: <http://www.w3.org/1999/02/22-rdf-syntax-ns#> .
@prefix rdfs: <http://www.w3.org/2000/01/rdf-schema#> .
@prefix owl: <http://www.w3.org/2002/07/owl#> .
@prefix xsd: <http://www.w3.org/2001/XMLSchema#> .
```

```
# SWRL imports
@prefix swrl: <http://www.w3.org/2003/11/swrl#> .
@prefix swrlb: <http://www.w3.org/2003/11/swrlb#> .

# Domain imports
@prefix ft: <http://semwebprogramming.org/2009/ftracker#> .
@prefix facebook: <http://www.facebook.com/ontology#> .

@prefix : <http://semwebprogramming.org:8099/ont/ft-facebook-mapping#> .

facebook:Friend owl:equivalentClass ft:Friend .
facebook:name owl:equivalentProperty ft:isNamed .
facebook:picture owl:equivalentProperty ft:hasPic .

:state a swrl:Variable .
:city a swrl:Variable .
:person a swrl:Variable .
:loc a swrl:Variable .
:origin a swrl:Variable .

:OriginRule a swrl:Imp ;
swrl:body
(
[ a swrl:IndividualPropertyAtom ;
  swrl:propertyPredicate facebook:location ;
  swrl:argument1 :person ;
  swrl:argument2 :loc
]
[ a swrl:DatavaluedPropertyAtom ;
  swrl:propertyPredicate facebook:city ;
  swrl:argument1 :loc ;
  swrl:argument2 :city
]
[ a swrl:DatavaluedPropertyAtom ;
  swrl:propertyPredicate facebook:state ;
  swrl:argument1 :loc ;
  swrl:argument2 :state
]
[ a swrl:BuiltinAtom ;
  swrl:builtin swrlb:stringConcat ;
  swrl:arguments (:origin :city  ", " :state )
]
) ;
swrl:head
(
[ a swrl:DatavaluedPropertyAtom ;
  swrl:propertyPredicate ft:isFrom ;
  swrl:argument1 :person ;
  swrl:argument2 :origin
]
) .
```

Now that there is an ontology to bridge the gap between the data source and the application ontology, we need to use it from within Java to convert between them. The `FacebookFriendSource` class is a subclass of `JenaSource`, which is able to create and populate FriendTracker Java objects based on instance data encoded in the Facebook ontology. There are three important methods in the `FacebookFriendSource` class, which are shown in the following code.

```
public class FacebookFriendSource extends JenaSource
   implements FriendSource {

   private FacebookRESTClient _client;
   private FacebookConfiguration _config;
   private String _authToken = null;

   @Override
   protected void createModel() {
     model =
     ModelFactory.createOntologyModel(PelletReasonerFactory.THE_SPEC);
   }

   @Override
   public void initialize(Object configurationObject) {

   // *Snip* Facebook client-specific configuration...

     String mappingLocation = _config.getMappingLocation();
     String friendtrackerOntologyLocation =
                 config.getFriendTrackerOntologyLocation();
     FileInputStream mappingStream = null;
     FileInputStream friendtrackerOntologyStream = null;
     try {
       mappingStream = new FileInputStream(mappingLocation);
       friendtrackerOntologyStream =
           new FileInputStream(friendtrackerOntologyLocation);
   // bring in the mapping stuff - OWL + rules...
       model.read(
         friendtrackerOntologyStream,
         "http://semwebprogramming.org/2009/ftracker#",
         "TURTLE");
       model.prepare();
       model.read(
         mappingStream,
         "http://semwebprogramming.org:8099/ont/ft-facebook-mapping#",
         "TURTLE");
       model.prepare();
     } catch (FileNotFoundException e) {
         throw new ProperException(e);
     }
   }
```

```
public List<Friend> getFriends() {
  List<Friend> toReturn;
  String friendUids;
  String authToken = getAuthToken();
  FacebookSession session;
  Collection<String> friends;
  session = _client.createSession(authToken);
  friends = _client.getFriendsList(session);
  friendUids = Utilities.concatenateStringSet(
              new HashSet<String>(friends));
  model.read(
    client.getPopulatedFriendsRdf(
      session, friendUids, config.getFields(), "TURTLE"),
    "",
    "TURTLE");
  toReturn = extractFriends();
  return toReturn;
  }
}
```

Within the FriendTracker application, the convention is for the methods to be called in order: `createModel`, `initialize`, and then, at some point later in the execution, `getFriends`. The `createModel` method is very short, and it simply initializes a new Jena model defined by the `JenaSource` parent class. It initializes that model using the Pellet reasoner because this class uses Pellet for its SWRL processing and inferencing.

The `initialize` method loads the location of the FriendTracker ontology and the mapping ontologies from the configuration objects, and then it uses the Jena model to load those two ontologies. At this point, with the model primed and Pellet engaged, any new statements in the Facebook data source ontology will allow Pellet to infer the correct statements in the application ontology. This is what happens upon a call to `getFriends`. The `getFriends` method calls the Facebook RDF client from Chapter 9 and loads that information into the model. Finally, a call to the `JenaSource` method `extractFriends` causes it to create and populate FriendTracker `Friend` objects based on the information in the model.

Aligning Ontologies with XSLT

If it is practical to serialize RDF encoded in a source ontology as RDF/XML, an Extensible Stylesheet Language Transformation (XSLT) can sometimes be used to map between ontologies. This can be a very desirable technique for mapping given the widespread availability of XSLT tools and expertise. However, be careful when considering this approach. It can be dangerous to use XSLTs for ontology alignment because the same RDF graph can be serialized in different ways. For example, consider the following two simple RDF/XML graphs:

```
<rdf:RDF
   xmlns:rdf="http://www.w3.org/1999/02/22-rdf-syntax-ns#"
   xmlns:rdfs="http://www.w3.org/2000/01/rdf-schema#"
   xmlns:owl="http://www.w3.org/2002/07/owl#"
   xml:base="http://example.org/example-ont#"
>
   <owl:Class rdf:ID="Person" />
</rdf:RDF>
<rdf:RDF
   xmlns:rdf="http://www.w3.org/1999/02/22-rdf-syntax-ns#"
   xmlns:rdfs="http://www.w3.org/2000/01/rdf-schema#"
   xmlns:owl="http://www.w3.org/2002/07/owl#"
   xml:base="http://example.org/example-ont#"
>
   <rdf:Description rdf:about="#Person">
      <rdf:type rdf:resource="http://www.w3.org/2002/07/owl#Class" />
   </rdf:Description>
</rdf:RDF>
```

Both define a new class called `Person` and in fact represent the exact same statement. An XSLT written to match the first serialization would not match the second. In cases where the RDF/XML serialization is consistent and well known, however, it is feasible to use an XSLT to do translations between RDF/XML documents.

An example of this is the WordPress source. The WordPress client code, based on the version in Chapter 9, uses Jena to perform the RDF/XML serialization, so it is always produced in a consistent way. The `WordPressSource` class implements both `FriendSource` and `PostSource` because it maintains information about the authors of the posts. Recall from Chapter 9 that the WordPress data source works by issuing a SPARQL query against a D2RQ-enabled Word-Press blog database. D2RQ translates the SPARQL query into SQL queries and then sends the results back as RDF. The query used to generate the results is reproduced here:

```
PREFIX wp: <http://www.semwebprogramming.net/wordpress/ontology#>
PREFIX rdfs: <http://www.w3.org/2000/01/rdf-schema#>
PREFIX rdf: <http://www.w3.org/1999/02/22-rdf-syntax-ns#>
PREFIX xsd: <http://www.w3.org/2001/XMLSchema#>

CONSTRUCT
{
   ?user    rdf:type wp:wp_users;
            wp:wp_users_ID ?uid;
            ?usersProp ?usersVal.
   ?post    rdf:type wp:wp_posts;
            wp:wp_posts_post_author ?uid;
            ?postProp ?postVal.
```

```
          }
          WHERE
          {
              ?user    rdf:type wp:wp_users;
                       wp:wp_users_ID ?uid;
                       ?usersProp ?usersVal.
              ?post    rdf:type wp:wp_posts;
                       wp:wp_posts_post_author ?uid;
                       wp:wp_posts_post_type "post";
                       wp:wp_posts_post_status "publish";
                       ?postProp ?postVal.
          }
```

FriendTracker can make use of only a subset of the many fields that are returned for posts and authors. In particular, the fields wp_posts_post_content, wp_posts_post_title, wp_posts_post_date, and wp_posts_ID are relevant for the Post objects, and the wp_users_ID, wp_users_user_nicename, wp_users_user_login, and wp_users_user_email fields are relevant for Friend objects. These properties map easily to properties in the FriendTracker application ontology. The following code shows the XSLT that FriendTracker uses to map from the WordPress data source ontology to the application ontology:

```xml
<?xml version="1.0"?>

<xsl:stylesheet xmlns:xsl="http://www.w3.org/1999/XSL/Transform"
  xmlns:rdf="http://www.w3.org/1999/02/22-rdf-syntax-ns#"
  xmlns:wp="http://www.semwebprogramming.net/wordpress/ontology#"
  xmlns:ft="http://semwebprogramming.org/2009/ftracker#"
  version="1.0">

  <xsl:output method="xml" version="1.0" encoding="UTF-8"
    indent="yes" />

<!-- match the root node (and add our own RDF root... -->
  <xsl:template match="/rdf:RDF">
    <rdf:RDF
      xmlns:rdf="http://www.w3.org/1999/02/22-rdf-syntax-ns#"
      xmlns:rdfs="http://www.w3.org/2000/01/rdf-schema#"
      xmlns:owl="http://www.w3.org/2002/07/owl#"
      xmlns:xsd="http://www.w3.org/2001/XMLSchema#"
      xmlns:ft=
          "http://semwebprogramming.org/2009/ftracker#"
      xmlns:time="http://www.w3.org/2006/time#"
      xml:base="http://semwebprogramming.org:8099/data/wordpress#"
      >


    <xsl:for-each select="rdf:Description">
<!-- Handle posts -->
```

```
        <xsl:if
          test="rdf:type/@rdf:resource =
'http://www.semwebprogramming.net/wordpress/ontology#wp_posts'">
<rdf:Description rdf:about="#post{wp:wp_posts_ID}">
  <rdf:type
          rdf:resource=
          "http://semwebprogramming.org/2009/ftracker#Post"
        />
  <ft:hasContent>
    <xsl:value-of select="wp:wp_posts_post_content" />
  </ft:hasContent>
  <ft:hasTitle>
    <xsl:value-of select="wp:wp_posts_post_title" />
  </ft:hasTitle>
  <ft:occursAt>
            <time:Instant>
              <time:inXSDDateTime>
                <xsl:value-of
                    select="wp:wp_posts_post_date" />
              </time:inXSDDateTime>
            </time:Instant>
          </ft:occursAt>
</rdf:Description>
        </xsl:if>


<!-- Handle users -->
      <xsl:if
          test="rdf:type/@rdf:resource =
'http://www.semwebprogramming.net/wordpress/ontology#wp_users'">
          <rdf:Description rdf:about="#user{wp:wp_users_ID}">
  <rdf:type rdf:resource=
"http://semwebprogramming.org/2009/ftracker#Friend" />
  <ft:isNamed>
    <xsl:value-of select="wp:wp_users_user_nicename"/>
  </ft:isNamed>
  <ft:isNamed>
    <xsl:value-of select="wp:wp_users_user_displayname"/>
  </ft:isNamed>
  <ft:hasHandle>
    <xsl:value-of select="wp:wp_users_user_login" />
  </ft:hasHandle>
  <ft:hasEmailAddress>
    <xsl:value-of select="wp:wp_users_user_email" />
  </ft:hasEmailAddress>
</rdf:Description>
        </xsl:if>
      </xsl:for-each>

<!-- Associate posts with users -->
    <xsl:for-each select="rdf:Description">
```

```
            <xsl:if test="rdf:type/@rdf:resource=
    'http://www.semwebprogramming.net/wordpress/ontology#wp_posts'">
             <rdf:Description rdf:about="#user{wp:wp_posts_post_author}">
        <ft:hasPost rdf:resource="#post{wp:wp_posts_ID}" />
    </rdf:Description>
            </xsl:if>
        </xsl:for-each>
        </rdf:RDF>
      </xsl:template>
    </xsl:stylesheet>
```

Because of the current state of SWRL and SWRL tool support, some ontology translation operations are significantly easier to accomplish with an XSLT as compared to SWRL rules. For example, in the WordPress XSLT, each resulting `Post` and `Friend` instance is assigned an IRI that is based on its primary key within the database. This is a valuable characteristic because that IRI is now consistent and unique. Subsequent queries to WordPress that return the same IRI will be describing the same users and blog posts. This is something that is not easily accomplished with the SWRL support of today. We can expect that as time passes and a Semantic Web rule standard settles, XSLT will become less relevant to ontology translation, but until that time it remains a valuable tool for Semantic Web application developers.

At this point, it is useful to turn back to the Java code, specifically to the `JenaSource` class. In the code that follows we see how the `JenaSource` class uses a SPARQL query against its internal model to generate new `Post` objects when requested:

```
protected List<Post> extractPosts() {
  List<Post> toReturn = new ArrayList<Post>();
  final String queryString =
"PREFIX ft: <" + FriendTracker.Base.getString() + "> \n" +
"PREFIX time: <" + Time.Base.getString() + "> \n" +
"SELECT ?post ?title ?content ?date \n" +
"WHERE { ?post a ft:Post ; ft:hasTitle ?title ; \n" +
    "        ft:hasContent ?content ; \n" +
    "        ft:occursAt [ time:inXSDDateTime ?date ]}";
  Query query;
  QueryExecution queryExecution;
  ResultSet rs;

  query = QueryFactory.create(queryString);
  queryExecution = QueryExecutionFactory.create(query, _model);
  rs = queryExecution.execSelect();
  while(rs.hasNext()){
QuerySolution solution = rs.nextSolution();
RDFNode temp;
PostImpl post = new PostImpl();
temp = solution.get("post");
```

```
post.setID(temp.asNode().getURI());
temp = solution.get("title");
post.setTitle(extractValueFromNode(temp));
temp = solution.get("content");
post.setContent(extractValueFromNode(temp));
temp = solution.get("date");
post.setPostDate(parseDate(extractValueFromNode(temp)));

toReturn.add(post);
  }
  return toReturn;
}
```

Just as the `FacebookFriendSource` called `JenaSource`'s `extractFriends` method, so does the `WordPressSource` call the `extractPosts` method. Here you can see the method in its entirety. It shows how to use SPARQL queries to navigate the graph of statements to quickly extract useful data.

Aligning Ontologies with Code

While external tools like SWRL and XSLT can simplify ontology alignment and translation, sometimes it is more appropriate to use code for this task. These tools are very helpful, but depending on the resource or performance constraints on your application, it may make sense to investigate optimizing translation code and implementing it by hand. The `UpcomingEventSource` has been implemented to manually perform an ontology mapping as an illustration of how to proceed in this situation.

The structure of the ontology translation code within the `Upcoming EventSource` models the structure of the data upon which it operates. Execution flows downward through the methods `performConversionFrom UpcomingOntToFriendTrackerOnt`, `convertOneEvent`, and `convertOneVenue` until all of the events and their associated venues have been re-expressed according to the FriendTracker application ontology. As a representative example of the way these methods work, the following example shows the `convertOneVenue` method:

```
private void convertOneVenue(Resource upcomingEvent, Individual venue) {
    String venueName;
    String venueLat;
    String venueLong;

    venueName = extractValueFromNode(
        getFirstNode(
            _model.listObjectsOfProperty(
                upcomingEvent,
                _model.createProperty(
                    Upcoming.getString(Upcoming.Base) + "VenueName"))));
```

```
venueLat = extractValueFromNode(
    getFirstNode(
        _model.listObjectsOfProperty(
            upcomingEvent,
            _model.createProperty(
                Upcoming.getString(Upcoming.Base) + "Latitude"))));
venueLong = extractValueFromNode(
    getFirstNode(
        _model.listObjectsOfProperty(
            upcomingEvent,
            _model.createProperty(
                Upcoming.getString(Upcoming.Base) + "Longitude"))));
if(null != venueName)
{
  _model.add(venue, getProperty(FriendTracker.isNamed), venueName);
}
if(null != venueLat)
{
  _model.add(venue, getProperty(Geo.latitude), venueLat);
}
if(null != venueLong)
{
  _model.add(venue, getProperty(Geo.longitude), venueLong);
}

_model.add(upcomingEvent, getProperty(FriendTracker.hasVenue), venue);
}
```

Navigating the graph this way can be very efficient, particularly when the structure of the classes and relationships in the data source ontology aligns closely with the structure of those in the application ontology. Without similar graph structures, the software must pass around so much context between methods that the code can become less efficient. This approach also has the drawback of a tight dependency on the framework. While a change of underlying framework would require changes to the data source even if SWRL or XSLT were used, in the case where the mapping occurs in external tools that conform to well-known standards, the dependency is just on the interface code and not on the business logic.

Aligning Simple Ontologies with RDFS

We've seen how OWL and SWRL can be used to align ontologies. In some cases, however, OWL and SWRL are more powerful tools than are required. Albert Einstein famously said, "Make everything as simple as possible, but no simpler." In the case of RDFS and OWL, following that advice and choosing to represent mappings in RDFS as opposed to OWL can net significant dividends. Tool support for RDFS is more widespread than for OWL, which means that avoiding OWL in favor of RDFS offers more choices of tool implementations. In addition, because RDFS is relatively less expressive than OWL, an inference engine that implements only RDFS reasoning can often be made to run faster than one that must also consider OWL semantics.

RDFS reasoning can be more useful for practical alignment than might immediately be obvious. Take, for instance, the case of the `owl:equivalentClass` and `owl:equivalentProperty` constructs. While these are invaluable for rigorous ontology alignment, in the case of an application like FriendTracker where the mapping between data source and application ontologies need only be one-way, `rdfs:subClassOf` and `rdfs:subPropertyOf` are sufficient. Consider the case of the Jabber data source ontology:

```
# Standard import statements
@prefix rdf: <http://www.w3.org/1999/02/22-rdf-syntax-ns#> .
@prefix rdfs: <http://www.w3.org/2000/01/rdf-schema#> .
@prefix owl: <http://www.w3.org/2002/07/owl#> .
@prefix xsd: <http://www.w3.org/2001/XMLSchema#> .

@prefix : <http://www.jabber.org/ontology#> .

:Contact a owl:Class .
:name a owl:DatatypeProperty .
:status a owl:DatatypeProperty .
:presenceType a owl:ObjectProperty .
:presenceMode a owl:ObjectProperty .
```

It is clear that there is an `owl:equivalentClass` relationship between the `Contact` class of the Jabber ontology and the `Friend` class of the FriendTracker ontology, as well as an `owl:equivalentProperty` relationship between `name` and `isNamed`. FriendTracker never uses the Jabber client in such a way as to need to represent contacts from Facebook or WordPress as Jabber objects. There would in fact be no point of doing that in this case, since we can query the Jabber service only with reference to Jabber users. In this case, it is sufficient to use the `rdfs:subClassOf` and `rdfs:subPropertyOf` statements instead of the OWL constructs. These will result in the proper assertions from the point of view of FriendTracker, which is sufficient here. The mapping for this class and property is as follows:

```
@prefix friendtracker:
        <http://semwebprogramming.org/2009/ftracker#> .
@prefix jabber: <http://www.jabber.org/ontology#> .

jabber:Contact rdfs:subClassOf friendtracker:Friend .
jabber:name rdfs:subPropertyOf friendtracker:isNamed .
```

Restricting the mapping vocabulary to RDFS and excluding OWL means that a wider range of reasoner implementations is available. Of course, while this mapping is sufficient for this property and class, it does not cover the `presenceType` and `presenceMode` predicates. These can be mapped explicitly using a lookup in code:

```
private Model performMappingQuery(String ftProp, String ftVal,
                        String jabProp, String jabVal) {
   String queryString = String.format(
      "CONSTRUCT {\n " +
      "?person <%1$s> <%2$s> .\n" +
      "}\n" +
      "WHERE {\n" +
      "?person <%3$s> <%4$s> .\n" +
      "}",
      ftProp,
      ftVal,
      jabProp,
      jabVal);
   Query query = QueryFactory.create(queryString);
   QueryExecution queryExec =
               QueryExecutionFactory.create(query, _model);

   return queryExec.execConstruct();
}

private void convertStatus() {
   final String jabberOnt = _config.getBaseOntologyUri();
 _model.add(
    performMappingQuery(
      FriendTracker.hasStatus.getString(),
      FriendTracker.AvailableStatus.getString(),
      jabberOnt + "presenceMode",
      jabberOnt + "Available"));
   // Perform similar mapping queries for Away, DoNotDisturb and
   // unavailable...
}
```

This approach is very practical in that it has no dependencies except for Jena, uses the simplest RDFS reasoning possible, and complements that with a few small queries. This code is easy to understand and performs well.

FriendTracker is an example of how easy Semantic Web technologies can make information integration. Careful design of the application ontology and a small amount of work to create the `JenaSource` class is all it took to establish a flexible system that can integrate new sources with minimal marginal work. Each new data source need only accomplish a mapping between its own ontology and the FriendTracker ontology to be used by the application.

Each source was essentially a thin wrapper around a shared Jena model. In the case of the Facebook and WordPress modules, there were not any direct dependencies on the ontologies that would require a recompilation should the data source ontologies be altered. The only ontology on which there was a significant dependency was the application ontology, which represents the mode of operation for the entire program itself.

This approach to software development has some advantages that reach beyond a single application. When designing a data source client, you can feel assured that if you use an ontology as your output format, then consumers of all sorts will be able to easily access your results. Ontological representations like those used in FriendTracker also update well. Because the mappings from the data source ontology to the application ontology care only about specific fields, it does not matter if new fields are added in the future. Using a standard format like OWL means that you can spend less of your time implementing each data source and be confident that you will be able to reuse your code in the future.

So far in the chapter, we've seen how to use Semantic Web technologies to align ontologies and integrate information. However, there remains another component to information integration that we have not mentioned: record linkage.

Record Linkage

Record linkage describes the issue of two entity descriptions that actually refer to the same entity. This is a widespread problem that is not specific to Semantic Web approaches to information integration; the term *record linkage* is used in relational database communities as well.

This problem has two dimensions. The first is the challenge of determining when two descriptions describe the same entity; the second is how to handle that situation once it is identified. There are sometimes easy solutions to both aspects, but often one or both present complications.

Sometimes characteristics of data sets can make it feasible to determine automatically that two entities are the same. Functional and inverse functional predicates (explained in detail in Chapter 4, "Incorporating Semantics"), for example, provide some support for automatically determining when two individuals are identical.

If entities can be uniquely identified by some characteristic, say a Social Security Number for people or a Universal Product Code for merchandise, and if that value is available from all of the data sources in an application, then the identification question becomes a trivial one. In fact, the `owl:hasKey` construct is designed to address precisely this situation:

```
@prefix rdf: <http://www.w3.org/1999/02/22-rdf-syntax-ns#> .
@prefix rdfs: <http://www.w3.org/2000/01/rdf-schema#> .
@prefix owl: <http://www.w3.org/2002/07/owl#> .
```

```
@prefix xsd: <http://www.w3.org/2001/XMLSchema#> .
@prefix : <http://semwebprogramming.org:8099/2009/chapter10/ex2#> .

:Product a owl:Class .
:PeanutButter a owl:Class ;
              rdfs:subClassOf :Product .
:hasName a owl:DatatypeProperty ;
         rdfs:range xsd:string .
:Crunchiness a owl:Class ;
             owl:oneOf (:Crunchy :Creamy) .
:Crunchy owl:differentFrom :Creamy .
:hasCrunchiness a owl:ObjectProperty ;
                rdfs:domain :Product ;
                rdfs:range :Crunchiness .
:hasSize a owl:DatatypeProperty .
:hasUPC a owl:DatatypeProperty ;
        rdfs:domain :Product ;
        rdfs:range xsd:string .
:Product owl:hasKey :hasUPC .

[] a :Product ;
   :hasName "JIF Peanut Butter" ;
   :hasSize "18" ;
   :hasUPC "051500241356" .

[] a :Product ;
   :hasName "JIF Peanut Butter" ;
   :hasSize "18" ;
   :hasUPC "051500241288" .

[] a :PeanutButter ;
   :hasName "Peanut Butter" ;
   :hasCrunchiness :Creamy ;
   :hasUPC "051500241288" .

[] a :PeanutButter ;
   :hasName "Peanut Butter" ;
   :hasCrunchiness :Crunchy ;
   :hasUPC "051500241356" .
```

The semantics of `owl:hasKey` are such that if two instances have the same key, then they are implied to be the same instance. The preceding code shows four instances: two that describe the crunchiness of the peanut butter and two that include a size in ounces. The `owl:hasKey` assertion helps to tie the instances together to give a more complete picture of the project. With the `owl:hasKey` statement, we can infer that there are in fact two instances as described: one creamy, one crunchy, and both 18 ounces.

If, however, no single identifying set of characteristics is available to serve as the role of a primary key, then things become much more difficult. The power of the Semantic Web is that it allows for the interchange of information from a multitude of heterogeneous sources that need not share any knowledge of one another, but those exact characteristics make it difficult to identify duplicate descriptions. This is a question for which there is no correct answer, and each application developer must consider it on a case-by-case basis depending on the particular situation.

Generally speaking, presenting users with the opportunity to identify duplicate entities is a useful approach, since their familiarity with the application domain should make them good judges. An enhancement of this basic idea is to flag entities as possible duplicates based on any number of similarity measures. Even if the available data is not sufficient to declare with certainty that two individuals are identical, reducing the burden placed on users to make these sorts of determinations is valuable. Which values are the most significant determinants of similarity depends on the application domain.

The picture is a little brighter once duplicates have been identified. OWL provides a construct for expressing that two individual entities are the same as one another: `owl:sameAs`. If two entities have been asserted to be `owl:sameAs` each other, then every statement for which either entity is the subject or object is equally valid for the other. For example, the following statements:

```
:A owl:sameAs :B .
:A :hasName "Adam" .
:B :hasName "Betty" .
:A :isTallerThan :B .
```

imply the following additional statements:

```
:A :hasName "Betty" .
:B :hasName "Adam" .
:B :isTallerThan :A .
:A :isTallerThan :A .
:B :isTallerThan :B .
:B owl:sameAs :A .
:A owl:sameAs :A .
:B owl:sameAs :B .
```

By virtue of the `owl:sameAs` statement, `:A` and `:B` have been identified as alternate names for the same individual entity. This can be a very powerful tool, but it can present issues as well. Suppose that the user who asserted `:A owl:sameAs :B` saw the additional statements and decided that there was a contradiction in the notion of `:A :isTallerThan :A` and wanted to change his mind. With a forward-chaining reasoner, the extra assertions could have been entailed and added to the knowledgebase in a way that would have made it difficult if not impossible to determine what the original set of statements was.

Another approach is to introduce your own concepts into the application ontology that represent the concept of sameness. For example, a predicate like `provisionallySameAs` could be used to express the idea that the present working assumption is that two individuals are identical. This method avoids the automatic entailment of statements that could be wrong, but at its own cost. Because OWL reasoners do not recognize this predicate as significant, they will not entail any extra statements based on it. This of course means that you will have to either modify the queries used by your system to accommodate this concept or implement some other method of behaving, treating `provisionallySameAs` entities appropriately. Using a custom property means that querying the model becomes more complicated, but it is often the right approach for long-lived systems.

Summary

In this chapter, you've learned about information integration via ontology alignment and seen the various techniques employed by the FriendTracker application. You've seen some of the benefits of a data-centered application design and the flexibility it affords. In Chapter 11, "Sharing Information," you'll learn ways to take integrated information and expose it to the wider world.

Sharing Information

"Share Everything."
—Robert Fulghum

Information was meant to be free and the Semantic Web gives us a powerful platform in which to share it. In this high-level section, you've learned about locating RDF information and integrating various RDF data providers into the FriendTracker application. This chapter will cover the different ways in which we can take the output of our application and share it with the global community. As you'll see, sharing isn't limited to standing up a SPARQL endpoint or placing a static RDF file on your web server. There are all sorts of ways to share semantic information so others can use it for their needs, quickly building a chain of use and reuse from data far removed from its original purpose. Additional topics like microformats and their relation to the Semantic Web will also be covered.

This chapter also covers:

- Microformats
- eRDF
- RDFa
- Tools and frameworks that expose RDF data
- Creating a web page with embedded RDFa data based on the Friend-Tracker ontology

Microformats

Microformats, in the simplest definition, are XML tags that are incorporated into XHTML web pages and support the declarative expression of semantics. The fundamental components of microformats are laid out in Figure 11-1 and are based on information located at www.microformats.org. The idea behind microformats is straightforward: By enriching existing websites with the addition of attributes such as `class` and `rel`, it is easy for both people and intelligent agents (such as web crawlers or a web scrapers) to determine semantics that otherwise aren't apparent. Microformats provide a quick and easy way for web authors to assist human or computer consumers in understanding intent. For example, if Matt's web page has a link to Ryan's web page, there was a reason why Matt added that link in the first place. Are they work associates? Perhaps Ryan has some online documents that Matt feels are important to his business? Are they friends? Close friends, simple acquaintances or are they somehow related? It is dangerous to infer any relationship based on other attributes, such as the number of hyperlinks Matt has to Ryan's pages or the use of contextually-ambiguous phrases such as, "Ryan is my brother" within the web page. However, if a tag was explicitly added by the author regarding that content, the intent of the data is clarified:

```
<a href= rel="friend co-worker">Ryan's page</a>
```

Matt's connection to Ryan is based on a professional and more-than-casual relationship given the presence of the relationship (`rel`) attribute and the `friend` and `co-worker` values, all of which are defined as part of the XFN (XHTML Friends Network) microformat. We did not need to infer any relationship as it was explicitly declared for us. There was no need for recreating data in a format such as OWL because the use of the `rel` tag is standard XHTML. There is a need to conform to a single vocabulary. In a nutshell, that is what microformats are all about: reuse, simplicity and support for embedded information (see Figure 11-1).

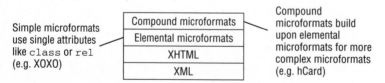

Figure 11-1 The building blocks of microformats

Note that the larger issues of trust (can I assume that the editor/author of Matt's web content is being truthful) or access (can I assume that proper permissions to manage Matt's data have been given to only those authorized individuals) are important but not necessary to understand the technology which is the focus here.

USING HCARD

We can quickly add our business card information to our website with a few small additions highlighted below. Information can be posted for machine harvesting but hidden from human eyes using the style="display: none;" entry:

```
<h1>Contact Information:</h1>
<div id="hcard-John-Doe" class="vcard">
<a class="url fn" href=http://example.org/johndoe
    style="display: none;">Johnathan Doe</a>
<div class="title" style="display: none;">
    Software Engineer</div>
<div class="url" style="display: none;">
    http://www.example.org</div>
<div class="org">Acme Systems</div>
<div class="adr">
  <div class="street-address">123 Main Street</div>
  <span class="locality">Arlington</span>,
  <span class="region">VA</span>,
  <span class="postal-code">12345</span>
  <div class="country-name">USA</div>
</div>
<div class="tel"><span class="type">work</span>:
  <span class="value">703-555-1234</span></div>
  <a class="email">jdoe@example.org</a>
</div>
```

Each of the class values such as tel and email are known hCard properties and very closely map to the vCard specification, RFC 2426.

Microformats were born from the desire to achieve some of the same goals as the Semantic Web: adding structure to web-based content, supporting decentralized knowledge management and developing community standards to encourage structure reuse. Yet they differ in several aspects. Microformats aren't driven by a single entity much like the Semantic Web is centered around the activities of the W3C. Sometimes referred to as the "lowercase semantic web", microformats are for human consumption first, machine readability second. They emphasize incorporating markup into existing web documents over the creation of new formats (e.g., OWL, RDF) which work well when the data is the same.

Our intent here is not to declare that microformats are better than the Semantic Web or vice versa. Both have their advantages and disadvantages and, more importantly, each helps illuminate issues that developers can work to address in both areas. We are not of the opinion that these two technologies are completely diametric. In fact, RDFa is examined in the next section as a technology to capitalize on some of the advantages of both worlds. In closing, some of the most popular microformats are listed below. Their adoption by such products such as Microsoft's Internet Explorer (version 8), Mozilla's Firefox (version 3), Google's Social Graph API and Yahoo's SearchMonkey strongly suggests that they will be around for quite a while:

- **XFN,** short for XHTML Friends Network, describes various relationships between people based on over fifteen different values, all using the `rel` XML attribute (`http://www.gmpg.org/xfn/`).

- **hCard** specifies information about people, locations, organizations or companies. Based on the vCard RFC 2426 standard, it supports several dozen attributes and values that map well to information found on a business card or stored in an address book (`http://microformats.org/wiki/hcard`).

- **hCalendar** relies on the iCalendar representation, as described in RFC 2445 to detail a calendar-dependent event. It covers all the fundamentals such as beginning and end dates and times (using ISO8601), event summary and locations using latitude and longitude values (`http://microformats.org/wiki/hcalendar`).

- **XOXO** describes outlines, numbered lists, and bulleted lists but enriches them with information such as titles, descriptions, and URLs (`http://microformats.org/wiki/xoxo`).

- **Rel-License** describes the use of `rel=license` attribute/value in a hyperlink to specify that the link's endpoint refers to a license (e.g., Creative Commons) for the content on that given page (`http://microformats.org/wiki/rel-license`).

- **hReview** is a microformat to detail reviews of anything. The syntax supports standard review information such as quantitative ratings (`http://microformats.org/wiki/hreview`).

eRDF

eRDF, shorthand for embedded RDF, is a subset of RDF that works well for placement in XHTML or HTML. By subset, we mean that several items that are part of the formal RDF Recommendation are not supported in eRDF:

- Blank nodes
- Containers Bag, Seq, and Alt

- Implicit typing such as RDFS subclassing
- Typed literals
- Arbitrary statements where either the subject or object can refer to URIs outside the superseding document

The basics of eRDF are straightforward. First, developers can declare their web pages as containing eRDF content by the use of the `profile` attribute in the `head` element of (X)HTML:

```
<html>
  <head profile="http://purl.org/NET/erdf/profile">
    ...
  </head>
</html>
```

The profile URL is an explicit declaration that the webpage's data has some amount of data described in eRDF as well as providing a resolvable endpoint for executable transformations (e.g., XSLT stylesheets) that can be applied against the web page.

Second, developers denote namespaces using the `link` element and the relationship attribute. Note that the `rel` attribute should always begin with the syntax, `schema.` and be followed by the namespace prefix:

```
<html>
  <head profile="http://purl.org/NET/erdf/profile">
    ...
  <link rel="schema.rdf"
   href="http://www.w3.org/1999/02/22-rdf-syntax-ns#" />
  <link rel="schema.rdfs"
   href="http://www.w3.org/2000/01/rdf-schema#" />
  <link rel="schema.dc"
   href="http://purl.org/dc/elements/1.1/" />
  <link rel="schema.foaf"
   href="http://xmlns.com/foaf/0.1/" />
  <link rel="schema.doap"
   href="http://usefulinc.com/ns/doap#" />
  <link rel="schema.wn"
   href="http://www.w3.org/2006/03/wn/wn20/schema/" />
  </head>
</html>
```

The third step involves the actual creation of statements. The following code gives various examples in both the head and the body of a document. For a definitive list of eRDF syntax, visit `http://research.talis.com/2005/erdf/wiki/Main/RdfInHtml`.

```
<html>
  <head profile="http://purl.org/NET/erdf/profile">
```

```
<base href="http://www.semwebprogramming.org/erdf" />
<link rel="schema.rdf"
 href="http://www.w3.org/1999/02/22-rdf-syntax-ns#" />
<link rel="schema.rdfs"
 href="http://www.w3.org/2000/01/rdf-schema#" />
<link rel="schema.foaf"
 href="http://xmlns.com/foaf/0.1/" />

<!-- Object property in the head section -->
<link rel="foaf.maker" href="#matt" />
<!-- contains the statement:
  <http://www.semwebprogramming.org/erdf>
  <http://xmlns.com/foaf/0.1/maker>
  <http://www.semwebprogramming.org/erdf#matt> -->

<!-- Datatype property in the head section -->
<meta name="rdf.label" content="eRDF info" />
<!-- contains the statement:
  <http://www.semwebprogramming.org/erdf>
  <http://www.w3.org/1999/02/22-rdf-syntax-ns#label>
  "eRDF info" -->

<!-- Two object properties in the head section
     Using rev to reverse the triple direction  -->
<link rev="foaf.made foaf.interest" href="#matt" />
<!-- contains the statements:
  <http://www.semwebprogramming.org/erdf#matt>
  <http://xmlns.com/foaf/0.1/made>
  <http://www.semwebprogramming.org/erdf>

  <http://www.semwebprogramming.org/erdf#matt>
  <http://xmlns.com/foaf/0.1/interest>
  <http://www.semwebprogramming.org/erdf> -->
</head>

<body>
<!-- object properties in the document body
     connecting Matt to John.  The leading hyphen
     denotes an RDF class affiliation (foaf:Person)
-->
<div id="matt" class="-foaf-Person">
  Matt used to work with
  <span class="-foaf-Person foaf-knows" id="john">
  John</span> on site.
</div>
<!-- contains the statements:
  <http://www.semwebprogramming.org/erdf#matt>
  <http://www.w3.org/1999/02/22-rdf-syntax-ns#type>
  <http://xmlns.com/foaf/0.1/Person>
```

```
    <http://www.semwebprogramming.org/erdf#john>
    <http://www.w3.org/1999/02/22-rdf-syntax-ns#type>
    <http://xmlns.com/foaf/0.1/Person>

    <http://www.semwebprogramming.org/erdf#matt>
    <http://xmlns.com/foaf/0.1/knows>
    <http://www.semwebprogramming.org/erdf#john> -->
  </body>
</html>
```

eRDF was spearheaded by Ian Davis, CTO and director of Talis, and saw most of its development activity in 2005 and 2006. There is no type of autogenerator available online (although given the inherent flexibility of RDF, this is understandable), but there are services available to extract RDF from eRDF documents. For example, `http://arc.semsol.org/docs/v2/extractors` provides PHP extraction code for eRDF and Talis provides both a webpage and the underlying XSLT stylesheet at `http://research.talis.com/2005/erdf/extract`.

RDFa

RDFa is a W3C Recommendation that permits embedded semantics in existing XHTML pages. If people have already taken the time to create web pages with limited semantics based on hyperlinks and layout tags such as `div` and `span`, why not reuse or enrich them? RDFa evolved after microformats and it attempts to take the best of microformats, such as enriching existing web content with semantics and removing the need of heavy Semantic Web knowledge via easy syntax, while overcoming some of their most visible issues, such as unscoped vocabularies as well as required community standardization stovepipes and mixing and matching various microformats. RDFa is interoperable with the RDF W3C Recommendations, supporting XML namespaces and CURIEs (Compact URIs).

RDFa supports distributed knowledge management, just like the Semantic Web. Since developers and knowledge engineers will want to (and regularly do) create their own vocabularies, taxonomies, and ontologies, RDFa enables these data providers to create and publish their information without restriction. From the RDFa Recommendation, we can get a sense of how web pages can embed RDF (`http://www.w3.org/TR/rdfa-syntax/`):

In RDFa, a subject [URI reference] is generally indicated using @about, and predicates are represented using one of @property, @rel, or @rev. Objects which are [URI reference]s are represented using @href, @resource or @src, whilst objects that are [literal]s are represented either with @content or the content of the element in question (with an optional datatype expressed using @datatype).

Supported Attributes

Here is the list of RDFa-friendly attributes with extracts of code examples:

xmlns

A prefix and qualified URL defining an XML namespace for the document.

```
<html xmlns="http://www.w3.org/1999/xhtml"
      xmlns:foaf="http://xmlns.com/foaf/0.1/"
      xmlns:cyc="http://www.cyc.com/2003/04/01/cyc/">
  ...
</html>
```

rel

A white space–separated list of reserved keywords (listed in the sidebar) or CURIEs, that details predicates between resources (no literals).

```
<html xmlns="http://www.w3.org/1999/xhtml"
      xmlns:foaf="http://xmlns.com/foaf/0.1/"
      xmlns:cyc="http://www.cyc.com/2003/04/01/cyc/">
  <head>
<title>rel example</title>
<link
      about="http://www.semwebprogramming.org#Matt"
      rel="foaf:knows cyc:likesAsFriend"
      href="http://www.semwebprogramming.org#Andrew"/>
  </head>
</html>
```

It results in triples:

```
<http://www.semwebprogramming.org#Matt>
<http://xmlns.com/foaf/0.1/knows>
<http://www.semwebprogramming.org#Andrew>

<http://www.semwebprogramming.org#Matt>
<http://www.cyc.com/2003/04/01/cyc/likesAsFriend>
<http://www.semwebprogramming.org#Andrew>
```

REL AND REV RESERVED KEYWORDS

The RDFa Recommendation details a list of reserved keywords for the `rel` and `rev` attributes and is placed here for quick reference. These keywords provide

(continued)

REL AND REV RESERVED KEYWORDS *(continued)*

shortcuts that derive from the XHTML Metainformation Vocabulary and utilize the `http://www.w3.org/1999/xhtml/vocab#` namespace.

Keyword	Meaning
alternate	Designates alternate versions for a resource
appendix	Refers to a resource serving as an appendix in a collection
bookmark	Refers to a bookmark. A bookmark is a link to a key entry point within an extended document.
cite	Refers to a resource that defines a citation
chapter	Refers to a resource serving as a chapter in a collection
contents	Refers to a resource serving as a table of contents
copyright	Refers to a copyright statement for the resource
first	Refers to the first item in a collection (see also start and top)
glossary	Refers to a resource providing a glossary of terms
help	Refers to a resource offering help (more information, links to other sources of information, etc.)
icon	Refers to a resource that represents an icon
index	Refers to a resource providing an index
last	Refers to the last resource in a collection of resources
license	Refers to a resource that defines the license associated with a resource
meta	Refers to a resource that provides metadata, for instance in RDF
next	Refers to the next resource (after the current one) in an ordered collection
p3pv1	Refers to a P3P Policy Reference File : `http://www.w3.org/TR/rdfa-syntax/#ref_P3P`
prev	Refers to the previous resource (before the current one) in an ordered collection
role	Indicates the purpose of the resource
section	Refers to a resource serving as a section in a collection
stylesheet	Refers to a resource acting as a stylesheet for a resource
subsection	Refers to a resource serving as a subsection in a collection
start	Refers to the first resource in a collection of resources. A typical use case might be a collection of chapters in a book
top	Synonym for start
up	Refers to the resource "above" in a hierarchically structured set

rev

A white space–separated list of reserved keywords (listed in the sidebar) or CURIEs that details predicates between resources (no literals) in a direction opposite of the `rel` attribute.

```
<html xmlns="http://www.w3.org/1999/xhtml"
      xmlns:foaf="http://xmlns.com/foaf/0.1/"
      xmlns:cyc="http://www.cyc.com/2003/04/01/cyc/">
  <head>
    <title>rev example</title>
    <link
      about="http://www.semwebprogramming.org#Matt"
      rev="foaf:knows cyc:likesAsFriend"
      href="http://www.semwebprogramming.org#Andrew"/>
  </head>
</html>
```

It results in triples:

```
<http://www.semwebprogramming.org#Andrew>
<http://xmlns.com/foaf/0.1/knows>
<http://www.semwebprogramming.org#Matt>

<http://www.semwebprogramming.org#Andrew>
<http://www.cyc.com/2003/04/01/cyc/likesAsFriend>
<http://www.semwebprogramming.org#Matt>
```

content

A plain literal (string) that is used to represent an object in an RDF triple.

```
<html xmlns="http://www.w3.org/1999/xhtml"
      xmlns:foaf="http://xmlns.com/foaf/0.1/">
  <head>
    <title>content example</title>
    <link
      about="http://www.semwebprogramming.org#Matt"
      property="foaf:family_name"
      content="Fisher"/>
  </head>
</html>
```

Results in triple:

```
<http://www.semwebprogramming.org#Matt>
<http://xmlns.com/foaf/0.1/family_name>
"Fisher"
```

href

A resource URI that is used to represent an object in an RDF triple. See `rel`, `rev` for an example.

src

A resource URI that is used to represent a subject in an RDF triple. Its function is identical to `about`.

```
<html xmlns="http://www.w3.org/1999/xhtml"
    xmlns:foaf="http://xmlns.com/foaf/0.1/">
  <body>
    <img
      src="http://www.semwebprogramming.org/Title.png"
      rev="foaf:depiction"
      href="http://www.semwebprogramming.org"/>
  </body>
</html>
```

Results in triple:

```
<http://www.semwebprogramming.org>
<http://xmlns.com/foaf/0.1/depiction>
<http://www.semwebprogramming.org/Title.png>
```

The following attributes have been introduced as part of RDFa:

about

A resource URI or CURIE that is used to represent a subject in an RDF triple. Its function is identical to `src` but is not limited to `img` elements. See `rel`, `rev`, or `content` for an example.

property

A white space–separated list of CURIEs that details predicates between a subject and a plain literal.

```
<html xmlns="http://www.w3.org/1999/xhtml"
    xmlns:foaf="http://xmlns.com/foaf/0.1/">
  <body>
    Here's the story of a man named
    <div about="http://www.semwebprogramming.org#Matt"
        property="foaf:firstName foaf:nick"
        content="Matt">
      <div property="foaf:title" content="Mr">Fisher
```

```
      </div>
    </div>
  </body>
</html>
```

It results in triples:

```
<http://www.semwebprogramming.org#Matt>
<http://xmlns.com/foaf/0.1/nick>
"Matt"

<http://www.semwebprogramming.org#Matt>
<http://xmlns.com/foaf/0.1/firstName>
"Matt"

<http://www.semwebprogramming.org#Matt>
<http://xmlns.com/foaf/0.1/title>
"Mr"
```

SAFE CURIES

For those attributes that support either URIs or CURIEs, specifically attributes `resource` and `about`, an RDFa parser needs to be able to differentiate between the two URI types, otherwise incorrect expansion could occur. By using safe CURIE notation, where the CURIE is surrounded by square brackets ([or]), an RDFa parser can interpret the proper type of URI used. A safe CURIE can be used anywhere a regular CURIE is supported. See `resource` for an example of the syntax.

resource

A resource URI or CURIE that is used to represent a subject in an RDF triple. Its function is identical to `href`, but the resource cannot be hyperlinked.

```
<html xmlns="http://www.w3.org/1999/xhtml"
      xmlns:foaf="http://xmlns.com/foaf/0.1/"
      xmlns:swp="http://www.semwebprogramming.org#">
  <body>
    Here's the story of a man named
    <div about="http://www.semwebprogramming.org#Ryan"
         rel="foaf:knows"
         resource="[swp:John]">
      <div rel="foaf:knows"
           resource=
             "http://www.semwebprogramming.org#Matt">Matt
```

```
      </div>
    </div>
  </body>
</html>
```

It results in triples:

```
<http://www.semwebprogramming.org#Ryan>
<http://xmlns.com/foaf/0.1/knows>
<http://www.semwebprogramming.org#John>


<http://www.semwebprogramming.org#John>
<http://xmlns.com/foaf/0.1/knows>
<http://www.semwebprogramming.org#Matt>
```

datatype

A compart URI, or CURIE, that represents a literal datatype.

```
<html xmlns="http://www.w3.org/1999/xhtml"
      xmlns:foaf="http://xmlns.com/foaf/0.1/"
      xmlns:swp="http://www.semwebprogramming.org#">
  <body>
  Thank you for purchasing Semantic Web Programming on
    <span about="http://www.semwebprogramming.org#Book"
          property="dc:date"
          datatype="xsd:date">2009-05-02
    </span>
   </body>
  </html>
```

It results in triples:

```
<http://www.semwebprogramming.org#Book>
<http://purl.org/dc/elements/1.1/date>
"2009-05-02"^^xsd:date
```

typeof

A white space–separated list of CURIEs that specify one or more RDF types that apply to the subject of the current triple.

```
<html xmlns="http://www.w3.org/1999/xhtml"
      xmlns:foaf="http://xmlns.com/foaf/0.1/"
      xmlns:cyc="http://www.cyc.com/2003/04/01/cyc/">
  <body>
```

```
        Matt Fisher wishes he had a killer chopper like
        <a about="http://www.semwebprogramming.org#Matt"
           typeof="foaf:Person cyc:AdultMalePerson
                   cyc:HomoGenus"
           rel="foaf:knows"
           href="http://www.semwebprogramming.org#Andrew">
           Andrew</a>
    </body>
</html>
```

It results in triples:

```
<http://www.semwebprogramming.org#Matt>
<http://www.w3.org/1999/02/22-rdf-syntax-ns#type>
<http://www.cyc.com/2003/04/01/cyc/HomoGenus>

<http://www.semwebprogramming.org#Matt>
<http://www.w3.org/1999/02/22-rdf-syntax-ns#type>
<http://www.cyc.com/2003/04/01/cyc/AdultMalePerson>

<http://www.semwebprogramming.org#Matt>
<http://www.w3.org/1999/02/22-rdf-syntax-ns#type>
<http://xmlns.com/foaf/0.1/Person>

<http://www.semwebprogramming.org#Matt>
<http://xmlns.com/foaf/0.1/knows>
<http://www.semwebprogramming.org#Andrew>
```

Blank Nodes

Based on its roots in RDF, RDFa has full support of blank nodes. In fact, an RDFa parser should not only guarantee that the creation of blank nodes is unique within a given document but that any implicit blank nodes will not clash with explicitly named blank nodes declared in a document. For example, creating RDFa for two FOAF people who know each other could look like:

```
<html xmlns="http://www.w3.org/1999/xhtml"
      xmlns:foaf="http://xmlns.com/foaf/0.1/">
  <body>
    <div typeof="foaf:Person">Matt
      <div property="foaf:firstName">Matt</div>
      <div property="foaf:family_name"
           content="Fisher"/>
      <div rel="foaf:knows"
           resource="[_:bNode1337]">knows
        <span property="foaf:firstName">Andrew</div>
        <span rel="foaf:interest"
              resource="http://www.w3.org/2001/sw/"/>
```

```
      </div>
    </div>
  </body>
</html>
```

It should produce the following triples:

```
_:bnode0
<http://www.w3.org/1999/02/22-rdf-syntax-ns#type>
<http://xmlns.com/foaf/0.1/Person>

_:bnode0
<http://xmlns.com/foaf/0.1/firstName>
"Matt"

_:bnode1
<http://xmlns.com/foaf/0.1/interest>
<http://www.w3.org/2001/sw/>

_:bnode1
<http://xmlns.com/foaf/0.1/firstName>
"Andrew"

_:bnode0
<http://xmlns.com/foaf/0.1/knows>
_:bnode1

_:bnode0
<http://xmlns.com/foaf/0.1/family_name>
"Fisher"
```

The RDFa specification isn't exactly clear as to whether or not the same blank node identifiers should be used (e.g., starting with _:bNode1337 but resulting in _:bnode1) but it is clear that uniqueness must be maintained.

Language Support

RDFa supports XML language tags as defined in the W3C XML Recommendation (http://www.w3.org/TR/REC-xml/#sec-lang-tag). Language tags can be dictated for an entire document or for a subset of triples. In the latter case, it is possible to override earlier language tags.

Borrowing from the example above, the next example supports English with one instance in U.S. English and two instances of British English:

```
<html xmlns="http://www.w3.org/1999/xhtml"
      xmlns:foaf="http://xmlns.com/foaf/0.1/"
      xml:lang="en">
  <body>
```

```
<div typeof="foaf:Person">
  <div property="foaf:firstName" xml:lang="en-US">
      Matt</div>
  <div property="foaf:family_name"
      content="Fisher"/>
  <div rel="foaf:knows" resource="[_:bNode1337]"
      xml:lang="en-GB">knows
    <span property="foaf:firstName">Andrew</span>
    <span rel="foaf:interest"
          resource="http://www.w3.org/2001/sw/"/>
  </div>
</div>
</body>
</html>
```

Tools and Frameworks

Publishing semantic data isn't limited to XHTML pages; there are other tools and frameworks for hosting RDF or converting datatypes, relational databases, iCalendar, Outlook, and Flickr metadata to RDF based on. Instead of describing the details of each one, we present a list of possible applications and converters that could be applicable for your data needs. One exception is the discussion of xOperator, a tool for connecting to SPARQL endpoints over XMPP. This list is far from complete but provides several good places to begin your search.

RDF Transformational Tools

Table 11-1 lists applications that transform data from their native formats into RDF, sometimes referred to as *RDFizers*. Visit `http://simile.mit.edu/wiki/RDFizers` and `http://esw.w3.org/topic/ConverterToRdf` for more sources.

SPARQL Endpoints

SPARQL endpoints were covered in detail in Chapter 6, "Discovering Information," and provide an ideal medium for retrieving RDF data given its design as an RDF query language. Typically, a data provider or data store provides a SPARQL endpoint on top of its data as another mechanism for retrieving semantic data. Table 11-2 lists some of the available tools that support SPARQL endpoints.

Table 11-1 Tools That Transform Native Formats into RDF

APPLICATION	WEBSITE	DESCRIPTION
Aperature	`http://aperture.sourceforge.net/`	Aperature is a framework for crawling, extracting and indexing data from a variety of formats, and allows developers to transform both data and metadata to an RDF format. There are currently over twenty extraction classes ranging from JPEG and MP3 files to PDF, Word, or Visio documents. Out-of-the-box crawlers include iCal, IMAP, and file systems.
Flickcurl	`http://librdf.org/flickcurl/`	Dave Beckett's C-based implementation for turning Flickr data such as photo metadata, tags, and places into RDF.
Javadoc RDFizer	`http://simile.mit.edu/wiki/Javadoc_RDFizer/`	Built by the Simile team at MIT, this project builds a doclet that will turn any javadoc-compliant data into RDF. A doclet is a program that implements the doclet API transforming javadocs into any format of your choosing. More information on doclets can be found at `http://java.sun.com/javase/6/docs/technotes/guides/javadoc/doclet/overview.html`.
RDF123	`http://rdf123.umbc.edu/`	This research project resulted in an application that can ingest simple spreadsheet information, such as those using HTML table tags and comma-separated files (CSVs), and return the data in RDF. It was developed at the University of Maryland, Baltimore County.
Torrent2RDF	`http://www.inf.unideb.hu/~jeszy/rdfizers/torrent2rdf-0.3.zip`	Torrent2RDF provides foundational Java code to read a torrent file or torrent URL and extract the information as RDF. The output currently goes to stdout but the GNU GPL license gives developers the flexibility to expand it as necessary.

Joseki Installation and Operation

As noted in Table 11-2, Joseki is one of the quickest ways to host a SPARQL endpoint. This section will outline the steps to install and run Joseki 3.2, the latest version at the time of this writing.

Table 11-2 Applications That Support SPARQL Endpoints

APPLICATION	WEBSITE	DESCRIPTION
Virtuoso Universal Server	http://virtuoso. openlinksw.com/	Built and supported by OpenLink Software, the universal server is billed as a complete data management solution. It handles XML, RDF, ODB, and RDB data stores as well as web services and an application server. A subset of the functionality is provided in OpenLink Virtuoso, an open source implementation hosted on SourceForge (http://sourceforge.net/projects/virtuoso/). Virtuoso provides the SPARQL endpoint for DBpedia that was explored in Chapter 6, "Discovering Information."
Joseki	http://www. joseki.org/	Joseki was developed by HP labs, the same team that developed Jena. Joseki is built on top of ARQ, Jena's multi-language query engine that supports SPARQL in addition to RDQL (RDF Query Language) and its own ARQ language. Given its ability to support any type of Jena Model, it is an ideal starting point for standing up your own endpoint.

Begin by downloading and unzipping the file http://downloads. sourceforge.net/joseki/joseki-3.2.zip. Directly off the newly installed Joseki-3.2 directory is a lib subdirectory. Either add each of the jar files in this lib directory to your CLASSPATH environment variable or you can pass each jar file in on the command line when you launch Joseki. In the sample below, Joseki is executed from the Joseki-3.2 directory via the latter method:

```
java -cp "lib/antlr-2.7.5.jar:lib/arq.jar:
        lib/arq-extra.jar:
        lib/commons-logging-1.1.jar:lib/concurrent.jar:
        lib/icu4j_3_4.jar:lib/iri.jar:lib/jena.jar:
        lib/jenatest.jar:lib/jetty-6.1.10.jar:
        lib/jetty-util-6.1.10.jar:lib/joseki.jar:
        lib/json.jar:lib/junit.jar:
        lib/log4j-1.2.12.jar:
        lib/lucene-core-2.3.1.jar:
        lib/servlet-api-2.5-6.1.10.jar:
        lib/slf4j-log4j12.jar:lib/stax-api-1.0.jar:
        lib/wstx-asl-3.0.0.jar:
        lib/xercesImpl.jar:lib/xml-apis.jar"
    joseki.rdfserver joseki-config-example.ttl
```

At this point, the output should resemble the following lines:

```
INFO [main] (Configuration.java:81) - ==== Configuration ====
INFO [main] (Configuration.java:164) - Loading : <joseki-config-
  example.ttl>
INFO [main] (ServiceInitSimple.java:25) - Init: Example initializer
INFO [main] (ServiceInitSimple.java:25) - Init: Example2
INFO [main] (Configuration.java:100) - ==== Datasets ====
INFO [main] (Configuration.java:610) - New dataset: Books
INFO [main] (Configuration.java:621) -    Default graph : books.n3
INFO [main] (Configuration.java:610) - New dataset: Dataset 1
INFO [main] (Configuration.java:621) -    Default graph : Model(plain)
INFO [main] (Configuration.java:637) -    Graph / named :
  <http://example.org/name1>
INFO [main] (Configuration.java:637) -    Graph / named :
  <http://example.org/name2>
INFO [main] (Configuration.java:610) - New dataset: Test
INFO [main] (Configuration.java:621) -    Default graph : <<blank node>>
INFO [main] (Configuration.java:102) - ==== Services ====
INFO [main] (Configuration.java:382) - Service reference: "books"
INFO [main] (Configuration.java:390) -    Class name:
  org.joseki.processors.SPARQL
INFO [main] (SPARQL.java:58) - SPARQL processor
INFO [main] (SPARQL.java:94) - Locking policy: multiple reader, single
  writer
INFO [main] (SPARQL.java:115) - Dataset description: false // Web loading:
  false
INFO [main] (Configuration.java:488) - Dataset: Books
INFO [main] (Configuration.java:382) - Service reference: "sparql"
INFO [main] (Configuration.java:390) -    Class name:
  org.joseki.processors.SPARQL
INFO [main] (SPARQL.java:58) - SPARQL processor
INFO [main] (SPARQL.java:104) - Locking policy: none
INFO [main] (SPARQL.java:115) - Dataset description: true // Web loading:
  true
INFO [main] (Configuration.java:104) - ==== Bind services to the server
  ====
INFO [main] (Configuration.java:521) - Service: <books>
INFO [main] (Configuration.java:521) - Service: <sparql>
INFO [main] (Configuration.java:106) - ==== Initialize datasets ====
INFO [main] (Configuration.java:122) - ==== End Configuration ====
INFO [main] (Dispatcher.java:122) - Loaded data source configuration:
  joseki-config-example.ttl
INFO [main] (?:?) - Logging to  via org.mortbay.log.Slf4jLog
INFO [main] (?:?) - jetty-6.1.10
INFO [main] (?:?) - NO JSP Support for /, did not find
  org.apache.jasper.servlet.JspServle
```

Direct your browser to `http://localhost:2020` and you will see the page as shown in Figure 11-2. Selecting the first link, *Form for SPARQL queries on a small books database,* will show a simple SPARQL query that can be run against a small RDF data set of book and title information. This data set is located in `Joseki-3.2/Data/books.n3` and is listed in `joseki-config-example.ttl`, the parameter file passed to the JVM when Joseki was launched. The second link, *General purpose SPARQL processor,* will display an input box for user queries like those used in Chapter 6.

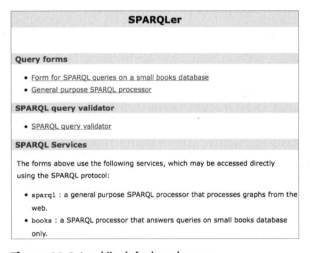

Figure 11-2 Joseki's default web page

To change the RDF data sets behind Joseki, modify `joseki-config-example .ttl` with data of your own choosing.

xOperator

xOperator isn't a SPARQL endpoint itself, but rather provides a medium for connecting to existing SPARQL endpoints. xOperator uses XMPP, a protocol discussed in Chapter 9, "Combining Information," and relies on the premise that people have one or more trusted groups of friends, contacts, or associates. One way people define these trusted groups is through their use of IM or creating chat groups and contacts based on different levels of trust and relationships. If some of these users had software agents (or intelligent agents) that provided access to their owners' data, then trusted individuals could freely search and obtain information from those users in an automated fashion. The inherent social network supports an environment of trust while the agents enable fast information navigation, searching, and querying.

This section briefly discusses how to install and work with xOperator in its current release, version 0.1. Note that there are stability issues with this tool but it is covered nonetheless so you can experiment with alternatives to SPARQL endpoints.

Installation and Operation

After downloading and unzipping xOperator from `http://xoperator` `.googlecode.com/files/xOperator-0.1.zip`, go to the installation's root directory and rename the `xoperator.properties-dist` file to `xoperator.` `properties`. Then edit the file to add your XMPP account information as well as the information for your agent (also called a proxy):

```
## your full jid, e.g. someuser@someserver.com
main_username=justadummy@jabber.org

## the password for this account
main_password=justadummypassword

## ***PROXY************
## if set to true, no proxy account is necessary and the
## main account is used for interaction
standalone=false

## enable inter-agent communication, not working properly
## at this moment.
p2penabled=false

## outcomment the following lines, in case you want to have
## a proxy and put standalone above on false
proxy_username= justadummyproxy@im.flosoft.biz
proxy_password= justadummyproxypassword
```

Next, start the proxy. There is a shell script for Unix/Linux and a batch file for Windows, shown below:

```
start.bat
```

Once started, your XMPP client should display an agent contact based on the `proxy_username` text entered in `xoperator.properties`. If you send the agent a 'help' message, you should get the following response (there are a few misspellings in this version of xOperator):

```
7:26:03 AM: The agent understands the following commands:
query executes a simple query. for example: 'query select distinct....'
help lists information about the implementes commands
list ds List all the available datastore of this agent.
add ds adds a datastore to the configuration of the client.
use: add ds <name> <uri>
del ds removes a prviously defined data store from the
```

```
system. usage del ds <name>
add template adds a template to the agent usage: add
template "<pattern>" "<query>". In the pattern section one
or more wildcards can be used via the * character, the
value of the wildcard can be adressed in the query by
inserting the position of the star, surrounded by four %-
symbols, for example %%2%% in the query adresses the second
wildcard in the pattern.
list templates Lists all the aiml templates in the system
del template deletes a previously stored aiml template,
usage: del template "<pattern>"
add ns adds a namespace defintion to the agents
configuration. namespaces defined herewith are
automatically added to the query if needed
del ns removes a namespace from the definition. Usage del
ns <name>
list ns lists all the defined namespaces
```

Example Query

At this point, we're ready to try a sample SPARQL query. Reusing a query from Chapter 6 (retrieving all of George Washington's namesakes from DBpedia) is a good place to start. However, we first tell our agent the endpoint of interest through the following command:

```
add ds dbpedia uri=http%3A%2F%2Fdbpedia.org
```

Then, run the query with a second command:

```
query SELECT ?location WHERE {
    ?person <http://www.w3.org/2000/01/rdf-schema#label>
        "George Washington"@en.
    ?location <http://dbpedia.org/property/namedFor> ?person
    }
```

The agent responds with:

```
7:39:17 AM: Store dbpedia answered:
        location
<http://dbpedia.org/resource/Grayson_County%2C_Kentucky>
<http://dbpedia.org/resource/Washington_County%2C_Idaho>
<http://dbpedia.org/resource/Washington_County%2C_Kentucky>
<http://dbpedia.org/resource/Washington_Parish%2C_Louisiana>
<http://dbpedia.org/resource/Washington_County%2C_Georgia>
<http://dbpedia.org/resource/Washington_County%2C_Minnesota>
<http://dbpedia.org/resource/Washington_County%2C_Ohio>
<http://dbpedia.org/resource/Washington_Township%2C_Clinton_
County%2C_Indiana>
<http://dbpedia.org/resource/Washington_County%2C_Utah>
```

For the sake of simplicity, namespaces weren't used but they are supported in xOperator. With the example working, you can move on to bigger items like templates and query scripts, which are described in detail in the doc folder off the root directory of your xOperator installation.

FriendTracker in RDFa

Advancing the work seen in Chapter 10, "Aligning Information," it's time to share our FriendTracker information with others on the Internet. However, instead of publishing this data solely in a Semantic Web medium using a SPARQL endpoint or a static web page without any semantic, machine-readable information, this section will show an example of automatically generating a web page in XHTML with RDFa embedded content.

Chapter 10 discussed a FriendTracker ontology upon which this sample instance data is based:

```
@prefix rdf: <http://www.w3.org/1999/02/22-rdf-syntax-ns#> .
@prefix xsd: <http://www.w3.org/2001/XMLSchema#> .
@prefix time: <http://www.w3.org/2006/time#> .
@prefix ftrack: <http://semwebprogramming.org/2009/ftracker#> .
@prefix : <http://semwebprogramming.org/2009/ftracker/example#> .

:Andrew rdf:type ftrack:Friend ;
    ftrack:isFrom "Virginia" ;
    ftrack:hasEmailAddress "andrew@semwebprogramming.org" ;
    ftrack:isFrom "United States" ;
    ftrack:isNamed "Andrew" ;
    ftrack:hasPost :Post00123 .

:John rdf:type ftrack:Friend ;
    ftrack:hasPic "http://www.semwebprogramming.org/images/john.png" ;
    ftrack:isFrom "Maryland" ;
    ftrack:isNamed "Johnny" ;
    ftrack:hasEmailAddress "john@semwebprogramming.org" ;
    ftrack:hasTitle "Head Honcho" ;
    ftrack:hasPost :Post00124 .

:Post00123 rdf:type ftrack:Post ;
    ftrack:hasContent "When in the Course of human events
      it becomes necessary ..." ;
    ftrack:hasTitle "All About Post00123" ;
    ftrack:occursAt :TimeSample1 .

:Post00124 rdf:type ftrack:Post ;
    ftrack:hasTitle "One day at a time" ;
    ftrack:hasContent "I have a dream that one day this
```

```
        nation will rise up and live out the true meaning of
        its creed: We hold these truths to be self-evident,
        that all men are created equal" ;
    ftrack:occursAt :TimeSample2 .

:TimeSample1 rdf:type time:Instant ;
    time:inXSDDateTime "2008-10-28T11:31:52"^^xsd:dateTime .

:TimeSample2 rdf:type time:Instant ;
    time:inXSDDateTime
        "2008-11-02T09:30:50+03:00,"^^xsd:dateTime .

:Matt rdf:type ftrack:Friend ;
    ftrack:hasPic
        "http://www.semweb.../images/matt.png"^^xsd:anyURI ;
    ftrack:hasTitle "Engineer At Large" ;
    ftrack:isNamed "Matt" ;
    ftrack:hasEmailAddress "mfisher@semwebprogramming.org" ,
                           "matt2@semwebprogramming.net" ;
    ftrack:hasStatus ftrack:Available .
```

This instance data is used as the input RDF to the abbreviated code that
follows. Note that while the directly writing HTML snippets to the Buffered-
Writer instance isn't ideal, it is used here for simplicity and to focus on the use
of RDFa.

```java
public class PublishRDFa {

  // Write any isNamed property values
  private void writeIsNamedProperty(Model model,
            BufferedWriter w, Resource person) throws
            IOException {
    Property prop = model.getProperty(defaultOntNS,
                                    "isNamed");
    if (person.hasProperty(prop)) {
      w.write("<tr>\n");
      w.write("<th colspan=\"2\"
            property=\"ftrack:isNamed\">");
      NodeIterator names =
        model.listObjectsOfProperty(person, prop);
      while (names.hasNext()) {
        RDFNode name = names.nextNode();
        w.write(name.toString() + " ");
      }
      w.write("\n</th>\n");
      w.write("</tr>\n");
    }
  }
```

```java
// Write any hasEmail property values
private void writeHasEmailAddressProperty(Model model,
            BufferedWriter w, Resource person) throws
            IOException {
  Property prop = model.getProperty(defaultOntNS,
                                    "hasEmailAddress");
  if (person.hasProperty(prop)) {
    w.write("<tr>\n");
    w.write("<td " + tableCellParams + ">Email:</td>\n");
    w.write("<td>");
    NodeIterator addrs =
      model.listObjectsOfProperty(person, prop);
    while (addrs.hasNext()) {
      RDFNode address = addrs.nextNode();
      w.write("\n<div rel=\"ftrack:hasEmailAddress\"
              href=\"" + address.toString() + "\">");
      w.write(address.toString() + " ");
      w.write("</div>\n");
    }
    w.write("</td>\n");
    w.write("</tr>\n");
  }
}

public static void main (String args[]) {

  PublishRDFa rdfaFactory = new PublishRDFa();

  // Read in our data
  Model model = rdfaFactory.readRDFInput();

  // Open the output RDFa file and output a standard
  // XHTML header
  BufferedWriter rdfaWriter = null;
  try {
    rdfaWriter = rdfaFactory.writePreAction();
  } catch (IOException e) {
    e.printStackTrace();
  }

  // Cycle through any friend instances and build
  // XHTML+RDFa syntax
  Resource friendClass = model.getResource(defaultOntNS +
                                    "Friend");
  ResIterator friendIter =
    model.listSubjectsWithProperty(RDF.type, friendClass);
  try {
    while (friendIter.hasNext()) {
```

```
    Resource person = friendIter.nextResource();
    rdfaWriter.write("<div about=\"" + owner +
      "\" rel=\"foaf:knows\">\n");
    rdfaWriter.write("<div about=\"" + defaultPrefix +
      ":" + person.getLocalName() + "\">\n");
    rdfaWriter.write("<p/><table " + tableParams +
      ">\n");

    // Do we have any isNamed information?
    rdfaFactory.writeIsNamedProperty(model,
      rdfaWriter, person);

    // Do we have any hasPic information?
    rdfaFactory.writeHasPicProperty(model,
      rdfaWriter, person);

    // Do we have any hasStatus information?
    rdfaFactory.writeHasStatusProperty(model,
      rdfaWriter, person);

    // Do we have any hasEmailAddress information?
    rdfaFactory.writeHasEmailProperty(model,
      rdfaWriter, person);

    // Do we have any isFrom information?
    rdfaFactory.writeIsFromProperty(model,
      rdfaWriter, person);

    rdfaWriter.write("</table>\n");
    rdfaWriter.write("</div>\n");
    rdfaWriter.write("</div>\n\n");
  }

  writePostAction(rdfaWriter);
} catch (IOException e) {
  e.printStackTrace();
  }
 }
}
```

The code acts like an agent for Ryan, inserting statements that he knows each of the people in the FriendTrack instance data. The resulting XHTML will look something like this abridged output:

```
<?xml version="1.0" encoding="utf-8"?>
<!DOCTYPE html PUBLIC "-//W3C//DTD XHTML+RDFa 1.0//EN"
  "http://www.w3.org/MarkUp/DTD/xhtml-rdfa-1.dtd">
<html version="XHTML+RDFa 1.0"
  xmlns="http://www.w3.org/1999/xhtml"
  xmlns:foaf="http://xmlns.com/foaf/0.1/"
```

```
    xmlns:owl="http://www.w3.org/2002/07/owl#"
    xmlns:rdf="http://www.w3.org/1999/02/22-rdf-syntax-ns#"
    xmlns:rdfs="http://www.w3.org/2000/01/rdf-schema#"
    xmlns:ftrack=
      "http://semwebprogramming.org/2009/ftracker#"
    xmlns:smp="
      http://semwebprogramming.org/2009/ftracker/example#"
    xmlns:xsd="http://www.w3.org/2001/XMLSchema#">
<head>
  <base href="smp:Ryan"/>
  <title>Sample RDFa page - Friend Tracker</title>
</head>
<body>
  <div about="smp:Ryan" rel="foaf:knows">
    <div about="smp:Andrew">
      <p/><table style="border: 5px solid black; width:
          500px;">
        <tr>
          <th colspan="2" property="ftrack:isNamed">Andrew
          </th>
        </tr>
        <tr>
          <td style="width: 23%;">Email:</td>
          <td>
            <div rel="ftrack:hasEmailAddress"
              href="andrew@semwebprogramming.org">
              andrew@semwebprogramming.org </div>
          </td>
        </tr>
        <tr>
          <td style="width: 23%;">Origin Location(s):</td>
          <td>
            <div rel="ftrack:isFrom"
                href="United States">United States
            </div>
            <div rel="ftrack:isFrom"
                href="Virginia">Virginia </div>
          </td>
        </tr>
      </table>
    </div>
  </div>

  <div about="smp:Ryan" rel="foaf:knows">
    <div about="smp:Matt">
      <p/><table style="border: 5px solid black; width:
          500px;">
        <tr>
          <th colspan="2" property="ftrack:isNamed">Matt
          </th>
```

```
      </tr>
      <tr>
        <td style="width: 23%;">Picture:</td>
        <td>
          <div rel="ftrack:hasPic"><img alt="none" src="
           http://www.semweb.../images/matt.png"/>
          </div>
        </td>
      </tr>
      <tr>
        <td style="width: 23%;">Online Status:</td>
        <td rel="ftrack:hasStatus"
         href="http://semwebprogramming.net#Available">
           Available
        </td>
      </tr>
      <tr>
        <td style="width: 23%;">Email:</td>
        <td>
          <div rel="ftrack:hasEmailAddress"
           href="mfisher@semwebprogramming.org">
           mfisher@semwebprogramming.org </div>
            <div rel="ftrack:hasEmailAddress"
             href="matt2@semwebprogramming.net">
             matt2@semwebprogramming.net </div>
        </td>
      </tr>
    </table>
  </div>
</div>

<div about="smp:Ryan" rel="foaf:knows">
  <div about="smp:John">
    <p/><table style="border: 5px solid black; width:
        500px;">
      <tr>
        <th colspan="2" property="ftrack:isNamed">Johnny
        </th>
      </tr>
      <tr>
        <td style="width: 23%;">Picture:</td>
        <td>
          <div rel="ftrack:hasPic"><img alt="none"
           src=" http://www.semweb.../images/john.png"/>
          </div>
        </td>
      </tr>
      <tr>
        <td style="width: 23%;">Email:</td>
        <td>
```

```
              <div rel="ftrack:hasEmailAddress"
                href="john@semwebprogramming.org">
                john@semwebprogramming.org </div>
            </td>
          </tr>
          <tr>
            <td style="width: 23%;">Origin Location(s):</td>
            <td>
              <div rel="ftrack:isFrom" href="Maryland">
                Maryland</div>
            </td>
          </tr>
        </table>
      </div>
    </div>
  </body>
</html>
```

This example is a simple one; there is no exceptional processing here. The code takes RDF input and embeds it into XHTML with the same namespaces and properties as originally supplied. Any RDFa extraction agent will get the same data. It is possible to imagine how the code could be embellished to translate triples to another namespace, perform ontology alignment or act as an information filter.

Existing HTML-generation frameworks, like those fashioned with PHP and Perl, need only to verify their architectures produce XHTML-compliant web pages to begin using RDFa. Their compliance can be tested at `http://validator.w3.org/`. At that point, RDFa tags can be inserted for semantic enrichment and data shared with others. RDFa extraction is available from the W3C at `http://www.w3.org/2007/08/pyRdfa/`.

Summary

This chapter covered some of the biggest ways to share semantic data, both in RDF and other formats, breaking out of the typical Semantic Web paradigm of triple stores and manually-generated RDF files. The developers of microformats and other semantic markups had the right focus: leverage the millions of pages of existing content but add machine-accessibility with minimal work and invasiveness.

RDFa has strong potential, especially with the backing of the W3C. It is unlikely that it will be the last technology for sharing semantics, as this burgeoning area hasn't seen the dust settle yet. Feel free to experiment with various syntaxes, tools, and frameworks until you find the ones that meet your needs.

Expanding Semantic Web Programming

The Semantic Web is big. It's fluid. It's dynamic and evolving. And today, it is at a point where early adopters are identifying and exploiting the nuggets in the field, and at the same time researchers are pushing the boundaries of the field. This book explores the Semantic Web from a programmer's perspective. We pragmatically approach the technologies and concepts behind the Semantic Web and identify along the way what works and what doesn't. This section completes the journey through Semantic Web programming by presenting useful extensions to Semantic Web programming including semantic-based services and spatial-temporal context, by exploring common architectures, patterns, and best practices of the Semantic Web, and by looking ahead to the future of the Semantic Web.

Chapter 12 covers the subject of semantic web services using the Semantic Web. Thus, the Semantic Web includes services as well as data. Exposing services via semantics offers machine readability to allow automatic composition and negotiations. A number of different technologies and protocols offer different approaches. This chapter discusses Semantic Web services such as the Web Service Modeling Ontology (WSMO), Semantic Web Services Framework (SWSF) and Semantic Annotations for WSDL and MDF. Each technology is discussed in detail.

The chapter wraps up with an example of MDF.

Chapter 13 explores spatial and temporal context in the Semantic Web. Most information involves some notion of space and time. Both are often extremely useful. Depending on the system, that notion, or context, may be assumed or it may be explicitly expressed in the data itself. This chapter presents the concept of spatial and temporal information and how it can be represented in the Semantic Web. Example applications are presented that integrate both a spatial and a temporal index into the Jena Semantic Web Framework in order to provide efficient query performance when information is described spatially and temporally.

Chapter 14 is a retrospective of sorts. It builds on everything that has been covered so far in the book by presenting a series of architecture patterns for constructing various Semantic Web applications. Each architecture is presented and decomposed with important components and protocols identified and discussed. Following the patterns, a series of commonly encountered issues is presented along with the best-practice solutions to each.

Chapter 15 concludes the book by looking to the future, which is most certainly bright! The chapter focuses on four critical, evolving areas for Semantic Web. First, the number, coverage, availability, and utility of ontologies are all being advanced through efforts to create ontology sharing and development technologies. Second, researchers are addressing the need to integrate data and ontologies automatically using distributed queries and automatic ontology alignment. The third area involves advances to reasoning capabilities that address uncertain and fuzzy information and provide provisions for integrating trust into the Semantic Web. The fourth and final area addresses visualizing the rich and voluminous data that becomes accessible with the Semantic Web.

## CHAPTER 12

Developing and Using Semantic Services

"Quality in a service or product is not what you put into it. It is what the client or customer gets out of it."
—Peter F. Drucker

Semantic Services (usually called Semantic Web Services, or SWS) are an additional step beyond today's web services, much like the Semantic Web itself is an extension of the original World Wide Web. *Web services* describe those services that support the traditional SOAP-based or RESTful architectures.

There exist thousands of traditional web services today. However, the ability to integrate and combine them into useful mash-ups requires extensive manual work. The developer must examine each service for its value or semantics and then determine how to extract that value through the correct syntax and protocol. This work severely limits the complexity of mash-ups using traditional web services. Most mash-ups limit the integration to a handful of services, such as Amazon, YahooMaps, or GoogleMaps. In addition, there is limited "contractual agreement" on the various web service interfaces. Interfaces can be modified or removed by their providers at any time, and developers who use these services may never know that changes have taken place until their dependent applications no longer work. This situation makes mash-ups brittle and vulnerable to a change in any of the underlying services.

Analogous to semantic information, SWS directly addresses these limitations by exposing a uniform, machine-readable way to interoperate with a web service—a Semantic Web Service.

SWS enables dynamic machine processing for discovery, invocation, negotiation, and composition of web services to achieve some end goal for users. Order-processing workflow, from order creation to final delivery, is a popular example. Today, workflow requires complex frameworks, such as those based on an enterprise service bus (ESB) or the sometimes-vague notion of a service-oriented architecture (SOA), as well as a high level of human intervention to properly construct the flow of data. The inability of service users to take advantage of a service provider's competitive edge (shortest response times, greatest mean time between failures, largest client user base) to dynamically choose one service over another is another disadvantage of traditional web services. Establishing services that are accessible via the Web is just a beginning step; the next challenge is capitalizing on these services and the data they provide to produce more meaningful data in a machine-accessible way.

This chapter focuses on some of the major technologies being proposed and used today. SWS is an evolving area where the balance of expressivity and usefulness hasn't been fully settled. We first examine the attributes of a Semantic Web Service and then examine three proposed solutions: Semantic Markup for Web Services (OWL-S), Web Service Modeling Ontology (WSMO), and Semantic Annotations for WSDL and XML Schema (SAWSDL). Each holds some insights into the challenge of SWS, and none of them has become the clear, uncontested winner in this field. Most likely SWS will continue to be refined and tweaked into the future. These three technologies form a path to understanding SWS. You can use them now because they address some of the needs previously mentioned; however, realize that the landscape is constantly changing. Like the Semantic Web, Semantic Services benefit from participation; the more participation, the more value.

In this chapter, you:

- Learn the fundamental components and value of Semantic Web Services
- Explore OWL-S, WSMO, and SAWSDL
- Investigate a sample SAWSDL service

Background

Presenting a single definition of a web service is difficult since there are many perceptions behind what precisely constitutes a web service. The W3C published a note (`http://www.w3.org/TR/ws-gloss/`) as part of its Web Services Architecture that includes the following definition:

> *A Web service is a software system designed to support interoperable machine-to-machine interaction over a network. It has an interface described in a machine-processable format (specifically WSDL). Other systems interact with the Web service in a manner prescribed by its description using SOAP-messages, typically conveyed using HTTP with an XML serialization in conjunction with other Web-related standards.*

This definition does not cover RESTful web services, but if you focus on the first sentence, it fits the bill: A web service is a software system designed to support interoperable machine-to-machine interaction over a network. A service must *do* something as part of this interaction: ingest, provide, or transform data, or possibly trigger an event, to name a few examples. A web service exists to provide a service.

NOTE Not all web service infrastructures use WSDL, but those systems that do utilize WSDL are generally considered to be part of a web service infrastructure.

The main issue with traditional web services is that while they specify the syntax of a service, they completely lack any semantics about their operations. In other words, they can declaratively list information about their required inputs, outputs, and how to handle communications. Yet it can be impossible to tell what data or data operations a web service provides solely based on its syntax. For example, a Bear News web service WSDL might specify a method that takes a `dateTime` parameter as input and returns a list of headlines as `string` types. Are these headlines about general news events, or are they the latest news about bears? Likewise, two services could be described very differently yet return similar data. As we have stated in previous chapters, semantics enrich our syntax with meaning.

The secondary issue with web services is that they don't support enough machine automation. While developers can code web services and deploy them in a Tomcat container, for example, it is incumbent upon the developers to utilize a service's endpoint in the application code or publish it to some registry, possibly using Universal Description, Discovery and Integration (UDDI). It is incumbent upon the developers to take the output of one web service (or other provider) and pass it as input to another web service (or other consumer)—a process known as *service chaining, service choreography,* or *service composition*. It is incumbent upon the developers and IT community to manage and maintain working web service frameworks on a daily basis.

Figure 12-1 shows the abridged lifecycle of a web service, focusing on those steps that benefit from semantic enrichment.

Starting with the requirement or the need for a web service, a new service is created. Services ideally go through a refinement loop whereby additional services that provide some sort of useful data are discovered, negotiated with, and composed. Once the pieces are satisfactorily assembled, the web service begins the process of calling these additional web services and ingesting their data. Besides the use of UDDI as a discovery mechanism and the request/response process, these steps require manual intervention and constant maintenance over the long term.

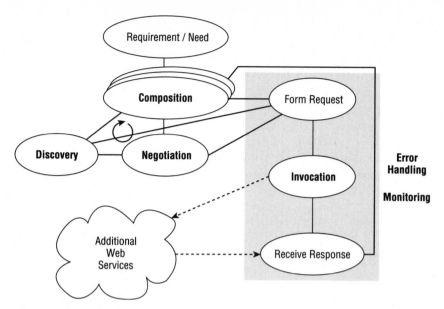

Figure 12-1 Web service lifecycle

The following sections break down the major steps illustrated in Figure 12-1: discovery, invocation, negotiation, error handling, monitoring, and composition.

Discovery

Services that could go to some set of well-defined information servers to self-register, inquire about other available services (including those that provided the same functionality as the inquiring service), or traverse a global network of service registrations would be ideal. Software agents are well suited for this role of discovery. This information would give a semantic service the data it needed to know when and how to register itself, under what topics/headings it should be included and organized, and where to find metadata about the service. Existing technologies aren't closing the gap. For example, public UDDI registries aren't as pervasive as originally hoped, and the centralized nature of UDDI isn't always well aligned to the decentralized nature of the Internet.

Invocation

Invocation describes how a service is triggered or executed. This includes knowing where the service resides (resolvable URIs detailed in a WSDL obtained via UDDI, for example), what inputs it requires, and what outputs it will return. However, a service may actually require a series of operations to achieve a desired outcome rather than a single method call. These steps could be declaratively stored for machine interpretation as well as include added semantics to determine when the steps should be called, how to interpret the output, and how to handle irregular data, to name a few ideas.

Negotiation

Negotiation covers a broad set of ideas, from trust negotiation to contract negotiation, with the latter covering the bartering and agreement of cost, service-level agreements (SLAs), data quality, data quantity, and the like. By embedding SWS, or the agents that run them, with negotiation algorithms, it is possible to have services act in the best interests of their customers. For example, say a user wants to get the latest weather every 5 to 10 minutes unless there is an emergency situation, such as a hurricane, and then the user wants weather information every 60 seconds. It is possible to use semantics to capture this information and determine what available services can meet this level of service as well as their associated cost, which can't be done with syntax alone.

Error Handling

Error handling could become much more robust with semantics. The idea of expanding from a syntactic-based error code or exception when a service fails, to providing a set of alternative services to call or procedures to execute is ideal. SWS could also take advantage of failed conditions to obtain different input (such as finding more recent data or additional data) and repeat service calls, thereby gaining success without manual intervention.

Monitoring

Capturing information about the success and failure rates of service calls, performance figures, data volume, and other indicators and semantically tagging this information to provide a feedback loop for service improvement cannot be done with syntax languages alone. In addition, larger, enterprise service–based systems could incorporate these semantics and, with the help of ontological mediation, present a fused view of service operations from a high level.

Composition

Service composition is a popular and often-cited reason for using SWS. To realize the goal of a global network of loosely coupled specialized services, it is necessary to compose services into a *workflow*. Returning to the order-processing example, building an order requires a customer to purchase an item, select a shipping option, and input payment—an oversimplification, of course. The provider must reserve, find, and package the item, have it shipped, and then process payment, all while managing the progress at each step in the process. It is hard to reuse any of these operations if the entire workflow is encapsulated in a monolithic system. SOAs boast of the ability to provide these frameworks, but the services and the infrastructure require regular specialized maintenance by skilled personnel. With SWS, the operations of such architectures could scale beyond enterprise networks while reducing the dependency on human intervention at the same time. Specifically, software agents rely on declarative semantics that enable them to react to, monitor, adjust, and fulfill services that manually would require many hours of information technology support.

Semantic Web Services burst onto the scene at the beginning of the decade, with many publications and publicized joint efforts appearing around 2002–2004. They didn't deliver all that was promised; however, they continue to attract strong academic research. The next sections will explore OWL-S, the Web Service Modeling Ontology (WSMO), and Semantic Annotations for WSDL and XML Schema (SAWSDL). Note the strong use of WSDL and other standards in all of these technologies. This reuse strengthens the notion that SWS uses evolutionary designs based on what developers are building today versus some out-of-touch revolutionary approach from scratch.

Implementing Semantic Services

Now we'll examine three approaches to SWS. Each technology constructs ontology statements to guide the semantics surrounding the outlined web service life cycle. These solutions take the first step in outlining the key data necessary to form a possible service that could discover, invoke, and monitor a set of web services automatically. The ontologies differ not only in their respective semantics but also in their expressivity and ease of integration with related web services standards like WSDL.

Note that the ontologies express the operations of a service via semantics, not just elements and attributes. Hence your application can use the semantic techniques outlined in the book, such as searching, navigating, and queries, to produce the correct match and operations on a desired service. This design goes well beyond exact keyword matches that are presented without a context. Using the power of SPARQL, your application could ask a precise service query that expresses not only a service's inputs and outputs but also its reliability, privacy details, and the like. The query remains constrained only by the power of the semantic description found in the available ontological instances or the level of available expressivity. However, as expressivity grows, so does its code complexity. If the description is too complex, participation and adoption become more of a challenge. Thus, the three solutions provide their own insight as to the proper balance between expressivity and complexity.

Adoption of these ontologies and the creation of corresponding services still remains largely unfulfilled. It remains to be seen whether these technologies have produced the right balance or if they might be replaced by other frameworks. In any case, it is important to understand these approaches because, whether they succeed or fail, they help guide the way to better managing the growing possibilities of SWS against the thousands of services offered throughout the Internet.

Semantic Markup for Web Services

OWL-S 1.1 is a 2004 W3C Submission found at `http://www.w3.org/Submission/OWL-S`. Its name is not an acronym for OWL services but is shorthand for Semantic Markup for Web Services. OWL-S is an upper ontology that is represented by three high-level concepts. An updated version, 1.2, is available from the DAML website (`http://www.daml.org/services/owl-s/1.2/`). This section will focus on version 1.1, as it was the original basis for the W3C Submission.

Figure 12-2 outlines the basic components implemented through OWL-S. The three concepts to the right of the diagram exist as distinct ontologies that address the semantics of a web service as connected to the main class, `Service`. `ServiceProfile` outlines what the service does. `ServiceGrounding` details how to access the service, while `ServiceModel` defines how the service operates.

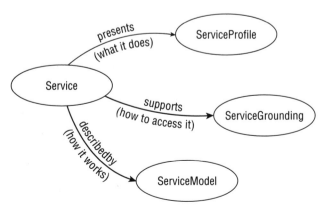

Figure 12-2 A high-level view of OWL-S from the W3C OWL-S Submission

ServiceProfile

ServiceProfile and its subclass Profile describe what a given service does. As a SWS client searches the network for particular services, a Profile provides the necessary data such that a client can determine whether or not a service meets its needs. A Profile may include information such as serviceParameters (referring to any sort of property about a service) and serviceCategorys (a generic method for housing classification system information that is not limited to OWL-S). The Profile class is defined in http://www.daml.org/services/owl-s/1.1/Profile.owl. Figure 12-3 shows the properties and references that are part of Profile.

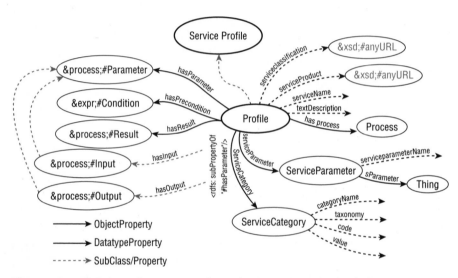

Figure 12-3 RDF view of a Profile from the W3C OWL-S Submission

ServiceModel

ServiceModel, and its subclass Process, enables potential clients to understand how a service operates and how it should be used. It provides abstract details such as parameters (with inputs and outputs as specific cases of parameters), participants, and preconditions. It was designed to handle simple, one-step services as well as service composition. The Process class is defined in http://www.daml.org/services/owl-s/1.1/Process.owl.

ServiceGrounding

ServiceGrounding details a mapping from the abstract ServiceProfile and ServiceModel classes into a concrete implementation, similar to a service binding. The only grounding realized for OWL-S 1.1 was WSDL 1.1 through class `WsdlGrounding` since WSDL 2.0 wasn't an accepted W3C Recommendation at the time. `ServiceGrounding` included direct mapping properties for inputs and outputs between an ontology and a WSDL in addition to mapping associated datatypes. `WsdlGrounding` is defined in `http://www.daml.org/services/owl-s/1.1/Grounding.owl`.

All three of these classes are defined in a separate, fourth OWL file located at `http://www.daml.org/services/owl-s/1.1/Service.owl`. OWL-S addresses the service composition through the `CompositeProcess` class. This class gives OWL-S the ability to execute web services in flexible ways such as in serial or parallel steps as well as the use of conditions.

The mindswap group at the University of Maryland created the de facto Java implementation of OWL-S, appropriately called the OWL-S API. This API is no longer actively maintained through the university, yet it remains a popular choice as an SWS implementation and is freely available through Google Code (`http://code.google.com/p/owl-s/`).

Web Service Modeling Ontology

WSMO starts with a similar approach to OWL-S in detailing semantic services ontologies. This technology extends beyond service description ontologies to address the full requirements in addressing automated, complex interactions with sets of web services. WSMO and its two counterparts, the Web Service Modeling Language (WSML) and the Web Service Execution Environment (WSMX), were submitted to the W3C for consideration in 2005 (`http://www.w3.org/Submission/WSMO/`, `http://www.w3.org/Submission/WSML/`, and `http://www.w3.org/Submission/WSMX`, respectively). WSMO details four main components: ontologies, web service descriptions, goals, and mediators. WSMO's ontologies provide the classes and properties that link all the WSMO concepts to one another in a WSMO implementation. Web service descriptions provide the necessary information about services (both functional and nonfunctional) around which a WSMO implementation can ground its operations. Goals are what users expect to achieve through the use of WSMO web services, and mediators can be thought of as the bridges across these components (mapping ontologies together or connecting goals, for example).

WSMO is not based on OWL but has its own language called the Web Service Modeling Language (WSML). WSML can be mapped to OWL-DL constructs, RDF, or XML for maximum flexibility. A reference implementation of WSMO, called the Web Service Execution Environment (WSMX), is available on SourceForge at `http://sourceforge.net/projects/wsmx`. It is briefly discussed here.

Building WSMX from the source is fairly straightforward and can be done from within Eclipse or the command line (assuming Java 1.6 and Ant 1.7.0 or greater). In this case, Eclipse will serve as the development environment.

Once the 0.5 distribution is downloaded and unzipped, you need to create a new Java project based on the `wsmx-0.5-src` directory. Verify that your ant classpath includes `ant-wsmx.jar` and the three necessary `jax*.jars` (set via Window ➤ Preferences ➤ Ant ➤ Runtime in Eclipse). A snapshot of the classpath is shown in Figure 12-4.

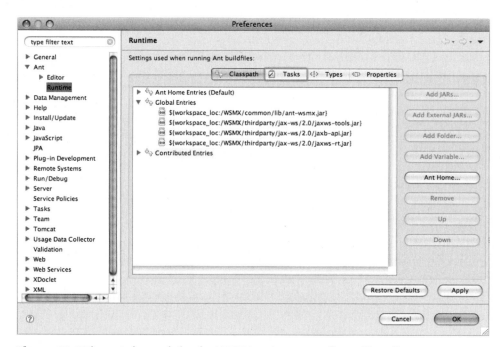

Figure 12-4 The ant classpath for the WSMX project as configured in Eclipse

Create the core and necessary subcomponents through the default Ant build target:

```
ant build.all.dist
```

Then execute the `run` target:

```
ant run
```

A series of web services, ontologies, goals, and mediators is loaded, and the environment is ready for the deployment of SWS. The default management portal is set to `http://localhost:8081` and is managed through JMX MBeans (Java Management Extensions Management Beans). A view of some of the server components is shown in Figure 12-5.

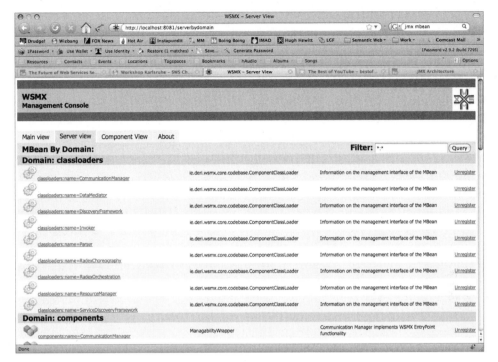

Figure 12-5 A web-based view of the WSMX Management Console

At this point, SWS can be developed and deployed in WSMX. Writing a WSMX-compliant SWS takes some effort and includes:

- The use of an existing WSDL-based web service or the creation of a service if it doesn't exist.

- The creation of WSMO constructs to support the SWS.

- An ontology that describes the selected web service.

- A goal that specifies the object of the SWS.

- A second ontology containing input instances that correspond to the named goal.

- Lowering and lifting adapters for service to conceptual transformations and vice-versa. Lowering and lifting adapters are the mappings that are used to go back and forth from WSMO to RDF or XML, for example.

More information on these steps is covered in the WSMX documentation (http://www.wsmx.org/papers/documentation/WSMXDocumentation.pdf). They are not covered here since the objective of this section is to present an introduction to WSMO and provide readers with a starting point toward development. Since the WSMO W3C submission, work continues on WSMO, specifically the creation of WSMO-Lite and MicroWSMO. WSMO-Lite uses

RDFS and SAWSDL to help realize the grounding of WSDLs to existing ontologies, and MicroWSMO covers semantic annotations in RESTful web services.

Semantic Annotations for WSDL

The final SWS framework is SAWSDL, originally an acronym for Semantic Annotations for WSDL, but which now stands for Semantic Annotations for WSDL and XML Schema. Like OWL-S, this W3C Recommendation, located at `http://www.w3.org/TR/sawsdl/`, has an uncomplicated approach to SWS, but unlike OWL-S and others, it does not force developers to use a particular conceptual representation such as OWL. SAWSDL provides a generic method of connecting WSDL objects, such as element declarations and type definitions, to some conceptual model based in OWL, RDF, RIF, WSML, or some other language. In addition, SAWSDL supports references to other artifacts (such as lifting and lowering attributes, detailed shortly) that can map data from a given element or attribute to the conceptual representation. In summary, SAWSDL is focused on achieving interoperability. The SAWSDL schema is limited to three simple attributes:

```
<xs:schema
  targetNamespace="http://www.w3.org/ns/sawsdl"
  xmlns="http://www.w3.org/ns/sawsdl"
  xmlns:xs="http://www.w3.org/2001/XMLSchema"
  xmlns:wsdl="http://www.w3.org/ns/wsdl">

<xs:simpleType name="listOfAnyURI">
  <xs:list itemType="xs:anyURI"/>
</xs:simpleType>

<xs:attribute name="modelReference" type="listOfAnyURI" />
<xs:attribute name="liftingSchemaMapping" type="listOfAnyURI" />
<xs:attribute name="loweringSchemaMapping" type="listOfAnyURI" />

<xs:element name="attrExtensions">
  <xs:complexType>
    <xs:annotation>
      <xs:documentation>This element is for use in WSDL 1.1 only.
        It does not apply to WSDL 2.0 documents.  Use in
        WSDL 2.0 documents is invalid.</xs:documentation>
    </xs:annotation>
    <xs:anyAttribute namespace="##any" processContents="lax" />
  </xs:complexType>
</xs:element>
</xs:schema>
```

`modelReference` is an annotation that informs an interpreter that the referenced URI is a link to some semantic model that corresponds to the annotated

WSDL object. The content, language, and syntax that belong to the URI are inconsequential to SAWSDL. The `liftingSchemaMapping` attribute provides a URI where the corresponding WSDL object is lifted from XML to a semantic model, while the `loweringSchemaMapping` attribute reverses the operation, lowering the semantic model into an XML format.

SAWSDL Example

Starting with a simple example, we will use an existing WSDL and create an association between some operation, the `operationname` web service, to an ontology that defines some model object, such as a `Request`:

```
<wsdl:operation name="operationname"
   sawsdl:modelReference="http://www.semwebprogramming.org#Request">
  <wsdl:input element="input"/>
  <wsdl:output element="output"/>
</wsdl:operation>
```

We can similarly use `modelReference` to map parameter names:

```
<xsd:element name="RequestService">
  <xsd:complexType>
    <xsd:sequence>
      <xsd:element name="itemCode" type="xsd:string"
sawsdl:modelReference="http://www.semwebprogramming.org#Parm1"/>
      <xsd:element name="date" type="xsd:string"
        sawsdl:modelReference="
              http://www.semwebprogramming.org#Parm2"/"/>
      <xsd:element name="qty" type="xsd:float"
        sawsdl:modelReference="
              http://www.semwebprogramming.org#Parm3"/"/>
    </xsd:sequence>
  </xsd:complexType>
</xsd:element>
```

With this mapping, elements `Parm1`, `Parm2`, and `Parm3` are enriched with semantics (such as the specific references in our model ontology) that are irrelevant to the WSDL itself yet provide disambiguation for machine-based clients of this service. If you look at the following code, you'll see that `Request` is defined as the object of `complexType` with a URI and associates a lifting operation that transforms `Request` elements into OWL via an XSLT:

```
<xsd:element name="Request">
  <xsd:complexType
     sawsdl:liftingSchemaMapping=
      "http://semwebprogramming.org/Request2Ont.xslt">
    <xsd:sequence>
```

```
       <xsd:element name="firstParam" type="xsd:string"/>
       <xsd:element name="secondParam" type="xsd:string"/>
   </xsd:sequence>
 </xsd:complexType>
 </xsd:element>
```

Sampling a section of `Request2Ont.xslt`, a SPARQL query is utilized to gather the data from a backend knowledgebase to populate a `Request` object. `firstParam` and `secondParam` provide the input needed for the query:

```
<lowering>
  <sparqlQuery>
    PREFIX semweb: <http://semwebprogramming.org/Request#>
    SELECT ?request
    WHERE {
       ?subject semweb:hasRequest ?request
    }
  </sparqlQuery>
</lowering>
```

This brief example shows one method to leverage existing technologies into a semantic framework.

SAWSDL Tools

The code behind the previous WSDL and XSLT is based on SAWSDL4J, an open-source API that provides Java objects as representatives for SAWSDL documents. The following source code provides a quick dump of our `modelReferences` (one) and its associated mapping messages:

```
// Get WSDL file
Definition def = SAWSDLUtility.getDefinitionFromFile
  (new File("wsdlfile.wsdl");
// Get Port Types
Map portTypes = def.getPortTypes();
for (Object key:portTypes.keySet()){
  PortType semanticPortType =
    def.getSemanticPortType((QName)key);

  System.out.println("Porttype QName ->" +
    semanticPortType.getQName());
  System.out.println("Model References ->" +
    semanticPortType.getModelReferences() );

  List operations = semanticPortType.getOperations();

  for (Object operation : operations) {
    System.out.println("Operation ->" +
      ((Operation) operation).getName());
  }
}
```

```
// Get Messages
Map messages = def.getMessages();
for (Object key:messages.keySet()){
  Message semanticMessage =
    def.getSemanticMessage((QName)key);

  System.out.println("Message QName ->" +
    semanticMessage.getQName());

  Map parts = semanticMessage.getParts();

  for (Object partKey : parts.keySet()) {
    Part semanticPart =
      semanticMessage.getSemanticPart((String) partKey);
  System.out.println("part ->" + semanticPart);
  System.out.println("part model references ->" +
    semanticPart.getModelReferences());
  }
}
```

SAWSDL4J is available at `http://lsdis.cs.uga.edu/projects/meteor-s/opensource/sawsdl4j/`. Another API, Woden4SAWSDL, provides WSDL 2.0 parsing abilities that enable SAWSDL artifacts to be generated from the given WSDL. It is available from `http://lsdis.cs.uga.edu/projects/meteor-s/opensource/woden4sawsdl/`.

There are also SAWSDL editors such as Radiant (`http://lsdis.cs.uga.edu/projects/meteor-s/downloads/index.php?page=1`) and WSMOStudio (`http://www.wsmostudio.org/`). Both are plug-ins for Eclipse.

Summary

Although none of the three technologies that you learned about in this chapter serve as a final answer to SWS, all three provide valuable insights into how Semantic Web Services will advance in the future. Clearly, as web services continue to gain critical mass, a solution beyond simple mash-ups will be needed. The inspection of these approaches provides the insights necessary to help get you there.

Semantic Web Services haven't reached the pinnacle of interoperability and automation that some advocates were touting several years ago. The tools to support SWS are limited, and some frameworks, such as WSMO, can require quite a bit of work to build the basics. Research continues at a steady pace, and with the acceptance of SAWSDL as a W3C Recommendation, additional implementations and extensions to these foundational languages and architectures aren't far away.

## CHAPTER 13

Managing Space and Time

Many modern software applications need to manage information about time or space, and applications for the Semantic Web are no different. Such information is called *spatial* or *temporal* if it relates to space or time, respectively, and *spatiotemporal* if it involves both space and time. This chapter presents a brief discussion of how software can manage spatiotemporal information and then discusses some of the challenges facing these systems. Next you'll learn some strategies for developing appropriate RDF and OWL representations of spatiotemporal data for your own applications. Finally, the chapter presents a pair of coding examples to show how you can optimize your Semantic Web systems for spatial and temporal data.

In this chapter, you will learn about:

- Spatial and temporal software
- Spatial and temporal data representations for the Semantic Web
- Extending Jena to exploit spatial and temporal information

Space and Time in Software

Notions of space and time are intimately related to everything that happens in the world because everything happens somewhere and some *when*. Almost every software system is concerned with the spatiotemporal aspect of data to some degree, though some deal only with the spatial or the temporal.

For some applications, the connection to space and time is very obvious. A package-tracking application, for example, clearly is designed to help answer some of the following questions: Where is the package coming from? To where is the package headed? When was it sent? When is it expected to arrive? Where is it now? These sorts of questions all explicitly involve space and time.

However, different sorts of applications use space or time more implicitly, more to contextualize an answer to a related query. Any system that maintains information that can change must at some level deal with time, for instance, and many questions include some assumptions of location as well. What does the company's organization chart look like? How much is the company spending on shipping? Which printer is best for this print job? The answers to these questions are not exclusively dependent on spatiotemporal data, but that information must be considered in order to give the best answer. Organization charts change over time, as do shipping costs and printer availability. In addition, given a companywide network of printers, the best printer is not necessarily the idlest one, but one that is also located at the same site as the person who initiated the job. Similarly, if a company ships to or from different warehouses, shipping costs may vary greatly from site to site depending on shipping method, fuel costs, and so forth. Being able to bound queries into a particular spatiotemporal region can be very useful.

Requirements about the data and the types of questions that will be asked of it always direct the design of an application. Whether the spatiotemporal aspect of a system is explicit or implicit can have significant impacts on the way that information is represented and managed. However, regardless of the application of the data, the concepts behind spatial and temporal data are the same.

Spatial Information

In general terms, spatial information describes regions of space. It is within these regions of space that entities of interest are located or where events of interest occur. Practically speaking, however, what is meant by "regions of space"? That definition is vague because it can cover a wide variety of different types of spatial information.

As examples, consider the following spatial descriptions: "the White House," "1600 Pennsylvania Avenue," "the caldera of Olympus Mons," and "latitude 42.359011, longitude -71.093512." Each of these descriptions defines a region in space, but they also serve to illustrate some of the important challenges to keep in mind when dealing with spatial information.

The first challenge is ambiguity. Take the first two examples: "the White House" and "1600 Pennsylvania Avenue." Both of these expressions define spatial regions. The first identifies a region by naming the structure that bounds it, the second by defining the region relative to the nation's road network. However, neither of these descriptions defines a region unambiguously. To a person in the United States, "the White House" describes the residence of the president of the United States at 1600 Pennsylvania Avenue in Washington, D.C. However, in Kyrgyzstan, the term "the White House" describes the residence of the president of that country, within the capital city of Bishkek. Similarly, "1600 Pennsylvania Avenue" could mean the residence of the U.S. president in Washington, D.C., but it could just as easily refer to an address in St. Louis, Missouri, or Dallas, Texas, both of which also have streets named Pennsylvania Avenue. This sort of ambiguity can be confusing even to humans and can easily cause errant behavior when machines are left to interpret it. Your design must combine software and data appropriately to unambiguously describe regions in your application.

A similar issue is raised by the latitude/longitude example. One given representation of a spatial region might be preferable to another equivalent representation. This can lead to complexity when trying to share information between systems that are designed for different purposes. For instance, the location described by the latitude/longitude pair is that of the mailing address of the Massachusetts Institute of Technology (MIT) at 77 Massachusetts Avenue in Cambridge, Massachusetts. Even though the mailing address and the latitude/longitude pair represent the same location, depending on whether a system intends to plot the location on a map or to send a letter there, one representation is more advantageous than the other. It is important to design a representation for spatiotemporal data that best suits the operations required of the data.

Another challenge is that of granularity, or resolution. Olympus Mons is a mountain on the planet Mars; it is the tallest known mountain in the solar system. At the top of the mountain is a depression, known as a caldera, that is 53 miles long and 37 miles across. This large region of space could reasonably be represented as a point from the perspective of Earth, but from the perspective of some future rover exploring that terrain, that type of representation would be insufficient. The amount of precision and sophistication of a spatiotemporal representation must be appropriate for the context in which that representation will be used.

Representations of spatial data also range in complexity based on the relevant frame of reference. A latitude/longitude system is a convenient way of referring to points on the surface of a planet, such as Earth or Mars. However, in either case, the latitude/longitude pair is only sufficient to describe surface locations with respect to one planet or the other, not both. A software system that managed the launching and landing of a spacecraft from MIT on Earth to Olympus Mons on Mars would need a richer representation than simple latitude/longitude pairs. More generally, the complexity of the representation for a given set of spatial data depends on the complexity of both the spatial region being described and the relevant frame of reference of that description.

Designers of spatial software systems must carefully choose a representation that takes into consideration the type of spatial data used by the system and the way in which that information will be used. They should take care to design an unambiguous representation that is flexible enough to support the full richness of the available data, but that is also optimized for the tasks that data will be used to perform. Without careful consideration of any of these points, it can be difficult to adequately represent and share spatiotemporal information.

Temporal Information

Just as spatial data describes regions in space, temporal data describe regions in time. Within these regions of time, entities of interest can interact with each other, and events of interest can occur. In some ways, temporal data is easier to conceptualize than spatial data, because time is only a single dimension. However, when designing a representation for temporal data, the fundamental challenges remain the same.

While time itself is only a single dimension, descriptions of entities in time require more complicated descriptions than a single point. As with space, temporal descriptions can refer to a zero-dimensional instant, like the moment you were born, a continuous period of time such as your lifespan, or a discrete set of periods in time, like the concept *Thursdays*. In addition, in the field of temporal databases, a distinction is drawn between two classes of time data. The first is called *valid time*, and the second is *transaction time*. These different types of temporal data have different characteristics and usually require different techniques for their management.

The valid time for a particular fact is that span of time for which the fact is true within the world modeled by the data. For example, consider a store that recognizes diligent workers with an "Employee of the Month" award. If you are the employee of the month for July, then from July 1 at 12:00 a.m. until July 31 at 11:59 p.m. the statement "You are the employee of the month" is valid. Outside that range, either before or after, the statement is invalid.

Transaction time has less to do with the facts themselves so much as with the current state of the information system that manages those facts. Transaction time describes the time during which a given fact is a part of the current state of the data model. For example, if the "Employee of the Month" award had been decided at the end of June instead of July, and the store manager had added that fact to her database on June 28, then that would be the beginning of the transactional time bound for that fact. If the fact were ever deleted from the database or replaced by a different fact, then that point would mark the end bound of that fact with respect to transaction time.

It takes a different conceptual approach to query a knowledgebase that is modeling information using valid time versus transaction time. Essentially, valid time queries allow users to ask questions about the passage of time within the world that is modeled by the data, and transaction time queries allow users to ask questions about the state of the data model through time.

Often it is valuable to be able to ask both kinds of questions. However, as with anything else, the more capabilities built into a software system, the more complicated that system must be.

Representing Spatiotemporal Data on the Semantic Web

Now that you've seen some of the challenges that must be addressed by different representations of spatiotemporal data, consider a few approaches to the issue in RDF and OWL. The representation must be based on the nature of the data and of the tasks your system will perform on it. With that in mind, it is valuable to recall the distinction between explicitly spatiotemporal data versus fundamentally non-spatiotemporal data that will be annotated with spatiotemporal context. If the information your system manages is dates or spatial regions, then your representation will focus on those. If your system focuses on other types of information and just annotates it with spatial or temporal values, then you first need a way to represent the spatiotemporal information, but you also need a way of associating that extra component with the bulk of the data.

Of course, before considering a new representation for spatial or temporal data, you should try to draw on existing conventions. It's often easier to find something already created than to develop it from scratch, and as with information on the Semantic Web in general, linking concepts together by reusing ontologies makes it much easier to interchange information. OWL does not include a standard representation for spatial data, and its support for describing time is limited to support for typed literal values. With typed literal values, you can take advantage of the standard XML Schema Definition (XSD) date, time, and dateTime types, but in some cases this is too limited a set of options.

While the OWL language's support for time is limited to typed literals, other representations for temporal data have been developed by members of the Semantic Web community. One such example is OWL-Time, which has been released by the World Wide Web Consortium (W3C), and is presently a working draft.

NOTE More information about OWL-Time is available at http://www.w3.org/TR/owl-time/.

OWL-Time includes the concept of a temporal entity, which can be either instantaneous, which is called an *instant*, or of some duration, called an *interval*. The duration of an interval is defined with an instance of the DurationDescription class, and it can be bound by instants with the hasBeginning and hasEnd properties. The DurationDescription instance uses predicates like weeks, days, hours, minutes, and seconds to specify the duration. A particular interval can be associated with multiple DurationDescription instances, each of which should be equivalent to the others. If an interval has the duration of a standard calendar unit, it can be a member of the DateTimeInterval class, and it is described with a DateTimeDescription instance. For example, "April 15" is an interval of 24 hours, but it also coincides with a date on the calendar. Therefore, that interval should be considered a DateTimeInterval. These DateTimeIntervals can be a day long, but they could also last a month, week, hour, minute, or second. The DateTimeDescription also allows for the definition of instants. Because an instant takes no time, it can never be exactly identified. The best that can be done is to identify an interval within which that instant falls. In OWL-Time, the inDateTime predicate is used to associate an instant with a DateTimeDescription in just this way.

The following is an example of describing a night's rest in OWL Time.

```
@prefix time: <http://www.w3.org/2006/time#> .
@prefix : <http://example.org/time#> .

# Person goes to sleep at :FallAsleepTime, and sleeps for
# 8 hours until :WakeUpTime
:NightsRest a time:TemporalEntity, time:Interval ;
            time:hasBeginning :FallAsleepTime ;
            time:hasEnding :WakeUpTime ;
            time:hasDurationDescription [ a time:DurationDescription ;
                                 time:hours "8"
                        ] .
# :FallAsleepTime is 10:27 on September 20th.
:FallAsleepTime a time:Instant ;
            time:inDateTime [ a time:DateTimeDescription ;
                        time:unitType time:unitMinute ;
                        time:month "9" ;
                        time:day "20" ;
                        time:hour "22" ;
                        time:minute "27" ;
                        time:second "0" ;
                        time:timeZone "-PT5H"
                    ] .
# :WakeUpTime is 6:27 on September 21st, 8 hours later
:WakeUpTime a time:Instant ;
            time:inDateTime [ a time:DateTimeDescription ;
                        time:unitType time:unitMinute ;
                        time:month "9" ;
                        time:day "21" ;
                        time:hour "6" ;
                        time:minute "27" ;
```

```
                              time:second "0" ;
                              time:timeZone "-PT5H"
             ] .
```

The example describes a night's rest of eight hours, beginning at 10:27 p.m. on September 20 and ending the next morning at 6:27 a.m. The precise instant of falling asleep and waking up is not defined in this example. Because the unitType of the DateTimeDescriptions is time:minute, only the fact that those instants fell within the minutes of 10:27 p.m. and 6:27 a.m., respectively, is preserved. OWL-Time also supports using XSD dateTime values directly, for those cases when succinctness is a priority. For instance, you can define an instant with an XSD dateTime value using the inXSDDateTime predicate for example:

```
@prefix time: <http://example.org/time#> .
@prefix : <http://example.org/time> .

:OneMomentInTime a time:Instant ;
   :inXSDDateTime "2008-09-21T22:27:00-5:00" .
```

This snippet is an alternate representation of the instant within the minute of 10:27 p.m. on September 20. If you need to express simple dates, times, and durations, you should consider using OWL-Time.

Work has been done in developing a way to express spatial regions on the Semantic Web as well. The GeoRSS project has created an abstract representation for spatial information so that it can be embedded into a Really Simple Syndication (RSS) feed.

NOTE More information about GeoRSS is available at http://georss.org/. RSS is an initialism for *Really Simple Syndication*, but it has historically also been an initialism for *RDF Site Summary*. More information about the history of RSS is available at http://cyber.law.harvard.edu/rss/rssVersionHistory.html.

The GeoRSS model supports the concepts of points, lines, boxes, and polygons. All of the points are latitude/longitude pairs according to the World Geodetic System from 1984 (WGS84). WGS84 is a standard way of representing points on the surface of the earth, and it is widely used in part because it is the encoding used by the Global Positioning System (GPS). GeoRSS's preferred representation for latitude/longitude pairs is a space-separated list of decimal-degreed values, for instance: "38.893754 -77.072568," or "42.390438 -71.148705," or for a collection of points, "38.893754 -77.072568 39.184543 -76.850706 42.390438 -71.148705." Collections of points are used to define multipoint regions like lines, boxes, and polygons.

DECIMAL DEGREES

Decimal degrees, like those used by GeoRSS, are a common way of conveniently representing latitude and longitude values as pairs of real-valued numbers. There is a straightforward translation between decimal degrees and standard latitude/longitude representation. Because there are 60 minutes in a degree of arc and 60 seconds in a minute of arc, to convert from a standard representation like 40° 44′ 55″ N, 73° 59′ 7″ W, to decimal degrees, simply divide the minutes by 60 and the seconds by 3600 to get the fractional portion of the degree. Add the fractional portion to the integer portion of the degree to generate the full decimal degree representation. By convention, positive latitudes are north of the equator and negative latitudes are south; positive longitudes are east of the prime meridian, and negative longitudes are west.

The latitude and longitude above, therefore, would be:

```
40 + 44/60 + 55/3600 = +44.748611
73 + 59/60 + 7/3600 = -73.985278
```

This pair, 40.748611, -73.985278, is the decimal degree representation of the Empire State Building in New York City.

Conceptually GeoRSS is a very convenient framework, but it can sometimes be difficult to work with this data in RDF because the values are concatenated as strings. In order to use this data, these strings must be parsed and the values extracted. For this reason, many Semantic Web systems use the Basic Geo Vocabulary.

NOTE More information about the Basic Geo Vocabulary is available at `http://www.w3.org/2003/01/geo/`.

The Basic Geo Vocabulary is a simple RDF encoding for WGS84 latitude and longitude values. It defines a `Point` class as well as `lat`, `long`, and `alt` predicates to describe a `Point`'s location in terms of latitude, longitude, and altitude.

If standard spatiotemporal representations like OWL-Time or GeoRSS and the Basic Geo Vocabulary are not a good fit for your application, then you can extend them or create your own. It is still always a good idea to ensure that even when it is not practical to use or extend an existing representation, you try to develop the new one in such a way as to be compatible with the existing representations. That makes it easy for data to be shared between your application and others'.

After you've decided on a representation for the spatiotemporal information, it remains to associate that component with the rest of the data in your system. For entities that are inherently spatiotemporal, this can be a simple process.

Take the example of a package-tracking application. A package is sent through a distribution network owned by a shipping company. At any point from the time the package is shipped until it arrives, it is either at a package depot or en route to the next one. Each time it arrives at a depot, it is scanned. In such a case, you could model it as shown in the following code:

```
@prefix time: <http://www.w3.org/2006/time#> .
@prefix geo: <http://www.w3.org/2003/01/geo/wgs84_pos#> .
@prefix owl: <http://www.w3.org/2002/07/owl#> .
@prefix : <http://example.org/package#> .

:Warehouse a owl:Class .
:Scan a owl:Class .

# This describes a package warehouse in Arlington, Virginia
:Warehouse1 a :Warehouse ;
  :name "Arlington Warehouse" ;
  :locatedAt [ a geo:Point ;
            geo:lat "38.893754" ;
            geo:long "-77.072568"
          ] .

# This describes a package warehouse in Columbia, Maryland
:Warehouse2 a :Warehouse ;
  :name "Columbia Warehouse" ;
  :locatedAt [ a geo:Point ;
            geo:lat "39.184543" ;
            geo:long "-76.850706"
          ] .

# This describes a package warehouse near Boston, Massachusetts
:Warehouse3 a :Warehouse ;
  :name "Boston Warehouse" ;
  :locatedAt [ a geo:Point ;
            geo:lat "42.390438" ;
            geo:long "-71.148705"
          ] .
# A package with package ID 1111, presumably other information about
# the package exists elsewhere
:Package1
   :id "1111" .

# A package with ID 2222
:Package2
   :id "2222" .

# A package scan, indicating that package 1 was in Arlington at 9:30 AM
# on September 24th, 2008
[] a :Scan ;
   :package :Package1 ;
```

```
    :location :Warehouse1 ;
    :time [ a time:Instant ;
            time:inXSDDateTime "2008-09-24T09:30:00-5:00"
          ] .


# A package scan, indicating that package 1 was in Columbia at 10:30 PM
# on September 24th, 2008
[] a :Scan ;
    :package :Package1 ;
    :location :Warehouse2 ;
    :time [ a time:Instant ;
            time:inXSDDateTime "2008-09-24T22:30:00-5:00"
          ] .


# A package scan, indicating that package 1 was in Boston at 6:08 PM
# on September 25th, 2008
[] a :Scan ;
    :package :Package1 ;
    :location :Warehouse3 ;
    :time [ a time:Instant ;
            time:inXSDDateTime "2008-09-25T18:08:00-5:00"
          ] .
```

In the code below you can see one possible representation for spatiotemporal information. The locations are represented using the `Point` class from the Basic Geo Vocabulary, and the scan times are represented using OWL-Time constructs. Then time and space are tied together using `Scan` instances. The `Scans` are blank nodes, and they are used in this case to represent a relationship with an arity of four (that is, a relationship of a higher order than the two of a binary relationship). This use of blank nodes is described in more detail in Chapter 3, ''Modeling Information.'' With a representation such as this, a system could easily track a package's progress through the distribution network.

For example, consider the following SPARQL query. When issued to an endpoint containing the package data, it will return the scan time and warehouse information (name, latitude, and longitude) for package 1111.

```
PREFIX time: <http://www.w3.org/2006/time#>
PREFIX geo: <http://www.w3.org/2003/01/geo/wgs84_pos#>
PREFIX owl: <http://www.w3.org/2002/07/owl#>
PREFIX pack: <http://example.org/package#>

SELECT ?name ?lat ?lon ?time
WHERE {
  ?scan a pack:Scan ;
        pack:package [ pack:id "1111" ] ;
        pack:location [ a pack:Warehouse ;
                        pack:name ?name ;
                        pack:locatedAt [ a geo:Point ;
                                         geo:lat ?lat ;
```

```
                                              geo:long ?lon
                                          ]
                          ] ;
          pack:time [ a time:Instant ;
                       time:inXSDDateTime ?time
                    ]
    }
```

Another type of application sees a collection of non-spatiotemporally oriented information that needs to be annotated with spatiotemporal data. In this case, reification can present a good strategy. Suppose that a shipping company has an organization chart detailing the executive structure of the company, as shown in Figure 13-1.

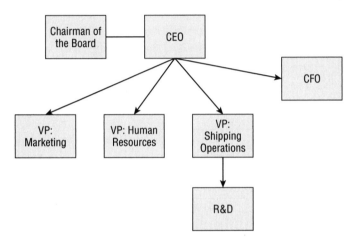

Figure 13-1 Organization chart for ACME Shipping

However, further suppose that in October of 2006, the organizational structure of the company changed. The Research and Development department of Shipping was restructured into its own independent division, and the position of Director of R&D was similarly changed to Vice President, reporting directly to the CEO. How could this fact be represented in OWL? The following code shows a portion of the chart from Figure 13-1:

```
@prefix owl: <http://www.w3.org/2002/07/owl#> .
@prefix time: <http://www.w3.org/2006/time#> .
@prefix rdf: <http://www.w3.org/1999/02/22-rdf-syntax-ns#type> .
@prefix : <http://example.org/organization#> .

:Company a owl:Class .
:Position a owl:Class .

:reportsTo a owl:ObjectProperty .
```

```
:CEO a :Position .
:VPShipping a :Position .
:DirectorRandD a :Position .

:AcmeShippingCompany a :Company ;
    :hasPosition :CEO , :VPShipping , :DirectorRandD .

:VPShipping :reportsTo :CEO .
:DirectorRandD :reportsTo :VPShipping .
```

This snippet describes two classes and one predicate: `Company`, `Position`, and `reportsTo`, respectively. It then describes the portion of the organization relating to research and development, with the `DirectorRandD` reporting to the `VPShipping`, and that vice president reporting to the `CEO` of the company. This is the state of affairs before the reorganization. The following code shows one approach to representing the company's structure after the October reorganization.

```
:AcmeShippingCompany :hasPosition :VPRandD .
:VPRandD :reportsTo :CEO .

:Reorganization a owl:Class .

:October2006Reorg a :Reorganization ;
    :removed ([ a rdf:Statement ;
            rdf:subject :AcmeShippingCompany ;
            rdf:predicate :hasPosition ;
            rdf:object :DirectoryRandD
          ]
          [ a rdf:Statement ;
            rdf:subject :DirectorRandD ;
            rdf:predicate :reportsTo ;
            rdf:object :VPShipping
          ]) ;
    :added ([ a rdf:Statement ;
            rdf:subject :AcmeShippingCompany ;
            rdf:predicate :hasPosition ;
            rdf:object :VPRandD
          ]
          [ a rdf:Statement ;
            rdf:subject :VPRandD ;
            rdf:predicate :reportsTo ;
            rdf:object :CEO
          ]) ;
    :effective [ a time:Instant ;
            :inXSDDateTime "2006-10-15T00:00:00-5:00"
          ] .
```

This section of code shows the change of the reorganization—the creation of the new position of Vice President for Research and Development (VPRandD in the section) and the fact that that new position reports to the CEO. The bulk of the code, however, is devoted to a description of the effect of the reorganization in the form of a Reorganization class and instance. October2006Reorg is an instance that is associated with two lists and an OWL-Time Instant instance. The lists describe the statements of the document that were removed and added, respectively, as a result of the reorganization, and the effective predicate indicates when the reorganization took effect.

In the previous code, reification is used to add temporal information to data that is not temporally oriented. It is important to note it was possible to enhance it with temporal data even though nothing about the way that the organizational chart was represented suggests that it was designed to accommodate that temporal information. Because reification allows for any statement to be described, it is a very powerful and flexible mechanism for adding temporal or spatial data to other information.

The flexibility that reification provides can come at a cost. While it makes it possible to annotate nontemporal information with temporal descriptions, reification, when used without special care, can significantly degrade the performance of an application. From the point of view of RDF triples, reification is a verbose way of expressing information. As shown, asserting that a statement should be removed requires five statements: the removed statement itself, the statement to declare the resource that is the object of the removed assertion, and then finally the rdf:subject, rdf:predicate, and rdf:object statements that define the statement to be removed. For triple stores, large amounts of reifications can slow down query processing unless they are specially optimized to handle reifications efficiently.

In addition, while reification makes temporal annotations possible, introducing temporal semantics to an application in this way is not sufficient to introduce any functionality related to time. Using reification to introduce temporal semantics in this way is tantamount to changing the underlying information representation, and making such a change without corresponding changes to queries and other software logic can lead to incorrect results. One good approach to solving this problem is to use temporally aware queries or program logic to generate a version of the underlying data that is consistent for a particular given time. This model can then be queried using the original queries. For example, if most applications are concerned only with the most current organizational hierarchy, a preprocessing step could be used to generate a model that strips out the reification and represents the most up-to-date structure of the organization.

Spatial and Temporal Software with Jena

Now that you've seen different ways to model spatiotemporal data in RDF and OWL, how can you work with this information efficiently in software? Treating spatiotemporal information just like other data values can lead to very inefficient system performance because of the nature of common queries. This leads to specialized data structures and approaches for dealing with space and time in software.

For example, in Table 13-1, consider a collection of addresses of restaurant locations and their latitudes and longitudes.

Table 13-1 Records with Restaurant Location Information

STREET ADDRESS	LATITUDE	LONGITUDE
1013 Richmond Ave, Staunton VA 24401	38.138948	-79.048496
107 N Fayette St, Alexandria VA 22314	38.805835	-77.052437
1304 W Main St, Salem VA 24153	37.289828	-80.078373
13580 Foulger Sq, Woodbridge VA 22192	38.656298	-77.304462
14001 Jefferson Davis Hwy, Woodbridge VA 22191	38.649417	-77.261204
1961 Chain Bridge Rd, Tysons Corner VA 22102	38.919611	-77.226403
2901 Richmond Ln, Alexandria VA 22305	38.83146	-77.069674
6541 Backlick Rd, Springfield VA 22150	38.777264	-77.184649
707 Southpark Blvd, Colonial Heights VA 23834	37.247886	-77.388923
750 Independence Blvd, Virginia Beach VA 23455	36.864308	-76.132557
931 W Broad St, Richmond VA 23220	37.55045	-77.450162

Imagine that sales are low at a store, and the manager of that store is wondering if his sales are being cannibalized by another location. He wants to know which stores are within three miles of his own. This is a challenging query to answer efficiently. Suppose you call the manager's store the base store. In order to answer this query, the system would need to calculate the distance between the base store and every other store each time the query was issued. This is potentially a very expensive operation, and it cannot be effectively precomputed. As you can see in Figure 13-2, the results of the query differ with respect to changes in both the search radius and the base store. In order to answer this query without significant calculation at runtime, every store would have to compute a result for each combination of base store and distance. This amount of work is infeasible even for reasonably sized data sets.

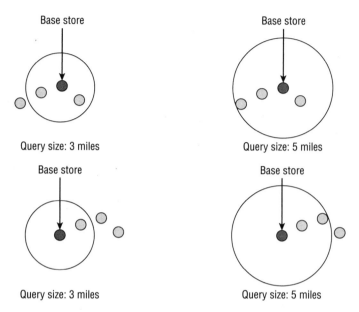

Query size: 3 miles   Query size: 5 miles

Query size: 3 miles   Query size: 5 miles

Figure 13-2 Spatial query results change based on both the center and the radius of the search region

Temporal data presents similar challenges. Information systems must be designed specifically in order to efficiently answer either transaction time or valid time queries. In the organization chart example, you saw that reification can be used effectively to associate temporal data with arbitrary sets of RDF statements. However, without specially designing a system to answer temporal queries, the only approach would be to reify every statement with a timestamp. This is possible, but it would clutter the knowledgebase with a great number of statements that are essentially just for bookkeeping and exacerbate the performance issues introduced by reification. Unless the application requires all those timestamps, that information should be kept out of the main knowledgebase.

Working with spatiotemporal data is challenging but by no means impossible. Special data structures have been and are being developed to efficiently answer some of the most common types of spatiotemporal queries. In this section, you'll see an example of how to take advantage of one such data structure, a spatial index.

Working with Spatial Data

While it is difficult to answer the spatial query about nearby restaurants without a special data structure, a spatial index can be integrated into a Jena model so as to make spatial queries efficient.

A *spatial index* is a special data structure that organizes information about objects in space based on their locations so that spatial queries can be answered efficiently. There are several algorithms typically used to index information in this way. A common approach is to build a tree-based data structure that partitions a region of space into smaller subsections. Each node in the tree represents a region of space, and its children represent smaller regions within the parent node. Each node also contains references to entities located within that node's region of space. Different algorithms use different criteria for partitioning space or for assigning entities to nodes. These varied approaches lead to different performance characteristics among spatial indices. In general, however, spatial indices greatly reduce the amount of computation required to answer queries like "find all entities within distance X of a reference location."

In order to answer that query, first the tree is traversed until the node that would contain the reference location is found. Once that node has been identified, the search algorithm steps back up the tree via parent nodes until the parent node's extent includes the search bounds. At that point, every entity within the subtree of that parent node is compared to determine whether the entity falls within the desired search region. Because the entities within the spatial index are organized according to their locations, it is not necessary to calculate the distances between every location at query time. Figure 13-3 shows a partitioning of the space on an island, with the entities marked as points within the grid.

Spatial indices are data structures that can be implemented separately from the main business logic of an application and distributed as libraries. One such library is the JTS Topology Suite (JTS).

> **NOTE** More information about the JTS Topology Suite is available at
> `http://tsusiatsoftware.net/jts/main.html`.

The JTS provides an API for developing spatial applications, and it includes an implementation of a spatial index called a quad tree. A *quad tree* is a spatial index in which each node represents a spatial region that is recursively subdivided into four quadrants, as shown in Figure 13-3. This recursion continues where necessary until a small number of node items are left in each square. In Figure 13-3, for example, any region with more than three points has been subdivided so that there is never a region with more than three points. In the following software example, a Jena model is enhanced with a quad tree to enable it to efficiently answer spatial queries.

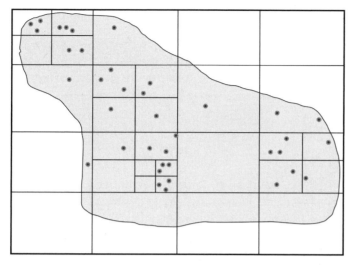

Figure 13-3 A spatial index partitions space and stores data according to its location

> **NOTE** The JTS Topology Suite uses Cartesian coordinates as opposed to latitude/longitude values. A Cartesian coordinate system describes locations on a flat surface, and latitude and longitude values describe locations along a collection of ellipses that represent the surface of the earth. A major impact of this difference is that on a Cartesian plane, the distance of one unit is the same everywhere, but the same is not true for latitude and longitude values. With latitude and longitude, the actual distance of a degree varies greatly depending on where the measurement is taken. For instance, at the north and south poles, all of the longitudinal lines converge. The distance between each degree line at those points is much less than it is near the equator. In spite of this issue, this example uses the JTS with latitude and longitude values for simplicity's sake. This, however, is not strictly correct.

Example: Spatial Queries

Consider the restaurant locations that were included in Table 13-1. If that information were encoded as RDF, how could it be ingested and indexed in such a way as to efficiently return the closest restaurants to a particular location?

Framing the Problem

Given a set of geospatial information in RDF, all of which are points, create a system that is capable of efficiently answering the query, "Return all of the points that are within a distance X of a given location."

Approach and Rationale

This program uses RDF data to answer spatial queries. The design of the software can therefore be broken into those two main groups: spatially oriented and RDF-oriented software components. The spatially oriented code makes use of the aforementioned quad tree implementation from the JTS, and the RDF-oriented software, like other examples in this book, uses the Jena API.

Components

The main classes used in this example are `JenaSpatialIndex` and `Spatial Graph`. `JenaSpatialIndex` wraps a JTS `Quadtree` object so that it can be easily used from Jena, serving as the bridge between the program and JTS. The `SpatialGraph` class implements Jena's `Graph` interface and is used to integrate the spatial indexing into the higher-level Jena constructs. The `Example` class serves as the main test harness program and simply uses a Jena `Model` backed by a `SpatialGraph` to read a data file and answer a query.

The `JenaSpatialIndex` class has two methods: `add(Node, Double, Double)` and `findWithin(double, double, double)`. The `add` method takes a `Node` representing an RDF resource and two double-valued numbers, representing the latitude and longitude, respectively, of the resource. As RDF statements are processed, the `JenaSpatialIndex` updates the latitude or longitude value for a given `Node` to collect a complete description of the location. Once an RDF resource has been fully defined with a latitude and longitude, it is added to the underlying spatial index. The `findWithin` method takes three parameters: a latitude, a longitude, and a search distance in meters. It creates a bounding box based on the search distance and uses the spatial index to return all `Nodes` within the bounding box.

The `SpatialGraph` class wraps an existing `Graph` object and uses the Delegation design pattern to avoid having to implement the entire interface. The two methods of significance in this class are `add(Triple)` and `getSpatialSubgraph(double, double, double)`. In the `SpatialGraph`, the add method inspects its parameter to determine if it is a statement that describes a latitude or longitude value. If it is, the `SpatialGraph` calls the `add` method on its `JenaSpatialIndex` object to register the value. The `getSpatialSubgraph` method is used to pose spatial queries of the model. Calling that method with latitude, longitude, and distance values returns another `Graph` object containing only statements about locations within the defined region (that is, the area within distance degrees of the latitude and longitude).

Now that you've seen how the program is structured, you'll be able to understand the code. Before tackling the code, however, you should see what some of the data looks like. The following example is a sample from a larger file that was generated from a restaurant chain's website using a screen-scraping program. The data can be found along with the source code at www.semwebprogramming.com.

```
@prefix dc: <http://purl.org/dc/elements/1.1/> .
@prefix ex: <http://semwebprogramming.net/example#> .
@prefix geo: <http://www.w3.org/2003/01/geo/wgs84_pos#> .

[]    a geo:Point ;
      dc:description "707 Southpark Blvd, Colonial Heights VA 23834" ;
      ex:hasPhoneNumber "(804) 526-4481" ;
      geo:lat "37.247886" ;
      geo:long "-77.388923" .

[]    a geo:Point ;
      dc:description "653 Center Point Way, Gaithersburg MD 20878" ;
      ex:hasPhoneNumber "(301) 926 9011" ;
      geo:lat "39.121925" ;
      geo:long "-77.234754" .

[]    a geo:Point ;
      dc:description "136 Lantana Dr, Hockessin DE 19707" ;
      ex:hasPhoneNumber "(302) 239-1270" ;
      geo:lat "39.776117" ;
      geo:long "-75.713017" .
```

The example that follows is an excerpt of the SpatialGraph class, showing all of the methods that are not simple delegations to the _innerGraph object:

```
package net.semwebprogramming.chapter13.spatial;

// Imports...

public class SpatialGraph implements Graph {
    private final Graph _innerGraph;

    private final JenaSpatialIndex _index;

    /**
     * Initializes a SpatialGraph.  This class will add a spatial
     * indexing capability to another graph.
     * @param graph a graph to which a spatial indexing capability
     * will be added
     */
    public SpatialGraph(Graph graph) {
        _innerGraph = graph;
        _index = new JenaSpatialIndex();
    }

    /**
     * Adds a triple to the graph, and adding any relevant portion to
```

```
     * to the spatial index.
     */
    public void add(Triple triple) throws AddDeniedException {
       _innerGraph.add(triple);

       String predicate = triple.getPredicate().getURI();

       if (WGS84.lat.equals(predicate) || WGS84.lon.equals(predicate)) {
          Node subjNode;
          Node objNode;
          Double value;

          subjNode = triple.getSubject();
          objNode = triple.getObject();

          if (WGS84.lat.equals(predicate)) {
             value = new Double(objNode.getLiteral().toString());
             _index.add(subjNode, value, null);
          } else if (WGS84.lon.equals(predicate)) {
             value = new Double(objNode.getLiteral().toString());
             _index.add(subjNode, null, value);
          }
       }
    }
    /**
     * Given a latitude, longitude and distance (measured in meters),
     * this method will return a Graph object containing only
     * statements where the subject is a point that falls within a
     * rectangular region centered on the latitude/longitude value.
     *
     * @param lat the latitude of the center of the search area
     * @param lon the longitude of the center of the search area
     * @param distance the maximum distance from the center point
     * for which values should be returned
     * @return a graph including only statements about locations
     * within the search region
     */
    public Graph getSpatialSubgraph(double lat, double lon,
                                    double distance) {
       Graph toReturn = new GraphMem();
       List<Node> validLocations;

       validLocations = _index.findWithin(lat, lon, distance);
       for (Node location : validLocations) {
          ExtendedIterator iterator =
                         _innerGraph.find(location, null, null);
          try {
             while (iterator.hasNext()) {
                toReturn.add((Triple) iterator.next());
             }
```

```
        } finally {
            if (null != iterator) {
                iterator.close();
            }
        }
    }

    return toReturn;
  }
  // Other methods to implement the Graph interface are delegated
  // to the _innerGraph object.
}
```

The constructor creates a `JenaSpatialIndex` object and then stores the value of the underlying graph to which the spatial indexing is applied. This `_innerGraph` object is the one to which the other methods of the `Graph` interface are delegated. They are not shown here in the interest of space, but the full code is available at `www.semwebprogramming.com`.

The first important method is `add`. The `add` method checks each statement to see if it is a latitude or longitude value describing a point. If it is either of these, then the method extracts either the latitude or longitude value and adds it to the `JenaSpatialIndex`. The `SpatialGraph`'s `add` method also delegates the call to the underlying graph's `add` method. This technique is useful—delegating the behavior to an underlying graph makes it possible to enhance a graph with only a small amount of code. It is a particularly advantageous approach in this case because it allows enhancements to be transparent to the rest of Jena.

The next method is `getSpatialSubgraph`. This method creates a new `Graph` implementation to return and then issues a spatial query to the `JenaSpatialIndex` based on the parameters passed as input to the method. The `JenaSpatialIndex` class returns a list of Jena `Node` objects that represent locations within the specified area. The `getSpatialSubgraph` method proceeds through the `Nodes`, retrieving all of the statements from the underlying graph where the `Node` is the subject of the statement. These statements are all added to the `Graph`, which is returned at the end of the method.

Now that you've seen how to integrate extra functionality into Jena with an enhanced `Graph` implementation, consider the spatial indexing itself by looking at the `JenaSpatialIndex` class in the following code:

```
package net.semwebprogramming.chapter13.spatial;

// Imports...
public class JenaSpatialIndex {
    class Location {

        private static final double AVG_MERIDONAL_RADIUS = 6367449;
        private static final double POLAR_RADIUS = 6356752.3142;
```

```java
    private Double _x = null;
    private Double _y = null;

    public double getX() {
        return _x.doubleValue();
    }
    public void setX(double d) {
        _x = new Double(d);
    }
    public boolean hasX() {
        return null != _x;
    }
    public double getY() {
        return _y.doubleValue();
    }
    public void setY(double d) {
        _y = new Double(d);
    }
    public boolean hasY() {
        return null != _y;
    }
}


/**
 * A collection of URIs to locations. This is used a
 * temporary staging ground so that complete locations
 * can be built up statement by statement.  I.e. because
 * the order of the statements is not known, it could be
 * that the statements saying:
 * _:x a Location ; hasX "10" ; hasY "25" .
 *
 * actually come in the opposite order. In that case, we
 * need to retain the information about the X value before
 * we can properly add it to the spatial index, which wants
 * only fully specified locations.
 */
private HashMap<Node, Location> _locations;

/**
 * A collection of the spatially indexed URIs.
 * The array index is the rectangle id used by the tree.
 * URIs are only spatially indexed if they have a valid X
 * and Y value.
 */
private final Set<Node> _indexedNodes;
private final SpatialIndex _index;
public JenaSpatialIndex() {
    _index = new Quadtree();
    _locations = new HashMap<Node, Location>();
    _indexedNodes = new HashSet<Node>(50);
}
```

```
public void add(Node node, Double x, Double y) {
   Location location;

   // Check to see if this is already spatially indexed. If
   // it is, we can ignore the add call, since it's already
   // been added.

   if (!_indexedNodes.contains(node)) {
      // if this is the first time we've seen this URI,
      // create a new entry for it in the map.
      if (!_locations.containsKey(node)) {
         location = new Location();
         _locations.put(node, location);
      } else {
         location = _locations.get(node);
      }
      // if we now know an x value, update the location
      if (null != x) {
         location.setX(x.doubleValue());
      }
      // if we now know a y value, update the location
      if (null != y) {
         location.setY(y.doubleValue());
      }
      // if the location is now fully specified, add it to the
      // spatial index
      if (location.hasX() && location.hasY()) {
         _indexedNodes.add(node);
         _index.insert(new Envelope(location.getX(), location.getX(),
               location.getY(), location.getY()), node);
      }
   }
}
private Envelope getSearchEnvelope(double lat, double lon,
                                    double distanceInMeters)
{
   Envelope toReturn = null;
   double metersPerDegreeLat, metersPerDegreeLon;
   double latOffsetInDegrees, lonOffsetInDegrees;

   metersPerDegreeLon = (Math.PI / 180) *
         Math.cos(Math.toRadians(lat)) * AVG_MERIDONAL_RADIUS;
   metersPerDegreeLat = (Math.PI * POLAR_RADIUS) / 180;
   lonOffsetInDegrees = distanceInMeters / (metersPerDegreeLon);
   latOffsetInDegrees = distanceInMeters / (metersPerDegreeLat);
   toReturn = new Envelope(
                  lon - lonOffsetInDegrees,
                  lon + lonOffsetInDegrees,
                  lat + latOffsetInDegrees,
                  lat - latOffsetInDegrees);
```

```
            return toReturn;
        }
    public List<Node> findWithin(Node uri,
            double maximumAllowedDistance) {
        List<Node> toReturn = new ArrayList<Node>(0);
        Location temp;
        if (_indexedNodes.contains(uri)) {
            temp = _locations.get(uri);
            toReturn = findWithin(temp.getX(), temp.getY(),
                maximumAllowedDistance);
        }
        return toReturn;
    }


    public List<Node> findWithin(double x, double y,
            double maximumAllowedDistance) {
        ArrayList<Node> toReturn = new ArrayList<Node>(0);
        Envelope searchEnvelope;
        final double offset = maximumAllowedDistance;
        List candidates = null;
        Node candidate;
        Location tempLocation;

        searchEnvelope = getSearchEnvelope(
                        latitude, longitude, maximumAllowedDistance);
        candidates = _index.query(searchEnvelope);
        for (Object o : candidates) {
            tempLocation = _locations.get(o);
            if (searchEnvelope.contains(
                    tempLocation.getX(),
                    tempLocation.getY())) {
                toReturn.add((Node) o);
            }
        }
        return toReturn;
    }
}
```

This class addresses the challenge that a statement expresses only a single datum, but the spatial index requires both latitude and longitude values before a point can be indexed. Since the existence of one statement is independent of all others, it is possible that there could be a set of statements with an incompletely defined point—only a latitude or a longitude. This means that the program must maintain a list of incompletely defined points, which is managed by the JenaSpatialIndex.

Looking at the preceding code, the first item to note is the inner class called Location. A Location object is used to represent the latitude and longitude values using objects so that they can be null. This way, it is possible to determine whether or not the point is complete.

The `JenaSpatialIndex` class itself maintains three collections of data. The first is a mapping, called `_locations`, of Jena `Node`s to `Location` objects. This allows the spatial index to answer spatial queries with useful results. The next is a set, called `_indexedNodes`, of `Node` objects that have been fully defined and added to the spatial index. The final data value is the spatial index itself, an object called `_index`.

The `add` method accepts three parameters: a `Node` and two `Double` objects, where the `Double`s can be null. The method simply creates a new `Location` for the `Node` if one does not already exist and then populates the `Location` with whichever value (latitude or longitude) is not `null`. If at the end of the method the `Location` object has both latitude and longitude values, then it is added to the spatial index and to the set of indexed nodes. This ensures that the spatial index is properly populated with valid `Location` objects.

The `findWithin` method is where the spatial index is used to retrieve values. Given a latitude, longitude, and distance, the method constructs a search bounding box. It uses the spatial index's `query` method to return a list of candidate matches. Recall that a spatial index can help to reduce the overall number of distance calculations required, but that it can sometimes return false positives. A final confirmation of all of the returned candidates is used to populate a list of `Node`s that is ultimately returned to the calling code.

This small set of classes can be used to extend Jena to efficiently answer queries about simple spatial data. The techniques, however, are not specifically limited to enhancing Jena for spatial data. In fact, a similar approach can be used to incorporate a temporal index, allowing for queries that are bounded in transaction time.

Example: Transaction Time–Bounded Queries

As discussed previously, transaction time–bounded queries can allow users to answer questions of the model as it changes over time. Consider the situation of a weather-tracking system. New readings are constantly arriving from a collection of different sensors around a geographic region. A meteorologist is testing a new predictive model and wants to issue a query against the system as it was at 8:30 last Friday evening. How can that query be answered correctly?

Framing the Problem

Given a Jena model to which new statements are being added over the course of a program's execution, create a system that can efficiently answer queries on data sets that are bounded by transaction time. A simplifying assumption of the model in this example is that it does not allow deletions. Therefore, the state of the model at any point in time is defined as the collection of statements added to the model before or at that point in time.

Approach and Rationale

In order to answer a query against the data as it existed at an arbitrary time, the software maintains a timestamp for each statement added to the model. Given a particular date and time, the system creates a derived model, including all of the statements added to the original model up until the designated time. There are two main classes: a `TemporalTripleIndex`, which manages a collection of statements and associates them with relevant timestamps, and a `TemporalGraph` class, which implements the `Graph` interface and incorporates a `TemporalTripleIndex`. The `TemporalGraph` class offers a method that will create a temporally bounded subgraph, which can be used as the basis of a new Jena model.

Components

In this example, the most important class is the `TemporalTripleIndex`. This class maintains a collection of statements and timestamps and provides an efficient means of collecting statements within a set of temporal bounds. There is only one complicated method in the `TemporalTripleIndex` class: `get Triples(Calendar, Calendar)`. Following is a section of the `TemporalTriple Index` class, showing the `getTriples` method as well as other ones:

```java
package net.semwebprogramming.chapter13.temporal;
// Imports...

public class TemporalTripleIndex {
    private class TemporalTriple implements Comparable<TemporalTriple> {
        private final Triple _triple;
        private final Calendar _time;
        public TemporalTriple(Triple trip, Calendar time) {
            _triple = trip;
            _time = time;
        }
        public Calendar getTime() {
            return _time;
        }
        public Triple getTriple() {
            return _triple;
        }
        public int compareTo(Object arg0) {
            int toReturn = _time.compareTo(arg0._time);
            return toReturn;        }
    }
    private final List<TemporalTriple> _triples;
    private boolean _sorted = true;
    public TemporalTripleIndex(int capacity) {
        _triples = new ArrayList<TemporalTriple>(capacity);
    }
```

```
    public void add(Triple triple) {
       _triples.add(new TemporalTriple(triple, Calendar.getInstance()));
    }
    public List<Triple> getTriples(Calendar lowerBound,
                                   Calendar upperBound) {
       int lower = 0;
       int upper = _triples.size() - 1;
       int returnSize = 0;
       boolean valid = true;
       List<Triple> toReturn;

       if (!_sorted) {
          Collections.sort(_triples);
       }

       if (null != lowerBound) {
          if (!_triples.get(_triples.size() - 1)
                 ._time.before(lowerBound)) {
             lower = findLower(search(0, upper, lowerBound));
          } else {
             valid = false;
          }
       }
       if (null != upperBound) {
          if (!_triples.get(0)._time.after(upperBound)) {
             upper = findUpper(search(0, upper, upperBound));
          } else {
             valid = false;
          }
       }
       if (valid) {
          if (upper > lower) {
             returnSize = upper - lower;
          }
          toReturn = new ArrayList<Triple>(returnSize);
          for (int i = lower; i < upper; i++) {
             toReturn.add(_triples.get(i)._triple);
          }
       } else {
          toReturn = new ArrayList<Triple>();
       }
       return toReturn;
    }
    // Other utility methods and convenience overloads are not shown
}
```

Before reviewing the getTriples method, inspect the rest of the class. The class starts with an inner class, TemporalTriple. A TemporalTriple ties together a Jena Triple and a Calendar date/time object. It implements the

Comparable<TemporalTriple> interface and sorts according to its Calendar object. The TemporalTripleIndex maintains a list of TemporalTriple objects, which it can use to answer temporally bounded queries. The add method creates a TemporalTriple to wrap the statement to be added, associating it with a new Calendar object. The new TemporalTriple is added to the class's collection, appending it to the end of the list.

The getTriples method takes an upper and lower temporal bound, defined by Calendar objects. Either bound, or both, can be left undefined. The algorithm is as follows:

1. If the list of TemporalTriples is not sorted, sort it by timestamp. The index supports adding statements from any time, not just the current time. If statements with a timestamp in the past have been added to the list of triples, the list will need to be sorted.

2. If the lower temporal bound is defined, check to make sure that it is not after the latest statement in the collection. If it is, no statements in the collection will be within the temporal bounds, so declare the operation invalid. If it is not, find the index of the first TemporalTriple with a timestamp that is either equal to or after the lower bound.

3. If the upper temporal bound is defined, check to make sure that it is not before the first statement in the collection. If it is, no statements in the collection will be within the temporal bounds, so declare the operation invalid. If it is not, find the index of the last TemporalTriple with a timestamp that is either equal to or before the upper bound.

4. Return a list consisting of every statement between the lower index and the upper index.

Now that you have seen a temporal index capable of maintaining basic transaction time information, consider the TemporalGraph class:

```
package net.semwebprogramming.chapter13.temporal;
// Imports...
public class TemporalGraph implements Graph {
    private final Graph _innerGraph;
    private final TemporalTripleIndex _index;
    public static TemporalGraph newInstance(){
        return new TemporalGraph(new GraphMem());
    }
    public TemporalGraph(Graph inner) {
        _innerGraph = inner;
        _index = new TemporalTripleIndex();
    }
    public Graph getTemporalSubgraph(Calendar start, Calendar end) {
        Graph toReturn = new GraphMem();
        List<Triple> triples = _index.getTriples(start, end);
```

```
        for(Triple t : triples)
        {
           toReturn.add(t);
        }
        return toReturn;
    }
    public void add(Triple t) throws AddDeniedException {
        _innerGraph.add(t);
        _index.add(t);
    }
    // Additional Graph methods delegated to the _innerGraph object.
}
```

This class is very similar to the SpatialGraph class from earlier because it supports the same usage model. The TemporalGraph class is also implemented using the same Delegation design pattern as the earlier SpatialGraph, delegating most calls to an inner graph. However, when Triples are added to the graph, they are additionally added to the temporal index. The TemporalGraph uses this index in its getTemporalSubgraph method, which issues a temporal query against the index and then populates a new Graph object. Jena's ModelFactory.createModelForGraph can use this newly created graph to construct a Model, which contains all the statements of the original model within the specified temporal bounds. That Model can then be used to answer queries as described in the problem statement.

Summary

This chapter presented an introduction to spatiotemporal development for the Semantic Web. You learned some of the basics of spatial and temporal systems and about some of the challenges associated with them. These challenges include not only abstract problems of information modeling but also practical concerns of program efficiency. You saw some approaches to overcome these challenges, with examples of RDF and OWL modeling for spatial and temporal data, and additional data structures. Finally, a walkthrough of example code helped to ground some of the discussion into something tangible. In the next chapter, you'll learn guidelines and tips for how to architect both large- and small-scale Semantic Web systems.

Notes

1. See C. S. Jensen, J. Clifford, S. K. Gadia, A. Segev, R. T. Snodgrass, "A glossary of temporal database concepts," *ACM SIGMOD Record*, Vol. 21, no. 3 (1992); http://portal.acm.org.

## CHAPTER 14

Semantic Web Patterns and Best Practices

"What's the point of wearing your favorite rocket ship underpants if nobody ever asks to see 'em?"

—Calvin (Calvin and Hobbes by Bill Watterson)

The quote may seem silly and off-topic, but the principles, architectures, and best practices by which a system are built often go unseen and unappreciated by those who use it. Developers tend to be the only ones who truly appreciate the importance of good design, reusable components, and standardized architectural patterns. So far, this book has covered the technologies and tools and protocols and standards and everything else that goes into programming with the Semantic Web. While a lot of time and attention is appropriately paid to the building blocks of systems and applications, most of the programming examples that have been presented are narrowly scoped and developed for demonstration purposes only. We included the FriendTracker reference application in this book to provide an example of integrating the technologies of the Semantic Web into a full-blown system, but it is only one such system. What is needed is a higher-level view of the major components and designs of real-world Semantic Web applications.

The purpose of this chapter is to provide a high-level perspective of Semantic Web programming by exploring a series of application architecture patterns. This chapter does not deal with software patterns per se; rather, it deals with common architectural idioms and system blueprints that are often used in Semantic Web applications. In a sense, this chapter represents a look back over the topics that we have covered so far. Only this time they are presented as they fit into larger, real-world applications. In addition to architecture patterns, this chapter explores a number of common issues encountered in Semantic Web applications and some suggested best-practice solutions to them.

The goals of this chapter are:

- To explore a series of Semantic Web application architectural patterns
- To provide a number of best-practice solutions to common challenges and issues encountered when programming on the Semantic Web

Aggregating Disparate Data Sources

The purpose of the first architecture is to aggregate data from multiple disparate data sources that have their own storage and representation format and knowledge model. The general flow of the architecture is from data source to the user via a multistep process that converts the data from each source into RDF and then translates it into a common ontology (often called a *domain ontology*). In this example, the data flows only from the data sources to the knowledgebase, but not back. This is essentially a read-only environment for aggregating data from disparate sources. More advanced architectures can incorporate the ability to write back changes to the data; however, such features introduce new challenges and considerations. Consider Figure 14-1, representing the high-level architecture of this system:

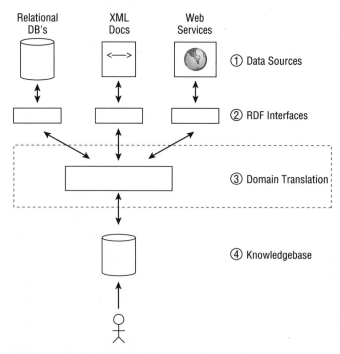

Figure 14-1 Architecture diagram representing a system that aggregates data from multiple disparate sources into RDF that is described by a single knowledge model

Figure 14-1 identifies by number each of the major components of the architecture. Following is a brief description of each component:

1. Data sources—Information starts in each of the data sources. In this example, the data sources are a relational database, a proprietary format flat file, and an XML file.

2. RDF interface—Each data source is exposed to the system using an RDF interface. This interface generates RDF from the data contained in the data source.

3. Domain translation—Each RDF interface generates ontologically described RDF. This component performs any ontology translation required to get the data into the user's or final application's knowledge model.

4. Knowledgebase—Once the data is in RDF and described according to the appropriate ontology, it is stored in a knowledgebase that is accessible to the user interface.

We'll discuss many subtle variations of this architecture throughout this section. In the following subsections, each of the components will be decomposed and discussed in depth. As you may have noticed, the FriendTracker application is based on this general architecture. In fact, the chapters that cover FriendTracker (Chapter 9, "Combining Information," and Chapter 10, "Aligning Information") cover the RDF interface and domain-translation components of this architecture. FriendTracker is just one specific instance of this architecture being applied to a particular set of requirements. Depending on the size and scale of the desired system, this architecture may exist entirely on a single system or within a single process, or it could span multiple servers and client machines.

Exposing Data Sources as RDF

Each data source in this architecture is exposed to the rest of the architecture via RDF interfaces. Each interface must meet a few fundamental requirements:

- It must accept a query or specification of the data to return.
- It must generate valid RDF that is described by one or more consistent ontologies.
- It must generate RDF that accurately reflects the data contained in the underlying source.

The specific requirements of the system dictate the sophistication of the interface. For example, a distributed query system that decomposes and routes SPARQL queries will require that each RDF interface is capable of satisfying SPARQL queries. A system in which provenance, or the ability to trace the source of a piece of information, is critical will require that each RDF interface expose RDF with resolvable URIs or metadata that allows a consumer to determine where the data came from.

There are a number of ways to expose an RDF interface as a service. SPARQL endpoints are services that accept SPARQL queries and return the result set according to the SPARQL protocol. An alternate is to provide the RDF interface as a SOAP or REST web service. These are not as ideal from a purist's perspective; however, it all depends on the requirements of the rest of the architecture. The issue with exposing an RDF interface using a nonstandard interface such as a customized web service is that it is nonstandard. Systems can't automatically ingest such an interface without some special-purpose adapter.

Many in the Semantic Web community anticipate that data source maintainers will ultimately expose and maintain RDF interfaces to their data sources. Many sites already expose XML web service–based APIs that allow web developers to access the data in their online applications. FriendTracker uses a number of these services by wrapping them in custom RDF interfaces.

The benefit to integrating data sources using RDF interfaces is that it decouples the data from the application. This makes it possible to swap existing data sources or integrate new ones without requiring substantial changes to the rest of the architecture.

Bringing Data into the Domain Knowledge Model

Once each data source is exposed as RDF and described by a source ontology, it must be brought into the domain's knowledge model. There are a number of ways to accomplish this task using ontology descriptions, SWRL rules, or SPARQL construct queries or by configuring the underlying RDF interface such that it produces RDF that is already described by the domain ontology.

The OWL Web Ontology Language provides a number of ways to relate the classes and properties of multiple ontologies. Two classes or two properties can be made equivalent using the `owl:equivalentClass` and `owl:equivalentProperty` predicates. In addition to the two equivalence predicates, any method of defining a class or property in terms of other classes and properties can be used to relate terms from disparate ontologies. The real goal of using ontology elements to map between ontologies is to establish adequate links between the two so that they essentially become a single ontology where all semantically related or equivalent terms are defined as such. Consider two ontologies with namespace prefixes `d1` and `d2`. The first domain contains the class `d1:canine`, and the second domain contains the class `d1:dog`. Asserting that `d1:canine owl:equivalentClass d2:dog` will make the two concepts semantically equivalent, any query for all instances of `d1:canine` against a knowledgebase that is performing OWL reasoning will return all instances of `d1:canine` and all instances of `d2:dog`. If the knowledgebase provides only RDFS reasoning, the same effect can be achieved by making each class `rdfs:subClassOf` the other.

The Semantic Web Rule Language (SWRL) is often used to translate data descriptions from one ontology to another. SWRL rules specify a conjunction of facts that, if met, imply some other set of facts. SWRL also includes an extensive library of built-in functions that provide mathematical operations, string manipulation, and logical operations over sets of variables. These can be used to generate new data based on existing data. This is something that cannot be done with OWL. OWL ontologies allow you to generate new metadata based on existing data, but ontology constructs are not quite as flexible as a rule language like SWRL. SWRL rules are useful for translation applications where structural changes must be made to data, such as converting units of measurement or formatting for literal values. As an example, consider one ontology in which all measurements are in metric units and another in which all units are English standard. There is no way to ontologically specify the conversion factor, but with relative ease a SWRL rule can make it happen. For more information on SWRL and its capabilities, refer to Chapter 7, "Adding Rules."

The SPARQL Query Language for RDF contains a query type called *construct*. A construct query allows a user to generate a new graph of RDF based on the results of a query. The benefit of this method is that no additional software is required. The only required component is a working SPARQL endpoint.

This is a simple operation of interpreting the data source ontology descriptions and generating the appropriate domain ontology descriptions. While SPARQL doesn't contain the same expressivity as SWRL in terms of generating and manipulating literal values, it does provide a much greater ability to specify the terms of the translation (in this case, the query itself, or in the case of SWRL, the body of the rule). SPARQL is covered in depth in Chapter 6, "Discovering Information."

Another way to bring data into the domain knowledge model is to simply configure the RDF interface to generate the data directly in the domain ontology. Chapter 9 introduces a number of ways of generating RDF that involve template files or translation files that essentially configure the translator to generate RDF in a specific format. If the translation file and system are expressive enough, it may be simplest to just modify the RDF interface to output the RDF described by the appropriate ontology. The drawback to this method is that it breaks the decoupling between the data source and the rest of the architecture. Multiple domains require multiple configurations.

Storing Information in the Knowledgebase

In most Semantic Web architectures the knowledgebase (KB) is a central component. The KB persists data, performs reasoning, provides APIs and query endpoints for data retrieval, and manages the state that drives the architecture. In aggregation architectures, the role of the KB is to store the results of the aggregation process and perform domain ontology reasoning.

Initiating the Flow of Data

Depending on the requirements of the application, the method by which the flow of data is initiated can vary. The user or controlling process may initiate each data source import directly at the data source. Since each source potentially has its own query method, this may require quite a bit of data source–specific configuration. Ideally, the data sources will be virtually integrated to the point that only a single query endpoint is needed, and queries can be issued against the domain ontology with no awareness of the underlying data source (unless this visibility is desired). In this kind of architecture, queries against the knowledgebase are decomposed and translated into a series of data source–specific queries against each of the RDF interfaces.

In this specific case, each interface is a SPARQL endpoint; however, different architectures may support RDF interfaces that take queries of any kind. Each endpoint processes the query against the underlying data source and returns the query results. These results are translated back into the domain ontology representation and aggregated into a complete result set that is persisted in the knowledgebase. This result set may be persisted permanently, or it may be treated as a transient query result that goes away once the query session is complete.

Annotating Unstructured Data

Tagging systems have become immensely popular during the Web 2.0 movement because they bring the user into the web experience. By giving users the ability to annotate pieces of data in ways that other users can benefit from, tagging became a way for users to enrich and expand web content. These systems take advantage of the fact that it is easy for a human to interpret images, videos, documents, and other forms of data, while it is very expensive and difficult for computers to do it with any kind of accuracy.

Tagging systems are immensely useful, but they have one significant drawback: tags have no intrinsic meaning. Figure 14-2 shows an example of an image that is tagged using simple keywords.

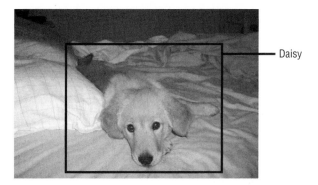

Figure 14-2 Tagging systems are used to help computers organize and index unstructured data by allowing users to describe the data using simple keywords.

These tags are merely words or phrases. They have no meaning beyond their potentially ambiguous language-based meaning. In Figure 14-2, *Daisy* could refer to a puppy or a flower. Unstructured text describing unstructured data sources may not be so great after all. A better solution is to allow users to tag data using semantic tags. These tags are defined in an organic ontology that grows and changes as users add to and extend it. Such a tag ontology is seeded with a basic set of common classes and properties. As users identify that required tags are missing, they simply add them and then expand the ontology to describe how the new concepts fit in. Such a system provides the basis for providing much better query capabilities as well as semantically valid and unambiguous description of data. A number of projects are emerging that take a similar approach to tagging data, and a lot of progress is being made on developing standardized annotation vocabularies and ontologies. Among these projects are Fuzzzy (`http://www.fuzzzy.com`) and Faviki (`http://www.faviki.com`). Fuzzzy (with three zs) is a collaborative tagging system for describing and sharing bookmarks. Faviki is a similar project that pulls its tag vocabulary from DBpedia.

The architecture in Figure 14-3 represents one approach to managing a semantic annotation system. The purpose of the system is to provide users with the ability to view unstructured data (maps, imagery, pictures, audio clips, videos, text documents, web pages, and so on) and make structured, ontology-based annotations that describe the data.

The general components of the architecture are numbered and introduced here. We'll describe each component in detail in the subsections that follow.

1. Annotation management—This component is responsible for providing the client application with a way to create and persist general-purpose annotations.

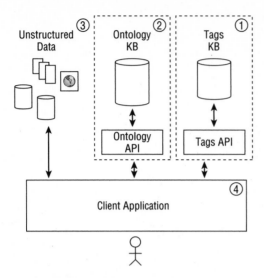

Figure 14-3 Semantic tagging architecture

2. Ontology management—This component provides the capability to build and extend ontologies that are used in annotations to describe the information that is being annotated.

3. Unstructured data sources—The system annotates data from unstructured sources.

4. Client application—The client application uses each of the other components to provide the user with an interface for creating and querying annotations.

Annotation Management

The annotation management component of the system can be broken down into two pieces: the persistence mechanism and the access API. In a distributed application, the persistence mechanism will likely be a knowledgebase server that provides a SPARQL query endpoint as well as an interface for modifying the knowledgebase contents. The access API is a client layer that provides the client application with a structured API for creating and retrieving annotations.

Annotations are RDF descriptions based on an annotation ontology. Annotation instances have both general and specific contextual information associated with them. General information includes spatial and temporal descriptions as well as the information necessary to index back into the unstructured source to which the annotation refers. Consider the example annotation in Figure 14-4.

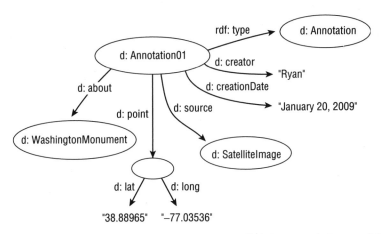

Figure 14-4 Example annotation of a satellite image of the Washington Monument in Washington, D.C.

As the example shows, there are elements of an annotation that are common to all annotations, such as the time stamp, the creator, the date of creation, and so on. There are also elements of the annotation that are specific to the media format and topic of the annotation data. The latter elements require that the system support a flexible set of ontologies so that users can express what they need to regardless of whether the concepts and relationships already exist in the ontology.

The annotation management component provides access to existing annotations. This is the component that allows the client application to query the full set of annotations for those that meet a set of parameters. In order to provide efficient querying for annotations, this component may incorporate specialized indices that provide quick access to annotations that have specific characteristics. Two examples are indices that provide quick access to all annotations within a specified spatial or temporal range. When searching a calendar-based system, a temporal index may be used to make it more efficient to retrieve annotations within a range of dates. Similarly, a spatial index may be used to retrieve all annotations for a spatial bounding box. Chapter 13 explored the topic of space and time on the Semantic Web in depth and presented examples of retrieval index implementations for each.

Ontology Management

In this architecture, ontology management plays two significant roles: to provide the client with the ontologies that can be used to build and query annotations and to provide the client with a system to incrementally build and extend those ontologies as needed. The ontology knowledgebase doesn't necessarily have to be separate from the annotations knowledgebase in implementation, but it is conceptually separate, and separation may simplify the implementation.

The first aspect of ontology management is to provide the client application with a set of concepts and relationships that can be used to generate annotations. This system provides the user with a set of terms that can be used to describe or tag each kind of unstructured data. This can also be the system that suggests to the client the types of annotations or metadata that may be relevant to a specific kind of unstructured data. In addition, each kind of unstructured data will have its own context for identifying the element of the data to which the annotation refers. Consider the following example contexts used by annotations to identify the *part* of the unstructured data to which they refer:

- Latitude and longitude coordinates identify a bounding box in satellite imagery.
- A time stamp identifies the offset or position within an audio stream.
- A character offset and length identify a word or phrase in a text file.
- A time range and a bounding box identify an object within a video stream.

The annotation structure of the ontology manages these data source–specific annotation classes and their relevant properties. It also manages the ontologies that can be used to associate general information with specific annotations. In other words, it manages the ontologies that specify the concepts and instances that the annotations are highlighting.

The second aspect of the ontology management is to provide the user with the ability to add new classes, properties, and instances to the ontology collection if needed. If a user is annotating an image of a Boeing 747, but the ontology doesn't contain one of the concepts needed to describe it, the system provides tools for adding the new concept and any properties that might be important to it. Once the new concepts are added, they are available to all users. By encouraging the reuse and sharing of concepts via a central knowledgebase, the system helps minimize ambiguity. In addition, when multiple similar concepts and properties do exist, users can identify how they are related so that the system can correctly process queries and users can see the available concepts and how they relate.

Unstructured Data Sources and the Client Application

There is no reason why an annotation system such as this cannot be used with a structured data source, but it is more common that it is applied to unstructured sources. Unstructured data sources can range from audio clips to radio stations, television feeds, web documents, text files, pictures, maps, satellite imagery, and the like. While the data varies, the concepts it represents are not singular to the source. Using a semantics-based approach to annotating data provides greater flexibility when incorporating new data sources and when distributing queries among the various sources of annotations.

While the data aggregation system was concerned with pulling together the actual data contained in each data source, this system is concerned only with pulling together annotations about each data source. As a result, there are no RDF interfaces exposing each data source. Instead, the application or an additional API must have a data source–specific access plug-in for retrieving and presenting data from each unstructured source. Given an annotation of a specific piece of satellite imagery, the client application must know how to go to the appropriate source, query for the piece of source imagery, render it to the user, and then overlay the appropriate annotation for user review. This kind of system still uses semantics and metadata to keep track of the required information, but it is interested only in the data at a meta level.

The client application must also provide search and retrieval capabilities so the user can build semantic queries for specific kinds of annotations or specific concepts associated with annotations, regardless of their source. Consider the example in Figure 14-5.

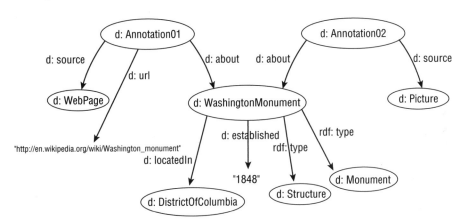

Figure 14-5 Example semantic annotations and the corresponding unstructured data

There are two annotations in this example: One is an annotation of a picture; another is of a Wikipedia article. Along with each piece of data is the corresponding annotation. Each annotation is about the Washington Monument and related concepts. A query for the Washington Monument will retrieve each of these annotations, which will be presented to the user in a single unified view. A user could also issue a query for all United States monuments, which would return these results and many more. Using the ontologically defined annotation terms, a much more intelligent, albeit more complex, system is possible.

Coordinating Semantic Services

Web services are nothing new. There are a ton of mature protocols, tools, and frameworks for managing web services throughout their full life cycle. Usually services are composed and integrated through an offline bootstrap process. In some cases, technologies are integrated that provide service advertisement and discovery. The goal of incorporating semantics into web service systems is to provide semantic descriptions of services and the data they provide. This enables more sophisticated methods of advertising and discovering services autonomously because even if a consumer can't interact directly with the service, he or she has the information necessary to see if there is another service or process that can act as an intermediary or a broker for the service, translating the service and data as necessary. Chapter 12 covered Semantic Web Services in depth and presented many of the tools and technologies critical to them. Figure 14-6 contains a pseudo-architecture illustrating how services can be composed to provide aggregate services.

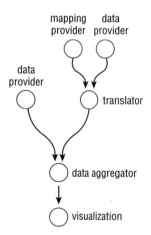

Figure 14-6 Services can be composed to perform complex actions or provide new services.

In this figure, there are nodes that play various roles: data provider, mapping provider, translator, aggregator, and visualization. This categorization is merely for illustration purposes, because any node in a system like this can play any role, and there are many more roles that we are not presenting in this discussion. The following list describes each of these node roles:

- Data provider—A data provider is any node that serves as a source of data. It can be an RDF interface to data sources, a knowledgebase, or any other source of information. These nodes don't necessarily have to be sources of RDF; they simply need to be sources of data.

- Mapping provider—A mapping provider is a node that provides information used to translate data. This can include SWRL rules, ontology axioms, or a custom configuration. Mapping providers feed translators, who act as intermediaries, translating data or service requests.

- Translator—A translator takes information from one representation or schema and converts it to another. Translators are both consumers and producers, because they consume data and mappings and produce the results of the translation.

- Aggregator—An aggregator combines data from multiple sources. In the case of RDF, it takes multiple documents and merges them into one (or the contents of multiple knowledgebases into one).

- Visualization—A visualization node takes data from any data provider and presents it to a user in visual form. Visualization is just one of many forms of user interface. Other nodes of this type could include any form of user interface, including visual, audio, and tactile.

This list of roles is incomplete. As we have already pointed out, there are essentially limitless roles that can exist in a service architecture. Notice that loosely coupled, component-based software systems can be mapped to a service architecture like this. Take, for example, the FriendTracker architecture. The RDF interfaces on each data source are data providers. The SWRL rules are mapping providers. The components that translate the data source ontology to the domain ontology are translators. The knowledgebase acts as an aggregator. Finally, the user interfaces are visualization components. The FriendTracker is like a service architecture that has a manual configuration.

The tools and technologies of the Semantic Web aim to make it easier to share information. One of the goals of Semantic Web Service architectures is to make it easier to automate configuration. When components are able to advertise and describe the operations they can perform and the data over which they operate, these components can be orchestrated automatically. Because this can occur automatically, systems can dynamically reconfigure themselves, enabling failure recovery and performance optimization. New roles can be implemented. Orchestrators can satisfy requests by pulling together multiple disparate services and resources. Directories can provide dynamic service lookup and ranking. This example architecture is fairly nonspecific because Semantic Web Services are far from fully developed. Because the hype surrounding service-oriented architectures (SOA) has subsided and many of their more extraordinary promises followed suit, semantic services have also lost some of their initial attention. It is unlikely that semantic services will tie your shoes for you and make your breakfast; however, on a small scale, these kinds of service architectures will be easier to implement using the technologies of the Semantic Web.

Applying Semantic Web Best Practices

In addition to architectural patterns for Semantic Web applications, there are a number of more targeted practices and philosophies. This section presents a series of topics that provide insight into potential problem areas of Semantic Web applications.

Creating URIs

URIs play a critical role in the Semantic Web. They make resources uniquely identifiable, provide the basis for the graph-like RDF data model, and enable distributed metadata creation. Creating URIs effectively and correctly is critical to Semantic Web programming.

URI management has been the subject of a lot of W3C work that has resulted in some useful documentation including Cool URIs Don't Change (`http://www.w3.org/Provider/Style/URI`) and Cool URIs for the Semantic Web (`http://www.w3.org/TR/cooluris`). These documents cover many of the important details that must be considered when generating RDF content for the Semantic Web, URIs and all. Among other things, they discuss the elements of a good URI, the difference between representation and description, and various approaches to making URIs resolvable.

This section presents a high-level overview of some of the most important aspects of generating URIs. You should review the documents just pointed out for a more in-depth exploration of the subject. Any application that is generating RDF or any developer who is creating an ontology will be responsible for generating URIs and should keep the following three best practices in mind when doing so.

- Make URIs unique.
- Make URIs consistent.
- Make URIs resolvable.

Making URIs Unique

URIs representing unique resources on the Semantic Web must be unique. It would be bad if a single URL addressed two separate web pages. In the same way, it would be bad if a single URI resolved to two distinct resources on the Semantic Web. Two resources sharing the same URI imply that the two are in fact the same resource. It is important to note that two unique URIs can each refer to the same unique concept. This is due to the no unique names assumption made by the semantics of OWL. URIs that aren't generated to be unique may collide when not intended to do so, which may have severe consequences. As an example, Figure 14-7 shows what happens when the two resources that go by the URI d:Thing1 are loaded into the same model.

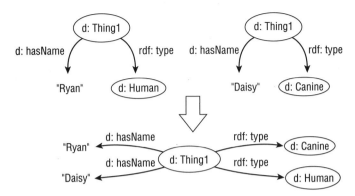

Figure 14-7 Two resources that are clearly unique are sharing the same URI. When they are loaded into the same model, they become the same resource.

The easiest way to manage generating unique URIs is to make sure to use a unique namespace URI as the basis of each ontology or for new URIs generated by an RDF interface or application that generates RDF. As long as the namespace URI is unique, any URI that uses that namespace will also be unique. A safe way to make sure a URI is unique is to base it on the web address at which the ontology or application is located. Since web URIs must be unique, it is safe to assume that no other resolvable ontology or application will be using that same URI. If no resolvable URI exists, then extra care must be taken to ensure uniqueness.

Many ontologies use a technique called *date spacing* when generating unique base URIs. The basis of the technique is to include the date on which the document was created or published in the base URI of the document. This convention can help decrease the probability of a URI collision when generating arbitrary URIs. Date spacing is illustrated here:

```
http://www.w3.org/1999/02/22-rdf-syntax-ns#type
```

The date is inserted after the host information and in the following order: YYYY/MM/DD.

Making URIs Consistent

In addition to making URIs unique, it is important to generate them in a consistent manner. Consider the process of exposing a document or database as RDF. The underlying data source contains a number of resources. What if the same process of exposing a set of data from the data source is performed twice in back-to-back fashion? Only a single set of unique URIs should be generated to represent those resources. The resources haven't changed. Why should the URIs?

This is an important feature of RDF interfaces. If URIs are not generated in a consistent manner, the same exposure process run twice will result in two different URIs. While still correct, this can be very inconvenient to consumers of the RDF data. They will have to determine that the two URIs actually refer to the same resource and deal with that information on their own. Consider the two representations of Mini in Figure 14-8.

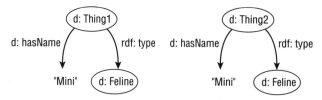

Figure 14-8 An RDF representation of the feline Mini is generated twice, but the URI that is generated is not consistent, resulting in two instances representing the same resource.

There are a number of useful strategies to generating consistent and unique URIs. When resources come from databases, the generated URIs usually consist of some permutation of the database URL, name, the table from which the resource was generated, and the column or columns that provide the primary key for the table. As long as the database is not regenerated or the schema changed, this type of method will always generate the same URI for the same record in a database. Regardless of where the data comes from, the idea is the same: URIs should be generated from characteristics of the data that uniquely identify the instance of the data while not changing during the regular life cycle of the data.

One interesting case to consider is creating URIs to represent statements involved in reification. In this case, the statement object itself is commonly modeled as an anonymous node without an explicit URI. Sometimes your implementation of reification may require that you assign the statement instance an explicit URI. In this case, it is useful to make the statement URI unique and consistent to simplify the generation of and retrieval of reification instances. One simple approach to solve each of these issues is to make the URI based on a hash of the concatenated subject, predicate, and object. As long as the hash doesn't produce a significant number of collisions, it will always generate the same unique URI for a given triple. This sort of technique can be used across systems as well because many hash algorithms are platform independent.

Making URIs Resolvable

The third best practice to consider when creating URIs is that URIs should be resolvable. In order for the vision of the Semantic Web to really come true, all this information and metadata and ontology descriptions need to be accessible to computers. If ontologies and resources aren't resolvable, it will be much harder for this to happen. The idea behind URI resolvability is that the namespace URI of an ontology or RDF document should resolve to that document. This way, a user or application can retrieve the RDF document that describes a resource by resolving it.

URI resolvability is a sticky subject because it is not always easy or practical to implement. On the one hand, it means that developers who create ontologies have to have somewhere to host the ontology where it will have a consistent and resolvable URL for its lifetime. On the other hand, consider how much less convenient ontology validation would be if ontologies weren't resolvable and tools couldn't just grab them off the Web using their URLs. Useful features like autocomplete and automatic syntax checking would be much more onerous to implement and use.

Specifying Units of Measurement

Everyone learned in science class that the units of a measurement are just as important as the value of the measurement itself. Knowing that the length of an object is five doesn't mean a whole lot by itself. It could be five inches, five meters, or five astronomical units. While in some situations, values have an implicit unit (for example, saying a person is 27 usually implies the unit years), these scenarios are difficult to codify and express in a way that computers can utilize.

OWL and RDF allow for the rich description of resources; the same is not true of literal values. The only description of literal values that is supported is the specification of datatype and in the case of strings, language. Arguably, this is a shortcoming of both RDF and OWL, as neither provides direct support. Support can be mimicked using some of the techniques that will be described in this section; however, each of the approaches described has its own benefits and drawbacks. The typical approaches to modeling literals with specific standard units of measurements include:

- Unit-specific properties
- Unit-specific datatypes
- Statement reification
- Value containers

With most of these approaches, there is a tension between expressivity and usability. Depending on the use case for the information, one approach may be better than the others. When a lot of computation is being performed, an efficient means of determining the unit of a literal may be very important. When literals are merely being displayed to humans without any interpretation, it may be adequate to express the unit as part of the literal value itself (5m to represent five meters). None of these methods is official or named in a specification. Thus, any application that uses one of these methods to maintain unit information will also have to interpret the units in order for them to have any bearing on the behavior of the application. The following subsections discuss each approach in brief.

Unit-Specific Properties and Datatypes

The idea behind using unit-specific properties and datatypes is to create a unique version of each that is made for a specific unit of measurement. A property representing *length* would become *length-feet*. A property representing *age* would become *age-years*. A datatype representing *floating point* values would become *float-feet*, or *integers* would become *int-years*.

Unit-specific properties have the negative impact that they create extra redundancy in ontologies. For example, an ontology that contains a property *height* will need a version of it for each unit of measurement used. This can get intractable quickly and can make it harder to reuse ontologies. Figure 14-9 illustrates the approach and the accompanying issues.

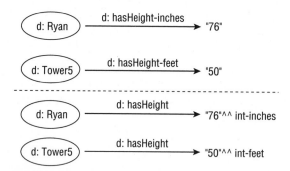

Figure 14-9 Unit-specific properties and datatypes create the need for extra versions of properties and datatypes and make it harder to work with the unit-specific concepts.

In addition, the conflation of property and unit implies that the two are connected when they are not. The unit of measurement is related to the literal value, not the property. On the other hand, unit-specific properties are very clear and don't add complexity to the data representation. Unit-specific datatypes have essentially the same benefits and drawbacks. However, not all frameworks support custom datatypes. As a result, they may introduce added complexity or incompatibility to an application.

Statement Reification

An alternate approach to annotating literals with the appropriate units is to annotate the reification resource of a statement with unit information that describes the value of the statement. The result is that a statement (subject, predicate, and object) is annotated with a unit of measurement. As Figure 14-10 shows, the statement *Ryan hasHeight 76* has a unit of measurement of *inches*.

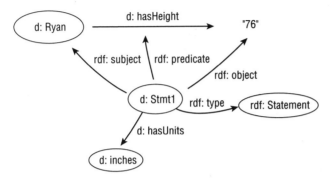

Figure 14-10 Unit of measurement information can be attached to the statement in which a value is used.

This approach is an improvement over unit-specific properties and datatypes in the sense that it eliminates potential redundancy in the data model; however, this is one of the only improvements to be had. Once again, the reification approach misplaces the unit information. Instead of just the literal or the literal and the property, now the units are associated with the entire statement. In addition, this method is complex and potentially expensive. Retrieving values and their units requires a much more complicated query than retrieving just the values, and creating new values now requires the generation and maintenance of reification information.

Value Containers

One of the most flexible, explicit, and correct approaches to associating units of measurement with literal values is the use of value containers. This approach replaces literal values with resources that represent the collection of a literal value and a unit of measurement. Figure 14-11 demonstrates the use of a value container to express that *Ryan hasHeight 72 inches.*

This is the first approach that has been presented that correctly associated the units with only the literal value. This method also represents units as resources themselves, meaning that the units could be richly described using an ontology, and reasoning could be performed and rules could be used to perform unit conversions. The drawback to this approach is that it is the most complex representation presented so far. Using this method to represent values essentially eliminates the practical use of datatype properties because all values will be stored in value containers that are associated with individuals using an object property. This also has the side effect of eliminating your ability to utilize OWL semantics with any of these kinds of properties. For example, data value restrictions and functional datatype properties will not work as expected because there is a level of indirection between instances and their attributes. In addition, this method is more complex and expensive to represent and to query, and like all the others it is nonstandard and may exacerbate interoperability issues.

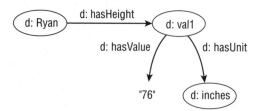

Figure 14-11 The value container associates the literal value *72* with the unit of measurement *inches*.

Representing N-ary Relationships

Relationships in RDF and OWL are binary. That is, a predicate can link only a single subject with a single object. Sometimes, relationships are *n-ary*; that is, an individual has multiple values for multiple properties whose pairing is significant. Consider a simple example of a building that has a geolocation. The geolocation is represented by a latitude value and a longitude value. The two values accurately convey the location of the building when they are interpreted as a pair. The best way to model this information is to introduce an intermediate object that acts as a container for the latitude and longitude values. Consider the following example RDF:

```
d:Person01 d:hasCoordinate d:coord1.
d:coord1   d:hasLatitude "38.88965";
           d:hasLongitude "-77.03536".
```

In this example, the person d:Person01 is associated with a coordinate that has a latitude and a longitude. Using restrictions, the ontology could even define a class that represents the coordinate based on the presence of the properties d:hasLatitude and d:hasLongitude. That would simplify queries for all coordinates.

Even though this point may seem straightforward, it is critically important. Since RDF is descriptive and any statement can be said about anything, there is nothing that says that `d:Person01` will not have another coordinate associated with it. Since people can move around, it is not uncommon that an individual may be associated with multiple sets of coordinates. Without using the intermediate object to group the latitude/longitude values, the values would get mixed up, as in the following example:

```
d:Person01    d:hasLatitude "38.88965";
              d:hasLatitude "39.88934";
              d:hasLongitude "-77.03536";
              d:hasLongitude "-10.00000";
```

In this example, it is unknown which latitude and longitude go together. This means that there are four possible pairings, two of which are completely inaccurate.

Managing Bad Data

This last section is not really a best practice. Rather, it's a warning. There is bad data out there: poorly formatted, invalid, and not adhering to its own schema. It is all out there, and inevitably it will have to be processed and used in Semantic Web applications. The question that must be answered when dealing with bad data is, when do you clean it? The answer may be to clean data when it is exposed from the data source via an RDF interface. It could be cleaned when any necessary translation is being performed on the data to bring it into the knowledge model of the application. It could be dealt with at the point when it is being displayed to the user.

When to fix bad data depends on the application and the developer and the client. There is no correct answer. Simply heed the warning, and be aware of the fact that it is out there and if not dealt with, it can wreak havoc on your Semantic Web applications, causing unexpected errors and unusual behavior.

Summary

This chapter is one of the capstones of this book. After everything that you've explored and learned about, this chapter provides a look back with an eye toward how everything fits together into a few sample architectures and in terms of some important best practices. Through this chapter you have seen where protocols and languages fit, how components go together and are arranged as part of a greater application, and how many of the different Semantic Web architectures are derived from the same set of building blocks. By using this chapter, you should be prepared to start high-level system designs that use these building blocks to meet your own requirements.

CHAPTER 15

Moving Forward

"When it comes to the future, there are three kinds of people: those who let it happen, those who make it happen, and those who wonder what happened."

—John M. Richardson, Jr.

This chapter exposes several representative advancements and extensions within the Semantic Web community. Clearly, the Semantic Web is active and growing in many directions—*a healthy sign*. In addition, the scale and scope of the Semantic Web itself and its supporting information base have opened up new challenges in harnessing the vastness of so much information from so many sources.

We explore these advancements not just by explanation but also, where possible, through working code examples and illustrations. You're encouraged to download and explore these approaches to gain hands-on confidence for future possibilities and direction. In many cases, these advancements strike at core challenges innate to large-scale, dynamic information exploitation—an area made possible only relatively recently by the vastness caused on one end by terabyte drives and on the other by the immensity of the Internet itself.

Virginia Tech has a nice slogan: "We invent the Future." In many ways this applies to the Semantic Web. The potential reach and expressive power of the Semantic Web offer entirely new opportunities to use and explore information. Traditional information applications are limited by both scope and expressivity. Traditional applications can neither tap into the enormity nor fully express its needs. This leaves systems struggling to put the pieces together or, more likely, remaining unaware of the larger possibilities. The two forces of scope and expressivity limit the vast potential to a small fraction of what is possible with traditional approaches. The challenge to

489

expose semantics to an application, à la machine readability, opens up this information to the power of Moore's Law and Metcalf's Law. Moore's Law predicts the growing power of computer resources. Metcalf's Law predicts the power of networks. Both of these laws can apply to the Semantic Web. The possibilities, and corresponding challenges, are just beginning to emerge.

Semantics form the next wave to improving our ability to manage and master the growing information base and its many relationships. The Semantic Web by no means addresses it all, but it is solidly on the right path.

We place these representative Semantic Web advancements into four categories:

- Advancing ontologies—The number and coverage of ontologies continue to grow. This creates the need for repositories to store them and registries to find them. In addition, new standards are emerging to link ontologies together. Finally, all these ontologies create a need to have versioning and metrics to determine quality and properly match an ontology with a given application.

- Advancing integration—Bringing two or more ontologies together creates new value through the combination of the information but also incurs some tough challenges because the ontologies may contain conflicts, duplication, and semantic differences. Here we'll look at distributed queries to bridge the integration and automatic alignment to aid in normalizing the semantics.

- Advancing reasoning—As machine readability improves with the increase in ontologies, reasoning capabilities can offer even more value. This creates several challenges for reasoning solutions. Reasoning must address the multitude of different rule engines and reasoners through standards. Reasoning must address the fuzziness of real life with probabilities and statistics. Reasoners must help establish trust among the many data sources, which is especially vital in large-scale integration. Finally, reasoners must improve their performance if they are to meet all these challenges effectively and handle the growing information base.

- Advancing visualization—Human readability is also important, and innovation continues to struggle with new ways to visualize the richness of the Semantic Web. Many of the interfaces are revealing information textures and views never before seen. It is uncertain whether these images are merely curious novelties or if they actually reveal deep secrets not yet understood. It is up to us to decide.

This chapter does not predict the future but rather hopes to ignite your interest and possible contributions to help the Semantic Web achieve its potential. The trends are clear—more data in more formats and in more locations. Semantics offer a path to make *more*, better.

Advancing Ontologies

The vastness and richness of available ontologies requires several advancements in order for you to fully take advantage of them. First you have to find them. For this you need methods to find and obtain the ontologies. Thus, ontology registries, repositories, and linked data offer a solution. Next you must verify that the ontology is compatible with your usage, hence the need for versioning. Finally, you need to determine the quality and appropriateness of your selected ontology, hence the need of absolute and relative metrics.

The growth in the number and types of ontologies produces a need to store them, find them, version them, measure them, and link them together.

Ontology Repositories and Registries

The number and types of ontologies continue to expand. This creates a significant challenge. How do you find a suitable ontology?

As you learned earlier, it is usually better to directly use or build on an existing ontology. Your application benefits from the existing work rather than starting from scratch. This is vital in both general, upper ontologies and specific domain ontologies. The upper ontologies struggle with definitions and relationships across a wide scope. The domain ontologies, dealing in depth within a given area, contain expertise possibly beyond your team. And, of course, if solutions reuse the same ontologies, integrating them later is much easier. These ontologies continue to advance, and your application can freely incorporate these advancements.

This challenge of finding suitable ontologies created several ongoing solutions for ontology repositories and registries. The repositories and registries vary based on two important factors: the searchable metadata they offer to find a suitable ontology, and whether they store or reference the ontology. Storing the ontology has the advantage of protecting it, possibly offering multiple versions. Referencing the ontology no longer requires storage at the repository site and provides linkage to the latest version of the ontology. This reference comes at the expense of losing control over the ontology. The linked ontology may be unavailable, be modified in an incompatible fashion, or simply be deleted. Correspondingly, the linked ontology may offer the most up-to-date version.

An ontology repository stores ontologies, whereas an ontology registry manages metadata and references the ontology rather than storing it. Typically an ontology repository contains a registry, but not the other way around. These guidelines are not rigidly followed by the various projects. You will find registries that also are repositories.

The OpenOntologyRepository (OOR) (`http://ontolog.cim3.net/cgi-bin/wiki.pl?OpenOntologyRepository_Scope`) aims to build a reference repository: a repository that allows the creation, sharing, searching, and management of ontologies as well as links to database and XML schema–structured data and documents. With similar goals to OOR, eXtended MetaData Registry (or XMDR, which is found at `http://www.xmdr.org/overview.html`) has similar aims. It employs the ISO/IEC metadata registry standards, which cover many knowledge representations including RDF and OWL. There is a demonstration of the registry at `http://bambam.lbl.gov:8080/xmdr/text.jsp`. You can search using several techniques, including a SPARQL query. Figure 15-1 illustrates XMDR search.

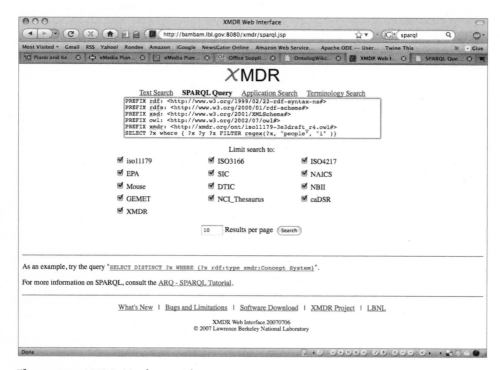

Figure 15-1 XMDR Ontology Registry

Linked Data

In addition to having repositories and registries, another approach to distributing the wealth of ontologies and related data is using best-practice methods to allow the creators to appropriately link them together. That is the goal of Linked Data, a project to create useful links to existing ontologies and data sources. The project was succinctly outlined by Tim

Berners-Lee (`http://www.w3.org/DesignIssues/LinkedData.html`). The links offer the pathways to follow an interesting direction intelligently. This type of exposure aims to enrich our Semantic Web navigation through practices that expose the data in a standard, accepted way. Linked Data outlines four key rules (taken directly from the preceding document):

1. Use URIs as names for things.
2. Use HTTP URIs so that people can look up those names.
3. When someone looks up a URI, provide useful information.
4. Include links to other URIs, so that they can discover more things.

Although vague, these basic guidelines have already forged large participation. This type of linking creates a browsable graph in a friendly, usable way. The Linked Data project uses the Tabulator to offer a friendly path through the linked data minus RDF vernacular and graphics. It makes extensive use of Gleaning Resource Descriptions from Dialects of Languages (GRDDL – see `http://www.w3.org/TR/grddl/`).

Instead of RDF graph images and URI-based statements, the Tabulator contains several views based on simple tables, maps, calendars, timelines, and any other friendly data exposure one can create. Figure 15-2 illustrates the FriendTracker ontology via the Tabulator.

Tabulator is a FireFox extension. The extension is activated when the browser receives an RDF file and displays it accordingly.

Versioning

As ontologies proliferate, versioning of ontologies becomes a challenge and a concern. The ease with which ontologies evolve, import other ontologies, and even possibly disappear makes versioning critical. The dynamics and growth of complex knowledge representations present a real challenge to maintain critical applications that depend on them. Several research efforts step up to this challenge.

As noted by Michel Klein in his ontology versioning talk (see `http://www.cs.vu.nl/~mcaklein/presentations/2001-07-31-SWWS-Stanford.pdf`), compatibility between versions falls into four categories:

- Fully compatible revisions—All combinations of instance data and ontologies provide correct operations.
- Backward compatible revisions—Newer schema versions can correctly use older instance data.
- Upward compatible revisions—New instances can use older ontologies.
- Incompatible revisions—The revision breaks all older versions.

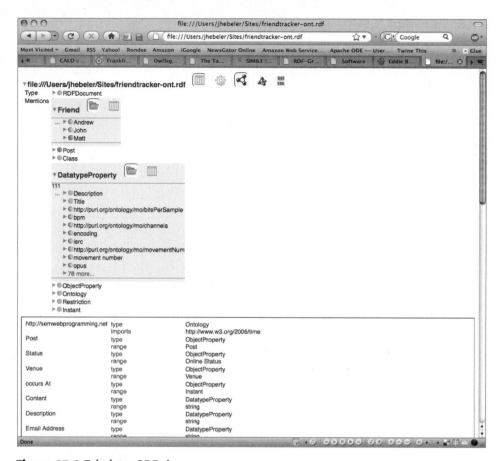

Figure 15-2 Tabulator RDF viewer

The OWL header provides the basic capture of critical versioning information with following constructs:

- `owl:versionInfo`—Basic information regarding the version.

- `owl:priorVersion`—Reference to another ontology noted as this ontology's predecessor.

- `owl:backwardCompatibleWith`—Similar to `priorVersion` but adds the notion that it maintains compatibility.

- `owl:incompatibleWith`—Specifically points out ontologies that this ontology is not compatible with. This is typically used when a new ontology is introduced that is not compatible with a previous ontology.

These fields provide the basic version information, but they rely on the implementation to carry out the necessary reaction. Tools will, no doubt, consume this information when the demand for using mixed versions increases.

Ontology Metrics

The "goodness" of an ontology is a controversial topic. The goodness measurement has two distinct types: absolute and relative. Absolute measurements can look for errors and conflicts—*does it follow the rules*. Relative measurements can determine an ontology's effectiveness for a given application—*does it do the job*. Both can help determine which ontology to select for your application.

Some efforts have stepped up to this large challenge. Although it has been around for a few years, OntoClean provides some absolute measurements, referring to them as *domain-independent properties*. These measurement properties are as follows.

- Identity—Enables the instance or individuals to remain unique despite possible changes. A substance that changes shape may retain unity because it is still the same substance. A person, john, remains the same, unique person despite growing up, getting married, moving to anther town, getting a different job, becoming a student, and the like. The ontology must respect this identity throughout all of its statements.

- Rigidity—A property is rigid if it is essential to *all* instances. Anti-rigid is the opposite. For example, "john is a person" would be rigid, whereas "john is a student" is not rigid. Thus, once an entity is declared a person, this cannot be changed, but declaring the person a student can.

- Unity—An individual represents a whole if and only if it is united by one or more properties that apply to all. The ontology must be clear in asserting unity. Either a set of parts is essential to the larger individual or it is not. For example, a marriage must contain two people. A married person cannot be by himself or herself in a marriage.

- Dependence—A property is dependent if each instance implies the existence of another instance. Therefore, the ontology cannot have one without the other. When a property or "part of" is essential to a containing class, the containing class is dependent on that property. For example, pizza must contain crust. It is dependent on crust for its very existence. Pizza is not dependent on tomato sauce, as a white pizza illustrates.

These dimensions help determine the quality of the ontology and identify inherent logical conflicts.

Protégé offers an implementation of OntoClean. Figure 15-3 displays the SIOC ontology.

OntoClean points out the discrepancies regarding the four traits listed previously. These refer to structural, absolute quality issues. OntoClean does not determine the usability of the ontology for a given application.

Matching an ontology to a given application offers a method as opposed to a tool. OntoMetric provides a relative measurement of an ontology's effectiveness for a given application. The OntoMetric methodology contains five steps (which are taken from "D1.2.3 Methods of Ontology Evaluation," Jens Hartmann et al, and found at `http://knowledgeweb.semanticweb.org/ semanticportal/deliverables/D1.2.3.pdf` :

1. Specify the objectives of the application.

2. Build a decision tree based on content, language, methodology, tool, and cost. This outlines the requirements.

3. Construct a pair-wise matrix within the decision tree.

4. For each ontology, assess its characteristics (currently the effort contains over 160 characteristics).

5. Combine vectors and weights to determine a solution.

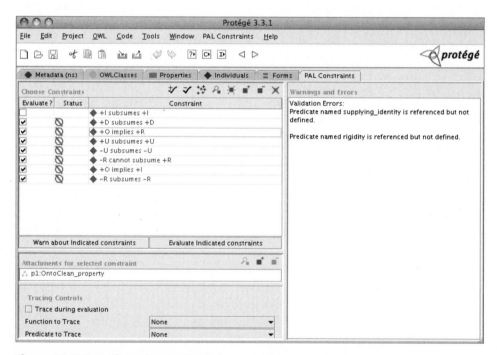

Figure 15-3 OntoClean view in Protégé

This method, although subjective and complex, can produce a useful answer.

Clearly much work needs to be done in evaluating and measuring ontologies. Formal methods provide value in forcing a hard look at the ontologies. Selecting an ontology is a fundamental factor in building a Semantic Web application. Time invested in studying the options for such a crucial component is time well spent.

Advancing Integration

Combining information from various ontologies and knowledgebases can greatly increase the value of the information. Fundamentally, the nature of the Semantic Web enables easy integration. These approaches help combine distributed ontologies and also align their semantics. Here we discuss several approaches to advance integration.

Semantic Pipes

Mash-ups are a favorite mechanism in Web 2.0 to integrate API-accessible applications and data sources. Yahoo Pipes took this a step further by providing a visual and programming metaphor—a pipe. Similar to Unix pipes, a pipe takes input, possibly transforms it, and then outputs it to another pipe. The chain continues until the set of pipes produces the desired end result.

Semantic pipes take this concept into the semantic realm. A group that's working on this concept is DERI Web Data Pipes (http://pipes.deri.org/). They have produced a working, open-source approach to richly combining, in real time, many available semantic sources.

Their site offers several examples and a working semantic pipe editor. Figure 15-4 illustrates a simple combination of two of our ontologies.

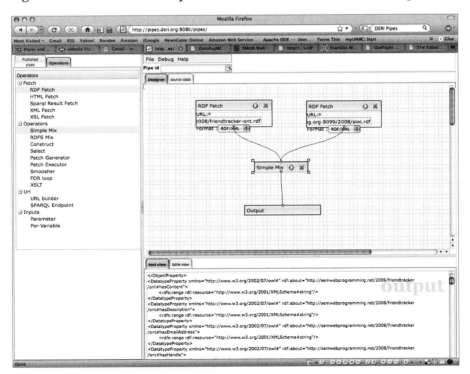

Figure 15-4 Simple semantic pipe

The left side of this screen lists the various assembly primitives. You simply drag them into the editor window. Reasoning can occur through direct reasoning processing or by using the graph generated from a CONSTRUCT query, as illustrated in Chapter 6, "Discovering Information." The DERI pipes can also use other types of data formats, including XML and RDFa.

Distributed Queries

Simply put, the Semantic Web is distributed. This gives an application two major choices in employing the vast amount of distributed Semantic Web data: copy to a single location or perform a distributed operation such as a query. The former is fraught with two major problems: latency and scale. Smaller applications may not suffer too much from these problems. Bigger applications may find them intractable.

Distributed queries address the distribution head-on. There are several methods to do this, and one of them you already have some familiarity with—D2RQ, seen in chapter 9.

The main factor regarding distributed queries is how involved or coupled you want your application to be with the multiple data sources. Highly coupled distributed queries are straightforward but form cumbersome and brittle solutions. Your application can individually query each data source using a CONSTRUCT query. The returned graphs aggregate in a local storage. After acquiring all the graphs, your application can ask a query of the aggregation. Of course, this requires your application to interact with each data source and detail its role in the aggregate model. This coupling inhibits change in both the queries and the data sources. Thus, if the data sources are out of your control (which is typical), the overall application will likely suffer from its brittleness.

D2RQ can extend the capability to relational databases. This allows you to query multiple databases. However, D2RQ still requires tight coupling between the databases and your application. The following code demonstrates how to create a D2RQ model from two databases:

```
MappingGenerator map1 = new MappingGenerator(jdbcURI1);
MappingGenerator map2 = new MapptingGenerator(jdcbcURI2);

// Set up FileOutputStream

map1.writeMapping(map1FS);
map2.writeMapping(map2FS);

relDB1 = new ModelD2RQ("map1.n3");
relDB1.add( new ModelD2RQ("map2.n3");
```

The example starts with generating the maps from each data source using the `MappingGenerator()` method. The mapping ontology has been written out. You can create the first model and then add the second to the first using the Jena method `add()`. Now a query aimed at `relDB1` could cross both data sources; the query must contain references to both. This is what creates the coupling.

In contrast, a loosely coupled distributed query creates a source and domain layer, as shown Figure 15-5.

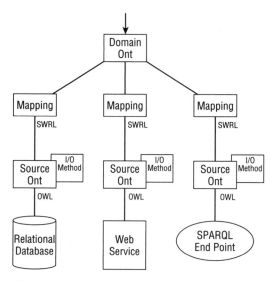

Figure 15-5 Loosely coupled distributed query

Each source has a source ontology that closely reflects the native source along with its access methods. The native source could be a web service, a relational database, SPARQL endpoint, or virtually any data source that could translate to an ontology. The source ontology not only has the data elements but also details the method necessary to get the data elements, such as a SQL call or web service call. On the user side, the distributed query starts with the domain ontology. The domain ontology remains the sole focus of the user. All questions and responses exist within this ontology. Now the answers all lie in the source ontologies. The missing piece maps the domain ontology to the various source ontologies. You can do this using SWRL rules or similar constructs. BBN maintains a working, deployed version of this approach called Asio (a species of OWL, see `http://asio.bbn.com`).

If you keep your data sources limited to SPARQL endpoints, DARQ (`http://darq.sourceforge.net`) provides a method to perform federated queries. DARQ extends the ARQ portion of Jena. The ARQ portion deals with query functionality. DARQ is still in an early release.

DARQ references a configuration file that describes each endpoint and its limitations, including available data, access pattern limitations, and statistical information useful for optimization. Once established, your application simply runs a query with Jena as before. The federation is transparent to the query, although there are limitations to the query, as noted at the DARQ website.

Alignment

As noted in the preceding ontology registry section, there is a growing list of ontologies, and we cited several examples. The various ontologies may capture general concepts or specific domains or combinations. Hopefully, a designed ontology serves its initial purpose well. But what if you want to combine information across multiple ontologies? In Chapter 10 we illustrated a situation in which the various ontologies were aligned for the FriendTracker application. It was a manual process using the various constructs of OWL and SWRL, such as `equivalentClass` to bind the two ontologies. Clearly, a manual approach limits the sharing of knowledge and services. It completely forestalls ad hoc, dynamic interrogation of multiple ontology-based sources and services.

Ontology alignment represents the constructs (such as adding an `equivalentClass` statement) required to bind two ontologies together. The alignment constructs can exist as their own ontology to be shared, improved, and reasoned over, independent from the ontologies aligned by the constructs.

Several efforts are under way to align ontologies *automatically*. In fact, there is a yearly competition to create useful alignment algorithms, sponsored by the Ontology Alignment Evaluation Initiative (OAEI is found at `http://oaei.ontologymatching.org/`).

Automatic alignment presents several problems if it is to work on a large scale, which, of course, is the only useful goal. The first issue is the need to express alignment in a standard way—a standard expression of alignment. The second is to create a programming framework to standardize the logistics of alignment. And third, the framework must offer a Plug and Play environment to hold various alignment algorithms. This environment not only allows experimentation but also allows the alignment methods to tune and sequence various algorithms depending on their specific alignment goals and the types of ontologies.

This is exactly what the Alignment API (which you can find at `http://alignapi.gforge.inria.fr/`) offers, which is sponsored by OAEI. The Alignment API offers a standard way to express alignment, standardizes the logistics of alignment, and offers a Plug and Play environment for various alignment algorithms.

Now let's examine a coding example that aligns the two ontologies. The OAEI website provides some excellent sample ontologies for the test. You can apply them to ontologies that we have used in previous examples in this book.

The API follows several steps to create an alignment:

1. Create two URI objects, one to reference each ontology.

2. Create the desired alignment process(es) associated with an alignment algorithm.

3. Bind each alignment process to the URI objects.

4. Compute the alignment.

5. Threshold the alignment results.

6. Output the alignment.

7. Optionally compare alignment results using different algorithms.

Here is a straightforward example of the alignment API:

```
public class BasicAlign {
    static String ont1 =
"http://semwebprogramming.org:8099/ontologies/friendtracker.rdf";
    static String ont2 = "http://semwebprogramming.org:8099/ontologies/
    sioc.rdf";

    static String ontDir = "/var/www/html/ontologies/";


    public static void main(String[] args) {
      System.out.println("Starting Alignment");
      try {
        URI uri1 = new URI(ont1);
        URI uri2 = new URI(ont2);

        Parameters parm = new BasicParameters();

        AlignmentProcess apSubsDistName =
                new SubsDistNameAlignment();
        apSubsDistName.init( uri1, uri2 );
        apSubsDistName.align((Alignment)null,parm);
        apSubsDistName.cut("prop", .6);

        // Set up PrintWriter(s)
        File fileHTML = new File(OntDir +
                "SubsDistNameAlignFT.html");
```

```
PrintWriter pwHTML = new PrintWriter(fileHTML);
File fileSWRL = new File(OntDir +
        "SubsDistNameAlignSWRLFT.xml");
PrintWriter pwSWRL = new PrintWriter(fileSWRL);
File fileOWL = new File(OntDir +
        "SubsDistNameAlignFT.owl");
PrintWriter pwOWL = new PrintWriter(fileOWL);

AlignmentVisitor avHTML =
        new HTMLRendererVisitor(pwHTML);
AlignmentVisitor avSWRL =
        new SWRLRendererVisitor( pwSWRL );
AlignmentVisitor avOWL =
        new OWLAxiomsRendererVisitor(pwOWL);

apSubsDistName.render(avHTML);
apSubsDistName.render(avSWRL);
apSubsDistName.render(avOWL);

// Flush and close the files
pwHTML.flush(); pwHTML.close();
pwSWRL.flush(); pwSWRL.close();
pwOWL.flush();  pwOWL.close();
} catch (Exception e) { e.printStackTrace(); }
System.out.println("Alignment Complete");
}
```

The example starts with creating two URIs, one for each of the ontologies. Here we use the `friendtracker.rdf` ontology and Semantically-Interlinked Online Communities (SIOC) ontology. We then declare an alignment process and use the SubsDistName algorithm. This computes a substring distance based on the class name. The `cut()` method filters out the lower-scored matches from the algorithm. Although it's used here for illustrative purposes, the algorithm still produces some useful results. The final step creates an AlignmentVisitor to enable output in the desired format of the alignment results.

We now examine three types of output:

- HTML format for human consumption
- SWRL rules
- OWL constructs

The latter two provide statements to bind the two ontologies together in a sharable, reusable format. The alignment process, illustrated in Figure 15-6, found five useful bindings between the two ontologies. Your application could choose to assert these statements to align the identified classes.

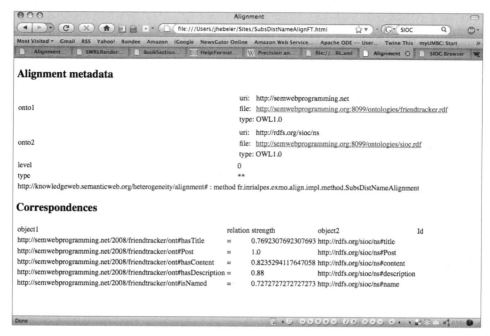

Figure 15-6 Alignment results via HTML

These bindings were all above our filter threshold of .6. Each match contains a relation strength ranging from .76 to 1 (a perfect match). Let's examine the results in more machine-usable formats, OWL and then SWRL. First, the OWL statements:

```
<owl:DatatypeProperty rdf:about="http://semwebprogramming.net/2008/
   friendtracker/ont#hasTitle">
  <owl:equivalentProperty rdf:resource="http://rdfs.org/sioc/
  ns#title"/>
</owl:DatatypeProperty>
<owl:Class rdf:about="http://semwebprogramming.net/2008/friendtracker/
  ont#Post">
  <owl:equivalentClass rdf:resource="http://rdfs.org/sioc/ns#Post"/>
</owl:Class>
<owl:DatatypeProperty rdf:about=
  "http://semwebprogramming.net/2008/friendtracker/ont#hasContent">
  <owl:equivalentProperty rdf:resource="http://rdfs.org/sioc/
  ns#content"/>
</owl:DatatypeProperty>
<owl:DatatypeProperty rdf:about=
  "http://semwebprogramming.net/2008/friendtracker/ont#hasDescription">
  <owl:equivalentProperty rdf:resource="http://rdfs.org/sioc/
```

```
            ns#description"/>
    </owl:DatatypeProperty>
      <owl:DatatypeProperty rdf:about=
        "http://semwebprogramming.net/2008/friendtracker/ont#isNamed">
        <owl:equivalentProperty rdf:resource="http://rdfs.org/sioc/ns#name"/>
      </owl:DatatypeProperty>
```

Here the alignment process used equivalence to map the classes and properties. Next are the corresponding SWRL rules:

```
    <ruleml:imp>
      <ruleml:_body>
        <swrl:datavaluedPropertyAtom swrlx:property=
         "http://semwebprogramming.net/2008/friendtracker/ont#hasContent"/>
          <ruleml:var>x</ruleml:var>
          <ruleml:var>y</ruleml:var>
        <swrl:datavaluedPropertyAtom>
      </ruleml:_body>
      <ruleml:_head>
        <swrl:datavaluedPropertyAtom swrlx:property="http://rdfs.org/sioc/
          ns#content"/>
          <ruleml:var>x</ruleml:var>
          <ruleml:var>y</ruleml:var>
        </swrl:datavaluedPropertyAtom>
      </ruleml:_head>
    </ruleml:imp>

    <ruleml:imp>
      <ruleml:_body>
        <swrl:datavaluedPropertyAtom swrlx:property=
        "http://semwebprogramming.net/2008/friendtracker/
          ont#hasDescription"/>
          <ruleml:var>x</ruleml:var>
          <ruleml:var>y</ruleml:var>
        <swrl:datavaluedPropertyAtom>
      </ruleml:_body>
      <ruleml:_head>
        <swrl:datavaluedPropertyAtom swrlx:property=
          "http://rdfs.org/sioc/ns#description"/>
          <ruleml:var>x</ruleml:var>
          <ruleml:var>y</ruleml:var>
        </swrl:datavaluedPropertyAtom>
      </ruleml:_head>
    </ruleml:imp>

    <ruleml:imp>
      <ruleml:_body>
        <swrl:datavaluedPropertyAtom swrlx:property=
```

```
        "http://semwebprogramming.net/2008/friendtracker/ont#isNamed"/>
        <ruleml:var>x</ruleml:var>
        <ruleml:var>y</ruleml:var>
      <swrl:datavaluedPropertyAtom>
    </ruleml:_body>
    <ruleml:_head>
      <swrl:datavaluedPropertyAtom swrlx:property=
        "http://rdfs.org/sioc/ns#name"/>
        <ruleml:var>x</ruleml:var>
        <ruleml:var>y</ruleml:var>
      </swrl:datavaluedPropertyAtom>
    </ruleml:_head>
  </ruleml:imp>
```

The SWRL rules declare the analogous equivalence compared with the OWL constructs. The SWRL rules are one-directional, but the OWL statements are bidirectional.

These formal alignment results can be shared, interrogated, or enriched in future efforts. This creates a need to store and find these alignments.

The Alignment API project has also produced a server to address the storage and retrieval of alignment artifacts. The server offers several interfaces: HTML, JADE/FIPA ACL, and HTTP/SOAP. The services include finding a similar ontology, aligning two ontologies, thresholding alignment results, storing the alignment, finding an alignment, and retrieving an alignment.

The API works with other types of tools such as WordNet (`http://wordnet.princeton.edu/`). WordNet is a large lexical database of English, essentially forming an excellent source of synonyms useful in alignment activities. You can take our basic example and change the `AlignmentProcess` to one that uses WordNet.

```
AlignmentProcess ap = new JWNLAlignment();
```

Finally, you can obtain statistics that compare various alignment techniques with each other. For this you use the `PRecEvaluator` class. The code is shown here:

```
PRecEvaluator eval =
        new PRecEvaluator(ap1, ap3);
eval.eval(p);
System.out.println(
    "Precision = " + eval.getPrecision() +
    " Recall = " + eval.getRecall() +
    " F = " + eval.getFmeasure() );
```

This approach illustrates the similarities between two alignment methods, with the first parameter passed to the `PRecEvaluator()` method being the basis for comparison. Once evaluated, methods return precision, recall, and F statistics. Precision demonstrates how many values in the second argument match with the first. Recall indicates how many values should have matched. The two together summarize into the F statistic. These values determine convergence or dissimilarity between multiple approaches. Also, keep in mind that you can use algorithms sequentially to improve results.

Advancing Reasoning

Reasoning amplifies information through logical deductions. Simply put, reasoning increases the information value. This section surveys three expanding areas: rule format standards, probabilistic reasoning, and trust reasoning.

Rule Interchange Format (RIF)

As you saw in our examples, several rule languages enable reasoning. We examined only a few and, given the adoption trends and fundamental differences, it is unlikely that one will become the standard. For many, the best rule language is simply the one that they know. This presents you with a dilemma—which one to pick?

RIF softens the blow of picking a rule language. Rather than fight it out and try to pick a winner, RIF approaches it in a different way by coming up with a standard interchange between rule languages. This way you could map rules from one language to another, analogous to a rule translator. W3C chartered a group in late 2005 to address this challenge.

The following is taken from the W3C mission charter (which you can find at `http://www.w3.org/2005/rules/wg/charter.html`):

> *The Working Group is to specify a format for rules, so they can be used across diverse systems. This format (or language) will function as an interlingua into which established and new rule languages can be mapped, allowing rules written for one application to be published, shared, and re-used in other applications and other rule engines.*

> *Because of the great variety in rule languages and rule engine technologies, this common format will take the form of a core language to be used along with a set of standard and non-standard extensions. The Working Group is chartered to first establish the extensible core and possibly a set of extensions, and then (in Phase 2) to begin to specify additional extensions based on user requirements. These extensions need not all be combinable into a single unified language.*

This mission is part of W3C's larger goal of enabling the sharing of information in forms suited to machine processing, as seen in several application areas presented at the 2005 W3C Workshop on Rule Languages for Interoperability:

■ *Rules themselves represent a valuable form of information for which there is not yet a standard interchange format, although significant progress has been made within the RuleML Initiative and elsewhere. Rules provide a powerful business logic representation, as business rules, in many modern information systems.*

■ *Rules are often the technology of choice for creating maintainable adapters between information systems.*

■ *As part of the Semantic Web architecture, rules can extend or complement the OWL Web Ontology Language to more thoroughly cover a broader set of applications, with knowledge being encoded in OWL or rules or both.*

W3C has made significant progress, which you can track at their wiki site: `http://www.w3.org/2005/rules/wiki/RIF_Working_Group`. Here you can find the use case and requirements documents, the core language, and other seminal documents dealing with translations to various rule implementations. The effort allows extensions, which eliminates merely producing a lowest-common denominator solution. This effort should at least allay some of your concerns in using a specific rule language.

Probabilistic Reasoning

A key reality of our world is the uncertainty that surrounds it. Few items are clearly black or white but rather maintain a degree of grayness. Probabilities quantify this grayness. Reasoning across probabilities for independent and dependent events presents valuable results. For example, you could calculate the simple probability of a specific flight arriving on time given its history. But how is this probability impacted by weather, other flights, the type of aircraft, and so on? This requires the aggregation of various probabilities, and that leads to the usefulness of probabilistic reasoning.

The native characteristics of OWL allow the insertion of probabilities in a relation, as with any attribute. Currently, no standard way exists to express it. Therefore, your application would have to do all the interpretations and calculations—a large task. Anyone who has taken a statistics course knows that the statistics surrounding data are not straightforward. Thankfully, several solutions have emerged to deal with this important part of expressivity—the uncertainty associated with a relationship. These approaches addresses three key areas: how to express probability, how to infer probabilities, and how to explain the inference. We'll examine three such solutions:

- Pronto, an extension of the Pellet reasoner
- PR-OWL, a Bayesian extension to OWL
- Fuzzy ontologies

Pronto, a partner to the Pellet reasoner discussed previously, is still in an early release but already has made significant progress in all three areas. Pronto offers the latest download along with documentation and examples at `http://pellet.owldl.com/pronto`. Pronto extends the Pellet reasoner that we used earlier in three ways:

- Adding probability statements to an OWL ontology
- Inferring new statements based on the probability
- Explaining the results

Pronto provides a useful example on breast cancer probabilities. First let's look at the ontology capture of probability expressions.

```
<!-- Any woman has a 12.3% risk of lifetime breast cancer -->
<owl:Axiom>
    <rdf:subject rdf:resource="#Woman"/>
    <rdf:predicate rdf:resource="&rdfs;subClassOf"/>
    <rdf:object rdf:resource="#WomanUnderLifetimeBRCRisk"/>
    <pronto:certainty>0;0.123</pronto:certainty>
</owl11:Axiom>
<!-- If a woman has BRCA mutation,
     then the risk is between 30% and 85% -->
<owl:Axiom>
    <rdf:subject rdf:resource="#WomanWithBRCAMutation"/>
    <rdf:predicate rdf:resource="&rdfs;subClassOf"/>
    <rdf:object rdf:resource="#WomanUnderLifetimeBRCRisk"/>
    <pronto:certainty>0.3;0.85</pronto:certainty>
</owl:Axiom>
<!--
    Relationships between risk factors  (from statistics)
-->
<owl:Axiom>
    <rdf:subject rdf:resource="#AshkenaziJewishWoman"/>
    <rdf:predicate rdf:resource="&rdfs;subClassOf"/>
    <rdf:object rdf:resource="#WomanWithBRCAMutation"/>
    <pronto:certainty>0.025;0.025</pronto:certainty>
</owl:Axiom>
```

The code demonstrates the expression of probabilities. The first case has a probability range for a woman of 0 to 12.3%. The second case has a range between 30% and 85% for a subclass of Woman—WomanWithBRCAMutation. The third case demonstrates the capture of relationship between risk factors.

Pronto supports five types of reasoning:

- Entailments between classes
- Entailments between individuals
- Satisfiability
- Consistency
- Improbability classes

Running Pronto to generate entailments between the two classes of AshkenaziJewishwoman and WomanUnderLifetimeBRCRisk results in the following output:

```
Query : entail
Result: http://clarkparsia.com/pronto/cancer_ra.owl#
   Helen:http://clarkparsia.com/pronto/cancer_ra.owl#
   WomanUnderModeratelyIncreasedBRCRisk[0.65;0.65]
Explanation:
Explaining the generic constraint 33:
   (WomanUnderModeratelyIncreasedBRCRisk|_TOP_)[0.65;0.65]:
Lower bound is because of:
[[15: (WomanTakingProgestin|_TOP_)[1.0;1.0], 16:
(WomanTakingEstrogen|_TOP_)[1.0;1.0], 0:
(WomanUnderModeratelyIncreasedBRCRisk|PostmenopausalWomanTaking-
   EstrogenAnd
Progestin)[0.65;0.65]]]
Upper bound is because of:
[[15: (WomanTakingProgestin|_TOP_)[1.0;1.0], 16:
(WomanTakingEstrogen|_TOP_)[1.0;1.0], 3:
(WomanUnderWeakelyIncreasedBRCRisk|
PostmenopausalWomanTakingEstrogenAndProgestin)[0.35;0.35]], [15:
(WomanTakingProgestin|_TOP_)[1.0;1.0], 16:
(WomanTakingEstrogen|_TOP_)[1.0;1.0], 0:
   (WomanUnderModeratelyIncreasedBRCRisk|
PostmenopausalWomanTakingEstrogenAndProgestin)[0.65;0.65]]]
```

The output provides the answer to the query plus its justification.

PR-OWL takes a different approach by introducing a Bayesian extension to OWL. It is an open research project at http://www.pr-owl.org. PR-OWL extends OWL to provide a framework for authoring probabilistic ontologies. It is based on the Bayesian first-order logic called Multi-Entity Bayesian Networks (MEBN). Bayesian inference uses continuously collected evidence to update the probability. The openness of OWL allows the consideration of incoming statements in forming a probability.

The PR-OWL effort offers an interesting example of a StarTrek ontology based on PR-OWL. The ontology deals with using probability to detect enemy ships (as opposed to James T. Kirk's or Jean-Luc Picard's intuition). Figure 15-7 offers a small view of the ontology that is reflected in Protégé.

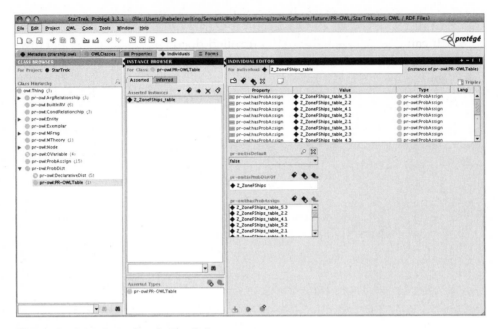

Figure 15-7 PR-OWL view in Protégé

PR-OWL addresses the first challenge—how to capture probabilities in OWL—and requires a reasoner to apply it.

Fuzzy ontologies take a slightly different approach by managing ill-structured, uncertain, or imprecise information that is contained in the knowledgebase ("A Fuzzy Ontology-Approach to Improve Semantic Information Retrieval" by Siliva Calegari and Elie Sanchez can be found at http://c4i.gmu.edu/URSW/2007/files/papers/URSW2007_P3_CalegariSanchez.pdf). Fuzzy ontologies relate information statistically with a semantic correlation. These correlations generate weights that associate various entities within the knowledgebase. This can more closely reflect real-world situations where the user expresses a "sort of" relationship.

Trust: Proof Markup Language

Trust is the cornerstone of any relationship. How much you trust a friend, a co-worker, or a spouse determines the value of the relationship. This is, of course, also true with data. The trust you put into the data determines the usefulness of that data to aid an objective, such as a critical decision.

Traditionally, systems created trust through careful protection of the data source. Databases were carefully protected in locked rooms and by observant administrators, who ensured high integrity and controlled access. This approach can extend somewhat to controlled documents and the like. However, modern distribution combined with many formats and a varying level of control erodes the traditions. These methods simply don't scale. Yet your applications still want to leverage all that information. This causes a new problem—how do you establish trust with dynamic, distributed sources combined with the deftness of the various reasoners?

This is exactly the area that Proof Markup Language (PML) sheds some light on—*trust*. It offers an approach to explain how results were obtained and what the results depended on. Collectively this is known as *transparency*. PML enables the representation of explanations and computations of trust issues, including aggregation of trust.

PML exists as three distinct ontologies to decompose trust:

- PML-P (pmlp prefix)—Providence ontology ties instances to its providence attributes, such as creation data, authors, owners, and the like.

- PML-J (pmlj prefix)—Justification ontology offers the encoding justifications for conclusions. This includes standard logic processing, inference steps, assumptions, extractions methods, and the like.

- PML-T (pmlt prefix)—Trust relation ontology explains belief assertions associated with instance information. PML-T complements the other two ontologies by providing explicit representations of trust assertions. This allows sharing of a trust conclusion.

PML-P provides the raw information or format to establish trust. PML-J provides a standard way to express a justification. PML-T ties the two together to establish a credible path to a given assertion for sharing. Your application still needs to interpret this information.

The PML Primer provides a useful example (see `http://inference-web.org/2007/primer/`). Following are some examples.

The scenario starts with a simple question: What type of food is Tony's specialty?

The following code contains PML-P:

```
<pmlp:Language rdf:about=
   "http://inference-web.org/registry/LG/KIF.owl#KIF">
    <pmlp:hasName rdf:datatype=
```

```
      "http://www.w3.org/2001/XMLSchema#string">
      Knowledge Interchange Format (KIF)</hasName>
      <pmlp:hasDescription>
        <pmlp:Information>
          <pmlp:hasURL rdf:datatype=
           "http://www.w3.org/2001/XMLSchema#anyURI">
            http://logic.stanford.edu/kif/kif.html</hasURL>
        <pmlp:/Information>
      <pmlp:/hasDescription>
      <pmlp:hasAuthorList>
        <pmlp:AgentList>
          <ds:first rdf:resource=
       "http://inference-web.org/registry/PER/MGENESERETH.owl
      #MGENESERETH"/>
          <ds:rest>
            <pmlp:AgentList>
              <ds:first rdf:resource=
               "http://inference-web.org/registry/PER/RFIKES.owl#RFIKES"/>
            <pmlp:/AgentList>
          </ds:rest>
        <pmlp:/AgentList>
      <pmlp:/hasAuthorList>
    </pmlp:Language>
```

PML-P provides ownership and other attributes useful to establish trust. Various conclusions help in answering the query. These steps are revealed via PML-J. An example of such follows, concluding that `TonysSpeciality` `SHELLFISH` has been directly assumed by the inference engine:

```
<pmlj:NodeSet rdf:about=
"http://inference-web.org/2007/primer/examples/proofs/tonys/
   assumption.owl
    #assumption">
    <pmlj:hasConclusion>
      <pmlp:Information>
        <pmlp:hasRawString rdf:datatype=
         "http://www.w3.org/2001/XMLSchema#string">
         (type TonysSpecialty SHELLFISH)</pmlp:hasRawString>
        <pmlp:hasLanguage rdf:resource=
         "http://inference-web.org/registry/LG/KIF.owl#KIF"/>
        </pmlp:Information>
    </pmlj:hasConclusion>
    <pmlj:isConsequentOf>
      <pmlj:InferenceStep>
        <pmlj:hasInferenceEngine rdf:resource=
          "http://inference-web.org/registry/IE/JTP.owl#JTP" />
        <pmlj:hasInferenceRule rdf:resource=
```

```
        "http://inference-web.org/registry/DPR/Assumption.owl#Assumption" />
            </pmlj:InferenceStep>
        </pmlj:isConsequentOf>
    </pmlj:NodeSet>
        This leads to sharing the trust in conclusions.
        The following code is the small example from preceding example.
<pmlt:FloatBelief rdf:about="#belief1">
    <pmlt:hasBelievingAgent rdf:resource= "#X" />
    <pmlt:hasBelievedInformation rdf:resource= "#info" />
    <pmlt:hasFloatValue>0.84</pmlt:hasFloatValue >
</pmlt:FloatBelief>
```

Trust is a critical factor in using the Semantic Web to address critical issues. Would you want answers for the Semantic Web directing your medical treatment or guiding financial decisions? Until trust is well established, many critical applications will rely on traditional, small-scale approaches and thus lose the advantages of a larger information base.

LarKC: The Large Knowledge Collider

No doubt you have seen by now that reasoning is powerful but also computationally expensive. This last dilemma limits the scope of reasoning to something less than the extremely large and dynamic data sources. Reasoning remains trapped in smaller, controlled data sources.

LarKC attacks this very challenge—large-scale, dynamic reasoning. A use case of the LarKC team requires reasoning across 10 billion triples in less than 100ms. ("Towards LarKC: A Platform for Web-Scale Reasoning" by D. Fensel et al; see http://www.larkc.eu/wp-content/uploads/2008/05 /larkc-icsc08.pdf). This wasn't just shown to generate large numbers but is based on realistic environments such as mobile phone reasoning needs.

The logical architecture consists of pluggable components that retrieve, abstract, select, reason, and decide. The basic algorithm that is detailed in the paper follows:

```
Loop
    Obtain a selection of data (RETRIEVAL)
    Transform to an appropriate representation (ABSTRACTION)
    Draw a Sample (SELECTION)
    Reason on the sample (REASONING)
    if more time is available
        And/or the result is not good enough (DECIDING) then
        Increase the sample size (RETRIEVAL)
```

```
    else
        exit
    end if
end loop
```

This provides a framework to reason across the entire Semantic Web and thus makes all the information even more valuable. LarKC not only makes large-scale reasoning doable but also lowers the bar on small-scale reasoning situations that compute in a much smaller window for faster decisions and lower costs.

Additional efforts are also taking on the reasoning scalability challenge. Part of these efforts include the IBM Scalable Highly Expressive Reasoner (better known as SHER, which you can find at `http://domino.research.ibm.com/comm/research_projects.nsf/pages/iaa.index.html`). SHER indexes the statements based on reasoning requirements. According to the website, SHER can reason across seven million triples in seconds.

Finally, the new additions to OWL 2, specifically the OWL 2 profiles, promote scalability by organizing its reasoning capabilities in better ways.

Advancing Visualization

Our exploration of the Semantic Web covered both machine and human interactions. Reasoning deals directly with machine readability. Visualization deals with human readability or human reasoning. The human ability to recognize subtle patterns in huge data sets is clear. Edward Tufte points out this capability throughout his series of excellent books on the visual displays of information. One graphic outlined in his book *The Visual Display of Quantitative Information*, barely an inch by an inch, effectively communicates over 25,000 data points. There is a lot of potential in visualizing portions of the Semantic Web.

The Semantic Web, with its many relationships, naturally forms into a rich graph. However, many attempts to provide a useful graph quickly become buried in the sheer number of relationships, many of which are irrelevant to a particular goal. Visualizing a large graph is challenging on several fronts, but real progress continues. We'll examine several solutions. They do not necessarily answer the question as to how to view the data but rather raise questions that have as yet been unanswered.

RDF-Gravity provides a visual tool with filters for RDF and OWL. It provides text search and queries. Figure 15-8 shows a graph of the FriendTracker ontology.

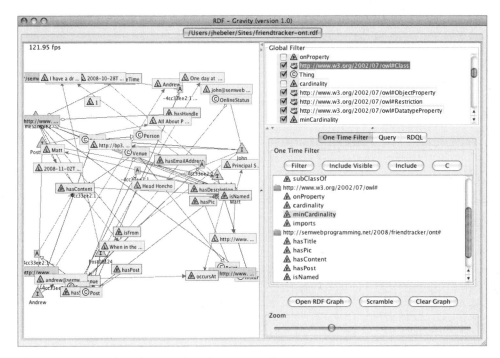

Figure 15-8 FriendTracker ontology in RDF-Gravity

The right side of the screen allows the removal of various ontology artifacts. Playing with this quickly illustrates the complexity even in a small ontology like FriendTracker.

Aduna Cluster Maps serve up hierarchical data in interesting ways. Figure 15-9 illustrates a cluster map.

In order to take advantage of the Aduna tool, your application must covert to Aduna's XML taxonomy. They supply an implementation API to assist in the conversion. Once your application is in their format, the tool allows several ways to filter and focus the data. The challenge here is converting a Semantic Web subset into a useful taxonomy. Some of the views are truly exciting, but that is not always the same as useful.

On the other hand, Semantic Interoperability of Metadata and Information in unLike Environments (SIMILE: `http://simile.mit.edu`) offers several tools, including Welkin and Longwell.

Welkin supplies a true macro view of an ontology and instance data. It focuses on the overall shape and clustering. It illustrates the interconnectivity and focus areas of the connections. Figure 15-10 shows the FriendTracker ontology and the SIOC ontology.

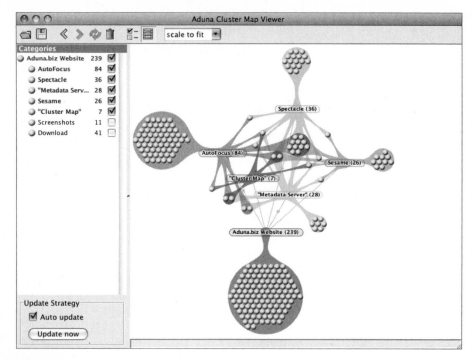

Figure 15-9 Cluster map

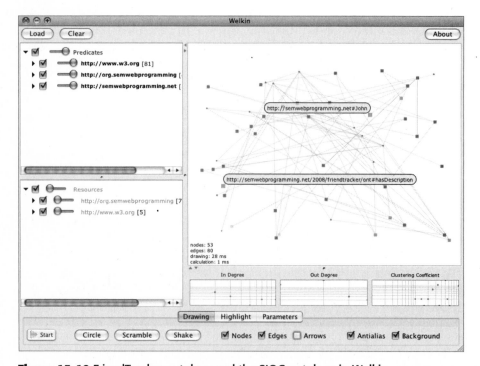

Figure 15-10 FriendTracker ontology and the SIOC ontology in Welkin

The bottom viewing area contains some interesting and overlooked perspectives on the data. In Degree provides the number of edges that point to the node. Out Degree provides the number of edges that start from the node. Clustering Coefficient indicates how many node associates are friends with one another, in other words, how tight the clustering is. This macro view can provide some interesting and curious views into the overall data.

Longwell provides a more micro view into RDF data. It is a faceted browser that allows emphasis based on more than one dimension. Figure 15-11 shows an example ontology from the Longwell site.

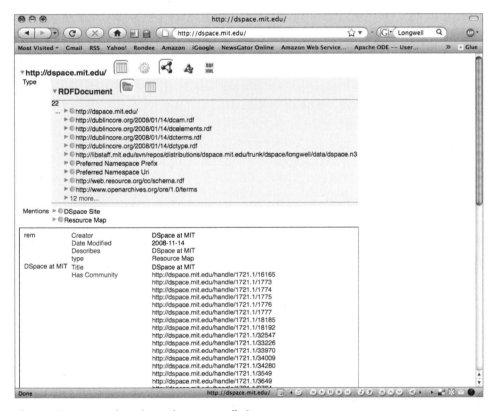

Figure 15-11 Ontology from the Longwell site

Visualization tackles a tough problem—how to make visual sense out of all the data and its relationships. No doubt this area will continue to expand as you experiment with the many visual methods to present and navigate the data. Although the tools we discussed are powerful representations, none tackle the tougher challenges of expressions beyond RDF into OWL.

Summary

Clearly the Semantic Web is active, flourishing, and evolving. This chapter briefly introduced some of the major development activities. Many of the advancements are a result of the new territory that has been established by the Semantic Web because of its scale, distributed nature, trust, and so on:

- Advancing ontologies illustrate the many techniques to manage the growing richness and volume of ontologies and their associated data. These include the registration and retrieval of the ontologies, linking standards between the ontologies, versioning ontologies, and ontology metrics.

- Advancing integration illustrates methods to fully leverage knowledgebases distributed across the Internet. These included semantic pipes to glue semantic sources together and distributed queries to gather the data from multiple sources without the need to copy all that data in one place or face the associated latency. Alignment aids in binding multiple ontologies and result sets into a unified knowledgebase.

- Advancing reasoning includes the standard effort to corral the many rule and reasoning languages. Probabilistic reasoning inserts the vagueness of the real world into ontologies. Trust tackles the need to have some assurance that the collected knowledge from various sources is credible and reliable. The knowledge collider addresses the need for improved performance on large reasoning efforts.

- Advancing visualization examines the success and challenges ahead to allow users and their advanced pattern recognition and curiosity skills to fully explore the richness of the Semantic Web. Clearly the richness of the Semantic Web and the innate human capabilities of pattern recognition offer much promise in revealing information value.

Of course, all of these noted advancements are just a, representative sample of the many Semantic Web development activities. Many more are out there, and hopefully, with the aid of this book, you will be making your own advancements.

This appendix describes the Resource Description Framework (RDF), an important technology for information representation that underlies many of the concepts and tools that are described in the book. This appendix is intended to serve as a concise refresher for the main RDF concepts and as a reference for the syntax and general usage for the most commonly used constructions in the book. RDF and the broader Semantic Web knowledge model are described in much more depth in Chapter 3, "Modeling Information."

Basic RDF takes a generalized graph-based approach to representing information so that it can be easily shared and mixed together. Like the notion of a graph itself, RDF is not a language per se but is an abstract information model that can be serialized in multiple ways. RDF represents information as a graph of related *statements*. A statement is made up of three elements, a *subject*, a *predicate*, and an *object*. In the graph, a statement represents a directed edge between two nodes, with the predicate (also referred to as a *property*) representing the edge, and the subject and object representing nodes. RDF defines two basic types of nodes: *literals* and *resources*. A literal is a concrete value, such as a string or a number, and literals cannot be the subjects of statements, only the objects. Resources represent, generally speaking, anything that can be assigned an International Resource Identifier (IRI). Examples of resources include people, things, locations, and concepts.

A special exception to this conceptualization of a resource is the special type of resource called a *blank node*. Blank nodes are existential variables used to express ideas that are not about particular resources. An example of an idea with an existential variable is "every book is written by a person." In this case, the "person" term in the sentence does not refer to any actual single person but rather is used to express the idea that for every book, there is an author who is a person. It would not preserve the meaning of the sentence to give that person a name, and so when representing these types of statements in RDF, we use a blank node.

RDF statements can be serialized in many different ways. Some of the most popular formats today are RDF/XML, the Terse RDF Triple Language (Turtle), and N-Triples. RDF/XML is an XML serialization, and it is the only normative format for RDF exchange. Turtle is compact and human friendly and is the preferred format used in this book. N-Triples is a line-based format that is easy to generate and easy to parse when streaming serialization is necessary, so it is often used in real-world Semantic Web software systems.

The RDF vocabulary is defined within the namespace `http://www.w3.org/1999/02/22-rdf-syntax-ns#`. For each RDF term, we present a description as well as a snippet of how it is serialized in RDF/XML and Turtle. For the examples in this appendix, the following declarations apply:

RDF/XML:

```
<rdf:RDF
xmlns:rdf="http://www.w3.org/1999/02/22-rdf-syntax-ns#"
xmlns:ex="http://example.org/ont#"
xml:base="http://example.org/base#">
```

Turtle:

```
@prefix rdf: <http://www.w3.org/1999/02/22-rdf-syntax-ns#> .
@prefix ex: <http://example.org/ont#> .
@prefix : <http://example.org/base#> .
```

Reification

Reification describes the process of making assertions about statements. The statement is represented by a resource of type `rdf:Statement`. The `rdf:subject`, `rdf:predicate`, and `rdf:object` predicates are used to identify the statement. For example:

"Witness Wally claims that Perpetrator Pete robbed the bank."

```
<rdf:Description rdf:about="#WitnessWally">
  <ex:claims>
```

```
    <rdf:Statement>
        <rdf:subject rdf:resource="#PerpetratorPete" />
        <rdf:predicate rdf:resource="http://example.org/ont#robbed" />
        <rdf:object rdf:resource="http://example.org/ont#bank" />
    </rdf:Statement>
  </ex:claims>
</rdf:Description>

:WitnessWally ex:claims [ a rdf:Statement ;
                         rdf:subject :PerpetratorPete ;
                         rdf:predicate ex:robbed ;
                         rdf:object ex:bank
             ] .
```

Containers

RDF containers and collections can be used to describe sets of resources. The basic types of containers are rdf:Bag, rdf:Seq, and rdf:Alt, and the basic type of RDF collection is rdf:List. The distinction between containers and collections is with *openness*. RDF containers are said to be *open* because there is no way to restrict the addition of extra resources to the sets they describe. The rdf:List construct, in contrast, is considered to be *closed*. Once defined, it is not possible to increase the set membership of an rdf:List.

The different types of containers have different meanings. The rdf:Bag, for example, groups resources together in an unordered fashion, while the rdf:Seq and rdf:List define ordered sequences of resources. The rdf:Alt is used to define a set of resources that can be considered equivalent for a particular circumstance. Consider the following sentence:

"The meal was cooked by two groups of individuals: James and Susan, and Brenda and William."

This sentence describes two sets of resources, but the order of the elements within those sets is not important. This is an excellent candidate for an rdf:Bag:

```
<ex:Meal>
 <ex:cookedBy>
    <rdf:Bag>
       <rdf:li rdf:resource="#James" />
       <rdf:li rdf:resource="#Susan" />
    </rdf:Bag>
 </ex:cookedBy>
 <ex:cookedBy>
    <rdf:Bag>
       <rdf:li rdf:resource="#Brenda" />
       <rdf:li rdf:resource="#William" />
    </rdf:Bag>
```

```
        </ex:cookedBy>
    </ex:Meal>

[ a ex:Meal ;
  ex:cookedBy [ a rdf:Bag ;
                rdf:_1 :James ;
                rdf:_2 :Susan
              ] ,
              [ a rdf:Bag ;
                rdf:_1 :Brenda ;
                rdf:_2 :William
              ]
] .
```

The following sentence describes a set of alternate, equivalent resources:

"To download the software, use either `dl1.example.com` *or* `dl2.example`
`.com.`*"*

This is represented with an `rdf:Alt`:

```
<ex:Software>
  <ex:available>
    <rdf:Alt>
      <rdf:li rdf:resource="http://dl1.example.com" />
      <rdf:li rdf:resource="http://dl2.example.com" />
    </rdf:Alt>
  </ex:available>
</ex:Software>

[ a ex:Software ;
  ex:available [ a rdf:Alt ;
                 rdf:_1 <http://dl1.example.com> ;
                 rdf:_2 <http://dl2.example.com>
               ]
] .
```

The following sentence can be represented with an `rdf:Seq`:

"This morning I woke up, brushed my teeth, and then had breakfast."

Significantly, we presume that other things happened during the day. While this sentence describes only up through breakfast, nothing can restrict extra assertions about things that happened that morning:

```
<ex:Person>
  <ex:activity>
    <rdf:Seq>
      <rdf:li rdf:resource="#WakeupActivity" />
      <rdf:li rdf:resource="#BrushTeethActivity" />
```

```
        <rdf:li rdf:resource="#EatBreakfastActivity" />
      </rdf:Seq>
    </ex:activity>
</ex:Person>


[ a ex:Person ;
  ex:activity [ a rdf:Seq ;
                rdf:_1 :WakeupActivity ;
                rdf:_2 :BrushTeethActivity ;
                rdf:_3 :EatBreakfastActivity
              ]
] .
```

When a collection of resources should be closed, use an `rdf:List`:

"The United States presidents from the Democratic-Republican party were Thomas Jefferson, James Madison, James Monroe, and John Quincy Adams."

Note how much more concise the Turtle representation is as compared to the RDF/XML serialization:

```
<ex:DemocraticRepublicanParty>
<ex:elected>
  <rdf:List>
    <rdf:first rdf:resource="#ThomasJefferson" />
    <rdf:rest>
      <rdf:List>
        <rdf:first rdf:resource="#JamesMadison" />
        <rdf:rest>
          <rdf:List>
            <rdf:first rdf:resource="#JamesMonroe" />
            <rdf:rest>
              <rdf:List>
                <rdf:first rdf:resource="#JohnQuincyAdams" />
                <rdf:rest>
                  <rdf:nil />
                </rdf:rest>
              </rdf:List>
            </rdf:rest>
          </rdf:List>
        </rdf:rest>
      </rdf:List>
    </rdf:rest>
  </rdf:List>
</ex:elected>
</ex:DemocraticRepublicanParty>


[ a ex:DemocraticRepublicanParty ;
  ex:elected (:John :Matt :Ryan :Andrew)
] .
```

The OWL Web Ontology Language

This appendix describes the OWL Web Ontology Language, the language used to build ontologies that describe information on the Semantic Web. OWL and its associated semantics are covered in depth in Chapter 4, "Incorporating Semantics." Appendix A, "RDF," presents the Resource Description Framework, its terse vocabulary of terms, and numerous illustrative examples. Because Chapter 4 already contains a lot of examples, this appendix focuses instead on providing a reference for the OWL vocabulary. The appendix is divided into major sections, each dealing with a different aspect of OWL. Each section contains a list of the OWL vocabulary terms and descriptions relevant to the topic of the section.

OWL extends RDF and RDF Schema (RDFS) to provide a vocabulary of properties and classes that have associated semantics. These classes and properties are used to build expressive ontologies that are in turn used to describe resources. Table B-1 contains the namespaces used by the OWL specification.

OWL requires adherence to two important assumptions:

Open world assumption—The open world assumption states that the truth of a statement is independent of whether it is known. In other words, not knowing that a statement is explicitly true does not imply that the statement is false.

No unique names assumption—The no unique names assumption states that unless explicitly stated otherwise, you cannot assume that resources that are identified by different URIs are different.

Table B-1 Namespaces Used In the OWL Web Ontology Language

NAMESPACE	PREFIX
http://www.w3.org/1999/02/22-rdf-syntax-ns#	rdf
http://www.w3.org/2000/01/rdf-schema#	rdfs
http://www.w3.org/2001/XMLSchema#	xsd
http://www.w3.org/2002/07/owl#	owl

These prefixes will be used in all examples without necessarily being defined explicitly.

OWL ontologies contain a header that is essentially the declaration of the ontology itself. After that, the ontology contains a series of class and property definitions, descriptions of individuals, and data range descriptions. A class is a collection of individuals. A property is a relationship, and it can be either between two individuals or between an individual and a literal value. An individual is an instance (also known as a member) of a class.

Annotation Properties

Annotation properties can be used to describe any axiom or resource in the ontology, including classes, properties, individuals, ontologies, and datatypes. The following is a list of the annotation properties that are provided in OWL as well as the class of annotation properties that can be used to describe new annotation properties.

owl:AnnotationProperty   The class of all annotation properties.

rdfs:label   Annotation property that provides a label that represents the resource. Often used by tools as a user interface substitute for a URI.

rdfs:comments   Annotation property that provides a text description of the resource.

rdfs:seeAlso   Annotation property that specifies a resource that provides additional information.

rdfs:isDefinedBy   Annotation property that specifies a resource that defines the subject resource.

owl:deprecated   Annotation property that specifies whether or not the subject URI is deprecated.

owl:DeprecatedClass   The class of all deprecated classes.

owl:DeprecatedProperty   The class of all deprecated properties.

owl:priorVersion   Annotation property that specifies a prior version of the ontology that is the subject of the statement.

owl:backwardCompatibleWith   Annotation property that specifies the URI of an ontology that is compatible with the ontology that is the subject of the statement.

owl:incompatibleWith   Annotation property that specifies the URI of an ontology that is not compatible with the ontology that is the subject of the statement.

Individuals

Individuals in OWL are members of classes. The following OWL vocabulary terms are used to describe individuals:

rdf:type   A relationship that specifies the class of which an individual is a member.

owl:sameAs   A relationship that specifies that two individuals are the same individual.

owl:differentFrom   A relationship that specifies that two individuals are not the same individual.

owl:AllDifferent   A class used with `owl:distinctMembers` to define a collection of individuals who are pair-wise different.

Classes

An OWL class definition consists of some optional annotations followed by zero or more constructs that restrict the membership of the class. These restrictions represent descriptions of the class and form the basis of the class definition. The various forms of class restriction include subclass relationships, explicit membership enumeration, property restrictions, and class-based set operations. The following OWL vocabulary terms can be used to describe a class:

rdfs:subClassOf   Relationship between two classes that states that one class is more specific than the other. If a class A is a subclass of a class B, any member of class A is also a member of class B. In addition, `rdfs:subClassOf` is transitive. If class A is a subclass of class B and B is a subclass of class C, then A is also a subclass of C.

owl:equivalentClass   Relationship that specifies that the extensions of two classes are equivalent.

owl:Thing   The class of all individuals.

owl:Nothing   The class that contains no individuals.

owl:oneOf   The membership of the class is limited to those members of the specified collection of individuals.

owl:intersectionOf   The members of this class are members of all of the specified classes.

owl:unionOf   The members of this class are members of at least one of the specified classes.

owl:complementOf   The members of this class are not members of the specified class.

owl:disjointWith   Relationship that specifies that the memberships of two classes share no individuals.

owl:AllDisjointClasses   A class used with `owl:members` to specify a set of classes that are pair-wise disjoint.

owl:disjointUnionOf   A relationship that specifies that this class is the union of the set of specified classes and that those classes are pair-wise disjoint.

Properties

OWL properties are used to establish relationships between resources. The following OWL vocabulary terms are used to define properties:

owl:ObjectProperty   The class of all properties that link two individuals.

owl:DatatypeProperty   The class of all properties that link an individual with a literal value.

owl:topObjectProperty   Property that connects all possible pairs of individuals.

owl:bottomObjectProperty   Property that connects no pairs of individuals.

owl:topDataProperty   Property that connects all possible individuals with all possible literals.

owl:bottomDataProperty   Property that does not connect any individual with a literal.

rdfs:domain   Specifies the domain of a statement that is using the property that is the subject of this domain statement.

rdfs:range   Specifies the range of a statement that is using the property that is the subject of this range statement.

rdfs:subPropertyOf   Relationship between two properties that specifies that one property is more specific than the other. If a property p1 is a subproperty of a property p2, the existence of a statement (A p1 B) implies the existence of the statement (A p2 B).

owl:equivalentProperty   Relationship that specifies that two properties are equivalent.

owl:inverseOf   Relationship that specifies that two properties are the inverse of each other. If a property p1 is the inverse of a property p2, the existence of a statement (A p1 B) implies the existence of the statement (B p2 A).

owl:propertyChain   Relationship that is used to build a chain of properties that represent the super property in a subproperty-of relationship.

owl:SymmetricProperty   The class of all properties that are symmetric. For all symmetric properties p, the statement (A p B) implies the existence of the statement (B p A).

owl:AsymmetricProperty   The class of all properties that are explicitly not symmetric. For all asymmetric properties p, the statement (A p B) implies the nonexistence of the statement (B p A).

owl:ReflexiveProperty   The class of all properties that are reflexive. For all reflexive properties p and individuals A, A is related to itself by p - (A p A).

owl:IrreflexiveProperty   The class of all properties that are not reflexive. For all irreflexive properties p and individuals A, there is no statement (A p A).

owl:TransitiveProperty   The class of all properties that are transitive. For all transitive properties p, (A p B) and (B p C) implies (A p C).

owl:FunctionalProperty   The class of all properties for which a given domain value has only a single range value.

owl:InverseFunctionalProperty   The class of all properties for which a given object of a statement has only a single subject value.

owl:propertyDisjointWith   Relationship that establishes that two properties are disjoint. If two properties p1 and p2 are disjoint, it implies that no two statements with the same subject and object can have the predicates p1 and p2 - (A p1 B) and (A p2 B).

owl:AllDisjointProperties   A class that is used with `owl:members` to describe collections of properties that are pair-wise disjoint.

In addition to conventional, positive property assertions, OWL provides the notion of negative property assertions. Negative property assertions specify that a particular relationship does not exist between two individuals or between an individual and a literal value. The following vocabulary terms are used to specify negative property assertions:

owl:NegativePropertyAssertion   The class of all negative property assertions.

owl:sourceIndividual   The individual that is the subject of the negative property assertion.

owl:assertionProperty   The property that is the predicate of the negative property assertion.

owl:targetIndividual   The individual that is the object of the negative property assertion.

owl:targetValue   The literal value that is the object of the negative property assertion.

Datatypes

Datatypes represent ranges of data values that are identified using URIs. OWL allows you to use a number of predefined datatypes, of which most are defined in the XML Schema Definition (xsd) namespace. In addition to the predefined datatypes, OWL 2 introduces the ability to define your own datatypes. There are two ways to do so: you can create a custom data range using facets (Table B-2), or you can define a datatype in terms of other datatypes.

Table B-2 Facets supported by OWL

FACET	DESCRIPTION
xsd:length	N is the exact number of items (or characters) allowed.
xsd:minLength	N is the minimum number of items (or characters) allowed.
xsd:maxLength	N is the maximum number items (or characters) allowed.
xsd:Pattern	A regular expression that defines allowed character strings.
xsd:minInclusive	Values must be greater than or equal to N.
xsd:minExclusive	Values must be strictly greater than N.
xsd:maxInclusive	Values must be less than or equal to N.
xsd:maxExclusive	Values must be strictly less than N.
xsd:totalDigits	The number of digits must be equal to N.
xsd:fractionDigits	N is the maximum number of decimal places allowed.

N refers to the value portion of the facet restriction.

This is the full set of vocabulary terms that can be used to define custom datatypes:

rdfs:Datatype   The class of all datatypes.

owl:onDatatype   Property that identifies the datatype to which the facet restrictions apply.

owl:withRestrictions   Property that identifies a collection of facet restrictions that describe the datatype.

owl:intersectionOf   Property that identifies a set of datatypes such that the datatype being described contains the values that are contained in all datatypes in the set.

owl:unionOf   Property that identifies a set of datatypes such that the datatype being described contains any value that is contained in at least one of the datatypes in the set.

owl:datatypeComplementOf   Property that specifies that the datatype being described contains all values that are not in the datatype that the property identifies.

owl:oneOf   Property that identifies a set of values that make up the datatype.

The following example demonstrates how to define an example datatype using facets. The first datatype represents all integers that have nine digits. Note that all custom datatypes must be anonymous resources.

```
@prefix ex: <http://example.org/>.
...
#integers with 9 digits
[] rdf:type rdfs:Datatype;
   owl:onDatatype xsd:integer;
   owl:withRestrictions (
      [
         xsd:totalDigits 9;
         ]
      ).
```

Property Restrictions

A property restriction describes the class of individuals that meet the specified property-based conditions. The restriction is declared using the construct `owl:Restriction`, and the property to which the restriction refers is identified using the property `owl:onProperty`. Restrictions are related to classes using either `rdfs:subClassOf` or `owl:equivalentClass`. They can also appear as the objects of statements that combine classes using set operators.

Similar to restrictions, OWL also provides a concept called *keys*. A key describes a set of properties whose collective values can be associated with only a single subject.

The following list of vocabulary terms can be used to build restrictions and keys:

owl:Restriction   The class of all restrictions.

owl:SelfRestriction   The class of all self-restrictions. Self-restrictions identify classes of individuals who are related to themselves by a property.

owl:onProperty   Property that identifies the property to which a restriction applies.

owl:allValuesFrom   Property that specifies that all instances in this class must have values only from the specified range for the specified property.

owl:someValuesFrom   Property that specifies that all instances of this class must have at least one property with a value from the specified range.

owl:hasValue   Property that specifies that all instances of this class must have the specified value for the specified property.

owl:minCardinality   Property that specifies there must be at least N of the specified properties on each instance of this class.

owl:maxCardinality   Property that specifies there must be at most N of the specified properties on each instance of this class.

owl:cardinality   Property that specifies there must be exactly N of the specified properties on each instance of this class.

owl:onClass   Property that identifies the class of which the subject of a qualified cardinality restriction is a member.

owl:minQualifiedCardinality   Property that specifies there must be at least N properties that each point to an instance of the specified class.

owl:maxQualifiedCardinality   Property that specifies there must be at most N properties that each point to an instance of the specified class.

owl:qualifiedCardinality   Property that specifies there are exactly N properties that each point to an instance of the specified class.

owl:hasKey   Property used to identify a collection of properties that constitute a key for a given class.

APPENDIX

C

SWRL

SWRL is an acronym for the *Semantic Web Rule Language*. This appendix presents several examples of SWRL and covers the namespaces, built-ins, and keywords in alphabetical order, which are part of the SWRL submission. In the case of keywords, a short description is given. A page number is listed if a keyword or example is described in finer detail in the book, and a reference URL is provided to obtain additional information from the W3C Submission.

SWRL Examples

Figure C-1 shows an example of deconstructed SWRL code in RDF concrete syntax. It is followed by another example in RDF concrete syntax as well as in Turtle.

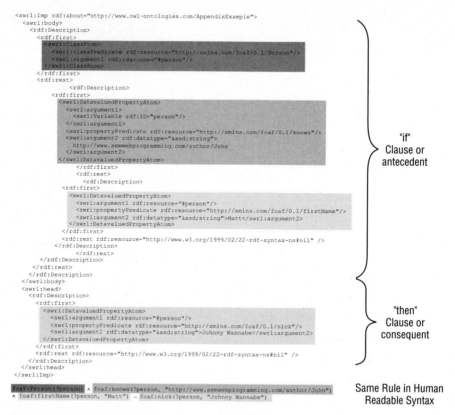

Figure C-1 A deconstructed SWRL sample in RDF concrete syntax

RDF concrete syntax:

```
<swrl:Imp rdf:about="http://www.semwebprogramming.com/dislikeRose
GrowingNeighborsRule">
  <swrl:body>
    <swrl:AtomList>
      <rdf:first>
        <rdf:Description>
          <rdf:type rdf:resource="&swrl;ClassAtom"/>
          <swrl:argument1>
            <rdf:Description rdf:about="#n"/>
          </swrl:argument1>
          <swrl:classPredicate
              rdf:resource="#Neighbor"/>
        </rdf:Description>
      </rdf:first>
      <rdf:rest>
        <swrl:AtomList>
          <rdf:first>
```

```
          <rdf:Description>
            <rdf:type
             rdf:resource="&swrl;ClassAtom"/>
            <swrl:argument1>
              <rdf:Description rdf:about="#r"/>
            </swrl:argument1>
            <swrl:classPredicate
              rdf:resource="#Rose"/>
          </rdf:Description>
        </rdf:first>
        <rdf:rest>
          <swrl:AtomList>
            <rdf:first>
              <rdf:Description>
                <rdf:type rdf:resource=
                   "&swrl;IndividualPropertyAtom"/>
                <swrl:argument2>
                  <rdf:Description rdf:about="#r"/>
                </swrl:argument2>
                <swrl:argument1>
                    <rdf:Description rdf:about="#n"/>
                </swrl:argument1>
                <swrl:propertyPredicate
                    rdf:resource="#plants"/>
              </rdf:Description>
            </rdf:first>
            <rdf:rest rdf:resource="&rdf;nil"/>
          </swrl:AtomList>
        </rdf:rest>
      </swrl:AtomList>
    </rdf:rest>
  </swrl:AtomList>
</swrl:body>
<swrl:head>
  <swrl:AtomList>
    <rdf:first>
      <rdf:Description>
        <rdf:type
         rdf:resource="&swrl;IndividualPropertyAtom"/>
        <swrl:argument2>
          <rdf:Description rdf:about="#n"/>
        </swrl:argument2>
        <swrl:argument1 rdf:resource="#me"/>
        <swrl:propertyPredicate
          rdf:resource="#dislike"/>
      </rdf:Description>
    </rdf:first>
    <rdf:rest rdf:resource="&rdf;nil"/>
  </swrl:AtomList>
```

```
        </swrl:head>
    </swrl:Imp>
```

Turtle:

```
:dislikeRoseGrowingNeighborsRule
    rdf:type swrl:Imp ;
    swrl:body
        [ rdf:type swrl:AtomList ;
          rdf:first
              [ rdf:type swrl:ClassAtom ;
                swrl:argument1 rose:n ;
                swrl:classPredicate rose:Neighbor
              ] ;
          rdf:rest
              [ rdf:type swrl:AtomList ;
                rdf:first
                    [ rdf:type swrl:ClassAtom ;
                      swrl:argument1 rose:r ;
                      swrl:classPredicate rose:Rose
                    ] ;
                rdf:rest
                    [ rdf:type swrl:AtomList ;
                      rdf:first
                          [ rdf:type swrl:IndividualPropertyAtom ;
                            swrl:argument1 rose:n ;
                            swrl:argument2 rose:r ;
                            swrl:propertyPredicate rose:plants
                          ] ;
                      rdf:rest ()
                    ]
              ]
        ] ;
    swrl:head
        [ rdf:type swrl:AtomList ;
          rdf:first
              [ rdf:type swrl:IndividualPropertyAtom ;
                swrl:argument1 rose:me ;
                swrl:argument2 rose:n ;
                swrl:propertyPredicate rose:dislike
              ] ;
          rdf:rest ()
        ] .
```

Namespaces

Table C-1 lists some of the namespaces that are typically used in files with SWRL statements.

Table C-1 Common SWRL Namespaces

PREFIX	URL
owlx	http://www.w3.org/2003/05/owl-xml
ruleml	http://www.w3.org/2003/11/ruleml
swrlb	http://www.w3.org/2003/11/swrlb
swrlx	http://www.w3.org/2003/11/swrlx

Built-ins

This section contains a list of all the built-ins with a short description of each as documented in the W3C SWRL Submission (http://www.w3.org/Submission/SWRL/#8).

Comparisons, Booleans

This section covers built-ins that are used for argument comparisons and boolean verification. Examples are provided in human-readable syntax.

booleanNot(?first, ?second)

Satisfied if and only if the first argument is true and the second argument is false, or vice versa.

booleanNot(?isFiveGreaterThanSix, true) will return true.

equal(?first, ?second)

Satisfied if and only if the first argument and the second argument are the same.

equal(6.1, ?height) will return true if height is set to 6.1.

greaterThan(?first, ?second)

Satisfied if and only if the first argument and the second argument are both in some implemented type and the first argument is greater than the second argument according to a type-specific ordering (partial or total), if there is one defined for the type.

greaterThan(1, 2) will return false.

greaterThanOrEqual(?first, ?second)

Satisfied if and only if the first argument and the second argument are both in some implemented type and the first argument is greater than or equal to the second argument according to a type-specific ordering (partial or total), if there is one defined for the type.

`greaterThanOrEqual(1, 2)` will return false.

lessThan(?first, ?second)

Satisfied if and only if the first argument and the second argument are both in some implemented type and the first argument is less than the second argument according to a type-specific ordering (partial or total), if there is one defined for the type.

`lessThan(1, 2)` will return true.

lessThanOrEqual(?first, ?second)

Satisfied if and only if the first argument and the second argument are both in some implemented type and the first argument is less than or equal to the second argument according to a type-specific ordering (partial or total), if there is one defined for the type.

`lessThanOrEqual(1, 2)` will return true.

notEqual(?first, ?second)

Satisfied if and only if the first argument and the second argument are not the same.

`notEqual(1, 2)` will return true.

Mathematics

This section covers mathematical operations for built-in arguments.

abs(?first, ?second)

Satisfied if and only if the first argument is the absolute value of the second argument.

`abs(1, ?value)` will return true if `?value` is set to 1 or −1.

add(?sum, ?second, ?third)

Satisfied if and only if the first argument (`?sum`) is equal to the arithmetic sum of the second and third arguments.

`add(?total, 85, 4)` will set the value of `?total` to 89.

ceiling(?first, ?second)

Satisfied if and only if the first argument is the smallest number with no fractional part that is greater than or equal to the second argument.

`ceiling(?c, 5.34)` will set the value of `?c` to 6.

cos(?first, ?second)

Satisfied if and only if the first argument is equal to the cosine of the radian value of the second argument.

`cos(?c, 3.14)` will set the value of `?c` to approximately −0.99999873172754.

divide(?quotient, ?second, ?third)

Satisfied if and only if the first argument (the quotient) is equal to the arithmetic quotient of the second argument divided by the third argument.

divide(?q, 15, 3) will set the value of ?q to 5.

floor(?first, ?second)

Satisfied if and only if the first argument is the largest number with no fractional part that is less than or equal to the second argument.

floor(?c, 5.34) will set the value of ?c to 5.

integerDivide(?quotient, ?second, ?third)

Satisfied if the first argument is the arithmetic quotient of the second argument divided by the third argument. If the numerator is not evenly divided by the divisor, then the quotient is the xsd:integer value obtained, ignoring any remainder that results from the division (that is, no rounding is performed).

integerDivide(?q, 16, 3) will set the value of ?q to 5.

mod(?remainder, ?dividend, ?divisor)

Satisfied if and only if the first argument represents the remainder resulting from dividing the second argument (the dividend) by the third argument (the divisor).

mod(?r, 16, 3) will set the value of ?r to 1.

multiply(?product, ?second, ?third)

Satisfied if and only if the first argument is equal to the arithmetic product of the second and third arguments.

multiply(?p, 75.3, 20) will set the value of ?p to 1506.

pow(?first, ?second, ?power)

Satisfied if and only if the first argument is equal to the result of the second argument raised to the third argument power.

pow(?f, 2, 3) will set the value of ?f to 8.

round(?first, ?second)

Satisfied if and only if the first argument is equal to the nearest number to the second argument with no fractional part.

round(?r, 22.3) will set the value of ?r to 22.

roundHalfToEven(?first, ?second, ?precision)

Satisfied if and only if the first argument is equal to the second argument rounded to the given precision. If the fractional part is exactly half, the result is the number whose least significant digit is even.

`roundHalfToEven(?r, 22.34582, 4)` will set the value of `?r` to 22.3458.

sin(?first, ?second)

Satisfied if and only if the first argument is equal to the sine of the radian value of the second argument.

`sin(?s, 3.14)` will set the value of `?s` to approximately .001592652916487.

subtract(?total, ?second, ?third)

Satisfied if and only if the first argument is equal to the arithmetic difference of the second argument minus the third argument.

`subtract(?t, 10, 4.2)` will set the value of `?t` to 5.8.

unaryMinus(?first, ?second)

Satisfied if and only if the first argument is equal to the second argument with its sign reversed.

`unaryMinus(?u, 10)` will set the value of `?u` to −10.

unaryPlus(?first, ?second)

Satisfied if and only if the first argument is equal to the second argument with its sign unchanged.

`unaryPlus(?u, 10)` will set the value of `?u` to 10.

Strings

This section covers string operations for built-in arguments.

contains(?first, ?second)

Satisfied if and only if the first argument contains the second argument (case sensitive).

`contains("SWRL", "wrl")` returns false.

containsIgnoreCase(?first, ?second)

Satisfied if and only if the first argument contains the second argument (case insensitive).

`containsIgnoreCase("SWRL", "wrl")` returns true.

endsWith(?first, ?second)

Satisfied if and only if the first argument ends with the second argument.

`endsWith("SWRL", "RL")` returns true.

lowercase(?first, ?second)

Satisfied if and only if the first argument is equal to the lowercase value of the second argument.

`lowercase(?l, "SWRL")` will set the value of `?l` to "swrl".

matches(?first, ?regex)

Satisfied if and only if the first argument matches the XML Schema-based regular expression presented in the second argument.

`matches("SWRL", "SW*")` returns true.

normalizeSpace(?first, ?second)

Satisfied if and only if the first argument is equal to the white space–normalized value of the second argument.

`normalizeSpace(?w, " Semantic Web ")` will set the value of ?w to "Semantic Web".

replace(?first, ?second, ?regex, ?replacement)

Satisfied if and only if the first argument is equal to the value of the second argument, with every substring matched by the regular expression (the third argument) replaced by the replacement string (the fourth argument).

`replace(?r, "Semantic Web Programming", "e? ", "xx")` will set the value of ?r to "Sxxmantic Wxxb Programming".

startsWith(?first, ?second)

Satisfied if and only if the first argument starts with the second argument.

`startsWith("SWRL", "SW")` returns true.

stringConcat(?concatenation, ?second, ?third)

Satisfied if and only if the first argument is equal to the string resulting from the concatenation of the strings of the second and third arguments.

`stringConcat(?c, "Semantic ", "Web")` will set the value of ?c to "Semantic Web".

stringEqualIgnoreCase(?first, ?second)

Satisfied if and only if the first argument is the same as the second argument (case insensitive).

`stringEqualIgnoreCase("SWRL", "sWrL")` returns true.

stringLength(?first, ?second)

Satisfied if and only if the first argument is equal to the length of the second argument.

`stringLength("ten", "two")` returns true.

substring(?first, ?second?, ?startingOffset, ?endingOffset)

Satisfied if and only if the first argument is equal to the substring based on the second argument, as restricted by the integers used in the third and fourth arguments.

substring(?s, "Semantic Web", 2, 5) will set the value of ?s to "emantic".

substringAfter(?first, ?second, ?third)

Satisfied if and only if the first argument is the characters of the second argument that follow the characters of the third argument.

substringAfter(?f, "Semantic Web", "Sem") will set the value of ?f to "antic Web".

substringBefore(?first, ?second, ?third)

Satisfied if and only if the first argument contains the characters of the second argument that precede the characters of the third argument.

substringBefore(?f, "Semantic Web", "tic Web") will set the value of ?f to "Seman".

tokenize(?first, ?second, ?regex)

Satisfied if and only if the first argument is a sequence of one or more strings whose values are substrings of the second argument separated by substrings that match the regular expression in the third argument.

tokenize(?t, "The Semantic Web", "\s+") will set ?t to "The", "Semantic" and "Web".

translate(?first, ?second, ?third, ?position)

Satisfied if and only if the first argument is equal to the second argument with occurrences of characters contained in the third argument replaced by the character at the corresponding position in the string of the fourth argument.

translate(?t, "The Semantic Web", "aei", "AqI") will set the value of ?t to "Thq SqmAntIc Wqb".

uppercase(?first, ?second)

Satisfied if and only if the first argument is equal to the uppercase value of the second argument.

uppercase(?u, "SwRl") will set the value of ?u to "SWRL".

Date, Time, Duration

This section covers date and time operations for built-in arguments.

addDayTimeDurations(?sum, ?second, ?third)

Satisfied if and only if the dayTimeDuration expressed in the first argument is equal to the arithmetic sum of the dayTimeDuration expressed in the second argument and the dayTimeDuration expressed in the last argument.

`addDayTimeDurations(?s, "P1Y6DT10H", "P3DT10H15M")` will set the value of `?s` to "P1Y9DT20H15M"^^xsd:duration.

addDayTimeDurationToDate(?sum, ?second, ?third)

Satisfied if and only if the `xsd:date` of the first argument is equal to the arithmetic sum of the `xsd:date` expressed in the second argument plus the `dayTimeDuration` expressed in the third argument.

`addDayTimeDurationToDate(?s, "2008-12-01", "P1Y9D")` will set the value of `?s` to "2009-12-10"^^xsd:date.

addDayTimeDurationToDateTime(?sum, ?second, ?third)

Satisfied if and only if the `xsd:dateTime` of the first argument is equal to the arithmetic sum of the `xsd:dateTime` expressed in the second argument plus the `dayTimeDuration` expressed in the third argument.

`addDayTimeDurationToDateTime(?s, "2008-12-01T06:30:00Z", "P1Y9DT15M")` will set the value of `?s` to "2009-12-10T06:45:00Z"^^xsd:dateTime.

addDayTimeDurationToTime(?sum, ?second, ?third)

Satisfied if and only if the `xsd:time` of the first argument is equal to the arithmetic sum of the `xsd:time` expressed in the second argument plus the `dayTimeDuration` expressed in the third argument.

`addDayTimeDurationToTime(?s, "06:30:00Z", "PT15M")` will set the value of `?s` to "06:45:00Z"^^xsd:time.

addYearMonthDurations(?sum, ?second, ?third)

Satisfied if and only if the `yearMonthDuration` of the first argument is equal to the arithmetic sum of the `yearMonthDuration` of the second argument and the `yearMonthDuration` of the third argument.

`addYearMonthDurations(?s, "P5Y10M", "P1Y1M")` will set the value of `?s` to "P6Y11M"^^xsd:duration.

addYearMonthDurationToDate(?sum, ?second, ?third)

Satisfied if and only if the `xsd:date` of the first argument is equal to the arithmetic sum of the `xsd:date` expressed in the second argument plus the `yearMonthDuration` expressed in the third argument.

`addYearMonthDurationToDate(?s, "2008-12-01", "P5Y11M")` will set the value of `?s` to "2014-11-01"^^xsd:date.

addYearMonthDurationToDateTime(?sum, ?second, ?third)

Satisfied if and only if the `xsd:dateTime` of the first argument is equal to the arithmetic sum of the `xsd:dateTime` expressed in the second argument plus the `yearMonthDuration` expressed in the third argument.

addYearMonthDurationToDateTime(?s, "2008-12-01T06:30:00Z", "P5Y11M") will set the value of ?s to "2014-11-01T06:30:00Z"^^ xsd:dateTime.

date(?fullDate, ?year, ?month, ?day, ?timezone)

Satisfied if and only if the first argument is the xsd:date representation consisting of the year in the second argument, the month in the third argument, the day in the fourth argument, and the timezone in the fifth argument.

date(?fd, 2008, 1, 1, 0) will set the value of ?fd to "2008-01-01"^^ xsd:date.

dateTime(?fullDateTime, ?year, ?month, ?day, ?hours, ?minutes, ?seconds, ?timezone)

Satisfied if and only if the first argument is the xsd:dateTime representation consisting of the year in the second argument, the month in the third argument, the day in the fourth argument, the hours in the fifth argument, the minutes in the sixth argument, the seconds in the seventh argument, and the timezone in the eighth argument.

dateTime(?fdt, 2008, 1, 1, 6, 45, 12, 0) will set the value of ?fdt to "2008-01-01T06:45:12Z"^^xsd:dateTime.

dayTimeDuration(?fullDayTime, ?days, ?hours, ?minutes, ?seconds)

Satisfied if and only if the first argument is the xsd:duration representation consisting of the days in the second argument, the hours in the third argument, the minutes in the fourth argument, and the seconds in the fifth argument.

dayTimeDuration(?fdt, 30, 66, 2, 51) will set the value of ?fdt to "P30DT66H2M51S"^^xsd:duration.

divideDayTimeDuration(?quotient, ?second, ?third)

Satisfied if and only if the dayTimeDuration of the first argument is equal to the arithmetic remainder of the dayTimeDuration of the second argument divided by the third argument.

divideDayTimeDuration(?q, "P2D15H32M17S", 2) will set the value of ?q to "P1D7H46M8.5S"^^xsd:duration.

divideYearMonthDurations(?quotient, ?second, ?third)

Satisfied if and only if the yearMonthDuration of the first argument is equal to the arithmetic remainder of the yearMonthDuration of the second argument divided by the third argument.

divideYearMonthDurations(?q, "P12Y6M", 1.5) will set the value of ?q to "P8Y4M"^^xsd:duration.

multiplyDayTimeDurations(?product, ?second, ?third)

Satisfied if and only if the dayTimeDuration of the first argument is equal to the arithmetic product of the dayTimeDuration of the second argument multiplied by the third argument.

multiplyDayTimeDurations(?p, "P2D15H32M17S", 2) will set the value of ?p to "P5D7H4M34S"^^xsd:duration.

multiplyYearMonthDuration(?product, ?second, ?third)

Satisfied if and only if the yearMonthDuration of the first argument is equal to the arithmetic product of the yearMonthDuration of the second argument multiplied by the third argument.

multiplyYearMonthDuration(?p, "P12Y6M", 1.5) will set the value of ?p to "P18Y9M"^^xsd:duration.

subtractDates(?difference, ?second, ?third)

Satisfied if and only if the dayTimeDuration of the first argument is equal to the arithmetic difference of the xsd:date of the second argument minus the xsd:date of the third argument.

subtractDates(?d, "2008-12-05", "2008-11-03") will set the value of ?d to "P1M2D"^^xsd:duration.

subtractDateTimesYieldingDayTimeDuration(?difference, ?second, ?third)

Satisfied if and only if the dayTimeDuration of the first argument is equal to the arithmetic difference of the xsd:dateTime of the second argument minus the xsd:dateTime of the third argument.

subtractDateTimesYieldingDayTimeDuration(?d, "2008-12-02T08:30:00Z", "2008-12-01T06:30:00Z") will set the value of ?d to "P1D2H"^^xsd:duration.

subtractDateTimesYieldingYearMonthDuration(?difference, ?second, ?third)

Satisfied if and only if the yearMonthDuration of the first argument is equal to the arithmetic difference of the xsd:dateTime of the second argument minus the xsd:dateTime of the third argument.

subtractDateTimesYieldingYearMonthDuration(?d, "2008-12-01T08: 30:00Z", "2007-12-01T06:30:00Z") will set the value of ?d to "P1Y"^^xsd:duration.

subtractDayTimeDurationFromDate(?difference, ?second, ?third)

Satisfied if and only if the xsd:date of the first argument is equal to the arithmetic difference of the xsd:date of the second argument minus the dayTimeDuration of the third argument.

subtractDayTimeDurationFromDate(?d, "2008-12-01", "P3DT2H30M") will set the value of ?d to "11-27-2008"^^xsd:date.

subtractDayTimeDurationFromDateTime(?difference, ?second, ?third)

Satisfied if and only if the xsd:dateTime of the first argument is equal to the arithmetic difference of the xsd:dateTime of the second argument minus the dayTimeDuration of the third argument.

subtractDayTimeDurationFromDateTime(?d, "2008-12-01T11:00:00", "P3DT2H30M") will set the value of ?d to "11-28-2008T08:30:00"^^xsd:dateTime.

subtractDayTimeDurationFromTime(?difference, ?second, ?third)

Satisfied if and only if the xsd:time of the first argument is equal to the arithmetic difference of the xsd:time of the second argument minus the dayTimeDuration of the third argument.

subtractDayTimeDurationFromTime(?d, "06:30:00Z", "PT2H30M") will set the value of ?d to "T04:00:00"^^xsd:time.

subtractDayTimeDurations(?difference, ?second, ?third)

Satisfied if and only if the dayTimeDuration of the first argument is equal to the arithmetic difference of the dayTimeDuration of the second argument minus the dayTimeDuration of the third argument.

subtractDayTimeDurations(?d, "P3DT12H30M54S", "P2DT6H-14M05S") will set the value of ?d to "P1D6H16M49S"^^xsd:duration.

subtractTimes(?difference, ?second, ?third)

Satisfied if and only if the dayTimeDuration of the first argument is equal to the arithmetic difference of the xsd:time of the second argument minus the xsd:time of the third argument.

subtractTimes(?d, "T12:30:54Z", "T11:05:05Z") will set the value of ?d to "P1H25M49S"^^xsd:duration.

subtractYearMonthDurationFromDate(?difference, ?second, ?third)

Satisfied if and only if the xsd:date of the first argument is equal to the arithmetic difference of the xsd:date of the second argument minus the yearMonthDuration of the third argument.

subtractYearMonthDurationFromDate(?d, "2008-12-01", "P1Y2M") will set the value of ?d to "2007-10-01"^^xsd:date.

subtractYearMonthDurationFromDateTime(?difference, ?second, ?third)

Satisfied if and only if the xsd:dateTime of the first argument is equal to the arithmetic difference of the xsd:dateTime of the second argument minus the `yearMonthDuration` of the third argument.

`subtractYearMonthDurationFromDateTime(?d, "2008-12-01T11:00:00", "P1Y2M")` will set the value of `?d` to "2007-10-01T11:00:00"^^xsd:dateTime.

subtractYearMonthDurations(?difference, ?second, ?third)

Satisfied if and only if the `yearMonthDuration` of the first argument is equal to the arithmetic difference of the `yearMonthDuration` of the second argument minus the `yearMonthDuration` of the third argument.

`subtractYearMonthDurations(?d, "P5Y10M", "P3Y2M")` will set the value of `?d` to "P2Y8M"^^xsd:duration.

time(?fullTime, ?hours, ?minutes, ?seconds, ?timezone)

Satisfied if and only if the first argument is the `xsd:time` representation consisting of the `hours` of the second argument, the `minutes` of the third argument, the `seconds` of the fourth argument, and the `timezone` of the fifth argument.

`time(?ft, 12, 14, 30, 0)` will set the value of `?ft` to "T12:14:30Z"^^xsd:time.

yearMonthDuration(?fullDuration, ?year, ?month)

Satisfied if and only if the first argument is the `xsd:duration` representation consisting of the `year` expressed in the second argument and the `month` in the third argument.

`yearMonthDuration(?d, 5, 11)` will set the value of `?d` to "P5Y11M"^^xsd:duration.

URIs

This section covers URI-related operations.

anyURI(?fullURI, ?scheme, ?host, ?port, ?path, ?query, ?fragment)

Satisfied if and only if the first argument is a URI reference consisting of the `scheme` in the second argument, the `host` in the third argument, the `port` in the fourth argument, the `path` in the fifth argument, the `query` in the sixth argument, and the `fragment` in the seventh argument.

`anyURI(?f, "http", "192.168.1.100", "8080", "/path/name", "?help", "=time")` will set the value of `?f` to `http://192.168.1.100:8080/path/name?help=time`.

resolveURI(?fullURI, ?referenceURI, ?baseURI)

Satisfied if and only if the URI reference of the first argument is equal to the value of the URI reference of the second argument resolved relative to the base URI of the third argument.

resolveURI(?u, "a/b", "http://www.semwebprogramming.com/path#") will set the value of ?u to "http://www.semwebprogramming.com/path#a/b".

Lists

This section covers list operations for built-in arguments.

empty(?list)

Satisfied if and only if the list in the first argument is an empty list.

empty("one" "two") returns false.

first(?firstMember, ?list)

Satisfied if and only if the first argument is the first member of the list in the second argument.

first(?f, "one" "two") will set the value of ?f to "one".

length(?length, ?list)

Satisfied if and only if the first argument is the length of the list in the second argument (the number of members of the list).

length(?l, "one" "two") will set the value of ?l to 2.

listConcat(?concatenation, ?second, ?third)

Satisfied if and only if the first argument is a list representing the concatenation of the lists of the second and third arguments.

listConcat(?c, "three" "four", "one" "two") will set the value of ?c to "three" "four" "one" and "two".

listIntersection(?intersection, ?second, ?third)

Satisfied if and only if the first argument is a list containing elements found in both the lists expressed in the second and third arguments.

listIntersection(?i, "one" "two", "two" "three" "four") will set the value of ?i to "two".

listSubtraction(?difference, ?second, ?third)

Satisfied if and only if the first argument is a list containing elements of the list in the second argument but that are not members of the list expressed the third argument.

`listSubtraction(?d, "one" "two" "three", "one" "two")` will set the value of `?d` to "three".

member(?member, ?list)

Satisfied if and only if the first argument is a member of the list in the second argument.

`member("one", "one" "two" "three")` will return true.

rest(?notHead, ?list)

Satisfied if and only if the first argument is a list containing all members of the list expressed in the second argument except the first member (the head).

`rest(?nH, "one" "two" "three")` will set the value of `?nH` to "two" "three".

sublist(?fullList, ?subList)

Satisfied if and only if the list in the first argument contains the list in the second argument.

`sublist("one" "two" "three", "one" "five")` returns false.

Keywords

This section covers SWRL keywords.

Atom

As part of the SWRL RDF namespace (`http://www.w3.org/2003/11/swrl`), `Atom` is the common ancestor for all types of SWRL atoms in the RDF concrete syntax. Formally defined at `http://www.w3.org/Submission/SWRL/swrl.rdf`.

argument1

As part of the SWRL RDF namespace (`http://www.w3.org/2003/11/swrl`), `argument1` is used as the first argument in various atom types (e.g., `ClassAtom`) and refers to an RDFS resource in the RDF concrete syntax. Formally defined at `http://www.w3.org/Submission/SWRL/swrl.rdf`.

argument2

As part of the SWRL RDF namespace (`http://www.w3.org/2003/11/swrl`), `argument2` is used as the second argument in various atom types (e.g., `DatavaluedPropertyAtom`) and refers to either an RDFS resource or a literal in the RDF concrete syntax. Formally defined at `http://www.w3.org/Submission/SWRL/swrl.rdf`.

arguments

As part of the SWRL RDF namespace (`http://www.w3.org/2003/11/swrl`), `arguments` is an RDF list of arguments for a `BuiltinAtom` in the RDF concrete syntax. Formally defined at `http://www.w3.org/Submission/SWRL/swrl.rdf`.

body

As part of the SWRL RDF namespace (`http://www.w3.org/2003/11/swrl`), `body` defines the antecedent (the `if` clause) of a SWRL rule in the RDF concrete syntax. Formally defined at `http://www.w3.org/Submission/SWRL/swrl.rdf`.

_body

As part of the RuleML namespace (`http://www.w3.org/2003/11/ruleml`), `_body` defines the antecedent (the `if` clause) of a SWRL rule in the XML concrete syntax. Described on page 239 as well as at `http://www.w3.org/Submission/SWRL/#owls_antecedent`.

Builtin

As part of the SWRL RDF namespace (`http://www.w3.org/2003/11/swrl`), `Builtin` defines the SWRL built-in as a class in the RDF concrete syntax. Formally defined at `http://www.w3.org/Submission/SWRL/swrl.rdf`.

builtin

As part of the SWRL XML namespace (`http://www.w3.org/2003/11/swrlx`), `builtin` is an attribute of `swrlx:builtinAtom` that specifies the URL of a particular built-in in the XML concrete syntax. Described on page 243, with a list of built-ins detailed at `http://www.w3.org/Submission/SWRL/#8`.

As part of the SWRL RDF namespace (`http://www.w3.org/2003/11/swrl`), `builtin` associates a `BuiltinAtom` with a given `Builtin` in the RDF concrete syntax. Formally defined at `http://www.w3.org/Submission/SWRL/swrl.rdf`.

BuiltinAtom

As part of the SWRL RDF namespace (`http://www.w3.org/2003/11/swrl`), `BuiltinAtom` defines a SWRL built-in and a list of arguments in the RDF concrete syntax. Formally defined at `http://www.w3.org/Submission/SWRL/swrl.rdf`.

builtinAtom

As part of the SWRL XML namespace (`http://www.w3.org/2003/11/swrlx`), `builtinAtom` declares the use of a SWRL built-in in the XML concrete syntax. Described on page 243 as well as at `http://www.w3.org/Submission/SWRL/#owls_builtinAtom`.

ClassAtom

As part of the SWRL RDF namespace (http://www.w3.org/2003/11/swrl), ClassAtom defines an OWL class in the RDF concrete syntax. Formally defined at http://www.w3.org/Submission/SWRL/swrl.rdf.

classAtom

As part of the SWRL XML namespace (http://www.w3.org/2003/11/swrlx), classAtom defines an OWL class in the XML concrete syntax. Described on page 240 as well as at http://www.w3.org/Submission/SWRL/#owls_classAtom.

classPredicate

As part of the SWRL RDF namespace (http://www.w3.org/2003/11/swrl), classPredicate relates a ClassAtom to a class in the RDF concrete syntax. Formally defined at http://www.w3.org/Submission/SWRL/swrl.rdf.

dataRange

As part of the SWRL RDF namespace (http://www.w3.org/2003/11/swrl), dataRange associates a DataRangeAtom with an owl:DataRange in the RDF concrete syntax. Formally defined at http://www.w3.org/Submission/SWRL/swrl.rdf.

DataRangeAtom

As part of the SWRL RDF namespace (http://www.w3.org/2003/11/swrl), DataRangeAtom defines a datarange atom in the RDF concrete syntax. It is used as the domain for the dataRange property. Formally defined at http://www.w3.org/Submission/SWRL/swrl.rdf.

datarangeAtom

As part of the SWRL XML namespace (http://www.w3.org/2003/11/swrlx) datarangeAtom associates a variable with a declared datatype or a range of literal values in the XML concrete syntax. Described on page 241 as well as at http://www.w3.org/Submission/SWRL/#owls_datarangeAtom.

datatype

As part of the OWL XML namespace (http://www.w3.org/2003/05/owl-xml), datatype is an attribute of owlx:DataValue that specifies the XML datatype of the DataValue's literal in the XML concrete syntax. Detailed at http://www.w3.org/Submission/SWRL/#8.

DataValue

As part of the OWL XML namespace (`http://www.w3.org/2003/05/owl-xml`), `DataValue` specifies a literal value in the XML concrete syntax. Described at `http://www.w3.org/TR/owl-xmlsyntax/#owls_DataValue`.

DatavaluedPropertyAtom

As part of the SWRL RDF namespace (`http://www.w3.org/2003/11/swrl`), `DatavaluedPropertyAtom` associates either a variable or an OWL individual with a datatype property in the RDF concrete syntax. Formally defined at `http://www.w3.org/Submission/SWRL/swrl.rdf`.

datavaluedPropertyAtom

As part of the SWRL XML namespace (`http://www.w3.org/2003/11/swrlx`), `datavaluedPropertyAtom` associates either a variable or an OWL individual with a datatype property in the XML concrete syntax. Described on page 242 as well as at `http://www.w3.org/Submission/SWRL/#owls_datavaluedPropertyAtom`.

DifferentIndividualsAtom

As part of the SWRL RDF namespace (`http://www.w3.org/2003/11/swrl`), `DifferentIndividualsAtom` relates two `owl:Thing` instances with an `owl:differentFrom` statement in the RDF concrete syntax. Formally defined at `http://www.w3.org/Submission/SWRL/swrl.rdf`.

differentIndividualsAtom

As part of the SWRL XML namespace (`http://www.w3.org/2003/11/swrlx`), `differentIndividualsAtom` relates two or more variables or OWL individuals with `owl:differentFrom` statements in the XML concrete syntax. Described on page 243 as well as at `http://www.w3.org/Submission/SWRL/#owls_differentIndividualsAtom`.

head

As part of the SWRL RDF namespace (`http://www.w3.org/2003/11/swrl`), `head` defines the consequent (the `then` clause) of a SWRL rule in the RDF concrete syntax. Formally defined at `http://www.w3.org/Submission/SWRL/swrl.rdf`.

_head

As part of the RuleML namespace (`http://www.w3.org/2003/11/ruleml`), `_head` defines the consequent (the `then` clause) of a

SWRL rule in the XML concrete syntax. Described on page 240 as well as at `http://www.w3.org/Submission/SWRL/#owls_consequent`.

Imp

As part of the SWRL RDF namespace (`http://www.w3.org/2003/11/swrl`), `Imp` defines a SWRL rule in the RDF concrete syntax. Formally defined at `http://www.w3.org/Submission/SWRL/swrl.rdf`.

imp

As part of the RuleML namespace (`http://www.w3.org/2003/11/ruleml`), `imp` defines a SWRL rule in the XML concrete syntax. Described on page 239 as well as at `http://www.w3.org/Submission/SWRL/#owls_Rule`.

Individual

As part of the OWL XML namespace (`http://www.w3.org/2003/05/owl-xml`), `Individual` specifies an OWL individual in the XML concrete syntax. Described at `http://www.w3.org/TR/owl-xmlsyntax/#owls_IndividualID`.

IndividualPropertyAtom

As part of the SWRL RDF namespace (`http://www.w3.org/2003/11/swrl`), `IndividualPropertyAtom` associates either a variable with an OWL individual or two OWL individuals with an object property in the RDF concrete syntax. Formally defined at `http://www.w3.org/Submission/SWRL/swrl.rdf`.

individualPropertyAtom

As part of the SWRL XML namespace (`http://www.w3.org/2003/11/swrlx`), `individualPropertyAtom` associates a variable with an OWL individual, two variables or two OWL individuals with an object property in the XML concrete syntax. Described on page 241 as well as at `http://www.w3.org/Submission/SWRL/#owls_individual-PropertyAtom`.

propertyPredicate

As part of the SWRL RDF namespace (`http://www.w3.org/2003/11/swrl`), `propertyPredicate` relates an `Atom` or any of its subclasses to a property in the RDF concrete syntax. Formally defined at `http://www.w3.org/Submission/SWRL/swrl.rdf`.

_rlab

As part of the RuleML namespace (`http://www.w3.org/2003/11/ruleml`), `_rlab` is an optional element for declaring a rule label in the XML concrete syntax. Described on page 239 as well as at `http://www.w3.org/Submission/SWRL/#owls_rlab`.

SameIndividualAtom

As part of the SWRL RDF namespace (`http://www.w3.org/2003/11/swrl`), `SameIndividualAtom` relates two `owl:Thing` instances with an `owl:sameAs` statement in the RDF concrete syntax. Formally defined at `http://www.w3.org/Submission/SWRL/swrl.rdf`.

sameIndividualAtom

As part of the SWRL XML namespace (`http://www.w3.org/2003/11/swrlx`), `sameIndividualAtom` relates two or more variables or OWL individuals with `owl:sameAs` statements in the XML concrete syntax. Described on page 242 as well as at `http://www.w3.org/Submission/SWRL/#owls_sameIndividualAtom`.

var

As part of the RuleML namespace (`http://www.w3.org/2003/11/ruleml`), `var` defines a SWRL variable declaration in the XML concrete syntax. Described on page 238 as well as at `http://www.w3.org/Submission/SWRL/#owls_Variable`.

Variable

As part of the SWRL RDF namespace (`http://www.w3.org/2003/11/swrl`), `Variable` defines a SWRL variable declaration in the RDF concrete syntax. Formally defined at `http://www.w3.org/Submission/SWRL/swrl.rdf`.

SPARQL is a recursive acronym for the *SPARQL Protocol and RDF Query Language*. This appendix contains several examples of the SPARQL query language and details, in alphabetical order, the operators and keywords that are part of the SPARQL recommendation. In the case of keywords, we give a short description. We list page numbers if a keyword or example is described in finer detail in the book. Also, we provide a reference URL to additional information in the W3C reference.

SPARQL Examples

The following examples can also be found in Chapter 6, "Discovering Information."

```
# George Washington's Namesakes
SELECT ?location
WHERE {
    ?person <http://www.w3.org/2000/01/rdf-schema#label>
        "George Washington"@en.
    ?location <http://dbpedia.org/property/namedFor> ?person
    }
```

```
# George Washington's Namesakes using prefixes
PREFIX rdfs: <http://www.w3.org/2000/01/rdf-schema#>
PREFIX dbprop: <http://dbpedia.org/property/>
SELECT ?location
WHERE {
    ?person rdfs:label "George Washington"@en.
    ?location dbprop:namedFor ?person
    }


# A sorted query for information on George Washington
PREFIX rdfs: <http://www.w3.org/2000/01/rdf-schema#>
PREFIX dbprop: <http://dbpedia.org/property/>
PREFIX foaf: <http://xmlns.com/foaf/0.1/>
SELECT ?job ?birthLoc ?picture
WHERE {
    ?person rdfs:label "George Washington"@en.
            dbprop:occupation ?job;
            dbprop:birthPlace ?birthLoc;
            foaf:img ?picture
} ORDER BY ?birthLoc DESC(?job)


# Information about Tim Berners-Lee's FOAF friends
PREFIX tbl: <http://www.w3.org/People/Berners-Lee/card#>
PREFIX foaf: <http://xmlns.com/foaf/0.1/>
PREFIX rdfs: <http://www.w3.org/2000/01/rdf-schema#>
PREFIX karl:
        <http://www.w3.org/People/karl/karl-foaf.xrdf#>
SELECT ?personName2 ?predicate ?object
FROM <http://www.w3.org/People/Berners-Lee/card>
FROM <http://www.w3.org/People/karl/karl-foaf.xrdf>
FROM <http://www.koalie.net/foaf.rdf>
FROM <http://heddley.com/edd/foaf.rdf>
FROM <http://www.cs.umd.edu/~hendler/2003/foaf.rdf>
FROM <http://www.dajobe.org/foaf.rdf>
FROM <http://www.isi.edu/~gil/foaf.rdf>
FROM <http://www.ivan-herman.net/foaf.rdf>
FROM <http://www.kjetil.kjernsmo.net/foaf>
FROM <http://www.lassila.org/ora.rdf>
FROM <http://www.mindswap.org/2004/owl/mindswappers>
WHERE {
    tbl:i foaf:knows ?person.
    ?person foaf:name ?personName1;
            rdfs:seeAlso ?iri.
    ?iri foaf:primaryTopic ?person2.
    ?person2 foaf:name ?personName2;
             ?predicate ?object
    FILTER(?personName1 = ?personName2).
}
```

```
# Various names of Tim Berners-Lee's FOAF friends
# using named graphs
PREFIX tbl: <http://www.w3.org/People/Berners-Lee/card#>
PREFIX foaf: <http://xmlns.com/foaf/0.1/>
PREFIX rdfs: <http://www.w3.org/2000/01/rdf-schema#>
PREFIX rdf: <http://www.w3.org/1999/02/22-rdf-syntax-ns#>
SELECT *
FROM NAMED <http://www.koalie.net/foaf.rdf>
FROM NAMED <http://heddley.com/edd/foaf.rdf>
FROM NAMED <http://www.cs.umd.edu/~hendler/2003/foaf.rdf>
FROM NAMED <http://www.dajobe.org/foaf.rdf>
FROM NAMED <http://www.isi.edu/~gil/foaf.rdf>
FROM NAMED <http://www.ivan-herman.net/foaf.rdf>
FROM NAMED <http://www.kjetil.kjernsmo.net/foaf>
FROM NAMED <http://www.lassila.org/ora.rdf>
FROM NAMED
      <http://www.mindswap.org/2004/owl/mindswappers>
WHERE {
    GRAPH ?originGraph {
        _:blank1 foaf:knows _:blank2.
        _:blank2 rdf:type foaf:Person;
                 foaf:nick ?nickname;
                 foaf:name ?realname
    }
}


# A filtered SPARQL query for any information regarding
# George Washington's last term as the President of the
# United States
PREFIX rdfs: <http://www.w3.org/2000/01/rdf-schema#>
PREFIX dbprop: <http://dbpedia.org/property/>
PREFIX xsd: <http://www.w3.org/2001/XMLSchema#>
SELECT ?prop ?object
WHERE {
    ?person rdfs:label "George Washington"@en;
            dbprop:presidentStart ?start;
            ?prop ?object.
    FILTER(xsd:integer(?start) + 4 <=
           xsd:integer(?object))
}


# An optional SPARQL query that may return an image,
# mailbox or last name of any given set of FOAF friends
PREFIX foaf: <http://xmlns.com/foaf/0.1/>
SELECT *
WHERE {
    ?person foaf:name ?name.
```

```
        OPTIONAL {
            ?person foaf:img ?img;
                    foaf:mbox ?mbox;
                    foaf:family_name ?fName
            }
    }


# Returning FOAF information with a CONSTRUCT statement
PREFIX foaf: <http://xmlns.com/foaf/0.1/>
PREFIX rdf: <http://www.w3.org/1999/02/22-rdf-syntax-ns#>
PREFIX ms: <http://www.mindswap.org/2003/owl/mindswap#>
CONSTRUCT {
   ?person rdf:type foaf:Person;
           foaf:name ?rname;
           foaf:homepage ?hpage;
           foaf:nick ?nick;
           foaf:mbox ?mbox.
}
FROM NAMED <http://www.kjetil.kjernsmo.net/foaf>
FROM NAMED <http://www.dajobe.org/foaf.rdf>
FROM NAMED <http://heddley.com/edd/foaf.rdf>
FROM NAMED <http://www.cs.umd.edu/~hendler/2003/foaf.rdf>
FROM NAMED <http://www.koalie.net/foaf.rdf>
FROM NAMED <http://www.isi.edu/~gil/foaf.rdf>
FROM NAMED <http://www.ivan-herman.net/foaf.rdf>
FROM NAMED <http://www.lassila.org/ora.rdf>
FROM NAMED
        <http://www.mindswap.org/2004/owl/mindswappers>
WHERE {
   GRAPH ?originGraph {
      # This pattern now returns information for everyone
      # except www.mindswap.org.
        {
          _:blank1 foaf:knows ?person.
          ?person rdf:type foaf:Person.
          # If we find a foaf:Person, then make sure we
          # either the nickname and/or the name and/or the
          # homepage.  If we had omitted the FILTER clause,
          # then we could have returned a query solution
          # containing ?orginGraph and no other
          # information!
          OPTIONAL { ?person foaf:nick ?nick }.
          OPTIONAL { ?person foaf:name ?rname }.
          OPTIONAL { ?person foaf:homepage ?hpage }.
          FILTER(bound(?nick) || bound(?rname) ||
                  bound(?hpage))
        }
      # Here's where we grab www.mindswap.org folks of
```

```
            # all stripes.  We are claiming that any friends we
            # find will have triples declaring his/her name,
            # homepage and mailbox.
            UNION {
                { ?person rdf:type ms:Affiliate }
                UNION
                { ?person rdf:type ms:Alumni }
                UNION
                { ?person rdf:type ms:Faculty }
                UNION
                { ?person rdf:type ms:Programmer }
                UNION
                { ?person rdf:type ms:Researcher }
                UNION
                { ?person rdf:type ms:GraduateStudent }
                UNION
                { ?person rdf:type ms:UndergraduateStudent } .
                ?person foaf:name ?rname;
                        foaf:homepage ?hpage;
                        foaf:mbox ?mbox
            }
    }
}


# Using a DESCRIBE statement for George Washington
PREFIX rdf:
        <http://www.w3.org/1999/02/22-rdf-syntax-ns#>
PREFIX dbpedia: <http://dbpedia.org/resource/>
DESCRIBE *
WHERE {
     ?person ?anyProperty dbpedia:George_Washington
}


# An ASK SPARQL query determining whether George
# Washington was president in the year 1795
PREFIX rdfs: <http://www.w3.org/2000/01/rdf-schema#>
PREFIX dbprop: <http://dbpedia.org/property/>
PREFIX xsd: <http://www.w3.org/2001/XMLSchema#>
ASK
WHERE {
    ?person rdfs:label "George Washington"@en;
            dbprop:presidentStart ?startDate;
            dbprop:presidentEnd ?endDate.
    FILTER(xsd:integer(?startDate) < xsd:integer('1795')
          &&
          xsd:integer(?endDate) > xsd:integer('1795'))
    }
```

Operators

This section contains a list of all supported SPARQL query language operators as documented in the W3C SPARQL Recommendation (http://www.w3.org/TR/rdf-sparql-query/#OperatorMapping). To avoid duplication, some operators are specified here while others are discussed in the "Keywords" section. We provide short examples of each operator.

Unary Operators

Unary operators are those operations that require only a single argument.

!boolExpr   Returns `true` if `boolExpr` is `false` and returns `false` if `boolExpr` is `true`.

!(true)   will return `false`.

+numericExpression   Returns the positive value of `numericExpression`.

   `xsd:integer(?startDate) < +xsd:integer('1795')`

-numericExpression   Returns the negative value of `numericExpression`.

   `xsd:integer(?startDate) > -xsd:integer('1795')`

BOUND(?variable)   Detailed in the "Keywords" section.

   `BOUND(?x)`

DATATYPE(iri)   Detailed in the "Keywords" section.

   `FILTER(DATATYPE(?startDate) = xsd:integer)`

isBLANK(iri)   Returns `true` if `iri` is a blank node; otherwise `false`.

   `isBLANK(?x)`

isLITERAL(lit)   Returns `true` if `lit` is an RDF literal; otherwise `false`.

   `isLITERAL(?x)`

isIRI(iri)   Detailed in the "Keywords" section.

   `isIRI(?x)`

isURI(iri)   Detailed in the "Keywords" section.

   `isURI(?x)`

LANG(iri)   Detailed in the "Keywords" section.

   `LANG(?x)`

STR(iri)   Detailed in the "Keywords" section.

   `STR(?x)`

Binary Operators

Binary operators are those operations that require two arguments. Any reference to types is specific to XML Schema datatypes.

boolExpr1 || boolExpr2   Returns `true` if either `boolExpr1` or `boolExpr2` is `true`; otherwise it returns `false`.

`FILTER(?x > 0 || ?y = 1)`

boolExpr1 && boolExpr2   Returns `true` if both `boolExpr1` and `boolExpr2` are `true`; otherwise it returns `false`.

`FILTER(?x > 0 && ?y = 1)`

expr1 = expr2   Returns `true` if `expr1` and `expr2` are equal in value; otherwise it returns `false`. `expr1` and `expr2` can be of numeric, literal, boolean, string, or dateTime types as well as RDF terms.

`FILTER(?x = ?y)`

expr1 != expr2   Returns `true` if `expr1` and `expr2` are not equal in value; otherwise it returns `false`. `expr1` and `expr2` can be of numeric, literal, boolean, string, or dateTime types as well as RDF terms.

`FILTER(?x != ?y)`

expr1 < expr2   Returns `true` if `expr1` is less than `expr2` in value; otherwise it returns `false`. `expr1` and `expr2` can be of numeric, literal, boolean, string, or dateTime types.

`FILTER(?x < ?y)`

expr1 > expr2   Returns `true` if `expr1` is greater than `expr2` in value; otherwise it returns `false`. `expr1` and `expr2` can be of numeric, literal, boolean, string, or dateTime types.

`FILTER(?x > ?y)`

expr1 <= expr2   Returns `true` if `expr1` is less than or equal to `expr2` in value; otherwise it returns `false`. `expr1` and `expr2` can be of numeric, literal, boolean, string, or dateTime types.

`FILTER(?x <= ?y)`

expr1 >= expr2   Returns `true` if `expr1` is greater than or equal to `expr2` in value; otherwise it returns `false`. `expr1` and `expr2` can be of numeric, literal, boolean, string, or dateTime types.

`FILTER(?x >= ?y)`

numericExpr1 * numericExpr2   Returns the product of `numericExpr1` and `numericExpr2`.

`FILTER(?x > ?y*5)`

numericExpr1 / numericExpr2   Returns the quotient of dividing
numericExpr1 by numericExpr2.

```
FILTER(?x > ?y/5)
```

numericExpr1 + numericExpr2   Returns the sum of numericExpr1 and
numericExpr2.

```
FILTER(?x > ?y+5)
```

numericExpr1 - numericExpr2   Returns the difference between
numericExpr1 and numericExpr2.

```
FILTER(?x > ?y-5)
```

langMATCHES(iri1, iri2)   Detailed in the "Keywords" section.

```
langMATCHES(?x, "en")
```

sameTERM(iri1, iri2)   Detailed in the "Keywords" section.

```
sameTERM(?x, ?y)
```

REGEX(string, pattern)   Returns true if pattern is found in string;
otherwise false. Both arguments must be simple literals.

```
REGEX(?input, "John")
```

Trinary Operators

Trinary (aka ternary) operators are those operations that require three arguments.

REGEX(string, pattern, flags)   Returns true if pattern is found in
string as dictated by the flags argument; otherwise false. Both
arguments must be simple literals. Flags, described in detail at
http://www.w3.org/TR/xpath-functions/#flags, is an xsd:string
of any of the following concatenated character arguments:

i   If present, then match pattern against string in a case-insensitive
manner.

m   If present, then match pattern against string where
string supports multiple lines. This affects how characters ^, $, and newline characters are interpreted.

s   If present, then match pattern against string where string supports
single lines.

x   If present, then remove all whitespaces in pattern before matching.
The sole exception is against any whitespaces present in a character
class exception (i.e., those delimited with a set of square brackets).

```
REGEX(?input, "John", "is")
```

Keywords

The SPARQL Recommendation notes the set of keywords that are part of the query language. They are listed here in alphabetical order along with a description of each. Note that there is some overlap with some of the operators described in the previous section (for example, REGEX, sameTERM), but they are listed here for completeness as part of the Recommendation's Extended Backus-Naur Form (EBNF).

a   A shortcut keyword that can be used in place of the predicate IRI http://www.w3.org/1999/02/22-rdf-syntax-ns#type. Described at http://www.w3.org/TR/rdf-sparql-query/#abbrevRdfType.

ASK   A SPARQL query form that tests whether or not a query has a matching graph pattern or not. Described on page 225 as well as http://www.w3.org/TR/rdf-sparql-query/#ask.

BASE   Defines a base IRI that resolves relative IRIs. Described on page 224 as well as http://www.w3.org/TR/rdf-sparql-query/#relIRIs.

BOUND   Returns true if the given variable is bound to a value, or else it returns false. Variables with values of NAN (not a number) or INF (infinity) are considered not bound. Described on page 220 as well as http://www.w3.org/TR/rdf-sparql-query/#func-bound.

CONSTRUCT   A SPARQL query form that returns a single RDF graph as specified by the query's graph template. Described on page 222 as well as http://www.w3.org/TR/rdf-sparql-query/#construct.

DATATYPE   This keyword returns the datatype of a given literal. Simple literals will always return xsd:string. Described at http://www.w3.org/TR/rdf-sparql-query/#func-datatype.

DESCRIBE   A SPARQL query form that returns a single RDF graph for a set of RDF resources. Described on page 224 as well as http://www.w3.org/TR/rdf-sparql-query/#describe.

DISTINCT   This keyword guarantees that duplicate query results that are bound to identical variables are removed. Described at http://www.w3.org/TR/rdf-sparql-query/#modDistinct.

false   A keyword that is shorthand for the literal "false"^^xsd:boolean. Described at http://www.w3.org/TR/rdf-sparql-query/#QSynLiterals.

FILTER   Restricts the number of solutions in a result set based on a given expression. Described on page 213 as well as http://www.w3.org/TR/rdf-sparql-query/#tests.

FROM   Specifies a default RDF dataset against which a query is performed. The dataset is identified by an IRI. Described on page 202 as well as `http://www.w3.org/TR/rdf-sparql-query/#specifyingDataset`.

FROM NAMED   Specifies a named RDF dataset against which a query is performed. The dataset is identified by an IRI. Described on page 202 as well as `http://www.w3.org/TR/rdf-sparql-query/#specifying Dataset`.

GRAPH   Used in conjunction with named graphs, `GRAPH` specifies both a variable and a graph pattern. The variable specifies the named graph against which the graph pattern is executed. Described on page 206 as well as `http://www.w3.org/TR/rdf-sparql-query/#queryDataset`.

isIRI   A SPARQL operator that returns `true` if the given value is an IRI or `false` otherwise. Described at `http://www.w3.org/TR/rdf-sparql-query/#func-isIRI`.

isLITERAL   A SPARQL operator that returns `true` if the given value is an RDF literal or `false` otherwise. Described at `http://www.w3.org/TR/rdf-sparql-query#func-isLiteral`.

isURI   Identical in functionality to `isIRI`, `isURI` returns `true` if the given value is an IRI or `false` otherwise. Described at `http://www.w3.org/TR/rdf-sparql-query/#func-isIRI`.

LANG   This keyword returns the language tag of a given literal; otherwise it returns an empty string. Described at `http://www.w3.org/TR/rdf-sparql-query/#func-lang`.

LANGMATCHES   A SPARQL operator that takes two arguments. `LANGMATCHES` returns `true` if the first argument is a member of the language tags passed in the second argument. Otherwise, it returns `false`. Described at `http://www.w3.org/TR/rdf-sparql-query/#func-langMatches`.

LIMIT   Places an upper bound on the number of results returned in a result set. Described on page 211 as well as `http://www.w3.org/TR/rdf-sparql-query/#modResultLimit`.

OFFSET   This keyword causes the solutions generated in a result set to begin after a given number of solutions. Described on page 211 as well as `http://www.w3.org/TR/rdf-sparql-query/#modOffset`.

OPTIONAL   Notes that certain portions of a graph pattern are not required as part of a query but should be included if there is a match. Described on page 215 as well as `http://www.w3.org/TR/rdf-sparql-query/#OptionalMatching`.

ORDER BY   This keyword enables solutions in a result set to be arranged by one or more variables in either an ascending or descending order. Described on page 210 as well as `http://www.w3.org/TR/rdf-sparql-query/#modOrderBy`.

PREFIX   Allows a prefix label to be associated with a given IRI. Described on page 197 as well as `http://www.w3.org/TR/rdf-sparql-query/#prefNames`.

REDUCED   A weaker version of `DISTINCT`, this keyword signals the SPARQL endpoint to optionally remove duplicate solutions. Described on page 210 as well as `http://www.w3.org/TR/rdf-sparql-query/#modReduced`.

REGEX   Specifies that the XPath function `fn:matches` should be used to match a given pattern against a given text string. Optional flags are also available. Described on page 215 as well as `http://www.w3.org/TR/rdf-sparql-query/#funcex-regex`.

sameTERM   This keyword returns `true` if the two given arguments are equal RDF terms. Otherwise it returns `false`. Described at `http://www.w3.org/TR/rdf-sparql-query/#func-sameTerm`.

SELECT   A SPARQL query form that returns a set of variables and their bindings in an XML result set. Described on page 197 as well as `http://www.w3.org/TR/rdf-sparql-query/#select`.

STR   A SPARQL operator that returns the string representation of a given literal or IRI. Described at `http://www.w3.org/TR/rdf-sparql-query/#func-str`.

true   A keyword that is shorthand for the literal `"true"^^xsd:boolean`. Described at `http://www.w3.org/TR/rdf-sparql-query/#QSynLiterals`.

UNION   Allows for the result sets of two or more graph patterns to be combined into a single result. Described on page 219 as well as `http://www.w3.org/TR/rdf-sparql-query/#alternatives`.

WHERE   This keyword precedes a graph pattern that is used to match RDF data against some set of RDF datasets. Described on page 193 as well as `http://www.w3.org/TR/rdf-sparql-query/#GraphPattern`.

Jena Reference Guide

The programming examples in this Appendix use the Jena Semantic Web Framework. This reference guide contains two parts: the key Jena classes and the main programming steps for using the Jena Semantic Web Framework.

The first part contains the key classes and presents them in alphabetic order. The second part contains the main Jena programming steps and presents them in life-cycle order.

NOTE The Jena class descriptions are adapted from the Javadocs that are available in the downloaded Jena zip file. The Javadocs also contain additional details regarding associated classes, methods, and parameters.

Key Jena Classes

The following sections describe the key Jena classes.

DIGReasoner Class

This reasoner is the generator of inference graphs (InfGraph) that can use an external DIG inference engine to perform DL reasoning tasks.

`bind()`, `bindSchema()` binds a given graph to the external reasoner.

`configure()` configures reasoner properties.

DIGReasonerFactory Class

This is a factory class for generating instances of DIG reasoners. It implements the singleton pattern.

`create()` creates a DIG reasoner.

Graph Interface

This is the interface that must be satisfied by implementations maintaining collections of RDF triples. The core interface is small (`add`, `delete`, `find`, `contains`) and is augmented by additional classes to handle more complicated matters such as reification, query handling, bulk update, event management, and transaction handling. It enables alternate persistence mechanisms through implementing the `Graph` methods.

IDBConnection Interface

This interface encapsulates the specification of a Java Database Connectivity (JDBC) connection, mostly used to simplify the calling pattern for `ModelRDB` factory methods.

InfModel Interface

This is an extension to the normal `Model` interface that supports access to any underlying inference capability.

In Jena the primary use of inference is to generate entailments from a set of RDF data. These entailments manifest as additional RDF data in the inferred model and are accessed through the normal API.

A few reasoner services cannot be made directly available in this way, and the `InfGraph` extension gives access to these, such as access to validation/consistency checking and derivation traces.

Model Interface

An RDF model is a set of statements. Methods are provided for creating resources, properties, and literals, and the statements that link them, for adding statements to and removing them from a model, for querying a model, and set operations for combining models.

Models may create resources (URI nodes and bnodes). Creating a resource does not make the resource visible to the model; resources are only "in" models if statements about them are added to the model. Similarly, the only way to "remove" a resource from a model is to remove all the statements that mention it.

When a resource or literal is created by a model, the model is free to reuse an existing resource or literal object with the correct values, or it may create a fresh one. (All Jena RDFNodes and statements are immutable, so this is generally safe.)

This interface defines a set of primitive methods. A set of convenience methods that extends this interface, for example, performing automatic type conversions and support for enhanced resources, is defined in ModelCon.

add() provides various ways to add statements and other models.

close() releases all computing resources and completes any pending operations.

createXXXX() enables the creation of various model resources, where xxxx can stand for Resource, Statements, Property, Literal, List, and more.

enterCriticalSection() and leaveCriticalSection() enable multithreading.

query() enables a basic matching query.

remove() removes statements.

write() outputs the model contents in various formats.

ModelFactory Class

This static class creates standard model objects.

createDefaultModel() creates an in-memory model with a standard reification style.

createFileModelmaker() creates an in-memory ModelMaker backed by a file store.

createInfModel() builds an inference model from parameter InfGraph.

createModelForGraph() builds a model from parameter Graph.

createRDBMaker() builds a model associated with IDBConnection database.

createOntologyModel() builds an OntModel.

ModelMaker Interface

A ModelMaker contains a collection of named models, methods for creating new models (both named and anonymous) and opening previously named models, removing models, and accessing a single default model for this maker.

■ createDefaultModel() is similar to the ModelFactory class method.

OntModelSpec Class

This class encapsulates a description of the components of an ontology model, including the storage scheme, reasoner, and language profile.

NOTE Refer to the Javadocs for specific settings.

Query Class

This is a class of graph queries, as well as some machinery for implementing them. The data structure for a query is presented externally. There are two ways of creating a query: using the parser to turn a string description of the query into the executable form, and the programmatic way (the parser is calling the programmatic operations driven by the query string). The declarative approach of passing in a string is preferred. Once a query is built, it can be passed to the `QueryFactory` to produce a query execution engine.

QueryExecution Interface

This interface results in a single execution of a query.

`execSelect()` executes a `SELECT` query.

`execConstruct()` executes a `CONSTRUCT` query.

`execDescribe()` executes a `DESCRIBE` query.

`execAsk()` executes an `ASK` query.

`close()` releases resources that are associated with the query.

QuerySolution Interface

This interface results in a single answer from a `SELECT` query.

`get()` returns the value of the named variable parameter.

`contains()` returns `true` if the named variable is in this binding.

`getLiteral()` returns the literal of the named variable parameter.

`varNames()` iterates over the variable names in the `QuerySolution`.

ObjectListener Class

This listener funnels all the changes into added/removed.

`added()` overrides base functionality to track all objects added to the model.

`addedStatement()` overrides base functionality to track the addition of a single statement.

`removed()` overrides base functionality to track any removal of objects from the model.

removedStatement() overrides base functionality to track the removal of a single statement.

OntClass Interface

This interface represents an ontology node characterizing a class description.

createIndividual() creates or finds an existing Individual given a URI parameter.

getSubClass() provides the subclass.

getSuperClass() provides the superclass.

addSuperClass() adds the parameter as a superclass.

OntModel Interface

This interface provides an enhanced view of a Jena model that is known to contain ontology data, under a given ontology vocabulary (such as OWL). This class does not by itself compute the deductive extension of the graph under the semantic rules of the language. Instead, we wrap an underlying model with this ontology interface, which presents a convenient syntax for accessing the language elements. Depending on the inference capability of the underlying model, the OntModel will bapp05ar to contain more or less triples.

In addition to the Model methods, OntModel adds an ontology for restrictions and logical relationships. Following is a sample—see the Javadocs for the complete method list.

createSymmetricProperty() sets the symmetric property to the URI parameter.

createTransitiveProperty() sets the transitive property to the URI parameter.

createOntResource() creates or finds an OntResource with the given URI parameter.

getOntology() gets an Ontology resource to provide metadata regarding the ontology.

Ontology Interface

This interface encapsulates the distinguished instance in a given ontology document; it presents metadata and other processing data about the document (including which other documents are imported by a document).

getBackwardCompatibleWith() obtains the ontology represented as a resource that is compatible with this model.

getPriorVersion() obtains the ontology that was superseded by the current ontology.

listImports() provides an iterator that lists all imports into this ontology.

OntProperty Interface

This interface encapsulates a property in an ontology. This is an extension to the standard Property interface, adding a collection of convenience methods for accessing the additional semantic features of properties in OWL, RDFS, and DAML+OIL, such as domain, range, or inverse. Not all such capabilities exist in all supported ontology languages.

addInverseOf() adds a property that is the inverse of the parameter property.

addSubProperty() adds a subproperty of this property.

convertToDatatypeProperty() converts to a datatype property.

convertToObjectProperty() converts to an object property.

OntResource Interface

This interface provides a common supertype for all of the abstractions in this ontology representation package.

RDFNode Interface

This interface covers RDF resources and literals. It allows probing whether a node is a literal (blank URI resource), moving nodes from model to model, and viewing them as different Java types using the .as() polymorphism.

isLiteral() is true if RDFNode is a literal.

as() converts to different implementations based on the Class parameter.

toString() provides a string representation.

Reasoner Interface

This is the minimal interface to which all reasoners (or reasoner adaptors) conform. This only supports attaching the reasoner to a set of RDF graphs that represent the rules or ontologies and instance data. The actual reasoner requests are made through the InfGraph, which is generated once the reasoner has been bound to a set of RDF data.

bind() attaches the reasoner to a parameter graph or model.

bindSchema() attaches the reasoner to a graph or model representing the ontology.

getReasonerCapabilities() returns a description of the reasoner
capabilities.

Resource Interface

This is an RDF resource. When created, the resource instances may be associated with a specific model. Resources created by a model will refer to
that model and support a range of methods, such as getProperty() and
addProperty(), which will access or modify that model. This enables the
programmer to write code in a compact and easy style.

Resources created by ResourceFactory will not refer to any model and
will not permit operations that require a model. Such resources are useful as
general constants.

This interface provides methods supporting typed literals. This means that
methods are provided that will translate a built-in type or an object to an RDF
literal. This translation is done by invoking the toString() method of the
object or its built-in equivalent. The reverse translation is also supported. This
is built in for built-in types. Factory objects, provided by the application, are
used for application objects.

addProperty() adds the property to this resource.

toString() provides a string representation of the resource.

getURI() returns the URI of the resource.

begin() begins a transaction in the associated model.

commit() commits the transaction in the associated model.

abort() aborts the transaction in the associated model.

ResultSet Interface

This interface provides results from a query in a table-like manner for SELECT
queries. Each row corresponds to a set of bindings that fulfill the conditions of
the query. You access the results by variable name.

hasNext() is true or false if there is an additional returned row.

next() moves to the next result possibility.

getResultVars() returns a list of variable names contained in the result set.

Statement Interface

This interface is an RDF statement. A statement is not a resource, but it can
produce a reified statement that represents it and from which the statement
can be recovered.

A statement instance tracks which model created it, if any. All the resource components of a statement are in the same model as the statement, if it has one, and are in no model if the statement isn't in a model.

changeObject() changes the object portion of the statement with the parameter.

createReifiedStatement() creates a reified statement that embodies this statement.

equals() determines whether two statements are equal.

getModel() gets the model in which this statement was created.

getResource() gets the object of the statement.

isReified() determines if the statement is reified.

StmtIterator Interface

This interface is an iterator that returns RDF statements. RDF iterators are standard Java iterators, except that they have extra methods to return specifically typed objects, in this case RDF statements, and have a close() method that should be called to free resources if the application does not complete the iteration.

nextStatement() returns the next statement in the iteration.

ValidityReport Interface

This interface is a data structure that is used to report the results of validation or consistency-checking operations. It is an array of reports, each of which has a severity, a type (string), and a description (string).

getReports() returns an iterator over ValidityReport.Report records.

isClean() returns true if the model is both valid (logically consistent) and has no warnings.

isValid() returns true if no logical inconsistencies exist.

Main Programming Steps

The following summary outlines each of the major programming steps for using the Jena Semantic Web Framework. Each step contains working code and uses the classes that were outlined previously.

Establishing the Model

```
OntModel ontmodel = ModelFactory.createOntologyModel();

ModelMaker maker = ModelFactory.createModelRDBMaker(conn);
Model modelTmp = maker.createModel("ModelName");
OntModelSpec spec = new OntModelSpec(OntModelSpec.OWL_MEM);
OntModel ontModelDB =
 ModelFactory.createOntologyModel(spec,modelTmp);
```

Populating the Model

```
ontmodel.read("http://xmlns.com/foaf/spec/index.rdf");
ontmodel.read("/ontologies/foaf.rdf");

ontmodel.add(otherModel);

 ontmodel.add(Resource, Property, Resource);
```

Querying the Model

```
Query query = QueryFactory.create("Select ?s ?p ?o WHERE {?s ?p ?o}");
QueryExecution qexec = QueryExecutionFactory.create(query,ontmodel);
ResultSet results = qexec.execSelect( );
While( results.hasNext()){
QuerySolution soln = response.nextSolution();
RDFNode name = soln.get("?o");
        System.out.println(name.toString());
}
```

Binding a Reasoner to the Model

```
Reasoner reasoner = PelletReasonerFactory.theInstance().create();
reasoner = reasoner.bindSchema(ontmodel);
InfModel inferredModel = ModelFactory.createInfModel(reasoner,ontmodel);
```

Exporting the Model

```
FileOutputStream outModel;
outModel = new FileOutputStream("/outputfile.turtle");
ontModel.write(outModel, "TURTLE.ttl");
```

Installation Reference Guide

This appendix offers a quick reference to all the software components used in the book. The list is alphabetized so that you can find items quickly.

D2RQ: Conversion from Relational Database to Jena Model

D2RQ converts a relational database to a Jena model. This allows direct Jena access to the database (found at `http://www4.wiwiss.fu-berlin.de/bizer/D2RQ/spec/`).

1. Download the `.zip` file for the D2RQ API at `http://sourceforge.net/project/showfiles.php?group_id=111002`.
2. Expand the `.zip` file in the desired directory.
3. Add the `.jar` files to the Java classpath. (You can also run commands in Windows, as described in Chapter 8.)

NOTE The complete Javadocs are found under `/doc`.

Eclipse Integrated Development Environment

Eclipse provides a full development environment for Java applications, including a code-aware editor, documentation reference, and debugger (found at `http://www.eclipse.org/downloads/`).

1. Select Eclipse IDE for Java Developers for your given operating system: Windows, Mac OS X, or Linux.
2. Expand the compressed file, a `.zip` file or `.tar` file, in the desired directory.
3. Run `eclipse.app` in Mac, `eclipse.exe` in Windows, or `eclipse` in Linux. When you run Eclipse for the first time, you need to select the editor in the Welcome window.
4. Select File ➢ New ➢ New Java Project, and you are ready to go.

Java Classpath

All of the programming libraries used throughout the book are in the Java programming language. Your application must be aware of the location of these library files. For that, the Java classpath indicates the location of all compiled files, which can be both in the native *class* structure file or an archived set of class files in a `.jar` file. The Java classpath contains directories of class files and locations of the specific `.jar` files. Each referenced Java class must be included in your Java program's classpath via a reference to its class directory or its `.jar` file. A missing reference generates the "Class Not Found" exception when the class is referenced at runtime.

There are several ways to set the classpath specific to each operating system. You can set the classpath in the command line when calling the Java program, set an environment variable in Windows and Unix/Mac, or have a Java IDE set it for you. We examine all three. (Note that you can also set the classpath within the `.jar` file. This is not demonstrated here.)

When executing your Java program, you invoke the Java virtual machine by using the `java` command. This command takes several options, including classpath settings. The following is an example:

```
$ java -classpath /directory1/common.jar:/directory2/gui.jar:
                   /directoryofclassfiles javaclass
```

Note that you separate multiple `.jar` file locations with a colon.

Setting an environment variable in Windows is done by opening the Windows Control Panel through the Start menu. Next, launch System Properties. Select the Advanced tab. Figure F-1 illustrates the Advanced tab of the System Properties window.

Figure F-1 Windows Advanced System Properties window

1. Click the Environment Variables button.

2. Click the New button under System Variables.

3. Enter the classpath variable name along with its value. Figure F-2 shows the classpath populated with both a `.jar` file and a directory of class files. Files and directories must be separated by a semicolon. You need to list every `.jar` file separately; this can get quite tedious, but it is necessary. Don't forget to include your own files in the classpath, or Java will fail immediately by not finding your application classes.

   Setting an environment variable in Unix requires a change to your profile generation. This can be done globally by adding a variable to `/etc/profile` or individually by adding the variable to your specific shell environment file in your home directory. The BASH shell is found in your home directory under the file `.base_profile`. In either case, you enter the following lines:

   ```
   CLASSPATH= \
     /directory/common.jar:/directory2/gui.jar:/directoryofclasses
   EXPORT CLASSPATH
   ```

   Note that CLASSPATH is all uppercase. You must remember to execute the file within your current shell or launch a new shell. You can execute the file by using `$ . ./base_profile` or `. /etc/profile`.

4. Test the proper setting by using the `echo` command (`echo $CLASSPATH`).

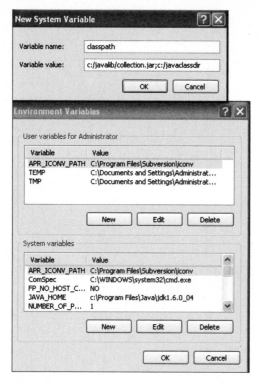

Figure F-2 Setting a new system variable in Windows

5. To set the classpath through the IDE (demonstrated here with Eclipse since Eclipse is used), right-click on the Java project for which you wish to set the classpath. This brings up a long menu.

6. Select Build Path ➤ Configure Build Path. A window opens, listing the current setting of the Java classpath, as shown in Figure F-3.

7. Select Add External JARs.

8. Select the appropriate .jar file(s) within your file system. (Eclipse also links to the documentation, which is very useful.)

JAXB-RI

JAXB provides a convenient way to process XML content using Java objects by binding its XML schema to a Java representation.

You can download the latest version from the Downloads link on the reference site (https://jaxb.dev.java.net/). The site also points to useful documentation and tutorials.

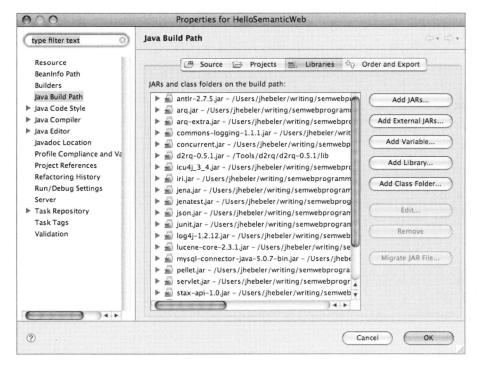

Figure F-3 Setting the classpath in Eclipse IDE

1. Download the .zip file, such as JAXB RI 2.1.9.zip.
2. Expand it in the desired directory.
3. Add the .jar files in the lib directory to the Java classpath.

Jena Semantic Web Framework

The RDF, RDFS, and OWL programming framework is found at http://jena.sourceforge.net/.

The download consists of a .zip file that contains all necessary .jar files contained in the lib directory as well as examples and documentation.

1. Download the jena.zip file.
2. Expand the .zip file in the desired directory.
3. Add the .jar files in the lib directory to the Java classpath.
4. Examine the various classes and methods by loading doc/javadoc/index.html into your browser.

JDBC Driver for MySQL

This driver enables JDBC access to a MySQL database and is found at
`http://dev.mysql.com/downloads/connector/j/5.1.html`.

1. Download the `.zip` file.
2. Expand the `.zip` file in the desired directory.
3. Add the `mysql-connector-java-5.1.7-bin.jar` file to the Java class-path.

NOTE The full documentation explains the various options.

Pellet Reasoner

This reasoner is exposed via `.jar` files or a remote DIG interface (found at
`http://clarkparsia.com/pellet/`).

1. Download the `.zip` file
2. Expand the `.zip` file in the desired directory
3. Add the `.jar` files to the `/lib` directory.
4. For the DIG interface, start the standalone pellet through `pellet-dig.sh`
   (`pellet.sh` for Pellet 2.x) for Linux/Mac or `pellet-dig.bat`
   (`pellet.bat` for Pellet 2.x) for Windows. The default port for
   DIG is port 8081. You can use another port by providing the
   argument `-port` *XXXX*, where *XXXX* is an available port.

Protégé Ontology Editor

This ontology editor can incorporate queries and reasoners (found at
`http://protege.stanford.edu/`).

1. Download for the appropriate operating system.
2. You have two choices: a `.zip` file you expand or an automatic installer.
3. Run `protege.app`.
4. You can link to the Pellet reasoner by selecting Pellet from the Reasoner menu.

Tar/Gzipped Files

Tar files consist of an archive of files. In addition, gzipped compresses files. Therefore, a tar/gzipped file contains an archive of compressed files. Uncompressing and unzipping such files is a two-step operation. First you unpack the archive, and second you expand the compressed files. The following commands do just that:

```
gunzip compressedfile.tar.gz
tar -xvf compressedfile.tar
or in one step
tar -xzvf compressedfile.tar.gz
```

Velocity: GUI Templates

This is a web template tool (found at `http://velocity.apache.org`).

1. Download the latest `.zip` file, `velocity-X.X.X.zip`.

2. Expand the `.zip` file in the appropriate directory.

3. Add the `/lib` `.jar` files to your classpath.

Index

Want to **EXPLORE** even more?

semantic universe

Educating the World About Semantic Technologies & Applications

The best online resource for ongoing information and education about Semantic Technologies is the Semantic Universe Network, a vibrant online community and communications hub for the global semantic technology marketplace. The Semantic Universe Network is the professional and educational resource for the people, companies, editorial content, events, products, advertising, research and initiatives within the high-growth semantics sector. The Network was developed and deployed on a sophisticated semantic application platform to facilitate the highest level of user engagement, contextual relevancy and editorial resource matching. At Semantic Universe, you will find:

- Blogs
- Webcasts
- Articles
- Audio & Video archives

- Product Listings
- Community Directories
- Educational Resources
- Live Events and Meetings

FREE MEMBERSHIP

MEMBERSHIP IS FREE!

Join today at: http://semanticuniverse.com/SemanticWebProgramming/